Twenty Questions for the Writer

A Rhetoric with Readings

SECOND EDITION

JACQUELINE BERKE
DREW UNIVERSITY

Harcourt Brace Jovanovich, Inc.
NEW YORK   CHICAGO   SAN FRANCISCO   ATLANTA

ISBN: 0-15-592399-4

Library of Congress Catalog Card Number: 75-35312

Printed in the United States of America

PICTURE CREDITS
- 51: Reprinted from *The Book of Popular Science* by permission of the publisher, Grolier, Incorporated.
- 55: André Kertész, Magnum
- 113: Edvard Munch, *The Cry* (1893), Nasjonalgalleriet, Oslo, Norway
- 115: Henri Cartier-Bresson, Magnum
- 145: Top, Brown Brothers, Sterling, Pennsylvania
  Bottom, Danny Lyons, Magnum
- 168: Wide World Photos, Inc.
- 219: Erika Stone, Peter Arnold Photo Archives
- 307–08: Copr. © 1948, James Thurber. From *The Beast in Me and Other Animals*, published by Harcourt Brace Jovanovich, Inc. Originally printed in The New Yorker
- 385: From Bess Sondel, *Power Steering with Words*, copyright © 1964 Follett Publishing Co.

PREFACE TO THE SECOND EDITION

"A preface," Charles Lamb once wrote, "is nothing more than a talk with the reader." Precisely so. And it is in this very spirit of talking—of making conversational reply—to those who have read and tested in their own classrooms the First Edition of *Twenty Questions for the Writer* that I approach this preface to the Second Edition. My purpose here is twofold: to thank those who have given the book such a favorable reception; and to point out the improvements designed to make the Second Edition still more useful, enjoyable, and self-contained than the First.

1. A compact but reasonably comprehensive section has been incorporated into Chapter 26, "Improving Sentences"—an outline of basic grammar, which serves as a reminder of the rules and conventions underlying rhetorical principles.

2. A new Chapter 28 has been added, "Revising and Editing," which provides an extensive editing checklist along with a punctuation chart and punctuation review to serve as a guide to revision. This chapter also outlines mechanical procedures: capitalization, italics, abbreviations and contractions, numbers, and spelling (a list of 101 commonly misspelled words stands as warning and—let us hope—prevention).

3. Approximately thirty-five new readings have been introduced, drawn from such lively and provocative writers as John Barth, Donald Barthelme, Simone de Beauvoir, John Fowles, Penelope Gilliatt, Ernest Hemingway, Mary McCarthy, Joyce Carol Oates, May Sarton, and James Thurber.

4. The assignment sections at the end of each chapter have been reorgan-

ized into two categories. The first provides "Class Discussion and Paragraph Suggestions," consisting of questions, lists of topics, and additional readings intended to stimulate discussion and writing in the classroom. The second category of assignments consists of "Essay Suggestions"—lists of topics on which students may draw for their longer papers.

5. New illustrations have been included, which are intended to enliven the text further and to communicate nonverbal messages that will elicit meaningful verbal responses.

6. Inside the back cover, a guide to the principles of style discussed in Part III, plus an extended Index, provide easier access to specific areas of interest.

Beyond these concrete changes, my underlying attitudes toward writing and what I consider an essentially common-sense approach to the teaching of writing remain the same. Since the publication of the First Edition I have received many helpful suggestions from instructors who have used the textbook. One waggish colleague proposed that I prepare an abridged "Ten Questions for the Part-time Writer." I enjoyed that suggestion (thank you, John Clark of the University of South Florida), but in view of the present state of unpreparedness among many writing students I must defer any such action, insisting instead that within the confines of their regular academic programs, students should write as nearly full-time as is humanly possible.

Others who have supported this textbook and helped me in various ways to smooth its rough edges include the following: Joan S. Agard, Madison Area Technical College; Lynn Z. Bloom, University of New Mexico; Charles T. Bown, Ferris State College; Isagani R. Cruz, University of Maryland; Gretchen Kidd Fallon, University of Maryland; Dennis D. Gartner, Frostburg State College; Roger B. Gillan, Robert Morris College; Myrna Goldenberg, Montgomery College; Richard Guertin, Normandale Community College; John M. Hansen, Catonsville Community College; Jon Hassler, Brainerd State Community College; Joe W. Leonard, Southwestern College; Samuel O. Monson; Brigham Young University; Margaret Moran, Westfield State College; John O'Brien, Aurora College; David L. Rankin, Winthrop College; David E. Sawyer; Sister Lois Sculco, Seton Hill College; Philip Skerry, Lakeland Community College; Mildred Steele, Drake University; Helen J. Throckmorton, Wichita State University; Sandra C. Vekasy, Evangel College; Arthur W. M. Voss, Lake Forest College; and Nancy T. Zuercher, University of South Dakota. My special thanks go to Robert M. Coogan of the University of Maryland for his valuable suggestions for improving the manuscript, particularly the new Chapter 28 and the new section on grammar in Chapter 26.

I also want to express special thanks to my colleagues in the Department of English at Drew University: to John Bicknell, author of the Letter to the Editor in Chapter 20 (only a scrupulously logical mind could have planted so many fallacies in so little space); to Janet Burstein, whose comments were always "golden"; to Robert Chapman for sharing his fine poem; to Nadine Ollman, who kept seeing new possibilities; to Robert Ready, for using the book so creatively and for testing and helping to improve illustrative materials; and to John Warner for asking an important question which set me thinking.

I also want to thank my daughter, Laura Berke, for expediting matters (like the whiz/which she is) and my husband, Philip Berke, for making a single but spectacular suggestion.

Finally, I want to express appreciation to my book's team at Harcourt Brace Jovanovich: to Juliana Koenig for careful, conscientious copy editing; to Anna Kopczynski for attractive and ingenious design; to Kenzi Sugihara for efficient supervision of production and scheduling; to Cecilia Gardner— especially—so subtle and sure in her editing that already I am half convinced that her judicious changes were my own; and—most especially—to Eben Ludlow, who navigated us all through this Second Edition with a singularly steady hand and seemingly imperturbable spirit.

JACQUELINE BERKE

PREFACE TO THE FIRST EDITION

During my twelve years of teaching writing I have found that procedure in a writing course is as important as content. And the simpler the procedure, the better. For me, then, the ideal textbook for a writing course would be—first of all—complete and self-contained. Instructors are thereby spared the job of correlating readings in one book with writing assignments in another, with a style guide and exercises in still another, with footnote rules in still another, and so on. Second, the ideal textbook would be sequentially organized, requiring no complicated rearranging of chapters by instructors in order to construct a workable frame for their course. The textbook itself would offer a frame, but, along with this, it would offer sufficient materials and resources to enable instructors to make a course that would satisfy their own preferences and the needs of their students. That is, the ideal writing textbook would be flexible as well as clearly organized.

While hardly pretending or even aspiring to write the ideal textbook, I have nonetheless tried in this book to meet the basic requirements of completeness, simplicity of procedure, and flexibility. *Twenty Questions for the Writer* is self-contained in that it may be used without any additional resources other than a recently edited standard dictionary: included are ample and varied readings; hundreds of suggested writing assignments; practice exercises (for use inside and outside the classroom); instructions for and illustrations of four different types of term paper; a chapter on research procedure and documentation; two chapters on language; a review of rhetorical principles involving the word, the sentence, and the paragraph.

During a three-year period of testing this material in my own classes at Drew University, I have discovered that it can be used simultaneously in two different sections of the course without duplicating either the readings or the writing assignments. To be sure, instructors using this textbook may choose to assign additional materials, but for most purposes they will not be forced to do so.

My organizing principle—again in the interest of simplicity and ease—has been sequential, roughly in an order of increasing complexity. Thus, instructors can move through the chapters of this textbook as they move through the weeks of the semester, choosing from among the twenty units of writing assignments those that best serve the needs of a particular class. Each unit of writing assignment, as the table of contents indicates, is presented in the form of a question. *The writer invariably begins with a question:* the book is rooted in this observation and the chapters are titled accordingly.

Each unit of writing (that is, each chapter, each question) includes illustrative essays on a variety of subjects and in a wide range of tones from the very earnest to the matter-of-fact to the frivolous and satiric. In each assignment students are required to assume the responsibility for answering a given question, but within that mold and the discipline that the mold requires, they may address themselves to whatever subject area engages their interest and speak in whatever tone their spirit dictates. I have tried, in other words, to establish in this book a balance between the discipline required to complete even the simplest piece of writing and the feeling of freedom required for a more than pedestrian performance. I consider the striking of such a balance essential to all good writing. Indeed, just as the organizing principle of the book is rooted in the concept of the question, so the basic operating principle (and faith) is rooted in the idea that freedom in writing, as Robert Frost said of freedom in general, means "moving easy in harness."

Applying this metaphor to *Twenty Questions for the Writer,* I would say that the nature of each question provides a particular harness ("How Is X Made or Done?" dictates chronological ordering; "What Are the Types of X?" requires systematic classification; and so on), whereas the discussions within the chapter, the illustrative essays, and the assignments encourage students to move naturally and easily in a chosen direction within the given confines.

Needless to say, instructors using this book will impose as loose or tight a harness as they see fit. Although the suggested assignments at the end of each chapter advise students to select their own topics, there may well be occasions when an instructor will want the entire class to focus its attention on one topic in particular. And then again maybe not. . . . What applies to students applies equally to instructors: in order to conduct a meaningful and reasonably rewarding course they too must have the opportunity of "moving easy in harness."

I want to thank the following people: for patiently and perceptively reviewing the manuscript at different stages, Barbara McKenzie of the University of Georgia; for mobilizing pages into an expertly turned out manuscript, Ruth Demaree and Nan Lemmerman of Drew University's very expert Stenographic Service; for counsel and guidance in gathering resource materials for Chapter 22, Evelyn Meyer—Reference Librarian at Drew University—herself an extraordinary resource. I also want to thank my students at Drew for their encouraging and constructive responses to preliminary drafts of this material. Finally I want to thank Harcourt editors Ronald Campbell for flexibility and faith, and Mildred Tackett for her consistently incisive and insightful editing throughout and for her particularly rich contribution to Chapter 22.

JACQUELINE BERKE

CONTENTS

Introduction

Writing as a
Human Activity

And how is clarity to be acquired? Mainly by taking trouble; and by writing to serve people rather than to impress them.[1]

—F. L. Lucas

It is only when we view writing in its broadest perspective—as an instrument through which people communicate with one another in time and space, transmitting their accumulated culture from one generation to another—that we can see how vitally related our written language is not only to the life of the individual but to the total life of the community: "Greece and Rome civilized by language," Ezra Pound tells us. "Rome rose with the idiom of Caesar, Ovid, and Tacitus; she declined in a welter of rhetoric, the diplomat's 'language to conceal thought'!"

Pound uses the term "rhetoric" in the pejorative sense to mean tricks that are designed to deceive and confuse the reader or listener. But the classical meaning of "rhetoric"—and the meaning insisted on by modern rhetoricians—is the art of using language to its best possible effect: to teach, to delight, to win assent, to "energize" the truth, to move an audience to action—not ill-chosen or precipitous action, but considered and significant action. This ancient and modern view is best expressed in Kenneth Burke's deeply moral definition of rhetoric as "the use of language to promote social

---

[1]From *Style*, by F. L. Lucas. Copyright © 1962, 1955 by F. L. Lucas. Reprinted by permission of The Macmillan Company and Cassell & Co. Ltd.

cooperation in the human jungle." Thus the modern rhetorician—dedicated to the effective and forceful use of language—shuns verbal trickery, sophistry, and all forms of sensationalism and harangue, leaving these to the demagogue, the professional agitator, the propagandist, and the supersalesman. The rest of us—particularly those of us in a college community where our special task is to search out truth—are also expected to make our major appeal to reason rather than emotion: to inform and explain by indicating precisely *how* and *why;* to organize material in logical patterns; to argue by carefully reasoned, consistent procedures; to support, illustrate, demonstrate, amplify, and wherever possible *prove* our points; to express ourselves clearly and accurately. These are the touchstones of responsible writing.

It is imperative, then, that we write clearly, cogently, compellingly; that we build bridges to one another with our written discourse; that we use it to unite and not divide us. Although, thanks to twentieth-century technology, we may be said to live in a global village where electronic media connect even the most remote areas of the world, we are still tied to the written word as the basic means of human communication and interaction. On a personal and political level we still write *to* and *for* one another, as is evidenced by the increasing number of newspapers, magazines, and books that pour off the presses. And we are still tied to written communication for conducting the business of the world: the machine makers and button pushers follow written instructions; radio and television programs originate in written proposals, recommendations, and scripts; diplomats negotiate—endlessly—by means of formal correspondence (witness the huge collections of presidential materials in the Truman, Eisenhower, Kennedy, and Johnson libraries). Supplemented by film, tape, and record, the written document still provides the copious details that constitute the archives of our civilization.

Developing the Ability to Write

There is no question, then, that the ability to write clearly, cogently, and persuasively is a basic need in our time—a need that, unfortunately, goes largely unfulfilled. The fact is that most people write poorly—and thus with great reluctance. As one student complained, pointing first to his head and then to the paper in front of him, "It's all up here; I just can't get it down there." Although he thought this was *his* unique problem, this student was actually voicing everyone's problem. Writing is the act of transmitting thoughts, feelings, and ideas from "up here" in the head to "down there" on paper. "Putting black on white," as one author described his work, is very exacting and—when it is done well—very exciting work that requires many composite skills: (1) *mental*—you must be able to think clearly and to organize your ideas in an orderly, logical sequence; (2) *psychological*—you must feel free and sufficiently relaxed so that ideas will in fact move from head to hand, so that they will not "block" or elude the cast of words; (3) *rhetorical*—you must know the fundamentals of the craft: the variety of ways sentences can be put together to make a smoothly flowing, readable composition; (4) *critical*—once you have written something, you must be able to judge it, to know whether it is good or bad, and if it is bad, to improve it.

Students often admit that they realize a paper is poor when they turn it in, but they cannot improve it. They do not know *specifically* what is weak, *specifically* how it can be strengthened. Unless we can evaluate our writing in a concrete and constructive way, unless we learn to be patient and painstaking almost to the limits of endurance, we cannot hope to reach a level of excellence, or even competence. Professional writers who recognize that "hard writing makes easy reading," resign themsevles to drudgery: "I can't write five words but that I change seven," complained Dorothy Parker. "There is no good writing, only re-writing," said James Thurber, always witty, urbane, and unbelievably facile (or so it seemed). Surely writing was second nature to him! Quite the opposite, as Thurber himself said:

> The first or second draft of everything I write reads as if it was turned out by a charwoman. . . . For me it's mostly a question of rewriting. . . . A story I've been working on—"The Train on Track Six," . . . was rewritten fifteen complete times. . . . It's part of a constant attempt on my part to make the finished version smooth, to make it seem effortless.

To make the finished version seem effortless: this is the mark of a supremely good style. It is *unobtrusively* good; it does not call attention to itself. In fact, readers are barely aware of *how* the writer has written; they are aware only of *what* has been written; the subject matter alone stands out, not the writing. The writing flows smoothly, like a river moving with the current—inevitably onward.

Many people who write are simply not aware of what is involved in the writing process: the thinking, planning, assembling, classifying, organizing—in short, the prewriting that is prerequisite to a clear presentation (not to mention the rewriting that comes later). Others do realize what is required but stubbornly refuse to take necessary pains. Their writing is obscure and hard to read because they will not submit to the demands of the discipline. Unfortunately, we are sometimes forced to read the work of such authors (they surround us, alas; sometimes they even write textbooks). Reading them means rereading and rereading, for their prose is like an obstacle course through which we wend a weary and uncertain way—as in the following passage:

> In conformity with the preceding point, if all the interacting parties in marriage, in minority-majority groups, in different occupational, religious, political, economic, racial, ethnic, and other interacting groups and persons view the given overtly similar (or dissimilar) traits: A,B,C,D,N (physical, biological, mental, socio-cultural) as negligible values or as no values at all, as comprising even no similarity (or dissimilarity), such overt similarities-dissimilarities are innocuous in the generation of either solidarity or antagonism.[2]

[2]Cited in Albert Kitzhaber, *Themes, Theories, and Therapy* (New York: McGraw-Hill, 1963), p. 129.

Whenever possible, of course, the sensible reader refuses to read such gibberish, just as the sensible person refuses to visit a doctor who is careless or a lawyer who is incompetent. Clearly, the writer of the above sentence-paragraph is both careless *and* incompetent. To begin with, his thoughts are addled (we wonder, "Does *he* know what he is talking about?"). One phrase tumbles out after another in no discernible order; parentheses interrupt the flow of thought; the endless listing of abstract words, curiously hyphenated words, jargon, and unnecessary coding (A, B, C, D, N) make the head spin. It is impossible to follow or even *guess* at the writer's meaning.

Admittedly, you cannot hope that a basic writing course—or even a four-year college education—will make you a first-rate writer, a master of the craft. But you can hope and expect that you will gain important insights into the act of writing, that you will learn how to analyze a page of prose, to see how it works: why it succeeds as a unit of communication or why it projects only a hazy and possibly distorted notion of the intended meaning. Most important, you will gain greater control of your own writing; you will learn to write better and still better, with greater fluency and flexibility.

The Qualities of Good Writing

Even before you set out, you come prepared by instinct and intuition to make certain judgments about what is "good." Take the following familiar sentence, for example: "I know not what course others may take, but as for me, give me liberty or give me death." Do you suppose this thought of Patrick Henry's would have come ringing down through the centuries if he had expressed this sentiment not in one tight, rhythmical sentence but as follows:

It would be difficult, if not impossible, to predict on the basis of my limited information as to the predilections of the public, what the citizenry at large will regard as action commensurate with the present provocation, but after arduous consideration I personally feel so intensely and irrevocably committed to the position of social, political, and economic independence, that rather than submit to foreign and despotic control which is anathema to me, I will make the ultimate sacrifice of which humanity is capable—under the aegis of personal honor, ideological conviction, and existential commitment, I will sacrifice my own mortal existence.

How does this rambling, "high-flown" paraphrase measure up to the bold "Give me liberty or give me death"? Who will deny that something is "happening" in Patrick Henry's rousing challenge that not only fails to happen in the paraphrase but is actually negated there? Would you bear with this long-winded, pompous speaker to the end? If you were to judge this statement strictly on its rhetoric (its choice and arrangement of words), you might aptly call it more boring than brave. Perhaps a plainer version will work better:

Liberty is a very important thing for a person to have. Most people—at least the people I've talked to or that other people have told me about—know this and therefore are very anxious to preserve their liberty. Of course I can't be absolutely sure about what other folks are going to do in this present crisis, what with all these threats and everything, but I've made up my mind that I'm going to fight because liberty is really a very important thing to me; at least that's the way I feel about it.

This flat, "homely" prose, weighted down with what Flaubert called "fatty deposits," is grammatical enough. As in the pompous paraphrase, every verb agrees with its subject, every comma is in its proper place; nonetheless it lacks the qualities that make a statement—of one sentence or one hundred pages—pungent, vital, moving, memorable.

Let us isolate these qualities and describe them briefly. (They are described in greater detail in Part III, "Principles of Style: A Guide.")

Economy

The first quality of good writing is *economy*. In an appropriately slender volume entitled *The Elements of Style*, authors William Strunk and E. B. White stated concisely the case for economy: "A sentence should contain no unnecessary words, a paragraph no unnecessary sentences, for the same reason that a drawing should have no unnecessary lines and a machine no unnecessary parts. This requires not that the writer make all his sentences short or that he avoid all detail . . . but that every word tell." In other words, economical writing is *efficient* and *aesthetically satisfying*. While it makes a minimum demand on the energy and patience of readers, it returns to them a maximum of sharply compressed meaning. You should accept this as your basic responsibility as a writer: that you inflict no unnecessary words on your readers—just as a dentist inflicts no unnecessary pain, a lawyer no unnecessary risk. Economical writing avoids strain and at the same time promotes pleasure by producing a sense of form and right proportion, a sense of words that fit the ideas that they embody—with not a line of "deadwood" to dull the reader's attention, not an extra, useless phrase to clog the free flow of ideas, one following swiftly and clearly upon another.

Simplicity

Another basic quality of good writing is *simplicity*. Here again this does not require that you make all your sentences primerlike or that you reduce complexities to bare bone, but rather that you avoid embellishment or embroidery. The natural, unpretentious style is best. But, paradoxically, simplicity or naturalness does not come naturally. By the time we are old enough to write, most of us have grown so self-conscious that we stiffen, sometimes to the point of rigidity, when we are called upon to make a statement in speech or in writing. It is easy to offer the kindly advice "Be yourself," but many people do not feel like themselves when they take a pencil in hand or sit down at a typewriter. Thus during the early days of the Second World War, when air raids were feared in New York City and blackouts were instituted, an anonymous writer—probably a young civil service worker at City Hall—produced and distributed to stores throughout the city the following poster:

Illumination
Is Required
to be
Extinguished
on These Premises
After Nightfall

What this meant, of course, was simply "Lights Out After Dark"; but apparently that direct imperative—clear and to the point—did not sound "official" enough; so the writer resorted to long Latinate words and involved syntax (note the awkward passives "*is* Required" and "*to be* Extinguished") to establish a tone of dignity and authority. In contrast, how beautifully simple are the words of the translators of the King James Version of the Bible, who felt no need for flourish, flamboyance, or grandiloquence. The Lord did not loftily or bombastically proclaim that universal illumination was required to be instantaneously installed. Simply but majestically "God said, Let there be light: and there was light. . . . And God called the light Day, and the darkness he called Night."

Most memorable declarations have been spare and direct. Abraham Lincoln and John Kennedy seemed to "speak to each other across the span of a century," notes French author André Maurois, for both men embodied noble themes in eloquently simple terms. Said Lincoln in his second Inaugural Address: "With malice towards none, with charity for all, with firmness in the right as God gives us the right, let us strive on to finish the work we are in. . . ." One hundred years later President Kennedy made his Inaugural dedication: "With a good conscience our only sure reward, with history the final judge of our deeds, let us go forth to lead the land we love. . . ."

Clarity

A third fundamental element of good writing is *clarity*. Some people question whether it is always possible to be clear; after all, certain ideas are inherently complicated and inescapably difficult. True enough. But the responsible writer recognizes that writing should not add to the complications nor increase the difficulty; it should not set up an additional roadblock to understanding. Indeed, the German philosopher Wittgenstein went so far as to say that "whatever can be said can be said clearly." If you understand your own idea and want to convey it to others, you are obliged to render it in clear, orderly, readable, understandable prose—else why bother writing in the first place? Actually, obscure writers are usually confused, uncertain of what they want to say or what they mean; they have not yet completed that process of thinking through and reasoning into the heart of the subject.

Suffice it to say here that whatever the topic, whatever the occasion, expository writing should be readable, informative, and, wherever possible, engaging. At its best it may even be poetic, as Nikos Kazantzakis suggests in *Zorba the Greek*, where he draws an analogy between good prose and a beautiful landscape:

To my mind the Cretan countryside resembled good prose, carefully ordered, sober, free from superfluous ornament, powerful and restrained. It expressed all that was necessary with the greatest economy. It had no flippancy nor artifice about it. It said what it had to say with a manly austerity. But between the severe lines one could discern an unexpected sensitiveness and tenderness; in the sheltered hollows the lemon and orange trees perfumed the air, and from the vastness of the sea emanated an inexhaustible poetry.

Even in technical writing, where the range of styles is necessarily limited (and poetry is neither possible nor appropriate), you must always be aware of "the reader over your shoulder." Take such topics as how to follow postal regulations for overseas mail, how to change oil in an engine, how to produce aspirin from salicylic acid. Here are technical expository descriptions that defy a memorable turn of phrase; here is writing that is of necessity cut and dried, dispassionate, and bloodless. But it need not be difficult, tedious, confusing, or dull to those who want to find out about mailing letters, changing oil, or making aspirin. Those who seek such information should have reasonably easy access to it, which means that written instructions should be clear, simple, spare, direct, and most of all, *human:* for no matter how technical a subject, all writing is done *for* human beings *by* human beings. Writing, in other words, like language itself, is a strictly human enterprise. Machines may stamp letters, measure oil, and convert acids, but only human beings talk and write about these procedures so that other human beings may better understand them. It is always appropriate, therefore, to be human in one's statement.

Rhetorical Stance

Part of this humanity must stem from your sense of who your readers are. You must assume a "rhetorical stance." Indeed this is a fundamental principle of rhetoric: *nothing should ever be written in a vacuum.* You should identify your audience, hypothetical or real, so that you may speak to them in an appropriate voice. A student, for example, should never "just write," without visualizing a definite group of readers—fellow students, perhaps, or the educated community at large (intelligent nonspecialists). Without such definite readers in mind, you cannot assume a suitable and appropriate relationship to your material, your purpose, and your audience. A proper rhetorical stance, in other words, requires that you have an active sense of the following:

1. Who you are as a writer.
2. Who your readers are.

3. Why you are addressing them and on what occasion.
4. Your relationship to your subject matter.
5. How you want your readers to relate to the subject matter.

"Courtship" Devices

In addition to establishing a rhetorical stance, the writer should draw upon those personal and aesthetic effects that will enhance a statement without distorting it and that will "delight" readers, or at least sustain their attention. "One's case," said Aristotle, "should, in justice, be fought on the strength of the facts alone." This would be ideal: mind speaking to mind. The truth is, however, that people cannot be appealed to solely on rational grounds, or, to quote Aristotle again in a more cynical mood, "External matters do count much, because of the sorry nature of an audience." Facing the realities, then, you should try to "woo" the reader through a kind of "courtship," to use another of Kenneth Burke's expressions. In other words, you should try to break down the natural barriers and fears that separate people, whether their encounter is face to face or on the printed page.

What you must do is personalize your relationship with the reader by using those rhetorical devices that will enable you to emerge from the page as a human being, with a distinctive voice and, in a broad sense, a personality. Somehow the occasion on which writer and reader come together must be recognized as a special occasion, marked by a special purpose and an element of pleasure.

Rhetoric provides a rich storehouse of "courting" devices, and we shall consider these in Part III. For example, the pleasant rhythm of a balanced antithesis is evident in President Kennedy's immortal statement, "Ask not what your country can do for you; ask what you can do for your country." The lilting suspense of a periodic sentence (one that suspends its predication until the end) appears in Edward Gibbon's delightful account of how he came to write the famous *Decline and Fall of the Roman Empire:*

It was at Rome, on the 15th of October 1764, as I sat musing amidst the ruins of the Capitol, while the barefooted friars were singing vespers in the temple of Jupiter, that the idea of writing the decline and fall of the city first started to my mind.

Modern scholar Simeon Potter has observed that the word-picture drawn by Gibbon, although brief, is "artistically perfect":

The rhythm is stately and entirely satisfying. The reader is held in suspense to the end.

Had he wished, and had he been less of an artist, Gibbon might have said exactly the same things in a different way, arranging them in their logical and grammatical order: "The idea of writing the decline and fall of the city first started to my mind as I sat musing amidst the ruins of the Capitol at Rome on the 15th of October 1764, while the barefooted friars were singing vespers in the temple of Jupiter." What has happened? It is not merely that a periodic sentence has been re-expressed as a loose one. The emphasis is now all wrong and the magnificent cadence of the original is quite marred. All is still grammatically correct, but "proper words" are no longer in "proper places." The passage has quite lost its harmonious rhythm.

In addition to economy, simplicity, and clarity, then—the foundations of sound, dependable rhetoric—there is this marvelous dimension of "harmonious rhythm," of proper words in proper places. If you are sensitive to these "strategies," you will delight as well as inform your reader, and in delighting reinforce your statement.

The Student Writer

As Erich Fromm has said of the child, "He must grow until finally he becomes his own father," so we can say of the student writer: you must grow until you become your own teacher, your own critic, your own editor. Slowly you will cultivate a sensitivity to good, clear, unpretentious prose; at the same time, you will develop a negative sensitivity—an intolerance—to prose that is awkward, pompous, jargon-ridden, diffuse, dull. You will, in other words, be able to view a passage of prose, your own or someone else's, with a keen, critical eye, capable of seeing what has gone into it and of judging what has emerged as a finished piece.

Most important, when you have reached maturity as a writer, you will know how to go about the job of writing, no matter what your assignment. You will not feel overwhelmed or intimidated by your material any more than the carpenter is overwhelmed or intimidated by the unworked wood from which a desk or a bookcase must be constructed. In much the same way, you will act on your raw material and shape it in accordance with your will and plan. You will know what you want to say, even as a carpenter knows before picking up a saw what the final product is to be; you will organize your ideas in a logical, orderly sequence, even as a carpenter assembles the tools and maps out the steps by which raw wood will be converted into smooth, polished furniture.

Always in control of what you are doing, you the writer—like the artisan and the artist—will experience a sense of creativity. For, in truth, you *will be* creating. Indeed, the term "creative writing" should not be limited, as it often is, to poetry, short stories, and novels. *All* writing is creative when the writer forges out of his or her raw material (poetic images, anecdotes, statistics, a set of facts) a new whole: a poem, an expository article, an essay, a term paper. Any writer who understands language as a medium of expression and uses it in a deliberate and disciplined way to shape his or her purposes, factual or fictional, and to address a chosen audience, is working creatively and thereby producing creative writing. You should, then, regard all writing assignments, expository or otherwise, as a creative challenge; you are being called upon to create out of isolated, separate elements (facts, feelings, memories, ideas, and so on) a new whole which will be, as John Stuart Mill described a chemical compound, "more than the sum of its parts."

ASSIGNMENTS

As a reader, respond to the following passages, indicating whether you think they are well written or poorly written and why.

1. The data, in general, suggest that neither similarity nor complementarity of needs appears to be particularly meaningful in the determination of adolescent friendships beyond the suggested importance of similarity in a case where an extreme difference in friendship choices exists. However, both of these need patterns are internally consistent phenomena and perhaps are related to other factors. Similarities in perceptual and cognitive phenomena appear to be promising leads for future research in this area.
   —From a doctoral dissertation in education,
   cited in Albert Kitzhaber, *Themes, Theories, and Therapy*

2. Becoming a doctor is by no means a recent notion, it is a goal which has lingered with me since high school. I am not interested in going into a field of research or teaching, although I am quite aware that without these professions, medicine would not have progressed much from Hippocrates' time. My purpose for obtaining a M.D. is to go into the practice of medicine. To treat patients with the best equipment at my disposal and to establish a personal patient-physician relationship. To me being a doctor is not a five day a week job, one's work is not completed after office hours. A good doctor will be available when he is needed. I want to become a doctor so I can instill a feeling of security and trust in my patients and to convey to them that a doctor can be more than just one who prescribes medication. He can be someone to trust and turn to in time of crisis—a healer in the broadest sense of the word.
   A doctor holds an admirable position in today's society and being a physician offers security for the future. There is no worry about having a job for next year or that a bad winter will cause financial difficulties. I am certainly looking forward to having a family some day and expect to send my children through school. As a doctor I would be assured the ability to send my children through school and establish a happy life for my family.
   —Student application to medical school

3. I suspect that we have a good deal to learn from the 18th-century travelers. First, they saw that their books were printed with dignity, with fine type and wide margins on paper that had some texture to it. Second, they took with them an attitude of mind that delighted in the extravagance and eccentricities of the people they met on their journeys; they were far from being moralists. Third, they had a fine feeling for monuments, by which they meant palaces and castles, towers, churches and gateways, and all carved stonework and woodwork wherever it met the eye. Finally, they were in no hurry.
   —Robert Payne, "Florence Was Exciting, Venice Overrated,"
   The New York Times Book Review, June 5, 1966, p. 3

4. Of the two types of crime, namely crime as deviant behavior and crime as learned behavior, the theory of deviant behavior is implicit or explicit in most predictive studies. Also, personality differences which are ignored or considered unimportant in the cultural approach to crime are considered relevant in most prediction instruments, whether devised by clinicians or by sociologists. For example, stud-

ies have emphasized that delinquent recidivism is the result of failure of personal and/or social controls, whether in the family or in the local community. But from a learning viewpoint of delinquency the emphasis would have been upon accessibility to delinquent associates and upon the continued influence by delinquents as against conventional persons.

According to this paragraph, studies in the prediction of crimes emphasize ____ . Fill in the correct letter, choosing from the following answers:

A. Complete reliance on measurable community factors in terms of continued relations with delinquent or criminal types.
B. Deviations from conventional behavior as key clues in prediction.
C. Personality factors as more significant than cultural factors.
D. Primarily the direct linkages between learned behavior and crime incidents.
E. The relationships between persons outside the home rather than inside the family.

—From a New York City Civil Service Exam

5. You might have known it was Sunday if you had only waked up in the farmyard. The cocks and hens seemed to know it, and made only crooning subdued noises; the very bull-dog looked less savage, as if he would have been satisfied with a smaller bite than usual. The sunshine seemed to call all things to rest and not to labour; it was asleep itself on the moss-grown cow-shed; on the group of white ducks nestling together with their bills tucked under their wings; on the old black sow stretched languidly on the straw, while her largest young one found an excellent spring-bed on his mother's fat ribs; on Alick, the shepherd, in his new smock-frock, taking an uneasy siesta, half-sitting half-standing on the granary steps. Alick was of opinion that church, like other luxuries, was not to be indulged in often by a foreman who had the weather and the ewes on his mind. "Church! nay—I'n gotten summat else to think on," was an answer which he often uttered in a tone of bitter significance that silenced further question. I feel sure Alick meant no irreverence; indeed, I know that his mind was not of a speculative negative cast, and he would on no account have missed going to church on Christmas Day, Easter Sunday, and "Whissuntide." But he had a general impression that public worship and religious ceremonies, like other non-productive employments, were intended for people who had leisure.

—George Eliot, *Adam Bede*

Finding
a Subject

It is not true—as is commonly supposed—that professional writers are people who have something vital and compelling to say that drives them to the typewriter so that they can say it and be *done* until another idea comes along to drive them to the typewriter again and still again when a third idea crops up, and so on and on. More often, writers are people who have chosen to write because they find writing to be a delight, a disease, or a bit of both. But once having made this decision, they are not perennially brimming over with things to write *about*.

Like all writers who do not work on given assignments (as reporters do), you are periodically faced with a blank page and an equally blank mind. From the "booming buzzing confusion" of the world around you, you must somehow locate and lay claim to one particular, self-contained topic. You must, as Cicero said, "hit upon what to say." Once you have done this, you can go on to "manage and marshal" your materials and finally "to array them in the adornments of style" (to continue quoting Cicero). But first—and there is no getting around this—*first you must hit upon what to say*. It is an obvious first step, and yet until recently, with the revival of rhetoric, it was virtually ignored as an integral part of the composition process. The assumption seemed to be that the getting of an idea was the writer's own private problem. Seek and you shall find. Somehow.

There is some truth to this, of course; getting an idea is indeed a private, inner process; and if you wish to find, you certainly should seek. But *how* to seek? *Where* to find? It is not easy, because in the beginning you don't even know exactly *what* you are seeking—just a good idea. "I wasted the entire week trying to decide what to write about," says a discouraged freshman. True enough: he spends hours at his desk staring into space in morose silence, lamenting his fate, moaning, groaning, and chewing erasers off pencils (a pleasantly self-pitying approach, but not especially productive). He submits the finished paper disconsolately; it was written between midnight and 4 A.M. and proofread on the way to class. He knows it is not very good, but at least it is *done.* How he hates to write! If only he could think of things to write about. . . .

This student should be introduced to what classical Greek and Roman rhetoricians called the art of invention—finding something to write about. He should be made to see that this first step in the composition process is an art in itself that must be consciously and conscientiously cultivated. Briefly, it may be described as knowing how to "invent" or "discover" (classical rhetoricians used both terms) the subject of a discourse by putting yourself in the way of stimulation, the kind of stimulation that will actively generate ideas in your mind and thereby produce a specific topic and things to say about the topic.

These are the two main aspects of the art of invention: finding a subject and developing it. Like every other stage of the composition process, this first stage of finding something to write about can be dealt with actively and systematically. Even more important, it can and must be dealt with *creatively,* for finding an idea and preparing to mold it into a new and original whole is a distinctly creative process.

The aim of this section, then, is to explain how to go about the creative process of invention with appropriate creative energy and purpose. To help accomplish this aim we shall draw upon basic principles of rhetoric,[1] and concern ourselves with common-sense techniques like trying to find an idea by *looking* for it and by using simple, easily accessible guides such as the dictionary, which, called into service in this cause, is a rich source of ideas.

Checklist of Subjects

Here, then, are twenty subjects chosen from the most familiar and available of all reference works—the dictionary. (An encyclopedia, reader's guide, or any alphabetically arranged subject index will do as well.) The procedure is simple: thumb through the pages starting with *A* and move on through the alphabet, jotting down whatever terms catch your eye and your interest— whatever you *respond* to. You can be certain that an unconscious as well as a

---

[1] In Chapter 22, "Gathering Information," we shall deal with methods of probing the mind to gather information for an essay using the insights of depth psychology, for it is from the psychologist rather than the rhetorician that we can learn how to reach into the "inner psyche" and thereby activate a stubborn memory or stimulate a seemingly empty mind. In this process we must learn how to probe our own ideas and feelings; how to concentrate deeply; how to be receptive to images that are "not thought out but beheld." (Wolfgang Pauli, cited in Ira Progoff, *Depth Psychology and Modern Man* [New York: The Julian Press, Inc., 1959], p. 236.)

conscious process of selection is at work here, guiding you to one or another
term that appeals to you and that will therefore provide a good starting point
for the invention process.

1. American Indian	11. Nature
2. Assassination	12. Patriotism
3. Books	13. Poetry
4. Creativity	14. Poverty
5. Education	15. Prejudice
6. Family	16. Propaganda
7. Holocaust	17. Science
8. Intellectual	18. Symbol
9. Language	19. Women
10. Literature	20. Writing

Limiting the Subject

Let us begin with the first item on the subject list—American Indian.
Surely we cannot approach this subject as such, for it is as vast and formless
as the Great Plains the Indians once inhabited. Where should we begin?
How can we hope to cover the American Indian in less than a volume?
Clearly, the only sensible procedure is to *limit the subject,* to concentrate on
one or another of its many aspects. For instance, we could consider one
particular tribe in one particular place (Navajos of New Mexico). We could
limit the subject still further (Navajos living in New Mexico *at the present
time*). The subject is now more manageable in scope, more amenable to
essay form, although it is still not sharply focused as to what we will say
about the Navajos living in New Mexico at the present time. This will come
later (as we shall see), when we address a specific question to the limited
topic; only then will we arrive at the *real* topic—the thesis, or *point of the
piece.*

Let us move on to the third item on the subject list—Books. Here again,
we cannot reasonably expect to write a short, coherent piece about books in
general. Why not reduce the subject numerically, then, to *one particular*
book? E. M. Forster once wrote a delightful and engaging essay on "A Book
That Influenced Me"; William Golding wrote nostalgically and vividly of his
response to one childhood favorite, *The Swiss Family Robinson.*

We are not concerned at this point with the actual finding of a real topic,
but rather with the preliminary process of narrowing down a subject area to
some aspect of it that is feasible and encompassable in a single essay of
approximately 500 to 750 words (the average weekly paper in a college
writing course). This conscious, deliberate narrowing-down process is an
imperative first step in invention; without it we are likely to wander over a
too-large and amorphous field, never to get our bearings. Only if we resist
such overwhelming subjects as "Science" and contemplate instead a limited
subject such as three specific characteristics of the scientific spirit (Robert

Millikan, "The Spirit of Modern Science," pp. 60–62) can we achieve a unified and coherent unit of discourse.

To summarize: in selecting a topic for a paper, we should try to view it in terms of such limiting factors as the following:

1. a specific *kind*	not art in general, but pop art
2. a specific *time*	not art in all periods, but the last decade of twentieth-century art
3. a specific *place*	not universal art but art in America
4. a specific *number*	not all pop artists, but representative pop artists
5. a specific *person*	Roy Lichtenstein, a well-known pop art pioneer
6. a specific *type*	not all kinds of pop art, but serigraphs (silk screen prints)
7. a specific *aspect*	not art as a whole, but art as communication
8. a specific *example*	not pop art, but Andy Warhol's *Marilyn Monroe*
9. a specific *experience*	the first time you saw a pop art exhibit

Admittedly, there are times when the normal processes of invention are telescoped, as if by miracle, into a sudden flash of inspiration ("Ah, *this* is what I want to say!"), followed by a few blissful hours of pouring forth what we do in fact *want to say at a particular moment*. It is an exhilarating experience, this "inspiration," but we cannot *depend* on it. We must proceed by plan and regular procedure, as writers have done throughout the many centuries when rhetoric was taught as a formal discipline.

The Classical Topics

Having found and limited our subject, we must now go on to the second stage of invention: finding something to say about our subject, developing it. Let us turn to the classical rhetoricians, for although they were concerned largely with writing speeches to be delivered in public, they recognized the full sweep of the composition process: that it begins in the mind and the way the mind looks *out* upon its subject matter and *in* upon itself. Thus the orator was encouraged to read widely and to study conscientiously in order to "stock" the mind with subject matter. Cicero specified that the ideal orator was a person of vast learning and liberal education, trained in techniques to set the mind in motion, to entreat thinking, to stir memory, to coax imagination. Through these concrete procedures the orator was spared the torments of the blank page, the frustration of just sitting back and waiting for a topic to present itself. Aristotle went so far as to codify the invention procedure by reducing all possible topics to four categories:

1. what is possible or impossible
2. what happened or did not happen

3. what will happen
4. questions of degree (greatness or smallness)

Aristotle's list may seem absurdly oversimplified, but notice that on any subject these four categories are excellent places to begin thinking about what a writer might want to say (thus the ancient designation *topoi:* a place or region of thinking where an argument might be located and developed). Take an example of *topoi*—or, as we now say, topic—1 (what is possible or impossible): "By mining the sea, we can derive more than sufficient food-stuff to feed the hungry people of the world." The writer is asserting that something is possible—a familiar type of proposition. Topic 2 (what happened or did not happen) also provides a familiar proposition: "The Treaty of Versailles laid the groundwork for the Second World War." Either this *did* or *did not* happen; the writer who asserts either position must prepare an argument. Topic 3 (what will happen) characterizes all prophetic writing, from the simple weather forecast to full-scale analyses of future develop-ments in any sphere: why candidate X will win the election, why urban areas are heading for decentralization. The possibilities are endless. Finally there is topic 4 (questions of degree): "Human organ transplants are too widely and sensationally publicized, thereby creating a circuslike atmosphere around a serious new medical specialty." The proposition stands as an argument for *less* of something and, by implication, *more* of something else—privacy, dignity.

Aristotle's four basic categories plus certain other modes of analysis recog-nized among the classical rhetoricians—cause-effect (X causes Y); similarity (X is like Y); dissimilarity (X is unlike Y); example (X illustrates Y); conse-quence (X is a result of Y)—provided a kind of checklist of mental acts orators might perform when investigating and collecting arguments on a subject. Having this checklist available, classical orators were never at a loss, never driven to passive despair; on the contrary, they always had before them the prescribed "discovery procedures" that they could calmly and confidently follow, secure in the knowledge that by doing so they would locate their arguments and line up their proofs.

The New Heuristic

Wisely, then, classical rhetoricians refused to leave the matter of invention to chance and haphazard improvisation. They insisted on a formal *heuristic*, that is, a systematic inquiry into a subject matter—and into one's mind as well—in order to discover the best possibilities for discourse. Modern rheto-ricians are evolving a comparable heuristic, rooted in the classical system but strongly influenced by new concepts drawn from modern science, especially linguistic theory. We shall not describe this new heuristic in full here; we shall simply incorporate some of its more helpful features into a heuristic of our own—a method of inquiry suited to our needs in this textbook.

Asking the Right Questions

Actually, the substance of our approach can be summed up in a single phrase: asking the right questions. By using the question as a probing instrument—turned inward to the mind (a repository of dormant ideas) and outward to the subject matter (a source of data and information)—we are able to make discoveries, ultimately to generate a sharply focused idea. In every case, as we shall see, *it is the question, posed and answered, that is at the heart of any single piece of discourse.* For what else does the writer do but ask questions and then answer them?

The writer may be telling newspaper readers who robbed whose house and what was stolen; explaining in a magazine advertisement why Brand X cosmetic cream will prevent "crow's feet" around the eyes; describing in a controversial book the death of a president or the reasons for violence in American cities; analyzing the Lost Generation of the 1920s or telling its story in novel or play form; revealing secret military alliances in the Middle East; or rhapsodizing over the song of a skylark. Whatever the subject, whatever the temper and tone of the piece, the writer is forever answering questions. "And a writer cannot answer a question," as one journalist pointed out, "unless he has first asked it."[2] Nor can the writer achieve a sharp focus or a unified thrust in a piece of writing unless he or she is aware of exactly what question or questions he or she is posing, making certain to hold firmly throughout to a steady line of development so that the finished piece answers precisely that single question or those several questions.

Like the journalist, then, applying to all events the perennial "who-what-when-where-why?" the writer must always be prepared with the right set of questions if he or she expects to find a way into a topic, to stimulate thinking, to stake out a special area of interest, and to glean enough information about it to make a new whole—a unified piece of writing that is distinctly his or her own.

What are the right questions specifically? We shall consider them below and elaborate on the many ways they may generate and focus a piece of discourse. But first it will be well to caution against viewing a modern set of *topoi* with the same complacency Aristotle felt toward the "commonplaces," that is, the common places where one might go in order to invent an argument. The seeming completeness of Aristotle's survey of topics was, as we now know, largely illusory. There is no fixed number of topics nor of topic categories; the number is endless. Discourse is a process; one idea generates another in ongoing, open-ended progression.

Checklist of Twenty Questions

In this cycle of question generating idea, idea generating question, further questions generating further ideas, and so on and on, the following twenty

[2]Norman Lobsenze, *Writing as a Career* (New York: Henry Z. Walck, Inc., 1963), p. 15.

basic questions have been compiled. Although they have been stripped of all concrete subject reference, you should not be put off by their faceless aspect: the topic is referred to as "X" in order to keep the discussion on an abstract level. These twenty questions present ways of *observing* or *thinking about* a subject as "thought starters" to set the wheels of invention turning. As such they apply to any subject matter.

Suppose, for example, you have been asked to write a paper on anything that interests you. *Where* will you find a wedge into *what* subject? We have already considered ways of locating and limiting a subject; now let us examine this checklist of questions, each of which can provide the final, focal point of departure for your essay. Each question generates the type of essay listed in the right-hand column.

1. What does X mean?	Definition
2. How can X be described?	Description
3. What are the component parts of X?	Simple Analysis
4. How is X made or done?	Process Analysis
5. How *should* X be made or done?	Directional Analysis
6. What is the essential function of X?	Functional Analysis
7. What are the causes of X?	Causal Analysis
8. What are the consequences of X?	Causal Analysis
9. What are the types of X?	Classification
10. How does X compare with Y?	Comparison
11. What is the present status of X?	Comparison
12. How can X be interpreted?	Interpretation
13. What are the facts about X?	Reportage
14. How did X happen?	Narration
15. What kind of person is X?	Characterization
16. What is my personal response to X?	Reflection
17. What is my memory of X?	Reminiscence
18. What is the value of X?	Evaluation
19. How can X be summarized?	Summary
20. What case can be made *for* or *against* X?	Argumentation

Before we proceed to put flesh and bone on X by referring to specific subjects, a few important points should be made about the questions themselves. First of all, as you can see, they are not comprehensive. There are more questions you can ask of a subject than have been indicated here. So be it; even the newest of the new heuristics does not pretend to cover *all* possible approaches. In this case your imagination can fill in any gaps you may encounter. You may, in other words, invent your own questions or frame them somewhat differently if that helps you to focus your idea more precisely.

Furthermore, it must be admitted that there is some overlapping within the twenty questions themselves. This is inevitable, as every list compiler ultimately discovers, whether the list contains principles, rules, regulations, or questions. (Even the Ten Commandments overlap to some extent, as do the Seven Deadly Sins.)

Admittedly, then, these questions are not meant to be complete but only suggestive of the way the mind regularly and automatically goes about its business of thinking and thereby exploring the universe. Like Aristotle's "commonplaces," these questions represent some of the common places that the mind naturally travels to when it encounters a person, object, event, or idea in the outside world, or an experience, thought, feeling, or sensation within. "What is it?" we wonder. "How does it work?" "Why?" We are forever wondering about things and searching for answers and explanations; this is a natural, ongoing process of the human mind.

Applying the Question to the Subject-Topic

As we have said, the special job of invention is to start up a specific line of questioning *at a given time* when the mind may not necessarily be ready to perform; when it may be tired or simply lazy; but when there are, nonetheless, demands on it to think up something to write about. For it is by asking a question that we find a topic and by answering it that we compose our paper. Our paper, in other words, is the reply we make to the question we pose. No question, no paper.

In Part I, the heart of this book, each chapter is concerned with one of the twenty questions posed above. The selections reprinted in each illustrate answers to the question. For example, in response to question 1, "What does X mean?" psychologist Gordon Allport addresses himself to the nature of prejudice (subject 15 on our checklist of subjects). He answers the question by presenting four specific instances (pp. 37–38). Look now at Chapter 2, "How Can X Be Described?" John V. Young's essay "Moonrise Over Monument Valley" (pp. 43–44) is a narrowed-down, sharply focused presentation of the broad subject area "Nature" (subject 11 on the checklist):

Nature:	limited to one type of habitat	the desert
	limited to one country	United States
	limited to one state	Arizona
	limited to one place in that state	Monument Valley
	limited to one time	when the moon rises

To this narrowed-down aspect of his subject area Young addresses the question, "How can it be described?" His answer is given in the very striking and evocative description of the moon rising over "a limitless expanse of tawny desert."

It is not necessary at this point to review the many ways in which a writer *invents* or *locates* a topic by addressing a pertinent question to some aspect of a subject area. The table of contents for Part I provides abundant illustrations of how this heuristic works. Suffice it to say here that the heuristic (indeed, the art of invention itself) is not so much a formal technique as it is plain common sense. But it is common sense *applied in a deliberate and disciplined manner* to help you fulfill a particular assignment at a particular time and to make you relatively independent of "inspiration"; to show you how to find a topic when you *need* one, not merely when the spirit moves you.

It demeans neither the art of invention nor the heuristic (that is, the question procedure) to admit that they are essentially intuitive processes; you have been asking similar questions and inventing topics all your life. The aim of the procedure described here is to help you invent topics "on call," with more precision, originality, and ease. Eventually you will come to feel toward the heuristic something of the confidence and assurance that the classical orators felt toward Aristotle's "commonplaces." Eventually the question procedure will serve you in the same efficient and dependable manner.

ASSIGNMENTS

1. Using a dictionary or any reference work of comparable scope, make up a list of twenty subjects that interest you. They may be fields of study (astronomy, astrology); hobbies (glassblowing, raising guppies); sports (rugby, ice hockey, tennis). Almost any subject area—provided you are interested in it or know something about it—will offer a good starting point for the invention process.

2. Using the list of limiting factors cited on page 17, narrow each of your subjects to one aspect of itself (one specific kind, time, place, experience).

3. Select five of your twenty subjects and carry them through progressive stages of limitation (as on p. 21). Formulate your *real* topic by posing a specific question chosen from the list on page 20 to some aspect of your limited topic.

Writing a Short Paper

1 What Does X Mean?

Cicero said that every discourse should begin with a definition in order to make clear what the subject under consideration *is*. True enough: whether the subject is basically a matter of dispute or merely of discussion, a definition helps to clarify the issues. Definition, then, is important when the discourse depends on a term or terms whose meaning must be understood if the rest of the piece is to make sense, if the writer and reader are to stand on common ground. Thus many essays, articles, and books begin with a statement indicating how the author intends to use a given word, *what he or she means* by it.

In his introduction to *A History of Western Philosophy,* for example, Bertrand Russell states that since the term "philosophy" is used in many different ways, he will explain what *he* means by it:

A Definition of Philosophy[1]

BERTRAND RUSSELL

"Philosophy" is a word which has been used in many ways, some wider, some narrower. I propose to use it in a very wide sense, which I will now try to explain.

Philosophy, as I shall understand the word, is something intermediate between theology and science. Like theology, it consists of speculations on matters as to which definite knowledge has, so far, been unascertainable; but like science, it

[1]From *A History of Western Philosophy,* by Bertrand Russell. Reprinted by permission of Simon & Schuster, Inc., and George Allen & Unwin Ltd.

25

appeals to human reason rather than to authority, whether that of tradition or that of revelation. All *definite* knowledge—so I should contend—belongs to science; all *dogma* as to what surpasses definite knowledge belongs to theology. But between theology and science there is a No Man's Land, exposed to attack from both sides; this No Man's Land is philosophy. Almost all the questions of most interest to speculative minds are such as science cannot answer, and the confident answers of theologians no longer seem too convincing as they did in former centuries. Is the world divided into mind and matter, and, if so, what is mind and what is matter? Is mind subject to matter, or is it possessed of independent powers? Has the universe any unity or purpose? Is it evolving towards some goal? Are there really laws of nature, or do we believe in them only because of our innate love of order? Is man what he seems to the astronomer, a tiny lump of impure carbon and water impotently crawling on a small and unimportant planet? Or is he what he appears to Hamlet? Is he perhaps both at once? Is there a way of living that is noble and another that is base, or are all ways of living merely futile? If there is a way of living that is noble, in what does it consist, and how shall we achieve it? Must the good be eternal in order to deserve to be valued, or is it worth seeking even if the universe is inexorably moving towards death? Is there such a thing as wisdom, or is what seems such merely the ultimate refinement of folly? To such questions no answer can be found in the laboratory. Theologies have professed to give answers, all too definite; but their very definiteness causes modern minds to view them with suspicion. The study of these questions, if not the answering of them, is the business of philosophy.

Russell has done more here than look up the word "philosophy" in the dictionary (that repository of all accepted, conventional meanings of words) and set forth the *one* meaning he liked best or found most useful. In a sense, Russell has gone beyond conventional meaning in this definition; certainly he has particularized and elaborated on the conventional meaning in a way that is both inventive and illuminating. Thus, we do not receive from Russell any of the routine dictionary definitions:

1. Philosophy is the love or pursuit of wisdom.
2. Philosophy is the search for underlying causes.
3. Philosophy is a critical examination of fundamental beliefs.
4. Philosophy is the study of the principles of human nature and conduct.

Instead, Russell begins by locating the word with almost geographical precision: "Philosophy . . . is something intermediate between theology and science." We can almost *see* it:

Theology ⟵⟶ Philosophy ⟵⟶ Science

This spatial placement of a word accords with the original meaning of "definition," for the term is derived from the Latin *definire:* to put boundaries around. Thus, when we define a term we set up boundaries or limits that separate it from other terms, just as a fence separates one piece of land from another. An agricultural metaphor lurks in the background here, and it is appropriate, since the definer does in fact stake out for his or her term a special territory of meaning. Under the "No Man's Land" of philosophy, for example, Russell has very skillfully included all the traditional concerns of the discipline: questions relating to the nature of reality ("Is the world divided into mind and matter?"); the problem of good and evil ("Is there a way of living that is noble and another that is base?"); the possibility of knowledge ("Is there such a thing as wisdom?"). Russell concludes his definition by further restricting the domain of the discipline by indicating that it is the *studying* of these questions rather than the *answering* of them that is "the business of philosophy."

Like Russell's definition, many definitions are really introductory essays to larger units of discourse, ranging in length from one paragraph to several pages. At the same time, the definition can exist as an independent form—an essay in definition.

Finding a Subject in Definition

Whatever its form or length, however, definition offers vast possibilities to the student writer, for you can hit upon your topic simply by asking "What does it mean?" or "What *should* it mean?" about any term that seems uncertain, mystifying, curious, provocative, troublesome, or simply in need of refurbishing (one might strip away a hard crust of connotation, for example, to find a more fundamental meaning). As we shall see (Chapter 24, "The Limits of Language"), there are many abstract and ambiguous words in our language that mean different things to different people: a word like "excellence," for example, about which John Gardner said, "It is a little like those ink blots that psychologists use to interpret personality. As the individual contemplates the word 'excellence' he reads into it his own aspirations, his own conceptions of high standards, his hopes for a better world."[2] The same is true of words such as "honor," "loyalty," "liberty," "progress," "courage," "justice," "democracy," "capitalism," "communism" (any -ism). They are all "ink blots" and as such create an opportunity for an essay which may establish common criteria of meaning or offer a personal meaning, as E. B. White does in his essay "Democracy" (pp. 36–37).

In addition to ambiguous terms, you may contemplate words that are, in your opinion, not widely or well understood either because their meaning has changed or because they have acquired connotations. Linguists have shown that language grows organically, moved by its own inner forces. No external pressure—not even the most determined efforts of the strictest purists—can dictate its destiny. This does not imply, however, that the users of language may not concern themselves with the way specific words are faring. Since meanings often blur, it is appropriate that periodically someone reappraise a word by recognizing and redefining its boundaries. It may even happen, as in the case of the word "grammar," that in the course of its development a word will radiate so widely from its original sense that it will come to mean several different things, thereby requiring several different

[2]John Gardner, *Excellence* (New York: Harper & Row, 1961), pp. xii–xiii.

definitions. W. Nelson Francis' essay "Three Meanings of Grammar" (below) illustrates this point.

"What does X mean?" You might address this question to a word that you believe should be recalled to itself, that should have its original and potential fullness of meaning reviewed and restored. An essay could be written on the word "discipline," for example, in which the commonly used negative and restrictive notion of punishment would be replaced by the wider meaning of training. In actual, etymological fact the derivation of "discipline" is the same as that of "disciple": "one who learns or voluntarily follows a leader." Seen in this light, the word "discipline" carries no stigma; it means "making a disciple." Similarly the words "welfare" (welfare state), "charity" (handout), "intellectual" (egghead), and "politician" (opportunist) have all taken on negative connotations that you might decide are objectionable. Thus in answer to the question "What does it mean?" you might try to rescue a word from its progressive "degradation" by redefining it in a more affirmative context. A dictionary definition merely sums up and informs, but an essay in definition may agitate for reform.

Methods of Developing a Definition

There are many ways to develop a definition. Bertrand Russell, as we have seen, lists the questions that in his view constitute the subject matter or "business" of philosophy. Allan Nevins (p. 31) develops his definition of "history" by contrasting it with what it is *not*. Thus these writers establish the boundaries of their subject. The essays that follow illustrate various methods whereby the writer may set boundaries and in so doing answer the question "What does X mean?" It is worth noting also that most of the essays are structured, roughly, in three parts:

1. The need for a definition is stated.
2. Past or current uses are reviewed and shown to be inadequate, inappropriate, or confusing.
3. The writer's definition (often a restatement of diversely held notions) is offered and its application demonstrated.

By Citing Different Meanings of X

Three Meanings of Grammar[3]

W. NELSON FRANCIS

A curious paradox exists in regard to grammar. On the one hand it is felt to be the dullest and driest of academic subjects, fit only for

[3] From "Revolution in Grammar," by W. Nelson Francis. Reprinted from *The Quarterly Journal of Speech*, October 1954, by permission of W. Nelson Francis and Speech Communication Association.

Need for
definition
stated
those in whose veins the red blood of life has long since turned to ink. On the other, it is a subject upon which people who would scorn to be professional grammarians hold very dogmatic opinions, which they will defend with considerable emotion. Much of this prejudice stems from the usual sources of prejudice—ignorance and confusion. Even highly educated people seldom have a clear idea of what grammarians do, and there is an unfortunate confusion about the meaning of the term "grammar" itself.

Hence it would be well to begin with definitions. What do people mean when they use the word "grammar"? Actually the word is used
Current
uses are
confusing
to refer to three different things, and much of the emotional thinking about matters grammatical arises from confusion among these different meanings.

The first thing we mean by "grammar" is "the set of formal patterns in which the words of a language are arranged in order to convey larger meanings." It is not necessary that we be able to
Three
meanings
isolated
discuss these patterns self-consciously in order to be able to use them. In fact, all speakers of a language above the age of five or six know how to use its complex forms of organization with considerable skill; in this sense of the word—call it "Grammar 1"—they are thoroughly familiar with its grammar.

The second meaning of "grammar"—call it "Grammar 2"—is "the branch of linguistic science which is concerned with the description, analysis, and formulization of formal language patterns." Just as gravity was in full operation before Newton's apple fell, so grammar in the first sense was in full operation before anyone formulated the first rule that began the history of grammar as a study.

The third sense in which people use the word "grammar" is "linguistic etiquette." This we may call "Grammar 3." The word in this sense is often coupled with a derogatory adjective: we say that the expression "he ain't here" is "bad grammar." What we mean is that such an expression is bad linguistic manners in certain circles. From the point of view of "Grammar 1" it is faultless; it conforms just as completely to the structural patterns of English as does "he isn't here." The trouble with it is like the trouble with Prince Hal in Shakespeare's play—it is "bad," not in itself, but in the company it keeps.
Why the new
three-part
definition
is better
(it unravels
confusion)
As has already been suggested, much confusion arises from mixing these meanings. One hears a good deal of criticism of teachers of English couched in such terms as "they don't teach grammar any more." Criticism of this sort is based on the wholly unproved assumption that teaching Grammar 2 will increase the student's proficiency in Grammar 1 or improve his manners in Grammar 3. Actually the form of Grammar 2 which is usually taught is a very inaccurate and misleading analysis of the facts of Grammar 1; and it therefore is of highly questionable value in improving a person's ability to handle the structural patterns of his language. It is hardly reasonable to expect that teaching a person some inaccurate grammatical analysis will either improve the effectiveness of his assertions or teach him what expressions are acceptable to use in a given social context.

Summary

These, then, are the three meanings of "grammar": Grammar 1, a form of behavior; Grammar 2, a field of study, a science; and Grammar 3, a branch of etiquette.

By Citing Examples of X

What Is a Symbol?[4]

M. H. ABRAMS

Definition

A symbol, in the broadest use of the term, is anything which signifies something else; in this sense, all words are symbols. As commonly used in criticism, however, "symbol" is applied only to a word or phrase signifying an object which itself has significance; that is, the object referred to has a range of meaning beyond itself.

Examples of public symbols

Some symbols are "conventional," or "public"; thus "the Cross," "the Red, White, and Blue," "the Good Shepherd" are terms which signify objects of which the symbolic meanings are widely known. Poets, like all of us, use these conventional symbols; but some poets also use "private symbols," which are not widely known, or which they develop for themselves (usually by expanding and elaborating pre-existing associations of an object), and these set a more difficult problem in interpretation.

Example of private symbol

Take as an example the word "rose," which in its literal meaning is a kind of flower. In Burns's line, "O my love's like a red, red rose," the word is used as a simile, and in the version, "O my love is a red, red, rose," it is used as a metaphor. William Blake wrote:

> O Rose, thou art sick!
> The invisible worm
> That flies in the night,
> In the howling storm,
>
> Has found out thy bed
> Of crimson joy,
> And his dark secret love
> Does thy life destroy.

This rose is not the vehicle for a simile or a metaphor, because it lacks the paired subject—"my love," in the examples just cited—which is characteristic of these figures. . . . Blake's rose *is* a rose—yet it is also something more; words like "bed," "joy," "love," indicate that the described object has a further range of significance which makes it a symbol. But Blake's rose is not, like the symbolic rose of Dante's *Paradise* and other medieval poems, an element in a complex set of traditional religious symbols which were widely known to contemporary readers. Only from the clues in Blake's poem itself, supplemented by a knowledge of parallel elements in his other poems, do we come to see that Blake's worm-eaten rose

[4]From *A Glossary of Literary Terms,* by Meyer H. Abrams. Reprinted by permission of Holt, Rinehart and Winston, Inc.

symbolizes such matters as the destruction wrought by furtiveness, deceit, and hypocrisy in what should be a frank and joyous relationship of physical love.

By Contrasting X with What It Is Not

What Is History?[5]
ALLAN NEVINS

Need for definition

What history is *not*

Inadequate definitions

New definition

    Because history has been approached from many different points of view, it has received more amusingly varied definitions than even the novel. The cynic's definition of it as a *mensonge convenu,* a lie agreed upon, may harmonize with the statement attributed to Disraeli that he preferred romances to history because they told more truth; but it is a piece of baseless flippancy. It is precisely the fact that historians are always ready to disagree with each other which makes any persistence of lies in history—that is, true history—unlikely. Carlyle, approaching the subject from his special predilection, which emphasized the role of the individual, termed history the essence of innumerable biographies. But obviously it is a good deal more than that; it takes account of many forces which are not personal at all. John Cotter Morison defined it as "the prose narrative of past events, as probably true as the fallibility of human testimony will allow." Good so far as it goes, that definition is too pedestrian to be wholly satisfactory. Conversely, a familiar modern statement that history is the record of everything in the past which helps explain how the present came to be, is too philosophical and priggish. It emphasizes too much the utilitarian role of history, which we often wish to read without any reference whatever to the present—even to get entirely away from the present.

    History is any integrated narrative or description of past events or facts written in a spirit of critical inquiry for the whole truth. A definition which attempts to be more precise than this is certain to be misleading. For above all, it is the historical point of view, the historical method of approach—*that is, the spirit of critical inquiry for the whole truth*—which, applied to the past, makes history. It will not do to lay down a more exclusive formula. There are as many different schools and theories of history as the schools of philosophy, of medicine, and of painting. But it will be agreed that a newspaper report of some current event, a debate in Congress, a diplomatic exchange between France and Germany, is not history, because it cannot be written as an inquiry into the *whole* truth. Only superficial sources of information, generally speaking, are open to newspapermen. It will also be agreed that a Democratic or Republican campaign-book reviewing events of the four years just preceding publication is not history; it is not written as a *critical* inquiry into the truth. A careful historical novel, like Charles Reace's *Cloister and*

[5]From *The Gateway to History* by Allan Nevins. Reprinted by permission of D. C. Heath and Company.

the Hearth, holds many historical values. But it will be agreed that it is not history, for it is not written primarily as an inquiry into past *truth* at all, but primarily to entertain and please by an artistic use of the imagination.

By Tracing the Historical Development of X

The Meaning of Humanism[6]

ERWIN PANOFSKY

Nine days before his death Immanuel Kant was visited by his physician. Old, ill and nearly blind, he rose from his chair and stood trembling with weakness and muttering unintelligible words. Finally his faithful companion realized that he would not sit down again until the visitor had taken a seat. This he did, and Kant then permitted himself to be helped to his chair and, after having regained some of his strength, said "Das Gefühl für Humanität hat mich noch nicht verlassen"—"The sense of humanity has not yet left me." The two men were moved almost to tears. For, though the word *Humanität* had come, in the eighteenth century, to mean little more than politeness or civility, it had, for Kant, a much deeper significance, which the circumstances of the moment served to emphasize: man's proud and tragic consciousness of self-approved and self-imposed principles, contrasting with his utter subjection to illness, decay and all that is implied in the word "mortality."

Historically the word *humanitas* has had two clearly distinguishable meanings, the first arising from a contrast between man and what is less than man; the second, between man and what is more. In the first case *humanitas* means a value, in the second a limitation.

The concept of *humanitas* as a value was formulated in the circle around the younger Scipio, with Cicero as its belated, yet most explicit spokesman. It meant the quality which distinguishes man, not only from animals, but also, and even more so, from him who belongs to the species *homo* without deserving the name of *homo humanus;* from the barbarian or vulgarian who lacks pietas and παιδεια—that is, respect for moral values and that gracious blend of learning and urbanity which we can only circumscribe by the discredited word "culture."

In the Middle Ages this concept was displaced by the consideration of humanity as being opposed to divinity rather than to animality or barbarism. The qualities commonly associated with it were therefore those of frailty and transcience: *humanitas fragilis, humanitas caduca.*

Thus the Renaissance conception of *humanitas* had a two-fold aspect from the outset. The new interest in the human being was based both on a revival of the classical antithesis between *humanitas* and *barbaritas,* or *feritas,* and on a survival of the mediaeval antithesis between *humanitas* and *divinitas.* When Marsilio Ficino defines man as a "rational soul participating in the intellect of God, but operating in a body," he defines him as the one being that is both autonomous and finite. And Pico's famous "speech," "On the Dignity of Man," is anything but a document of paganism. Pico says that God placed man in the center of the universe so that he

---

[6]From *Meaning in the Visual Arts* (New York: Doubleday–Anchor Books, 1955), pp. 1–2. Copyright © 1955 by Erwin Panofsky. Reprinted by permission of Doubleday & Company, Inc.

might be conscious of where he stands, and therefore free to decide "where to turn." He does not say that man *is* the center of the universe, not even in the sense commonly attributed to the classical phrase, "man the measure of all things."

It is from this ambivalent conception of *humanitas* that humanism was born. It is not so much a movement as an attitude which can be defined as the conviction of the dignity of man, based on both the insistence on human values (rationality and freedom) and the acceptance of human limitations (fallibility and frailty); from this two postulates result—responsibility and tolerance.

By Enlarging the Meaning of X

The Security of Discipline[7]
FRANKLIN S. DU BOIS, M.D.

General introduction

From time immemorial discipline has been recognized as an essential ingredient of man's life. Experience has demonstrated that objectives can be achieved and individuals can be happy only if human energies are directed in an orderly fashion. Since a person's desires often conflict with the desires of others, society has set up regulations for the common good, to which each member of the group must adhere or suffer a penalty. Fortunate is the individual who can so govern the expression of his instinctive drives as to experience the least conflict in adaptation. Attainment of such adequate self-direction leads to the inner security, the preservation of mental health, and the integrity of personality necessary for wise decisions and ethical conduct. The well-disciplined person is guided by certain principles in which he believes, and he follows those principles because he has been taught by example, by training, and by experience, that intelligent action based on practical ideals brings satisfaction to him and to others.

Need for definition

Background meanings

New definition

To arrive at helpful conclusions, one must first have an understanding of what is meant by discipline. The immediate and restrictive connotation is apt to be what is done *to* an individual when he is disturbing to others, but we shall deal with the broader concept that *discipline is a process of training and learning that fosters growth and development.* Its derivation is the same as that of disciple: "one who learns or voluntarily follows a leader" (Webster). Discipline is, therefore, primarily the process of "making a disciple." Parents attempt to help their children become disciples of a way of life that leads to usefulness and happiness. They teach by precept and example, and their children learn by imitation and practice; consequently, techniques of discipline are less significant than the spirit of the relationship between parents and children. And in this relationship it is the warmth and genuine affection of both the father and the mother that is most important because, as Rose has said, "learned parenthood" is ineffective as contrasted with spontaneous feeling

[7]From *Mental Hygiene,* 36, No. 3 (July 1952), pp. 353–72. Reprinted by permission.

states of parents that make children feel wanted and secure in their efforts to develop independence.

How new definition applies

While discipline may carry with it an idea of punishment, this should be only the discomfort that logically follows the pursuance of a selected course of action and is voluntarily accepted as incidental to the attainment of a desired goal.

One speaks of the discipline of medicine, of art, of athletic training, when one refers to hardships foreseen and endured in an undertaking that leads to the chosen objective. Like the athlete, the child in training must learn to accept the restriction of many of his impulses. Discipline, in essence, means adherence to the rules of life; not a hardship to be endured intolerantly, but an educational opportunity to be welcomed enthusiastically, since it is only through discipline that lasting satisfactions can be obtained.

A child cannot be expected to see discipline in this light, but his parents must so view it. Parents must think in terms not only of the immediate behavior at two, six, or sixteen years—even though mismanagement of reactions in childhood can lead to fundamental character disturbances—but also of the ultimate results of discipline at twenty, forty, and sixty, when parental control is no longer in force. Then the individual must be constructively self-directed or else suffer remorse because of violation of his personal code, or be punished by society when his conduct is contrary to its laws. Hence, one should think of discipline as the educational process by which parents lead the child to independent self-discipline and the inner security of the wholesome, well-integrated personality that is characteristic of the emotionally mature adult.

You will agree that the enlargement of the term "discipline" is not altogether out of bounds; it does not strain either our credibility or the limits of language itself. This is a prerequisite, of course, of all definition: although it may depart from ordinary meaning, it must remain in the neighborhood of common usage. Because Humpty Dumpty's definition of "glory" in *Through the Looking Glass* was *not* within the neighborhood of common usage ("I meant," he told Alice, "'there's a nice knockdown argument for you!'"), Alice was forced to reject the word. Even in Wonderland it carried too private a meaning to have any exchange value.

Thus in trying to control or qualify the common meaning of a word, we may attempt to restore its original luster; or we may attempt to sharpen, deepen, enlarge, or enrich its current domain of denotation and connotation; but we may *not* try to rewrite the dictionary.

Formal Definition

If you examine the above definitions carefully, you will note that at the core of most of them is a three-part "formal" or "logical" definition (so called by rhetoricians). According to this pattern, a term to be defined is placed in a larger category or class; it is then distinguished from other members of the class by noting "differentiae." This process is illustrated below:

Term (to be defined)	*Class* (or genus)	*Differentiae* (distinguishing characteristics)
philosophy	is a field of study	that speculates on matters for which there is no definite knowledge and that appeals to reason rather than authority
grammar 1	is a set of formal patterns	whereby the words of a language are arranged to convey a larger meaning
grammar 2	is a branch of linguistic science	concerned with the description, analysis, and formularization of formal language patterns
grammar 3	is a branch of language study	concerned with etiquette
a symbol	is any "thing"	that stands for something else
history	is an integrated narrative of past events	written in a spirit of inquiry for the whole truth
humanism	is an attitude	marked by a conviction of human dignity
discipline	is a process of training and learning	that helps children become "disciples" of a way of life that leads to usefulness and happiness

Unlike the logician, the writer is not obliged to follow the logical formula *exactly*. Yet most good expository definitions have the three-part formal pattern, even if it is implicit rather than explicit. And most rhetorical definitions satisfy the basic *logical* prerequisites of a good definition: that the differentiae be neither too broad nor too narrow and that the definition be the equivalent of the term defined.

In any case, it is helpful for both the writer and reader to search out and apply to the rhetorical definition the basic logical patterning of a term, for nothing marks off an area of meaning with greater precision than the formal one-sentence definition. It often provides a foundation and thesis for the entire piece that may then be extended, as we have seen in the illustrations above, by any number of methods. Thus it may be stated as a general principle that whenever possible, the question "What does X mean?" should be answered by developing a formal, logical definition.

Experiential Definition

Formal definition is not always possible, however; some words are too inextricably tied to an individual vantage point: too subjective, too relative, too experiential. One such word, as Abraham Lincoln pointed out, is "liberty":

The world has never had a good definition of the word liberty. . . . We all declare for liberty, but using the same word we do not mean the same thing. With some, the word liberty may mean for each man to do as he pleases with himself and the product of his labor; while with others the same word may mean for some men and the product of other men's labor. . . .

The shepherd drives the wolf from the sheep's throat, for which the sheep thanks the shepherd as his liberator, while the wolf denounces him for the same act. . . . Plainly the sheep and the wolf are not agreed upon a definition of liberty.

—Abraham Lincoln, "Definition of Liberty"

What should the writer do, then, with such subjective words? The answer is simple. He or she can write an essay containing *not* a formal definition, worked out against fixed, objective standards, but rather a personal definition worked out on the basis of his or her own beliefs, feelings, and experiences. Thus the eloquent Judge Learned Hand had this to say about the spirit of liberty:

What then is the spirit of liberty? I cannot define it; I can only tell you my own faith. The spirit of liberty is the spirit which is not too sure that it is right; the spirit of liberty is the spirit which seeks to understand the minds of other men and women; the spirit of liberty is the spirit which weighs their interests alongside its own without bias; the spirit of liberty remembers that not even a sparrow falls to earth unheeded; the spirit of liberty is the spirit of Him who, near two thousand years ago, taught mankind that lesson it has never learned, but has never quite forgotten: that there may be a kingdom where the least shall be heard and considered side by side with the greatest.

—Learned Hand, "The Spirit of Liberty"

Similarly, E. B. White was moved, during the Second World War, to define "democracy" *not* by following formal procedures, but by exploring his own experiences and associations.

Democracy[8]

E. B. WHITE

We received a letter from the Writers' War Board the other day asking for a statement on "The Meaning of Democracy." It presumably is our duty to comply with such a request, and it is certainly our pleasure.

Surely the Board knows what democracy is. It is the line that forms on the right. It is the don't in don't shove. It is the hole in the stuffed shirt through which the

[8]This editorial first appeared in *The New Yorker*. It is reprinted with permission of the author from his book, *The Wild Flag*, Houghton Mifflin 1946. Copyright by E. B. White, 1943–46.

sawdust slowly trickles; it is the dent in the high hat. Democracy is the recurrent suspicion that more than half of the people are right more than half of the time. It is the feeling of privacy in the voting booths, the feeling of communion in the libraries, the feeling of vitality everywhere. Democracy is a letter to the editor. Democracy is the score at the beginning of the ninth. It is an idea that hasn't been disproved yet, a song the words of which have not gone bad. It's the mustard on the hot dog and the cream in the rationed coffee. Democracy is a request from a War Board, in the middle of a morning in the middle of a war, wanting to know what democracy is.

According to political scientist Anatol Rapoport, the personal definition is no less valuable than the formal; in fact, it is sometimes the best, perhaps the *only* way to formulate certain definitions—by indicating the feelings, experiences, and ideas associated with the term in question. What *happens* in connection with it? What is done? What is thought, felt? In Rapoport's view the question "What do you mean?" is essentially a request to share the experiences associated with the words you are using. In the following definition of "prejudice," for example, psychologist Gordon Allport achieves this form of "sharing" by citing four instances in which prejudice was "happening." Thus he establishes—as no formal definition alone could—the experiential common denominator of "prejudice":

The Nature of Prejudice[9]
GORDON ALLPORT

Before I attempt to define prejudice, let us have in mind four instances that I think we all would agree are prejudice.

The first is the case of the Cambridge University student, who said, "I despise all Americans. But," he added, a bit puzzled, "I've never met one that I didn't like."

The second is the case of another Englishman, who said to an American, "I think you're awfully unfair in your treatment of Negroes. How *do* Americans feel about Negroes?" The American replied, "Well, I suppose some Americans feel about Negroes just the way you feel about the Irish." The Englishman said, "Oh, come now! The Negroes are human beings!"

Then there's the incident that occasionally takes place in various parts of the world (in the West Indies, for example, I'm told). When an American walks down the street the natives conspicuously hold their noses till the American gets by. The case of odor is always interesting. Odor gets mixed up with prejudice because odor has great associative power. We know that some Chinese deplore the odor of Americans. Some white people think Negroes have a distinctive smell and vice versa. An intrepid psychologist recently did an experiment; it went as follows. He brought to a gymnasium an equal number of white and colored students and had them take shower baths. When they were nice and clean he had them exercise vigorously for fifteen minutes. Then he put them in different rooms, and he put a clean white sheet over each one. Then he brought his judges in, and each went to the sheeted figures and sniffed. They were to say, "white" or "black," guessing at the identity of the subject. The experiment seemed to prove that when we are sweaty we all smell bad in the same way. It's good to have experimental demonstration of the fact.

[9]From "Reading the Nature of Prejudice," by Gordon W. Allport, in the *Claremont College Reading Conference 17th Yearbook*. Reprinted by permission of The Claremont College Curriculum Laboratory.

The fourth example I'd like to bring before you is a piece of writing that I quote. Please ask yourselves who, in your judgment, wrote it. It's a passage about the Jews.

> The synagogue is worse than a brothel. It's a den of scoundrels. It's a criminal assembly of Jews, a place of meeting for the assassins of Christ, a den of thieves, a house of ill fame, a dwelling of iniquity. Whatever name more horrible to be found, it could never be worse than the synagogue deserves.
>
> I would say the same things about their souls. Debauchery and drunkenness have brought them to the level of lusty goat and pig. They know only one thing; to satisfy their stomachs and get drunk, kill, and beat each other up. Why should we salute them? We should have not even the slightest converse with them. They are lustful, rapacious, greedy, perfidious robbers.

Now who wrote that? Perhaps you say Hitler, or Goebbels, or one of our local anti-Semites? No, it was written by Saint John Chrysostom, in the fourth century A.D. Saint John Chrysostom, as you know, gave us the first liturgy in the Christian church still used in the Orthodox churches today. From it all services of the Holy Communion derive. Episcopalians will recognize him also as the author of that exalted prayer that closes the offices of both matin and evensong in the *Book of Common Prayer.* I include this incident to show how complex the problem is. Religious people are by no means necessarily free from prejudice. In this regard be patient even with our saints.

What do these four instances have in common? You notice that all of them indicate that somebody is "down" on somebody else—a feeling of rejection, or hostility. But also, in all these four instances, there is indication that the person is not "up" on his subject—not really informed about Americans, Irish, Jews, or bodily odors.

So I would offer, first a slang definition of prejudice: *Prejudice is being down on somebody you're not up on.* If you dislike slang, let me offer the same thought in the style of St. Thomas Aquinas. Thomists have defined prejudice as *thinking ill of others without sufficient warrant.*

You notice that both definitions, as well as the examples I gave, specify two ingredients of prejudice. First there is some sort of faulty generalization in thinking about a group. I'll call this the process of *categorization.* Then there is the negative, rejective, or hostile ingredient, a *feeling* tone. "Being down on something" is the hostile ingredient; "that you're not up on" is the categorization ingredient; "Thinking ill of others" is the hostile ingredient; "without sufficient warrant" is the faulty categorization.

Parenthetically I should say that of course there is such a thing as *positive* prejudice. We can be just as prejudiced *in favor of* as we are *against.* We can be biased in favor of our children, our neighborhood or our college. Spinoza makes the distinction neatly. He says that *love prejudice* is "thinking well of others, through love, more than is right." *Hate prejudice,* he says, is "thinking ill of others, through hate, more than is right."

In summary it might be said that the way you answer the question "What does X mean?" depends on what X *is* and what your purpose is in defining it. If you are trying to communicate what "prejudice" means *experientially,* then of course illustrations will best serve your purpose, for they bridge the gap most directly between words and experience. If, however, your purpose is to evaluate an alleged violation of the Fair Employment Practices Act, you need a general, working definition of "prejudice"; not the feeling or experience of prejudice, but the category of practice into which it may be classified and further described in terms of its "differentiae" (those distinguishing characteristics that, added together, could fairly be viewed as constituting "prejudicial treatment" of a job applicant). In this instance, formal, fixed, and objective criteria must be set up to indicate what constitutes prejudice toward a job applicant—formally, logically, and legally.

ASSIGNMENTS

Reminder: A definition, as pointed out above, is never written in a vacuum but always within a specific rhetorical stance, within a given context established by the writer to meet the needs of a given occasion. Thus, before you begin an assignment in definition you should visualize or (if the assignment is merely an exercise) *invent* the occasion that calls it forth. As a writer you should keep in mind a particular problem or situation, a specific audience, and a fixed point of view.

Class Discussion and Paragraph Suggestions

(See Chapter 27 for methods of composing unified, adequately developed paragraphs.)

1. Read the following definition and evaluate its structure, stated purpose, and the degree of success with which it fulfills that purpose.

What Is an Intellectual?[10]

THOMAS P. NEILL

In certain ways the word "intellectual" is not a happy choice in America, for it seems to set aside the individual falling within this category from the rest of society. But no substitute can be found for the term. We use "intellectual" here in a functional sense, as seems to be the common practice in this country. Thus Merle Curti uses it to include all who "are dedicated to the pursuit of truth in some special field or to the advancement of learning in general." This would include scholars, teachers, and perhaps others such as editorial writers, columnists, and serious journalists who are concerned with the advancement of learning. More specifically, Peter Viereck tells us: "I define intellectuals as all who are full-time servants of the Word or of the word. This means educators in the broadest sense: philosophers, clergymen, artists, professors, poets, and also such undreamy and uncloudy professions as editors and the more serious interpreters of news." In an attempt to separate the true intellectual from his pseudo counterpart or the "egghead"—from the blind specialist, who knows nothing but his specialty, and from the dilettante, who purveys what he does not really understand—Professor Charles Frankel describes the intellectual thus: "He has, in fact, become increasingly rare. He is the man who has made himself master of some definite intellectual skill or field of learning, and who knows from his own first-hand experience what the difference is between solid thinking and empty vaporizing. But while he cultivates his own private garden, he is also a man who looks beyond its walls occasionally and comments on the public world as it looks from his angle of vision." This definition excludes many scholars who are obviously engaged in intellectual activity but do not possess the broadness of view that Frankel would like all those deserving the term "intellectual" to have.

[10]Reprinted by permission of the publisher from "The Social Function of the Intellectual," *Thought,* 32, No. 125 (New York: Fordham University Press, 1957), Copyright © 1957 by Fordham University Press, pp. 199–223 at 200–01; abridged.

Let us accept as a functional definition of the term "intellectual" one who is engaged professionally in the pursuit or the propagation of the truth. This includes those who may be mistaken in their view of the truth as long as they believe they are pursuing or propagating the truth in their professional capacity. Just as the incompetent or dishonest physician does not discredit medicine as a profession, nor can it be denied that he is a physician, neither does the incompetent or dishonest intellectual discredit intellectuals as a class or intellectual activity as a profession.

2. Write a one-sentence formal or logical definition of each of the following terms. Compare your definitions with those of classmates, noting relative merits of each.

lawyer	idiot	navy
doctor	imbecile	marines
rhetoric	needle	psychotic
biology	pencil	neurotic
botany	rock	jet
archeology	rock music	star
photosynthesis	radar	book
fireplace		

3. Expand one of your definitions into a paragraph of 100–150 words, using the definition as your topic sentence.

4. Compare Bertrand Russell's definition of "philosophy" with Allan Nevins' definition of "history." How are they similar? Note their basic organization or structure. Examine each paragraph, noting its topic sentence, method of development, ordering principle, coordinate and subordinate sequences, transitional devices, tone, and point of view.

5. In a paragraph (150–250 words) trace recent changes in the meaning of one of the following words:

survey	affluent	computer
recession	retarded	beat
stoned	cool	tough
center	liquidate	loophole

6. About the spirit of liberty, Judge Learned Hand said "I cannot define it; I can only tell you my own faith." In a paragraph (150–300 words) tell your "own faith" in the spirit of one of the following words:

justice	honor	brotherhood
courage	sportsmanship	democracy
love	loyalty	idealism
freedom	charity	neighborliness

Essay Suggestions

1. In a form comparable to that of Russell's definition of "philosophy" or Nevins' definition of "history," write a definition (500–750 words) of one of the following disciplines:

literature	chemistry	sociology
music	physics	anthropology
history	geology	political science
economics		

2. Write a definition (500–750 words) of one of the following general terms, using the one-sentence, formal definition (explicitly stated or implicit) as a base or thesis:

patriotism	public opinion	mass media
plagiarism	libel	isolationist
atheism	heresy	internationalist
communism	reactionary	myth
(any) –ism	liberal	jazz
censorship	radical	temperance
poverty	religion	nature

3. In an essay (500–750 words) restore one of the following words to respectability by stripping it of negative connotations and redefining it in a more respectable light:

gang	exploit	censorship
politician	charity	slang
bookworm	cliché	militarist
shrewd	informer	welfare
manipulator	gossip	intellectual
idle		

4. In the manner of Erwin Panofsky's essay on humanism, write an essay (500–750 words) tracing the history of one of the following words:

romance	grammar	hussy	serious
tragedy	citizen	pride	undertaker
comedy	boor	science	scruple
epic	boycott	atomic	lynch
gossip	affair	bunk	corporation
logic	cad	scissors	rifle
rhetoric			

5. In an essay (500–750 words) written in the manner of Dr. Du Bois's essay on discipline suggest an enlarged definition of one of the following terms:

politician	bookworm	atheist
miser	cheat	agnostic
preacher	hero	religious person
soldier	coward	heretic
militarist	explorer	adventurer

6. In an essay (500–750 words) written in the manner of Gordon Allport's essay on prejudice, establish the common denominator for a term by citing three or four instances in which it clearly has application:

courage	wisdom	freedom
cowardice	intelligence	oppression
wit	genius	tyranny
love	patriotism	maturity
hate	discrimination	beauty
happiness	peace	violence

2 How Can X Be Described?

For the student who reportedly said that he would "have to run out and get run over by a truck in order to find something to write about," there is a simpler and safer alternative: address the question "How can it be described?" to some aspect of the environment—a person, a place, an object, or an event. Look at the sky and the stars; look at the school gymnasium and the used-car lot at the edge of town (your subject need not be poetic). Look up from your desk, look across the room, look at the window, look *out* the window, look out and *beyond*. Look and then answer the question "What does it look like?" Describe what you see, hear, smell, feel. Describe your sensations and impressions. Is it a dark and eerie night (scary?); a gray and bleak day (depressing?); a sunny and warm day, alive with people and laughter? Whatever is happening out there, take careful note; for as poet John Ciardi has said, whatever is looked at carefully is worth looking at— and, he might have added, worth writing about as well.

Like a definition, a description may be an essay in itself or part of a longer work (short story, novel, article, biography). Description is a necessary adjunct to all types of writing, because it reconstructs for the reader how something or someone *appears*. This above all, then, in writing description: you must have a keen eye; in fact, all your senses must be alert if you are to take in the scene and then reproduce it in a verbal picture that will come alive for the reader.

Sensory Description

The conscientious writer tries to probe beneath the surface not only to see what is there, but also to discover what can only be felt or surmised: the underlying mood or atmosphere, the sense as well as the sight of the subject.

Creating Mood in Description

Notice how successfully, yet how simply, the writer of the following essay has accomplished this deeper dimension of description through his skillful use of words that communicate not merely the visual and physical quality of the event but also its underlying mood and magic.

Words such as "mysterious" and "lonely," for example, evoke in their very sound a sense of mystery and loneliness; the descriptive term "diminutive wraith" (a succession of short, light "i's" followed by the emphatic and vaguely archaic monosyllable "wraith") suggests a small, other-worldly creature, a wisp and not an overweight chunk of a girl. Similarly, words such as "fantastically," "limitless," "towering," "enormous," and "massive" introduce a scene that is unmistakably larger than life, a blowup of the ordinary in which time itself is extended far back to an "ancient sea." Note the color words at work in this description: "red and yellow sandstone," "tawny desert," "silver ornaments," "darkening shades of orange," "pale saffron." Note the very precise shapes: "giant's chess pieces," "twin pinnacles," "miniature ocean waves," a "golden globe," a "massive disk," a "ragged skyline."

All these details, embedded in the sound and contour as well as in the meaning of the words, contribute to the total impact of the piece: we *see* the colors; we *hear* the rustle of the night wind; we *feel* the texture of the surrounding sandstone; we *sense* in our own muscles the relentless thrust upward to the sky where, soon, the moon will rise.

Moonrise Over Monument Valley[1]

JOHN V. YOUNG

We were camped here in early spring, by one of those open-faced shelters that the Navajos have provided for tourists in this part of their vast tribal park on the Arizona-Utah border, 25 miles north of Kayenta. It was cool but pleasant, and we were alone, three men in a truck.

We were here for a purpose: to see the full moon rise over this most mysterious and lonely of scenic wonders, where fantastically eroded red and yellow sandstone shapes soar to the sky like a giant's chess pieces and where people—especially white strangers—come quickly to feel like pretty small change indeed.

Because all Navajo dwellings face east, our camp faced east—toward the rising sun and the rising moon and across a limitless expanse of tawny desert, that ancient

[1]From "When the Full Moon Shines Its Magic Light Over Monument Valley," by John V. Young. © 1965–69 by The New York Times Company. Reprinted by permission.

sea, framed by the towering nearby twin pinnacles called The Mittens. We began to feel the magic even before the sun was fully down. It occurred when a diminutive wraith of a Navajo girl wearing a long, dark, velvet dress gleaming with silver ornaments drifted silently by, herding a flock of ghostly sheep to a waterhole somewhere. A bell on one of the rams tinkled faintly, and then its music was lost in the soft rustle of the night wind, leaving us with an impression that perhaps we had really seen nothing at all.

Just then, a large woolly dog appeared out of the gloom, seeming to materialize on the spot. It sat quietly on the edge of the glow from our camp-fire, its eyes shining like mirrors. It made no sound but when we offered food, it accepted the gift gravely and with much dignity. The dog then vanished again, probably to join the girl and her flock. We were not certain it was not part of the illusion.

As the sun disappeared entirely, the evening afterglow brush tipped all the spires and cliffs with magenta, deepening to purple, and the sand ripples stood out like miniature ocean waves in darkening shades of orange. Off to the east on the edge of the desert, a pale saffron glow told us the moon was about to rise behind a thin layer of clouds, slashed by the white contrail of an invisible jet airplane miles away.

We had our cameras on tripods and were fussing with light meters, making casual bets as to the exact place where the moon would first appear, when it happened— instant enchantment. Precisely between the twin spires of The Mittens, the enormous golden globe loomed suddenly, seeming as big as the sun itself, behind a coppery curtain on the rim of creation.

We were as totally unprepared for the great size of the moon as we were for its flaming color, nor could we have prepared ourselves for the improbable setting. We felt like the wizards of Stonehenge, commanding the planets to send their light through the magic orifices in line at the equinox. Had the Navajo medicine men contrived this for our benefit?

The massive disk of the moon seemed to rise very fast at first, an optical effect magnified by the crystalline air and the flatness of the landscape between us and the distant, ragged skyline. Then it seemed to pause for a moment, as if it were pinioned on one of the pinnacles or impaled on a sharply upthrusting rocky point. Its blazing light made inky shadows all around us, split by the brilliant wedge of the moon's path between the spires. The wind had stopped. There was not a sound anywhere, not even a whisper. If a drum had sounded just then, it would not have been out of place, I suppose, but it would have frightened us half to death.

Before the moon had cleared the tops of The Mittens, the show was over and the magic was gone. A thin veil of clouds spread over the sky, ending the spell as suddenly as it had come upon us. It was as if the gods had decided that we had seen enough for mere mortals on one spring night, and I must confess it was something of a relief to find ourselves back on mundane earth again, with sand in our shoes and a chill in the air.

In this strikingly vivid description we are there with the writer, sharing his campsite and his physical point of view—that is, his angle of vision, facing east across the limitless expanse of tawny desert. With him, we are turned toward the rising moon, and never—from the opening to the closing paragraph—do we turn away. Our position in relation to the subject is fixed throughout, even when we are momentarily distracted from the scenery by the appearance of "a Navajo girl wearing a long, dark, velvet dress gleaming with silver ornaments." Note that these few details enable us to see her as the writer saw her; note also that she reinforces the mood that is beginning to overtake the writer as he settles down in this "mysterious and lonely" place.

The girl could have been a distraction if the writer had presented her as clomping onto the scene. Instead she is silent throughout; her sheep are a "ghostly" flock, and the small bell on the neck of a ram tinkles only "faintly." (We can *hear* it blending with "the soft rustle of the night wind.") No wonder, then, that as she vanishes into the distance followed by the large, woolly dog—silent, grave, and dignified, with "its eyes shining like mirrors" as if to foreshadow the still brighter shining to come—we are left with the impression that they never in actual fact passed by; they were illusions, the work of a magician.

As the sun begins to sink there is a sudden cascade of color: magenta, purple, darkening shades of orange, and a pale saffron "glow." The stage is set for the instant enchantment that will accompany the rise—at long last—of the full moon, an "enormous golden globe . . . as big as the sun itself." The writer is obviously moved at this point, but happily he does not rhapsodize nor lapse into purple prose (" . . . its blinding light burned deep into my eyes with its illimitable luster and swept through my being like a spear of fire . . ."). Instead, he gives a calm, controlled, accurate, and unembellished report that rings true:

We were as totally unprepared for the great size of the moon as we were for its flaming color, nor could we have prepared ourselves for the improbable setting. We felt like the wizards of Stonehenge, commanding the planets to send their light through the magic orifices in line at the equinox.

How apt is the analogy to the "wizards of Stonehenge"; how well it develops the sense of mystery and magic.

So too does the sudden "still picture" of the moon as it seems to pause for a moment "pinioned on one of the pinnacles." (Note the arresting alliteration of "p's" that themselves cause a moment's pause.) We move in, as if for a camera close-up, to see what it looks like: "Its blazing light made inky shadows all around us, split by the brilliant wedge of the moon's path between the spires."

The massive disk of the moon clears the tops of The Mittens and abruptly disappears: "The show was over and the magic was gone." As a thin veil of clouds passes over, the writer returns us to earth, telling us that we are "mere mortals" after all, and proving his point by evoking the concrete image (and thereby the tactile sensation) of "sand in our shoes and a chill in the air."

Effective Selection of Detail

Clearly, a good description must evoke sensory impressions, for only then can the reader begin to respond totally. Although several senses may be called into play, the visual will usually predominate, since most of us use our eyes as a primary guide and as a check or verifier of our other senses. (Thus Shakespeare, in *A Midsummer Night's Dream,* has Bottom rush into the woods "to see a noise that he heard.") It is not surprising, then, that most descriptions focus on how something or someone looked.

Take, for example, Sophia, the lovely heroine of *Tom Jones:*

Sophia, ... the only daughter of Mr. Western, was a middle-sized woman; but rather inclining to tall. Her shape was not only exact, but extremely delicate; and the nice proportion of her arms promised the truest symmetry in her limbs. Her hair, which was black, was so luxuriant that it reached her middle, before she cut it to comply with the modern fashion; and it was now curled so gracefully in her neck that few could believe it to be her own. If envy could find any part of the face which demanded less commendation than the rest, it might possibly think her forehead might have been higher without prejudice to her. Her eyebrows were full, even, and arched beyond the power of art to imitate. Her black eyes had a lustre in them which all her softness could not extinguish.

Fielding does not give all the details of Sophia's physical appearance; an overly detailed listing would be tedious and dull. Just as in "Moonrise Over Monument Valley" the writer selects those details that help to create the dominant mood of the piece, in the description of Sophia we are given a selection of details that enables us to see her in our mind's eye: she is tall, with nice proportions (the overall contour of the person); she is delicate (the texture or "aura" of her); her black hair curls gracefully on her neck; she has a relatively low forehead (perhaps a *slight* imperfection to make her seem more human); she has lovely arched eyebrows and lustrous black eyes (proverbially "the windows of the soul"). One need not carry the description further; for all practical purposes, Sophia has been described. The first principle of description, then, is careful selection of detail.

Arrangement: Physical Point of View

The second basic principle of description is to arrange details methodically, not in haphazard or random fashion, but in a given order that is either inherent in the subject or dictated by the context. In "Moonrise Over Monument Valley," for example, the description is organized so that the writer tells "what it looked like" by relating "how it happened," a step-by-step description of a process (the rising of the moon) *necessarily* arranged in chronological order.

Another important aspect of arrangement of details is to maintain a consistent physical point of view—that is, to describe the subject as it is observed and to include only what can be observed. There are basically two physical points of view: the fixed and the moving. Fielding's description of Sophia, for example, is written from the point of view of a person standing in front of her (a fixed observer); Fielding does not tell us what Sophia's back looks like. The following short passage presents a scene from the viewpoint of an observer whose eyes move from left to right. (An example of the moving observer is found in the Mark Twain selection reprinted below.)

View from Rochester Bridge

CHARLES DICKENS

On the left of the spectator lay the ruined wall, broken in many places, and in some, overhanging the narrow beach below in rude and heavy masses. Huge knots of sea-weed hung upon the jagged and pointed stones, trembling in every breath of wind; and the green ivy clung mournfully round the dark and ruined battlements. Behind it rose the ancient castle, its towers roofless, and its massive walls crumbling away, but telling us proudly of its own might and strength, as when, seven hundred years ago, it rang with the clash of arms, or resounded with the noise of feasting and revelry. On either side, the banks of the Medway, covered with corn-fields and pastures, with here and there a windmill, or a distant church, stretched away as far as the eye could see, presenting a rich and varied landscape, rendered more beautiful by the changing shadows which passed swiftly across it, as the thin and half-formed clouds skimmed away in the light.of the morning sun. The river, reflecting the clear blue of the sky, glistened and sparkled as it flowed noiselessly on; and the oars of the fishermen dipped into the water with a clear and liquid sound, as the heavy but picturesque boats glided slowly down the stream.

Tone: Psychological Point of View

In addition to maintaining a consistent physical point of view toward the subject, the writer of description must maintain a consistent attitude—a psychological point of view—to ensure unity of effect. In the following passage from *Life on the Mississippi,* note first how Mark Twain uses the physical point of view of the moving observer. We move at his elbow on a tour of "the house beautiful" of the Midwest in mid–nineteenth-century America; we move from outside to inside to hallway to parlor to bedrooms. Unlike Dickens surveying Rochester Bridge, from one stationary point, Twain keeps us moving.

Note also that the details in this sketch are overwhelming—and deliberately so. The house itself, certainly the main parlor, is overwhelmingly and outrageously overcrowded, incredibly elaborate, and essentially uncomfortable (with its horsehair sofa "which keeps sliding from under you"), lacking in taste, originality, or restraint. Nothing less than a total description will reveal it for what it is: a middle-class monstrosity. This description, then—amusing and entertaining as it is—is actually more than description; it presents an attitude toward and a commentary on a way of life. And these, in turn, establish the special tone of the piece.

The House Beautiful

MARK TWAIN

Every town and village along that vast stretch of double river frontage had a best dwelling, finest dwelling, mansion,—the home of its wealthiest and most conspicuous citizen. It is easy to describe it: large grassy yard, with paling fence painted white—in fair repair; brick walk from gate to door; big, square, two-story "frame" house, painted white and porticoed like a Grecian temple—with this difference, that the imposing fluted columns and Corinthian capitals were a pathetic sham, being made of white pine, and painted; iron knocker; brass door knob—discolored, for lack of polishing. Within, an uncarpeted hall, of planed boards; opening out of it, a parlor, fifteen feet by fifteen—in some instances five or ten feet larger; ingrain carpet; mahogany center-table; lamp on it, with green paper shade—standing on a gridiron, so to speak, made of high-colored yarns, by the young ladies of the house, and called a lamp mat; several books, piled and disposed, with cast-iron exactness, according to an inherited and unchangeable plan; among them, Tupper, much penciled; also, *Friendship's Offering,* and *Affection's Wreath,* with their sappy inanities illustrated in die-away mezzotints; also, Ossian; *Alonzo and Melissa;* maybe *Ivanhoe;* also *Album,* full of original "poetry" of the Thou-hast-wounded-the-spirit-that-loved-thee breed; two or three goody-goody works—*Shepherd of Salisbury Plain,* etc.; current number of the chaste and innocuous *Godey's Lady's Book,* with painted fashion plate of wax-figure women with mouths all alike—lips and eyelids the same size—each five-foot woman with a two-inch wedge sticking from under her dress and letting on to be half of her foot. Polished airtight stove (new and deadly invention), with pipe passing through a board which closes up the discarded good old fireplace. On each end of the wooden mantel, over the fireplace, a large basket of peaches and other fruits, natural size, all done in plaster, rudely, or in wax, and painted to resemble the originals—which they don't. Over middle of mantel, engraving—Washington Crossing the Delaware; on the wall by the door, copy of it done in thunder-and-lightning crewels by one of the young ladies—work of art which would have made Washington hesitate about crossing, if he could have foreseen what advantage was going to be taken of it. Piano—kettle in disguise—with music, bound and unbound, piled on it, and on a stand near by: "Battle of Prague"; "Bird Waltz"; "Arkansas Traveler"; "Rosin the Bow"; "Marseilles Hymn"; "On a Lone Barren Isle" (St. Helena); "The Last Link Is Broken"; "She Wore a Wreath of Roses the Night When Last We Met"; "Go, Forget Me, Why Should Sorrow o'er that Brow a Shadow Fling"; "Hours There Were to Memory Dearer"; "Long, Long Ago"; "Days of Absence"; "A Life on the Ocean Wave, a Home on the Rolling Deep"; "Bird at Sea"; and spread open on the rack, where the plaintive singer has left it, *Ro*-holl on, silver *moo*-hoon, guide the *trav*-el-lerr his way, etc. Tilted pensively against the piano, a guitar—guitar capable of playing the Spanish fandango by itself, if you give it a start. Frantic work of art on the wall—pious motto, done on the premises, sometimes in colored yarns, sometimes in faded grasses: progenitor of the "God Bless Our Home" of modern commerce. Framed in black moldings on the wall, other works of art, conceived and committed on the premises, by the young ladies; being grim black-and-white crayons; landscapes, mostly: lake, solitary sailboat, petrified clouds, pre-geological trees on shore, anthracite precipice; name of criminal conspicuous in the corner. Lithograph, Napoleon Crossing the Alps. Lithograph, The Grave at St. Helena. Steel plates, Trumbull's Battle of Bunker Hill, and the Sally from Gibraltar. Copperplates, Moses Smiting the Rock, and Return of the Prodigal Son. In big gilt frame, a slander of the family in oil: papa holding a book ("Constitution of the United States"); guitar leaning against Mama, blue ribbons fluttering from its neck; the young ladies, as children, in slippers and scalloped pantalettes, one embracing toy horse, the other beguiling kitten with ball of yarn, and both simpering up at Mama, who simpers back. These persons all fresh, raw, and red—apparently skinned. Opposite, in gilt frame, grandpa and grandma, at thirty and twenty-two, stiff, old-fashioned, high-collared, puff-sleeved, glaring pallidly out from a background of solid Egyptian night. Under a glass French clock dome, large bouquet of stiff flowers done in corpsy white wax. Pyramidal whatnot in the corner, the shelves occupied chiefly with bric-a-brac of the period, disposed with an eye to best effect: shell, with the Lord's Prayer carved on it; another shell—of the long-oval sort, narrow, straight orifice, three inches long, running from end to end—portrait of Washington carved on it; not well done; the shell had Washington's mouth, originally—artist should have built to that. These two are memorials of the long-ago bridal trip to New Orleans and the French Market. Other bric-a-brac: Californian "specimens"—quartz, with gold wart adhering; old Guinea-gold locket, with circlet of ancestral hair in it; Indian arrowheads, of flint; pair of bead moccasins, from uncle who crossed the Plains; three "alum" baskets of various colors—being skeleton frame of wire, clothed-on with cubes of crystallized alum in the rock-candy style—works of art which were achieved by the young ladies; their doubles and duplicates to be found upon all whatnots in the land; convention of desiccated bugs and butterflies pinned to a card; painted toy dog, seated upon bellows attachment—drops its under jaw and squeaks when pressed upon; sugar-candy rabbit—limbs and features merged together, not strongly defined; pewter presidential-campaign medal; miniature cardboard wood sawyer, to be attached to the stovepipe and operated by the heat; small Napoleon, done in wax; spread-open daguerreotypes of dim children, parents, cousins, aunts and friends, in all attitudes but customary ones; no templed portico at back, and manufactured landscape stretching away in the distance—that came in later, with the photograph; all these vague figures lavishly chained and ringed—metal indicated and secured from doubt by stripes and splashes of vivid gold bronze; all of them too much combed, too much fixed up; and all of them uncomfortable in inflexible Sunday clothes of a pattern which the spectator cannot realize could ever have been in fashion; husband and wife generally grouped together—husband sitting, wife standing, with hand on his shoulder—and both preserving, all these fading years, some traceable effect of the daguerreotypist's brisk "Now smile, if you please!" Bracketed over whatnot—place of special sacredness—an outrage in water color, done by the young niece that came on a visit long ago, and died. Pity, too; for she might have repented of this in time. Horsehair chairs, horsehair sofa which keeps sliding from under you. Window shades of oil stuff, with milkmaids and ruined castles stenciled on them in fierce colors. Lambrequins dependant from gaudy boxings of beaten tin, gilded. Bedrooms with rag carpets; bedstead of the "corded" sort, with a sag in the middle, the cords needing tightening; snuffy feather bed—not aired often enough; cane-seat chairs, splint-bottomed rocker; looking glass on wall, school-slate size, veneered frame; inherited bureau; washbowl and pitcher, possibly—but not certainly; brass candlestick, tallow candle, snuffers. Nothing else in the room. Not a bathroom in the house; and no visitor likely to come along who has ever seen one.

That was the residence of the principal citizen, all the way from the suburbs of New Orleans to the edge of St. Louis.

To produce a unified effect, then, a description should embody a consistent psychological as well as physical point of view—that is, the writer should generate throughout the piece a particular tone and a consistent attitude toward the subject: a sense of awe and wonder ("Moonrise Over Monument Valley"); of appreciative delight ("Sophia"); of amusement ("The House Beautiful"). Obviously there are no restrictions as to tone; the only imperative is that the tone be maintained consistently throughout.

Technical Description

In addition to sensory or impressionistic description there is another type: technical or scientific description, which focuses exclusively on what is literally, physically, and palpably there; what can be objectively perceived, measured, checked, and verified. The describer tries to be objective, dispassionate, reliable, and fair, respecting the subject as it is, for what it is; adding no comments or asides; offering no personal interpretation or aesthetic judgment. Technical description appeals to the understanding rather than the senses or the emotions. It is limited in scope, but it is also very useful and important, especially for students in the sciences, technology, and business, for they will be asked to describe subjects such as an amoeba under a microscope, a Diesel engine, a computer program. Each of these requires a detached approach, a clear eye, and an equally clear, direct, matter-of-fact style of writing—with no rhetorical flourishes or personal digressions.

Take the following description, for example. This, says the writer, is what the common grasshopper looks like:

The Grasshopper[2]

JOHN C. PALLESTER

Grasshopper species are distributed in a wide belt around the world, extending from the cold regions of the north to those of the south. They range up to the snow fringes of mountains and have reached many isolated oceanic islands. These insects are generally large, averaging about two inches in length; the range is from a half inch to six inches. About 18,000 species are known.

The head is rather large and solidly built; the forewings are usually strong. There are two rather compound eyes, three ocelli (simple eyes), two short antennae—less

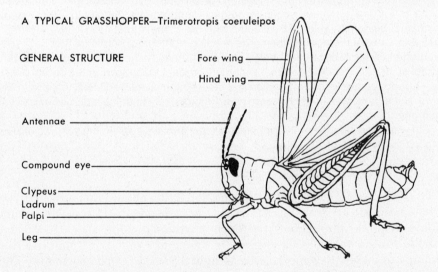

A TYPICAL GRASSHOPPER—Trimerotropis coeruleipos

GENERAL STRUCTURE

Fore wing
Hind wing

Antennae
Compound eye
Clypeus
Ladrum
Palpi
Leg

[2]Reprinted from *The Book of Popular Science* by permission of the publishers, Grolier Incorporated, New York.

than half the length of the body—and a powerful set of jaws. The front wings cover the more delicate rear wings when the insect is at rest. The front and middle pair of legs are short and are used for walking. The rear legs, which serve for leaping, are large and strongly muscled. They catapult the insect several feet into the air. Here the powerful wings take over, sometimes for extended flights of many miles. The legs are armed with rows of spines. These aid the insect in pushing through thick vegetation and also serve as defensive armament against a pursuing enemy.

Along the inner surface of each upper hind leg of many grasshoppers is an elevated, sharp ridge. This may be smooth or notched. There is also a raised vein on each tegmen, or forewing. When the grasshopper scrapes his legs against his tegmina, he produces the familiar rasping noise we associate with his kind.

In contrast, then, to the sensory or impressionistic description, the technical description is addressed exclusively to the mind, providing data that even a camera would miss: the ridge on the inner surface of each of the grasshopper's upper hind legs. It omits details that would strike us immediately in a photograph or that would be essential in a sensory description: the color and texture of the skin, the shape of the eyes. Although the technical description does not give us a visual impression of the grasshopper, it serves its own unique purpose. It enables us, without any further aids but the attributes included in the description, to identify an unknown insect as a grasshopper.

It is worth noting, finally, that like many technical or scientific descriptions, this one uses an illustration to supplement the verbal picture, providing both an overall perspective and a set of details that words alone cannot communicate. Thus, whenever possible, the writer of a technical description should try to include a diagrammatic representation or illustration of what is being described.

As is true of many types of writing, the distinction between technical and sensory description is not always sharp. Occasionally, in a scientific description the writer uses details mainly for sensory effect, and more frequently the writer of a sensory description includes technical details that appeal to our understanding rather than our senses. In James Agee's description of a Southern cemetery, below, the details are so strange and unfamiliar as to be barely believable. Yet we are moved to belief because the painstakingly rendered details and the matter-of-fact tone give the piece a documentary solidity. On the one hand, the description offers objective data ("The graveyard is about fifty by a hundred yards . . ."); on the other hand, it offers vivid sense impressions ("It is heavily silent and fragrant and all the leaves are breathing slowly . . ."). For many reasons, and on many levels, this essay in description will repay close study.

ASSIGNMENTS

Class Discussion and Paragraph Suggestions

(See Chapter 27 for methods of composing unified, adequately developed paragraphs.)

1. Read the following descriptive essay.

Shady Grove, Alabama, July 1936[3]

JAMES AGEE

The graveyard is about fifty by a hundred yards inside a wire fence. There are almost no trees in it: a lemon verbena and a small magnolia; it is all red clay and very few weeds.

Out at the front of it across the road there is a cornfield and then a field of cotton and then trees.

Most of the headboards are pine, and at the far end of the yard from the church the graves are thinned out and there are many slender and low pine stumps about the height of the headboards. The shadows are all struck sharp lengthwise of the graves, toward the cornfield, by the afternoon sun. There is no one anywhere in sight. It is heavily silent and fragrant and all the leaves are breathing slowly without touching each other.

Some of the graves have real headstones, a few of them so large they must be the graves of landowners. One is a thick limestone log erected by the Woodmen of the World. One or two of the others, besides a headpiece, have a flat of stone as large as the whole grave.

On one of these there is a china dish on whose cover delicate hands lie crossed, cuffs at their wrists, and the nails distinct.

On another a large fluted vase stands full of dead flowers, with an inch of rusty water at the bottom.

On others of these stones, as many as a dozen of them, there is something I have never seen before: by some kind of porcelain reproduction, a photograph of the person who is buried there; the last or the best likeness that had been made, in a small-town studio, or at home with a snapshot camera. I remember one well of a fifteen-year-old boy in Sunday pants and a plaid pull-over sweater, his hair combed, his cap in his hand, sitting against a piece of farm machinery and grinning. His eyes are squinted against the light and his nose makes a deep shadow down one side of his chin. Somebody's arm, with the sleeve rolled up, is against him; somebody who is almost certainly still alive: they could not cut him entirely out of the picture. Another is a studio portrait, close up, in artificial lighting, of a young woman. She is leaned a little forward, smiling vivaciously, one hand at her cheek. She is not very pretty, but she believed she was; her face is free from strain or fear. She is wearing an evidently new dress, with a mail-order look about it; patterns of beads are sewn over it and have caught the light. Her face is soft with powder and at the wings of her nose lines have been deleted. Her dark blonde hair is newly washed and professionally done up in puffs at the ears which in that time, shortly after the first great war of her century, were called cootie garages. This image of her face is split across and the split has begun to turn brown at its edges.

I think these would be graves of small farmers.

There are others about which there can be no mistake: they are the graves of the poorest of the farmers and of the tenants. Mainly they are the graves with the pine headboards; or without them.

When the grave is still young, it is very sharply distinct, and of a peculiar form. The clay is raised in a long and narrow oval with a sharp ridge, the shape exactly of an inverted boat. A fairly broad board is driven at the head; a narrower one, sometimes only a stob, at the feet. A good many of the headboards have been sawed into the flat simulacrum of an hourglass; in some of these, the top has been roughly rounded off, so that the resemblance is more nearly that of a head and shoulders sunken or risen to the waist in the dirt. On some of these boards names and dates have been written or printed in hesitant letterings, in pencil or in crayon, but most of them appear never to have been touched in this way. The boards at some of the graves have fallen slantwise or down; many graves seem never to have been marked except in their own carefully made shape. These graves are of all sizes between those of giants and of newborn children; and there are a great many, so many they seem shoals of minnows, two feet long and less, lying near one another; and of these smallest graves, very few are marked with any wood at all, and many are already so drawn into the earth that they are scarcely distinguishable. Some of the largest, on the other hand, are of heroic size, seven and eight feet long, and of these more are marked, a few, even, with the smallest and plainest blocks of limestone, and initials, once or twice a full name; but many more of them have never been marked, and many, too, are sunken half down and more and almost entirely into the earth. A great many of these graves, perhaps half to two thirds of those which are still distinct, have been decorated, not only with shrunken flowers in their cracked vases and with bent targets of blasted flowers, but otherwise as well. Some have a line of white clam-shells planted along their ridge; of others, the rim as well is garlanded with these shells. On one large grave, which is otherwise completely plain, a blown-out electric bulb is screwed into the clay at the exact center. On another, on the slope of clay just in front of the headboard, its feet next the board, is a horseshoe; and at its center a blown bulb is stood upright. On two or three others there are insulators of blue-green glass. On several graves, which I presume to be those of women, there is at the center the prettiest or the oldest and most valued piece of china: on one, a blue glass butter dish whose cover is a setting hen; on another, an intricate milk-colored glass basket; on others, ten-cent-store candy dishes and iridescent vases; on one, a pattern of white and colored buttons. On other graves there are small and thick white butter dishes of the sort which are used in lunch-rooms, and by the action of rain these stand free of the grave on slender turrets of clay. On still another grave, laid carefully next the headboard, is a corncob pipe. On the graves of children there are still these pretty pieces of glass and china, but they begin to diminish in size and they verge into the forms of animals and into homuncular symbols of growth; and there are toys: small autos, locomotives and fire engines of red and blue metal; tea sets for dolls, and tin kettles the size of thimbles: little effigies in rubber and glass and china, of cows, lions, bulldogs, squeaking mice, and the characters of comic strips; and . . . what two parents have done here for their little daughter: not only a tea set, and a cocacola bottle, and a milk bottle, ranged on her short grave, but a stone at the head and a stone at the foot, and in the headstone her six month image as she lies sleeping dead in her white dress, the head sunken delicately forward, deeply and delicately gone, the eyes seamed, as that of a dead bird, and on the rear face of this stone the words:

> We can't have all things to please us,
> Our little Daughter, Joe An, has gone to Jesus.

a. Evaluate this description of Shady Grove cemetery in the following terms:
   1. technical elements that give the piece documentary solidness
   2. sensory images, personal impressions, judgments
   3. point of view
   4. selection, arrangement, and significance of details
   5. organization
   6. dominant mood or atmosphere

      7. choice of words and images

      8. tone

      9. aptness of subject (Do you agree with poet John Ciardi that anything looked at carefully is worth looking at?)

  b. Do you think this cemetery is worth looking at? Why?

  c. Write a one-paragraph answer (150–250 words) to the following question: Do you think a comment ("thematic statement") on human nature and life in general is being made in this essay? State your position in an opening topic sentence; then support that position with concrete details.

2. For each of the following descriptions, evaluate the dominant mood or impression the writer creates and how he creates it (choice of words, sounds, sense images, projection of feeling):

I gazed upon the schoolroom into which he took me, as the most forlorn and desolate place I had ever seen. I see it now. A long room, with three long rows of desks, and six of forms, and bristling all around with pegs for hats and slates. Scraps of old copy-books and exercises litter the dirty floor. Some silkworms' houses, made of the same materials, are scattered over the desks. Two miserable little white mice, left behind by their owner, are running up and down in a fusty castle made of pasteboard and wire, looking in all the corners with their red eyes for anything to eat. A bird, in a cage very little bigger than himself, makes a mournful rattle now and then in hopping on his perch, two inches high, or dropping from it, but neither sings nor chirps. There is a strange unwholesome smell upon the room, like mildewed corduroys, sweet apples wanting air, and rotten books. There could not well be more ink splashed about it, if it had been roofless from its first construction, and the skies had rained, snowed, hailed, and blown ink through the varying seasons of the year.

      —Charles Dickens, *David Copperfield*

It was a beautiful college. The vines and the roads gracefully winding, lined with hedges and wild roses that dazzled the eyes in the summer sun. Honeysuckle and purple wisteria hung heavy from the trees and white magnolias mixed with their scents in the bee-humming air. I've recalled it often, here in my hole: How the grass turned green in the springtime and how the mocking birds fluttered their tails and sang, how the moon shone down on the buildings, how the bell in the chapel tower rang out the precious short-lived hours; how the girls in bright summer dresses promenaded the grassy lawn. Many times, here at night, I've closed my eyes and walked along the forbidden road that winds past the girls' dormitories, past the hall with the clock in the tower, its windows warmly aglow, on down past the small white Home Economics practice cottage, whiter still in the moonlight, and on down the road with its sloping and turning, paralleling the black powerhouse with its engines droning earth-shaking rhythms in the dark, its windows red from the glow of the furnace, on to where the road became a bridge over a dry riverbed, tangled with brush and clinging vines; the bridge of rustic logs, made for trysting, but virginal and untested by lovers; on up the road, past the buildings, with the southern verandas half-a-city-block long, to the sudden forking, barren of buildings, birds, or grass, where the road turned off to the insane asylum.

      —Ralph Ellison, *The Invisible Man*

3. In a paragraph (150–250 words) describe a *person, place, setting,* or *event* in such a way that you project one of the following moods or atmospheres:

bustling activity	poverty	loneliness
calm and quiet	beauty	despair
sloppiness	luxury	gaiety
cleanliness	fear	ugliness
deprivation	suspicion	

4. In a paragraph (150–250 words), describe a season of the year, an aspect of a season, or a particular mood or emotion associated with a particular month ("April is the cruelest month," wrote T. S. Eliot, "mixing memory and desire"). Try to place your topic sentence at the beginning of one paragraph (as George Eliot did in the descriptive paragraph on p. 13 of the Introduction) and at the end of the other. If you think no topic sentence is necessary, be prepared to defend your decision.

5. Write a technical description (150–250 words) comparable to "The Grasshopper." Illustrate if you wish.

6. Study the picture below, noting every feature and detail. Then write a one-paragraph objective or technical description (150–250 words) in which you describe the "facts" of the picture: what it looks like to an objective observer who adds no personal opinion or judgment.

7. Write a second description (150–250 words) in which you respond personally and emotionally to the picture, projecting into it your own thoughts and feelings (as did Agee).

8. Write one-paragraph (150–250 words) descriptions of a room, a building, a street, a lake, a mountain, or the like from two different physical points of view: regarding your subject from a fixed position ("View from Rochester Bridge"), and moving *through* your subject, beginning with an overall view from the perimeter (a long shot) and then coming progressively closer to note the finer details ("The House Beautiful").

9. Point to the humorous and ironic details in "The House Beautiful" that reveal Mark Twain's attitude toward this "residence of the principal citizen." Include such mocking touches (evident in the "voice" of the author) as "Pity, too; for she might have repented of this in time. . . ."

Essay Suggestions

1. Adopt the satirical point of view of the observer-commentator, in the manner of Twain in "The House Beautiful." Describe an "event" (500–750 words)—a party, a person, a meeting, a family gathering, a class session—that you think lends itself to satire.

2. Write a descriptive essay (500–750 words) in which you adopt a suitable psychological point of view and maintain this attitude throughout.

3. In the manner of "Moonrise Over Monument Valley," write a description (500–750 words) of a natural event as you watch it happen or as you imagine it, organizing your material chronologically.

4. Write an essay (500–750 words) in which you describe both the physical aspects and the psychological implications of the picture on the preceding page, combining objective description with subjective impression and response.

5. Write a description (500–750 words) of any place, person, or event that captures your imagination.

3 What Are the Component Parts of X?

To ask about the component parts of something, to find out what they are and how they are related to one another—this is analysis. We are, of course, forever analyzing things, simply because the only way to understand a person, an object, an idea, an event, a process, or an organization is to take it apart in a systematic manner to try to see what makes it tick, what made it happen, why it is as it is. Thus analysis is a natural function of the human mind, going on all the time as we explore the world around us in order to understand it better. Thinking itself is impossible without analysis; every subject we contemplate with any seriousness—whether we write or talk about it—is necessarily analyzed.

All the questions in this book, but particularly the next ten, deal with analysis in that they attempt to break down a total subject into its parts. Logicians call this process *division;* it is a necessary first step in problem-solving and in writing as well. Before we can deal with a subject we must see its internal divisions.

Analysis of a Physical Structure

The organization of an analysis is more or less given to the writer; once you have answered the question "What are the component parts of X?" you have already outlined your essay: the parts of the subject become the parts of your piece. In the following essay the three kinds of blood cells plus the plasma constitute the four basic units of the discourse, which are in turn broken down into subunits, as each of the components of blood is analyzed into *its* respective parts.

The Composition of Blood[1]

LOUIS FAUGERES BISHOP

Introduction (states component elements)

Under the microscope we can see that [blood] is composed of a watery fluid called plasma, in which certain formed elements are suspended. The formed elements are different types of cells—red blood cells, white blood cells and platelets.

1. Red blood cells

The red blood cells are the most numerous of the formed elements. There are normally about 5,000,000 in each cubic millimeter of blood in men and about 4,500,000 in women during the child bearing years. Each cell is about $\frac{1}{3500}$ of an inch in diameter. Normally the cells are in the form of disks, both sides of which are concave.

Red blood cells are developed in the red marrow, found in the ends of the long bones and throughout the interior of flat bones, such as the vertebrae and ribs. The cells have definite nuclei in the early stages of their formation; in man and the other mammals the nuclei are lost by the time the cells have become mature and before they are released into the blood stream.

(Broken down into their elements)

Each mature red blood cell has a structural framework called the stroma, which is made up chiefly of proteins and fatty materials. It forms a mesh extending into the interior of the cell; it gives the cell its shape and flexibility. The most important chemical substance in the cell is hemoglobin, which causes blood to have a red color. Hemoglobin is composed of an iron-containing pigment called heme and a protein called globin; there are about four parts of heme to ninety-six parts of globin. In man the normal amount of hemoglobin is 14 to 15.6 grams per 100 cubic centimeters of blood; in woman it is 11 to 14 grams.

Hemoglobin combines with oxygen in the lungs after air has been inhaled; the resulting compound is called oxyhemoglobin. When the red blood cells later make their way to other parts of the body deficient in oxygen, the oxygen in the compound breaks its bonds and makes its way by diffusion to the tissues of the oxygen-poor areas. Thus the red blood cells draw oxygen from the lungs, transport it in the blood stream and release it to the tissues as needed.

2. White blood cells

The white blood cells are the body's military force, attacking disease organisms such as staphylococci, streptococci and meningococci. These cells are far less numerous than the red variety; the proportion of white to red under normal conditions is 1 to 400 or 500. The white cells are semitransparent bodies. They differ from red cells in several important respects; among other things, they contain no hemoglobin and they always have nuclei.

[1]"The Life Stream: What Blood Is and What It Does," *The Book of Popular Science*, III (Canada: The Grolier Society, 1971), pp. 325–31.

(Indication
of the
varieties)
There are several easily distinguished varieties of white cells: neutrophils, lymphocytes, basophils, eosinophils and monocytes. Neutrophils, basophils and eosinophils are formed in the bone marrow. Lymphocytes are made in the lymphatic tissues; monocytes, in the reticulo-endothelial system.

The neutrophils are by far the most numerous of the white blood cells, making up from 65 to 70 per cent of the total. They derive their name from the fact that they readily take the color of a neutral dye. These cells are about half as large again as red blood cells.

3. Platelets
Platelets are tiny circular or oval disks, which are derived from certain giant cells in the bone marrow, called megakaryocytes. Their number ranges from 200,000 per cubic millimeter to 500,000 or more. The platelets, which are much smaller than the blood cells, serve several useful purposes. When they disintegrate, they liberate a substance called thrombokinase or thromboplastin, which is vital in the blood-clotting process. They also help to plug leaks in the tiny blood vessels called capillaries.

4. Analysis
of
plasma
The plasma is the watery part of the blood, making up from 50 to 60 per cent of the total. It is a clear yellow fluid, serving as a vehicle for the transportation of red blood cells, white blood cells, platelets and various substances necessary for the vital functioning of the body cells, for clotting and for the defense of the body against disease. After clotting occurs, a straw-colored fluid called serum is left; this retains its liquid form indefinitely.

About 90 per cent of plasma is water, in which a great variety of substances are held in suspension or in solution. These include proteins, such as fibrinogen, albumin and the globulins, and also sugar, fat and inorganic salts derived from food or from the storage depots of the body. Plasma contains urea, uric acid, creatine and other products of the breakdown of proteins. There are enzymes, such as adrenal hormones, thyroxine and insulin, derived from the glands of internal secretion. There are also various gases: oxygen and nitrogen, diffused into the blood from the lungs; and carbon dioxide, diffused into the blood from the tissues.

Analysis of an Intellectual Structure

Just as objects and substances may be broken down into their physical parts, ideas and concepts may be divided into their conceptual and psychological components: for example, the thoughts, attitudes, and feelings that make up the concept of "patriotism." Conceptual analysis is more common than physical analysis. Most people regularly try to "figure things out" in their heads, whereas relatively few want to know about "taking things apart" (like a television set or a clock).

Ultimately, if one is determined enough, no concept is too abstract for analysis. The renowned physicist Robert Andrew Millikan, for example, believed that most people do not understand the conceptual whole called the "scientific spirit," and he wrote the following essay to analyze what it is by describing its three basic elements.

The Spirit of Modern Science[2]

ROBERT ANDREW MILLIKAN

The spirit of modern science is something relatively new in the history of the world, and I want to give an analysis of what it is. I want to take you up in an aeroplane which flies in time rather than in space, and look down with you upon the high peaks that distinguish the centuries, and let you see what is the distinguishing characteristic of the century in which we live. I think there will be no question at all, if you get far enough out of it so that you can see the woods without having your vision clouded by the proximity of the trees, that the thing which is characteristic of our modern civilization is the spirit of scientific research,—a spirit which first grew up in the subject of physics, and which has spread from that to all other subjects of modern scientific inquiry.

That spirit has three elements. The first is a philosophy; the second is a method; and the third is a faith.

Look first at the philosophy. It is new for the reason that all primitive peoples, and many that are not primitive, have held a philosophy that is both animistic and fatalistic. Every phenomenon which is at all unusual, or for any reason not immediately intelligible, used to be attributed to the direct action of some invisible personal being. Witness the peopling of the woods and streams with spirits, by the Greeks; the miracles and possession by demons, of the Jews; the witchcraft manias of our own Puritan forefathers, only two or three hundred years ago.

That a supine fatalism results from such a philosophy is to be expected; for, according to it, everything that happens is the will of the gods, or the will of some more powerful beings than ourselves. And so, in all the ancient world, and in much of the modern, also, three blind fates sit down in dark and deep inferno and weave out the fates of men. Man himself is not a vital agent in the march of things; he is only a speck, an atom which is hurled hither and thither in the play of mysterious, titanic, uncontrollable forces.

Now, the philosophy of physics, a philosophy which was held at first timidly, always tentatively, always as a mere working hypothesis, but yet held with ever increasing conviction from the time of Galileo, when the experimental method may be said to have had its beginnings, is the exact antithesis of this. Stated in its most sweeping form, it holds that the universe is rationally intelligible, no matter how far from a complete comprehension of it we may now be, or indeed may ever come to be. It believes in the absolute uniformity of nature. It views the world as a mechanism, every part and every movement of which fits in some definite, invariable way into the other parts and the other movements; and it sets itself the inspiring task of studying every phenomenon in the confident hope that the connections between it and other phenomena can ultimately be found. It will have naught of caprice. Such is the spirit, the attitude, the working hypothesis of all modern science; and this philosophy is in no sense materialistic, because good, and mind, and soul, and moral values,—these things are all here just as truly as are any physical objects; they must simply be inside and not outside of this matchless mechanism.

Second, as to the method of science. It is a method practically unknown to the ancient world; for that world was essentially subjective in all its thinking, and built up its views of things largely by introspection. The scientific method, on the other hand, is a method which is ready for the discard the very minute that it fails to work. It is the

[2]From pp. 311–12 in *Science in Literature,* edited by Frederick H. Law (Harper, 1929). Reprinted by permission of Harper & Row, Publishers.

method which believes in a minute, careful, wholly dispassionate analysis of a situation; and any physicist or engineer who allows the least trace of prejudice or preconception to enter into his study of a given problem violates the most sacred duty of his profession. This present cataclysm, which has set the world back a thousand years in so many ways, has shown us the pitiful spectacle of scientists who have forgotten completely the scientific method, and who have been controlled simply by prejudice and preconception. This fact is no reflection on the scientific method; it merely means that these men have not been able to carry over the methods they use in their science into all the departments of their thinking. The world has been controlled by prejudice and emotionalism so long that reversions still occur; but the fact that these reversions occur does not discredit the scientist, nor make him disbelieve in his method. Why? Simply because that method has worked; it is working to-day, and its promise of working to-morrow is larger than it has ever been before in the history of the world.

Do you realize that within the life of men now living, within a hundred years, or one hundred and thirty years at most, all the external conditions under which man lives his life on this earth have been more completely revolutionized than during all the ages of recorded history which preceded? My great-grandfather lived essentially the same kind of life, so far as external conditions were concerned, as did his Assyrian prototype six thousand years ago. He went as far as his own legs, or the legs of his horse, could carry him. He dug his ditch, he mowed his hay, with the power of his own two arms, or the power of his wife's two arms, with an occasional lift from his horse or his ox. He carried a dried potato in his pocket to keep off rheumatism, and he worshipped his God in almost the same superstitious way. It was not until the beginning of the nineteenth century that the great discovery of the ages began to be borne in upon the consciousness of mankind through the work of a few patient, indefatigable men who had caught the spirit which Galileo perhaps first notably embodied, and passed on to Newton, to Franklin, to Faraday, to Maxwell, and to the other great architects of the modern scientific world in which we live,—the discovery that man is not a pawn in a game played by higher powers, that his external as well as his internal destiny is in his own hands.

You may prefer to have me call that not a discovery but a faith. Very well! It is the faith of the scientist, and it is a faith which he will tell you has been justified by works. Take just this one illustration. In the mystical, fatalistic ages, electricity was simply the agent of an inscrutable Providence: it was Elijah's fire from Heaven sent down to consume the enemies of Jehovah, or it was Jove's thunderbolt hurled by an angry god; and it was just as impious to study so direct a manifestation of God's power in the world as it would be for a child to study the strap with which he is being punished, or the mental attributes of the father who wields the strap. It was only one hundred and fifty years ago that Franklin sent up his famous kite, and showed that thunderbolts are identical with the sparks which he could draw on a winter's night from his cat's back. Then, thirty years afterward Volta found that he could manufacture them artificially by dipping dissimilar metals into an acid. And, thirty years farther along, Oersted found that, when tamed and running noiselessly along a wire, they will deflect a magnet: and with that discovery the electric battery was born, and the erstwhile blustering thunderbolts were set the inglorious task of ringing house bells, primarily for the convenience of womankind. Ten years later Faraday found that all he had to do to obtain a current was to move a wire across the pole of a magnet, and in that discovery the dynamo was born, and our modern electrical age, with its electric transmission of power, its electric lighting, its electric telephoning, its electric toasting, its electric foot warming, and its electric milking. All that is an immediate and inevitable consequence of that discovery,—a discovery which grew out of the faith of a few physicists that the most mysterious, the most capricious, and the most terrible of natural phenomena is capable of a rational explanation, and ultimately amenable to human control.

At the [Pennsylvania state] Capitol in Harrisburg is a picture by Sir Edwin Abbey, which is entitled, "Wisdom, or the Spirit of Science." It consists of a veiled figure with the forked lightnings in one hand, and in the other, the owl and the serpent, the symbols of mystery; and beneath is the inscription:

> I am what is, what hath been, and what shall be.
> My veil has been disclosed by none.
> What I have brought forth is this: The sun is born.

It is to lighten man's understanding, to illuminate his path through life, and not merely to make it easy, that science exists.

Here again the essay, like most essays in simple analysis, is organized at the moment the writer indicates what the component parts of the subject are: the elements of the "spirit" are also the units of the piece. Thus Millikan's essay can be outlined as follows:

INTRODUCTION:
>The spirit of modern science is relatively new; has three elements: philosophy, method, and faith.
>>I. Philosophy
>>II. Method
>>III. Faith

CONCLUSION:
>As the picture "Wisdom, or the Spirit of Science" illustrates, science exists to illuminate life, not merely to make it easy.

Principles of Analysis

Analysis is a challenging and demanding form of writing in that it requires systematic and rigorously logical thinking conducted in the light of clear and consistent principles. We cannot concern ourselves here with formal logic, but neither can we ignore three basic logical principles that are fundamental to all analysis, whether performed by a logician or by a writer:

1. Analysis (or division) must be made according to the structure of the thing analyzed. In logical terms, to smash a glass is not to divide it, because a glass is not composed of fragments of glass. To determine the component parts of a glass it is necessary to make a chemical analysis.

2. The kind of structure being analyzed depends on the interest of the analyzer. Thus, English literature can be analyzed as a chronological structure into Old, Middle, Modern, or it can be analyzed into various genres— poetry, drama, essays, and so on. Whatever structure you might choose to work with, you must be consistent if you are to achieve the primary purpose of analysis: to keep component parts clear and distinct. Thus, you cannot analyze literature into Old, Middle, and poetry; such an analysis shifts its basis of division from chronology to genre.

3. A logical analysis should also be complete—that is, X should be divided into *all* its component parts, not just some of them. In scientific or technical analysis this is mandatory; in a general essay on a nonscientific subject, however, you need not be quite as strict. You may choose to deal with only the main part or selected aspects of your subject, in which case you should indicate that the analysis is partial and incomplete, thereby letting the reader know you have not inadvertently overlooked the elements you have not mentioned. One simple device for completing a division with dispatch is to include the category "others" or "miscellaneous." Thus, in analyzing the body of an author's works, you might divide them into novels, plays, short stories, and "miscellaneous writings." In this way nothing is left out.

The essays by Bishop and Millikan amply fulfill these prerequisites of logical analysis. In "The Composition of Blood" Bishop analyzes blood in terms of its natural components; he never shifts the basis of division (to "rich" or "poor" blood, color of blood, rate of flow). The analysis is also complete; although Bishop does not name every protein or enzyme found in plasma, he indicates that there are other substances ("other products," "also various gases") that fall into the explicitly stated main categories. Similarly, in his essay on modern science, Millikan analyzes this vast and complex subject in terms of his special interest—namely, its spirit. At no point does he shift his ground to contemplate the various types of sciences (biology, chemistry), their degree of "purity," their difficulty. And Millikan's analysis is complete: as he sees it, there are three and no more than three "basic elements" of the scientific spirit.

Skillfully written analysis can reveal the essence of a seemingly difficult or esoteric subject. Take music, for example, which many people enjoy, but relatively few understand. Hoping to increase enjoyment by promoting understanding, musicologist David Randolph wrote the following analysis, in which he considers the totality "music" from his chosen point of view: what the listener responds to. The analysis is strictly logical in that Randolph sticks scrupulously throughout to the special ground on which the analysis rests. He never shifts to types of music, individual instruments, and so on. There is also no question as to whether it is complete. There are five and only five important elements to respond to in music. Even "if we wanted to be rigid about definitions," Randolph assures us, "we could say that music consists of nothing but the manipulation of the five elements."

Five Basic Elements of Music[3]

DAVID RANDOLPH

Let us see what it is that you respond to in music.

Do you find something appealing about the famous tune from Schubert's Unfinished Symphony? If so, then you are responding to one of the most important elements of music—*melody*.

Do you find that you feel like tapping your foot during the march movement of

Tchaikovsky's Pathetique Symphony? If so, then you are responding to another extremely important element—*rhythm.*

Yet observe that rhythm is present in the melody of Schubert's Unfinished (just tap out the melody on a table with your finger, without singing, and you will isolate the rhythm), and that melody is present in even the most rhythmic portion of the Tchaikovsky march. Therefore, in the process of merely "liking" one of these works, you are actually appreciating *two* musical elements at once. While this example may not impress you by its profundity, the *principle*—being aware of what it is that you respond to—is at the root of all genuine music appreciation.

Now imagine how much less satisfying Schubert's melody would be if it were buzzed through a tissue-papered comb, instead of being played by the entire cello section of an orchestra. The melody and the rhythm would still be present as before; the difference would lie only in the quality of the sound that reached your ears. Therefore, when you enjoy the richness of the sound of the massed cellos playing the melody, you are responding to another of the basic elements—*tone color.* Your appreciation, then, really involves *three* elements.

Now, let us suppose that a pianist is playing one of your favorite songs—the melody in the right hand, the accompanying chords in the left. Suppose that his finger slips as he plays one of the chords, causing him to play a sour note. Your immediate awareness of that wrong note comes from your response to another of the basic elements—*harmony.*

Let us briefly consider the more positive implications of harmony. Whether you are attracted by barbershop-quartet singing, or by an atmospheric work by Debussy, or by the powerful, forthright ending of Beethoven's Fifth Symphony, *part* of your reaction stems from your response to the harmony, which may be defined as the simultaneous sounding of two or more notes (usually more than two, as in these three examples). Thus we have found a *fourth* element in your appreciation.

Do you have a sense of completeness at the conclusion of a performance of (we will use only one of countless possible examples) Beethoven's Ninth Symphony? Are you left with a feeling of satisfaction as well as of elation? If so, part of that sense of satisfaction—of completion—comes from your feeling for *form,* which is the last of the five basic elements of music. . . .

If we wanted to be rigid about definitions, we could say that music consists of nothing but the manipulation of the five elements. The statement is correct in that there is no music in the world, regardless of the time or place of its origin, that can be based upon anything other than some combination of these five elements. Thus, to offer the most extreme contrast possible, what we may imagine as the ritual stamping on the ground by the savage appealing to his god partakes of some of the same basic elements as does Bach's *Passion According to St. Matthew,* notably rhythm and tone color, and certainly, to a degree, form.

ASSIGNMENTS

Class Discussion and Paragraph Suggestions

(See Chapter 27 for methods of composing unified, adequately developed paragraphs.)

1. Analyze the three essays in this chapter in terms of the following rhetorical issues:
   a. As you can infer it from the essays themselves, describe the rhetorical stance of

each writer: his purpose and his relationship to subject, occasion, and reader. Is each identical to, similar to, or different from the other two?

    b. Evaluate paragraph structure according to where "breaks" occur. Indicate how they do or do not coincide with steps in the unfolding and development of the ideas in each essay. Are the paragraphs themselves unified? internally consistent? Reconstruct what you perceive to have been the writer's "working outline" (see the sample outline of Millikan's essay on p. 62).

    c. Comment on the appropriateness of tone in these essays.

2. Read the essay below and answer the questions that follow.

The Credo of the Intellectuals[4]

FREDERICK LEWIS ALLEN

What was the credo of the intellectuals during these years of revolt [against middle-class conformity in the 1920's]? Not many of them accepted all the propositions in the following rough summary; yet it suggests, perhaps, the general drift of their collective opinion:

1. They believed in a greater degree of sex freedom than had been permitted by the strict American code; and as for discussion of sex, not only did they believe it should be free, but some of them appeared to believe it should be continuous. They formed the spearhead of the revolution in manners and morals. . . . From the early days of the decade, when they thrilled at the lackadaisical petting of F. Scott Fitzgerald's young thinkers and at the boldness of Edna St. Vincent Millay's announcement that her candle burned at both ends and could not last the night, to the latter days when they were all agog over the literature of homosexuality and went by the thousands to take Eugene O'Neill's five-hour lesson in psychopathology, *Strange Interlude,* they read about sex, talked about sex, thought about sex, and defied anybody to say No.

2. In particular, they defied the enforcement of propriety by legislation and detested all the influences to which they attributed it. They hated the Methodist lobby, John S. Sumner, and all other defenders of censorship; they pictured the Puritan, even of Colonial days, as a blue-nosed, crack-voiced hypocrite; and they looked at Victorianism as half indecent and half funny. The literary reputations of Thackeray, Tennyson, Longfellow, and the Boston *literati* of the last century sank in their estimation to new lows for all time. Convinced that the era of short skirts and literary dalliance had brought a new enlightenment, the younger intellectuals laughed at the "Gay Nineties" as depicted in *Life* and joined Thomas Beer in condescending scrutiny of the voluminous dresses and fictional indirections of the Mauve Decade. Some of them, in fact, seemed to be persuaded that all periods prior to the coming of modernity had been ridiculous—with the exception of Greek civilization, Italy at the time of Casanova, France at the time of the great courtesans, and eighteenth-century England.

3. Most of them were passionate anti-prohibitionists, and this fact, together with their dislike of censorship and their skepticism about political and social regeneration, made them dubious about all reform movements and distrustful of all reformers. They emphatically did not believe that they were their brothers' keepers; anybody who did not regard tolerance as one of the supreme virtues was to them intolerable.

If one heard at a single dinner party of advanced thinkers that there were "too many laws" and that people ought to be let alone, one heard it at a hundred. In 1915 the word reformer had been generally a complimentary term; in 1925 it had become—among the intellectuals, at least—a term of contempt.

4. They were mostly, though not all, religious skeptics. If there was less shouting agnosticism and atheism in the nineteen-twenties than in the eighteen-nineties it was chiefly because disbelief was no longer considered sensational and because the irreligious intellectuals, feeling no evangelical urge to make over others in their own image, were content quietly to stay away from church. It is doubtful if any college undergraduate of the 'nineties or of any other previous period in the United States could have said "No intelligent person believes in God any more" as blandly as undergraduates said it during the discussions of compulsory college chapel which raged during the 'twenties. Never before had so many books addressed to the thinking public assumed at the outset that their readers had rejected the old theology.

5. They were united in a scorn of the great bourgeois majority which they held responsible for prohibition, censorship, Fundamentalism, and other repressions. They emulated Mencken in their disgust at Babbitts, Rotarians, the Ku Klux Klan, Service-with-a-Smile, boosters, and super-salesmen. Those of them who lived in the urban centers prided themselves on their superiority to the denizens of the benighted outlying cities and towns where Babbittry flourished; witness, for example, the motto of the *New Yorker* when it was first established in the middle of the decade: "Not for the old lady from Dubuque." Particularly did they despise the mobs of prosperous American tourists which surged through Europe; one could hardly occupy a steamer chair next to anybody who had Aldous Huxley's latest novel on his lap without being told of a delightful little restaurant somewhere in France which was quite "unspoiled by Americans."

6. They took a particular pleasure in overturning the idols of the majority; hence the vogue among them of the practice for which W. E. Woodward, in a novel published in 1923, invented the word "debunking." Lytton Strachey's *Queen Victoria,* which had been a best seller in the United States in 1922, was followed by a deluge of debunking biographies. Rupert Hughes removed a few coats of whitewash from George Washington and nearly caused a riot when he declared in a speech that "Washington was a great card-player, a distiller of whisky, and a champion curser, and he danced for three hours without stopping with the wife of his principal general." Other American worthies were portrayed in all their erring humanity, and the notorious rascals of history were rediscovered as picturesque and glamorous fellows; until for a time it was almost taken for granted that the biographer, if he were to be successful, must turn conventional white into black and *vice versa.*

7. They feared the effect upon themselves and upon American culture of mass production and the machine, and saw themselves as fighting at the last ditch for the right to be themselves in a civilization which was being leveled into monotony by Fordismus and the chain-store mind. Their hatred of regimentation gave impetus to the progressive school movement and nourished such innovations in higher education as Antioch, Rollins, Meiklejohn's Experimental College at Wisconsin, and the honors plan at Swarthmore and elsewhere. It gave equal impetus to the little-theater movement, which made remarkable headway from coast to coast, especially in the schools. The heroes of current novels were depicted as being stifled in the air of the home town, and as fleeing for their cultural lives either to Manhattan or, better yet, to Montparnasse or the Riviera. In any café in Paris one might find an American expatriate thanking his stars that he was free from standardization at last, oblivious

of the fact that there was no more standardized institution even in the land of automobiles and radio than the French sidewalk café. The intellectuals lapped up the criticisms of American culture offered them by foreign lecturers imported in record-breaking numbers, and felt no resentment when the best magazines flaunted before their eyes, month after month, titles like "Our American Stupidity" and "Childish Americans." They quite expected to be told that America was sinking into barbarism and was an altogether impossible place for a civilized person to live in—as when James Truslow Adams lamented in the *Atlantic Monthly,* "I am wondering, as a personal but practical question, just how and where a man of moderate means who prefers simple living, simple pleasures, and the things of the mind is going to be able to live any longer in his native country."

Few of the American intellectuals of the nineteen-twenties, let it be repeated, subscribed to all the propositions in this credo; but he or she who accepted none of them was suspect among the enlightened. He was not truly civilized, he was not modern. The prosperity band-wagon rolled on, but by the wayside stood the high-brows with voices upraised in derision and dismay.

   a. What is a "credo"?
   b. Into how many constituent parts is this subject divided? What are they?
   c. Is the division complete? or complete *enough?*
   d. Comment on the organization of the essay. Are the parts arranged logically? Can you detect any particular principle of order?
   e. Is there a single quality or "spirit" that runs through all the parts?
   f. Does the credo of the intellectuals appear to be *thoughtful, moderate, fair-minded?* or *pretentious, close-minded, intolerant?* What qualities of heart and mind do you feel run through the separate "propositions" of this credo? Cite specific words and phrases that seem to be clues.

3. Write a one-paragraph (150–250 words) description of the tone of voice (reverent? disdainful? amused? flippant? angry? ironic?) that emerges in the Allen essay. Be sure to state your judgment in an opening topic sentence; then cite specific items—words, phrases, images, manner of expression, and so on—that help to create this tone.

Essay Suggestions

1. Write an essay (500–750 words) analyzing the credo of intellectuals today (or of feminists, radicals, some other group in which you have an interest).

2. Assuming a rhetorical stance similar to Randolph's and using the informal direct "you" address to the reader, write an essay (500–750 words) in which you isolate the elements of one of the following:

Arts	*Sports*
ballet	baseball
painting	football
architecture	soccer
photography	tennis
opera	golf
literature	skiing

3. As Robert Millikan analyzes the spirit of modern science by breaking it down into its three elements, write an essay (500–750 words) in which you describe the "spirit" of one of the subjects listed below by analyzing it in terms of its basic elements—features, qualities, beliefs. Note the organization of Millikan's essay

and draw up a working outline that is adapted to the needs of your piece. Try to include subheadings and sub-subheadings (see Chapter 23): the more accurately you draw up your "map" of a projected piece, the more likely it is to have shape and a logical, smoothly flowing sequence of parts.

the spirit of modern art
the spirit of the new morality
the spirit of dissent
the spirit of revolution
the spirit of liberal education

4 How Is X Made or Done?

If you were to ask how something is done or made, you would be entering into a special form of analysis that rhetoricians call *process analysis*. Here, instead of dividing a given subject into its component parts, you divide an ongoing process into its successive stages.

An essay of this kind presents an orderly, step-by-step, chronologically arranged description of how a process of some kind takes place: how a poem is written (a creative process); how a clock keeps time (a mechanical process); how plants make chlorophyll (a natural process); how bread is baked (a manufacturing process); how women won the franchise (a social process); how the Russian Revolution began (a historical process). An essay in process analysis is likely to be readable and lively, for by its very nature it keeps moving from stage one to stage two to stage three, and so on.

Suppose, for example, you address the question "How is X done?" to one aspect of creativity (subject 4 in the checklist on page 19): the creative art of choreography. In this case you might write an essay like the following vividly descriptive analysis by choreographer Agnes DeMille of how she composes a ballet.

Composing a Ballet[1]

AGNES DE MILLE

To make up a dance, I still need . . . a pot of tea, walking space, privacy and an idea. . . .

When I first visualize the dance, I see the characters moving in color and costume.

[1]Copyright 1951, 1952 by Agnes DeMille. From *Dance to the Piper* by Agnes DeMille, by permission of Atlantic–Little, Brown and Co.

Before I go into rehearsal, I know what costumes the people wear and generally what color and texture. I also, to a large extent, hear the orchestral effects. Since I can have ideas only under the stress of emotion, I must create artificially an atmosphere which will induce this excitement. I shut myself in a studio and play gramophone music, Bach, Mozart, Smetana, or almost any folk music in interesting arrangements. At this point I avoid using the score because it could easily become threadbare.

I start sitting with my feet up and drinking pots of strong tea, but as I am taken into the subject I begin to move and before I know it I am walking the length of the studio and acting full out the gestures and scenes. The key dramatic scenes come this way. I never forget a single nuance of them afterwards; I do usually forget dance sequences.

The next step is to find the style of gesture. This is done standing and moving, again behind locked doors and again with a gramophone. Before I find how a character dances, I must know how he walks and stands. If I can discover the basic rhythms of his natural gesture, I will know how to expand them into dance movements.

It takes hours daily of blind instinctive moving and fumbling to find the revealing gesture, and the process goes on for weeks before I am ready to start composing. Nor can I think any of this out sitting down. My body does it for me. It happens. That is why the choreographic process is exhausting. It happens on one's feet after hours of work, and the energy required is roughly the equivalent of writing a novel and winning a tennis match simultaneously. This is the kernel, the nucleus of the dance. All the design develops from this.

Having established a scenario and discovered the style and key steps, I then sit down at my desk and work out the pattern of the dances. If the score is already composed, the dance pattern is naturally suggested by and derived from the pattern of the music. If it remains to be composed as it does in all musical comedies, the choreographer goes it alone. This, of course, is harder. Music has an enormous suggestive power and the design of the composer offers a helpful blueprint. . . .

Through practice I have learned to project a whole composition in rough outline mentally and to know exactly how the dancers will look at any given moment moving in counterpoint in as many as five groups. As an aid in concentration, I make detailed diagrams and notes of my own arbitrary invention, intelligible only to me and only for about a week, but they are not comparable in exactness to music notation.

At this point, I am ready, God help me, to enter the rehearsal hall.

Obviously it is not difficult to organize an essay in process analysis, because it generally organizes itself in a time sequence. What *is* difficult is dividing the process into logical sequential stages, and making certain that each stage is accurately described, for if there is one weak link in the chain, the entire explanation can collapse, leaving the reader in confusion.

Notice how carefully DeMille has divided the choreographic act into its component parts—namely, the six successive steps through which it is carried out:

step one: getting the ideas (and the conditions for developing them: a pot of tea, walking space)

step two: visualizing the dancers "moving" in color and costume and "hearing" the music

step three: establishing key dramatic scenes

step four:	discovering the basic gestures, rhythms, and style of charac-ter ("My body does it for me.")
step five:	writing down the pattern of the dances (detailed diagrams and notes)
step six:	entering the rehearsal hall (with God's help!)

Notice also that the six steps *flow* into one another. At no point do readers wonder what stage they are at, for "time" words (plus "place" words, pronouns that refer to earlier nouns, repetition of key words) keep them oriented and moving steadily *ahead:*

When I *first* visualize the dance . . .
Before I go into rehearsal . . .
At this point I avoid using the score . . .
I *begin* to move and *before* I know it . . .
I never forget a single nuance . . . *afterwards* . . .
The *next* step is to find the style . . .
. . . *again* behind locked doors and *again* with a gramophone . . .
Before I find how a character dances . . .
. . . the process *goes on for weeks* . . .
. . . *after* hours of work . . .
I *then* sit down at my desk . . .
At this point, I am ready . . .

The creative process, as it has been described by many scientists and artists, falls roughly into four stages: *preparation*—the stage of deliberate and conscious planning, training, and effort; *incubation*—the stage in which you are not *consciously* dwelling on a problem but are nonetheless "mulling it over" on a subconscious level; *illumination*—the "flash" wherein you see, as Bertrand Russell says in the following essay, "exactly what I had to say"; *verification*—the stage in which you check and test your newly discovered hypothesis and review and revise what you have "made."

How I Write[2]

BERTRAND RUSSELL

I cannot pretend to know how writing ought to be done, or what a wise critic would advise me to do with a view to improving my own writing. The most that I can do is to relate some things about my own attempts.

Until I was twenty-one, I wished to write more or less in the style of John Stuart Mill. I liked the structure of his sentences and his manner of developing a subject. I had, however, already a different ideal, derived, I suppose, from mathematics. I wished to say everything in the smallest number of words in which it could be said clearly. Perhaps, I thought, one should imitate Baedeker rather than any more literary model. I would spend hours trying to find the shortest way of saying something without

[2]From *Portraits from Memory,* by Betrand Russell. Copyright © 1951, 1952, 1953, 1956 by Bertrand Russell. Reprinted by permission of Simon and Schuster and George Allen & Unwin Ltd.

ambiguity, and to this aim I was willing to sacrifice all attempts at aesthetic excellence.

At the age of twenty-one, however, I came under a new influence, that of my future brother-in-law, Logan Pearsall Smith. He was at that time exclusively interested in style as opposed to matter. His gods were Flaubert and Walter Pater, and I was quite ready to believe that the way to learn how to write was to copy their technique. He gave me various simple rules, of which I remember only two: "Put a comma every four words," and "never use 'and' except at the beginning of a sentence." His most emphatic advice was that one must always re-write. I conscientiously tried this, but found that my first draft was almost always better than my second. This discovery has saved me an immense amount of time. I do not, of course, apply it to the substance, but only to the form. When I discover an error of an important kind, I re-write the whole. What I do not find is that I can improve a sentence when I am satisfied with what it means.

Very gradually I have discovered ways of writing with a minimum of worry and anxiety. When I was young each fresh piece of serious work used to seem to me for a time—perhaps a long time—to be beyond my powers. I would fret myself into a nervous state from fear that it was never going to come right. I would make one unsatisfying attempt after another, and in the end have to discard them all. At last I found that such fumbling attempts were a waste of time. It appeared that after first contemplating a book on some subject, and after giving serious preliminary attention to it, I needed a period of sub-conscious incubation which could not be hurried and was if anything impeded by deliberate thinking. Sometimes I would find, after a time, that I had made a mistake, and that I could not write the book I had had in mind. But often I was more fortunate. Having, by a time of very intense concentration, planted the problem in my sub-consciousness, it would germinate underground until suddenly the solution emerged with blinding clarity, so that it only remained to write down what had appeared as if in a revelation.

The most curious example of this process, and the one which led me subsequently to rely upon it, occurred at the beginning of 1914. I had undertaken to give the Lowell Lectures at Boston, and had chosen as my subject "Our Knowledge of the External World." Throughout 1913 I thought about this topic. In term time in my rooms at Cambridge, in vacations in a quiet inn on the upper reaches of the Thames, I concentrated with such intensity that I sometimes forgot to breathe and emerged panting as from a trance. But all to no avail. To every theory that I could think of I could perceive fatal objections. At last, in despair, I went off to Rome for Christmas, hoping that a holiday would revive my flagging energy. I got back to Cambridge on the last day of 1913, and although my difficulties were still completely unresolved I arranged, because the remaining time was short, to dictate as best I could to a stenographer. Next morning, as she came in at the door, I suddenly saw exactly what I had to say, and proceeded to dictate the whole book without a moment's hesitation.

I do not want to convey an exaggerated impression. The book was very imperfect, and I now think that it contains serious errors. But it was the best that I could have done at that time, and a more leisurely method (within the time at my disposal) would almost certainly have produced something worse. Whatever may be true of other people, this is the right method for me. Flaubert and Pater, I have found, are best forgotten so far as I am concerned.

Although what I now think about how to write is not so very different from what I thought at the age of eighteen, my development has not been by any means rectilinear. There was a time, in the first years of this century, when I had more florid and rhetorical ambitions. This was the time when I wrote The Free Man's Worship, a work of which I do not now think well. At that time I was steeped in Milton's prose, and his rolling periods reverberated through the caverns of my mind. I cannot say that I no longer admire them, but for me to imitate them involves a certain insincerity. In fact, all imitation is dangerous. Nothing could be better in style than the Prayer Book and the Authorized Version of the Bible, but they express a way of thinking and feeling which is different from that of our time. A style is not good unless it is an intimate and almost involuntary expression of the personality of the writer, and then only if the writer's personality is worth expressing. But although direct imitation is always to be deprecated, there is much to be gained by familiarity with good prose, especially in cultivating a sense of prose rhythm.

X as a Historical-Social Process

As was mentioned above, process analysis is relatively easy to organize because it falls naturally into a chronological progression. What happens, however, when the process being analyzed is so complex (as in many historical events or in complicated scientific processes) that dozens, maybe hundreds, of stages are involved? In such a case, it would be unwieldy, if not impossible, to analyze each stage. One solution is to "block out" the process into three or four key units around which a multitude of events can be arranged.

In historical analysis, then, your main challenge is to find an appropriate way of grouping the stages of a given event, for the limitless day-by-day, minute-by-minute details involved in any historical occurrence could easily swamp you. Certainly you cannot include everything. You must group your facts around particular "centers"; you must also be scrupulously clear about chronology. Notice how the writer of the following historical process sweeps through centuries of history in a single paragraph by clustering all the events of the prehistoric period around three main groups of migrants who arrived in Britain in three waves (note also the time transitions: *"first," "next,"* and *"later"*).

First wave   *First* were the paleolithic men, or men of the rough-stone age, who used rude weapons, ornaments, and implements of stone and bone. They probably lived in caves and depended for their subsistence on Second wave the wild beasts they captured and the vegetable products they found growing wild. *Next* were the neolithic men, or men of the polished-stone age, who used the well-shaped stone, bone, and horn implements that are frequently found, and probably lived in some kind of artificial buildings, raised crops, kept domestic animals, knew how Third wave to weave cloth and to make pottery, and perhaps traded with other peoples. They built and deposited their dead in long burial mounds such as those whose remains still exist. They were small men, perhaps of the same race as is now represented by the Basques of Spain. *Later* than these came a race who knew the use of bronze, who buried their dead in small, round burial mounds, and who were probably the builders of Stonehenge, Kit's Coty House, and the other mysterious groups of standing stones which are found scattered through England. These are known as men of the bronze age, and may have been the earliest immigrants of the race dominant in Britain when our written knowledge of it begins.[3]

X as a Technical-Natural Process

Another common type of process analysis involves description of natural or technical operations. Here again transitional devices are especially important, for they link the stages of a process that might otherwise seem fragmented or discontinuous. What keeps the stages clearly sequential are "time" words, "place" words (such as "here"), pronouns that refer to nouns in preceding sentences, and repetition of key words. Observe how these several factors work in the following paragraph, a brief—but clear and precise—analysis of a physiological process: how blood circulates. (Key transitions and repetitions are italicized.)

Part of the *blood* in the heart [receives] a fresh store of *oxygen* from the *lungs.* This *blood* is pumped into a large *artery*—the *aorta*—and from the *aorta* it is carried into a branched system of smaller *arteries.* From the *arteries* it passes into the capillaries. *Here oxygen* and food materials (which have been absorbed from the small intestine and liver) are given up to the tissues. Waste materials, including the gas carbon dioxide, are received. The *blood then* passes to the *veins.* It is returned to the heart by way of two large *veins.*

Next, the *blood* is pumped from the heart through the large *pulmonary artery* to the *lungs.* (*Pulmonary* comes from the Latin *pulmo:* "lung.") In the *lungs* carbon dioxide is discharged and *oxygen* is received. The *blood* is *then* returned to the heart through the *pulmonary veins,* and another cycle begins.[4]

The two analyses that follow are also technical, although they are very different in both tone and style. The first is a straightforward factual explanation of the working of a thermostat, described in terms of the natural laws that underlie it—specifically the fact that liquid expands when it is heated. This account is dry and somewhat difficult to read, for it is an uncompromisingly detailed description of an uncompromisingly natural-mechanical process.

The second analysis, "The Process of Riveting," though also technical, is easier to read because *the process is humanized.* It is written from the point of view of the people involved in the process. Thus the collective effort of the riveters at each step—their skillful and risky manipulation of the rivet— introduces an element of life and suspense into an otherwise mechanical procedure.

[3]From *A Short History of England,* revised and enlarged edition, by Edward P. Cheyney. Reprinted by permission of Ginn and Company.
[4]Reprinted from *The Book of Popular Science* by permission of the publishers, Grolier Incorporated, New York.

The Way Things Work: A Thermostat[5]

A thermostat is a device for maintaining a temperature constant at a desired value. For this purpose it is equipped with a temperature sensing unit which detects any deviation of the actual temperature from the desired value and transmits information on this to a device which cancels the deviation. The sensing unit may be a tube filled with a liquid, a bimetallic strip or a spring bellows. The simplest device of this kind is the direct-acting thermostat. It makes use of the fact that nearly all liquids expand on heating (Fig. 1). The thermostat itself consists of a tube filled with a liquid which expands very considerably when it is heated (Fig.2). The connection to the control device which actuates the valve in the hot-water supply pipe (for example) is established by a capillary tube which is also filled with liquid. If the air temperature in the room under thermostatic control rises above the desired level, the liquid in the sensing unit expands, overcomes the restraining force of a spring on the valve, and throttles or closes the latter. As a result of this, the flow of hot water (or other heating medium) is reduced and less heat is supplied to the room. Because of this the temperature in the room will go down after a time, so that the liquid cools and contracts. The spring load on the valve once again exceeds the pressure exerted by the liquid and opens the valve. In this way the temperature in the room is kept

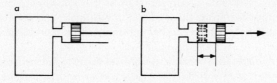

Fig. 1   PRINCIPLE OF THERMOSTATIC CONTROL

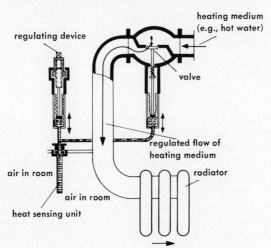

Fig. 2   THERMOSTAT FOR SPACE HEATING CONTROL
(*direct action*)

[5] From *The Way Things Work: An Illustrated Encyclopedia of Technology*. Copyright © 1967, by George Allen & Unwin, Ltd. Reprinted by permission of Simon and Schuster.

constant within fairly narrow limits. The desired value of the temperature is set on a graduated scale which has been calibrated by the makers. By rotation of the screw on the control device the valve spring is compressed to a greater or less extent by the liquid, so that the valve correspondingly opens more or less. The low rate of the hot water thus increases or decreases, causing the temperature level in the room to rise or to fall (Fig. 2).

The Process of Riveting[6]

The actual process of riveting is simple—in description. Rivets are carried to the job by the rivet boy, a riveter's apprentice whose ambition it is to replace one of the members of the gang—which one, he leaves to luck. The rivets are dumped into a keg beside a small coke furnace. The furnace stands on a platform of loose boards roped to steel girders which may or may not have been riveted. If they have not been riveted there will be a certain amount of play in the temporary bolts. The furnace is tended by the heater or passer. He wears heavy clothes and gloves to protect him from the flying sparks and intense heat of his work, and he holds a pair of tongs about a foot and a half long in his right hand. When a rivet is needed, he whirls the furnace blower until the coke is white-hot, picks up a rivet with his tongs, and drives it into the coals. His skill as a heater appears in his knowledge of the exact time necessary to heat the steel. If he overheats it, it will flake, and the flakes will permit the rivet to turn in its hole. And a rivet which gives in its hole is condemned by the inspectors.

When the heater judges that his rivet is right, he turns to face the catcher, who may be above or below him or fifty or sixty or eighty feet away on the same floor level with the naked girders between. There is no means of handing the rivet over. It must be thrown. And it must be accurately thrown. And if the floor beams of the floor above have been laid so that a flat trajectory is essential, it must be thrown with considerable force. The catcher is therefore armed with a smallish, battered tin can, called a cup, with which to catch the red-hot steel. Various patented cups have been put upon the market from time to time but they have made little headway. Catchers prefer the ancient can.

The catcher's position is not exactly one which a sportsman catching rivets for pleasure would choose. He stands upon a narrow platform of loose planks laid over needle beams and roped to a girder near the connection upon which the gang is at work. There are live coils of pneumatic tubing for the rivet gun around his feet. If he moves more than a step or two in any direction, he is gone, and if he loses his balance backward he is apt to end up at street level without time to walk. And the object is to catch a red-hot iron rivet weighing anywhere from a quarter of a pound to a pound and a half and capable, if he lets it pass, of drilling an automobile radiator or a man's skull 500 feet below as neatly as a shank of shrapnel. Why more rivets do not fall is the great mystery of skyscraper construction. The only reasonable explanation offered to date is the reply of an erector's foreman who was asked what would happen if a catcher on the Forty Wall Street job let a rivet go by him around lunch hour. "Well," said the foreman, "he's not supposed to."

There is practically no exchange of words among riveters. Not only are they averse to conversation, which would be reasonable enough in view of the effect they have on the conversation of others, but they are averse to speech in any form. The catcher faces the heater. He holds his tin can up. The heater swings his tongs, releasing one

[6]"Riveting a Skyscraper," by the Editors of *Fortune* (October 1930). Courtesy of *Fortune* magazine.

handle. The red iron arcs through the air in one of those parabolas so much admired by the stenographers in the neighboring windows. And the tin can clanks.

Meantime the gun-man and the bucker-up have prepared the connection—aligning the two holes, if necessary, with a drift pin driven by a pneumatic hammer—and removed the temporary bolts. They, too, stand on loose-roped boards with the column or the beam between them. When the rivet strikes the catcher's can, he picks it out with a pair of tongs held in his right hand, knocks it sharply against the steel to shake off the glowing flakes, and rams it into the hole, an operation which is responsible for his alternative title of sticker. Once the rivet is in place, the bucker-up braces himself with his dolly bar, a short heavy bar of steel, against the capped end of the rivet. On outside wall work he is sometimes obliged to hold on by one elbow with his weight out over the street and the jar of the riveting shaking his precarious balance. And the gun-man lifts his pneumatic hammer to the rivet's other end.

The gun-man's work is the hardest work, physically, done by the gang. The hammers in use for steel construction work are supposed to weigh around thirty pounds and actually weigh about thirty-five. They must not only be held against the rivet end, but held there with the gun-man's entire strength, and for a period of forty to sixty seconds. (A rivet driven too long will develop a collar inside the new head.) And the concussion to the ears and to the arms during that period is very great. The whole platform shakes and the vibration can be felt down the column thirty stories below. It is common practice for the catcher to push with the gun-man and for the gun-man and the bucker-up to pass the gun back and forth between them when the angle is difficult. Also on a heavy rivet job the catcher and the bucker-up may relieve the gun-man at the gun.

The weight of the gun is one cause, though indirect, of accidents. The rivet set, which is the actual hammer at the point of the gun, is held in place, when the gun leaves the factory, by clips. Since the clips increase the weight of the hammer, it is good riveting practice to knock them off against the nearest column and replace them with a hank of wire. But wire has a way of breaking, and when it breaks there is nothing to keep the rivet set and the pneumatic piston itself from taking the bucker-up or the catcher on the belt and knocking him into the next block.

X as an Intellectual Process

When you try to present a "train of thought" or a line of reasoning—in order to explain your views, or to argue a case for or against something—you are attempting to describe an intellectual or logical process, one that is based on the laws of reasoning. No finer essay has been written in this category than Thomas Huxley's eminently readable analysis of the act of thinking itself: how we use the inductive and deductive modes in our everyday lives.

Thinking Scientifically[7]
THOMAS HENRY HUXLEY

There is a well-known incident in one of Molière's plays, where the author makes the hero express unbounded delight on being told that he had been talking prose during the whole of his life. In the same way, I trust, that you will take comfort, and be

[7]From *Collected Works*, by Thomas H. Huxley (1825–1895).

delighted with yourselves, on the discovery that you have been acting on the principles of inductive and deductive philosophy during the same period. Probably there is not one here who has not in the course of the day had occasion to set in motion a complex train of reasoning, of the very same kind, though differing of course in degree, as that which a scientific man goes through in tracing the causes of natural phenomena.

A very trivial circumstance will serve to exemplify this. Suppose you go into a fruiterer's shop, wanting an apple,—you take up one, and, on biting it, you find it sour; you look at it, and see that it is hard and green. You take up another one, and that too is hard, green, and sour. The shopman offers you a third; but, before biting it, you examine it, and find that it is hard and green, and you immediately say that you will not have it, as it must be sour, like those that you have already tried.

Nothing can be more simple than that, you think; but if you will take the trouble to analyse and trace out into its logical elements what has been done by the mind, you will be greatly surprised. In the first place you have performed the operation of induction. You found that, in two experiences, hardness and greenness in apples went together with sourness. It was so in the first case, and it was confirmed by the second. True, it is a very small basis, but still it is enough to make an induction from; you generalise the facts, and you expect to find sourness in apples where you get hardness and greenness. You found upon that a general law, that all hard and green apples are sour; and that, so far as it goes, is a perfect induction. Well, having got your natural law in this way, when you are offered another apple which you find is hard and green, you say, "All hard and green apples are sour; this apple is hard and green, therefore this apple is sour." That train of reasoning is what logicians call a syllogism, and has all its various parts and terms,—its major premiss, its minor premiss, and its conclusion. And, by the help of further reasoning, which if drawn out, would have to be exhibited in two or three other syllogisms, you arrive at your final determination, "I will not have that apple." So that, you see, you have, in the first place, established a law by induction, and upon that you have founded a deduction, and reasoned out the special conclusion of the particular case. Well now, suppose, having got your law, that at some time afterwards, you are discussing the qualities of apples with a friend: you will say to him, "It is a very curious thing,—but I find that all hard and green apples are sour!" Your friend says to you, "But how do you know that?" You at once reply, "Oh, because I have tried them over and over again, and have always found them to be so." Well, if we were talking science instead of common sense, we should call that an experimental verification. And if still opposed, you go further, and say, "I have heard from the people in Somersetshire and Devonshire, where a large number of apples are grown, that they have observed the same thing. It is also found to be the case in Normandy, and in North America. In short, I find it to be the universal experience of mankind wherever attention has been directed to the subject." Whereupon, your friend, unless he is a very unreasonable man, agrees with you, and is convinced that you are quite right in the conclusion you have drawn. He believes, although perhaps he does not know he believes it, that the more extensive verifications are,—that the more frequently experiments have been made, and results of the same kind arrived at,—that the more varied the conditions under which the same results are attained, the more certain is the ultimate conclusion, and he disputes the question no further. He sees that the experiment has been tried under all sorts of conditions, as to time, place and people, with the same result; and he says with you, therefore, that the law you have laid down must be a good one, and he must believe it.

In science we do the same thing;—the philosopher exercises precisely the same faculties, though in a much more delicate manner. In scientific inquiry it becomes a matter of duty to expose a supposed law to every possible kind of verification, and to take care, moreover, that this is done intentionally, and not left to a mere accident, as in the case of the apples. And in science, as in common life, our confidence in a law is in exact proportion to the absence of variation in the result of our experimental verifications. For instance, if you let go your grasp of an article you may have in your hand, it will immediately fall to the ground. That is a very common verification of one of the best established laws of nature—that of gravitation. The method by which men of science establish the existence of that law is exactly the same as that by which we have established the trivial proposition about the sourness of hard and green apples. But we believe it in such an extensive, thorough, and unhesitating manner because the universal experience of mankind verifies it, and we can verify it ourselves at any time; and that is the strongest possible foundation on which any natural law can rest.

ASSIGNMENTS

Class Discussion and Paragraph Suggestions

(See Chapter 27 for methods of composing unified, adequately developed paragraphs.)

1. Answer the following questions based on the essay "The Process of Riveting."
   a. Outline the main stages involved in riveting steel.
   b. How does the writer move us through the stages? (Note his point of view.)
   c. What additional information, i.e., additional to the "outline of stages," does the writer include in this analysis (biographical data, descriptive details, suggestion of attitudes, anecdotes, description of people)? Why does he include them?
   d. Comment on the writer's style: length of paragraphs and unity; choice of words (technical? plain?); length and difficulty of sentences; transitional devices; general flow and readability, appropriateness of tone.
   e. Comment specifically on the following sentences. In what way do they contribute to the overall tone of the piece?
      1. "It must be thrown. And it must be accurately thrown."
      2. "Catchers prefer the ancient can."
      3. "The catcher's position is not exactly one which a sportsman catching rivets for pleasure would choose."
      4. "Well, he's not supposed to."
      5. "And the tin can clanks."

2. In a paragraph of 150 to 250 words support or challenge the rhetorician who called "The Process of Riveting" "a justly admired example of description of a process."

3. Consider Huxley's examples of scientific thinking in everyday life.

   a. Write a paragraph (150–250 words) called "Thinking Scientifically," in which you illustrate your own everyday use of inductive and deductive reasoning.
   b. Write another paragraph of equal length supporting Dr. Samuel Johnson's counterobservation that "most men think indistinctly." Cite examples of the illogical, the irrational, the impulsive, the half-thought-through. Suggested title: "Thinking Unscientifically."

4. Answer the following questions based on the essay "The Way Things Work: A Thermostat."

   a. Describe the stages in the action of a thermostat.
   b. Are the stages clearly indicated in this essay, or must they be inferred?

c. Before describing the *action* of a thermostat, what information must the writer offer?

d. What purpose do the illustrations serve?

e. Does this description of a process convey *attitudes* of any kind?

5. Write a paragraph comparable to this one (150–250 words) in which you describe (in terms of the natural laws underlying the process) how one of the following works:

a camera   a radio
a microscope   a barometer
a telegraph   a parachute
a magnet   a mirror

Essay Suggestions

1. Creative Process

a. Write an essay (500–750 words) describing a creative experience you have had—the composition of a poem, story, or piece of music; the painting of a picture; the design of a room or a piece of furniture.

or

b. Describe in an essay (500–750 words) the process of learning how to do something (as Russell learned to write). Any accomplishment will provide a suitable topic: how you learned to swim, ski, speak French, play bridge— maybe even how you learned "to think," that is, to think *rigorously*.

2. Historical Process

Write an essay (500–750 words) on one of the following topics, chosen from one of the following groups:

a. Discoveries and Inventions

How Schliemann discovered Troy
How Columbus discovered America
How Salk discovered the polio vaccine
How Pasteur discovered the pasteurization process
How the Curies discovered radium
How Bell invented the telephone
How Edison invented the electric light

b. General Historical Events

Beginnings:

How Alaska became a state
How the Great Wall of China was built
How the Third Reich rose

Endings:

How Belgium lost the Belgian Congo
How the French Revolution ended
How the Roman Empire fell

c. Social and Political Processes

How Congress conducts investigations
How a U.S. president is elected
How women won the vote
How Prohibition was repealed

d. General Enterprises

> How a newspaper or magazine is "put to bed"
> How the paper is delivered (from press to doorstep)
> How a class is conducted
> How a party is organized
> How a paper is written
> How a trip is planned
> How traffic is regulated
> How a university (or any part thereof) is run

3. Technical and Natural Processes

a. Write an essay (500–750 words) on one of the following complex processes, *humanizing* it in the manner of "The Process of Riveting":

> How explosives are manufactured
> How glass is blown
> How skyscraper windows are washed
> How paintings are restored
> How tobacco is cured

b. Write an essay (500–750 words) explaining one of the following natural processes:

1. Physiology (how X is done)

> How we see
> How we hear
> How we maintain balance
> How we breathe
> How we digest food
> How we think
> How we remember
> How we fall asleep

2. Botany (how X is made)

> How plants manufacture chlorophyll
> How plants manufacture oxygen
> How plants manufacture food
> How plants reproduce
> How plants evolve
> How trees develop "rings"

5 How Should X Be Made or Done?

With this question we come to the most practical type of writing: the "how-to" piece, a form of process analysis that tells readers not only how a particular process *is* made or done, but how it *should be* made or done. Thus it becomes a set of directions from you to your readers, telling them precisely how to move through a series of steps toward a given goal. All recipes are instances of the "how-to" form, as are all inside-the-package instructions. We conduct much of the business of the world by means of this kind of writing. Here, for example, is a straightforward account of how to perform a relatively simple operation.

How to Sharpen Your Knife[1]
FLORENCE H. PETTIT

If you have never done any whittling or wood carving before, the first skill to learn is how to sharpen your knife. You may be surprised to learn that even a brand-new knife needs sharpening. Knives are never sold honed (finely sharpened), although some gouges and chisels are. It is essential to learn the firm stroke on the stone that will keep your blades sharp. The sharpening stone must be fixed in place on the table, so that it will not move around. You can do this by placing a piece of rubber inner tube or a thin piece of foam rubber under it. Or you can tack four strips of

[1]From *How to Make Whirligigs and Whimmy Diddles* by Florence H. Pettit. Copyright © 1972 by Florence H. Pettit. Reprinted with the permission of Thomas Y. Crowell Company, Inc., publisher.

wood, if you have a rough worktable, to frame the stone and hold it in place. Put a generous puddle of oil on the stone—this will soon disappear into the surface of a new stone, and you will need to keep adding more oil. Press the knife blade flat against the stone in the puddle of oil, using your index finger. Whichever way the cutting edge of a knife faces is the side of the blade that should get a little more pressure. Move the blade around three or four times in a narrow oval about the size of your fingernail, going *counterclockwise* when the sharp edge is facing right. Now turn the blade over in the same spot on the stone, press hard, and move it around the small oval *clockwise,* with more pressure on the cutting edge that faces left. Repeat the ovals, flipping the knife blade over six or seven times, and applying lighter pressure to the blade the last two times. Wipe the blade clean with a piece of rag or tissue and rub it flat on the piece of leather strop at least twice on each side. Stroke *away* from the cutting edge to remove the little burr of metal that may be left on the blade.

Qualities of Good "How-to" Writing

"How-to," or directional, writing automatically puts you in the authoritative position of instructor, telling your "less informed" reader-students exactly what to do and how to do it. Imperatives are common in a "how-to" piece: *put* a puddle of oil; *press* the knife blade flat; *move* the blade around. With the sense of self-importance that inevitably accompanies this form of writing, however, you should feel an equal sense of responsibility, for in assuming the role of teacher and counselor, you must make certain you are teaching well and counseling wisely.

Your first responsibility, of course, is to be accurate and clear. If, for example, you are instructing readers in "the art of winning at bridge," you should be absolutely certain first that you have your facts right, and second that you explain them clearly, not leaving out a single step or important detail, taking nothing for granted, allowing for no uncertainties or ambiguities as to what is meant. These are the cardinal virtues of directional writing: accuracy, clarity, and *conciseness.* No extra words should clog the free flow of information. Instructions should be written in a systematic, lucid, and readable manner.

"How-to" pieces present no serious organizational problems, since directions must be given in strict chronological order (first do this, then do that, and so on) and the mode of address, as we have seen, is invariably imperative.

Variety in "How-to" Writing

The "how-to" form clearly lends itself to an extraordinarily wide range of subject matter and an equally wide variety of tones. In general, the writer and reader are brought together in intimate contact (direct address from *me* to *you*), thereby establishing a situation in which the deeper humanistic purposes of writing have an excellent opportunity to fulfill themselves:

increasing understanding among people, sharing knowledge and skills, helping one another.

The most helpful "how-to" pieces often deal with concrete and important activities that people should know about. Thus a book like *What to Do Till the Doctor Comes* performs a public service by providing a series of "how-to" essays explaining the essentials of first-aid treatment for a variety of ills, such as bleeding.

How to Control Bleeding by Pressure Bandage[2]

As a rule, bleeding which is not severe can be controlled by placing a compress (pad of sterile gauze, clean handkerchief, or similar material) over the wound and applying pressure by means of a bandage or adhesive-tape strapping. If the pressure bandage does not control the bleeding, hand pressure applied on the compress directly over the wound may stop it. When bleeding has been controlled by a pressure bandage, do not remove the dressing if it soaks through. By doing so you will disturb the blood clots which are forming and may hurt the patient, thus increasing the danger of shock. Put another dressing on top of the first one and bandage tightly.

Less concrete as to physical action, but useful in their own way (provided they are not too pat), are advice pieces such as the following:

How to Get More Work Done[3]

JOHN KORD LAGEMANN

Whenever I meet anyone with a special flair for getting things done, I make a point of asking, "How do you do it?" The answers, I have found, are rules of thumb which belong in the category of practical wisdom rather than scientific research—but they work. Here are the techniques that busy men and women in a wide variety of professions have told me that are most helpful.

Get started. "There are two steps in getting any task done," said the late Adlai Stevenson when I asked him how he managed to write all his own speeches in addition to carrying on his official duties as U.S. Ambassador to the United Nations. "The first step is to begin. The second is to begin again. The first is the hardest."

Making a good start on any new project is like taking your first parachute jump—it requires boldness. At 40, Winston Churchill took up painting as a hobby. "Very gingerly," Churchill recalled, "I mixed a little blue paint with a very small brush, and then with infinite precaution made a mark about as big as a small bean upon the affronted snow-white shield." At that moment, a friend who was a painter's wife entered the room and exclaimed, "But what are you hesitating about?" Seizing a brush, she walloped the canvas with large, fierce strokes. "The spell was broken," Churchill concluded. "I have never felt any awe of a canvas since. This beginning with audacity is a great part of the art of painting." It is also a large part of tackling and mastering any new job.

Just getting into the posture for work may put you in the mood. Pianist Ania

[2]*What to Do Till the Doctor Comes,* by Donald B. Armstrong, M.D., and Grace T. Hallock. Copyright © 1943, by Simon and Schuster, Inc. Reprinted by permission of the publisher.
[3]Reprinted with permission from the May 1967 *Reader's Digest.* Copyright 1967 by the Reader's Digest Assn., Inc. Also reprinted by permission of Mrs. John Kord Lagemann.

Dorfman said that the hardest part of practicing was sitting down at the keyboard. After that, habit and discipline took over and set her in motion. . . .

Choose a pacesetter. Every coach knows that the best way to improve the performance of a player is to expose him to pacesetters—outstanding players who set high standards of skill and endurance. In tennis, for example, it is impossible for even an ace to show what he can do if he is matched with a dud. Dennis Ralston, three times the top-ranking U.S. amateur tennis player before recently turning pro, says, "In training, the main problem is to find the opponent who is a little better than you are, and learn how to beat him at his own game." . . .

Manage your time. Time is our working capital. "Managing it is everybody's No. 1 problem," says the well-known management consultant, Peter F. Drucker, in his recent book, *The Effective Executive.* "Those who really get things done don't start with their work; they start with their time."

Like money, time has a way of disappearing—a dribble here, a dribble there, until you find yourself asking at the end of a busy day, "Where did it go?" It's only by budgeting the hours and minutes of the day that you can have time left over for your own personal use. It's this "discretionary time" that buys freedom from harassment and a sense of mastery in getting a job done.

One of the most effective techniques of time management is the simple one of setting a deadline. Once my two sons and I spent a week by ourselves in the country. We had to do all the housework, but we put off doing the domestic chores until the house was a mess. One night I bet the boys a dollar I could do the supper dishes in ten minutes. They took me up on it, and I finished just under the wire. Next night my sons shaved two minutes off my record. We assigned time limits to the other daily housekeeping tasks, and found that we could keep things shipshape with no more than an hour of concentrated work. The rest of the day was ours to do with as we pleased.

. . . One day the editor dropped in to see how the work was going and, realizing that I was getting nowhere, said, "Did you ever notice that one of the first things that strikes you about a girl is her perfume? After you've been with her a while, the perfume seems to disappear. But if you leave her and come back, the scent is as vivid as ever. Maybe that's what you should do with this article. Leave it for a while and do something else. Then come back to it."

I took his advice, and the article was finished. Since then, I've noticed that most people who work with ideas use this same device. They work on one problem until they start losing the feel of it, then turn to something else. Later they return to the first problem with fresh interest.

Filter out the irrelevant. Imagine yourself surrounded by an invisible bubble within which you are shielded from distraction. The outside world is still there, but the wall of your bubble filters out everything irrelevant to the task at hand.

Concentration doesn't mean a narrowing down of interest. It means the widening out and fullest use of all one's powers—a comprehensive problem under consideration. Emerson called this kind of concentration "the secret of strength in politics, in war, in trade—in short, in all management of human affairs."

Find your own work rhythm. The conventional way of breaking up the day is so many hours for work and so many for play, relaxation and sleep. But if you feel like working after dinner—or, for that matter, at 3 A.M.—why not? A lot of creative work can be done at odd times and places.

The great Canadian physician Sir William Osler, between his teaching, his medical writings and practice, had very little time to pursue his lifelong interest in books. However, he set aside 15 minutes every night to compile an annotated bibliography of his huge library. When he died his ambitious *Bibliotheca Osleriana* contained 7787 entries.

Finish the job. Jobs, like stories, have a beginning, a development and an end. Having started work on a project, many of us don't know when or where to stop. The solution is to plan your work in advance so that when you come to the point where your plan is fulfilled, you can say, "That's that."

Don't be like the futile politician of whom philosopher George Santayana once said, "Having lost sight of his goal, he redoubles his effort." Define your goal precisely, so that once it is attained you can move on to other projects. . . .

For humorists as well as serious advice-givers, the "how-to" piece opens up vast possibilities, as can be seen in the delightfully zany piece that follows:

How to Dismount from an Elephant[4]
RICHARD L. THOMAS

Anyone can manage to get down from an elephant, in the sense of scrambling around without the least regard for appearances or proper form. Indeed, falling off is one surefire method. But people of poise and breeding do not feel the end justifies the means—they insist on dismounting in style. They are the natural aristocrats who have so mismanaged their lives that now they're marooned atop an elephant and not at all sure what to do about it.

I

The first thing you do in dismounting from an elephant is to compose yourself.

II

In step II, we begin to familiarize ourselves with the beast. I know this sounds remote from your current needs and aspirations, and perhaps even a trifle academic. Nonetheless, I must ask you to have confidence in me and place yourself completely in my hands.

Very well then. Now, there are many ways you can go about familiarizing yourself with your host. I'll merely advise you to try to obtain this personal information about him without his knowledge. Many elephants chafe under close scrutiny, and others become sullen and withdrawn, so it's best to employ an extremely tactful, circuitous approach.

III

Our next step will be to learn the nomenclature of the elephant. This kind of careful preparation will help you avoid getting rattled and losing your composure in the hectic hours ahead. . . .

Now, the elephant is an animal of many parts, but we will confine ourselves to those portions which directly concern us here. This should not lead you to think there is nothing more to it. In fact, *the elephant is a very complex animal, mentally and emotionally, and should never be dismissed lightly.*

Notice how I have not bothered to mention the elephant's eye. This was a precautionary measure, not an oversight. You see, it is important to avoid, at all costs, *any* contact with the eye. The reasons for this are fascinating:

(a) An elephant does not see very well to begin with.

(b) But he is *not* blind, for heaven's sake, and if you were suddenly to appear before him on your way down, it could startle him, especially if he hasn't been aware that you were on him.

(c) Elephants do not like people sneaking on and off them.

IV

Try to decide in advance from which side you want to dismount, and then *stick to your decision!* If you put off making up your mind until the last possible minute or keep changing your plans, you may find yourself unable to decide at all and end up running around in a flurry of indecision. It is surprising how quickly any panic you feel can communicate itself to the elephant, who in turn may decide to go berserk.* But that's nothing compared with how quickly *his* panic can communicate itself to you.

Once you've settled on a point of debarkation, walk quietly and casually to the site you have chosen. By now the elephant will surely know something is up, even if he is not sure it is you. But if you have been following these rules diligently, the news should not rankle him.

V

Generally speaking, it's best to select one of the orthodox ways of dismounting— the Right Side Descent, the Prefrontal Slide, the Posterial Crawl, etc. Do *not* attempt anything fancy your first time down, such as swinging grandly from the elephant's ear . . . and alighting with a springly little leap onto the ground. Even the experts can't carry off this sort of thing with much success. Running starts and other grandstand plays should similarly be eschewed.

VI

Miscellaneous Hints and Caveats

1. Wait until the elephant stops before dismounting. This is *not* a boxcar or a trolley you are dealing with, but a flesh-and-blood animal with hopes, fears, and ambitions not so very different from your own.

If the elephant happens to be sprinting at the time you decide to make your move, you'll especially want to wait for him to stop. For those of you to whom this would be an intolerable delay, at least wait until he slows down to a canter. This is no time to become impatient or hotheaded, even if you *have* whipped yourself into a frenzy of courage to prepare for the moment of truth. Besides, he won't run forever, so it won't be a long wait anyway. He's probably just remembered something he meant to do earlier.

2. Better yet, wait until he is asleep if you can hold out that long, the better to avoid any acrimonious confrontations. It's always politic to avoid showdowns of *any* kind with an elephant, but most particularly when the time and place are not of your own choosing.

If you wait until dusk or later before starting your descent, the elephant isn't so likely to see you and take umbrage at your effrontery. However, you increase your chances of running into things and tipping him off that you're up to something. If

---

*The elephant is very high-strung, a condition normally attributed to his deep-seated (but probably mistaken) feeling of inadequacy.

you've never groped around at night on the back of an elephant, perhaps you shouldn't start now.

3. Do not leave anything behind, such as camera equipment, clothing, or magazines. These give the elephant a cluttered appearance, which he is likely to resent, and may also give him a clue to your present whereabouts, a fact you'll of course want to keep from him.

4. If he's one of those elephants who wear a lot of expensive jewelry and trappings, leave it all alone. It means the animal belongs to somebody, and you'll have enough trouble as it is trying to explain what you were doing up there, without being caught red-handed like a common second-story man.

5. Don't kick the elephant after you're down, or use similar crude techniques to vent your ill feelings on him. On the other hand, don't stop and chat with him in a fit of camaraderie, or chuck him affectionately under the tusks, or make a fuss about how glad you are to be down. Some elephants have very thin skins and are quick to detect a slur in the most harmless remarks. A waspish elephant is no laughing matter. If you *must* communicate with him, be sure to choose your words carefully, using pleasing gestures, and try to keep your tone of voice civil and well modulated. Above all, don't be condescending.

If you can manage all right now, I must be on my way.

Carrying the "How-to" Too Far

Some people feel that as a prose form, "how-toism" has been extended to ridiculous extremes, that it threatens to run our lives:

How to eat, talk, breathe, sleep, cook with sour cream, play canasta, give a church supper, raise parakeets, and bet on the horses. How to be healthy, wealthy, wise, and happily married. How to become popular, articulate, refined, charming, virile, cultured, and couth. How to cope with children, sex, religion, old age, Christmas, in-laws, and other common problems of life.[5]

More disturbing, "how-toism" often distorts a difficult process by depicting it in a rosy glow of simplicity ("there's nothing to it!"). Two actual titles establish this point clearly enough: "You Can Make a Stradivarius Violin" and "The Art of Becoming an Original Writer in Three Days."

Most of us have read similar pieces that simplify, to the point of simple-mindedness, the intricacies of real life. Take, for example, the following:

How to Stop Worrying[6]
DALE CARNEGIE

Rule 1: Get the facts. Remember that Dean Hawks of Columbia University said that "half the worry in the world is caused by people trying to make decisions before they have sufficient knowledge on which to base a decision."

[5]Dwight Macdonald, *Against the American Grain* (New York: Random House, 1962), p. 361.
[6]From *How to Stop Worrying and Start Living* by Dale Carnegie. Copyright © 1944, 1945, 1946, 1947, 1948 by Dale Carnegie. Reprinted by permission of Simon and Schuster, Inc.

Rule 2: After carefully weighing all the facts, come to a decision.

Rule 3: Once a decision is carefully reached, act! Get busy carrying out your decision—and dismiss all anxiety about the outcome.

Rule 4: When you, or any of your associates, are tempted to worry about a problem, write out and answer the following questions:

    a. What is the problem?

    b. What is the cause of the problem?

    c. What are all possible solutions?

    d. What is the best solution?

There is probably nothing wrong with these suggestions as sensible thumbnail guides for the average "worrywart." But in the face of the complexities of human nature and human predicaments, such guides are pathetically pat and superficial. Indeed, anyone who sincerely believes that he or she can solve the problem of worrying simply by following Dale Carnegie's four basic rules has in fact something to worry about!

ASSIGNMENTS

Class Discussion and Paragraph Suggestions

See Chapter 27 for methods of composing unified, adequately developed paragraphs.)

1. Discuss whether each of the "how-tos" in this section fulfills the following principles of writing:

    a. *accuracy* (Are the facts correct? Indicate in what ways the writer may have oversimplified or overcomplicated the process.)

    b. *clarity* (Are the steps clearly presented?)

    d. *economy* (Are there any unnecessary words or information?)

    d. *rhetorical stance* (To whom is the piece addressed? What is the writer's point of view? tone? purpose in writing the piece?)

2. Read the following paragraph by Benjamin Franklin, describing a technical process for which he was famous.

How to Make Lightning Rods[7]
BENJAMIN FRANKLIN

Prepare a steel rod about five or six feet long, about half an inch thick at its largest end, and tapering to a sharp point. This point should be gilded to prevent its rusting. Secure to the big end of the rod a strong eye or a ring half an inch in diameter. Fix the rod upright to the chimney or the highest part of a house. It should be fixed with some sort of staples or special nails to keep it steady. The pointed end should extend upward, and should rise three or four feet above the chimney or building to which the rod is fixed. Drive into the ground an iron rod about one inch in diameter, and ten or twelve feet long. This rod should also have an eye or ring fixed to its upper end. It is best to place the iron rod some distance from the foundation of the house. Ten feet away is a good distance, if the size of the property permits. Then take as much length

[7]From a letter to David Hume, dated in London, January 24, 1762.

of iron rod of a smaller diameter as will be necessary to reach from the eye on the rod above to the eye of the rod below. Fasten this securely to the fixed rods by passing it through the eyes and bending the ends to form rings too. Then close all the joints with lead. This is easily done by making a small bag of strong paper around the joints, tying it tight below, and then pouring in the molten lead. It is useful to have these joints treated in this way so that there will be a considerable area of contact between each piece. To prevent the wind from shaking this long rod, it may be fastened to the building by several staples. If the building is especially large or long, extending more than one hundred feet for example, it is wise to erect a rod at each end. If there is a well sufficiently near to the building to permit placing the iron rod in the water, this is even better than the use of the iron rod in the ground. It may also be wise to paint the iron to prevent it from rusting. A building so protected will not be damaged by lightning.

    a. In what ways has Franklin made each step clear and distinct?
    b. Comment on Franklin's choice of verbs, transitional devices, qualifications, and explanations.
    c. Write a paragraph (150–250 words) comparable to Franklin's in which you explain to a friend how to make something. Suggestions:

a loudspeaker	a ceramic bowl
a bookcase	a decal
a tray	a blanket
a wax figure	a basket
a lamp	a bracelet
pickles (or any other food)	a string of beads
a sweater	a leather belt
a slipcover	a dress (or any other article of clothing)
a potholder	

2. Write a short self-help piece (150–250 words) in which you:

    a. Offer concrete suggestions on how to treat the following physical ills:

high fever	hangover
cold	first-degree burn
frostbite	bee sting
poison ivy	dog bite
acne	muscle strain
athlete's foot	

    b. Offer concrete, sensible, and restrained suggestions on how to deal with the following psychological problems:

attempts to stop smoking	anxiety
insomnia	dreams
hysteria	fatigue
shock	guilt
depression	drug abuse

    c. Offer sweepingly oversimplified advice on the problems listed above.

Essay Suggestions

1. Write an essay (500–750 words) in which you present basic instructions for one of the following:

stamp collecting	diving
bird watching	hiking
folk dancing	pitching horseshoes
tightrope walking	mountain climbing
hunting an alligator	kite flying
bicycle riding	pitching a tent
serving a tennis ball	fishing
playing billiards	

2. Write a set of instructions (500–750 words) for improving any skill, craft, art, or sport in which you are proficient.

3. Write a "how-to" essay (500–750 words) on a topic as compelling and instructive as "How to Dismount from an Elephant."

6 What Is the Essential Function of X?

In discussing questions 3, 4, and 5 in the preceding chapters, we dealt with various kinds of analysis: breaking something down into its component parts; describing the steps in a process; explaining "how to" go about a process. There is still another kind of analysis, especially useful in dealing with a complex concept or entity, in which we seek to explain our subject by locating its essential function.

The Function of an Institution

As an example, let us take subject 5 on the checklist of subjects—Education—narrow this down to *College* Education, and ask: "What is its essential function?" In other words, what main purpose does—and *should*—a college serve, particularly a liberal arts college? Replying to this question, poet-educator John Ciardi develops his "enrichment of life" principle through a long and lively illustration, and William James speaks with eloquence and passion in behalf of college education as "the sifting of human creations."

Another School Year—Why?[1]

JOHN CIARDI

Let me tell you one of the earliest disasters in my career as a teacher. It was January of 1940 and I was fresh out of graduate school starting my first semester at the University of Kansas City. Part of the reading for the freshman English course

---

[1]"Another School Year—Why?" by John Ciardi from the *Rutgers Alumni Monthly*, November 1954. Reprinted by permission.

was *Hamlet.* Part of the student body was a beanpole with hair on top who came into my class, sat down, folded his arms, and looked at me as if to say: "All right, damn you, teach me something." Two weeks later we started *Hamlet.* Three weeks later he came into my office with his hands on his hips. It is easy to put your hands on your hips if you are not carrying books, and this one was an unburdened soul. "Look," he said, "I came here to be a pharmacist. Why do I have to read this stuff?" And not having a book of his own to point to, he pointed at mine which was lying on the desk.

New as I was to the faculty, I could have told this specimen a number of things. I could have pointed out that he had enrolled, not in a drugstore-mechanics school, but in a college, and that at the end of his course he meant to reach for a scroll that read Bachelor of Science. It would not read: Qualified Pill-Grinding Technician. It would certify that he had specialized in pharmacy and had attained a certain minimum qualification, but it would further certify that he had been exposed to some of the ideas mankind has generated within its history. That is to say, he had not entered a technical training school but a university, and that in universities students enroll for both training and education.

I could have told him all this, but it was fairly obvious he wasn't going to be around long enough for it to matter: at the rate he was going, the first marking period might reasonably be expected to blow him toward the employment agency.

Nevertheless, I was young and I had a high sense of duty and I tried to put it this way: "For the rest of your life," I said, "your days are going to average out to about twenty-four hours. They will be a little shorter when you are in love, and a little longer when you are out of love, but the average will tend to hold. For eight of these hours, more or less, you will be asleep, and I assume you need neither education nor training to manage to get through that third of your life.

"Then for about eight hours of each working day you will, I hope, be usefully employed. Assume you have gone through pharmacy school—or engineering, or aggie, or law school, or whatever—during those eight hours you will be using your professional skills. You will see to it during this third of your life that the cyanide stays out of the aspirin, that the bull doesn't jump the fence, or that your client doesn't go to the electric chair as a result of your incompetence. These are all useful pursuits, they involve skills every man must respect, and they can all bring you good basic satisfactions. Along with everything else, they will probably be what sets your table, supports your wife, and rears your children. They will be your income, and may it always suffice.

"But having finished the day's work what do you do with those other eight hours— with the other third of your life? Let's say you go home to your family. What sort of family are you raising? Will the children ever be exposed to a reasonably penetrating idea at home? We all think of ourselves as citizens of a great democracy. Democracies can exist, however, only as long as they remain intellectually alive. Will you be presiding over a family that maintains some basic contact with the great continuity of democratic intellect? Or is your family life going to be strictly penny-ante and beer on ice? Will there be a book in the house? Will there be a painting a reasonably sensitive man can look at without shuddering? Will your family be able to speak English and to talk about an idea? Will the kids ever get to hear Bach?"

That is about what I said, but this particular pest was not interested. "Look," he said, "you professors raise your kids your way; I'll take care of my own. Me, I'm out to make money."

"I hope you make a lot of it," I told him, "because you're going to be badly stuck for something to do when you're not signing checks."

Fourteen years later, I am still teaching, and I am here to tell you that the business of the college is not only to train you, but to put you in touch with what the best human minds have thought. If you have no time for Shakespeare, for a basic look at philosophy, for the continuity of the fine arts, for that lesson of man's development we call history—then you have no business being in college. You are on your way to being that new species of mechanized savage, the Push-button Neanderthal. Our colleges inevitably graduate a number of such life-forms, but it cannot be said that they went to college; rather the college went through them—without making contact.

No one gets to be a human being unaided. There is not time enough in a single lifetime to invent for oneself everything one needs to know in order to be a civilized human.

Assume, for example, that you want to be a physicist. You pass the great stone halls of, say, M.I.T., and there cut into the stone are the names of the master scientists. The chances are that few if any of you will leave your names to be cut into those stones. Yet any one of you who managed to stay awake through part of a high school course in physics, knows more about physics than did many of those great makers of the past. You know more because they left you what they knew. The first course in any science is essentially a history course. You have to begin by learning what the past learned for you. Except as a man has entered the past of the race he has no function in civilization.

And as this is true of the techniques of mankind, so is it true of mankind's spiritual resources. Most of these resources, both technical and spiritual, are stored in books. Books, the arts, and the techniques of science, are man's peculiar accomplishment. When you have read a book, you have added to your human experience. Read Homer and your mind includes a piece of Homer's mind. Through books you can acquire at least fragments of the mind and experience of Virgil, Dante, Shakespeare—the list is endless. For a great book is necessarily a gift: it offers you a life you have not time to live yourself, and it takes you into a world you have not time to travel in literal time. A civilized human mind is, in essence, one that contains many such lives and many such worlds. If you are too much in a hurry, or too arrogantly proud of your own limitations, to accept as a gift to your humanity some pieces of the minds of Sophocles, of Aristotle, of Chaucer—and right down the scale and down the ages to Yeats, Einstein, E. B. White, and Ogden Nash—then you may be protected by the laws governing manslaughter, and you may be a voting entity, but you are neither a developed human being nor a useful citizen of a democracy.

I think it was La Rochefoucauld who said that most people would never fall in love if they hadn't read about it. He might have said that no one would ever manage to become human if he hadn't read about it.

I speak, I am sure, for the faculty of the liberal arts college and for the faculties of the specialized schools as well, when I say that a university has no real existence and no real purpose except as it succeeds in putting you in touch, both as specialists and as humans, with those human minds *your* human mind needs to include. The faculty, by its very existence, says implicitly: "We have been aided by many people, and by many books, and by the arts, in our attempt to make ourselves some sort of storehouse of human experience. We are here to make available to you, as best we can, that experience."

What Is a College Education For?[2]

WILLIAM JAMES

The sifting of human creations!—nothing less than this is what we ought to mean by the humanities. Essentially this means biography; what our colleges should teach

[2]From "The Social Value of the College Bred" from *Memories and Studies* by William James.

is, therefore, biographical history, ... not of politics merely, but of anything and everything so far as human efforts and conquests are factors that have played their part. Studying in this way, we learn what types of activity have stood the test of time; we acquire standards of the excellent and durable. All our arts and sciences and institutions are but so many quests of perfection on the part of men; and when we see how diverse the types of excellence may be, how various the tests, how flexible the adaptations, we gain a richer sense of what the terms "better" and "worse" may signify in general. Our critical sensibilities grow both more acute and less fanatical. We sympathize with men's mistakes even in the act of penetrating them; we feel the pathos of lost causes and misguided epochs even while we applaud what overcame them.

Such words are vague and such ideas are inadequate, but their meaning is unmistakable. What the colleges—teaching humanities by examples which may be special, but which must be typical and pregnant—should at least try to give us, is a general sense of what, under various disguises, *superiority* has always signified and may still signify. The feeling for a good human job anywhere, the admiration of the really admirable, the disesteem of what is cheap and trashy and impermanent—this is what we call the critical sense, the sense for ideal values. It is the better part of what men know as wisdom. Some of us are wise in this way naturally and by genius; some of us never become so. But to have spent one's youth at college, in contact with the choice and rare and precious, and yet still to be a blind prig or vulgarian, unable to scent out human excellence or to divine it amid its accidents, to know it only when ticketed and labelled and forced on us by others, this indeed should be accounted the very calamity and shipwreck of a higher education.

The sense for human superiority ought, then, to be considered our line, as boring subways is the engineer's line and the surgeon's is appendicitis. Our college ought to have lit up in us a lasting relish for the better kind of man, a loss of appetite for mediocrities, and a disgust for cheapjacks. We ought to smell, as it were, the difference of quality in men and their proposals when we enter the world of affairs about us. Expertness in this might well atone for some of our awkwardness at accounts, for some of our ignorance of dynamos. The best claim we can make for the higher education, the best single phrase in which we can tell what it ought to do for us, is then, exactly what I said: it should enable us to *know a good man when we see him. . . .*

The notion that a people can run itself and its affairs anonymously is now well known to be the silliest of absurdities. Mankind does nothing save through initiatives on the part of inventors, great or small, and imitation by the rest of us—these are the sole factors active in human progress. Individuals of genius show the way, and set the patterns, which common people then adopt and follow. *The rivalry of the patterns is the history of the world.* Our democratic problem thus is statable in ultra-simple terms: Who are the kind of men from whom our majorities shall take their cue? Whom shall they treat as rightful leaders? We and our leaders are the x and the y of the equation here; all other historic circumstances, be they economical, political, or intellectual, are only the background of occasion on which the living drama works itself out between us.

In this very simple way does the value of our educated class define itself: we more than others should be able to divine the worthier and better leaders. The terms here are monstrously simplified, of course, but such a bird's-eye view lets us immediately take our bearings. In our democracy, where everything else is shifting, we alumni and alumnae of the colleges are the only permanent presence that corresponds to the aristocracy in older countries. We have continuous traditions, as they have; our motto, too, is *noblesse oblige;* and, unlike them, we stand for ideal interests solely, for we have no corporate selfishness and wield no powers of corruption. We ought to have our own class-consciousness. "Les intellectuels"! What prouder club-name could there be than this one, used ironically by the party of "red blood," the party of every stupid prejudice and passion, during the anti-Dreyfus craze, to satirize the men in France who still retained some critical sense and judgment! Critical sense, it has to be confessed, is not an exciting term, hardly a banner to carry in processions. Affections for old habit, currents of self-interest, and gales of passion are the forces that keep the human ship moving; and the pressure of the judicious pilot's hand upon the tiller is a relatively insignificant energy. But the affections, passions, and interest are shifting, successive, and distraught; they blow in alternation, while the pilot's hand is steadfast. He knows the compass, and, with all the leeways he is obliged to tack toward, he always makes some headway. A small force, if it never lets up, will accumulate effects more considerable than those of much greater forces if these work inconsistently. The ceaseless whisper of the more permanent ideals, the steady tug of truth and justice, give them but time, *must* warp the world in their direction.

The Function of an Intellectual

Let us apply the question of function to another aspect of the general subject of Education: What is the function of a critic—a person educated beyond the level of most people, an interpreter and evaluator, a tastemaker? How does the critic serve the ordinary person? Poet W. H. Auden has answered this question simply and practically, first by pointing out what he believes to be the critic's essential function, and then by developing his opinion, point by point—the same organizational procedure followed by the other essays in this chapter.

The Function of a Critic[3]

W. H. AUDEN

What is the function of a critic? So far as I am concerned, he can do me one or more of the following services:

1. Introduce me to authors or works of which I was hitherto unaware.
2. Convince me that I have undervalued an author or a work because I had not read them carefully enough.
3. Show me relations between works of different ages and cultures which I could never have seen for myself because I do not know enough and never shall.
4. Give a "reading" of a work which increases my understanding of it.
5. Throw light upon the process of artistic "Making."
6. Throw light upon the relation of art to life, to science, economics, ethics, religion, etc.

The first three of these services demand scholarship. A scholar is not merely someone whose knowledge is extensive; the knowledge must be of value to others.

[3]From *The Dyer's Hand and Other Essays,* by W. H. Auden. Copyright © 1962 by W. H. Auden. Reprinted by permission of Random House, Inc.

One would not call a man who knew the Manhattan Telephone Directory by heart a scholar, because one cannot imagine circumstances in which he would acquire a pupil. Since scholarship implies a relation between one who knows more and one who knows less, it may be temporary; in relation to the public, every reviewer is, temporarily, a scholar, because he has read the book he is reviewing and the public has not. Though the knowledge a scholar possesses must be potentially valuable, it is not necessary that he recognize its value himself; it is always possible that the pupil to whom he imparts his knowledge has a better sense of its value than he. In general, when reading a scholarly critic, one profits more from his quotations than from his comments.

The last three services demand, not superior knowledge, but superior insight. A critic shows superior insight if the questions he raises are fresh and important, however much one may disagree with his answers to them. Few readers, probably, find themselves able to accept Tolstoi's conclusions in "What is Art?", but, once one has read the book, one can never again ignore the questions Tolstoi raises.

The one thing I most emphatically do not ask of a critic is that he tell me what I "ought" to approve of or condemn. I have no objection to his telling me what works and authors he likes and dislikes; indeed, it is useful to know this for, from his expressed preferences about works which I have read, I learn how likely I am to agree or disagree with his verdicts on works which I have not. But let him not dare to lay down the law to me. The responsibility for what I choose to read is mine, and nobody else on earth can do it for me.

Related to both the educated man and the critic, as Auden points out, is the scholar. No one has described the scholar's role with greater eloquence or a firmer grasp of the "ideal" to be aspired to than has Ralph Waldo Emerson in his famous Phi Beta Kappa address of 1837, an address that Oliver Wendell Holmes called "our intellectual Declaration of Independence."

The Role of the Scholar

RALPH WALDO EMERSON

The office of the scholar is to cheer, to raise, and to guide men by showing them facts amidst appearances. He plies the slow, unhonored, and unpaid task of observation. Flamsteed and Herschel, in their glazed observatories, may catalogue the stars with the praise of all men, and, the results being splendid and useful, honor is sure. But he, in his private observatory, cataloguing obscure and nebulous stars of the human mind, which as yet no man has thought of as such,—watching days and months, sometimes, for a few facts; correcting still his old records;—must relinquish display and immediate fame. In the long period of his preparation, he must betray often an ignorance and shiftlessness in popular arts, incurring the disdain of the able who shoulder him aside. Long he must stammer in his speech; often forego the living for the dead. Worse yet, he must accept,—how often! poverty and solitude. For the ease and pleasure of treading the old road, accepting the fashions, the education, the religion of society, he takes the cross of making his own, and, of course, the self-accusation, the faint heart, the frequent uncertainty and loss of time, which are the nettles and tangling vines in the way of the self-relying and self-directed; and the state of virtual hostility in which he seems to stand to society, and especially to educated society. For all this loss and scorn, what offset? He is to find consolation in exercising the highest functions of human nature. He is one, who raises himself from private considerations, and breathes and lives on public and illustrious thoughts. He is the world's eye. He is the world's heart. He is to resist the vulgar prosperity that retrogrades ever to barbarism, by preserving and communicating heroic sentiments, noble biographies, melodious verse, and the conclusions of history. Whatsoever oracles the human heart, in all emergencies, in all solemn hours, has uttered as its commentary on the world of actions,—these he shall receive and impart. And whatsoever new verdict Reason from her inviolable seat pronounces on the passing men and events of to-day,—this he shall hear and promulgate.

These being his functions, it becomes him to feel all confidence in himself, and to defer never to the popular cry. He and he only knows the world. The world of any moment is the merest appearance. Some great decorum, some fetish of a government, some ephemeral trade, or war, or man, is cried up by half mankind and cried down by the other half, as if all depended on this particular up or down. The odds are that the whole question is not worth the poorest thought which the scholar has lost in listening to the controversy. Let him not quit his belief that a popgun is a popgun, though the ancient and honorable of the earth affirm it to be the crack of doom. In silence, in steadiness, in severe abstraction, let him hold by himself; add observation to observation, patient of neglect, patient of reproach, and bide his own time,—happy enough, if he can satisfy himself alone, that this day he has seen something truly. Success treads on every right step. For the instinct is sure, that prompts him to tell his brother what he thinks. He then learns, that in going down into the secrets of his own mind, he has descended into the secrets of all minds. He learns that he who has mastered any law in his private thoughts, is master to that extent of all men whose language he speaks, and of all into whose language his own can be translated. The poet, in utter solitude remembering his spontaneous thoughts and recording them, is found to have recorded that, which men in crowded cities find true for them also. The orator distrusts at first the fitness of his grand confession,—his want of knowledge of the persons he addresses,—until he finds that he is the complement of his hearers;—that they drink his words because he fulfills for them their own nature; the deeper he dives into his privatest, secretest presentiment, to his wonder he finds, this is the most acceptable, most public, and universally true. The people delight in it; the better part of every man feels, This is my music; this is myself.

ASSIGNMENTS

Class Discussion and Paragraph Suggestions

(See Chapter 27 for methods of composing unified, adequately developed paragraphs.)

1. Compare the essays by John Ciardi and William James.
    a. In a sentence or two apiece, summarize each writer's view of the function or purpose of education.
    b. Are the two views mutually exclusive, or do they overlap?
    c. Do you subscribe to one view more than the other? Explain.
    d. Consider the statement by Carl Becker that the chief merit of any college course is "that it unsettles students, makes them ask questions." How does this observation relate to the essays by Ciardi and James?

2. Compare the Ciardi and James essays on the basis of
    a. general readability, tone, and style
    b. specific structure and organization:

paragraphs (locate topic sentences)
sentence construction
choice of words; level of usage (for example, how do you respond to Ciardi's phrase "this particular pest"?)
mechanics (for example, what function is served by the exclamation point in James's first sentence?)

3. Consider the Auden essay on "The Function of a Critic."

   a. Do you agree with the six basic services of the critic as Auden states them? Explain.
   b. Compare Auden's critic with Arnold Bennett's "passionate few" ("Why a Classic Is a Classic," pp. 108–11). What is the relationship of both the critic and the passionate few to the general reader?
   c. In what category do you think Auden belongs: critic, passionate few, general reader?
   d. Comment on Auden's statement: "But let him [the critic] not dare to lay down the law to me."

4. Compose a paragraph (150–250 words) using as your topic sentence "Let the critic not dare to lay down the law to me."

5. There is much to contemplate in Emerson's statement on the function of the scholar.

   a. Do you agree that "The office of the scholar is to cheer, to raise, and to guide men by showing them facts amidst appearances"?
   b. To what do "facts" and "appearances" refer?
   c. In what sense is the scholar "the world's eye" and "the world's heart"?
   d. To what sort of "oracles" uttered by the human heart is Emerson referring?
   e. Considering Emerson's description of the functions of the scholar, do you agree with him that the scholar should "defer never to the popular cry"? Is this a democratic principle?
   f. Does the statement "he and he only knows the world" refer to *all* knowledge?
   g. Do you think it is true today (as Emerson says of the scholar of his time) that the scholar will be "happy enough, if he can satisfy himself alone, that this day he has seen something truly"?
   h. Do you agree that the scholar fulfills for the public "their own nature"?
   i. Do you think the scholar described by Emerson is a real person or an ideal?
   j. Comment on Emerson's prose style, noting sentence structure, rhythm and flow of sentences, choice of words, images, and tone. (Note especially the last two sentences.)

6. Write a paragraph (150–250 words) in which you respond to one of Emerson's observations, indicating specific reasons why you agree or disagree.

Essay Suggestions

1. In an essay (500–750 words) describe the main function of higher education as you view it, drawing on the essays reprinted here and on any other sources you wish to consult.

2. As Auden describes the function of the critic, write an essay (500–750 words) in which you describe the function of one of the following professionals:

scientist	minister, rabbi, priest, or nun
artist	police officer
musician	lawyer
writer	doctor
teacher	philosopher

3. In an essay (500–750 words) compare the function of James's educated man with that of Emerson's scholar, showing how they are alike and unlike one another. You may wish to add a third person—a member of Bennett's "passionate few," for example.

4. Write an essay (500–750 words) in which you explain the essential function, as you view it, of any aspect of your life or environment: a hobby, sport, or recreation; a person or place; an object. If you are scientifically inclined, you might consider, in a less personal manner, the essential function of some element of nature, such as the moon or sun; or of some organ of the body, such as the heart or spleen; or of some social ritual, such as courtship or the cocktail party.

7 What Are the Causes of X?

Surely there is no more provocative question than the simple "Why?" Why is the sky dark at night? Why are we more or less intelligent? Why is a classic a classic?

When asking "Why?" the writer is preparing to write a causal analysis— that is, seeking to locate and explain the causes for a given act, idea, feeling, condition, or event. As Aristotle pointed out, human beings are naturally curious; almost as soon as we begin to think, we begin to wonder "Why?" As early as the fifth century B.C. the Greek philosopher Leucippus said: "Nothing happens without a ground but everything through a cause and of necessity." Here, then, is the "principle of universal causation," believed to run through all things, confirming us in our impulse to ask "Why?"

The First Principle of Causation: Uniformity

Why, for instance, do natural events occur as they do—why the tides of the sea, why the movement of the planets, why the cycle of seasons? There will be little guesswork or speculation in answering these questions, for the course of nature is regarded as uniform: natural events proceed by natural, uniform law. Thus, under the same circumstances, the same things will always happen in the same way. The leaves fall from the trees every autumn, and the first leaf and the last fall for the same reasons as all the billions of leaves in between.

We refer, then, to the "law of causation," which establishes that two events (X and Y) are so closely and unconditionally connected that one *cannot* occur without the other. That is, Y can take place only if X has previously occurred; if X occurs, then Y necessarily and inevitably follows. In such an instance we say that X is the cause of Y.

In writing about natural events, your first responsibility is to familiarize yourself fully with the uniform laws that govern the event in question. Firmly in command of this information, you can then explain the event clearly and engagingly so that the reader can understand and enjoy the explanation, even if it is necessarily complicated—as many scientific explanations are. Certainly the writer of the following essay (not a scientist but a journalist) has managed to render an extraordinarily lucid and vivid account of a complicated natural process.

Why Is the Sky Dark at Night?[1]

BRUCE BLIVEN

Since the childhood of our race, mankind has accepted the darkness of the nighttime sky as an unquestioned commonplace fact of life on earth. The sun rises each morning, bringing with it daylight. When the sun sets, the one major source of light is gone. Hence the sky can no longer be bright. So have reasoned generation upon generation of men—but their reasoning overlooked something.

The first man who seems to have thought deeply about this phenomenon was a German physician, Heinrich W. M. Olbers, who lived in Bremen and who, in 1826, set out to produce a scientific and mathematical answer to the question: *Why is the world dark at night?*

Dr. Olbers had a lifelong passion for astronomy. Even during the years when he was practicing medicine he spent the greater part of each night in his homemade observatory on top of his house, studying the heavens. He located the comet of 1815, which was named for him; he took part in the rediscovery of Ceres and discovered Pallas and Vesta—three tiny planets that circle the sun. But his greatest achievement was to ask this seemingly obvious question.

The sun, Olbers figured, provides only about half the light we on earth should theoretically be receiving; the other half should come from the billions of stars in the heavens. With all that starlight, why is midnight not as bright as day?

Dr. Olbers would have been even more puzzled had he had today's knowledge of the incredible vastness of the universe, the uncounted billions of light-giving stars in the depths of space. Our sun and its planets are only a microscopic part of the Milky Way, an average-size galaxy containing 100 billion stars—which are on the average as bright as our sun. And the Milky Way itself is only one of a seemingly limitless number of galaxies. Radio telescopes can now "hear" several billion light-years out into space; and however far they penetrate, in every direction, the galaxies continue to appear.

The number of the stars is, in fact, far beyond the power of the mind to grasp; yet so great is space that it is sparsely populated.

Though he was aware of only a small part of the stellar universe, the total number of stars known to Dr. Olbers was yet huge indeed. Taking into account their

[1]Reprinted with permission from the July 1963 *Reader's Digest*. Copyright 1963 by the Reader's Digest Assn., Inc. Also reprinted by permission of Bruce Bliven.

numbers, brightness and distance, making painstaking calculations, he came to an amazing conclusion: with light streaming from so many stars, the sky should *not* be dark at night. The earth even at midnight should be blazing with light and heat. It should, in fact, be frying.

How did he figure this? Suppose, said Dr. Olbers, you think of the universe as a vast hollow ball studded with stars and trillions of miles in diameter, with the earth at its center. Light will reach the earth from a multitude of stars; and while the rays from those far away will be very faint, this will be offset because the farther out you go, the greater the number of stars. In fact, the number of stars increases much faster than the distance (just as the volume of a sphere increases in proportion to its radius). Thus the weakening of the light at greater distances is *more than offset* by the greater number of stars there are when such distances are taken into account. No matter how weak the effect of any one star, therefore, if the number is large enough and the elapsed time long enough, the planet at the center should be ablaze with light and heat.

Why is this not so? Why then *is* the sky dark at night? The good doctor thought that interstellar fog must absorb almost all the starlight. But other astronomers were not satisfied that this was a sufficient explanation, and the question became famous as "Olbers' paradox."

For 100 years astronomers tried to solve the paradox. A clue came only 16 years after Olbers had raised the question, but nobody at the time recognized its relevance.

In 1842, an Austrian professor of mathematics, Christian Doppler, discovered what has ever after been known as the Doppler effect. Stand by a railroad track; as a train comes toward you the pitch of its whistle sounds high, but after it has passed, the whistle sounds lower. Doppler found the clue. As the train approaches, the sound waves it sends toward you seem, to you, shortened or "crowded"—and since short-wave sounds are higher pitched, the whistle sounds higher. Conversely, when the train speeds *away* from you, the sound waves must travel a greater distance; so they seem to you to be farther apart and therefore sound lower.

The Doppler effect applies to light waves, too. Light waves appear to the eye as longer when they come from an object moving away from us; they seem shorter and "crowded" if the object is approaching us.

With light the effect shows up in color. Light waves are longer (and weaker) at the red end of the color spectrum, shorter at the violet end. So light waves from a source that is moving away tend to be shifted down the spectrum toward the red end, a phenomenon called the "Red Shift." Thus astronomers came to realize that a slight redness in the light coming from a celestial body means that it is moving away from the observer.

Among those in this century who pondered Olber's paradox, knowing there *must* be an answer to it, was Dr. Edwin P. Hubble of California's Mount Wilson Observatory. In 1924, with the superior instruments available, Dr. Hubble found that light from distant sources, from distant galaxies outside the Milky Way, showed the Red Shift. This, he reasoned, could only mean that their light waves were being stretched out—hence these stars, these whole galaxies of stars, must be traveling away from us at tremendous speed.

Could it be? Hubble continued to watch the sky, and the evidence mounted that this was so. He found that the farther out he looked, the redder was the light that his telescope picked up. In fact, he saw, the galaxies were escaping from us with speeds that increased in a mathematically precise manner with their distance.

Hubble concluded that the whole universe is expanding—everything in it is moving farther and farther apart from everything else. Other observers confirmed his theory, and "the expanding universe" became the fundamental, though almost unbelievable, discovery of modern astronomy.

With this discovery Dr. Olbers' question at last was answered. *The sky is dark at night because the universe expands!* The galaxies are moving away from us so fast as to weaken the radiation we receive from them. This is what gives us our restful nocturnal darkness, and also saves us from being vaporized in the never-ending shower of hot starlight. Were it not for this fact, life on earth would not be possible.

Note that in this essay the author explains the phenomenon of the dark sky as the necessary result of three natural laws: the Doppler effect, the Red Shift, and, underlying both, the expanding universe. It is possible, of course, to extend the principle of uniformity beyond scientific causal analysis. Thus, even in everyday reasoning, we tend to search for a principle of uniformity: "Why did Johnny break his truck?" "Because he was tired." Generalization (principle of uniformity): "Tired children tend to break their toys."

The Second Principle of Causation: Sufficiency

Cause-and-effect sequences are of several types.

1. Cause ——————————→ Effect (Single cause, Single effect)

2. Cause 1
   Cause 2 ——————————⤳ Effect (Multiple causes, Single effect)
   Cause 3

3. Cause ⟨——————————→ Effect 1
                       → Effect 2 (Single cause,
                       → Effect 3 Multiple effects)

4. Cause 1 → Cause 2 → Cause 3 → Effect (Causal chain)

The following essay begins by suggesting the possibility of one cause for a given effect, but demonstrates that on the basis of the evidence, one cause is not sufficient explanation for the event in question. There are, in fact, *two* equally important causes at work.

The Heredity–Environment Question[2]

DONALD OLDING HEBB

The classical view in psychology was that intelligence is determined essentially by heredity. This view seemed to be supported by such experiments as the following:

Learning ability was tested in a large number of laboratory rats. The brightest males and females, those with the fewest errors, were then bred with each other, and the dullest likewise. The second generation was tested and the brightest males and females of the bright group were bred with each other, and the dullest males and

---

[2]From *Textbook of Psychology*, 3rd ed., by Donald Olding Hebb (Philadelphia: W. B. Saunders, 1972), pp. 161–63. Reprinted by permission of W. B. Saunders Company and the author.

females of the dull group. This was continued till by the seventh generation it was found that there was little or no overlap in the scores of the bright and dull groups; practically all of the bright strain made better scores in maze learning than any of the dull strain (R. C. Tryon).

This experiment appears to show that intelligence is dependent on heredity alone. However, there are other experiments that contradict the conclusion. We can take litters of rats and divide them in two groups. Bring up one group in a restricted environment, each animal alone in a small cage which he cannot see out of, containing no objects and presenting no opportunity for problem solving. Bring up the other group in a "free environment," a large cage containing the whole group, and laid out as a sort of amusement park for rats with a variety of barriers to give experience with varied paths from point to point (B. Hymovitch; Forgays and Forgays). Or rear dogs . . . , some in restricted cages, some as pets in normal homes (another form of free environment). Then compare the restricted rats or dogs at maturity with those reared in the wider environment. When such experiments have been done, the animals reared in restriction show marked deficiencies in maze learning and the solution of simple problems. These experiments show that intelligence is determined by environment, not by heredity.

But do they? Look again at the two kinds of experiments. . . . In the breeding experiment all the animals were reared in identical small cages; this keeps environmental differences from affecting the results. In the study of restricted vs. free environment, heredity is prevented from having any systematic effect by splitting litters. In effect, the two groups (as groups) have the same heredity, just as in the other experiment the two groups had the same environment. What the experiments show, therefore, is that both heredity and environment determine adult intelligence. If one source of variability in adult performance is held constant, all the variability (the difference between individuals or groups) comes from the other source, as one might expect.

With this point in mind, we can examine the result of a related investigation of human intelligence. Identical twins are twins that originate from a single fertilized ovum and thus, according to genetics, have the same hereditary characteristics. If they are brought up in different environments, we should be able to see what kind of effect variations of environment have upon intelligence. Psychologists have therefore been very interested in identical twin orphans adopted by different families. It has been found that their IQ's are very similar, and this fact has sometimes been used as argument that man's adult intelligence is determined by heredity and not by environment.

But when we look at the evidence, we find that most of these pairs of children have been brought up in very similar environments. When a pair of twins is orphaned, one of two things happens. They may be adopted by the neighbors, which implies similar environments—the same community, plus the fact that all the families in one neighborhood are apt to have about the same economic and social status. Or the twins may be taken charge of by a social agency, to oversee adoption, and this again means that they will get into environments that have much in common, social workers having strong ideas about who is fit to bring up children. In this kind of "experiment" differential effects of environment are minimized, and it is hardly surprising to find similar IQ's in identical twins with similar environments. The fact that identical twins have IQ's which are more alike than those of fraternal twins shows that heredity is important, just as the rat breeding experiment did; but it does not show that heredity is the only variable.

Sometimes it is recognized that heredity and environment both affect intelligence, but the writer then goes on to say *how* important each is. The student may find it said, for example, that 80 per cent of intelligence is determined by heredity, 20 per cent by environment. This statement is, on the face of it, nonsense. It means that a man would have 80 per cent of the problem-solving ability he would otherwise have had, if he were never given the opportunity to learn a language, to learn how people behave, and so forth. Conversely, it means that any animal would develop 20 per cent of a man's capacity for thought if reared in a good environment, no matter what its heredity, be it that of a mouse or a cow. What we must say is that both these variables are of 100 per cent importance; their relation is not additive, but multiplicative. That is, asking how much heredity contributes to man's intelligence is like asking how much the width of a field contributes to its area, and how much its length contributes. Neither can contribute anything by itself.

Though we cannot experiment with the effect of environment on the intelligence of the growing child, there are cases in which its importance has been unequivocally demonstrated. Goldfarb . . . showed that an orphanage environment may be sufficiently unstimulating to account for a deficiency of 23 points in the IQ, comparing orphanage children with foster-home children. Also, children who grew up about 1920 on canal boats in England, removed from many of the normal experiences of other children, showed a sharp decline in intelligence. Their mean IQ was 90 at the age of six, 77 at age seven and a half, 60 at age twelve. An IQ below 70 is ordinarily considered to mean mental deficiency, whereas 90 is within the range of normal ability. Again, a very similar picture (mean IQ for seven-year-olds, 84; for fifteen-year-olds, 60) was found for children growing up in isolated mountain communities in the United States. The higher IQ's for the younger children show that the low IQ's at later ages do not mean deficient heredities—if they did, all the scores would be low. Instead, it appears that the social and cultural environment is sufficiently stimulating for a normal development of intelligence in the first four or five years of life, but progressively inadequate from then on.

It is implied by these facts that the child at birth has a certain capacity or potential for intellectual development, but a stimulating environment is needed if the potential is to be realized. The extent to which intelligence can be developed may be low, in which case no environment can produce a high IQ; then heredity sets a limit on the development. But the child may have inherited a better brain, capable of developing a high IQ, and yet in a poor environment his IQ remains low—just as with a child that inherited a poorer brain

In establishing causal connections, you must think carefully and rigorously, recognizing that it is easy to fall into such common fallacies as *post hoc ergo propter hoc* (after this, therefore because of this). Only to the simple mind (or the mind intent on deceiving) is any event that follows another necessarily the *result* of it. Thus, as Mark Twain once pointed out in a humorous *post hoc* application: "I joined the Confederacy for two weeks. Then I deserted. The Confederacy fell."

Most superstitions grow out of this fallacy: "A black cat crossed my path. Later that day I twisted my ankle. The black cat *caused* my twisted ankle. Black cats are therefore unlucky." And: "John eats a lot of fish. John is smart. Eating fish is good for the brain."

The writer who wishes to be taken seriously must guard against superstitious, oversimplified cause-and-effect connections. The first question a critical mind addresses to an assertion of causal relationship should be: "Was the supposed cause *sufficient* to produce the given effect?" Obviously a black cat cannot be sufficient cause for a twisted ankle, fish cannot stimulate the brain, and a four-leaf clover cannot bring luck. In each case the stated cause (however colorful) is *insufficient* to produce the given effect.

Cause and Condition

Thus, as a careful thinker and writer, you must make certain that you consider *all* possible causes for any given event. You must recognize not only that there *can* be more than one cause behind any given situation (war, recession, racial unrest), but that there usually *is,* that the world of events is rarely characterized by

Single Cause → Single Effect

More than that, you must be aware that for every individual effect there are—in addition to multiple causes—countless *conditions* that must also be taken into account if a causal explanation is to be reasonably accurate and complete. Let us say that the direct cause of my answering the telephone is that it rings:

Cause ————————————→ Effect
(telephone ringing)   (I answer the telephone)

One could view this event in this linear manner; it is accurate, but only roughly. In actual fact, countless conditions enter into this situation that enable it to occur: the telephone is in good repair (each small part is working); my ears are "attuned" (here again, each small part is working); I am within hearing distance (I might have stepped outside for a moment). And so on. If any one of these numerous small conditions had not held to its exact course at the precise moment the telephone rang, I would not have answered it: the given effect would *not* have followed the supposed cause.

With this in mind, we can look back to Bliven's essay on nighttime darkness and note that many conditions had to remain equal and constant in order for the law of causation to operate in its ordinary manner. Of course the sun rises each morning, as stated—but only if no untoward occurrences take place in the solar system that throw the entire causal chain out of gear. Similarly, the environment, as described in Hebb's essay, will influence the development of certain individuals in certain ways—but only if the individual nervous system remains within the normal range of functioning, and the environment continues to be the environment as we know it.

The careful thinker and writer, then, will take into account not only the basic *causes* of a given effect, but the surrounding *conditions* as well.

Speculating on Reasons

Many essays in causal analysis are little more than nonsense because they assert causal connections that have no basis in fact or logical inference. The two essays reprinted above are not guilty of what logicians call "forced" or unwarranted hypotheses, because the explanation (Why darkness? Why intelligence?) is based on concrete evidence drawn from the orderly realm of science and not merely from heady speculation.

In contrast, the following essay is based on speculation. Novelist Arnold Bennett tries to explain how and why a classic becomes and remains a classic. He cannot *know* for certain, because there are no controlled studies, surveys, or experiments yielding definite information or objective data on this subject. Thus Bennett has no alternative but to speculate, and he does this by establishing a causal sequence that (according to his observation and experience) seems accurate:

$$\text{Cause A} \rightarrow \text{Cause B} \rightarrow \text{Cause C} \rightarrow \text{Effect}$$

As you read, note that Bennett begins with Cause C and works backward. Classics survive, he tells us, because of a devoted minority, the "passionate few," who love literature (Cause C). And *why* do they love literature? Because they find in it the kind of "keen and lasting pleasure" that some people find in beer. It is the "recurrence of this pleasure" that keeps their interest in literature alive (Cause B).

And *why* does literature give this pleasure? No answer! Bennett tells us that the passionate few can no more resist literature than the bee can neglect a flower. *But they can no more tell you why!* In other words, at this point (Cause A) causation breaks down.

Why a Classic Is a Classic[3]

ARNOLD BENNETT

Introduction: the problem stated
The large majority of our fellow citizens care as much about literature as they care about archaeology or the program of the Legislature. They do not ignore it; they are not quite indifferent to it. But their interest in it is faint and perfunctory; or, if their interest happens to be violent, it is spasmodic. Ask the two hundred thousand persons whose enthusiasm made the vogue of a popular novel ten years ago what they think of that novel now, and you will gather that they have utterly forgotten it, and that they would no more dream of reading it again than of reading Bishop Stubb's *Select Charters*. Probably if they did read it again they would not enjoy it—not because the said novel is a whit worse now than it was ten years ago; not because their taste has improved—but because they have not had sufficient practice to be able to rely on their taste as a means of permanent pleasure. They simply don't know from one day to the next what will please them.

The question posed: *why?*
In the face of this one may ask: Why does the great and universal fame of classical authors continue? The answer is that the fame of classical authors is entirely independent of the majority. Do you

[3]From *Literary Taste and How to Form It* by Arnold Bennett, 1927, reprinted by permission of Doubleday & Company, Inc.

Cause C
(described)

suppose that if the fame of Shakespeare depended on the man in the street it would survive a fortnight? The fame of classical authors is originally made, and it is maintained, by a passionate few. Even when a first-class author has enjoyed immense success during his lifetime, the majority have never appreciated him so sincerely as they have appreciated second-rate men. He has always been reinforced by the ardor of the passionate few. And in the case of an author who has emerged into glory after his death the happy sequel has been due solely to the obstinate perseverance of the few. They could not leave him alone; they would not. They kept on savoring him, and talking about him, and buying him, and they generally behaved with such eager zeal, and they were so authoritative and sure of themselves, that at last the majority grew accustomed to the sound of his name and placidly agreed to the proposition that he was a genius; the majority really did not care very much either way.

And it is by the passionate few that the renown of genius is kept alive from one generation to another. These few are always at work. They are always rediscovering genius. Their curiosity and enthusiasm are exhaustless, so that there is little chance of genius being ignored. And, moreover, they are always working either for or against the verdicts of the majority. The majority can make a reputation, but it is too careless to maintain it. If, by accident, the passionate few agree with the majority in a particular instance, they will frequently remind the majority that such and such a reputation has been made, and the majority will idly concur: "Ah, yes. By the way, we must not forget that such and such a reputation exists." Without that persistent memory-jogging the reputation would quickly fall into oblivion which is death. The passionate few only have their way by reason of the fact that they are genuinely interested in literature, that literature matters to them. They conquer by their obstinacy alone, by their eternal repetition of the same statements. Do you suppose they could prove to the man in the street that Shakespeare was a great artist? The said man would not even understand the terms they employed. But when he is told ten thousand times, and generation after generation, that Shakespeare was a great artist, the said man believes—not by reason, but by faith. And he too repeats that Shakespeare was a great artist, and he buys the complete works of Shakespeare and puts them on his shelves, and he goes to see the marvellous stage effects which accompany *King Lear* or *Hamlet,* and comes back religiously convinced that Shakespeare was a great artist. All because the passionate few could not keep their admiration of Shakespeare to themselves. This is not cynicism; but truth. And it is important that those who wish to form their literary taste should grasp it.

Cause B
(described)

What causes the passionate few to make such a fuss about literature? There can be only one reply. They find a keen and lasting pleasure in literature. They enjoy literature as some men enjoy beer. The recurrence of this pleasure naturally keeps their interest in literature very much alive. They are forever making new researches, forever practising on themselves. They learn to understand themselves. They learn to know what they want. Their taste becomes surer and surer as their experience lengthens. They do not enjoy today what will seem tedious to them tomorrow. When they find a book tedious, no amount of popular clatter will persuade them that it is pleasurable; and when they find it pleasurable no chill silence of the street crowds will affect their conviction that the book is good and permanent. They have faith in themselves. What are the qualities in a book which give keen and lasting pleasure to the passionate few? This is a question so difficult that it has never yet been completely answered. You may talk lightly about truth, insight, knowledge, wisdom, humor, and beauty, but these comfortable words do not really carry you very far, for each of them has to be defined, especially the first and last. It is all very well for Keats in his airy manner to assert that beauty is truth, truth beauty, and that that is all he knows or needs to know. I, for one, need to know a lot more. And I shall never know. Nobody, not even Hazlitt nor Sainte-Beuve, has ever finally explained why he thought a book beautiful. I take the first fine lines that come to hand—

> The woods of Arcady are dead,
> And over is their antique joy—

and I say that those lines are beautiful, because they give me pleasure. But why? No answer! I only know that the passionate few will, broadly, agree with me in deriving this mysterious pleasure from those lines. I am only convinced that the liveliness of our pleasure in those and many other lines by the same author will ultimately cause the majority to believe, by faith, that W. B. Yeats is a genius. The one reassuring aspect of the literary affair is that the passionate few are passionate about the same things. A continuance of interest does, in actual practice, lead ultimately to the same judgements. There is only the difference in width of interest. Some of the passionate few lack catholicity, or, rather, the whole of their interest is confined to one narrow channel; they have none left over. These men help specially to vitalize the reputations of the narrower geniuses: such as Crashaw. But their active predilections never contradict the general verdict of the passionate few; rather they reinforce it.

A classic is a work which gives pleasure to the minority which is intensely and permanently interested in literature. It lives on because the minority, eager to renew the sensation of pleasure, is eternally curious and is therefore engaged in an eternal process of rediscovery. A classic does not survive for any ethical reason. It does not survive because it conforms to certain canons, or because neglect would not kill it. It survives because it is a source of pleasure, and because the passionate few can no more neglect it than a bee can neglect a flower. The passionate few do not read "the right things" because they are right. That is to put the cart before the horse. "The right things" are the right things solely because the passionate few *like* reading them. Hence—and I now arrive at my point—the one primary essential to literary taste is a hot interest in literature. If you have that, all the rest will come. It matters nothing that at present you fail to find pleasure in certain classics. The driving impulse of your

Cause A

(declared
a mystery)

interest will force you to acquire experience, and experience will teach you the use of the means of pleasure. You do not know the secret ways of yourself: that is all. A continuance of interest must inevitably bring you to the keenest joys. But, of course, experience may be acquired judiciously or injudiciously, just as Putney may be reached via Walham Green or via Moscow.

Presenting Personal Reasons

A still more subjective type of causal analysis is that in which the writer tries to explain why he or she has felt or acted a certain way. In this case the causes are personal and therefore cannot be evaluated objectively as accurate or inaccurate, but rather as sincere or insincere, convincing or unconvincing, logically consistent or inconsistent, and reasonable or unreasonable in terms of themselves. Thus Simone de Beauvoir explains her reasons for becoming a writer.

Why I Decided to Be a Writer[4]
SIMONE DE BEAUVOIR

Why did I decide to be a writer? As a child, I had never taken my scribblings very seriously; my real aim had been to acquire knowledge; I enjoyed doing French compositions, but my teachers objected to my stilted style; I did not feel I was a "born" writer. Yet at the age of fifteen when I wrote in a friend's album the plans and preferences which were supposed to give a picture of my personality, I answered without hesitation the question "What do you want to do later in life?" with "To be a famous author." As far as my favorite composer and my favorite flower were concerned I had invented more or less factitious preferences. But on that one point I had no doubts at all: I had set my heart on that profession, to the exclusion of everything else.

The main reason for this was the admiration I felt for writers: my father rated them far higher than scholars, philosophers, and professors. I, too, was convinced of their supremacy: even if his name was well-known, a specialist's monograph would be accessible to only a small number of people; but everyone read novels: they touched the imagination and the heart; they brought their authors universal and intimate fame. As a woman, these dizzy summits seemed to me much more accessible than the lowlier slopes; the most celebrated women had distinguished themselves in literature.

I had always had a longing to communicate with others. In my friend's album I cited as my favorite hobbies reading and conversation. I was a great talker. I would recount, or try to, everything that had struck me in the course of the day. I dreaded night and oblivion; it was agony to condemn to silence all that I had seen, felt, and liked. Moved by the moonlight, I longed for pen and paper and the ability to describe my feelings. When I was fifteen I loved volumes of letters, intimate journals—for example, the diary of Eugénie de Guérin—books that attempted to make time stand

---

[4]Simone de Beauvoir, *Memoirs of a Dutiful Daughter* (New York: Harper & Row, 1974), pp. 141–142. Copyright © 1958 by Librairie Gallimard. Translation © 1959 by The World Publishing Company. Reprinted by permission.

still. I had also realized that novels, short stories, and tales were not divorced from life but that they are, in their own way, expressions of it.

If at one time I had dreamed of being a teacher it was because I wanted to be a law unto myself; I now thought that literature would allow me to realize this dream. It would guarantee me an immortality that would compensate for the loss of heaven and eternity; there no longer was a God to love me, but I would burn as a beacon in millions of hearts. By writing a work based on my own experience I would re-create myself and justify my existence. At the same time I would be serving humanity: what finer offering could I make to it than books? I was concerned at the same time with myself and with others; I accepted the individuality of my "incarnation," but I did not wish to surrender membership in the universal. This writing project reconciled everything; it gratified all the aspirations which had been unfolding in me during the past fifteen years.

ASSIGNMENTS

Class Discussion and Paragraph Suggestions

(See Chapter 27 for methods of composing unified, adequately developed paragraphs.)

1. While keeping in mind the fact that the writer of an informal causal analysis is permitted more latitude than formal logic would allow, we should nonetheless examine carefully the basic assumptions and reasoning of Bennett's "Why a Classic Is a Classic."

   a. Do you think Bennett's basic assumption is sound—that the majority of people do not know or care about literature and that they are simply intimidated by the reputation of a Shakespeare? Do *you* like Shakespeare? Why or why not?

   b. Do you agree that only the "passionate few" are genuinely appreciative of literature and that it is preserved only through their zealous support?

   c. Is Bennett correct in his assertion that most people have not read enough to rely on their own taste either as a standard of judgment or as a means of pleasure ("They simply don't know from one day to the next what will please them")? Do you think you have read enough to trust your own taste? Do you feel that the observation made about a liberal education—that it aims to increase the area of potential appreciation—is relevant here? How so?

   d. Do you know anybody who "enjoys literature as some men enjoy beer"? Do you? If not, do you think anybody does?

   e. Is it, as Bennett asserts, impossible to analyze completely the reasons why a book gives pleasure or why it is great ("Nobody has ever finally explained why he thought a book beautiful")? Can you explain why you thought a given work was beautiful? Are there human (in addition to literary) reasons Bennett has not indicated (perhaps not thought of) that contribute to making a book "great," valued by generations of readers?

   f. How do you interpret Bennett's term "hot interest in literature"? Do you agree that "if you have that, all the rest will come"?

   g. Do you agree with Bennett's definition of a classic as "a work which gives pleasure to the minority which is intensely and permanently interested in literature"? Could this definition be seen as "begging the question" (see Logical Fallacies, Chapter 20)? Suggest your own definition and cite examples.

2. Examine each of the paragraphs in de Beauvoir's essay, "Why I Decided to Be a Writer." Note topic sentence, method of development, ordering principle, coordinate and subordinate sequences (see Chapter 27), transitional devices, tone, and

point of view. Also note sentence construction: subordination and coordination, use of semicolons and commas.

3. Study Edvard Munch's *The Cry*, below, trying to imagine or infer the causes of the "cry." Write a one-paragraph explanation (150–250 words). Try using your general judgment as a topic sentence, placing it at the beginning of the paragraph, and supporting it with specific details.

4. Consider this Sufi parable:

"What is Fate?" Nasrudin was asked by a scholar.
"An endless succession of intertwined events, each influencing the other."
"That is hardly a satisfactory answer. I believe in cause and effect."
"Very well," said the Mulla, "Look at that." He pointed to a procession passing in the street. "That man is being taken to be hanged. Is that because someone gave him a silver piece and enabled him to buy the knife with which he committed the murder; or because someone saw him do it; or because nobody stopped him?"[5]

Write a one-paragraph comment (150–250 words) on the nature of these questions and suggest a possible reply.

[5]From Idries Shah, *The Exploits of the Incomparable Nasrudin* (New York: E. P. Dutton, 1972).

Essay Suggestions

1. Write an essay (500–750 words) in which you support Bennett's reasoning or show it to be inadequate.

   or

   Write an essay of equal length in which you explain why you regard one of the following works as a classic:

   > *The Adventures of Huckleberry Finn*
   > *David Copperfield*
   > *Pride and Prejudice*
   > *Romeo and Juliet*
   > *Peter Pan*

2. Write an essay (500–750 words) indicating the main causes for any one of the following:

   a. Natural phenomena

   > green grass
   > rain
   > blue sky
   > white clouds
   > appearance of stars at night
   > revolution of the earth around the sun
   > sunrise
   > sunset
   > movement of the tides

   b. Biological-psychological conditions

   Disorders

headaches	hay fever
arteriosclerosis	stuttering
high blood pressure	schizophrenia
diabetes	suicide
cirrhosis	aphasia
epilepsy	amnesia
hiccoughing	

   Accidents

   > automobile accidents
   > home accidents
   > fires
   > airplane crashes
   > mining accidents

   c. Architecture

   > the construction of one of the Seven Wonders of the World
   > the construction of cathedrals (or one particular cathedral) in
   >   the Middle Ages
   > the popularity of prefabricated houses
   > the evolution of the skyscraper in the United States
   > the belief that Frank Lloyd Wright was a great architect

3. Write an essay (500–750 words) in which you explain why you believe or disbelieve in any one of the following:

a. Law

> the death penalty
> legal abortion
> civil rights legislation
> present divorce laws
> alimony
> the jury system
> immigration quotas
> the presumption of innocence until guilt is proved
> diplomatic immunity
> present income tax laws
> inheritance tax
> Executive privilege
> treating prostitution as a crime
> treating drug abuse as a crime
> conscientious objectors

b. Religion

> religion *per se*
> God as "giver"
> going to church
> the Bible as revelation
> the Bible as literature
> the Immaculate Conception
> immortality
> heaven and hell
>
> missionaries
> papal infallibility
> the Trinity
> salvation
> Day of Judgment
> original sin
> free will
> doctrine of the elect

4. Study the photograph below. In an essay (500–750 words), speculate on—or simply invent—the causes of this situation.

5. Write an essay (500–750 words) in which you offer your personal reasons for making an important decision in your life. Consider an organization like that of de Beauvoir's "Why I Decided to Be a Writer":

> Introductory paragraph: provides background information
> Paragraph two: provides a second reason, again supported by details
> Paragraph four: provides a final reason, with further details and a summing-up comment and conclusion

8 What Are the Consequences of X?

Just as we are naturally curious about the causes of various ideas, acts, or events, so we are naturally curious about consequences.[1] Thus whereas the previous question ("What Are the Causes of X?") started with *effects* and traced them back to *causes*, we now start with *causes* and trace them forward to *effects*. The following essay, for example, contemplates the consequences of brain transplantation on identity.

Brain Transplantation and Personal Identity[2]

ROLAND PUCCETTI

I begin without introduction. We have a patient dying of some wasting general disease, such as cancer, which as far as we can tell has not yet affected his brain. Let us call him X. At the same time we have an emergency admission, Y, where massive cerebral damage was incurred in an accident, though his body is unhurt and in good general health. We keep Y alive for hours using a respirator machine, adrenalin injections, and so on, but it is quite clear he will never recover consciousness or control over his body. X and Y are of the same blood group. So with X's consent, and with permission of Y's nearest kin, we prepare to transplant X's brain into Y's body, sacrificing thereby one fatally-diseased body and one fatally-damaged brain. On the

---

[1] In tracing consequences, as in tracing reasons, it is important to establish a clear cause-and-effect relationship, especially when dealing with social and historical topics. For a consideration of the logical foundations for sound causal analysis, see the preceding chapter, pp. 101–07.

[2] From *Analysis*, Vol. 29, No. 3, January 1969. Reprinted by permission of Basil Blackwell, Publisher.

level of medical ethics I cannot see how this is much different from heart transplantation. However, there are formidable surgical and logical differences, as we shall see.

The actual operation is easier stated than described, but I shall give its general lines. First we cut the vertebral artery and clamp it in both X and Y. We do the same with the carotid artery, except that in X's case we withdraw blood from the brain, chill it, and pump it back. This freezes the hypothalamus slightly, lowers the temperature and metabolic rate within the brain, and reduces danger of tissue damage by oxygen starvation. Then we cut through X's scalp, lay it back, and section the cranium in large arcs. Next the brainstem is severed in the *medulla oblongata,* where it passes through the *foramen magnum* and merges with the spinal cord. Finally we cut all twelve cranial nerves where they join the brainstem, and lift X's brain out. Exactly the same having been done with Y's brain, we now place X's brain in Y's empty cranial cavity. Y's brain, of course, we discard along with X's body. The ends of the two arteries are now sutured, the twelve cranial nerves are butted and sheathed in arterial tubes made for this purpose, and the lower brainstem–spinal cord fitted together. Then we rewire the sections of Y's cranium, replace the cerebrospinal fluid by injection, sew back the scalp, and dose Y's body heavily with immuno-suppressive drugs. . . .

We now have X's brain comfortably installed in Y's body, hooked up and ready to go. This is where our logical difficulties begin. To avoid prejudicing the outcome, let us call the composite organism Z. The question arises, *Who* is Z? Is Z just Y with a new brain? Or X with a new body? Or have we created a third person, "Z"? And depending on our answer here, to what extent is our concept of a particular person linked to possession of a particular body or brain? To a particular sex, for that matter?

. . .

Suppose we let six months go by, during which time Z heals nicely and is discharged from the hospital. We now find Z in his favourite pub of a late afternoon, toasting his new health. A youngish man enters, slaps him on the back, and starts addressing him as Y.

> Joel Andrews, you say? I'm terribly sorry. My name is Weatherby.
> Oh, come off it, Joel. I know you like a brother.
> Clarence Weatherby.
> We roomed together at school!
> I had all my schooling in Australia.
> But I was best man at your wedding, just two years ago!
> Two years ago I was in South Africa, long since married.
> This is incredible! You even have that scar on the bridge of your nose.
> What about it?
> I gave it to you, with a cricket bat. Don't you remember?
> Never played cricket in my life.

Nothing in this dialogue comes as a surprise. After all, how *could* Z, i.e. Y's body with X's brain, remember things Y did? Memories are stored in the cerebral cortex and brainstem, not the body. What the young man is asking Z to remember perished with Y's brain. So Z cannot be Y, even if he has Y's body. You might say, Yes, but people sometimes lose memories—even all memories prior to a cerebral accident— yet they are the same people. True, but Z is not a general amnesiac. Unless he's lying he has a very definite set of memory traces to draw upon, quite different from Y's.

To whom do these memories belong? Surely not to Z as a distinct person. If Z were a distinct person, newly created by the juncture of X's brain and Y's body, his memory could extend no further back in time than six months ago. Indeed, as a new person he would not even have the store of unconscious traces the amnesiac has. He would not know how to walk and talk, for example. He would be on the intellectual level of the infant toddler. But Z is not like that at all. Thus Z cannot be "Z," that is a novel person, any more than he can be Y. Then who *is* Z? Only one alternative remains. He must be X.

> Look, I think there's something you should know. Your friend is dead.
> Joel dead? Good God! How did it happen?
> I'm told he dived into an empty swimming pool on his head.
> How did you learn this? Did you know him?
> We never actually met. I mean, we weren't introduced.
> How's Kitty taking it?
> His wife? I owe my life to that woman.
> I don't follow.
> You've heard of brain transplantation, haven't you? Well . . .

Will the young man accept Z as X, even if he hears the whole story from Y's lips? Or will he think he is the victim of some kind of elaborate joke? No one can say in advance, but assuming that brain transplants are not unknown by this time, it seems to me he would.

> So there she sat, vaguely hoping I was her husband after all.
> Poor Kitty.
> Yes, she even kissed me goodbye on her last visit. I actually cried.
> And your own wife? It must have been equally weird to her.
> Well, of course. *(Smiling.)* But on the whole I'd say she's pleased with the change.
> What do you mean?
> I was 48 and your friend only 29. A most vigorous young man too, if I must say so.
> Joel was an excellent skier.
> That won't help me. I don't know how to stand in the bloody things.
> Do you like any sports?
> Tennis. I can play a match of singles without breathing hard now.
> That's funny. Joel never played tennis.
> Should have taken it up. What stamina! And his reflexes.

Everything above is consistent with the hypothesis of brain transplantation, once one realises exactly what is being transplanted.

For instance, while he's talking Z will probably reveal a slight Australian accent. When appropriate he would throw in some Australian expression. But his voice production would be Y's, because that's not in X's brain. Similarly, his sexual interests and associations would remain X's, but reinforced by Y's hormone production and better general health. Since the memory storage is in the brain, he could hardly be expected to have acquired Y's learned responses along with that body. These are stored in the reticular activating system in the upper brainstem, and in the cerebellum. Thus he wouldn't be able to ski, though if he knew tennis he would find he has become a better player because the reflexes, muscle response to nerve impulses, and supporting organ efficiency—heart, lungs, *etc.*—would be far superior to what he had before he acquired Y's body. No doubt the first few months of post-operative recovery would require Z to get used to these differences. Where he used to drag himself out of bed he will now bound, as if he had been transported to a planet subject to lesser gravitational forces. It is the reverse of a healthy person having to walk very carefully after a long confinement in bed, when his muscular response, *etc.,* became weakened. Since the reticular activating system and cerebellum embody a feedback mechanism enabling us to make adjustments between sensory input and motor output unconsciously, the new situation requires conscious adjustment. But soon it is effected. X learns, in brief, to take over Y's body successfully.

But then why should we continue to speak of Z? Z is not, as we saw, really "Z," a new person. Z is the organic composite of X's brain and Y's body, which in terms of personal identity is really X. We sometimes say someone is "a new person" where we mean he's undergone *sauna* treatments, psychoanalysis, Dr. Reich's orgone box, transcendental meditation, hormone injections, conversion to Roman Catholicism, Communism, Zen Buddhism or what have you. These are all weak senses of the term "new person." In the strong sense they remain the same person nevertheless. So does X, even though his transformation is more drastic on the corporeal side. Old acquaintances who knew him not long before the transplant would find it hard, as his wife did, to believe this is Clarence Weatherby. But he could provide convincing evidence he is, in the form not only of specific memories but also of continued likes and dislikes, emotional responses, character traits—everything that goes to make up a real individual person.

One can fancy X standing in the graveyard, in Y's body, watching a double funeral. Alongside him are Y's wife and his son. There are two coffins being lowered into the grave together. One is very small—shoebox size. That is Y's dead brain. The other is very big, X's former body. Everyone is grieving. But not for X. Why should they, since he is standing there, alive and happier than he has been for years? Only Y is being buried, in that tiny box. If you asked X how it felt to witness his own funeral he would perhaps laugh, and rightly so. He might even point to the shoebox-sized coffin and say "ask Y that."

By addressing the question of consequences to almost any subject, you will consistently be able to locate a topic, especially if you begin by asking, "What would happen *if* . . . ?" What would happen, for example, if a law were suddenly to go into effect whereby the *opposite* of what you wished or expected to happen would happen? An editorial writer with a gift for whimsical contemplation of consequences developed this notion into an amusing essay.

Gumperson's Law[3]

January is a good time to think about the law of perverse opposites. This law will not be found on any statute books but it is fully explained in a recent issue of Changing Times magazine. To most laymen, the law is known as Gumperson's Law, named after a famous divicist who spent most of his life in research on a number of irritating events that might otherwise be put down to mere chance.

It is Gumperson's Law, for example, that causes grass to grow in the cracks of concrete sidewalks but not on lawns. This, and similar phenomena, have long been known to scientists but until Dr. Gumperson went to work had been considered only curiosities.

Gumperson's Law accounts for the fact that you can toss a lighted match from

[3]From the Summit (N.J.) *Herald,* January 1963. Reprinted by permission of the publisher.

your car window and start a three-state forest fire but it will take two boxes of kitchen matches, a can of lighter fluid and the entire Sunday issue of the New York Times to start a fire in the fireplace.

The Law, simply stated, is that the contradictory of a welcome probability will assert itself whenever such an eventuality is likely to be most frustrating.

Examples of the Law at work include the following:

That after a raise in salary you will have less money at the end of each month than you had before.

That children have more energy after a hard day of play than they do after a good night's sleep.

That the person who buys the most raffle tickets has the least chance of winning.

That the dishwasher will break down the evening you give a dinner party for ten people.

That when the plumbing breaks down it will always be on a Sunday.

That good parking places are always on the other side of the street.

That a child can be exposed to mumps for weeks without catching them but can catch them without exposure the day before the family starts its vacation.

That the U.S. Weather Bureau, despite its vast personnel and advanced equipment, is not as good as the Old Farmer's Almanack.

Familiarity with Gumperson's Law will do much to refresh one's understanding of the universe and steel one for the uncertainties of the New Year.

ASSIGNMENTS

Class Discussion and Paragraph Suggestions

See chapter 27 for methods of composing unified, adequately developed paragraphs.)

1. Comment on the bizarre speculations and projected problems suggested in the essay on brain transplantation. Can you envision still further consequences and complications of such surgery?

2. Consider the several ways in which both of the following "meditations" are studies in cause and consequence.

Two Meditations[4]

JOHN BARTH

1. Niagara Falls

She paused amid the kitchen to drink a glass of water; at that instant, losing a grip of fifty years, the next-room-ceiling-plaster crashed. Or he merely sat in an empty study, in March-day glare, listening to the universe rustle in his head, when suddenly the five-foot shelf let go. For ages the fault creeps secret through the rock; in a second, ledge and railings, tourists and turbines all thunder over Niagara. Which snowflake triggers the avalanche? A house explodes; a star. In your spouse, so apparently resigned, murder twitches like a fetus. At some trifling new assessment, all the colonies rebel.

[4]From *Lost in the Funhouse* (New York: Doubleday & Co., 1968), p. 104. Copyright © 1966 by John Barth.

2. Lake Erie

The wisdom to recognize and halt follows the know-how to pollute past rescue. The treaty's signed, but the cancer ticks in your bones. Until I'd murdered my father and fornicated my mother I wasn't wise enough to see I was Oedipus. Too late now to keep the polar cap from melting. Venice subsides; South America explodes.

Let's stab out our eyes.

Too late: our resolve is sapped beyond the brooches.

3. Write "two meditations" of your own in which you attempt to project consequences of what you presently observe as significant events. Treat your details either metaphorically (as Barth does) or with literal directness.

4. Read the following poem, which explores the consequences of "a dream deferred."

Dream Deferred[5]

LANGSTON HUGHES

What happens to a dream deferred?

Does it dry up
like a raisin in the sun?

Or fester like a sore—
And then run?

Does it stink like rotten meat?
Or crust and sugar over—
like a syrupy sweet?

Maybe it just sags
like a heavy load.

Or does it explode?

    a. List the various similes used by Hughes and indicate in what ways they are effective.

4. b. Why, do you suppose, are all but one of the possible consequences framed as questions?

    c. What is gained by italicizing the last line?

    d. Does the poet provide an answer to his original question?

5. Write a paragraph (150–250 words) in which you contemplate the possible consequences of repressing any strong feeling or desire; base your speculations on your own experience or that of someone you know; shape your topic sentence in the form of a question and develop the paragraph in terms of specific possibilities.

Essay Suggestions

1. Write an essay (500–750 words) in which you project your brain into the body of some well-known public figure—a political or professional person whose actions

would have wide and noteworthy consequences; begin with this topic sentence: "My brain was guiding his (or her) actions."

2. Write an essay (500–750 words) indicating what you think were, are, or will be the major effects or consequences of any one of the following (on the individual, the family, or society at large):

a. Inventions

    the automobile
    the telephone
    the television
    the airplane
    the electric light

b. Social changes

space travel	increased mixed marriages
human organ transplants	increased urbanization
war on poverty	increased automation
fight against pollution	increased income tax
increased drug usage	increased leisure
increased divorce rate	the new morality

3. In an essay (500–750 words) describe the effect on your mind or sensibilities of one of the following:

the moon	prejudice
the sun	current fashions
long hair and beards	nightmares
hot weather	fatigue
cold weather	religion
noise	advertising
silence	

4. Write an editorial (300–500 words) entitled "Gumperson's Law," using examples drawn from your own observation and experience. Use as your opening sentence "January is a good time to think about the law of perverse opposites"; or write an equally timely and suitable opening sentence of your own.

5. Write an essay (500–750 words) in which you answer the question "What would happen if . . . ?"

9 What Are the Types of X?

Another common and popular type of analysis is classification: seeing the subject as consisting of or belonging to classes, or "types."

Classification is a highly methodical and sophisticated form of analysis and an indispensable condition of systematic thought, for it involves a sorting process that groups things into categories based on similar characteristics, thereby bringing order out of chaos. Indeed, Adam did precisely this when he classified the beasts of the field and the fowl of the air; in the multiplicity of creatures on the earth he saw common characteristics that entitled them to be grouped together.

Ever since then, human beings have been classifying things, arranging them in order to see their similarities and differences more clearly, and in that way to learn more about them.

We frequently use classification in our daily living; for example, we may sort our daily mail into three categories: bills, junk mail, and letters (an incomplete but still useful system of classification). We put the bills to one side, throw away the junk mail unopened, and give our time to the letters. Or a friend may say to us: "I have just met your neighbor Joe Smith. What kind of man is he?" The friend is asking us to classify Joe Smith. We may reply: "Oh, Joe is the aggressive junior-executive-on-the-make type, but very friendly." If our friend knows other junior executives on the make, he will have some idea of the characteristics of Joe Smith.

In using classification we can either start with the individual member and put it into a class (as we did with Joe Smith) or (as in the following piece) start with a class and divide it into its constituent members. Thus, Paul Bohannan observes that there are—roughly—three kinds of human needs:

The Needs of the Human Infant[1]

PAUL BOHANNAN

When a baby is born he is a bundle of needs [which] must be satisfied. The psychiatrist, Harry Stack Sullivan, has divided the needs of the human infant (and, indeed, of all human beings) into three main groups. The first of these is the need for the chemicals and the proper temperature to maintain life and growth. The infant [like] any other human being, feels these needs as the tensions of hunger and cold, and as the need for oxygen.

The second type of need is . . . for sleep. This need is one that we do not yet understand totally, although our present scientific knowledge of sleep is more extensive than it was even a few years ago. This is a difficult subject, and I shall say no more about the need for sleep than that it includes a need to dream, that the proportion of time one spends sleeping is reduced as one grows older, and that the way in which people sleep is greatly affected by their cultural customs.

The third kind of need has been called many things, but there is no real need for a euphemism—it is the need for love. This need is a response to a kind of tension quite different from the tensions of chemical demands. It is what doctors call the tension of anxiety. The tension of anxiety does not pertain to physical needs, but to the fear of punitive social relationships or of the loss of gratifying relationships.

The personality of the human animal is rooted as deeply in this need for love—at least, personal interaction—as his physical well-being is rooted in his chemical needs.

Bohannan equates the third need, for love, with the first two because like them it is "a response to tension." That is, the common characteristic that makes these needs a genuine class is that they are all "responses to tension." But it might be argued that since the need for love does not, like the other needs, have a purely physical basis, Bohannan's classification is not valid, and his discussion falls apart.

This is the essential point about classification: it must be based on shared characteristics of the individual members of the class. Simply to group things is not to classify them. If we put 100 people in a room, we do *not* have a class; if we put 100 airline pilots or 100 engineers or 100 Americans of Italian descent in a room, then we *do* have a class.

Classification According to Purpose

What characteristics you use as the basis of a classification depend on your own interest and purpose. Thus, you can classify the 100 people politically, socially, economically, or even by the color of their eyes, depending on what special point you want to make.

[1]From *Love, Sex, & Being Human* by Paul Bohannan, copyright © 1969 by Paul Bohannan. Reprinted by permission of Doubleday & Company, Inc.

You are, of course, free to choose whatever basis of classification best suits your purpose, but once you have chosen you must not switch midway to a different ground. If you do, you will be committing the logical error of cross-ranking, that is, producing overlapping rather than mutually exclusive categories. Someone who classifies the types of houses in a town as Victorian, colonial, ranch, and two-story is guilty of cross-ranking because Victorian and colonial style houses can have two stories.

When properly envisioned, classification is an extraordinarily useful method of inventing an essay, for there is always a "story" in the designation of types—as you choose to depict them. And the choice will depend on *why* you are making the classification in the first place, and on what new insights or refinements of understanding you hope to provide by analyzing your subject in terms of a given set of categories.

Complete Classification

In the following paragraph, Joseph Addison divides bodily labor into two kinds; he makes a dichotomous (two-part) classification. All labor is of either one kind or the other.

Bodily labor is of two kinds, either that which a man submits to for his livelihood, or that which he undergoes for his pleasure. The latter of them generally changes the name of labor for that of exercise, but differs only from ordinary labor as it rises from another motive.[2]

A dichotomous classification is necessarily complete because it divides everything into either A or B (X or not X). However, completeness is more difficult to achieve in a complex classification such as a scientific classification or the Dewey Decimal System for classifying books in a library.

A scientific classification, like a simple analysis, must be complete; that is, each separate item must fall into its designated group with no loose ends. Thus zoology has a place in its classification for *every* form of animal life; botany does the same for plant life. Similarly, under the Dewey Decimal System a library assigns every one of its holdings a general "number" heading: 900 if it is a history book, 700 if it deals with the arts, and so on. These numbers are then broken down further: 930 for ancient history; 940 for medieval and modern European history; and so on. A good classification embodies the dictum "a place for everything and everything in its place." Thus in the Dewey system, small items that are too specialized to have individual headings are grouped into categories such as "General Works," "Miscellaneous," and "Literature of Other Languages" (the "other" includes all languages that have not been specifically named, so that no language spoken or written anywhere is overlooked; each has a theoretical place into which it fits within the library's classification system). The Dewey Decimal

[2]"Recreation," *The Spectator*, No. 115, July 12, 1711.

System, then, is a valid scientific classification because it is *complete* and the groups are *mutually exclusive* (there is no overlapping).

In using classification for rhetorical reasons—as the formal basis of an essay—you are, of course, allowed more latitude than scientific classification would permit. Even so, note that in the following essay—a nonscientific classification—the author makes a gesture toward completeness:

Different Types of Composers[3]

AARON COPLAND

I can see three different types of composers in musical history, each of whom conceives music in a somewhat different fashion.

The type that has fired public imagination most is that of the spontaneously inspired composer—the Franz Schubert type, in other words. All composers are inspired, of course, but this type is more spontaneously inspired. Music simply wells out of him. He can't get it down on paper fast enough. You can almost tell this type of composer by his prolific output. In certain months, Schubert wrote a song a day. Hugo Wolf did the same.

In a sense, men of this kind begin not so much with a musical theme as with a completed composition. They invariably work best in the shorter forms. It is much easier to improvise a song than it is to improvise a symphony. It isn't easy to be inspired in that spontaneous way for long periods at a stretch. Even Schubert was more successful in handling the shorter forms of music. The spontaneously inspired man is only one type of composer, with his own limitations.

Beethoven symbolizes the second type—the constructive type, one might call it. This type exemplifies my theory of the creative process in music better than any other, because in this case the composer really does begin with a musical theme. In Beethoven's case there is no doubt about it, for we have the notebooks in which he put the themes down. We can see from his notebooks how he worked over his themes—how he would not let them be until they were as perfect as he could make them. Beethoven was not a spontaneously inspired composer in the Schubert sense at all. He was the type that begins with a theme; makes it a germinal idea; and upon that constructs a musical work, day after day, in painstaking fashion. Most composers since Beethoven's day belong to this second type.

The third type of creator I can only call, for lack of a better name, the traditionalist type. Men like Palestrina and Bach belong in this category. They both exemplify the kind of composer who is born in a particular period of musical history, when a certain musical style is about to reach its fullest development. It is a question at such a time of creating music in a well-known and accepted style and doing it in a way that is better than anyone has done it before you.

Beethoven and Schubert started from a different premise. They both had serious pretensions to originality: After all, Schubert practically created the song form singlehanded; and the whole face of music changed after Beethoven lived. But Bach and Palestrina simply improved on what had gone before them.

The traditionalist type of composer begins with a pattern rather than with a theme. The creative act with Palestrina is not the thematic conception so much as the personal treatment of a well-established pattern. And even Bach, who conceived

[3]From *What to Listen For in Music,* Revised Edition, by Aaron Copland, copyright © 1957 by McGraw-Hill, Inc., used with permission of McGraw-Hill Book Company.

forty-eight of the most varied and inspired themes in his *Well Tempered Clavichord,* knew in advance the general formal mold that they were to fill. It goes without saying that we are not living in a traditionalist period nowadays.

One might add, for the sake of completeness, a fourth type of composer—the pioneer type: men like Gesualdo in the seventeenth century, Moussorgsky and Berlioz in the nineteenth, Debussy and Edgar Varèse in the twentieth. It is difficult to summarize the composing methods of so variegated a group. One can safely say that their approach to composition is the opposite of the traditionalist type. They clearly oppose conventional solutions of musical problems. In many ways, their attitude is experimental—they seek to add new harmonies, new sonorities, new formal principles. The pioneer type was the characteristic one at the turn of the seventeenth century and also at the beginning of the twentieth century, but it is much less evident today.

Organizing the Classification

You can see that an essay concerned with "the types of X" presents no serious problem in organization, because the organization is more or less given: the three or four (or however many) designated "types" generally make up the three or four sections of the piece.

This organization underlies the Copland essay reprinted above and the essay that follows, a description of Carl Jung's classic division of people into two personality types (extravert and introvert). Note that in this essay, even more than in Copland's, the types are regarded not as mutually exclusive, with discernibly fixed personalities (an imperative of the scientific or technical classification), but rather as poles on the scale of personality (people are predominantly one or the other; no one is purely extravert or introvert). Thus in this essay, as in all rhetorical rather than strictly logical classifications, the categories may overlap to some extent.

Jung's Psychological Types[4]

FRIEDA FORDHAM

Introduction   Jung's contribution to the psychology of the conscious mind is largely embodied in his work on psychological types. The attempt to classify human beings according to type has a long history; it is nearly two thousand years since the Greek physician, Galen, tried to distinguish four fundamental temperamental differences in men, and his descriptive terms (though psychologically naive)—the sanguine, the phlegmatic, the choleric, and the melancholic—have passed into common speech. There have been various attempts which, taking modern knowledge into account, aim at a more precise formulation—for instance, Kretschmer's—and [Carl] Jung's division of people into extraverts and introverts has already come to be widely known, if not fully understood. Jung distinguishes two

[4]From *An Introduction to Jung's Psychology* by Frieda Fordham. Copyright 1953, 1959, 1966 by Frieda Fordham. Reprinted by permission of Penguin Books Ltd.

differing attitudes to life, two modes of reacting to circumstances which he finds sufficiently marked and widespread to describe as typical.

> There is a whole class of men [he says] who at the moment of reaction to a given situation at first draw back a little as if with an unvoiced "No," and only after that are able to react; and there is another class who, in the same situation, come forward with an immediate reaction, apparently confident that their behavior is obviously right. The former class would therefore be characterized by a certain negative relation to the object, and the latter by a positive one . . . the former class corresponds to the introverted and the second to the extraverted attitude.

Type one

The extraverted attitude is characterized by an outward flowing of libido, an interest in events, in people and things, a relationship with them, and a dependence on them; when this attitude is habitual to anyone Jung describes him or her as an *extraverted type.* This type is motivated by outside factors and greatly influenced by the environment. The extraverted type is sociable and confident in unfamiliar surroundings. He or she is generally on good terms with the world, and even when disagreeing with it can still be described as related to it, for instead of withdrawing (as the opposite type tends to do) they prefer to argue and quarrel, or try to reshape it according to their own pattern.

Type two

The introverted attitude, in contrast, is one of withdrawal; the libido flows inward and is concentrated upon subjective factors, and the predominating influence is "inner necessity." When this attitude is habitual Jung speaks of an "introverted type." This type lacks confidence in relation to people and things, tends to be unsociable, and prefers reflection to activity. Each type undervalues the other, seeing the negative rather than the positive qualities of the opposite attitude, a fact which has led to endless misunderstanding and even in the course of time to the formulation of antagonistic philosophies.

Conclusion

In the West we prefer the extraverted attitude, describing it in such favourable terms as outgoing, well-adjusted, &c., while on the other hand, in the East, at least until recent times, the introverted attitude has been the prevailing one. On this basis one may explain the material and technical development of the Western Hemisphere as contrasted with the material poverty but greater spiritual development of the East.

ASSIGNMENTS

Class Discussion and Paragraph Suggestions

(See Chapter 27 for methods of composing unified, adequately developed paragraphs.)

1. Evaluate Aaron Copland's essay on "Different Types of Composers."
   a. Is the classification complete?
   b. Comment on the repetition of the words "type" and "composer." Could you eliminate any of this repetition? Would this improve the piece rhetorically?

    c. Note the repetition of the word "case" in paragraph four, sentences two and three. Is it necessary? Could you eliminate one use of "case"? What would you substitute? Would it be better?

    d. Compare Copland's rhetorical stance in this piece with Randolph's in "Five Basic Elements of Music" (pp. 63–64).

2. Write a paragraph (150–250 words), opening with the topic sentence "I can see three different types of students in this room." Instead of devoting a paragraph to each type (as in the full-length Copland essay), devote only two sentences. The first naming the type, the second adding specific details or examples of the type. In Francis Christensen's terms (see Chapter 27), this will be a coordinate sequence paragraph—one that moves from general to specific:

    1 Topic sentence (general)
      2 First type (specific)
        3 Details or examples (more specific)
      2 Second type (specific)
        3 Details or examples (more specific)
      2 Third type (specific)
        3 Details or examples (more specific)

Essay Suggestions

1. Using Aaron Copland's first sentence, "I can see three different types of composers in musical history, each of whom conceives music in a somewhat different fashion," substitute for "composers in musical history" one of the following and write an essay (500–750 words). You may have to vary the number of types.

painters	photographers
dancers	artists
poets	students
playwrights	teachers
novelists	doctors
architects	

2. In an essay (500–750 words) classify people you know or know of into Jung's *extravert* and *introvert* types. You may wish to add a third category, the *ambivert* (one who balances or oscillates between extraversion and introversion).

3. Write an essay (500–750 words) in which you warn against oversimplification by describing the many types of one of the following (as you have observed or experienced it):

intelligence	beauty
freedom	goodness
truth	loyalty
happiness	charity
love	courage

4. In an essay (500–750 words) indicate the "common types" of any one of the following:

    a. Psychology/Sociology

dreams	propaganda
memories	conformity
mental disturbances	class conflict
talent or aptitude	fads
ambition	pressure groups
success	communities
prejudice	status seekers

b. Anthropology (customs in a given group)

marriage	suicide
mourning	drinking
burials	hospitality
courtship	taboos

c. Travel

railroad
road
motor vehicle

d. Law

law courts	crime prevention
law specialties	assaults
crimes	evidence
prisons	misdemeanors

e. Zoology

whales	reptiles
goats	monkeys
crabs	snakes
elephants	ants

10 How Does X Compare to Y?

Take any two people, objects, events, ideas, books, disciplines, countries, continents, planets; take any two periods of time, works of art, artists, *anything* (provided there is a logical basis of comparison), and ask of your double subject: How does one compare with the other? How are they similar? How different? In this way you will be "inventing" a study in comparative analysis.[1] Read the following example, a short comparison of two Presidents that shows how they were alike:

Kennedy has been compared to Franklin Delano Roosevelt and he liked to pose in front of an F.D.R. portrait. In fact, some of his qualities more nearly recall Theodore Roosevelt, the apostle of the big stick, the strenuous life and the bully pulpit. Like T.R., for instance, Kennedy had a perhaps undue regard for Harvard and a craving for its approval. The only election he ever lost was one of the ones he wanted most to win—his first try for a seat on the Harvard Board of Overseers. He grimly ran again and his election to the Board was a cherished triumph. Like T.R., too, Kennedy fancied himself in the role of national taste maker—Roosevelt picked up Edwin Arlington Robinson and Kennedy adopted Robert Frost. Roosevelt let his rather rigid

[1]Strictly speaking, *comparison* refers to the drawing of similarities and *contrast* to dissimilarities; but in popular usage the term "comparison" encompasses both processes and means "bringing things together in order to examine them and to see how they are related to one another." Also strictly speaking, a comparison may involve more than two subjects: X could theoretically be set alongside not only Y but also S, T, U, and V; or X could be compared with Y in the light of Z; and so on. We will confine ourselves to the double subject, since most of what should be said about comparison fits under this heading.

literary ideas get about and the Kennedys thought they ought to provide White House examples—Casals, Shakespeare and opera in the East Room—for the cultural uplift of the nation. . . .[2]

Note that in this paragraph the two men are compared not merely *in general* but on the basis of *two specific qualities*. This is the basis of all good comparison. You should not simply say X is like Y; instead you should say X is like Y on the basis of the following specific points: 1, 2, 3, etc.—which is to say, in this case:

Kennedy was like Theodore Roosevelt in that both
1. regarded Harvard highly.
2. regarded themselves as tastemakers.

Now note another comparison, this one showing—through an analogy—how two Presidents were *different:*

Lyndon Johnson's father once told him that he did not belong in politics unless he could walk into a roomful of men and tell immediately who was for him and who was against him. In fact, even the shrewd LBJ has not quite such occult power, but his liking for the story tells us something useful about him: he sets much store by instinct. No wonder, then, that it would be to his instincts—honed in the Texas hill country, sharpened in a life of politics, confirmed in his successful Congressional career—that he would often turn in the White House.

This reliance on instinct enabled Johnson to put on the Presidency like a suit of comfortable old clothes. John Kennedy, on the other hand, came to it with a historical, nearly theoretical view of what was required of a strong President; he knew exactly what Woodrow Wilson had said about the office and he had read Corwin and Neustadt and he was unabashedly willing to quote Lincoln: "I see the storm coming and I know His hand is in it. If He has a place and work for me, I believe that I am ready."

And Kennedy would add: "Today I say to you that if the people of this nation select me to be their President, I believe that I am ready." With eager confidence, Kennedy acquired a Presidential suit off the rack and put on a little weight to make himself fit it.[3]

Similarity and Difference in Comparison

As a form of analysis, comparison is not merely a rhetorical technique; it is a natural, instinctive process that goes on constantly in everyone's mind. We think and learn by comparing the unfamiliar with the familiar; we come to terms with a new situation by comparing it with an old one; we get our bearings by comparing the past with the present. Whether we are more

[2]From *Kennedy Without Tears: The Man Beneath the Myth* by Tom Wicker. Copyright © 1964 by Tom Wicker. First published in *Esquire Magazine.* Reprinted by permission of William Morrow and Company, Inc.
[3]Reprinted by permission of William Morrow and Company, Inc., from *JFK and LBJ: The Influence of Personality Upon Politics* by Tom Wicker, copyright © 1968 by Tom Wicker.

impressed by the *similarities* between two situations or the *differences* depends, of course, on the situations themselves. The ability to see through the differences to the underlying similarities—or through the similarities to the underlying differences—is the mark not only of critical intelligence but of the creative mind at work. Psychologist William James wrote, "Some people are far more sensitive to resemblances and far more ready to point out wherein they consist, than others are. They are the wits, the poets, the inventors, the scientific men, the practical geniuses." Speaking specifically of Newton and Darwin, James said, "The flash of similarity between an apple and the moon, between the rivalry for food in nature and the rivalry for man's selection, was too recondite to have occurred to any but exceptional minds."

One need not be a Newton or a Darwin, however, to be discriminating, to cut through to "the heart of the matter." Thus you, concentrating full attention on your topic, may note that two seemingly similar things are, in one or more discernible and significant respects, *different* (X is *not* like Y). Literary critic Mark Schorer makes this point about two Southern writers, Truman Capote and Carson McCullers. Their names, he tells us, are "frequently coupled," but "the differences are greater than the similarities." Schorer documents this observation by citing several specific points of contrast, beginning with the doctrine of "love."

Two "Southern" Writers[4]
MARK SCHORER

First point of difference

If Truman Capote is also a writer who comes from the South, he is not a "Southern writer" in the sense that Mrs. McCullers is: he is equally at home and perhaps even more at home in very different settings. The doctrine of love [is] given different interpretations. In Capote's *The Grass Harp,* the Judge speaks as follows:

> "We are speaking of love. A leaf, a handful of seed—begin with these, learn a little what it is to love. First, a leaf, a fall of rain, then someone to receive what a leaf has taught you, what a fall of rain has ripened. No easy process, understand, it would take a lifetime, it has mine; and still I've never mastered it—I only know how true it is: that love is a chain of love, as nature is a chain of life."

And later in the novel, Dolly recalls this speech:

> "Charlie said that love is a chain of love. I hope you listened and understood him. Because when you can love one thing," she held the blue egg as preciously as the Judge had held a leaf, "you can love another, and that is owning, that is something to live with. You can forgive everything."

The difference is that in the Capote world, love does make for communion and even community in a way that Mrs. McCullers can

---

[4]Reprinted by permission of Farrar, Straus & Giroux, Inc., from *The World We Imagine* by Mark Schorer. Copyright © 1963, 1968 by Mark Schorer.

Second
point
of difference

rarely permit. His is the gentler view, hers the more disabused. And if both like to write about children and grotesques, freaks and cripples and perverts, Mrs. McCullers seems to view them as representative of the human race whereas for Capote they are exemplars of a

Third point
of difference

private world within the world at large, and of a private view. And finally, if both are novelists of sensibility, Mrs. McCullers' sensibility, as we have observed, expresses itself most fully in the objective forms of parable and fable, while Capote's sensibility moves in two different directions—into the most subjective drama of all, the psychic drama far below the level of reason, on the one hand, and, on the other, into objective social drama, often fanciful, and always indifferent to "social problems" in the usual sense.

Conclusion

Close readers could probably find many minor similarities of detail (the crossed eyes of Miss Amelia Evans [in McCullers' *Ballad of the Sad Cafe*], for example, "exchanging with each other one long and secret gaze of grief," and the crossed eyes of Verena in *The Grass Harp,* peering "inward upon a stony vista"), but these make for no important similarity. In the end they are two quite different writers.

In the same way, the writer may make the point that apparent opposites are reconciled on a deeper level by common, shared qualities. Such is the case, says Civil War historian Bruce Catton, with Generals Ulysses S. Grant and Robert E. Lee—"oddly different" men on the surface, representing "two conflicting currents," but "under everything else" the same type of man.

Grant and Lee: A Study in Contrasts[5]

BRUCE CATTON

When Ulysses S. Grant and Robert E. Lee met in the parlor of a modest house at Appomattox Court House, Virginia, on April 9, 1865, to work out the terms for the surrender of Lee's Army of Northern Virginia, a great chapter in American life came to a close, and a great new chapter began.

These men were bringing the Civil War to its virtual finish. To be sure, other armies had yet to surrender, and for a few days the fugitive Confederate government would struggle desperately and vainly, trying to find some way to go on living now that its chief support was gone. But in effect it was all over when Grant and Lee signed the papers. And the little room where they wrote out the terms was the scene of one of the poignant, dramatic contrasts in American history.

They were two strong men, these oddly different generals, and they represented the strengths of two conflicting currents that, through them, had come into final collision.

Back of Robert E. Lee was the notion that the old aristocratic concept might somehow survive and be dominant in American life.

Lee was tidewater Virginia, and in his background were family, culture, and tradition . . . the age of chivalry transplanted to a New World which was making its own legends and its own myths. He embodied a way of life that had come down

[5]From *The American Story*, edited by Earl S. Miers. Copyright 1956 by Broadcast Music, Inc. Reprinted by permission of Broadcast Music, Inc.

through the age of knighthood and the English country squire. America was a land that was beginning all over again, dedicated to nothing much more complicated than the rather hazy belief that all men had equal rights and should have an equal chance in the world. In such a land Lee stood for the feeling that it was somehow of advantage to human society to have a pronounced inequality in the social structure. There should be a leisure class, backed by ownership of land; in turn, society itself should be keyed to the land as the chief source of wealth and influence. It would bring forth (according to this ideal) a class of men with a strong sense of obligation to the community; men who lived not to gain advantage for themselves, but to meet the solemn obligations which had been laid on them by the very fact that they were privileged. From them the country would get its leadership; to them it could look for the higher values—of thought, of conduct, of personal deportment—to give it strength and virtue.

Lee embodied the noblest elements of this aristocratic ideal. Through him, the landed nobility justified itself. For four years, the Southern states had fought a desperate war to uphold the ideals for which Lee stood. In the end, it almost seemed as if the Confederacy fought for Lee; as if he himself was the Confederacy ... the best thing that the way of life for which the Confederacy stood could ever have to offer. He had passed into legend before Appomattox. Thousands of tired, underfed, poorly clothed Confederate soldiers, long past the simple enthusiasm of the early days of the struggle, somehow considered Lee the symbol of everything for which they had been willing to die. But they could not quite put this feeling into words. If the Lost Cause, sanctified by so much heroism and so many deaths, had a living justification, its justification was General Lee.

Grant, the son of a tanner on the Western frontier, was everything Lee was not. He had come up the hard way and embodied nothing in particular except the eternal toughness and sinewy fiber of the men who grew up beyond the mountains. He was one of a body of men who owed reverence and obeisance to no one, who were self-reliant to a fault, who cared hardly anything for the past but who had a sharp eye for the future.

These frontier men were the precise opposites of the tidewater aristocrats. Back of them, in the great surge that had taken people over the Alleghenies and into the opening Western country, there was a deep, implicit dissatisfaction with a past that had settled into grooves. They stood for democracy, not from any reasoned conclusion about the proper ordering of human society, but simply because they had grown up in the middle of democracy and knew how it worked. Their society might have privileges, but they would be privileges each man had won for himself. Forms and patterns meant nothing. No man was born to anything, except perhaps to a chance to show how far he could rise. Life was competition.

Yet along with this feeling had come a deep sense of belonging to a national community. The Westerner who developed a farm, opened a shop, or set up in business as a trader, could hope to prosper only as his own community prospered—and his community ran from the Atlantic to the Pacific and from Canada down to Mexico. If the land was settled, with towns and highways and accessible markets, he could better himself. He saw his fate in terms of the nation's own destiny. As its horizons expanded, so did his. He had, in other words, an acute dollars-and-cents stake in the continued growth and development of his country.

And that, perhaps, is where the contrast between Grant and Lee becomes most striking. The Virginia aristocrat, inevitably, saw himself in relation to his own region. He lived in a static society which could endure almost anything except change. Instinctively, his first loyalty would go to the locality in which that society existed. He would fight to the limit of endurance to defend it, because in defending it he was defending everything that gave his own life its deepest meaning.

The Westerner, on the other hand, would fight with an equal tenacity for the broader concept of society. He fought so because everything he lived by was tied to growth, expansion, and a constantly widening horizon. What he lived by would survive or fall with the nation itself. He could not possibly stand by unmoved in the face of an attempt to destroy the Union. He would combat it with everything he had, because he could only see it as an effort to cut the ground out from under his feet.

So Grant and Lee were in complete contrast, representing two diametrically opposed elements in American life. Grant was the modern man emerging; beyond him, ready to come on the stage, was the great age of steel and machinery, of crowded cities and a restless, burgeoning vitality. Lee might have ridden down from the old age of chivalry, lance in hand, silken banner fluttering over his head. Each man was the perfect champion of his cause, drawing both his strengths and his weaknesses from the people he led.

Yet it was not all contrast, after all. Different as they were—in background, in personality, in underlying aspiration—these two great soldiers had much in common. Under everything else, they were marvelous fighters. Furthermore, their fighting qualities were really very much alike.

Each man had, to begin with, the great virtue of utter tenacity and fidelity. Grant fought his way down the Mississippi Valley in spite of acute personal discouragement and profound military handicaps. Lee hung on in the trenches at Petersburg after hope itself had died. In each man there was an indomitable quality . . . the born fighter's refusal to give up as long as he can still remain on his feet and lift his two fists.

Daring and resourcefulness they had, too; the ability to think faster and move faster than the enemy. These were the qualities which gave Lee the dazzling campaigns of Second Manassas and Chancellorsville and won Vicksburg for Grant.

Lastly, and perhaps greatest of all, there was the ability, at the end, to turn quickly from war to peace once the fighting was over. Out of the way these two men behaved at Appomattox came the possibility of a peace of reconciliation. It was a possibility not wholly realized, in the years to come, but which did, in the end, help the two sections to become one nation again . . . after a war whose bitterness might have seemed to make such a reunion wholly impossible. No part of either man's life became him more than the part he played in their brief meeting in the McLean house at Appomattox. Their behavior there put all succeeding generations of Americans in their debt. Two great Americans, Grant and Lee—very different, yet under everything very much alike. Their encounter at Appomattox was one of the great moments of American history.

Organization of a Comparison

There are several forms into which comparative analysis may conveniently be organized. There are also many variations within each form, for the forms are flexible, giving you ample freedom to shape your essay as you wish. What is important is that the essay always *have a shape*—a definite plan or pattern of development—so that it does not shift haphazardly back and forth: from X to Y; back to *part* of X; then more about Y; back to *another* part of X; and so on. Whatever shifting takes place must follow an orderly procedure.

Catton's piece, for example, represents a *comparison of wholes* wherein one total subject is compared with another total subject, so that the two may be regarded side by side, as follows:

I. Lee
    A. personal background
    B. leadership of the Confederate army
II. Grant
    A. personal background
    B. leadership of the Union army

If your main intention is not to compare two total subjects one against the other, but rather to demonstrate how parts of one "play off" against parts of the other, then you will structure your piece according to those specific points of concern. Thus in the final third of his essay, Catton considers— point by point—the fighting qualities of Grant and Lee, noting that they were remarkably similar in regard to:

1. tenacity
2. fidelity to cause
3. daring
4. resourcefulness
5. ability to convert from war to peace

This type of structure is called *comparison of parts*. It generally involves many parts, one following another in rapid succession with intricate (though always orderly) weaving back and forth between X and Y, sometimes within a single sentence, as in the following essay.

Stanley and Livingstone[6]

EMIL LUDWIG

If we compare Stanley with Livingstone, it is hard to say which of them gains by the comparison.

Both were self-made men, the one beginning as a cotton spinner, the other as a shepherd, sailor, and clerk. The one was a missionary, the other a journalist. But when they got down to work, Stanley remained what he was whereas Livingstone forgot the missionaries for his mission.

Both explored great rivers. Livingstone was a monomaniac in the grip of a misanthropic passion for the Nile, and he even had a peculiar love for its name. Stanley on the other hand was always actuated by some specific purpose.

Livingstone groped with a mystical urge towards enigmatic headwaters; Stanley broke himself a new path to an unpeopled estuary. Stanley was trying to fulfill a task; Livingstone was in search of Africa's marvels. The two men are alike in that they followed the two largest streams of a continent, the one going upstream to the source, the other going downstream to the mouth. Livingstone, loving Africa, wanted to explore. Stanley, loving his work, wanted to have explored.

Livingstone went for years without uttering a word. He wanted to remain alone

[6]From *Genius and Character*, pp. 64–67, by Emil Ludwig, copyright, 1927, by Harcourt Brace Jovanovich, Inc.; renewed 1955, by Kenneth Burke. Reprinted by permission of the publisher.

with his savages, whom he loved as fellow beings. His wife traveled with him for twelve years, until she died in the wilderness—and thereafter he remained alone. When he heard that white men were near, he would retire deeper into the interior. It is amusing to observe the elaborate precautions which Stanley took to keep his expedition in search of Livingstone a secret, lest his quarry should learn of it in time to escape. Stanley drew a breath of relief each time he left Africa. Livingstone firmly refused to accompany Stanley to England or to the coast.

Stanley always sent word—and as promptly as possible. He was continually writing, whereas Livingstone hardly ever wrote. He was taciturn, and grew old and gray in the wilderness while maintaining silence. Stanley also possessed the great virtue of silence, but only when some important undertaking had to be kept in the dark. Livingstone's silence was philosophical, Stanley's was shrewd.

Stanley advanced by force of arms, a whole train of people surrounding him. He nearly always looked upon the black man as an enemy. But Livingstone, when a negro became angry, acted like a wise old gentleman who merely frowned to show that he was offended.

Stanley gives a famous account of their meeting, when he finally came upon Livingstone after an eight months' march: "As I advanced towards him I noticed he was pale, looked wearied. . . . I would have run to him, only I was a coward in the presence of such a mob—would have embraced him, only, he being an Englishman, I did not know how he would receive me." Stanley took off his cap and said:

"Dr. Livingstone, I presume?"

"Yes."

"I thank God, Doctor, I have been permitted to see you."

"I feel thankful that I am here to welcome you."

Livingstone records the incident in his journal: "It was Henry Moreland Stanley, the traveling correspondent of the New York 'Herald,' sent by James Gordon Bennett, junior, at an expense of more than   4000, to obtain accurate information about Dr. Livingstone if living, and if dead, to bring home my bones."

The seeker: young, ambitious, optimistic, thoroughly pleased with his job. The sought: an old explorer, skeptical, mature, misanthropic, kind-hearted, eternally restless. The messenger of God, and the messenger of America.

Soon after this Livingstone died, alone in the primitive forests, at the heart of Africa. Black men brought his body to the coast, but England buried him in Westminster Abbey. Stanley died near London fifteen years after leaving Africa for the last time. He died well off, with wife and child at his bedside. But England refused to bury him.

Which of them should be ranked the higher?

From the standpoint of drama, it could only be Livingstone. Yet if I had the palm to award, I should lay it upon that rough stone on which is inscribed . . .

HENRY MORTON STANLEY
BULA–MATARI
1841–1904
AFRICA

In the following essay we find a variation of these two basic organizational patterns: first a comparison for similarities, then for differences. In most cases writers will present the position they want to stress in the second, more emphatic, half of the essay, following a principle that applies at every level of English discourse, whether it be sentence, paragraph, or whole essay: that which comes last is fixed most forcibly in readers' minds. Observing this psychological truth, Northrop Frye moves from the obvious similarities between myth and folk tale to the not-so-obvious differences.

Myth and Folk Tale[7]
NORTHROP FRYE

By a myth . . . I mean primarily a certain type of story . . . in which some of the chief characters are gods or other beings larger in power than humanity. Very seldom is it located in history: its action takes place in a world above or prior to ordinary time. . . . Hence, like the folk tale, it is an *abstract story-pattern.* The characters can do what they like, which means what the story-teller likes: there is no need to be plausible or logical in motivation. The things that happen in myth are things that happen only in stories; they are in a self-contained literary world. Hence myth would naturally have the same kind of appeal for the fiction writer that folk tales have. It presents him with a ready-made framework, hoary with antiquity, and allows him to devote all his energies to elaborating its design. Thus the use of myth in Joyce or Cocteau, like the use of folk tale in Mann, is parallel to the use of abstraction and other means of emphasizing design in contemporary painting; and a modern writer's interest in primitive fertility rites is parallel to a modern sculptor's interest in primitive woodcarving.

The differences between myth and folk tale, however, also have their importance. Myths, as compared with folk tales, are usually in a special category of seriousness: they are believed to have "really happened," or to have some exceptional significance in explaining certain features of life, such as ritual. Again, whereas folk tales simply interchange motifs and develop variants, myths show an odd tendency to stick together and build up bigger structures. We have creation myths, fall and flood myths, metamorphosis and dying-god myths, divine-marriage and hero-ancestry myths, etiological myths, apocalyptic myths; and writers of sacred scriptures or collectors of myth like Ovid tend to arrange these in a series. And while myths themselves are seldom historical, they seem to provide a kind of containing form of tradition, one result of which is the obliterating of boundaries separating legend, historical reminiscence, and actual history that we find in Homer and the Old Testament.

As a type of story, myth is a form of verbal art, and belongs to the world of art. Like art, and unlike science, it deals, not with the world that man contemplates, but with the world that man creates. The total form of art, so to speak, is a world whose content is nature but whose form is human; hence when it "imitates" nature it assimilates nature to human forms. The world of art is human in perspective, a world in which the sun continues to rise and set long after science has explained that its rising and setting are illusions. And myth, too,

Similarities noted — (margin note)

Differences noted — (margin note)

[7]From "Myth, Fiction, and Displacement," by Northrop Frye. Reprinted by permission from *Daedalus,* Journal of the American Academy of Arts and Sciences, Boston, Massachusetts, Volume 90, Number 1.

makes a systematic attempt to see nature in human shape: it does not simply roam at large in nature like the folk tale.

Note that in contrasting the two types of stories, myth and folk tale, Frye accentuates the qualities of each. This is one of the important rhetorical advantages of the comparative approach: each side of the comparison is more clearly delineated by the other, each *highlights* the other by bringing out distinctive points of similarity or difference.

Comparison as a Natural Process

Because the mind naturally tends to make comparisons, because comparative situations are common in everyday life (before and after, then and now, loss and gain, here and there, promise and fulfillment), and because there is no clearer indication of how well a person has grasped a subject than his or her ability to detect similarities and differences among its parts (hence the popularity of "How does X compare to Y?" as an essay-type examination question), you should make an extra effort to master this form of discourse. It is not a difficult form if it is approached systematically; more than that, it can be relied on to produce interesting and engaging essays.

In the following piece of reportage, written soon after the First World War, the young Ernest Hemingway—then a foreign correspondent for *The Toronto Star Weekly*—provides a vividly described and delicately evoked setting and highly compressed but emotionally charged dialogue to help the reader understand the difference between a closed-in Christmas in a foreign land and an old-fashioned family Christmas at home. The contrast is never explicitly developed point by point, for Christmas at home needs no description: most readers can fill in details from their own homes. Within the contrast we find a metaphor for the emotion that dominates this story: a gnawing loneliness, as unrelenting as the snow that is falling in the opening line of the piece and still falling at the end.

Christmas in Paris[8]
ERNEST HEMINGWAY

Paris with the snow falling. Paris with the big charcoal braziers outside the cafes, glowing red. At the cafe tables, men huddled, their coat collars turned up, while they finger glasses of *grog Americain* and the newsboys shout the evening papers.

The buses rumble like green juggernauts through the snow that sifts down in the dusk. White house walls rise through the dusky snow. Snow is never more beautiful than in the city. It is wonderful in Paris to stand on a bridge across the Seine looking up through the softly curtaining snow past the grey bulk of the Louvre, up the river spanned by many bridges and bordered by the grey houses of old Paris to where Notre Dame squats in the dusk.

It is very beautiful in Paris and very lonely at Christmas time.

[8]"Christmas in Paris" is reprinted by permission of Charles Scribner's Sons from *By-Line: Ernest Hemingway*. Copyright © 1967 Mary Hemingway.

The young man and his girl walk up the Rue Bonaparte from the Quai in the shadow of the tall houses to the brightly lighted little Rue Jacob. In a little second floor restaurant, The Veritable Restaurant of the Third Republic, which has two rooms, four tiny tables and a cat, there is a special Christmas dinner being served.

"It isn't much like Christmas," said the girl.

"I miss the cranberries," said the young man.

They attack the special Christmas dinner. The turkey is cut into a peculiar sort of geometrical formation that seems to include a small taste of meat, a great deal of gristle, and a large piece of bone.

"Do you remember turkey at home?" asks the young girl.

"Don't talk about it," says the boy.

They attack the potatoes which are fried with too much grease.

"What do you suppose they're doing at home?" says the girl.

"I don't know," said the boy. "Do you suppose we'll ever get home?"

"I don't know," the girl answered. "Do you suppose we'll ever be successful artists?"

The proprietor entered with the dessert and a small bottle of red wine.

"I had forgotten the wine," he said in French.

The girl began to cry.

"I didn't know Paris was like this," she said. "I thought it was gay and full of light and beautiful."

The boy put his arm around her. At least that was one thing you could do in a Parisian restaurant.

"Never mind, honey," he said. "We've been here only three days. Paris will be different. Just you wait."

They ate the dessert, and neither one mentioned the fact that it was slightly burned. Then they paid the bill and walked downstairs and out into the street. The snow was still falling. And they walked out into the streets of old Paris that had known the prowling of wolves and the hunting of men and the tall old houses that had looked down on it all and were stark and unmoved by Christmas.

The boy and the girl were homesick. It was their first Christmas away from their own land. You do not know what Christmas is until you lose it in some foreign land.

ASSIGNMENTS

Class Discussion and Paragraph Suggestions

(See Chapter 27 for methods of composing unified, adequately developed paragraphs.)

1. In "Grant and Lee: A Study in Contrasts" the two generals are shown to be different *and* alike. Cite the specific points of difference and likeness, indicating whether they are organized methodically and logically. Do the same with "Stanley and Livingstone."

2. a. Read the "Christmas in Paris" piece, noting the following:
   1. Opening and closing paragraphs: how do they function?
   2. Concrete details cited in paragraphs one and two. Note also and comment on the effectiveness of modifiers and verbs: "the softly *curtaining* snow," and "Notre Dame *squats* in the dusk."
   3. The restaurant scene, which constitutes the middle section: in what way do the setting and dialogue convey a specific mood?

4. Neither the man nor the woman mentions the fact that the dessert was slightly burned; why do they not speak of this?

5. "The boy and the girl were homesick": in what sense does the last sentence generalize their homesickness? in what sense does it *explain* their homesickness?

b. Compare this piece of reportage with the short story "Birthday Party" (pp. 155–56).

1. In what ways are they similar? In what ways different?

2. From what point of view is each story told?

3. Does Hemingway express any feelings of his own in this piece? Explain.

c. Write a one- to two-paragraph comparison of "Christmas in Paris" and "Birthday Party."

3. Consider the following three poems, noting specific points of similarity and difference; then write a one- or two-paragraph report of your findings. Be prepared to describe and explain your choice of organizational pattern—for example, comparison of parts or of wholes.

Death Be Not Proud

JOHN DONNE

Death, be not proud, though some have called thee
Mighty and dreadful, for thou art not so;
For those whom thou think'st thou dost overthrow
Die not, poor Death, nor yet canst thou kill me.
From rest and sleep, which but thy pictures be,
Much pleasure; then from thee much more must flow,
And soonest our best men with thee do go,
Rest of their bones, and soul's delivery.
Thou art slave to fate, chance, kings, and desperate men,
And dost with poison, war, and sickness dwell,
And poppy or charms can make us sleep as well
And better than thy stroke; why swell'st thou then?
One short sleep past, we wake eternally
And death shall be no more; Death, thou shalt die.

Do Not Go Gentle into That Good Night[9]

DYLAN THOMAS

Do not go gentle into that good night,
Old age should burn and rave at close of day;
Rage, rage against the dying of the light.

Though wise men at their end know dark is right,
Because their words had forked no lightning they
Do not go gentle into that good night.

[9]Dylan Thomas, *Collected Poems*. Copyright 1952 by Dylan Thomas. Reprinted by permission of New Directions Publishing Corporation, J. M. Dent & Sons Ltd., and the Trustees for the Copyrights of the late Dylan Thomas.

Good men, the last wave by, crying how bright
Their frail deeds might have danced in a green bay,
Rage, rage against the dying of the light.

Wild men who caught and sang the sun in flight,
And learn, too late, they grieved it on its way,
Do not go gentle into that good night.

Grave men, near death, who see with blinding sight
Blind eyes could blaze like meteors and be gay,
Rage, rage against the dying of the light.

And you, my father, there on the sad height,
Curse, bless, me now with your fierce tears, I pray.
Do not go gentle into that good night.
Rage, rage against the dying of the light.

Timor Mortis Conturbat Me[10]

R. L. CHAPMAN

My Lord Death, hear this petition:
You are (Thou art?) a goodly lord,
I know cerebrally;
Handsomer than that grinning clanky clown
We show you as;
Goodly, opulently velvety dark
And somberly lovely.

Pray, Lord, when you extinguish me,
Do it micro-fast and from behind,
So he did not know what hit him.
And wait, if you can manage
In your cleansing economy,
Until I am old enough to be the elegant
Rarefied abstraction of a man,
A paper person so fined by abrasive years
As to be more symbolic than real.

Then strike, and hear him rustle as he falls.

4. Write a one- or two-paragraph comparison of the pair of pictures opposite.

5. Write a one-paragraph essay (150–250 words) showing that X is *not* like Y, on the basis of specific points. Choose one pair of topics from one of the following categories. (Note: The specific points of difference need not be factual details in every case; a "point" may be an example, an analogy, an attitude, as in the comparison of Kennedy and Johnson. The "points" may also be the ramifications of *one* main point.)

  a. Warfare

      conventional/guerrilla
      Korea/Vietnam

[10]From *The Nation*, 5 April 1975, p. 414.

> atomic weapons/conventional weapons
> atomic warfare/germ warfare
> offensive/defensive

b. Astronomy

> astronomy/astrology
> dawn/dusk
> sun/moon
> Earth/Mars
> planet/star

c. Eating

> appetite/hunger
> home cooking/college cafeteria
> eating to live/living to eat
> eating in the tropics/eating in the Arctic
> eating/dining

d. Fact and Fiction

> detectives/detectives in movies and television
> American Indians/Indians in movies and television
> family life/family life on a television series
> Marine Corps/movie marines
> courtroom/courtroom on television

6. The paired terms listed below are close in meaning and therefore have to be distinguished from each other (either denotatively or connotatively—see Chapter 24). Write one or two paragraphs in which you cite the essential difference or differences between the terms in one of the following pairs:

talent/genius	induction/deduction
aptitude/talent	libel/slander
conscience/guilt	liberty/license
knowledge/wisdom	class/caste
intelligence/knowledge	dissent/rebellion
cooperate/collaborate	wit/humor

Essay Suggestions

1. Write an essay (500–750 words) in which you compare two men or two women, using as your organizational plan either comparison of wholes or comparison of parts.

2. Drawing on your own experience, write an essay (500–750 words) on one of the following topics:

    a. Two things mistakenly believed to be alike
    b. A similarity (or difference) between two authors or two literary works (or two of *anything*) that has not, to your knowledge, been observed before

3. Expand one of the paragraph exercises above into an essay of 500–750 words.

4. Write about a holiday away from home (500–750 words), indicating in what ways it was different from your normal holiday with the family. As an exercise in imagination, project your feelings onto a couple; let them speak for you (as, in a sense, Hemingway does in "Christmas in Paris"). Organize your piece accordingly:

    I. Opening scene (in "foreign" place)
    II. Conversation (overheard)
    III. Closing scene (a comment on how it feels to be away from home)

11 What Is the Present Status of X?

In every professional field or discipline, as well as in every area of ordinary life, we are periodically required to bring things up to date, to ask "What is the present status of X?" or, in words we are more likely to use, "What is new about X?" or "What is happening with X?" or "How do people feel about X at the present moment?" or "How do *I* feel at the present time?" Whatever form it takes, the question leads to a special kind of comparison (Chapter 10, "How Does X Compare to Y?") in which *then* is compared to *now*.

We may properly ask the question, "What is its present status?" of almost any thing, idea, habit, custom, condition, or belief. Is it "in" or "out"? Timely or obsolete? How is it different from or similar to what it was—and why? As Heraclitus pointed out more than two thousand years ago, the world is in a constant state of flux; nothing stands still; one never steps into the same stream twice. Thus there is always a story in an assessment of the present status of something.

Not surprisingly, then, in the summer of 1958—thirteen years after the defeat of Nazi Germany—an American correspondent went to Auschwitz, the most hideous of the Nazi concentration camps (where four million prisoners, mostly Jews, were murdered during the Second World War), to describe its present status. What is it like *now?* This was the question that he answered in the following news story, whose impact rests on the contrast between the ghastly activity of the past and the peaceful stillness of the present.

No News from Auschwitz[1]

A. M. ROSENTHAL

The most terrible thing of all, somehow, was that at Brzezinka the sun was bright and warm, the rows of graceful poplars were lovely to look upon and on the grass near the gates children played.

It all seemed frighteningly wrong, as in a nightmare, that at Brzezinka the sun should ever shine or that there should be light and greenness and the sound of young laughter. It would be fitting if at Brzezinka the sun never shone and the grass withered because this is a place of unutterable terror.

And yet, every day, from all over the world, people come to Brzezinka, quite possibly the most grisly tourist center on earth. They come for a variety of reasons— to see if it could really have been true, to remind themselves not to forget, to pay homage to the dead by the simple act of looking upon their place of suffering.

Brzezinka is a couple of miles from the better-known southern Polish town of Oswiecim. Oswiecim has about 12,000 inhabitants, is situated about 171 miles from Warsaw and lies in a damp, marshy area at the eastern end of the pass called the Moravian Gate. Brzezinka and Oswiecim together formed part of that minutely organized factory of torture and death that the Nazis called Konzentrationslager Auschwitz.

By now, fourteen years after the last batch of prisoners was herded naked into the gas chambers by dogs and guards, the story of Auschwitz has been told a great many times. Some of the inmates have written of those events of which sane men cannot conceive. Rudolf Franz Ferdinand Hoess, the superintendent of the camp, before he was executed wrote his detailed memoirs of mass exterminations and the experiments on living bodies. Four million people died here, the Poles say.

And so there is no news to report about Auschwitz. There is merely the compulsion to write something about it, a compulsion that grows out of a restless feeling that to have visited Auschwitz and then turned away without having said or written anything would be a most grievous act of discourtesy to those who died here.

Brzezinka and Oswiecim are very quiet places now; the screams can no longer be heard. The tourist walks silently, quickly at first to get it over with and then, as his mind peoples the barracks and the chambers and the dungeons and flogging posts, he walks draggingly. The guide does not say much either, because there is nothing much for him to say after he has pointed.

For every visitor, there is one particular bit of horror that he knows he will never forget. For some it is seeing the rebuilt gas chamber at Oswiecim and being told that this is the "small one." For others it is the fact that at Brzezinka, in the ruins of the gas chambers and the crematoria the Germans blew up when they retreated, there are daisies growing. There are visitors who gaze blankly at the gas chambers and the furnaces because their minds simply cannot encompass them, but stand shivering before the great mounds of human hair behind the plate glass window or the piles of babies' shoes or the brick cells where men sentenced to death by suffocation were walled up.

One visitor opened his mouth in a silent scream simply at the sight of boxes—great stretches of three-tiered boxes in the women's barracks. They were about six feet wide, about three feet high, and into them from five to ten prisoners were shoved for the night. The guide walks quickly through the barracks. Nothing more to see here.

A brick building where sterilization experiments were carried out on women prisoners. The guide tries the door—it's locked. The visitor is grateful that he does not have to go in, and then flushes with shame.

A long corridor where rows of faces stare from the walls. Thousands of pictures, the photographs of prisoners. They are all dead now, the men and women who stood before the cameras, and they all knew they were to die.

They all stare blank-faced, but one picture, in the middle of a row, seizes the eye and wrenches the mind. A girl, 22 years old, plumply pretty, blonde. She is smiling gently, as at a sweet, treasured thought. What was the thought that passed through her young mind and is now her memorial on the wall of the dead at Auschwitz?

Into the suffocation dungeons the visitor is taken for a moment and feels himself strangling. Another visitor goes in, stumbles out and crosses herself. There is no place to pray at Auschwitz.

The visitors look pleadingly at each other and say to the guide, "Enough."

There is nothing new to report about Auschwitz. It was a sunny day and the trees were green and at the gates the children played.

In a light, spoofing mood (with an undertone of seriousness), writer-editor Theodore M. Bernstein addresses the question of present status to the conventional but perennially confusing use of the word *whom.* "Who needs it?" he decides, in a beguiling essay that contains a fine argumentative edge.

I Favor *Whom's* Doom[2]

THEODORE M. BERNSTEIN

If I have anything to say about it, the pronoun *whom* will be dropped from the English language except in one context. And I do have something to say about it in what follows.

Not only is *whom* useless and senseless; it is in addition a complicated nuisance. Think, for example, of the puzzle-solving needed to determine the proper pronoun to use in each of these sentences:

"A suspect *whom* the police identified as John Jones was arrested."

"A suspect *who* the police said was John Jones was arrested."

"*Whomever* [*whoever?*] she marries will not be the boss in her home."

The pronoun in the objective case form serves no purpose in the language and should be banished, except when it follows immediately after a preposition and "sounds natural" even to the masses, as in "To *whom* it may concern" or "He married the girl for *whom* he had risked his life." Except for such postprepositional uses of *whom,* forget it.

Dropping *whom* will be neither radical nor unprecedented. The wiping out of case declensions of pronouns began centuries ago. The seven Indo-European cases were reduced to four, then by the time of the Middle English period the four were cut down to three with the disappearance of the distinction between the dative and the accusative. More than a century and a half ago Noah Webster denounced *whom* as useless and argued that common sense was on the side of "*Who* did he marry?" And half a century ago H. L. Mencken in "The American Language" said, "Although the schoolma'am continues the heroic task of trying to teach the difference between *who* and *whom, whom* is fast vanishing from Standard American; in the vulgar language it is virtually extinct."

Mencken made a valid point when he said that *whom* was fast vanishing, but the real point is the vanishing point: How can we speed its arrival? How can we escape from this pedagogical perplexity?

It seemed to me that the first step was to find out what experts on English thought about *whom's* doom. So I drew up a list of a couple of dozen teachers, consultants on dictionaries, writers and knowledgeable linguists, striving, so far as I was able, to achieve a balance between liberals and conservatives. A copy of the foregoing argument was sent to each of them along with a letter asking each to indicate agreement or disagreement with it by a vote of "yea" or "nay" and inviting any comments the recipient cared to make. Not to keep you in suspense, the results were 6 "nays," 15 "yeas" and 4 in-betweens, most of which leaned more to the "yea" side than the "nay" side.

Among the "nay"-sayers, Prof. Lionel Trilling of Columbia University commented, "Difficult though the correct use of *whom* often is, it seems to me that the difficulty it entails is of a kind the confrontation of which tends to build character, and in our cultural situation we need all the character we can get." Other "nay"-sayers were Russell Baker, New York *Times* columnist; Herbert Brucker, former editor of The Hartford *Courant;* Rudolf Flesch, writer on English style; Marya Mannes, author and critic, and Walter W. (Red) Smith, New York *Times* sports columnist.

There isn't space to quote all 15 "yea"-sayers, but Dwight Macdonald, author and critic, said, "YES, a thousand times YES on your proposal to deep-six *whom.* One of the practical beauties of English is its delightful poverty of inflection (ditto its confining of gender to sex). English has replaced French as the world's second language precisely because of its lack of such archaic frills. So do let's excise this vermiform appendix."

William F. Buckley Jr., editor of *National Review,* commented, "Your distinction is exactly correct. Where 'who' *sounds* right, it should be retained . . . You are aware of the Leo Durocher answer to a tough question at a banquet speech? (Pause) 'Whom knows?'"*

Norman Cousins, editor of *Saturday Review,* was one of the in-betweens. "Admittedly," he said, "there are cases when insistence on correct usage is stuffy and pedantic; I see no reason why *who* shouldn't suffice. But if you abolish *whom,* as you propose, will you not therefore be judging those who use the word correctly? In this case, you are abolishing sin for the sinner but superimposing it on the virtuous."

"Naturally I agree with the general purport of your treatment of *whom,*" said another of the "in-betweens," Emeritus Prof. Albert H. Marckwardt of Princeton University, "but . . . I doubt that advocacy, in the form of a solemn pronouncement that *whom* is dead or should die, will have much effect one way or the other." Other in-betweens were David B. Guralnik, editor of *Webster's New World Dictionary,* and Jess Stein, editor of the *Random House Dictionary.*

---

*The other "yeas" came from Prof. Robert L. Allen, Teachers College, Columbia University; Prof. Sheridan Baker, University of Michigan; Prof. Jacques Barzun, Columbia Unversity; Margaret M. Bryant, professor of English emeritus, City University of New York; Roy H. Copperud, the *Editor & Publisher* columnist; Prof. Bergen Evans, Northwestern University; Prof. S. I. Hayakawa, president emeritus, San Francisco State College; Jessica Mitford, author; William Morris, editor of the *American Heritage Dictionary;* Prof. Maxwell Nurnberg, New York University; Eric Partridge, English lexicographer; Prof. Mario Pei, Columbia University, and Vermont Royster, contributing editor of *The Wall Street Journal.*

Among the replies there is little defense of *whom* on the ground of "correctness" or necessity. There is some on the ground of discipline and building of character. But most interesting to me is the feeling suggested in two or three of the responses that the banishment of *whom* is not the kind of thing that can be legislated. It is true that changes in the language in the past have come about by themselves without anyone's doing anything about them. But does that mean that nothing can be done? Has anyone—including Mencken and Webster—ever attempted to do anything beyond commenting on the need for a change?

I propose a course of action. To begin with, I propose that teachers of English drop the obviously futile attempt to implant into pupils' minds the senseless rules about *whom.* I suggest that such bodies as the National Council of Teachers of English and the Council for Basic Education decide that such rules are null, void, useless, trouble-making and from now on to be ignored. For the present the existing text-books can remain in use with the teachers pointing out that what the books say about *whom* is in the same class as what some of they say about the split infinitive or about ending a sentence with a preposition. But from now on the textbooks should note that those rules are archaic.

But what about the grown-up who agrees that *whom* should go, but shrinks from doing anything about the matter himself for fear the "purists" will think him ignorant? For you who feel that way I have a gimmicky solution. No matter who you are writing to don't use a *whom* except after a preposition and, so he or she won't think you are ignorant, write at the bottom of the letter "I favor Whom's Doom except after a preposition." Better yet, get yourself a rubber stamp (cost: about $1) and stamp that declaration on your stationery.

Who knows, after enough of us have used such a stamp maybe the bumper-sticker people will grab the idea, spread it far and wide, and our cause will be whom free.

ASSIGNMENTS

Class Discussion and Paragraph Suggestions

(See Chapter 27 for methods of composing unified, adequately developed paragraphs.)

1. Answer the following questions about "No News from Auschwitz."
    a. In A. M. Rosenthal's grimly moving essay what is the basic and ironic contrast that makes everything seem "frighteningly wrong"?
    b. Point to other contrasting elements in this piece and show how they function as an organizing principle.
    c. Evaluate the function and effectiveness of the opening and closing paragraphs.
    d. In what way is the tone of this essay subdued?
    e. Discuss "restraint" as the fundamental rhetorical device of this essay. Cite specific examples of understatement, and speculate on what the piece might be like if the writer had not exercised restraint. Explain why the story would have been more or less effective.
    f. Discuss the simplicity of diction and the structure of the following sentences. Explain why you do or do not find them powerful.

    > And so there is no news to report about Auschwitz.
    > The guide does not say much either, because there is nothing much for him to say after he has pointed.
    > Nothing more to see here.

  g. Explain the grammatical structure of the following sentences and indicate what rhetorical function they serve:

> A brick building where sterilization experiments were carried out on women prisoners.
> A long corridor where rows of faces stare from the walls.
> Thousands of pictures, the photographs of prisoners.

  h. Why does the writer single out and ponder the photograph of one prisoner—the "plumply pretty" blonde?

  i. What is the significance of the visitor who "crosses herself"? What extra dimension of meaning is introduced by this detail?

2. Write a one-paragraph (150–250 words) response to Rosenthal's essay. Consider the advantages and disadvantages of using a topic sentence at either the beginning (movement from general to specific) or the end of the paragraph (movement from specific to general). Be prepared to explain your decision.

3. Consider Bernstein's essay on *whom*. How do you feel about this usage? Would you like to see *whom* abandoned? Why?

4. Write a one-paragraph (150–250 words) defense of your position. Open the paragraph with a topic sentence beginning "I do [or do not] favor *whom's* doom." Develop the paragraph with specific reasons, examples, and details.

Essay Suggestions

1. In an essay (500–750 words) describe the present status of a place that has changed drastically—for better or worse—since you first knew or heard about it.

2. In an essay (500–750 words) take a position on the present status of some current point of usage, as Bernstein does with *whom*. The *it is I/it is me* controversy may provide a provocative point of departure. For additional suggestions consult Margaret M. Bryant's *Current American Usage* or Margaret Nicholson's *A Dictionary of American-English Usage*.

3. In an essay entitled "On the Status of the Soul," Bertrand Russell once pointed out that we are losing such "fine old simplicities" as the belief in an immortal soul. In an essay (500–750 words) describe the present status, as you view it, of one of the following established "simplicities":

> Be it ever so humble, there's no place like home.
> Honor thy father and thy mother.
> Love conquers all.
> You can't keep a good man down.
> There's always room at the top.
> Cleanliness is next to godliness.
> The good go to heaven and the bad go to hell.

12 How Should X Be Interpreted?

Beyond definition, description, and analysis—and to a large extent dependent on these basic processes—is the more subtle and complex business of interpretation, of explaining what is not immediately apparent: the deeper meaning or significance of a subject, the relationship of particulars to a general principle, the truth that lies beneath the surface.

Interpreting an Activity

Take the subject of football, for example. On the face of it, football is simply a popular spectator sport, a national pastime, a "he-man" game filled with action and excitement. On a deeper level, however—as the writer of the following essay points out—football is more than a game. It is an acting-out of basic and primitive human aggression, of a compulsion to gain and hold on to property. Note how the writer supports his interpretation by explaining explicit facts about the game on the basis of an implicit general principle.

Football—the Game of Aggression[1]
GEORGE STADE

There are many ways in which professional football is unique among sports, and as many others in which it is the fullest expression of what is at the heart of all sports.

---

[1]From "Game Theory" by George Stade. Reprinted from *The Columbia Forum*, Fall 1966, Volume IX, Number 4. Copyright 1966 by The Trustees of Columbia University in the City of New York.

There is no other major sport so dependent upon raw force, nor any so dependent on a complex and delicate strategy; none so wide in the range of specialized functions demanded from its players; none so dependent upon the undifferentiated athletic *sine qua non,* a quickwitted body; none so primitive; none so futuristic; none so American.

Football is first of all a form of play, something one engages in instinctively and only for the sake of performing the activity in question. Among forms of play, football is a game, which means that it is built on communal needs, rather than on private evasions, like mountain climbing. Among games it is a sport; it requires athletic ability, unlike croquet. And among sports, it is one whose mode is violence and whose violence is its special glory.

In some sports—basketball, baseball, soccer—violence is occasional (and usually illegal); in others, like hockey, it is incidental; in others still, car racing, for example, it is accidental. Definitive violence football shares alone with boxing and bullfighting, among major sports. But in bullfighting a man is pitted not against another man, but against an animal, and boxing is a competition between individuals, not teams, and that makes a great difference. If shame is the proper and usual penalty for failures in sporting competitions between individuals, guilt is the consequence of failing not only oneself and one's fans, but also one's teammates. Failure in football, moreover, seems more related to a failure of courage, seems more unmanning than in any other sport outside of bullfighting. In other sports one loses a knack, is outsmarted, or is merely inferior in ability, but in football, on top of these, a player fails because he "lacks desire," or "can't take it anymore," or "hears footsteps," as his teammates will put it.

Many sports, especially those in which there is a goal to be defended, seem enactments of the games animals play under the stimulus of what ethologists, students of animal behavior, call *territory*—"the drive to gain, maintain, and defend the exclusive right to a piece of property," as Robert Ardrey puts it. The most striking symptom of this drive is aggressiveness, but among social animals, such as primates, it leads to "amity for the social partner, hostility for the territorial neighbor." The territorial instinct is closely related to whatever makes animals establish pecking orders: the tangible sign of one's status within the orders is the size and value of the territory one is able to command. Individuals fight over status, groups over *lebensraum* and a bit more. These instincts, some ethologists have claimed, are behind patriotism and private property, and also, I would add, codes of honor, as among ancient Greeks, modern Sicilians, primitive hunters, teen-age gangs, soldiers, aristocrats, and athletes, especially football players.

The territorial basis of certain kinds of sports is closest to the surface in football, whose plays are all attempts to gain and defend property through aggression. Does this not make football *par excellence* the game of instinctual satisfactions, especially among Americans, who are notorious as violent patriots and instinctive defenders of private property? (At the same time, in football this drive is more elaborated than in other sports by whatever turns instinct into art; football is more richly patterned, more formal, more complex in the functions of its parts, which makes football *par excellence* the game of esthetic satisfactions.) Even the unusual amity, if that is the word, that exists among football players has been remarked upon, notably by Norman Mailer. And what is it that corresponds in football to the various feathers, furs, fins, gorgeous colors by means of which animals puff themselves into exaggerated gestures of masculine potency? The football player's equipment, of course. His cleats raise him an inch off the ground. Knee and thigh pads thrust the force lines of his legs forward. His pants are tight against his rump and the back of his thighs, portions of his body which the requirements of the game stuff with muscle. Even the tubby guard looks slim of waist by comparison with his shoulders, extended half a foot on each side by padding. Finally the helmet, which from the esthetic point of view most clearly expresses the genius of the sport. Not only does the helmet make the player inches taller and give his head a size proportionate to the rest of him; it makes him anonymous, inscrutable, more serviceable as a symbol. The football player in uniform strikes the eye in a succession of gestalt shifts: first a hooded phantom out of the paleolithic past of the species; then a premonition of a future of spacemen.

In sum, and I am almost serious about this, football players are to America what tragic actors were to ancient Athens and gladiators to Rome: models of perennially heroic, aggressive, violent humanity, but adapted to the social realities of the times and places that formed them.

Interpreting a Story

Whereas analysis breaks down a subject, interpretation synthesizes or puts together. To formulate a convincing interpretation, then, the writer must see the scattered parts of a subject as contributing on a deeper level to a unified whole. Seen in this light, all of literary criticism involves interpretation, a probing into the individual elements of a poem or story to see how they are related to one another and to the whole. What is the writer trying to tell us beyond the surface details? What larger statement is he or she making? How do the single details contribute to that statement? Take a relatively simple short story such as the following, for example, and then judge one critic's interpretation of what the surface details add up to. Do you think it would be possible to defend an entirely different (maybe even an opposite) interpretation of this story?

Birthday Party[2]

KATHERINE BRUSH

They were a couple in their late thirties, and they looked unmistakably married. They sat on the banquette opposite us in a little narrow restaurant, having dinner. The man had a round, self-satisfied face, with glasses on it; the woman was fadingly pretty, in a big hat. There was nothing conspicuous about them, nothing particularly noticeable, until the end of their meal, when it suddenly became obvious that this was an Occasion—in fact, the husband's birthday, and the wife had planned a little surprise for him.

It arrived, in the form of a small but glossy birthday cake, with one pink candle burning in the center. The headwaiter brought it in and placed it before the husband, and meanwhile the violin-and-piano orchestra played "Happy Birthday to You" and the wife beamed with shy pride over her little surprise, and such few people as there were in the restaurant tried to help out with a pattering of applause. It became clear at once that help was needed, because the husband was not pleased. Instead he was hotly embarrassed, and indignant at his wife for embarrassing him.

You looked at him and you saw this and you thought, "Oh, now, don't *be* like that!"

[2]Copyright © 1946 by Katherine Brush. Originally published in *The New Yorker*, 16 March 1946. Reprinted by permission of Thomas S. Brush.

But he was like that, and as soon as the little cake had been deposited on the table, and the orchestra had finished the birthday piece, and the general attention had shifted from the man and woman, I saw him say something to her under his breath—some punishing thing, quick and curt and unkind. I couldn't bear to look at the woman then, so I stared at my plate and waited for quite a long time. Not long enough, though. She was still crying when I finally glanced over there again. Crying quietly and heartbrokenly and hopelessly, all to herself, under the gay big brim of her best hat.

An Interpretation of "Birthday Party"[3]

B. BERNARD COHEN

In "Birthday Party," the private emotions of an inconspicuous couple burst momentarily into public view. From the point of view of the observer we learn the circumstances which ignite the emotional tension. But, more important, the narrator's observations prepare us for the conflicting responses of the husband and wife.

In fact, the narrator's first impressions of the couple are remarkably sound without [her] realizing their validity. The husband's face is classified as "self-satisfied" with the clear implication of an egotistical and possibly arrogant character behind it. The wife, on the other hand, is extremely feminine and both fragile and meek. She is "fadingly pretty," an indication that she is like a beautiful piece of fragile china somewhat marred by aging. In addition, when the cake is presented and the birthday song is played, the wife is pictured as beaming with "shy pride." These details clearly stress the subdued nature of her character. Obviously the occasion is a sentimental one for her, yet her emotions in responding to her prepared surprise are not excessive.

Her husband's reactions to her "little surprise" are excessive: he is "hotly embarrassed" and indignant at his wife for embarrassing him. In his reaction there is something cruel—something sadistic—for when he feels affronted by her public display of the occasion, he deliberately hurts her with a statement described as "some punishing thing, quick and curt and unkind." Thus the meek, shy fragility of the wife is crushed by the overwhelmingly powerful emotional response of the husband.

Only when she is terribly hurt by his actions and words, do her emotions pour forth in tears. Yet her tears are fully understandable: what she had intended as a sentimental tribute to her husband has turned into a bruising emotional nightmare. The reversal is painfully ironic and is graphically described in the last sentence: " ... crying quietly and heartbrokenly and hopelessly, all to herself, under the gay big brim of her best hat." She is not big but beaten; she is not gay; the word "best" may be applicable to her hat, but not to her life.

That "gay big brim" is obviously a cover-up, a symbol perhaps of a hopeless attempt by the wife to conceal the basic incompatibility of two people whose characters and emotional make-up are vastly different. The story as presented through the observer is thus a conflict between her fragile meekness and his hard-heartedness, her sentimentality and his cold fury, her feeble attempt to please him and his sadistic desire to crush her. Behind this incompatibility there must be a long untold series of similar expressions of arrogance by the husband, who apparently knows that there is one person whom his ego can dominate and destroy—his wife. Even during his birthday party he defeats her.

[3] From *Writing About Literature* by B. Bernard Cohen. Copyright © 1963 by Scott, Foresman and Company.

Interpreting a Poem

Since poetry is the most compressed and cryptic of all literary forms, it must be carefully interpreted in order to be experienced in its deepest and fullest sense. The e. e. cummings poem reprinted below, for example, may appear on the surface to be mere nonsense, yet as critic R. W. Stallman points out, it is actually "rich in meanings." At the literal level it is a miniature short story; at the thematic level it makes a profound observation about how we live and how we love.

anyone lived in a pretty how town[4]

E. E. CUMMINGS

anyone lived in a pretty how town
(with up so floating many bells down)
spring summer autumn winter
he sang his didn't he danced his did.   4

Women and men(both little and small)
cared for anyone not at all
they sowed their isn't they reaped their same
sun moon stars rain   8

children guessed(but only a few
and down they forgot as up they grew
autumn winter spring summer)
that noone loved him more by more   12

when by now and tree by leaf
she laughed his joy she cried his grief
bird by snow and stir by still
anyone's any was all to her   16

someones married their everyones
laughed their cryings and did their dance
(sleep wake hope and then)they
said their nevers they slept their dream   20

stars rain sun moon
(and only the snow can begin to explain
how children are apt to forget to remember
with up so floating many bells down)   24

one day anyone died i guess
(and noone stooped to kiss his face)
busy folk buried them side by side
little by little and was by was   28

all by all and deep by deep
and more by more they dream their sleep
noone and anyone earth by april
wish by spirit and if by yes.   32

Women and men(both dong and ding)   .
summer autumn winter spring
reaped their sowing and went their came
sun moon stars rain   36

An Interpretation of e. e. cummings' "anyone lived in a pretty how town"[5]

R. W. STALLMAN

This poem, apparently obscure nonsense, is rich in meanings; and though it may appear difficult at first glance, it is actually very simple to understand. Cummings uses language "reflexively," every word being counterpointed against another. At the literal level of the language there is a narrative plot, a miniature short story. What makes the poem seem so strange or seemingly incomprehensible is its uncommon arrangement of common words, its wrenched syntax, and its coining of new words from old ones by reconverting their dictionary meaning and usage.

Cummings's case study is a certain anonymous fellow, a citizen of How* Town. The town disowns him. Why? Well, for one thing their conventions are shocked by his unconventional way of life. He simply does not conform. Of course they don't care for Mr. Anyone because they "cared for anyone not at all" (line 6); they care only selfishly for themselves alone. These people "both little [*i.e.,* children] and small" (5) are small spiritually; which is why "*noone* loved him more by more" (12). And socially he didn't count because "anyone" married "noone." As for Miss "noone," she "loved him more by more." The non-lovers are the Someones who "married their everyones" (17). They play the social game, which is why they are Someones, but in conforming like "everyones" they have lost out in living, in loving life for its own sake. These Someones and Everyones do the conventional things in the conventional ways, and their life is a deadness and a monotony—"sleep wake hope and then"—because they live not at all spontaneously. And that is what sets them apart from Mr. Anyone. They "*did* their dance" (18), whereas he "*danced* his did" (4). They "*said* their nevers" (20), said their neverthelesses, talked about what they didn't do and made excuses; whereas he "*sang* his didn't" (4). In short, "anyone *lived.*" For him How Town was "pretty how town," beautiful; beautiful "with up so floating many bells down"—life in both its up's and down's, it was all singsong to him. Anyone and Noone lived happily forever in the point-present now—not in How Town so much as in Now Town. She loved him "by now and tree by leaf" (13), all of him by every part of

---

[5]R. W. Stallman and R. T. Watters; *The Creative Reader,* 2nd ed. Copyright © 1962, The Ronald Press Company, New York. Used by permission.

*The dictionary lists eight variant meanings for the word *how,* and all eight reverberate throughout the poem. Cummings uses the word as a noun. In the noun-sense the word means manner or method. But the meanings of *how* as adverb equally apply:—1. In what manner or way; 2. to what number or degree; 3. in what state or condition; 4. for what reason; 5. with what meaning, to what effect; 6. at what price, how dear; and 7. *how* meaning "what," as how about it? How Town is the conventional town of conformity to convention, where what counts is social manner or method, social degree, state or condition. In How Town what counts is how you do it, and the price is dear. In the sense of *how* as "why," the question asked by the person is what meaning has this way of life?

him; "anyone's any [thing] was all to her" (16). She "laughed his joy she cried his grief" (14); whereas the Someones married to their Everyones "laughed [at] their cryings" (18); their marriage is no marriage, merely an empty form. Even in death the lovers "dream their sleep" (30), belong to eternity and are reborn ("earth by april"); whereas the non-lovers even while living seem dead—"they slept their dream" (20). Caring "for anyone not at all/they sowed their isn't they reaped their same" (6–7). Their routine, clocked existence repeats itself through the cycles of time—"autumn winter spring summer"—with one season the same as another and later generations repeating the same old stenciled way of life (stanza 9). Time passes, mechanical time clocked by "sun moon stars rain" (lines 8 and 36), with the variant—"stars rain sun moon" (21)—to indicate the passing of time. The life of Someones and Everyones is never punctuated by memorable moments. No comma halts these "busy folk." And their children repeat the same blurred, indiscriminate, humdrum existence; they too "went their came" (35), wasting their coming by their busy going. Thus the bells, symbolizing Time, sound to them only as "dong and ding" (33), which is as dead men hear it, hollow; whereas to Mr. Anyone the bells sang, and he danced his life in lilt with them. Himself childlike in spontaneity, "children guessed" *how to live,* by his example—"but only a few/and down they forgot as up they grew" (9–10). Living is by loving, and loving is by losing oneself in another:

> little by little and was by was

> all by all and deep by deep
> and more by more they dream their sleep
> noone and anyone

But like Someones and Everyones, children become time-busy and "forget to remember" how to live, how to love. And that is how it goes in How to Live Town. The day Anyone died (stanza 7) "noone stooped to kiss his face."

Interpreting a Myth

Still another broad area open to interpretation is the myth—biblical, classical, anthropological. Every culture has its myths, narratives which were once widely believed to be true explanations of why the world is the way it is and how it came to be that way. Many myths can be regarded today as fragments of dead religions, primitive science, or personifications of philosophical or abstract ideas. The Adam and Eve story, for example, has often been cited as an illustration of woman as temptress—weak, wayward, vain, treacherous, responsible for the loss of Eden. Not at all, says novelist John Fowles, who interprets the Adam and Eve episode in a highly unconventional and provocative manner, making woman the evangelist of progress.

Adam and Eve[6]
JOHN FOWLES

The male and female are the two most powerful biological principles; and their smooth inter-action in society is one of the chief signs of social health. In this respect

[6]From *The Aristos,* rev. ed. (Boston: Little, Brown & Co., 1970). Signet ed., pp. 165–67. Copyright © 1964, 1968, 1970 by John Fowles.

our world shows, in spite of the now general political emancipation of women, considerable sickness; and most of this sickness arises from the selfish tyranny of the male.

I interpret the myth of the temptation of Adam in this way. Adam is hatred of change and futile nostalgia for the innocence of animals. The Serpent is imagination, the power to compare, self-consciousness. Eve is the assumption of human responsibility, of the need for progress and the need to control progress. The Garden of Eden is an impossible dream. The Fall is the essential *processus* of evolution. The God of Genesis is a personification of Adam's resentment.

Adam is stasis, or conservatism; Eve is kinesis, or progress. Adam societies are ones in which the man and the father, male gods, exact strict obedience to established institutions and norms of behaviour, as during a majority of the periods of history in our era. The Victorian is a typical such period. Eve societies are those in which the woman and the mother, female gods, encourage innovation and experiment, and fresh definitions, aims, modes of feeling. The Renaissance and our own are typical such ages.

There are of course Adam-women and Eve-men; singularly few, among the world's great progressive artists and thinkers, have not belonged to the latter category.

The petty, cruel and still prevalent antifeminism of Adam-dominated mankind (the very term "*man*kind" is revealing) is the long afterglow of the male's once important physical superiority and greater utility in the battle for survival. To the Adam in man, woman is no more than a rapable receptacle. This male association of femininity with rapability extends far beyond the female body. Progress and innovation are rapable; anything not based on brute power is rapable. All progressive philosophies are feminist. Adam is a princeling in a mountain castle; raids and fortifications, his own power and his own prestige, obsess him.

But if Eve had the intelligence to trick Adam out of his foolish dream in the Garden of Eden, she had also the kindness to stick by him afterwards; and it is this aspect of the female principle—tolerance, a general scepticism towards the Adam belief that might is right—that is the most valuable for society. Every mother is an evolutionary system in microcosm; she has no choice but to love what is—her child, ugly or arrogant, criminal or selfish, stupid or deformed. Motherhood is the most fundamental of all trainings in tolerance; and tolerance, as we have still to learn, is the most fundamental of all human wisdoms.

Satirical Interpretation

Interpreters often insist on making heavy, one-sided, and sometimes ridiculous interpretations of relatively lightweight, innocent subject matter. A spoof of such heavy-handed interpretations follows.

Interpretations on a Tuffet[7]
RUSSELL BAKER

Little Miss Muffet, as everyone knows, sat on a tuffet eating her curds and whey when along came a spider who sat down beside her and frightened Miss Muffet

[7]From *The New York Times*, 25 March 1969. © 1969/1975 by the New York Times Company. Reprinted by permission.

away. While everyone knows it, the significance of the event had never been analyzed until a conference of thinkers recently brought their special insights to bear upon it. Following are excerpts from the transcript of their discussion:

Sociologist: We are clearly dealing with a prototypical illustration of a highly tensile social structure's tendency to dis- or perhaps even de-structure itself under the pressures created when optimum minimums do not obtain among the disadvantaged. Miss Muffet is nutritionally underprivileged, as evidenced by the subminimal diet of curds and whey upon which she is forced to subsist, while the spider's cultural disadvantage is evidenced by such phenomena as legs exceeding standard norms, odd mating habits and so forth.

In this instance, spider expectations lead the culturally disadvantaged to assert demands to share the tuffet with the nutritionally underprivileged. Due to a communications failure, Miss Muffet assumes without evidence that the spider will not be satisfied to share her tuffet, but will also insist on eating her curds and whey. Thus, the failure to pre-establish selectively optimum norm structures leads to. . . .

Militarist: Second-strike capability, sir! That's what was lacking. If Miss Muffet had developed a second-strike capability instead of squandering her resources on curds and whey, no spider on earth would have dared launch a first strike capable of carrying him right to the heart of her tuffet. I am confident that Miss Muffet had adequate notice from experts that she could not afford both curds and whey and at the same time support an early-spider-warning system. Yet curds alone were not good enough for Miss Muffet. She had to have whey, too. Tuffet security must be the first responsibility of every diner. . . .

Book Reviewer: Written on several levels, this searing, sensitive exploration of the arachnid heart illuminates the agony and splendor of Jewish family life with a candor that is at once breath-taking in its simplicity and soul-shattering in its implied ambiguity. Some will doubtless be shocked to see such subjects as tuffets and whey discussed without flinching, but hereafter writers too timid to call a tuffet a tuffet will no longer. . . .

Editorial Writer: Why has the Government not seen fit to tell the public all it knows about the so-called curds-and-whey affair? It is not enough to suggest that this was merely a random incident involving a lonely spider and a young diner. In today's world, poised as it is on the knife edge of. . . .

Psychiatrist: Little Miss Muffet is, of course, neither little, nor a miss. These are obviously the self she has created in her own fantasies to escape the reality that she is a gross divorcee whose superego makes it impossible for her to sustain a normal relationship with any man, symbolized by the spider, who, of course, has no existence outside her fantasies. She may, in fact, be a man with deeply repressed Oedipal impulses who sees in the spider the father he would like to kill, and very well may some day unless he admits that what he believes to be a tuffet is, in fact, probably the dining room chandelier and that the whey he thinks he is eating is, in fact, probably. . . .

Flower Child: This beautiful kid is on a bad trip. Like. . . .

Student Demonstrator: Little Miss Muffet, tuffets, curds, whey and spiders are what's wrong with education today. They're all irrelevant. Tuffets are irrelevant. Curds are irrelevant. Whey is irrelevant. Meaningful experience! How can you have relevance without meaningful experience? And how can there ever be meaningful experience without understanding? With understanding and meaningfulness and relevance, there can be love and good and deep seriousness, and education today will be freed of slavery and Little Miss Muffet, and life will become meaningful. . . .

Child: This is about a little girl who gets scared by a spider.

(The child was sent home when the conference broke for lunch. It was agreed that the child was too immature to add anything to the sum of human understanding and should not come back until he had grown up.)

ASSIGNMENTS

Class Discussion and Paragraph Suggestions

(See Chapter 27 for methods of composing unified, adequately developed paragraphs.)

1. Like "Birthday Party," the following story involves two people, a man and a woman, and can be interpreted in more than one way. Indeed, because of its richer texture, this story can be interpreted on more than one level.

The Waltz[8]

DOROTHY PARKER

Why, thank you so much. I'd adore to.

I don't want to dance with him. I don't want to dance with anybody. And even if I did, it wouldn't be him. He'd be well down among the last ten. I've seen the way he dances; it looks like something you do on Saint Walpurgis Night. Just think, not a quarter of an hour ago, here I was sitting, feeling so sorry for the poor girl he was dancing with. And now *I'm* going to be the poor girl. Well, well. Isn't it a small world?

And a peach of a world, too. A true little corker. Its events are so fascinatingly unpredictable, are not they? Here I was, minding my own business, not doing a stitch of harm to any living soul. And then he comes into my life, all smiles and city manners, to sue me for the favor of one memorable mazurka. Why, he scarcely knows my name, let alone what it stands for. It stands for Despair, Bewilderment, Futility, Degradation, and Premeditated Murder, but little does he wot. I don't wot his name, either; I haven't any idea what it is. Jukes, would be my guess from the look in his eyes. How do you do, Mr. Jukes? And how is that dear little brother of yours, with the two heads?

Ah, now why did he have to come around me, with his low requests? Why can't he let me lead my own life? I ask so little—just to be left alone in my quiet corner of the table, to do my evening brooding over all my sorrows. And he must come, with his bows and his scrapes and his may-I-have-this-ones. And I had to go and tell him that I'd adore to dance with him. I cannot understand why I wasn't struck right down dead. Yes, and being struck dead would look like a day in the country, compared to struggling out a dance with this boy. But what could I do? Everyone else at the table had got up to dance, except him and me. There was I, trapped. Trapped like a trap in a trap.

What can you say, when a man asks you to dance with him? I most certainly will *not* dance with you, I'll see you in hell first. Why, thank you, I'd like to awfully, but I'm having labor pains. Oh, yes, *do* let's dance together—it's so nice to meet a man who isn't a scaredy-cat about catching my beri-beri. No. There was nothing for me to do, but say I'd adore to. Well, we might as well get it over with. All right, Cannonball, let's run out on the field. You won the toss; you can lead.

Why, I think it's more of a waltz, really. Isn't it? We might just listen to the music a second. Shall we? Oh, yes, it's a waltz. Mind? Why, I'm simply thrilled. I'd love to waltz with you.

I'd love to waltz with you. I'd love to waltz with you. I'd love to have my tonsils out, I'd love to be in a midnight fire at sea. Well, it's too late now. We're getting under way. *Oh.* Oh, dear. Oh, dear, dear, dear. Oh, this is even worse than I thought it would be. I suppose that's the one dependable law of life—everything is always worse than you thought it was going to be. Oh, if I had any real grasp of what this dance would be like, I'd have held out for sitting it out. Well, it will probably amount to the same thing in the end. We'll be sitting it out on the floor in a minute, if he keeps this up.

I'm so glad I brought it to his attention that this is a waltz they're playing. Heaven knows what might have happened, if he had thought it was something fast; we'd have blown the sides right out of the building. Why does he always want to be somewhere that he isn't? Why can't we stay in one place just long enough to get acclimated? It's this constant rush, rush, rush, that's the curse of American life. That's the reason that we're all of us so—*Ow!* For God's sake, don't *kick*, you idiot; this is only second down. Oh, my shin. My poor, poor shin, that I've had ever since I was a little girl!

Oh, no, no, no. Goodness, no. It didn't hurt the least little bit. And anyway it was my fault. Really it was. Truly. Well, you're just being sweet, to say that. It really was all my fault.

I wonder what I'd better do—kill him this instant, with my naked hands, or wait and let him drop in his traces. Maybe it's best not to make a scene. I guess I'll just lie low, and watch the pace get him. He can't keep this up indefinitely—he's only flesh and blood. Die he must, and die he shall, for what he did to me. I don't want to be of the over-sensitive type, but you can't tell me that kick was unpremeditated. Freud says there are no accidents. I've led no cloistered life, I've known dancing partners who have spoiled my slippers and torn my dress; but when it comes to kicking, I am Outraged Womanhood. When you kick me in the shin, *smile.*

Maybe he didn't do it maliciously. Maybe it's just his way of showing his high spirits. I suppose I ought to be glad that one of us is having such a good time. I suppose I ought to think myself lucky if he brings me back alive. Maybe it's captious to demand of a practically strange man that he leave your shins as he found them. After all, the poor boy's doing the best he can. Probably he grew up in the hill country, and never had no larnin'. I bet they had to throw him on his back to get shoes on him.

Yes, it's lovely, isn't it? It's simply lovely. It's the loveliest waltz. Isn't it? Oh, I think it's lovely, too.

Why, I'm getting positively drawn to the Triple Threat here. He's my hero. He has the heart of a lion, and the sinews of a buffalo. Look at him—never a thought of the consequences, never afraid of his face, hurling himself into every scrimmage, eyes shining, cheeks ablaze. And shall it be said that I hung back? No, a thousand times no. What's it to me if I have to spend the next couple of years in a plaster cast? Come on, Butch, right through them! Who wants to live forever?

Oh. Oh, dear. Oh, he's all right, thank goodness. For a while I thought they'd have to carry him off the field. Ah, I couldn't bear to have anything happen to him. I love him. I love him better than anybody in the world. Look at the spirit he gets into a dreary, commonplace waltz; how effete the other dancers seem, beside him. He is youth and vigor and courage, he is strength and gaiety and—*Ow!* Get off my instep, you hulking peasant! What do you think I am, anyway—a gangplank? *Ow!*

No, of course it didn't hurt. Why, it didn't a bit. Honestly. And it was all my fault. You see, that little step of yours—well, it's perfectly lovely, but it's just a tiny bit tricky to follow at first. Oh, did you work it up yourself? You really did? Well, aren't you amazing! Oh, now I think I've got it. Oh, I think it's lovely. I was watching you do it when you were dancing before. It's awfully effective when you look at it.

It's awfully effective when you look at it. I bet I'm awfully effective when you look at me. My hair is hanging along my cheeks, my skirt is swaddling about me, I can feel the cold damp of my brow. I must look like something out of the "Fall of the House of Usher." This sort of thing takes a fearful toll of a woman my age. And he worked up his little step himself, he with his degenerate cunning. And it was just a tiny bit tricky at first, but now I think I've got it. Two stumbles, slip, and a twenty-yard dash; yes. I've got it. I've got several other things, too, including a split shin and a bitter heart. I hate this creature I'm chained to. I hated him the moment I saw his leering, bestial face. And here I've been locked in his noxious embrace for the thirty-five years this waltz has lasted. Is that orchestra never going to stop playing? Or must this obscene travesty of a dance go on until hell burns out?

Oh, they're going to play another encore. Oh, goody. Oh, that's lovely. Tired? I should say I'm not tired. I'd like to go on like this forever.

I should say I'm not tired. I'm dead, that's all I am. Dead, and in what a cause! And the music is never going to stop playing, and we're going on like this, Double-Time Charlie and I, throughout eternity. I suppose I won't care any more, after the first hundred thousand years. I suppose nothing will matter then, not heat nor pain nor broken heart nor cruel, aching weariness. Well. It can't come too soon for me.

I wonder why I didn't tell him I was tired. I wonder why I didn't suggest going back to the table. I could have said let's just listen to the music. Yes, and if he would, that would be the first bit of attention he has given it all evening. George Jean Nathan said that the lovely rhythms of the waltz should be listened to in stillness and not be accompanied by strange gyrations of the human body. I think that's what he said. I think it was George Jean Nathan. Anyhow, whatever he said and whoever he was and whatever he's doing now, he's better off than I am. That's safe. Anybody who isn't waltzing with this Mrs. O'Leary's cow I've got here is having a good time.

Still if we were back at the table, I'd probably have to talk to him. Look at him—what could you say to a thing like that! Did you go to the circus this year, what's your favorite kind of ice cream, how do you spell cat? I guess I'm as well off here. As well off as if I were in a cement mixer in full action.

I'm past all feeling now. The only way I can tell when he steps on me is that I can hear the splintering of bones. And all the events of my life are passing before my eyes. There was the time I was in a hurricane in the West Indies, there was the day I got my head cut open in the taxi smash, there was the night the drunken lady threw a bronze ash-tray at her own true love and got me instead, there was that summer that the sailboat kept capsizing. Ah, what an easy, peaceful time was mine, until I fell in with Swifty, here. I didn't know what trouble was, before I got drawn into this *danse macabre*. I think my mind is beginning to wander. It almost seems to me as if the orchestra were stopping. It couldn't be, of course; it could never, never be. And yet in my ears there is a silence like the sound of angel voices. . . .

Oh, they've stopped, the mean things. They're not going to play any more. Oh, darn. Oh, do you think they would? Do you really think so, if you gave them twenty dollars? Oh, that would be lovely. And look, do tell them to play this same thing. I'd simply adore to go on waltzing.

a. Who is telling this story?
b. What is the setting?
c. Comment on the significance of the following lines from the story:

. . . a peach of a world, too.
Why, he scarcely knows my name, let alone what it stands for.
Why can't he let me lead my own life?
. . . I'm having labor pains.
. . . let's run out on the field.
Why can't we stay in one place just long enough to get acclimated?
He can't keep this up indefinitely—he's only flesh and blood.
I've led no cloistered life.
I've been locked in his noxious embrace for the thirty-five years this waltz
    has lasted.
. . . I'm not tired. I'm dead, that's all I am.
. . . in my ears there is a silence like the sound of angel voices.
I'd simply adore to go on waltzing.

    d. In addition to a dance, what does the waltz represent in this story?

2. Write a one-paragraph (150–250 words) interpretation of "The Waltz."

3. Read the following two poems carefully at least three times; read them aloud; note their images, line by line.

Winter Trees[9]

SYLVIA PLATH

The wet dawn inks are doing their blue dissolve.
On their blotter of fog the trees
Seem a botanical drawing—
Memories growing, ring on ring,
A series of weddings.

Knowing neither abortions nor bitchery,
Truer than women,
They seed so effortlessly!
Tasting the winds, that are footless,
Waist-deep in history—

Full of wings, otherworldliness.
In this, they are Ledas.
O mother of leaves and sweetness
Who are these pietas?
The shadows of ringdoves chanting, but easing nothing.

Your Departure Versus the Hindenburg[10]

RICHARD BRAUTIGAN

Everytime we say good-bye
I see it as an extension of
the Hindenburg:

[9]"Winter Trees" from *Winter Trees* by Sylvia Plath. Copyright © 1963 by Ted Hughes. Reprinted by permission of Harper & Row, Publishers, Inc. Published by Faber & Faber, London. Copyright © 1971 by Ted Hughes.

[10]"Your Departure Versus the Hindenburg" excerpted from *The Pill Versus the Springhill Mine Disaster* by Richard Brautigan. Reprinted by permission of Delacorte Press/Seymour Lawrence.

> that great 1937 airship exploding
> in medieval flames like a burning castle
>   above New Jersey.
> When you leave the house, the
> shadow of the Hindenburg enters
>   to take your place.

4. Write a two-paragraph interpretation (300–500 words) of one of the above poems, citing words, images, and lines to support your view (as Stallman does in his interpretation of the cummings poem).

5. Evaluate Cohen's interpretation of "Birthday Party." Can you interpret the story in a way that makes the man a more sympathetic character? Discuss.

6. Sigmund Freud said that all behavior is a gesture—an "acting-out" of deep-seated feelings and needs. Thus what we see on the surface is often (if not always) an expression of underlying "deeper meanings"; for example, football may be an expression of aggression. Speculate on what larger human purposes are being "acted out"—and satisfied—in five of the following activities:

stealing	baseball	wrestling
suicide	knitting	ventriloquism
alcoholism	dancing	Bingo
stuttering	sailing	bullfighting
lying	automobile racing	fishing
swearing	skiing	playing pool
dreaming	gambling	mountain climbing
smoking	hunting	singing
promiscuity	boxing	working
ice skating	hiking	a crossword puzzle
playing a musical instrument	kite flying	

7. Write a paragraph (150–250 words) in which you interpret one of the above activities. Open with a general topic sentence; develop it into a coordinate sequence paragraph, a subordinate sequence, or a mixed construction (see examples in Chapter 27). Be prepared to explain your choice.

Essay Suggestions

1. Expand the paragraph you wrote in exercise 7 above into a full-length essay (500–1,000 words) interpreting "the deeper meaning" of a particular activity.

2. Expand your interpretation of "The Waltz" into an essay (500–750 words).

3. Write an interpretation (500–1,000 words) of a poem of your own choosing.

4. Write an essay (500–750 words) defending an interpretation of "Birthday Party" in which the man rather than the woman is viewed sympathetically, citing supporting evidence from the story.

5. Write your own interpretation (500–1,000 words) of a well-known myth (for example, the story of the Minotaur, the Tower of Babel, the Golden Fleece, Noah's Ark).

6. Write a satirical interpretation (500–750 words), in the manner of Russell Baker's piece, of a popular nursery rhyme (for example, "Mary, Mary, Quite Contrary," "Little Bo Peep," "Jack and Jill," or "Old King Cole").

13 What Are the Facts About X?

An essay presenting "the facts about X" is basically informative (as compared to descriptive, narrative, argumentative). Neither systematic nor complete in the formal sense, it is not analysis strictly speaking; yet in a looser sense it serves the same purpose.

Viewed journalistically, the factual piece may take many forms: the news story, which tells readers what is going on in the world; the interview, which offers information (or, at its worst, the latest gossip) about a person in the news; the feature story, which is like the regular news story in that it presents a factual word picture of some current happening, but goes beyond the facts to sketch in elements of human interest or social commentary. Let us examine some of these journalistic forms, for they provide the student writer with useful and challenging exercises in craft.

The Feature Story

The Photographic Feature

The simplest type of feature story merely points out an interesting factual item and accompanies it with a photograph. Thus the picture on the following page, with title and one-sentence caption, might be viewed as an essentially pictorial feature story.

HELPING HANDS (MERRITT ISLAND, FLA., SEPT. 26)—Gale Fritch, right, and Ricki Eskenez, both of Orlando, Fla., spotted a wounded pelican on a busy causeway in Merritt Island, Fla., and caught the bird with a picnic cloth to keep it from being hit by a passing car. (AP Wirephoto 1975)[1]

The Prose Feature

A longer feature story is designed to present its facts in such a way as to elicit an emotional response: to amuse us, amaze us, or warm our hearts. A group of orphans are treated to a free day at the circus; a young man delivers his valentine by parachuting onto his sweetheart's front lawn; a waitress in the local diner wins $50,000 in a lottery. The following feature story is typical in that it inspires as well as informs: not only are these four old women still active (as indicated by facts that help to dispel the misconception that old people are useless); they are also shown to be alert, cheerful, indomitable. Note how careful the reporter has been to provide the kinds of concrete facts that make these women come alive in a special and memorable way.

Old Hands Are Showing They're Young at Heart[2]

ALDEN WHITMAN

What age has not withered, nor custom staled are feelings of youthful zest that imbue four remarkable New York women active in volunteer work. Apart from their yeastiness, what distinguishes these women are their extraordinary years. The youngest is 87, the eldest 92. And they are all going strong. Without exception, these

---

[1]From Wide World Photos, 1975.
[2]From *The New York Times*, 20 June 1975, p. 19. © 1969/1975 by The New York Times Company. Reprinted by permission.

women belie their chronological ages. They are physically spry; they are up to the minute on current events; they can't wait for morning to get up and be busy; and they have a variety of social and cultural interests. The eldest is Irma Davis, who tells questioners that "I'm 92 and a half." Next is Marjorie Dana Barlow, who has just marked her 91st birthday. Elizabeth Dodge Clarke will celebrate her 91st in August. The "baby" is Hortense Mayer Hirsch, a mere 87.

For these women, doing volunteer work for good causes was part of their upbringing. Children in families of some means, they were taught the importance of sharing, of giving part of their time and energy to community projects.

Moreover, they grew up in an era when American women, products of the new higher educational institutions after the Civil War, were fired with a public mission.

Desire to Serve

In the last years of the 19th century and the first years of this, Jane Addams, Lillian Wald, Vida Scudder, Florence Kelley, Ellen Starr, Mary Rozet Smith and a score of other women stamped their ideals of community service on secure, middle-class American families. It was proper for daughters of these families to engage in some form of social work.

These women were liberated long before the modern feminist movement took hold. "Oh, I've been liberated for years," Mrs. Clarke said with a laugh while sitting at a garden picnic for about 80 Japanese women and their children on the grounds of her Riverdale home.

"I was brought up to believe that women should share part of their lives with the community," she added.

Her sharing these days involves her directly in the International Group, a loosely organized committee of Riverdale women, who have undertaken to act as friends to the neighborhood's Japanese women, wives of businessmen posted to New York for three to five years. The committee meets with the Japanese periodically at the Riverdale Presbyterian Church, of which Mrs. Clarke has been a member for 75 years.

"We try to help the women with their English, teach them to shop in supermarkets and to take advantage of the city's cultural life," Mrs. Clarke said, adding:

"They are all young women, and being with them keeps me young."

Mrs. Clarke, whose income derives from the Phelps Dodge mining interests, has been a widow for 15 years. Her first husband, George Huntington, taught at Roberts College in Istanbul. His students and their families are part of "my millions of nieces and nephews that I keep in touch with," Mrs. Clarke said. Dumont Clarke, her second husband, worked with farmers in North Carolina, and his family has joined the ranks of Mrs. Clarke's nieces and nephews.

"Oh, everything's so exciting, just keeping up with my 'family' and with what's going on in the news," Mrs. Clarke said.

Aid Spans 55 Years

Another who was taught as a child that "it's a duty and a pleasure to do volunteer work" is Mrs. Davis, who was born Irma Lewyn. Fifty-five years ago she was helping the Jewish Board of Guardians and the American Red Cross. Then the wife of Allen Bernstein, she was the mother of three children, one of them the late Aline Saarinen, the art critic, and another, Peter Bernstein, the economist. After her husband's death, she married G. Richard Davis, who died about 15 years ago.

"I had to find something to do that didn't concern myself," Mrs. Davis recalled, "so

I thought I'd teach painting." And for the last 11 years she's been an instructor at the 92d Street Y.W.–Y.M.H.A. with classes of mostly senior citizens.

"It's difficult teaching these older people—they're so set in their ideas," she remarked. "Me, I'm quite flexible. I've just taken up watercolors and collages, and I enjoy creating things."

Next fall Mrs. Davis plans to teach for two hours twice a week at the Lenox Hill Neighborhood House, not far from her home on the Upper East Side.

"I have an inordinate love of life," she remarked in accounting for her youthful outlook. "I just love to feel the blood go through my veins because there's so much that interests me—Zen, for one thing, going to the museums for another, traveling, as I'm going to do, to a Bach festival in Carmel, Calif., this summer.

"And I read all the time. I'm just now re-reading Henry James and a biography of Lizst. My legs are not so good, but my head's all right."

In addition, Mrs. Davis spends part of the day in her studio, a room in her apartment given over to an easel, canvases and oils and brushes. Her sole concession to years is that she sits at the easel.

Still Works at Hospital

To thousands of patients who have passed through Bellevue Hospital in the last 42 years Mrs. Barlow is synonymous with books. "Our longest and most faithful volunteer," a hospital spokesman said of her.

Three times a week until recently (it's twice now), Mrs. Barlow wheels books and magazines from the patient library to bedsides. Some of the books are donations from publishers, others are purchased by the hospital's auxiliary.

The daughter of Dr. Charles L. Dana, a Bellevue neurosurgeon, and the wife of William Tait Barlow, a retired shipping line executive, Mrs. Barlow has always lived among books and an aura of personal freedom.

Barred from the Grolier Club, which does not accept women members, Mrs. Barlow became a founder of the Hrosewitha Club, a women's bibliophilic group. Recently, she completed work on a long account of women printers in America, and discovered that there were thousands of them, including one who printed the Declaration of Independence and another who printed the Bill of Rights.

In her younger years a boxing fan ("I used to go to all the fights in Madison Square Garden, Yankee Stadium and Ebbets Field") and a tennis player and horsewoman, Mrs. Barlow is still vigorous enough to ride the bus to Bellevue from her Upper East Side apartment house.

"What keeps me young? Doing things that interest me—and everything I touch interests me," she commented. "I'm fond, of course, of the patients at Bellevue. I think I like those in the prison wards the best. You've got to be smart to be a crook, yes?"

For Mrs. Hirsch, the wife of a lawyer who died in 1938, volunteer work "has been my salvation." Chiefly she is associated with Mount Sinai Hospital, where she sits on the Auxiliary Board.

Mrs. Hirsch, who describes herself as "very liberal and very liberated," never seems to lack for good works. In addition to Mount Sinai, she helps the Play Schools Association, the United Hospital Fund and the Federation of Jewish Philanthropies.

Outlines Philosophy

"I've always held the firm conviction that if one lives in a community, one should contribute and work for the welfare of that community," she said in explaining the source of her energy and how it is that "women of 63 seem like debutantes to me."

"Being with young people—even younger than these 'debutantes'—keeps me youthful," Mrs. Hirsch said. "I'm not interested in medieval people."

In spare moments from volunteer work, Mrs. Hirsch attends concerts, the ballet and the theater.

"I attend lots of theater benefits—most of the plays are bum—but I can't wait to see 'Chorus Line,'" she said. "I hear it's a very youthful musical—and that's my style."

Reportage

Longer than the feature story and generally of more lasting significance is the report by a seasoned, socially aware observer whose sense of an event is so keen that his or her report amounts to a commentary. Two examples of such *reportage* follow. One was written in Toronto in 1923 by Ernest Hemingway and represents the old school of dynamic, on-the-spot reporting, told largely in narrative rather than expository style. Once Hemingway— "the reporter"—has given us his almost painfully factual, word-by-word conversations with various pawnbrokers, we no longer need ask "What is the market price of valor?" We *know*, for the reporter (present in the story simply as an interrogator) has *shown* us.

The second example of reportage is by Joan Didion, who uses to its best effect the "new nonfiction" technique (see p. 190) of piling fact upon fact, detail upon detail, and of combining these facts and details in such a way as to make a statement or social comment—in this case for the purpose of leading the reader to recognize the devastating absurdity of getting married in the bizarre, commercial atmosphere of Las Vegas.

War Medals for Sale[3]

ERNEST HEMINGWAY

What is the market price of valor? In a medal and coin shop on Adelaide street the clerk said: "No, we don't buy them. There isn't any demand."

"Do many men come in to sell medals?" I asked.

"Oh, yes. They come in every day. But we don't buy medals from this war."

"What do they bring in?"

"Victory medals mostly, 1914 stars, a good many M.M.'s, and once in a while a D.C.M., or an M.C. We tell them to go over to the pawnshops where they can get their medal back if they get any money for it."

So the reporter went up to Queen street and walked west past the glittering windows of cheap rings, junk shops, two-bit barber shops, second-hand clothing stores, and street hawkers, in search of the valor mart.

Inside the pawnshop it was the same story.

"No, we don't buy them," a young man with shiny hair said from behind a counter of unredeemed pledges. "There is no market for them at all. Oh, yes. They come in here with all sorts. Yes, M.C.'s. And I had a man in here the other day with a D.S.O. I send them over to the second-hand stores on York street. They buy anything."

---

[3]"War Medals for Sale" is reprinted by permission of Charles Scribner's Sons from: *By-Line: Ernest Hemingway.* Copyright © 1967 by Mary Hemingway.

"What would you give me for an M.C.?" asked the reporter.

"I'm sorry, Mac. We can't handle it."

Out on to Queen street went the reporter, and into the first second-hand shop he encountered. On the window was a sign, "We Buy and Sell Everything."

The opened door jangled a bell. A woman came in from the back of the shop. Around the counter were piled broken door bells, alarm clocks, rusty carpenters' tools, old iron keys, kewpies, crap shooters' dice, a broken guitar and other things.

"What do you want?" said the woman.

"Got any medals to sell?" the reporter asked.

"No. We don't keep them things. What do you want to do? Sell me things?"

"Sure," said the reporter. "What'll you give me for an M.C.?"

"What's that?" asked the woman, suspiciously, tucking her hands under her apron.

"It's a medal," said the reporter. "It's a silver cross."

"Real silver?" asked the woman.

"I guess so," the reporter said.

"Don't you know?" the woman said. "Ain't you got it with you?"

"No," answered the reporter.

"Well, you bring it in. If it's real silver maybe I'll make you a nice offer on it." The woman smiled. "Say," she said, "it ain't one of them war medals, is it?"

"Sort of," said the reporter.

"Don't you bother with it, then. Them things are no good!"

In succession the reporter visited five more second-hand stores. None of them handled medals. No demand.

In one store the sign outside said, "We Buy and Sell Everything of Value. Highest Prices Paid."

"What you want to sell?" snapped the bearded man back of the counter.

"Would you buy any war medals?" the reporter asked.

"Listen, maybe those medals were all right in the war. I ain't saying they weren't, you understand? But with me business is business. Why should I buy something I can't sell?"

The merchant was being very gentle and explanatory.

"What will you give me for that watch?" asked the reporter.

The merchant examined it carefully, opened the case and looked in the works. Turned it over in his hand and listened to it.

"It's got a good tick," suggested the reporter.

"That watch now," said the heavily bearded merchant judicially, laying it down on the counter. "That watch now, is worth maybe sixty cents."

The reporter went on down York street. There was a second-hand shop every door or so now. The reporter got, in succession, a price on his coat, another offer of seventy cents on his watch, and a handsome offer of forty cents for his cigaret case. But no one wanted to buy or sell medals.

"Every day they come in to sell those medals. You're the first man ever ask me about buying them for years," a junk dealer said.

Finally, in a dingy shop, the searcher found some medals for sale. The woman in charge brought them out from the cash till.

They were a 1914–15 star, a general service medal and a victory medal. All three were fresh and bright in the boxes they had arrived in. All bore the same name and number. They had belonged to a gunner in a Canadian battery.

The reporter examined them.

"How much are they?" he asked.

"I only sell the whole lot," said the woman, defensively.

"What do you want for the lot?"

"Three dollars."

The reporter continued to examine the medals. They represented the honor and recognition his King had bestowed on a certain Canadian. The name of the Canadian was on the rim of each medal.

"Don't worry about those names, Mister," the woman urged. "You could easy take off the names. Those would make you good medals."

"I'm not sure these are what I'm looking for," the reporter said.

"You won't make no mistake if you buy those medals, Mister," urged the woman, fingering them. "You couldn't want no better medals than them."

"No, I don't think they're what I want," the reporter demurred.

"Well, you make me an offer on them."

"No."

"Just make me an offer. Make me any offer you feel like."

"Not to-day."

"Make me any kind of an offer. Those are good medals, Mister. Look at them. Will you give me a dollar for all the lot?"

Outside the shop the reporter looked in the window. You could evidently sell a broken alarm-clock. But you couldn't sell an M.C.

You could dispose of a second-hand mouth-organ. But there was no market for a D.C.M.

You could sell your old military puttees. But you couldn't find a buyer for a 1914 star.

So the market price of valor remained undetermined.

Marrying Absurd[4]
JOAN DIDION

To be married in Las Vegas, Clark County, Nevada, a bride must swear that she is eighteen or has parental permission and a bridegroom that he is twenty-one or has parental permission. Someone must put up five dollars for the license. (On Sundays and holidays, fifteen dollars. The Clark County Courthouse issues marriage licenses at any time of the day or night except between noon and one in the afternoon, between eight and nine in the evening, and between four and five in the morning.) Nothing else is required. The State of Nevada, alone among these United States, demands neither a premarital blood test nor a waiting period before or after the issuance of a marriage license. Driving in across the Mojave from Los Angeles, one sees the signs way out on the desert, looming up from that moonscape of rattlesnakes and mesquite, even before the Las Vegas lights appear like a mirage on the horizon: "GETTING MARRIED? Free License Information First Strip Exit." Perhaps the Las Vegas wedding industry achieved its peak operational efficiency between 9:00 P.M. and midnight of August 26, 1965, an otherwise unremarkable Thursday which happened to be, by Presidential order, the last day on which anyone could improve his draft status merely by getting married. One hundred and seventy-one couples were pronounced man and wife in the name of Clark County and the State of Nevada that night, sixty-seven of them by a single justice of the peace, Mr. James A. Brennan. Mr. Brennan did one wedding at the Dunes and the other sixty-six in his office, and charged each couple eight dollars. One bride lent her veil to six others. "I got it down from five to three minutes," Mr. Brennan said later of his feat. "I could've married them *en masse,* but they're people, not cattle. People expect more when they get married."

What people who get married in Las Vegas actually do expect—what, in the largest sense, their "expectations" are—strikes one as a curious and self-contradictory business. Las Vegas is the most extreme and allegorical of American settlements, bizarre and beautiful in its venality and in its devotion to immediate gratification, a place the tone of which is set by mobsters and call girls and ladies' room attendants with amyl nitrite poppers in their uniform pockets. Almost everyone notes that there is no "time" in Las Vegas, no night and no day and no past and no future (no Las Vegas casino, however, has taken the obliteration of the ordinary time sense quite so far as Harold's Club in Reno, which for a while issued, at odd intervals in the day and night, mimeographed "bulletins" carrying news from the world outside); neither is there any logical sense of where one is. One is standing on a highway in the middle of a vast hostile desert looking at an eighty-foot sign which blinks "STARDUST" or "CAESAR'S PALACE." Yes, but what does that explain? This geographical implausibility reinforces the sense that what happens there has no connection with "real" life; Nevada cities like Reno and Carson are ranch towns, Western towns, places behind which there is some historical imperative. But Las Vegas seems to exist only in the eye of the beholder. All of which makes it an extraordinarily stimulating and interesting place, but an odd one in which to want to wear a candlelight satin Priscilla of Boston wedding dress with Chantilly lace insets, tapered sleeves and a detachable modified train.

And yet the Las Vegas wedding business seems to appeal to precisely that impulse. "Sincere and Dignified Since 1954," one wedding chapel advertises. There are nineteen such wedding chapels in Las Vegas, intensely competitive, each offering better, faster, and, by implication, more sincere services than the next: Our Photos Best Anywhere, Your Wedding on a Phonograph Record, Candelight with Your Ceremony, Honeymoon Accommodations, Free Transportation from Your Motel to Courthouse to Chapel and Return to Motel, Religious or Civil Ceremonies, Dressing Rooms, Flowers, Rings, Announcements, Witnesses Available, and Ample Parking. All of these services, like most others in Las Vegas (sauna baths, payroll-check cashing, chinchilla coats for sale or rent) are offered twenty-four hours a day, seven days a week, presumably on the premise that marriage, like craps, is a game to be played when the table seems hot.

But what strikes one most about the Strip chapels, with their wishing wells and stained-glass paper windows and their artificial bouvardia, is that so much of their business is by no means a matter of simple convenience, of late-night liaisons between show girls and baby Crosbys. Of course there is some of that. (One night about eleven o'clock in Las Vegas I watched a bride in an orange minidress and masses of flamecolored hair stumble from a Strip chapel on the arm of her bridegroom, who looked the part of the expendable nephew in movies like *Miami Syndicate.* "I gotta get the kids," the bride whimpered. "I gotta pick up the sitter, I gotta get to the midnight show." "What you gotta get," the bridegroom said, opening the door of a Cadillac Coupe de Ville and watching her crumple on the seat, "is sober.") But Las Vegas seems to offer something other than "convenience"; it is merchandising "niceness," the facsimile of proper ritual, to children who do not know how else to find it, how to make the arrangements, how to do it "right." All day and evening long on the Strip, one sees actual wedding parties, waiting under the harsh lights at a crosswalk, standing uneasily in the parking lot of the Frontier while the photographer hired by The Little Church of the West ("Wedding Place of the Stars") certifies the occasion, takes the picture: the bride in a veil and white satin pumps, the bridegroom usually in a white dinner jacket, and even an attendant or two, a sister or a best friend in hot-pink *peau de soie,* a flirtation veil, a carnation nosegay. "When I Fall in Love It Will Be Forever," the organist plays, and then a few bars of Lohengrin. The mother cries; the stepfather, awkward in his role, invites the chapel hostess to join them for a drink at the Sands. The hostess declines with a professional smile; she has already transferred her interest to the group waiting outside. One bride out, another in, and again the sign goes up on the chapel door: "One moment please—Wedding."

I sat next to one such wedding party in a Strip restaurant the last time I was in Las Vegas. The marriage had just taken place; the bride still wore her dress, the mother her corsage. A bored waiter poured out a few swallows of pink champagne ("on the house") for everyone but the bride, who was too young to be served. "You'll need something with more kick than that," the bride's father said with heavy jocularity to his new son-in-law; the ritual jokes about the wedding night had a certain Panglossian character, since the bride was clearly several months pregnant. Another round of pink champagne, this time not on the house, and the bride began to cry. "It was just as nice," she sobbed, "as I hoped and dreamed it would be."

The Brochure

The fact piece need not serve any larger purpose beyond itself. Facts for their own sake are justification enough for an essay, provided that the facts are interesting and that they satisfy what Aristotle called "natural curiosity."

Certainly the following piece fulfills these conditions. *Everyone* is interested in the weather—especially its more violent moods. Here, then, are the facts about hurricanes, as set down in a brochure—a small, factual pamphlet designed to provide basic information on a given subject. This brochure was issued by the world's most prolific publisher—the United States government.

Hurricanes[5]

Hurricanes are tropical cyclones in which winds reach speeds of 74 miles per hour or more, and blow in a large spiral around a relatively calm center—the eye of the hurricane. Every year, these violent storms bring destruction to coastlines and islands in their erratic path. Tropical cyclones of the same type are called typhoons in the North Pacific, baguios in the Philippines, and cyclones in the Indian Ocean.

Stated very simply, hurricanes are giant whirlwinds in which air moves in a large, tightening spiral around a a center of extreme low pressure, reaching maximum velocity in a circular band extending outward 20 or 30 miles from the rim of the eye. This circulation is counterclockwise in the Northern Hemisphere, and clockwise in the Southern Hemisphere. Near the eye, hurricane winds may gust to more than 200 miles per hour, and the entire storm dominates the ocean surface and lower atmosphere over tens of thousands of square miles.

[5]From *Hurricane*, United States Department of Commerce, Environmental Science Services Administration, 1969.

The eye, like the spiral structure of the storm, is unique to hurricanes. Here, winds are light and skies are clear or partly cloudy. But this calm is deceptive, bordered as it is by hurricane-force winds and torrential rains. Many persons have been killed or injured when the calm eye lured them out of shelter, only to be caught in the hurricane winds at the far side of the eye, where the wind blows from a direction opposite to that in the leading half of the storm.

Hurricane winds do much damage, but drowning is the greatest cause of hurricane deaths. As the storm approaches and moves across the coastline, it brings huge waves, raising tides some 15 feet or more above normal. The rise may come rapidly, and produce flash floods in coastal lowlands, or may come in the form of giant waves—which are mistakenly called "tidal waves." Waves and currents erode beaches and barrier islands, undermine waterfront structures, and wash out highway and railroad beds. The torrential rains produce sudden flooding; as the storm moves inland and its winds diminish, floods constitute the hurricane's greatest threat.

The hurricanes that strike the eastern United States are born in the tropical and subtropical North Atlantic Ocean, the Caribbean Sea, and the Gulf of Mexico. Most occur in August, September, and October, but the six-month period from June 1 to November 30 is considered the Atlantic hurricane season.

The principal regions of tropical cyclone origin vary during the season. Most early (May and June) storms originate in the Gulf of Mexico and western Caribbean. In July and August, the areas of most frequent origin shift eastward, and by September are located over the larger area from the Bahamas southeastward to the Lesser Antilles, and thence eastward to south of the Cape Verde Islands, near the west coast of Africa. After mid-September, the principal areas of origin shift back to the western Caribbean and Gulf of Mexico.

On average, six Atlantic hurricanes occur per year. However, there are significant deviations from this average. In 1916 and 1950, 11 hurricanes were observed, and no hurricanes were observed in 1907 and 1914. During 1893, 1950, and 1961 seasons, four hurricanes were observed in progress at the same time.

Hurricanes also form along the west coast of Mexico and Central America, but their effects are seldom felt as far north as California. These threaten shipping and aviation, however, and are watched as carefully as their Atlantic cousins.

Hurricanes begin as relatively small tropical cyclones which drift gradually to the west-northwest (in the Northern Hemisphere), imbedded in the westward-blowing tradewinds of the tropics. Under certain conditions these disturbances increase in size, speed, and intensity until they become full-fledged hurricanes.

The storms move forward very slowly in the tropics, and may sometimes hover for short periods of time. The initial forward speed is usually 15 miles per hour or less. Then, as the hurricane moves farther from the Equator, its forward speed tends to increase; at middle latitudes it may exceed 60 miles per hour in extreme cases.

The great storms are driven by the heat released by condensing water vapor, and by external mechanical forces. Once cut off from the warm ocean, the storm begins to die, starved for water and heat energy, and dragged apart by friction as it moves over the land.

The Aphorism

Little nuggets of factual wisdom—usually only a sentence or two in length—are called *aphorisms*. No matter what the subject, you can be sure that some sage has made a succinct, often witty pronouncement about it, as the following potpourri indicates.

On humor:

Every man is important if he loses his life; and every man is funny if he loses his hat and has to run after it.

—G. K. Chesterton

On writing:

We write, knowing we are licked before we start.

—Henry Miller

On love and hate:

We may hate and love the same person, nay even at the same moment.

—William Hazlitt

On work:

When you have a great and difficult task, something perhaps almost impossible, if you only work a little at a time, every day a little—*without faith and without hope*—suddenly the work will finish itself.

—Isak Dinesen

On nature:

The world was made to be inhabited by beasts, but studied and contemplated by man.

—Thomas Browne

On life:

Life is the art of drawing sufficient conclusions from insufficient premises.

—Samuel Butler

On human nature:

There may be said to be two classes of people in the world: those who constantly divide the people of the world into two classes, and those who do not.

—Robert Benchley

Organizing the Factual Essay

The factual essay, like any other piece of expository writing, requires careful organization (see Chapter 23, "Organizing the Paper"). Sometimes, if there is an overwhelming number of small, separate facts to contend with, you may have trouble trying to fit everything in, finding a format to accommodate the host of details. Here again, as always, your purpose and your overall rhetorical stance must be your guide.

The essay on hurricanes, for example, has an appropriately simple format that might be outlined as follows:

1. What hurricanes are
2. Dangers of the hurricane
3. Location and frequency of occurrence
4. How hurricanes form

In each of these sections the writer has included numerous details, which are easy to follow because of their logical arrangement and intrinsic interest.

Another method of organizing a fact piece is through "question and answer" presentation, a lively approach to a subject (everyone's curiosity is stirred by the presentation of a question) and serviceable in that readers can turn immediately to the specific aspect of the subject they are interested in. The following essay was published by the President's Special Action Office for Drug Abuse Prevention.

Questions About Marihuana[6]

What Is Marihuana?

Marihuana is the Indian hemp plant *(Cannabis sativa)*. Delta-9-tetrahydrocannabinol (THC) is the principal psychoactive ingredient in marihuana. The parts with the highest THC content are the flowering tops of the plant.

Hashish (hash) is the dark brown resin that is collected from the tops of potent *Cannabis sativa*. It is much stronger than crude marihuana since it contains more THC. The effect on the user is naturally more intense, and the possibility of side effects is greater.

Does Marihuana Vary in Strength?

Yes. Some marihuana may produce no effect whatsoever. A small amount of strong marihuana may produce marked effect. The THC content of the plant determines its mind-altering activity. Because THC is somewhat unstable, its content in marihuana decreases as time passes.

The plant strain that grows wild in the United States is low in THC content compared to cultivated marihuana, or the Mexican, Lebanese, Southeast Asian or Indian varieties. Plant strain, climate, soil conditions, the time of harvesting and other factors determine the potency.

Is Marihuana a Stimulant or a Depressant?

The effects of marihuana vary so widely that it can be either a stimulant or a depressant. THC is generally considered a hallucinogen with some sedative properties.

[6]From *Special Action Office for Drug Abuse Prevention Answers the Most Frequently Asked Questions About Drug Abuse* (Washington, D.C.: U.S. Government Printing Office, 1972), pp. 22–25.

Does Marihuana Have Any Medical Uses?

Marihuana has no general medical use in the U.S. at the present time. However, researchers are attempting to determine whether THC and other components may have appetite-enhancing, anticonvulsant, antidepressant, or other capabilities which may be clinically useful.

What Are the Immediate Physical Effects of Smoking Marihuana?

Reddening of the whites of the eyes, increasing heart rate, and coughing due to the irritation effects of the smoke on the lungs are the most frequent and consistent physical effects. Hunger or sleepiness is reported by some individuals.

How Long Do the Effects of Marihuana Last?

This depends upon the dose and the person. A few inhalations of strong marihuana act quickly and can affect a person for several hours. Weak marihuana may produce minimal effects for perhaps an hour. When a large amount is swallowed, the effects start later but persist longer than when the same quantity is smoked.

What Are the Long-Term Effects of Extended Marihuana Use?

The Report of the National Commission on Marihuana and Drug Abuse indicates that very heavy users show clear cut behavioral changes and that, furthermore, there is a greater incidence of physical injury the longer they use the drug.

Does the Individual's Tolerance to Marihuana Vary with Repeated Use?

Studies in animals show that tolerance to marihuana does occur. While tolerance does not seem to develop in the occasional user, the heavy user seems able to take large amounts without the expected effects. Interestingly, there is reason to expect that some recurrent users may begin to require less marihuana in order to obtain the desired effect. This may be a matter of learning how to smoke the drug, and of learning what effects to look for.

Do Heavy Users Suffer Physical Withdrawal Symptoms Like the Narcotic Addict?

As ordinarily used in the U.S., marihuana does not lead to physical dependence; therefore it cannot be considered addicting. Furthermore, it is not a narcotic. Chronic users may become psychologically dependent upon the effects of marihuana. Thus, it is classified as habituating. The fact that a drug is not addicting does not mean that it has no potential for harm, since dependence, whether psychological or physical, is a serious matter.

Sudden cessation of use may provoke restlessness and anxiety in some persons who daily smoke large amounts, but withdrawal symptoms as seen in the heroin addict do not develop.

Is There Anything in Marihuana That Leads to the Use of Other Drugs?

There is nothing in marihuana itself that produces a need to use other drugs. Most marihuana smokers do not progress to stronger substances, but some do. Surveys supported by the National Institute of Mental Health show that the chronic users tend to experiment with other drugs. Hashish is frequently tried, and large numbers of chronic users also try strong hallucinogens, amphetamines, and occasionally, barbiturates. Some try opium and heroin. It may be that the very act of experimenting with one mind-altering substance makes people a little less hesitant about experimenting with others.

What Are the Psychological Effects of Marihuana?

The psychological effects of marihuana are quite variable. They include distortions of hearing, vision and sense of time. Thought becomes dreamlike and the belief that one is thinking better is not unusual. Performance may be hampered or unchanged. Illusions (misinterpretation of sensations) are often reported but hallucination (experiencing nonexistent sensations) and delusions (false beliefs) are rare except at very high doses. Inexperienced users may develop unfounded suspicions which may be accompanied by anxiety. In some cases the individual tends to withdraw into himself. Marihuana also appears to interfere with short-term memory.

What Kinds of Emotional and Psychological Problems Can Result from the Use of Marihuana?

Anxiety reactions and panic states have been noted. Accidents have occurred due to impaired judgment and time-space distortions. The user, especially if he is inexperienced, may become suspicious of people and take action that leads to injury. A toxic psychosis consisting of mental confusion, loss of contact with reality, and memory disturbances has been recorded; however, such extreme reactions are relatively uncommon.

Does the Heavy Use of Marihuana Affect the Personality Development of the Young Person?

A number of researchers believe that it can. By making marihuana use a significant part of his life style, the young person may avoid normal life stresses and the problems that are an intrinsic part of growing up. He therefore can miss the opportunity to mature to his full physical and mental potential.

Recently, heavy chronic marihuana use in the United States has sometimes been associated with a type of social maladjustment called the amotivational syndrome. This syndrome has been described as a loss of desire to work, to participate, to compete and to face challenges. As the interests and major concerns of the individual become centered around marihuana, drug use becomes of paramount interest.

How Are Teenagers Introduced to Marihuana?

In general, adolescents are introduced to marihuana by others in their group. There is little evidence to confirm the belief that it is usually a pusher who introduces the nonuser to marihuana.

Is Marihuana Less Harmful Than Alcohol?

The results of intoxication by either drug can be harmful. We know that alcohol is a dangerous drug physically, psychologically and socially for millions of people. There is not enough information to estimate the adverse effects of marihuana if it were to be used on the same scale as alcohol.

If Alcohol Is Legal, Why Not Marihuana?

Only during the past 5 years has systematic, scientific study of marihuana been underway. Whether another intoxicant of unknown long-range health consequences should be accepted into the culture is the basic question. Since it seems to be true that once a drug becomes an accepted part of the social fabric it is almost impossible to prohibit its use, many concerned citizens feel it is prudent to await the results of ongoing and planned studies before treating marihuana in the same way as alcohol.

What Research Is Being Done on Marihuana?

In current research, studies are being conducted to:

1. Ascertain the consequences of long-term use of marihuana in humans;
2. Determine the effects of marihuana on acts requiring physical and mental skills;
3. Determine in greater detail the pharmacological properties of marihuana, its toxicity, and its effects on the body and behavior of animals and humans.

ASSIGNMENTS

Class Discussion and Paragraph Suggestions

(See Chapter 27 for methods of composing unified, adequately developed paragraphs.)

1. One of the great compilers of facts was the journalist John Gunther (*Inside Europe, Inside U.S.A.*), who tells in his autobiography how he regarded and approached facts.

I try to report facts as I see them and to tell the truth, but truth is an elusive concept. I think it was Frank Lloyd Wright who once said, "The truth is more important than the facts." I would hesitate to recommend this maxim unreservedly to a school of journalism, but surely what Mr. Wright meant is clear—that selection of facts can be as important as the facts themselves. No man, not even Christopher Isherwood, is a camera—and the camera, as a matter of fact, is one of the greatest liars of our time. There is no such thing as *purely* objective journalism, although plenty of us try to get close. A reporter with no bias at all would be a vegetable. I myself have always had a strong, unalterable liberal bent; I believe in decency and progress, in tomorrow as against yesterday. But I am not often swayed or shaken by events. I have little messianic blood in my veins, and I seldom editorialize. On most issues I take a somewhat detached, even cold, old-fashioned middle view, although I stand more to the left than to the right. *Why* do I write? I suppose the best answer to this is that basically I write for myself, to satisfy my own multiple curiosities. In other words, my work has been a kind of exercise in self-education at the public's expense. I myself am a fairly good average guinea pig, and if something interests me I am reasonably sure it will interest the general reader too. I can only hope that the public has had its money's worth.

My colleague the late Raymond Clapper once said, "Never underestimate a reader's intelligence; never overestimate what he knows." I always try to be readable (and readability, to repeat, depends on pace and euphony) and I greatly enjoy making lists and summaries in my attempts to synthesize large masses of material, but I want to be solid as well and I do not believe in being too simple. It is a good thing to make the reader reach up. On the other hand, he has an absolute right to have terms defined; I try hard never to use a word or a phrase, from "apartheid" to "Common Market," without doing my best to explain exactly what it means.[7]

a. Gunther says that "truth is an elusive concept." Do you think the various writers in this section regard truth in the same light?

[7]From pp. 112–13 in *A Fragment of Autobiography* by John Gunther. Copyright © 1961, 1962 by John Gunther. Reprinted by permission of Harper & Row, Publishers.

b. Do you think a distinction can be made between truth and facts? Could "Questions About Marihuana" have just as easily been called either "The Truth About Marihuana" or "The Facts About Marihuana"?

c. What do you think Frank Lloyd Wright meant by his observation that "the truth is more important than the facts"?

d. Which pieces in this chapter suggest or embody a distinction between truth and facts?

e. Discuss the difference between "expression" and "communication." Does Gunther take both into account?

f. How do you think the subjective "new journalists" would respond to the following comments by Gunther? How do you respond?

... I seldom editorialize. On most issues I take a somewhat detached, even cold, old-fashioned middle view....

No man ... is a camera. ..There is no such thing as *purely* objective journalism....

... if something interests me I am reasonably sure it will interest the general reader too.

I always try to be readable....

... readability ... depends on pace and euphony....

... I greatly enjoy making lists and summaries....

2. Write a paragraph (150–250 words) using as a topic sentence Raymond Clapper's statement, "Never underestimate a reader's intelligence; never overestimate what he knows."

3. Use the photograph of the early cyclists on p. 145 as the basis for a three- or four-sentence photographic feature story.

4. Consider Hemingway's "War Medals for Sale."

a. How do the opening and closing sentences serve as a frame? What form does the body of the reportage take?

b. Comment on the quality of the description (for example, of the shops along Queen Street). Cite other passages of description. What kinds of specific details does Hemingway provide? How are they effective?

c. What does Hemingway mean by "the valor mart"?

d. Comment on the quality of the dialogue and on the fact that the reporter simply reports what is said without describing his feelings.

e. Does "the market price of valor" remain "undetermined," as Hemingway flatly states in the last sentence? What larger comment or deeper meaning do you find in this statement? In the story as a whole?

5. Write a paragraph of 150–250 words in which you develop your answers to the above question.

6. Consider Didion's essay, "Marrying Absurd."

a. What is suggested by the simple declarative sentence early in the piece: "Nothing else is required"?

b. What is ironic about the statement by the justice of the peace: "I could've married them *en masse*, but they're people, not cattle. People expect more when they get married."

c. Why do you suppose the writer put quotation marks around the word "expectations" ("What people who get married in Las Vegas actually do expect—what, in the largest sense, their 'expectations' are ...")?

d. What is "curious and self-contradictory" about these expectations?

e. In what sense does the writer mean that what happens here has no connection with "'real' life"?

f. In what sense does Las Vegas exist "in the eye of the beholder"?

g. Explain the contradiction: it is "an extraordinarily stimulating and interesting place, but an odd one in which to want to wear a candlelight satin Priscilla of Boston wedding dress with Chantilly lace insets, tapered sleeves and a detachable modified train."

h. Why do you think the writer describes the wedding dress in such detail? Do you know exactly what "a candlelight satin Priscilla of Boston" is? What "Chantilly lace" is? Does it matter whether you know or not? Do these details create a rhetorical effect independent of literal meaning? Comment on the following words:

candlelight	Chantilly
satin	lace
Priscilla of Boston	modified

i. Does the listing of chapel advertisements ("Our Photos Best Anywhere," "Your Wedding on a Phonograph Record," and so on) become tedious? Does it serve any purpose?

j. Evaluate the effectiveness of the simile " . . . marriage, like craps, is a game to be played when the table seems hot."

k. There are two illustrative incidents in this essay; comment on their rhetorical impact—that is, indicate how they develop and reinforce the point the writer is trying to make throughout her exposition.

l. Comment on the effectiveness of the phrases "merchandising 'niceness'" and "the facsimile of proper ritual."

m. Discuss irony as the prevailing tone and unifying principle of this essay.

7. Write three aphorisms.

Essay Suggestions

1. Write a feature story (500–750 words) in which you develop the human-interest aspect of some person or event in the news. See "Elephant Boy" (pp. 216–17) for an example of the interview feature. Consider also such possibilities as the seasonal story (the first day of spring, Groundhog Day), the local story (a town resident who has an unusual hobby), the inspirational (a daring rescue). You might try a satiric piece in which you spoof some widely revered custom or convention that you think is ridiculous (beauty contests or TV game shows, perhaps).

2. Write a feature story (500–750 words) on one of the following widely misunderstood topics (see Chapter 22, "Gathering Information"). Organize your essay either in lists (presenting first the misconception and then the facts about each aspect of your topic) or in question-and-answer form (like the marijuana piece).

hypnotism	conservation
group therapy	capital punishment
missionaries	abortion
conscientious objectors	chemical warfare
alcoholism	Daughters of the American Revolution
drug addiction	parochial schools
Zen	sex education
pollution	pesticides
homosexuality	smoking

3. Write an essay (500–750 words) correcting the causal fallacies at the root of the medical superstitions listed below; in other words, cite the *facts* behind the superstition.

Night air is unhealthy.
Insanity is inherited.

Green apples cause a stomachache.
Children born of married cousins will be defective or deformed.
Frogs and toads cause warts.
Feed a cold, starve a fever.

4. Write a piece of reportage (500–1,000 words) in which you pose a question (as Hemingway did) and search for an answer by interviewing various people.

5. In an essay (750–1,000 words) describe a place, procedure, situation, or event that you have observed or have participated in, characterizing it indirectly through your presentation of the objective, observable facts rather than through explicit comment (as in "Marrying Absurd"). The tone of your piece should be appropriate to the subject matter and to the conclusion you want the reader to draw.

6. Write a brochure (500–1,000 words) on one of the following subjects. Use either a straight expository or a question-and-answer form.

cosmic rays	digestion	fire
inertia	coral reefs	haunted houses
gravity	opera	tobacco
mirages	pigeons	hara-kiri
cyclotrons	drought	sea serpents
glaciers	buried treasure	falling stars
earthquakes	dwarfs and midgets	clowns
Arctic Ocean	giants	astrology
wind	lullabies	sundials
cavemen	gypsies	ice fishing
cavewomen	magic	
chromosomes	voodoo	

7. Write a series of aphorisms on eight to ten subjects.

14 How Did X Happen?

When you ask the question "How Did X Happen?" you are preparing to write narration, a story about how something happened. We shall confine our attention here (as elsewhere in this book) to what *actually did happen*—not in the imagination of the writer but in real life; that is, we shall deal with factual rather than fictional narrative. In both kinds of narrative there are characters and ongoing actions: a series of events unfolding against a specific setting, causally related and moving steadily forward in time and through stages of action. Unlike process analysis, which merely *explains* an event, narration attempts to *re-create* it by putting readers in the very flow of the happening so that they may see and hear and feel exactly what it was like; so that they may (vicariously) *have* the experience, not merely learn about it. To achieve this, the narrator must present the events in the form of a story; there must be both a teller and a tale. For a piece of writing to qualify as narrative, no more and no less than this is required.

Autobiographical Narration

In the following selection Dick Gregory, comedian and civil rights activist, tells how hate and shame entered his life. Note how, in a good narrative such as this, the story flows smoothly and easily—as if the events were taking place at the very moment of telling—and how the dialogue rings true: the easy, colloquial speech of the narrator, the cold, unbending tones of the teacher, the flustered repetitions of the child.

Not Poor, Just Broke[1]

DICK GREGORY

I have never learned hate at home, or shame. I had to go to school for that. I was about seven years old when I got my first big lesson. I was in love with a little girl named Helene Tucker, a light-complected little girl with pigtails and nice manners. She was always clean and she was smart in school. I think I went to school then mostly to look at her. I brushed my hair and even got me a little old handkerchief. It was a lady's handkerchief, but I didn't want Helene to see me wipe my nose on my hand. The pipes were frozen again, there was no water in the house, but I washed my socks and shirt every night. I'd get a pot, and go over to Mister Ben's grocery store, and stick my pot down into his soda machine. Scoop out some chopped ice. By evening the ice melted to water for washing. I got sick a lot that winter because the fire would go out at night before the clothes were dry. In the morning I'd put them on, wet or dry, because they were the only clothes I had.

Everybody's got a Helene Tucker, a symbol of everything you want. I loved her for her goodness, her cleanness, her popularity. She'd walk down my street and my brothers and sisters would yell, "Here comes Helene," and I'd rub my tennis sneakers on the back of my pants and wish my hair wasn't so nappy and the white folks' shirt fit me better. I'd run out on the street. If I knew my place and didn't come too close, she'd wink at me and say hello. That was a good feeling. Sometimes I'd follow her all the way home, and shovel the snow off her walk and try to make friends with her Momma and her aunts. I'd drop money on her stoop late at night on my way back from shining shoes in the taverns. And she had a Daddy, and he had a good job. He was a paper hanger.

I guess I would have gotten over Helene by summertime, but something happened in that classroom that made her face hang in front of me for the next twenty-two years. When I played the drums in high school it was for Helene and when I broke track records in college it was for Helene and when I started standing behind microphones and heard applause I wished Helene could hear it, too. It wasn't until I was twenty-nine years old and married and making money that I finally got her out of my system. Helene was sitting in that classroom when I learned to be ashamed of myself.

It was on a Thursday. I was sitting in the back of the room, in a seat with a chalk circle drawn around it. The idiot's seat, the troublemaker's seat.

The teacher thought I was stupid. Couldn't spell, couldn't read, couldn't do arithmetic. Just stupid. Teachers were never interested in finding out that you couldn't concentrate because you were so hungry, because you hadn't had any breakfast. All you could think about was noontime, would it ever come? Maybe you could sneak into the cloakroom and steal a bite of some kid's lunch out of a coat pocket. A bite of something. Paste. You can't really make a meal of paste, or put it on bread for a sandwich, but sometimes I'd scoop a few spoonfuls out of the paste jar in the back of the room. Pregnant people get strange tastes. I was pregnant with poverty. Pregnant with dirt and pregnant with smells that made people turn away, pregnant with cold and pregnant with shoes that were never bought for me, pregnant with five other people in my bed and no Daddy in the next room, and pregnant with hunger. Paste doesn't taste too bad when you're hungry.

The teacher thought I was a troublemaker. All she saw from the front of the room was a little black boy who squirmed in his idiot's seat and made noises and poked the kids around him. I guess she couldn't see a kid who made noises because he wanted someone to know he was there.

It was on a Thursday, the day before the Negro payday. The eagle always flew on Friday. The teacher was asking each student how much his father would give to the Community Chest. On Friday night, each kid would get the money from his father, and on Monday he would bring it to the school. I decided I was going to buy me a Daddy right then. I had money in my pocket from shining shoes and selling papers, and whatever Helene Tucker pledged for her Daddy I was going to top it. And I'd hand the money right in. I wasn't going to wait until Monday to buy me a Daddy.

I was shaking, scared to death. The teacher opened her book and started calling out names alphabetically.

"Helene Tucker?"

"My Daddy said he'd give two dollars and fifty cents."

"That's very nice, Helene. Very, very nice indeed."

That made me feel pretty good. It wouldn't take too much to top that. I had almost three dollars in dimes and quarters in my pocket. I stuck my hand in my pocket and held onto the money, waiting for her to call my name. But the teacher closed her book after she called everybody else in the class.

I stood up and raised my hand.

"What is it now?"

"You forgot me."

She turned toward the blackboard. "I don't have time to be playing with you, Richard."

"My Daddy said he'd . . ."

"Sit down, Richard, you're disturbing the class."

"My Daddy said he'd give . . . fifteen dollars."

She turned around and looked mad. "We are collecting this money for you and your kind, Richard Gregory. If your Daddy can give fifteen dollars you have no business being on relief."

"I got it right now, I got it right now, my Daddy gave it to me to turn in today, my Daddy said . . ."

"And furthermore," she said, looking right at me, her nostrils getting big and her lips getting thin and her eyes opening wide, "we know you don't have a Daddy."

Helene Tucker turned around, her eyes full of tears. She felt sorry for me. Then I couldn't see her too well because I was crying, too.

"Sit down, Richard."

And I always thought the teacher kind of liked me. She always picked me to wash the blackboard on Friday, after school. That was a big thrill, it made me feel important. If I didn't wash it, come Monday the school might not function right.

"Where are you going, Richard?"

I walked out of school that day, and for a long time I didn't go back very often. There was shame there.

Now there was shame everywhere. It seemed like the whole world had been inside that classroom, everyone had heard what the teacher had said, everyone had turned around and felt sorry for me. There was shame in going to the Worthy Boys Annual Christmas Dinner for you and your kind, because everybody knew what a worthy boy was. Why couldn't they just call it the Boys Annual Dinner, why'd they have to give it a name? There was shame in wearing the brown and orange and white plaid mackinaw the welfare gave to 3,000 boys. Why'd it have to be the same for everybody so when you walked down the street the people could see you were on relief? It was a nice warm mackinaw and it had a hood, and my Momma beat me and called me a little rat when she found out I stuffed it in the bottom of a pail full of garbage way over on Cottage Street. There was shame in running over to Mister Ben's at the end of the day and asking for his rotten peaches, there was shame in asking Mrs. Simmons for a spoonful of sugar, there was shame in running out to meet the relief truck. I hated that truck, full of food for you and your kind. I ran into the house and hid when it came. And then I started to sneak through alleys, to take the long way home so the people going into White's Eat Shop wouldn't see me. Yeah, the whole world heard the teacher that day, we all know you don't have a Daddy.

Structure in Narration

A narrative begins at a specifically designated point in time ("Once upon a time" is the best-known fictional opening) and ends at an equally specific time. In the following episode by Nikos Kazantzakis, the action of the story begins at nightfall and ends the next morning. In between, the author provides us with "markers" indicating where we are located in the progression of the incident ("almost nightfall," "suddenly," "finally," "as soon as"). Note how at the outset Kazantzakis establishes a mood of tension, anxiety, and suspense by describing the deserted streets, bolted doors, and atmosphere of enveloping gloom. We are being prepared for a conflict that the narrator fearfully anticipates, and we follow him with mounting suspense as he moves into danger—or is it danger? The story unfolds quietly toward its gentle climax, revealed in the last line.

A Night in a Calabrian Village[2]
NIKOS KAZANTZAKIS

It was almost nightfall. The whole day: rain, torrents of rain. Drenched to the bone, I arrived in a little Calabrian village. I had to find a hearth where I could dry out, a corner where I could sleep. The streets were deserted, the doors bolted. The dogs were the only ones to scent the stranger's breath; they began to bark from within the courtyards. The peasants in this region are wild and misanthropic, suspicious of strangers. I hesitated at every door, extended my hand, but did not dare to knock.

O for my late grandfather in Crete who took his lantern each evening and made the rounds of the village to see if any stranger had come. He would take him home, feed him, give him a bed for the night, and then in the morning see him off with a cup of wine and a slice of bread. Here in the Calabrian villages there were no such grandfathers.

Suddenly I saw an open door at the edge of the village. Inclining my head, I looked in: a murky corridor with a lighted fire at the far end and an old lady bent over it. She seemed to be cooking. Not a sound, nothing but the burning wood. It was fragrant; it must have been pine. I crossed the threshold and entered, bumping against a long table which stood in the middle of the room. Finally I reached the fire and sat down on a stool which I found in front of the hearth. The old lady was squatting on another stool, stirring the meal with a wooden spoon. I felt that she eyed me rapidly, without turning. But she said nothing. Taking off my jacket, I began to dry it. I sensed

[2]From *A Report to Greco* by Nikos Kazantzakis. Copyright © 1965 by Simon and Schuster, Inc. Reprinted by permission of the publisher.

happiness rising in me like warmth, from my feet to my shins, my thighs, my breast. Hungrily, avidly, I inhaled the fragrance of the steam rising from the pot. The meal must have been baked beans; the aroma was overwhelming. Once more I realized to what an extent earthly happiness is made to the measure of man. It is not a rare bird which we must pursue at one moment in heaven, at the next in our minds. Happiness is a domestic bird found in our own courtyards.

Rising, the old lady took down two soup plates from a shelf next to her. She filled them, and the whole world smelled of beans. Lighting a lamp, she placed it on the long table. Next she brought two wooden spoons and a loaf of black bread. We sat down opposite each other. She made the sign of the cross, then glanced rapidly at me. I understood. I crossed myself and we began to eat. We were both hungry; we did not breathe a word. I had decided not to speak in order to see what would happen. Could she be a mute, I asked myself—or perhaps she's mad, one of those peaceful, kindly lunatics so much like saints.

As soon as we finished, she prepared a bed for me on a bench to the right of the table. I lay down, and she lay down on the other bench opposite me. Outside the rain was falling by the bucketful. For a considerable time I heard the water cackle on the roof, mixed with the old lady's calm, quiet breathing. She must have been tired, for she fell asleep the moment she inclined her head. Little by little, with the rain and the old lady's rhythmical respiration, I too slipped into sleep. When I awoke, I saw daylight peering through the cracks in the door.

The old lady had already risen and placed a saucepan on the fire to prepare the morning milk. I looked at her now in the sparse daylight. Shriveled and humped, she could fit into the palm of your hand. Her legs were so swollen that she had to stop at every step and catch her breath. But her eyes, only her large, pitch-black eyes, gleamed with youthful, unaging brilliance. How beautiful she must have been in her youth, I thought to myself, cursing man's fate, his inevitable deterioration. Sitting down opposite each other again, we drank the milk. Then I rose and slung my carpetbag over my shoulder. I took out my wallet, but the old lady colored deeply.

"No, no," she murmured, extending her hand.

As I looked at her in astonishment, the whole of her bewrinkled face suddenly gleamed.

"Goodbye, and God bless you," she said. "May the Lord repay you for the good you've done me. Since my husband died I've never slept so well."

Although the action of Kazantzakis' little tale is low-keyed and essentially leisurely, it moves steadily toward its culmination. This is a basic element of good narration: the story must move steadily forward. It should never slacken or bog down in unessential details or issues not directly related to what it is primarily about. Some beginning writers deliberately try to "draw the story out," on the mistaken notion that this creates suspense. On the contrary, suspense is created (indeed, interest can only be maintained) when the story has pace, when it moves without undue interruption toward its climax—the revelation of what happened.

Point of View in Narration

In narration as in description, you must clearly establish your point of view, the vantage point from which you are telling the story: What is your relation to the events? How much do you know? What is your purpose in telling the story? As a narrator, you may assume any one of several points of view. You may be an outsider, telling your story in the third person and knowing everything that is happening, including what goes on in everybody's head. This is called the *omniscient* point of view, and has generally been used by writers of fiction rather than nonfiction (obviously, since no one is really omniscient). Recently, however, a group of "new nonfiction" writers such as Tom Wolfe in *The Electric Kool-Aid Acid Test* and Truman Capote in *In Cold Blood* (which he called a "nonfiction novel") have borrowed the techniques of the novelist and short story writer in order to give their reportage a deeper dimension of vitality and reality. Thus they either speculate on what various persons are thinking, or find out (usually through intensive interviews) what they actually were thinking and feeling during the time of a reported happening.

You may also tell your story from the viewpoint of one character, seeing and knowing only what that character sees and knows. This is called the *limited* point of view. Or, as we have seen, you may tell your story in the first person. Or you may move like a sound camera, recording only what can be seen and heard, never delving into anyone's mind or heart—the *objective* or *dramatic* point of view.

It is a truism to say that the same events seen through different eyes or from different perspectives produce a different story. Thus no single element in a narrative is more significant than the narrator; as such, you are part of the story, the lens through which what happens is refracted. Consider, for example, the following brief yet complete narrative, in which an accident is observed by the narrator from the window of a commuter train moving through the South Bronx slums (the setting of the story). The impact of the accident on the narrator is explicitly stated: "a sight I would never be able to forget"; but the larger truth it reveals about human nature is embodied in a few lines of dialogue, which the narrator, refusing to intrude, allows to speak for themselves.

The Accident[3]

WILLIE MORRIS

One afternoon in late August, as the summer's sun streamed into the car and made little jumping shadows on the windows, I sat gazing out at the tenement-dwellers, who were themselves looking out of their windows from the gray crumbling buildings along the tracks of upper Manhattan. As we crossed into the Bronx, the train unexpectedly slowed down for a few miles. Suddenly from out of my window I saw a large crowd near the tracks, held back by two policemen. Then, on the other side, from my window, I saw a sight I would never be able to forget: a little boy almost severed in halves, lying at an incredible angle near the track. The ground was covered with blood, and the boy's eyes were opened wide, strained and disbelieving in his sudden oblivion. A policeman stood next to him, his arms folded, staring straight ahead at the windows of our train. In the orange glow of late afternoon the policemen, the crowd, the corpse of the boy were for a brief moment immobile,

[3]From Willie Morris, *North Toward Home* (Boston: Houghton Mifflin, 1967).

motionless, a small tableau to violence and death in the city. Behind me, in the next row of seats, there was a game of bridge. I heard one of the four men say as he looked out at the sight, "God, that's horrible." Another said, in a whisper, "Terrible, terrible." There was a momentary silence, punctuated only by the clicking of the wheels on the track. Then, after a pause, I heard the first man say: "Two hearts."

Immediacy in Narration

Narration clearly enables you to do more than talk about your subject. Through a well-chosen illustration, ranging in length from a paragraph—like "The Accident"—to a full-length factual narrative, you can embody your points in a dramatic presentation that is often far more meaningful and memorable than simple analysis would have been. "Two hearts," the bridge player says, and in these two words—pointing simultaneously to the game and to the silenced heart of the dead child (also to the heart of the narrator? to *any* two hearts?)—the pain and poignancy and essential isolation of human beings are embodied.

In much the same way, George Orwell in a longer essay is able to say more about the inhumanity of capital punishment by presenting his point in a brief narrative account than he might have said in a long treatise on the subject. Similarly, the essay indicts the dehumanizing effect of colonialism on the colonizers as well as on the subjugated colonials, an effect that finds devastating expression in the irritable complaint of the supervising army doctor who is anxious to get on with the execution (then to breakfast). "For God's sake," he says to his lackey, "the man ought to have been dead by this time."

A Hanging[4]

GEORGE ORWELL

It was in Burma, a sodden morning of the rains. A sickly light, like yellow tinfoil, was slanting over the high walls into the jail yard. We were waiting outside the condemned cells, a row of sheds fronted with double bars, like small animal cages. Each cell measured about ten feet by ten and was quite bare within except for a plank bed and a pot for drinking water. In some of them brown silent men were squatting at the inner bars, with their blankets draped round them. These were the condemned men, due to be hanged within the next week or two.

One prisoner had been brought out of his cell. He was a Hindu, a puny wisp of a man, with a shaven head and vague liquid eyes. He had a thick, sprouting moustache, absurdly too big for his body, rather like the moustache of a comic man on the films. Six tall Indian warders were guarding him and getting him ready for the gallows. Two of them stood by with rifles and fixed bayonets, while the others handcuffed him, passed a chain through his handcuffs and fixed it to their belts, and lashed his arms tight to his sides. They crowded very close about him, with their hands always on him in a careful, caressing grip, as though all the while feeling him

[4]From *Shooting an Elephant and Other Essays* by George Orwell, copyright 1945, 1946, 1949, 1950 by Sonia Brownell Orwell. Reprinted by permission of Harcourt Brace Jovanovich, Inc. Also reprinted by permission of A. M. Heath.

to make sure he was there. It was like men handling a fish which is still alive and may jump back into the water. But he stood quite unresisting, yielding his arms limply to the ropes, as though he hardly noticed what was happening.

Eight o'clock and a bugle call, desolately thin in the wet air, floated from the distant barracks. The superintendent of the jail, who was standing apart from the rest of us, moodily prodding the gravel with his stick, raised his head at the sound. He was an army doctor, with a grey toothbrush moustache and a gruff voice. "For God's sake hurry up, Francis," he said irritably. "The man ought to have been dead by this time. Aren't you ready yet?"

Francis, the head jailer, a fat Dravidian in a white drill suit and gold spectacles, waved his black hand. "Yes sir, yes sir," he bubbled. "All iss satisfactorily prepared. The hangman iss waiting. We shall proceed."

"Well, quick march, then. The prisoners can't get their breakfast till this job's over."

We set out for the gallows. Two warders marched on either side of the prisoner, with their rifles at the slope; two others marched close against him, gripping him by arm and shoulder, as though at once pushing and supporting him. The rest of us, magistrates and the like, followed behind. Suddenly, when we had gone ten yards, the procession stopped short without any order or warning. A dreadful thing had happened—a dog, come goodness knows whence, had appeared in the yard. It came bounding among us with a loud volley of barks, and leapt round us wagging its whole body, wild with glee at finding so many human beings together. It was a large woolly dog, half Airedale, half pariah. For a moment it pranced round us, and then, before anyone could stop it, it had made a dash for the prisoner and, jumping up, tried to lick his face. Everyone stood aghast, too taken aback even to grab at the dog.

"Who let the bloody brute in here?" said the superintendent angrily. "Catch it, someone!"

A warder, detached from the escort, charged clumsily after the dog, but it danced and gambolled just out of his reach, taking everything as part of the game. A young Eurasian jailer picked up a handful of gravel and tried to stone the dog away, but it dodged the stones and came after us again. Its yaps echoed from the jail walls. The prisoner, in the grasp of the two warders, looked on incuriously, as though this was another formality of the hanging. It was several minutes before someone managed to catch the dog. Then we put my handkerchief through its collar and moved off once more, with the dog still straining and whimpering.

It was about forty yards to the gallows. I watched the bare brown back of the prisoner marching in front of me. He walked clumsily with his bound arms, but quite steadily, with that bobbing gait of the Indian who never straightens his knees. At each step his muscles slid neatly into place, the lock of hair on his scalp danced up and down, his feet printed themselves on the wet gravel. And once, in spite of the men who gripped him by each shoulder, he stepped slightly aside to avoid a puddle on the path.

It is curious, but till that moment I had never realized what it meant to destroy a healthy, conscious man. When I saw the prisoner step aside to avoid the puddle I saw the mystery, the unspeakable wrongness of cutting a life short when it is in full tide. This man was not dying, he was alive just as we are alive. All the organs of his body were working—bowels digesting food, skin renewing itself, nails growing, tissues forming—all toiling away in solemn foolery. His nails would still be growing when he stood on the drop, when he was falling through the air with a tenth-of-a-second to live. His eyes saw the yellow gravel and the grey walls, and his brain still remembered, foresaw, reasoned—reasoned even about puddles. He and we were a party of men walking together, seeing, feeling, understanding the same world; and in two minutes, with a sudden snap, one of us would be gone—one mind less, one world less.

The gallows stood in a small yard, separate from the main grounds of the prison, and overgrown with tall prickly weeds. It was a brick erection like three sides of a shed, with planking on top, and above that two beams and a crossbar with the rope dangling. The hangman, a grey-haired convict in the white uniform of the prison, was waiting beside his machine. He greeted us with a servile crouch as we entered. At a word from Francis the two warders, gripping the prisoner more closely than ever, half led half pushed him to the gallows and helped him clumsily up the ladder. Then the hangman climbed up and fixed the rope around the prisoner's neck.

We stood waiting, five yards away. The warders had formed in a rough circle round the gallows. And then, when the noose was fixed, the prisoner began crying out to his god. It was a high, reiterated cry of "Ram! Ram! Ram! Ram!" not urgent and fearful like a prayer or cry for help, but steady, rhythmical, almost like the tolling of a bell. The dog answered the sound with a whine. The hangman, still standing on the gallows, produced a small cotton bag like a flour bag and drew it down over the prisoner's face. But the sound, muffled by the cloth, still persisted, over and over again: "Ram! Ram! Ram! Ram! Ram!"

The hangman climbed down and stood ready, holding the lever. Minutes seemed to pass. The steady, muffled crying from the prisoner went on and on, "Ram! Ram! Ram!" never faltering for an instant. The superintendent, his head on his chest, was slowly poking the ground with his stick; perhaps he was counting the cries, allowing the prisoner a fixed number—fifty, perhaps, or a hundred. Everyone had changed color. The Indians had gone grey like bad coffee, and one or two of the bayonets were wavering. We looked at the lashed, hooded man on the drop, and listened to his cries—each cry another second of life; the same thought was in all our minds: oh, kill him quickly, get it over, stop that abominable noise!

Suddenly the superintendent made up his mind. Throwing up his head he made a swift motion with his stick. "Chalo!" he shouted almost fiercely.

There was a clanking noise, and then dead silence. The prisoner had vanished, and the rope was twisting on itself. I let go of the dog, and it galloped immediately to the back of the gallows; but when it got there it stopped short, barked, and then retreated into a corner of the yard, where it stood among the weeds, looking timorously out at us. We went round the gallows to inspect the prisoner's body. He was dangling with his toes pointed straight downwards, very slowly revolving, as dead as a stone.

The superintendent reached out with his stick and poked the bare brown body; it oscillated slightly. "*He's* all right," said the superintendent. He backed out from under the gallows, and blew out a deep breath. The moody look had gone out of his face quite suddenly. He glanced at his wrist-watch. "Eight minutes past eight. Well, that's all for this morning, thank God."

The warders unfixed bayonets and marched away. The dog, sobered and conscious of having misbehaved itself, slipped after them. We walked out of the gallows yard, past the condemned cells with their waiting prisoners, into the big central yard of the prison. The convicts, under the command of warders armed with lathis, were already receiving their breakfast. They squatted in long rows, each man holding a tin panikin, while two warders with buckets marched round ladling out rice; it seemed quite a homely, jolly scene, after the hanging. An enormous relief had come upon us now that the job was done. One felt an impulse to sing, to break into a run, to snigger. All at once everyone began chattering gaily.

The Eurasian boy walking beside me nodded toward the way we had come, with a knowing smile: "Do you know, sir, our friend [he meant the dead man] when he heard his appeal had been dismissed, he pissed on the floor of his cell. From fright. Kindly take one of my cigarettes, sir. Do you not admire my new silver case, sir? From the boxwalah, two rupees eight annas. Classy European style."

Several people laughed—at what, nobody seemed certain.

Francis was walking by the superintendent, talking garrulously: "Well, sir, all hass passed off with the utmost satisfactoriness. It was all finished—flick! like that. It iss not always so—oah, no! I have known cases where the doctor wass obliged to go, beneath the gallows and pull the prissoner's legs to ensure decease. Most disagreeable!"

"Wriggling about, eh? That's bad," said the superintendent.

"Ach, sir, it iss worse when they become refractory! One man, I recall, clung to the bars of hiss cage when we went to take him out. You will scarcely credit, sir, that it took six warders to dislodge him, three pulling at each leg. We reasoned with him. 'My dear fellow,' we said, 'think of all the pain and trouble you are causing to us!' But no, he would not listen! Ach, he wass very troublesome!"

I found that I was laughing quite loudly. Everyone was laughing. Even the superintendent grinned in a tolerant way. "You'd better all come out and have a drink," he said quite genially. "I've got a bottle of whisky in the car. We could do with it."

We went through the big double gates of the prison into the road. "Pulling at his legs!" exclaimed a Burmese magistrate suddenly, and burst into a loud chuckling. We all began laughing again. At that moment Francis' anecdote seemed extraordinarily funny. We all had a drink together, native and European alike, quite amicably. The dead man was a hundred yards away.

Historical Narration

All historical accounts are, in a sense, answers to the question "How did it happen?" But only some historical accounts can be called "narrative," for only some writers present history not merely as a record of the past (wars, treaties, dates) but as an unfolding drama, a direct presentation of human experience. One master of historical narrative was Winston Churchill, whose four-volume *A History of the English-Speaking Peoples* moves with novel-like rapidity across the centuries, to describe the sweep and flow of events that shaped the English nation.

In the passage below, reprinted from the first volume, Churchill describes the Battle of Hastings (1066). He brings this military action—the climax of William the Conqueror's invasion—to life through the steady accumulation of concrete details that dramatize the butchery of battle; the slyness of William's feigned retreat; the terrible bloodiness of Harold's defeat; the pathos of his death as his naked body is "wrapped only in a robe of purple," and as his grief-stricken mother pleads in vain for permission to bury her son in holy ground. Note also a masterful touch: Churchill opens the battle scene by focusing (as in a movie close-up) on the fate of one man—Ivan Taillefer, "the minstrel knight who had claimed the right to make the first attack." With the "astonished English," we watch this impetuous adventurer fling his sword into the air and catch it again with all the jauntiness of a juggler performing before a wide-eyed audience. As he charges into the English ranks, he is immediately slain. Thus, in a four-line vignette, Churchill creates an unforgettable paradigm of human pride and futility.

In the Battle of Hastings[5]

WINSTON CHURCHILL

At the first streak of dawn William set out from his camp at Pevensey, resolved to put all to the test; and Harold the Saxon King, eight miles away, awaited him in resolute array.

As the battle began Ivan Taillefer, the minstrel knight who had claimed the right to make the first attack, advanced up the hill on horseback, throwing his lance and sword into the air and catching them before the astonished English. He then charged deep into the English ranks, and was slain. The cavalry charges of William's mail-clad knights, cumbersome in manoeuvre, beat in vain upon the dense, ordered masses of the English. Neither the arrow hail nor the assaults of the horsemen could prevail against them. William's left wing of cavalry was thrown into disorder, and retreated rapidly down the hill. On this the troops on Harold's right, who were mainly the local "fyrd," broke their ranks in eager pursuit. William, in the centre, turned his disciplined squadrons upon them and cut them to pieces. The Normans then reformed their ranks and began a second series of charges upon the English masses, subjecting them in the intervals to severe archery. It has often been remarked that this part of the action resembles the afternoon at Waterloo, when Ney's cavalry exhausted themselves upon the British squares, torn by artillery in the intervals. In both cases the tortured infantry stood unbroken. Never, it was said, had the Norman knights met foot-soldiers of this stubbornness. They were utterly unable to break through the shield-walls, and they suffered serious losses from deft blows of the axe-men, or from javelins, or clubs hurled from the ranks behind. But the arrow showers took a cruel toll. So closely were the English wedged that the wounded could not be removed, and the dead scarcely found room in which to sink upon the ground.

The autumn afternoon was far spent before any result had been achieved, and it was then that William adopted the time-honoured ruse of a feigned retreat. He had seen how readily Harold's right had quitted their positions in pursuit after the first repulse of the Normans. He now organised a sham retreat in apparent disorder, while keeping a powerful force in his own hands.

The house-carls around Harold preserved their discipline and kept their ranks, but the sense of relief to the less trained forces after these hours of combat was such that seeing their enemy in flight proved irresistible. They surged forward on the impulse of victory, and when half-way down the hill were savagely slaughtered by William's horsemen. There remained, as the dusk grew, only the valiant bodyguard who fought round the King and his standard. His brothers, Gyrth and Leofwine, had already been killed. William now directed his archers to shoot high into the air, so that the arrows would fall behind the shield-wall, and one of these pierced Harold in the right eye, inflicting a mortal wound. He fell at the foot of the royal standard, unconquerable except by death, which does not count in honour. The hard-fought battle was now decided. The last formed body of troops was broken, though by no means overwhelmed. They withdrew into the woods behind, and William, who had fought in the

[5]From *A History of the English-Speaking Peoples: The Birth of Britain* by Sir Winston Churchill. Reprinted by permission of Dodd, Mead & Company, Inc., and The Canadian Publishers, McClelland and Stewart Limited, Toronto.

foremost ranks and had three horses killed under him, could claim the victory. Nevertheless the pursuit was heavily checked. There is a sudden deep ditch on the reverse slope of the hill of Hastings, into which large numbers of Norman horsemen fell, and in which they were butchered by the infuriated English lurking in the wood.

The dead king's naked body, wrapped only in a robe of purple, was hidden among the rocks of the bay. His mother in vain offered the weight of the body in gold for permission to bury him in holy ground. The Norman Duke's answer was that Harold would be more fittingly laid upon the Saxon shore which he had given his life to defend. The body was later transferred to Waltham Abbey, which he had founded. Although here the English once again accepted conquest and bowed in a new destiny, yet ever must the name of Harold be honoured in the Island for which he and his famous house-carls fought indomitably to the end.

The Diary as Narration

Of the several types of narrative essay—personal, reportorial, biographical, and historical—the personal is probably the most common and popular. Certainly it is the most intimate, for in it the writer talks directly to readers of his or her own experiences. Especially intimate is the journal, or diary, which is sometimes written to be read by others (for publication after the author's death in some cases) and sometimes "just written" with no audience in mind.

Clearly it was chance that brought to light the diary of Carolina Maria De Jesus, a short section of which is reprinted below. This is one of the strangest diaries ever written, for Carolina originally set down her words on scraps of paper and litter picked up in the gutters and garbage pails of a Brazilian *favela* (slum). In the diary she tells how she lives with her three children (each born of a different father), trying day by day to scrape together enough food to keep the family alive. One of the most compelling documents of human poverty ever published, it was written by a woman with only two years of schooling.

The Diary of Carolina Maria De Jesus[6]

May 2, 1958   I'm not lazy. There are times when I try to keep up my diary. But then I think it's not worth it and figure I'm wasting my time.

I've made a promise to myself. I want to treat people that I know with more consideration. I want to have a pleasant smile for children and the employed.

I received a summons to appear at 8 P.M. at police station number 12. I spent the day looking for paper. At night my feet pained me so I couldn't walk. It started to rain. I went to the station and took José Carlos with me. The summons was for him. José Carlos is nine years old.

May 3   I went to the market at Carlos de Campos Street looking for any old thing. I got a lot of greens. But it didn't help much, for I've got no cooking fat. The children are upset because there's nothing to eat.

---

[6]From *Child of the Dark: The Diary of Carolina Maria De Jesus*, translated by David St. Clair. Copyright, ©, 1962 by E. P. Dutton & Co., Inc., and Souvenir Press, Ltd. Reprinted by permission of the publishers. (Published in England as *Beyond All Pity*.)

May 6 In the morning I went for water. I made João carry it. I was happy, then I received another summons. I was inspired yesterday and my verses were so pretty, I forgot to go to the station. It was 11:00 when I remembered the invitation from the illustrious lieutenant of the 12th precinct.

My advice to would-be politicians is that people do not tolerate hunger. It's necessary to know hunger to know how to describe it.

They are putting up a circus here at Araguaia Street. The Nilo Circus Theater.

May 9 I looked for paper but I didn't like it. Then I thought: I'll pretend that I'm dreaming.

May 10 I went to the police station and talked to the lieutenant. What a pleasant man! If I had known he was going to be so pleasant, I'd have gone on the first summons. The lieutenant was interested in my boys' education. He said the favelas have an unhealthy atmosphere where the people have more chance to go wrong than to become useful to state and country. I thought: if he knows this why doesn't he make a report and send it to the politicians? To Janio Quadros, Kubitschek,* and Dr. Adhemar de Barros? Now he tells me this, I a poor garbage collector. I can't even solve my own problems.

Brazil needs to be led by a person who has known hunger. Hunger is also a teacher.

Who has gone hungry learns to think of the future and of the children.

May 11 Today is Mother's Day. The sky is blue and white. It seems that even nature wants to pay homage to the mothers who feel unhappy because they can't realize the desires of their children.

The sun keeps climbing. Today it's not going to rain. Today is our day.

Dona Teresinha came to visit me. She gave me 15 cruzeiros and said it was for Vera to go to the circus. But I'm going to use the money to buy bread tomorrow because I only have four cruzeiros.

Yesterday I got half a pig's head at the slaughterhouse. We ate the meat and saved the bones. Today I put the bones on to boil and into the broth I put some potatoes. My children are always hungry. When they are starving they aren't so fussy about what they eat.

Night came. The stars are hidden. The shack is filled with mosquitoes. I lit a page from a newspaper and ran it over the walls. This is the way the favela dwellers kill mosquitoes.

May 13 At dawn it was raining. Today is a nice day for me, it's the anniversary of the Abolition. The day we celebrate the freeing of the slaves. In the jails the Negroes were the scapegoats. But now the whites are more educated and don't treat us any more with contempt. May God enlighten the whites so that the Negroes may have a happier life.

It continued to rain and I only have beans and salt. The rain is strong but even so I sent the boys to school. I'm writing until the rain goes away so I can go to Senhor Manuel and sell scrap. With that money I'm going to buy rice and sausage. The rain has stopped for a while. I'm going out.

I feel so sorry for my children. When they see the things to eat that I come home with they shout:

"Viva Mama!"

Their outbursts please me. But I've lost the habit of smiling. Ten minutes later they

---

* President of Brazil from 1956 to 1961.

want more food. I sent João to ask Dona Ida for a little pork fat. She didn't have any. I sent her a note:

"Dona Ida, I beg you to help me get a little pork fat, so I can make soup for the children. Today it's raining and I can't go looking for paper. Thank you, Carolina."

It rained and got colder. Winter had arrived and in winter people eat more. Vera asked for food, and I didn't have any. It was the same old show. I had two cruzeiros and wanted to buy a little flour to make a virado.* I went to ask Dona Alice for a little pork. She gave me pork and rice. It was 9 at night when we ate.

And that is the way on May 13, 1958, I fought against the real slavery—hunger!

How Carolina's diary was discovered and brought to publication, and what happened to Carolina as a result, constitutes a story in itself, part of which is reprinted below.

The Story of Carolina Maria De Jesus[7]
DAVID ST. CLAIR

In April of 1958, Audalio Dantas, a young reporter, was covering the inauguration of a playground near Caninde for his newspaper. When the politicians had made their speeches and gone away, the grown men of the favela began fighting with the children for a place on the teeter-totters and swings. Carolina, standing in the crowd, shouted furiously: "If you continue mistreating these children, I'm going to put all your names in my book!"

Interested, the reporter asked the tall black woman about her book. At first she didn't want to talk to him, but slowly he won her confidence and she took him to her shack. There in the bottom drawer of a dilapidated dresser she pulled out her cherished notebooks. . . .

. . . Published, her diary became the literary sensation of Brazil. Over a thousand people swamped the bookshop on the first day of sales. . . . Carolina signed 600 copies that afternoon, and would have done more if she hadn't stopped to talk to each of the buyers. She asked what their names were, where they lived, and if they were happy. When a state senator appeared with flash bulbs popping, Carolina wrote in his book: "I hope that you give the poor people what they need and stop putting all the tax money into your own pocket. Sincerely, Carolina Maria De Jesus."

Never had a book such an impact on Brazil. In three days the first printing of 10,000 copies was sold out in São Paulo alone. In less than six months 90,000 copies were sold in Brazil and today it is still on the best-seller list, having sold more than any other Brazilian book in history.

Carolina was invited to speak about the favela problem on radio and television, and she gave lectures on the problem in Brazilian universities. Her book has become required reading in sociology classes and the São Paulo Law University has given her the title of "Honorary Member," the first such person so honored who has not had a university education. The title was originally slated for Jean-Paul Sartre, but the students decided that Carolina was "far worthier in the fight for freedom" than the French philosopher.

*A dish of black beans, manioc flour, pork, and eggs.

[7]From *Child of the Dark: The Diary of Carolina Maria De Jesus,* translated by David St. Clair. Copyright, ©, 1962 by E. P. Dutton & Co., Inc., and Souvenir Press, Ltd. Reprinted by permission of the publishers. (Published in England as *Beyond All Pity.*)

ASSIGNMENTS

Class Discussion and Paragraph Suggestions

(See Chapter 27 for methods of composing unified, adequately developed paragraphs.)

1. Evaluate Dick Gregory's "Not Poor, Just Broke."
   a. Why does Gregory use this title? Does "Broke" have more than one meaning here?
   b. How do the two opening sentences function in the story?
   c. Are the characters convincingly drawn? Cite specific details.
   d. Outline the "plot." What is the central conflict? What additional conflicts are implied in the story?
   e. How does the writer establish and maintain an element of suspense?
   f. How does paragraph three function? What rhetorical device unifies the second sentence? What rhetorical purpose does it serve?
   g. List descriptive details that seem to you especially well-selected and evocative in helping you to see, hear, feel, and understand what is going on.
   h. Does the crucial event or climax of the story have sufficient impact? Explain.
   i. Where and how does the mood of the story change? Is there a reversal?

2. An interesting companion piece to Kazantzakis' "A Night in a Calabrian Village," is John Steinbeck's "A Night in a Maine Motel." It is taken from *Travels with Charley*, an account of Steinbeck's cross-country tour "in search of America." Like Kazantzakis, Steinbeck is "on the road" when we meet him, in need of shelter for the night.

A Night in a Maine Motel[8]

JOHN STEINBECK

Not far outside of Bangor I stopped at an auto court and rented a room. It wasn't expensive. The sign said "Greatly Reduced Winter Rates." It was immaculate; everything was done in plastics—the floors, the curtain, table tops of stainless burnless plastic, lamp shades of plastic. Only the bedding and the towels were of natural material. I went to the small restaurant run in conjunction. It was all plastic too—the table linen, the butter dish. The sugar and crackers were wrapped in cellophane, the jelly in a small plastic coffin sealed with cellophane. It was early evening and I was the only customer. Even the waitress wore a sponge-off apron. She wasn't happy, but then she wasn't unhappy. She wasn't anything. But I don't believe anyone is a nothing. There has to be something inside, if only to keep the skin from collapsing. This vacant eye, listless hand, this damask cheek dusted like a doughnut with plastic powder, had to have a memory or a dream.

On a chance I asked, "How soon you going to Florida?"

"Nex' week," she said listlessly. Then something stirred in that aching void. "Say, how do you know I'm going?"

"Read your mind, I guess."

She looked at my beard. "You with a show?"

"No."

"Then how do you mean read my mind?"

"Maybe I guessed. Like it down there?"

"Oh sure! I go every year. Lots of waitress jobs in the winter."

"What do you do down there, I mean for fun?"

"Oh, nothing. Just fool around."

"Do you fish or swim?"

"Not much. I just fool around. I don't like that sand, makes me itch."

"Make good money?"

"It's a cheap crowd."

"Cheap?"

"They rather spen' it on booze."

"Than what?"

"Than tips just the same here with the summer."

Strange how one person can saturate a room with vitality, with excitement. Then there are others, and this dame was one of them, who can drain off energy and joy, can suck pleasure dry and get no sustenance from it. Such people spread a grayness in the air about them. I'd been driving a long time, and perhaps my energy was low and my resistance down. She got me. I felt so blue and miserable I wanted to crawl into a plastic cover and die. What a date she must be, what a lover! I tried to imagine that last and couldn't. For a moment I considered giving her a five-dollar tip, but I knew what would happen. She wouldn't be glad. She'd just think I was crazy.

I went back to my clean little room. I don't ever drink alone. It's not much fun. And I don't think I will until I am an alcoholic. But this night I got a bottle of vodka from my stores and took it to my cell. In the bathroom two water tumblers were sealed in cellophane sacks with the words: "These glasses are sterilized for your protection." Across the toilet seat a strip of paper bore the message: "This seat has been sterilized with ultraviolet light for your protection." Everyone was protecting me and it was horrible. I tore the glasses from their covers. I violated the toilet-seat seal with my foot. I poured half a tumbler of vodka and drank it and then another. Then I lay deep in hot water in the tub and I was utterly miserable, and nothing was good anywhere.

Compare the Steinbeck and Kazantzakis essays on the basis of the following:

   a. point of view (voice, tone, rhetorical stance)
   b. setting (locale, atmosphere)
   c. characters (compare their respective moods at the beginning and end of the narrative)
   d. action (sequence and development of events, climax)
   e. theme (suggestions about human nature, economic values, and the impact of chance encounters)
   f. style (sentence structure, choice of words, images)

3. Write a one-paragraph comparison (150–250 words) of the women in the Kazantzakis and Steinbeck essays.

4. In a paragraph (150–250 words), retell "The Accident" from one of the following points of view:

   a. the bridge player
   b. the policeman
   c. the dead child

5. a. Show how the following images from "A Hanging" contribute to the total effect and thesis of the piece:

1. A "sickly light" slants into the jail yard.
2. The prisoner is held as if he were "a fish which is still alive and may jump back into the water."
3. " . . . a bugle call, desolately thin in the wet air, floated from the distant barracks."
4. The dog ("half Airedale, half pariah") licks the prisoner's face.
5. The prisoner cries "Ram! Ram! Ram! Ram!"
6. The superintendent examines the body and says, "*He's* all right."
7. " . . . everyone began chattering gaily."

   b. Why do you suppose Orwell does not indicate what crime the prisoner committed? Is it important?
   c. How effective is the one paragraph of explicit protest against capital punishment? Explain its rightness or wrongness in the middle of the narrative. Does it contribute to the horror of what is happening?
   d. What mood do you feel upon reading of the laughing and drinking that follow the hanging? Explain.

6. Consider the diary of Carolina Maria De Jesus.

   a. List the reasons why you think Carolina's diary became a best seller ("Never had a book such an impact on Brazil"). Do you think its relevance extends beyond Brazil? Explain.
   b. In what ways would a formal tract against poverty be more or less effective than this diary?
   c. What aspects of Carolina's style suggest a "natural" rather than a trained writer? Evaluate the effectiveness of her writing.
   d. Comment on the personality, character, and attitudes of Carolina. Is she bitter, resigned, hopeful?
   e. What qualities contribute to making this a "touchingly beautiful" document (as one critic has called it)?

7. Write narrative diary entries for two or three days in your life.

Essay Suggestions

1. Write a narrative essay (750–1,000 words) in which you describe how some dimension of feeling or understanding entered your life (as in Dick Gregory's "Not Poor, Just Broke"). Make certain your description is cast within the frame of a *story* in which there is a specific setting, characters (let them speak in normal, natural tones), and action. You may wish to follow the general structure of Gregory's essay:

   Introduction
   Background situation described (conflict)
   Crucial incident (climax)
   Long-term effect (resolution)

   Be sure to choose an appropriate tone for your narrative.

2. Write an essay (750–1,000 words) in which you tell the story of your encounter with another person, describing how you were affected, for either good or ill (as in the Kazantzakis and Steinbeck narratives).

3. Write a dramatization (750–1,000 words) of an event you have witnessed in which you suggest rather than explicitly state your judgment of its meaning and moral significance (as in "A Hanging").

4. Write a narrative essay (750–1,000 words) in which you describe a historical event, using the panoramic point of view as Winston Churchill does in "The Battle of

Hastings." He sweeps across the battlefield, moving from one event to another, closing in briefly here and there for a close-up, then moving on again.

a. Historic incidents:
      Boston Tea Party
      Chicago Fire
      Declaration of Independence is signed
      Pocahontas saves John Smith (fact and fiction)
      "Star-Spangled Banner" is composed
      the first humans walk on the moon
      Charlemagne is crowned emperor of the Holy Roman Empire
      Napoleon dies
      Balboa views the Pacific Ocean
      Fulton takes his steamboat up the Hudson River
      the Wright brothers fly at Kitty Hawk

b. Battles

Gettysburg	Crécy	Bunker Hill
Bull Run	Poitiers	Thermopylae
Shiloh	Waterloo	Dunkirk

5. Write an entry or a series of entries in a diary (500–1,000 words) describing in narrative fashion your activities (or state of mind, or both) for a week.

15 What Kind of Person Is X?

Many artists can create the "sense" of a person by simply setting down on their sketch pads a few swift, well-placed lines, thereby pictorially answering the question, "What kind of person is X?" So it is with the writer. By concentrating on a few well-selected, representative characteristics of the subject (a few broad brush strokes), he or she gives a character sketch, a word-picture, of what that person essentially is—or is from the writer's point of view.

To write of a person so that readers can "see him live, and 'live o'er each scene with him, as he actually advanced through the several stages of his life'": this is Boswell's definition of biography. Clearly, the essayist cannot do as much, although he or she must obviously try to bring the subject to life on the pages. The character essay can merely point to the thread that runs through a life and that thereby defines it, or to the single quality that seems to sum it up—to what Mary McCarthy calls (in reference to her fictional characters) the "key" that turns the lock.

Writing a character study is, then, another form of analysis, for it involves breaking down an individual personality into its component parts in order to discover its motivating forces. Thus the writer draws upon those questions we have considered that deal with analysis—for example, question 2, "How can X be described?" or question 3, "What are the component parts of X?"

A Member of the Family

The following two essays deal with uncles. In each the writer tries to sum up his uncle through one dominant characteristic; one is the classic "average" man; the other is a smug, mean-spirited bully. Note that in their essays both writers blend description and narration in varying proportions: the first essay is almost totally descriptive, and the second is cast within a narrative frame.

My Average Uncle[1]

ROBERT P. TRISTRAM COFFIN

He stood out splendidly above all my uncles because he did not stand out at all. That was his distinction. He was the averagest man I ever knew.

You would never pick him out in a crowd. He became just another man the minute he was in one. So many more pounds of man. Good solid pounds, but just pounds. You would never remember his hair or his chin, or the shape of his ears. If he said something, you would agree with it, and, an hour later, you would be sure you had said it yourself.

Sometimes I think men like that get along about the best. They are the easiest on their houses, their wives, and their children. They are easiest on the world. They slide along without having to do anything about it as small boys do on their breeches after they have slid on them enough to wear them down smooth. The world is all so much pine needles under them.

Uncle Amos was easy on his wives and children. He had three of them, in all. Wives, I mean. I never did get the count of his children straight, there were too many assortments of them. Three wives. It seemed surprising to me at the time. With all the trouble I had, myself, having to stand on my head and work my legs, or bung stones at cherrybirds, to keep the attention of just one girl for a month, I often wondered how Uncle Amos, who never stood on his head or whittled out even a butterpat, could attract so many women as he did. With hair a little thin on his head, and legs that could not possibly do more than three and a half miles an hour on the road, there he was, with three families behind him. Of course, he had the families spaced. The wives of Uncle Amos did not come all at once. They were drawn out. One batch of children grew pretty well up by the time the next batch hove in sight, waddling and falling on their faces—to save their hands—as waddling children do.

I knew my *Bible,* especially the marital parts, in which I took deep interest. I had read the *Bible* through many times under the eye of one particular aunt. I knew a lot about matrimony from that. But Uncle Amos had me puzzled. He had broken no commandments. All his marriages were open and aboveboard. He wasn't like the patriarchs who didn't always wait for one wife to go before another came. Yet Uncle Amos's status and his children's status were rather complicated.

The women must have been drawn to him because he was so much like what an average fair husband would seem to a woman to be.

This man made no flourishes to attract anybody. He never drove a fast horse. He never wore trousers with checks any larger than an inch square—which, for the time, was conservative. His house never got afire and burned down just after the fire insurance had run out. Not one of his boys and girls ever got drowned or run over by the steam-cars. The few that died growing up died of diphtheria or scarlet fever, which were what children died of then, the usual ways.

Uncle Amos never had a fight.

[1]Reprinted with permission of The Macmillan Company from *Book of Uncles* by Robert P. Tristram Coffin. Copyright 1942 by The Macmillan Company, renewed 1970 by Margaret Coffin Halvosa.

Uncle Amos never lost a pocket-book. At least not one with much money in it. Uncle Amos never went even as far as Boston.

But there he was, never making much money, but with all the comforts of home around him, eating his stewed eels, sitting in his galluses out in the orchard in the cool of the evening, with a plump baby to climb up in his lap, whenever he felt like having a baby on his lap and had his old trousers on and didn't care much what happened to him. There he was, shingling his house only when it got to leaking so it put the kitchen fire out. Drinking a little ale now and then, when he came by it easy. No big hayfields to worry about. No wife that craved more than one new dress a year, and that one she generally ran up herself on her sewing machine. One best pair of trousers to his name, which the moths got into, but not so deep but what they could be healed up with a needle. Not many books to excite him and keep him awake nights, or put ideas into his head and make him uneasy. No itch ever spreading out upon him to go out and take the world by its horns. There he was, in clover!

Amos was a Republican. But then, most everybody around was. It was an average condition. Uncle Amos didn't have much to do except carry a torchlight when the Republican Presidents got elected, as they did regularly. And if Uncle Amos got grease on him, it never was very much grease, and his current wife took it out of him with her hot iron. Politics passed him by. Great events passed him by. And big taxes.

But we nephews did not pass him by. We were strangely drawn to him. Especially when some of our specialist uncles wore us down with their crankiness and difference. I spent some of the quietest Sundays of my life in Uncle Amos's yard, lying under apple trees and listening to bees and not listening to Uncle Amos who was bumbling away at something he did not expect me to listen to at all. And caterpillars came suddenly down on fine wires shining like gold, and hit Uncle Amos on his bald spot, and he brushed them off and went on bumbling. The heat was a burden, and the apple blossoms fell to pieces and drifted down on me, and I could see the roof of the world over the black twigs they came from. These were my solidest hours of pure being. I did not have to do anything to live up to this quiet, friendly man. He did not expect me to stand on my head and show off, or go after his pipe, or keep the flies from lighting on his bald spot. And he always had lemon drops somewhere deep in his roomy pockets, fore or aft, and he liked to give them to me.

The only trouble Uncle Amos had in his life was after he had got through with it. When they came to bury him, they could not fix it so he could lie next to all his three women. He had liked them all equally well. But there was not enough of Uncle Amos to go round. So they put him on the end of the row.

Uncle Amos did not mind, I am sure. I am sure he sleeps average well.

Uncle Aram and the Poem[2]

WILLIAM SAROYAN

I had fought everybody for so long at school, at home, and everywhere else that I was sick of it, and sick of myself. I believed the way to become healed was to get out of town.

It was July, 1926.

Soon I'd be eighteen years old, but still I was in Fresno, which I now hated.

I went up to Aram's office to see about getting paid for the occasional office work I had done for a year or more, which I can't pretend I had especially *minded* doing,

[2]From *Here Comes There Goes You Know Who* by William Saroyan. Copyright © 1961, by William Saroyan. Reprinted by permission of Trident Press, division of Simon & Schuster, Inc.

which in fact I had enjoyed doing. It had been better than nothing, so to say, but at the same time I had actually written a great many letters for him on the typewriter, I had run errands for him, I had announced his clients, I had asked them to wait when he was busy, and in general I had made myself useful.

Still, he hadn't ever handed me any money, except when he had sent me out for a cold watermelon from Long John, or a pound of pistachio nuts, or a leg of lamb for him to take home. Even when I had handed him the change he had invariably accepted all of it.

He was alone in his office when he looked up and saw me. I couldn't help noticing that he knew my visit was not a routine one. And I knew he was ready for me.

"Sit down," he said. "What's on your mind?"

"I want to get out of town."

"I think that's a good idea. You've been giving my sister a bad time long enough. Get out and stay out. When are you leaving?"

"Right away, but I haven't got any money."

"You don't need any money. Bums don't need any money. Go out to the S.P. and grab a freight, the way all the bums do."

"I thought you might pay me."

"For what?"

"For the work I did for you."

"Work *you* did for *me*? This place has been a college for you. You should pay me."

"Well, maybe, then, you'd *lend* me five dollars."

Well, here, for some reason, he went a little berserk, shouting first in English, then in Armenian, and finally in Turkish and Kurdish.

His voice was being heard all over the Rowell Building. The dentist next door stuck his head into the office expecting to say he had a very delicate piece of work to do and Aram was disturbing his patient, but Aram shouted at him before he could open his mouth, which soon enough fell open with astonishment.

"Get out, you dentist. Don't come into this office. This is a place of business. Get back where you belong, and drill your rotten teeth."

And now he felt required to imitate the sound of the drill, saying, "Bzzzz, bzzzz, bzzzz, all day long. Open wider, please. Wider, please. Bzzzz, bzzzz, bzzzz. Get out of here with your dainty little washed hands."

The instant the dentist's face disappeared, before the door was even fully shut, he came right back at me.

Inside, in spite of the anger I felt, I was laughing, because the man was crazy, but very funny.

Now, though, when he renewed the attack, I couldn't take it in silence any more, and I began to shout back at him, only louder than he was shouting.

"For God's sake, what kind of a man are you, anyway? You made a fortune last year and you're going to make a bigger fortune this year. I worked for you. Every penny I've earned I gave to my mother. I can't go to her and ask her for money. What are you shouting at me for?"

Now, after I said each of these things, he shouted a nullifying reply, making a kind of ridiculous duet.

All of the windows on the court of the Rowell Building were being lifted by typists, bookkeepers, dentists, lawyers, fruit shippers, and others, and everybody knew who was shouting: the Armenians, the Saroyans, Aram and his nephew Willie.

When I said, "For God's sake, what kind of a man are you?", Aram said, "A great man, you jackass, not a jackass like you."

"You made a fortune last year."

"Bet your life I did, more than you or anybody else will ever know."

"And you're going to make a bigger fortune this year."

"The biggest yet in every way, shape, manner and form."

"I worked for you."

"You *shit—that's* what you did."

"Every penny I've ever earned I gave to my mother."

"That poor girl has been driven mad by your foolishness. You want to be a writer. Get money in a bank and write *checks,* that's the way to be a writer. That's the kind of writer *I* am, not a stupid poem writer. *The moon is sinking in the sea.* The moon is sinking in your empty head, that's where the moon is sinking. (This of course was his swiftest idea of poetry, and of course there's no telling where he had gotten it from.) You gave her a few pennies, so you could eat six or seven times a day; and sleep in a warm bed in your own room, and get free hotel service. Don't talk to me about giving my sister money. Your *pennies?*"

"I can't go to her and ask her for money."

"Bet your life you can't. You've got to go to the bank for money, the way I do. Tell them what you want it for—to be a bum—and they'll give it to you. But if they don't, they'll give you a blotter. You can always use a blotter, can't you?"

"What are you shouting at me for?"

"Because you're a disgrace to my family. To my sister. To the Saroyan family. Now, get out of here."

For some reason all of a sudden I thought of my father. Surely nobody had ever spoken to him that way, if in fact anybody had ever shouted at him, but I got the feeling that they had actually. Who wanted *The moon is sinking in the sea?* Who wanted any part of such nonsense? This was America. This was California. This was Fresno. This was the real world, not the world of the moon and the sea.

I knew I wasn't going to get any money, so there was no point in shouting any more. I just didn't know how to get money, even money I had earned, or at any rate *believed* I had earned, but perhaps I was mistaken, perhaps he was right, perhaps I owed him money for having gone to college in his office, and so the first thing I must do is earn some money and pay him. It didn't help at all that he was famous all over town as the most open-handed man of wealth among the Armenians. He donated, officially, to everything that came along, and he made generous handouts to all kinds of needy Armenians because they knew how to get money from him. They knew how to get him to write a check, and they always cried out with feigned astonishment, "A hundred dollars, Aram? Really, I had hoped for no more than ten."

Hushed, earnest, a little astonished, but still respectful, I left his office and sneaked out of the building, taking the stairs so I wouldn't have to face the elevator operator or anybody who might be in the elevator.

Despite their feelings about their uncles, writers Robert Coffin and William Saroyan were able to achieve a degree of objectivity, to stand back and observe their subjects' strengths and weaknesses. In writing about a closer relative, such detachment is rarely possible, for in viewing them the writer sees and feels the edges of his or her own life. Thus, a character sketch of a parent or grandparent is likely to be emotional—a paean of praise, perhaps, as in the e. e. cummings piece that follows; or a projection of past miseries, as in W. B. Yeats's essay about his grandfather; or a biting candor, as in Mary

McCarthy's piece about her grandmother. Interestingly and typically, all three essays tell us something about the writers as well as about the persons being written about.

My Father[3]

E. E. CUMMINGS

My father . . . was a New Hampshire man, 6 foot 2, a crack shot & a famous fly-fisherman & a firstrate sailor (his sloop was named The Actress) & a woodsman who could find his way through forests primeval without a compass & a canoeist who'd still-paddle you up to a deer without ruffling the surface of a pond & an ornithologist & taxidermist & (when he gave up hunting) an expert photographer (the best I've ever seen) & an actor who portrayed Julius Caesar in Sanders Theatre & a painter (both in oils & watercolors) & a better carpenter than any professional & an architect who designed his own houses before building them & (when he liked) a plumber who just for the fun of it installed all his own waterworks & (while at Harvard) a teacher with small use for professors—by whom (Royce, Lanman, Taussig, etc.) we were literally surrounded (but not defeated)—& later (at Doctor Hale's socalled South Congregational really Unitarian church) a preacher who announced, during the last war, that the Gott Mit Uns boys were in error since the only thing which mattered was for man to be on God's side (& one beautiful Sunday in Spring remarked from the pulpit that he couldn't understand why anyone had come to hear him on such a day) & horribly shocked his pewholders by crying "the Kingdom of Heaven is no spiritual roofgarden: it's inside you" & my father had the first telephone in Cambridge & (long before any Model T Ford) he piloted an Orient Buckboard with Friction Drive produced by the Waltham watch company & my father sent me to a certain public school because its principal was a gentle immense coalblack negress & when he became a diplomat (for World Peace) he gave me & my friends a tremendous party up in a tree at Sceaux Robinson & my father was a servant of the people who fought Boston's biggest & crookedest politician fiercely all day & a few evenings later sat down with him cheerfully at the Rotary Club & my father's voice was so magnificent that he was called on to impersonate God speaking from Beacon Hill (he was heard all over the common) & my father gave me Plato's metaphor of the cave with my mother's milk.

Grandfather[4]

WILLIAM BUTLER YEATS

Some of my misery was loneliness and some of it fear of old William Pollexfen my grandfather. He was never unkind, and I cannot remember that he ever spoke harshly to me, but it was the custom to fear and admire him. He had won the freedom of some Spanish city, for saving life perhaps, but was so silent that his wife never knew it till he was near eighty, and then from the chance visit of some old sailor. She asked him if it was true and he said it was true, but she knew him too well to question and his old shipmate had left the town. She too had the habit of fear. We knew that he had

[3]Reprinted by permission of the publishers from e. e. cummings, *i: Six Nonlectures*. Cambridge, Mass.: Harvard University Press, Copyright, 1953, by E. E. Cummings.

[4]Reprinted with permission of The Macmillan Company from *Autobiographies* by William Butler Yeats. Copyright 1916, 1936 by The Macmillan Company, renewed 1944 by Bertha Georgie Yeats.

been in many parts of the world, for there was a great scar on his hand made by a whaling-hook, and in the dining-room was a cabinet with bits of coral in it and a jar of water from the Jordan for the baptizing of his children and Chinese pictures upon rice-paper and an ivory walking-stick from India that came to me after his death. He had great physical strength and had the reputation of never ordering a man to do anything he would not do himself. He owned many sailing ships and once, when a captain just come to anchor at Rosses Point reported something wrong with the rudder, had sent a messenger to say "Send a man down to find out what's wrong." "The crew all refuse," was the answer, and to that my grandfather answered, "Go down yourself," and not being obeyed, he dived from the main deck, all the neighbourhood lined along the pebbles of the shore. He came up with his skin torn but well informed about the rudder. He had a violent temper and kept a hatchet at his bedside for burglars and would knock a man down instead of going to law, and I once saw him hunt a party of men with a horsewhip. He had no relation for he was an only child and, being solitary and silent, he had few friends. He corresponded with Campbell of Islay who had befriended him and his crew after a shipwreck, and Captain Webb, the first man who had swum the Channel and who was drowned swimming the Niagara Rapids, had been a mate in his employ and a close friend. That is all the friends I can remember and yet he was so looked up to and admired that when he returned from taking the waters at Bath his men would light bonfires along the railway line for miles; while his partner William Middleton whose father after the great famine had attended the sick for weeks, and taken cholera from a man he carried in his arms into his own house and died of it, and was himself civil to everybody and a cleverer man than my grandfather, came and went without notice. I think I confused my grandfather with God, for I remember in one of my attacks of melancholy praying that he might punish me for my sins, and I was shocked and astonished when a daring little girl—a cousin I think—having waited under a group of trees in the avenue, where she knew he would pass near four o'clock on the way to his dinner, said to him, "If I were you and you were a little girl, I would give you a doll."

Yet for all my admiration and alarm, neither I nor any one else thought it wrong to outwit his violence or his rigour; and his lack of suspicion and something helpless about him made that easy while it stirred our affection. When I must have been still a very little boy, seven or eight years old perhaps, an uncle called me out of bed one night, to ride the five or six miles to Rosses Point to borrow a railway-pass from a cousin. My grandfather had one, but thought it dishonest to let another use it, but the cousin was not so particular. I was let out through a gate that opened upon a little lane beside the garden away from ear-shot of the house, and rode delighted through the moonlight, and awoke my cousin in the small hours by tapping on his window with a whip. I was home again by two or three in the morning and found the coachman waiting in the little lane. My grandfather would not have thought such an adventure possible, for every night at eight he believed that the stable-yard was locked, and he knew that he was brought the key. Some servant had once got into trouble at night and so he had arranged that they should all be locked in. He never knew, what everybody else in the house knew, that for all the ceremonious bringing of the key the gate was never locked.

Even to-day when I read *King Lear* his image is always before me and I often wonder if the delight in passionate men in my plays and in my poetry is more than his memory. He must have been ignorant, though I could not judge him in my childhood, for he had run away to sea when a boy, "gone to sea through the hawse-hole" as he phrased it, and I can but remember him with two books—his Bible and Falconer's *Shipwreck,* a little green-covered book that lay always upon his table.

My Grandmother[5]

MARY McCARTHY

Luckily, I am writing a memoir and not a work of fiction, and therefore I do not have to account for my grandmother's unpleasing character and look for the Oedipal fixation or the traumatic experience which would give her that clinical authenticity that is nowadays so desirable in portraiture. I do not know how my grandmother got the way she was; I assume, from family photographs and from the inflexibility of her habits, that she was always the same, and it seems as idle to inquire into her childhood as to ask what was ailing Iago or look for the error in toilet-training that was responsible for Lady Macbeth. My grandmother's sexual history, bristling with infant mortality in the usual style of her period, was robust and decisive: three tall, handsome sons grew up, and one attentive daughter. Her husband treated her kindly. She had money, many grandchildren, and religion to sustain her. White hair, glasses, soft skin, wrinkles, needlework—all the paraphernalia of motherliness were hers; yet it was a cold, grudging, disputatious old woman who sat all day in her sunroom making tapestries from a pattern, scanning religious periodicals, and setting her iron jaw against any infraction of her ways.

Combativeness was, I suppose, the dominant trait in my grandmother's nature. An aggressive churchgoer, she was quite without Christian feeling; the mercy of the Lord Jesus had never entered her heart. Her piety was an act of war against the Protestant ascendancy. The religious magazines on her table furnished her not with food for meditation but with fresh pretexts for anger; articles attacking birth control, divorce, mixed marriages, Darwin, and secular education were her favorite reading. The teachings of the Church did not interest her, except as they were a rebuke to others; "Honor thy father and thy mother," a commandment she was no longer called upon to practice, was the one most frequently on her lips. The extermination of Protestantism, rather than spiritual perfection, was the boon she prayed for. Her mind was preoccupied with conversion; the capture of a soul for God much diverted her fancy—it made one less Protestant in the world. Foreign missions, with their overtones of good will and social service, appealed to her less strongly; it was not a *harvest* of souls that my grandmother had in mind.

This pugnacity of my grandmother's did not confine itself to sectarian enthusiasm. There was the defense of her furniture and her house against the imagined encroachments of visitors. With her, this was not the gentle and tremulous protectiveness endemic in old ladies, who fear for the safety of their possessions with a truly touching anxiety, inferring the fragility of all things from the brittleness of their old bones and hearing the crash of mortality in the perilous tinkling of a tea cup. My grandmother's sentiment was more autocratic: she hated having her chairs sat in or her lawns stepped on or the water turned on in her basins, for no reason at all except pure officiousness; she even grudged the mailman his daily promenade up her sidewalk. Her home was a center of power, and she would not allow it to be derogated by easy or democratic usage. Under her jealous eye, its social properties had atrophied, and it functioned in the family structure simply as a political headquarters. Family conferences were held there, consultations with the doctor and the clergy; refractory children were brought there for a lecture or an interval of thought-taking; wills were read and loans negotiated and emissaries from the Protestant faction on state occasions received. The family had no friends, and entertaining was held to be a foolish and unnecessary courtesy as between blood relations. Holiday dinners fell, as a duty, on the lesser members of the organization: the daughters and daughters-in-law (converts from the false religion) offered up Baked Alaska on a platter, like the head of John the Baptist, while the old people sat enthroned at the table, and only their digestive processes acknowledged, with rumbling, enigmatic salvos, the festal day.

A Famous Person

The following essay on a famous composer, whose identity is concealed until almost the end of the piece, is a study in monstrous egotism. Filled with biographical details that hold the reader in fascinated suspense, the essay concludes with a controversial view of genius.

The Monster[6]

DEEMS TAYLOR

He was an undersized little man, with a head too big for his body—a sickly little man. His nerves were bad. He had skin trouble. It was agony for him to wear anything next to his skin coarser than silk. And he had delusions of grandeur.

He was a monster of conceit. Never for one minute did he look at the world or at people, except in relation to himself. He was not only the most important person in the world, to himself; in his own eyes he was the only person who existed. He believed himself to be one of the greatest dramatists in the world, one of the greatest thinkers, and one of the greatest composers. To hear him talk, he was Shakespeare, and Beethoven, and Plato, rolled into one. And you would have had no difficulty in hearing him talk. He was one of the most exhausting conversationalists that ever lived. An evening with him was an evening spent in listening to a monologue. Sometimes he was brilliant; sometimes he was maddeningly tiresome. But whether he was being brilliant or dull, he had one sole topic of conversation: himself. What *he* thought and what *he* did.

He had a mania for being in the right. The slightest hint of disagreement, from anyone, on the most trivial point, was enough to set him off on a harangue that might last for hours, in which he proved himself right in so many ways, and with such exhausting volubility, that in the end his hearer, stunned and deafened, would agree with him, for the sake of peace.

It never occurred to him that he and his doing were not of the most intense and fascinating interest to anyone with whom he came in contact. He had theories about almost any subject under the sun, including vegetarianism, the drama, politics, and music; and in support of these theories he wrote pamphlets, letters, books . . . thousands upon thousands of words, hundreds and hundreds of pages. He not only wrote these things, and published them—usually at somebody else's expense—but he would sit and read them aloud, for hours, to his friends and his family.

He wrote operas; and no sooner did he have the synopsis of a story, but he would invite—or rather summon—a crowd of his friends to his house and read it aloud to them. Not for criticism. For applause. When the complete poem was written, the friends had to come again, and hear *that* read aloud. Then he would publish the poem, sometimes years before the music that went with it was written. He played the piano like a composer, in the worst sense of what that implies, and he would sit down at the piano before parties that included some of the finest pianists of his time, and play for them, by the hour, his own music, needless to say. He had a composer's voice. And he would invite eminent vocalists to his house, and sing them his operas, taking all the parts.

He had the emotional stability of a six-year-old child. When he felt out of sorts, he would rave and stamp, or sink into suicidal gloom and talk darkly of going to the East to end his days as a Buddhist monk. Ten minutes later, when something pleased him, he would rush out of doors and run around the garden, or jump up and down on the sofa or stand on his head. He could be grief-stricken over the death of a pet dog, and he could be callous and heartless to a degree that would have made a Roman emperor shudder.

He was almost innocent of any sense of responsibility. Not only did he seem incapable of supporting himself, but it never occurred to him that he was under any obligation to do so. He was convinced that the world owed him a living. In support of this belief, he borrowed money from everybody who was good for a loan—men, women, friends, or strangers. He wrote begging letters by the score, sometimes groveling without shame, at others loftily offering his intended benefactor the privilege of contributing to his support, and being mortally offended if the recipient declined the honor. I have found no record of his ever paying or repaying money to anyone who did not have a legal claim upon it.

What money he could lay his hands on he spent like an Indian rajah. The mere prospect of a performance of one of his operas was enough to set him to running up bills amounting to ten times the amount of his prospective royalties. On an income that would reduce a more scrupulous man to doing his own laundry, he would keep two servants. Without enough money in his pocket to pay his rent, he would have the walls and ceilings of his study lined with pink silk. No one will ever know—certainly he never knew—how much money he owed. We do know that his greatest benefactor gave him $6,000 to pay the most pressing of his debts in one city, and a year later had to give him $16,000 to enable him to live in another city without being thrown into jail for debt.

He was equally unscrupulous in other ways. An endless procession of women marches through his life. His first wife spent twenty years enduring and forgiving his infidelities. His second wife had been the wife of his most devoted friend and admirer, from whom he stole her. And even while he was trying to persuade her to leave her first husband he was writing to a friend to inquire whether he could suggest some wealthy woman—*any* wealthy woman—whom he could marry for her money.

He was completely selfish in his other personal relationships. His liking for his friends was measured solely by the completeness of their devotion to him, or by their usefulness to him, whether financial or artistic. The minute they failed him—even by so much as refusing a dinner invitation—or began to lessen in usefulness, he cast them off without a second thought. At the end of his life he had exactly one friend left whom he had known even in middle age.

He had a genius for making enemies. He would insult a man who disagreed with him about the weather. He would pull endless wires in order to meet some man who admired his work, and was able and anxious to be of use to him—and would proceed to make a mortal enemy of him with some idiotic and wholly uncalled-for exhibition of arrogance and bad manners. A character in one of his operas was a caricature of one of the most powerful music critics of his day. Not content with burlesquing him, he invited the critic to his house and read him the libretto aloud in front of his friends.

The name of this monster was Richard Wagner. Everything that I have said about him you can find on record—in newspapers, in police reports, in the testimony of people who knew him, in his own letters, between the lines of his autobiography. And the curious thing about this record is that it doesn't matter in the least.

Because this undersized, sickly, disagreeable, fascinating little man was right all the time. The joke was on us. He *was* one of the world's great dramatists; he *was* a great thinker; he *was* one of the most stupendous musical geniuses that, up to now, the world has ever seen. The world did owe him a living. People couldn't know those things at the time, I suppose; and yet to us, who know his music, it does seem as though they should have known. What if he did talk about himself all the time? If he had talked about himself for twenty-four hours every day for the span of his life he would not have uttered half the number of words that other men have spoken and written about him since his death.

When you consider what he wrote—thirteen operas and music dramas, eleven of them still holding the stage, eight of them unquestionably worth ranking among the world's great musico-dramatic masterpieces—when you listen to what he wrote, the debts and heartaches that people had to endure from him don't seem much of a price. Eduard Hanslick, the critic whom he caricatured in *Die Meistersinger* and who hated him ever after, now lives only because he was caricatured in *Die Meistersinger*. The women whose hearts he broke are long since dead; and the man who could never love anyone but himself has made them deathless atonement, I think, with *Tristan und Isolde.* Think of the luxury with which for a time, at least, fate rewarded Napoleon, the man who ruined France and looted Europe; and then perhaps you will agree that a few thousand dollars' worth of debts were not too heavy a price to pay for the *Ring* trilogy.

What if he was faithless to his friends and to his wives? He had one mistress to whom he was faithful to the day of his death: Music. Not for a single moment did he ever compromise with what he believed, with what he dreamed. There is not a line of his music that could have been conceived by a little mind. Even when he is dull, or downright bad, he is dull in the grand manner. There is greatness about his worst mistakes. Listening to his music, one does not forgive him for what he may or may not have been. It is not a matter of forgiveness. It is a matter of being dumb with wonder that his poor brain and body didn't burst under the torment of the demon of creative energy that lived inside him, struggling, clawing, scratching to be released; tearing, shrieking at him to write the music that was in him. The miracle is that what he did in the little space of seventy years could have been done at all, even by a great genius. Is it any wonder that he had no time to be a man?

A Type

Up to this point, the essays cited in this chapter have dealt with individuals; we have yet to examine the *type,* or *character.* Character writing is a very old and popular literary form, going back to the fourth century B.C., when the Greek philosopher Theophrastus wrote probing analyses of the different types of people he observed around him—"both good and bad." Unfortunately, the good portraits have been lost, and we are left with such tiresome but familiar types as the following:

The Unseasonable Man[7]
THEOPHRASTUS

Unseasonableness is an annoying faculty for choosing the wrong moment.

The unseasonable man is the kind who comes up to you when you have no time to spare and asks your advice. He sings a serenade to his sweetheart when she has influenza. Just after you have gone bail for somebody and had to pay up, he approaches you with a request that you will go bail for him. If he is going to give evidence he turns up when judgement has just been pronounced. When he is a guest at a wedding he makes derogatory remarks about the female sex. When you have just reached home after a long journey he invites you to come for a stroll. He is certain to bring along a buyer who offers more, when you have just sold your house. When people have heard a matter and know it by heart, he stands up and explains the whole thing from the beginning. He eagerly undertakes a service for you which you don't want performed but which you have not the face to decline. When people are sacrificing and spending money, he arrives to ask for his interest on a loan. When a friend's slave is being beaten he will stand there and tell how he once had a slave who hanged himself after a similar beating. If he takes part in an arbitration, he will set everyone at blows again just when both sides are ready to cry quits. And after dancing once he will seize as partner another man who is not yet drunk.

An up-to-date version of a tiresome type, the self-consciously modern, oh-so-chic reader of that self-consciously modern, oh-so-chic *Cosmopolitan* magazine, is scathingly satirized in the following essay.

That Cosmopolitan Girl[8]
DONALD BARTHELME

Must a girl always be protected by a man? Not this girl! When I lived in California I sometimes picked a man up in *my* car for a date if his was in the garage, loaned to a friend or—my car was in better shape! (No, he wasn't emasculated and we stayed friends.) Last week at J.F.K. I carried one of *Stephen's* bags. He was loaded with golf clubs and I only had a garment bag and a Vuitton. (No, I *didn't* throw my back out and Stephen and I are still together!) Isn't it silly to try to preserve old clichés when naturalness and freedom are so much better?
—*Adv. for* Cosmopolitan *in* The N.Y. Times.

Of course the next day when *Stephen* picked me up for dinner at Vuitton, looking *hysterically* handsome in his Vuitton coveralls, I was a shade taken aback when he literally *demanded* that I pay for the cab. (He always used to do little things like that as a matter of course!) Well, I paid cheerfully, because I have this magazine I read that teaches me how to be *natural* and *healthy* and *resilient,* but then when we got out of the cab he *loaded* this *immense* steamer trunk on my back. I said, "*Stephen,* what are you *doing?*" He said, "Just get it inside, dollbaby." Well, I don't know if

---

[7]From *The Characters* by Theophrastus, translated by Philip Vellacott. Copyright 1967 by Philip Vellacott. Reprinted by permission of Penguin Books Ltd.

[8]Reprinted with the permission of Farrar, Straus & Giroux, Inc., from *Guilty Pleasures* by Donald Barthelme, Copyright © 1963, 1964, 1965, 1966, 1968, 1969, 1970, 1971, 1972, 1973, 1974 by Donald Barthelme; "That Cosmopolitan Girl" originally appeared in *The New Yorker*.

you've ever marched into Vuitton with a Vuitton steamer trunk on your back, huffing and puffing and bent half double, but I can tell you *this,* it makes you feel kind of *weird.* But I *coped*—I just pretended I was some kind of super-soigné woman *mover!* (It's *silly* to preserve the old clichés about roles and such when *naturalness* and *freedom* and *health* are so much better but this time I *did* throw my back out!) We got a good table in spite of the steamer trunk because *Stephen* has this absolutely *wizardly* way with the V. headwaiters, and we ordered our own very special-together drink, nitroglycerin and soda (because of Stephen's really abso-lutely *unique* heart condition—he's the only person in the *whole world* who has it!), and I was beginning to feel all glow-y and comfortable, except that my back was positively *ruined,* because of carrying the steamer trunk. "Why are you twitching like that?" Stephen asked (a tiny bit crossly, I thought) and I explained to him that my back hurt. Usually he is the living *soul* of *compassion*—really *sweet*—but this time all he said was "If you didn't spend all your time reading that damned *magazine,* and *italicizing* every third word in your sentences, you'd have a *strong, healthy* back, just like your mother did. I'm going to get you a *washtub* and a wash*board* for your birthday. I bet you don't even know what a washboard *looks* like. I bet you never even saw one outside of a *jug band.*" (I thought that bit about my *italicizing* words was a bit *cruel,* because *he* does it *too*—all the *time!*) But I just gave him a quick grin and an impish, sort of *California* look, and asked if I could have another N & S. "You picking up the bloody *tab?*" he asked, a teeny bit viciously, I thought. But then I remembered that *men* have their little moods, just like women, and that *Stephen* is in very heavy trouble at the *office* right now, due to that nasty S.E.C. investigation, just because he tipped off a couple of hundred clients about the receivership ahead of time, but for heaven's sake, he was just trying to be *loyal* to his *friends.* So I just said offhandedly, "Sure." But then he reached over and began to unlatch the steamer trunk, which was still standing by the table, and I noticed that all the waiters and captains and *busboys* had begun to gather around, to see what was *inside!* (I guess their curiosity was normal and healthy and lovable, but it made me feel just the least most microcosmic bit *itchy!*) And what *was* inside you would never fathom in a thousand years! It was *another woman!* "Get up," Stephen said to me. "This is Elberta and I want to sit next to her." Well, I almost crumbled into *matchsticks,* as you can *imagine,* but I just acted *natural* as hard as I could, and that was easier because she was *wearing* the most peculiar *creation* you could possibly conjure up in your wildest dreams—I think it's called a *housedress.* I nearly *died* laughing, inside of course (outside I was still being natural and healthy, even though my back was giving me *pure unshirted hell*), and even smiled at the thought that my carrying the steamer trunk into the restaurant on my back hadn't emasculated Stephen *one little bit*—as a matter of fact he was sort of *feeling* Elberta's handbag, which looked like it was made of an old armadillo shell or something, in a manner that was downright *lascivious.* Well, I must admit that I was in the most *infinitesimal* bit of a twit, so I dipped into my Vuitton and brought out my copy of the current issue of the magazine to see if the advice columns had anything à *propos,* if there was any strong, natural, *lovable* way to deal with this rather *hideous* situation, but all of the writers seemed to be *preoccupied* with the problems of unmarried mothers this month, and that wasn't my problem, and *Stephen* was talking with Elberta in low tones that I couldn't hear, although I tried, so I reached over and patted Elberta on the hand, the hand that was curled around one of *our* drinks, and asked her in the *nicest* possible way what magazine she read, what magazine she identified with, what magazine *defined* her, because of course I was *insanely* curious about how she achieved that really *phony* wholesomeness that she *exuded* all over Stephen like a *web* or something. She just looked at me and said, "*Scientific American,* dearie."

An Interview Subject

Another way to describe a person, popular in newspapers and magazines, is through the interview, a form of feature story which focuses on a single individual, pointing out those distinguishing qualities which make that person special and newsworthy. The interview generally contains a liberal sampling of direct quotations, which give readers a sense of the subject's speech and presence. The interview below, for example, will appeal to everyone who has ever enjoyed elephants at the circus (which probably means everyone!). More than that, this interview provides a picture of a person whose affection for elephants is so intense that it has literally become his dominant trait, the trait that defines him.

Elephant Boy, 65, Remembers 50 Years with Circus[9]
IRVING SPIEGEL

For most of the year, Ray Moreau, wearing a flame-proof suit and goggles, stands over vats of sodium at the Du Pont plant in Niagara Falls. But yesterday, when the circus opened at Madison Square Garden, Ray Moreau was Sabu the Elephant Boy. It is a role he has been playing for the last 50 years.

Is there a better way to spend a vacation [than by taking care of elephants—] talking to them, living with them?

"People like to go fishing, I like elephants," he explains. "Tigers are beautiful, but what is to compare to elephants, first, last, and always? They are personalities, they're unique, and they care more about each other than people do."

While the fearless men and women in spangled costume fly above the throngs, the 65-year-old Sabu with his jaunty beret, his goatee and elephant boots is backstage, unheard by the crowds, saying to the elephants: "Easy Puppe, now, now Rani, move up Eva, good girl, Mary."

"Remember, I'm not a trainer. I'm a tender," the volunteer elephant boy says. "I shoveled for six years before they let me use the hook. I got to know the big fellows individually by their rear ends and it was a long time before I knew what they looked like up front."

In this role, Mr. Moreau has traveled the continent as far west as Anaheim, Calif., and as far south as Mexico City. He has worked under the direction of such elephant trainers as Walter McLean, Benny White, Arkie Scott, Hugo Schmitt, Axel Gauntier and now Gunther Gebel-Williams, the leading animal trainer of the circus's bicentennial edition.

"When I join my big friends, they remember me. They take one sniff and they know it is me," he says.

To his wife, Betty, and his daughter, Margaret, he is "our Sabu." He is "Sabu" to the circus family. "I bathe the elephants in mineral oil to preserve their skin. I dust them, they love me, I love them," he says. "My home is a cot near them."

Ray Moreau was born in Auburn, N.Y., in a tent when the circus was in town. His father, the late Georges Moreau, was the Big Show's bookkeeper. When he was 12, he was taken in tow by the elephant trainer, who dubbed him Sabu—a name dating to the original Sanskrit meaning "elephant boy."

Ray Moreau will be back with the sodium vats in Niagara Falls in two weeks, but not for long. The circus is going there, too.

"It's a nice feeling," he said, "parading with the elephants in your hometown and all your friends shouting 'There goes our Sabu.'"

An interviewer like Rex Reed, another of the "new journalists," will probe more deeply into a subject, trying to extract not only the motivating force but the subtlest essence of his or her personality, which the interviewer may then use as the basis of a story. Reed's interview with actress Ava Gardner, excerpted below, has become a classic of its kind. Indeed, Tom Wolfe has said of Rex Reed that he

raised the celebrity interview to a new level through his frankness and his eye for social detail. He has also been a master at capturing a story line in the interview situation itself—in this case by picturing Ava Gardner as the aging star demanding star treatment. Reed occasionally uses the first person but never obtrusively; more on the order of Nick Carraway in *The Great Gatsby,* even when, as in this case, the interviewer—himself—becomes a factor in the story. Reed is excellent at recording and using dialogue.[10]

Ava: Life in the Afternoon[11]

REX REED

She stands there, without benefit of a filter lens against a room melting under the heat of lemony sofas and lavender walls and cream-and-peppermint-striped movie-star chairs, lost in the middle of that gilt-edge birthday-cake hotel of cupids and cupolas called the Regency. There is no script. No Minnelli to adjust the Cinema-Scope lens. Ice-blue rain beats against the windows and peppers Park Avenue below as Ava Gardner stalks her pink malted-milk cage like an elegant cheetah. She wears a baby-blue cashmere turtleneck sweater pushed up to her Ava elbows and a little plaid mini-skirt and enormous black horn-rimmed glasses and she is gloriously, divinely barefoot.

Elbowing his way through the mob of autograph hunters and thrill seekers clustered in the lobby, all the way up in the gilt-encrusted elevator, the press agent Twentieth Century-Fox has sent along murmurs, "She doesn't see *anybody,* you know," and "You're very lucky, you're the only one she asked for." Remembering, perhaps, the last time she had come to New York from her hideout in Spain to ballyhoo *The Night of the Iguana* and got so mad at the press she chucked the party and ended up at Birdland. And nervously, shifting feet under my Brooks Brothers polo coat, I remember too all the photographers at whom she allegedly threw champagne glasses (there is even a rumor that she shoved one Fourth Estater off a balcony!), and—who could forget, Charlie?—the holocaust she caused the time Joe Hyams showed up with a tape recorder hidden in his sleeve.

Now, inside the cheetah cage without a whip and trembling like a nervous bird, the press agent says something in Spanish to the Spanish maid. "Hell, I've been there ten years and I still can't speak the goddam language," says Ava, dismissing him with a wave of the long porcelain Ava arms. "*Out!* I don't need press agents." The eyebrows

[10]From *The New Journalism* (New York: Harper & Row, 1973), p. 56.
[11]From *Do You Sleep in the Nude?* (New York: New American Library, 1968).

angle under the glasses into two dazzling, sequined question marks. "Can I trust him?" she asks, grinning that smashing Ava grin, and pointing at me. The press agent nods, on his way to the door: "Is there anything else we can do for you while you're in town?"

"Just get me *out* of town, baby. Just get me *outta* here."

ASSIGNMENTS

Class Discussion and Paragraph Suggestions

(See Chapter 27 for methods of composing unified, adequately developed paragraphs.)

1. Consider Coffin's "average" uncle.

   a. In the first paragraph the author calls his uncle the "averagest" man he ever knew. Is there such a word? In what way does its use establish the tone and point of view of the piece?
   b. Characterize the kind of person who could make you agree with something he said and, an hour later (as Coffin tells us in paragraph two), make you think *you* had said it.
   c. List the "average" characteristics attributed to the uncle. Are there any suggestions that he may not have been so average after all?

2. Compare the sketches of the two uncles.

   a. What kind of person was each (personality, distinctive traits of character)?
   b. What was the impact of each uncle on his nephew's life?
   c. What is the tone and style of each essay?

3. Contemplate and comment upon cummings' virtuoso one-sentence essay, noting in particular the striking selection of details, the parenthetic additions, and the final statement: "my father gave me Plato's metaphor of the cave with my mother's milk." What does this mean?

4. Write a one-sentence paragraph characterizing an unusual person you know.

5. Consider Yeats's "Grandfather."

   a. What is formidable and what is helpless about the grandfather?
   b. What does the "daring little girl" who asks for a doll contribute to the narration?
   c. In what ways is the grandfather like King Lear?

6. Consider "My Grandmother" by Mary McCarthy.
   a. What is "unpleasant" about the grandmother?
   b. Does she have any redeeming features?
   c. What do you infer to be McCarthy's attitude toward her grandmother?

7. Consider "The Monster" by Deems Taylor.

   a. Evaluate the effectiveness of paragraph one: concrete details, length of sentences.
   b. Do the succeeding paragraphs build suspense? In what way? Cite specific points of interest.
   c. Does the piece lose anything when the identity of the subject is revealed?
   d. Do you agree with Taylor's conclusion that because Wagner was a genius, "The world did owe him a living"?

8. Write a one-paragraph statement (150–250 words) of your opinion on the subject of whether the world owed Wagner a living. State your position in an opening topic sentence; develop it with specific reasons and details.

9. Write a twentieth-century version (150–250 words) of "The Unseasonable Man" or of a comparable type.

10. Itemize the characteristics of the "Cosmopolitan Girl" that Barthelme is spoofing.

11. Reread the "Elephant Boy" interview, inferring, from the information given and the direct quotations, what specific questions the interviewer addressed to his subject.

12. Make up a list of questions designed to draw out a particular aspect of the personality of someone in your class (five minutes). Ask these questions of your neighbor in an adjoining seat (five minutes); think about what you have discussed, framing more specific questions which could help you to round out the tentative impressions you have gleaned (five minutes); address these questions to your neighbor, jotting down direct quotes or relevant bits of information (five minutes). Write a one- or two-paragraph interview-sketch (150–250 words, ten minutes). Present it to the class.

13. Analyze the Reed interview, noting details of setting, descriptive details, background information, direct quotations, tone, voice of writer.

14. Write a character sketch (150–250 words) based on the photograph below.

Essay Suggestions

1. In an essay (500–1,000 words) explain what kind of person a friend or relative is. Try to focus on one dominant quality that, in your view, characterizes the person (as avariciousness characterized Uncle Aram). Present your character in action (as does Saroyan). In other words, set your character sketch within the form of narration.

2. Write an essay (500–750 words) about someone you both fear and admire, as Yeats did his grandfather.

3. Write a character sketch (500–1,000 words) of a well-known, widely admired musical or artistic genius (like Wagner).

4. Write a character sketch (500–750 words) based on one of the following types, using seventeenth-century style if you choose.

Virtues	*Vices*
The Reliable	The Fool
The Efficient	The Opportunist
The Mature	The Chronic Complainer
The Generous	The Calamity Jane
The Sincere	The Hypocrite
The Learned	The Bore
The Wise	The Flirt
The Helpful	
The Fun-loving	
The Courageous	
The Independent	

5. Write a satirical sketch (500–1,000 words) of a character comparable to "That Cosmopolitan Girl."

6. Interview someone whose personality or occupation makes him or her seem a promising candidate for a character sketch. Write up the interview as a feature story (500–750 words).

16 What Is My Personal Response to X?

One of the most common and popular types of writing is the so-called personal or familiar essay, an informal, discursive piece in which you describe your response to some aspect of your surroundings: an object, situation, or event; a fleeting thought or observation; an emotion, opinion, or reaction. This type of essay is friendly, perhaps intimate in tone; personal, perhaps even confessional in nature. The writer, rather than the subject of the essay, is of central significance. Indeed, the success of your personal essays will depend largely on your personality. Are you sensitive and perceptive? Do you see things with a fresh eye and clear spirit? Do you respond in a recognizably human way? Can readers feel for you—and with you?

An essay revolving around one's own personal responses is not easy to write, but it is generally rewarding and may even be therapeutic. People need to "talk," to tell their secrets within the frame of literary form. Here, then, is another human use of writing: the personal or familiar essay. At its best it enables people to see the many ways in which they are essentially alike.

The Personal or Familiar Essay

A Mood Essay

Consider the following essay, for example, by a master of the form, J. B. Priestley. A curious and fragile situation has created a mood of deep melancholy. Through an open window he has heard the strains of a harmonica, or "mouth organ" as the British call it. Somehow he is filled with indescribable longing and sadness, the kind all of us have felt at different times.

On a Mouth-Organ[1]

J. B. PRIESTLEY

For the past half hour, someone, probably a small boy, has been playing a mouth-organ underneath my window. I know of no person under this roof peculiarly susceptible to the sound of a mouth-organ, so that I cannot think that the unknown musician is serenading. He is probably a small boy who is simply hanging about, after the fashion of his mysterious tribe, and whiling away the time with a little music. Why he should choose a raw day like this on which to do nothing but slide his lips over the cold metal of a mouth-organ must remain a mystery to me; but I have long realised that unfathomable motives may be hidden away behind the puckered fact and uncouth gestures of small boyhood.

I have not been able to recognise any of the tunes, or the snatches of tunes, which have come floating up to my window. Possibly they are all unknown to me. But I think it is more likely that they are old acquaintances, coming in such a questionable shape that my ear cannot find any familiar cadence; they have been transmuted by the mouth-organ into something rich and strange; for your mouth-organ is one of the great alchemists among musical instruments and leaves no tune as it finds it.

It has been pointed out that whatever material Dickens used, however rich and varied it might be, it was always mysteriously transformed into the Dickens sub-stance, lengths of which he cut off and called Novels. It seems to me that the mouth-organ, though a mechanical agent, has something of this strange power of transfor-mation; whatever is played upon it seems to come out all of a piece; whatever might be the original character of the tunes, gay, fantastical, meditative, stirring, as their sounds are filtered through the little square holes of the instrument, their character changes, and they all become more or less alike. "Rule, Britannia!" "Annie Laurie," and the latest ditty of the music-halls somehow or other lose their individuality and flow into one endless lament, one lugubrious strain, that might very well go on for ever.

For this reason, the sound of a mouth-organ has always succeeded in depressing me. It must have been invented by an incorrigible pessimist, who sought to create a musical instrument that would give to every tune, no matter how lively, some touch of his own hopeless view of life; and probably the only time that he laughed was when he realised that he could leave this thing as a legacy to the world. I have never played a mouth-organ because I know that my own native optimism would not be strong enough to resist the baneful influence of the music it makes. To hear it now and again is more than enough for me.

To one who is filled with the joy of life—a small boy, for example—such hopeless strains may prove only invigorating, may serve as a wholesome check upon his ebullient spirits, like the skeleton at the Egyptian feasts. But to most of us weaker brethren, frail in spirit, music that is unillumined by even a glimmer of hope is intolerable.

For the past half hour, I have been trying to concentrate all my attention upon some fairly cheerful matter, and I have failed. It has been impossible to keep out the

---

sound of this mouth-organ. Its formless, unknown, unending tune, only fit for bewailing a ruined world, has gradually invaded my room, penetrated through the ear into my brain, and coloured or discoloured all the thoughts there. There is in it no trace of that noble sadness which great music, like great poetry, so often brings with it; the mouth-organ knows nothing of "divine despair." It seems to whimper before "the heavy and the weary weight of all this unintelligible world."

"Oh de-ar!" I seem to hear it crying, "No hope for yo-ou and yo-ours; me-eserable world! Oh de-ear!" It has brought with it a fog of depression; my spirits have been sinking lower and lower; and under the influence of this evil mangler of good, heartening tunes I have begun to think that life is not worth living.

Most music worthy of the name has such beauty that it will either raise us to a kind of ecstasy or give us a feeling of vague sadness, which some delicate persons prefer to wild joy. Sir Thomas Browne, you remember, has something to say on this point, in a passage that can never become hackneyed no matter how many times it is quoted: "Whosoever is harmonically composed delights in harmony; which makes me much distrust the symmetry of those heads which declaim against all church music. For myself, not only from my obedience, but my particular genius, I do embrace it; for even that vulgar and tavern-music, which makes one man merry, another mad, strikes in me a deep fit of devotion, and a profound contemplation of the first composer."

But these mouth-organ strains will make a man neither mad nor merry, nor yet strike in him a deep fit of devotion; but if his ear is like mine, they will make him sink into depression and dye his world a ghastly blue.

It is curious that certain other popular musical instruments seem to have the same characteristics as the mouth-organ. The concertina and the accordion, good friends of the sailor, the lonely colonist, and rough, kindly fellows the world over, seem to me to possess the same power of transforming all the tunes played upon them into one long wail. I have read about their "lively strains," but I have never heard them. The sound of a concertina a quarter of a mile away is enough to shake my optimism. An average accordion could turn the Sword Theme from *Siegfried* into a plea for suicide. A flageolet or a tin-whistle has not such a shattering effect; nevertheless, both of them can only give a tune a certain subdued air, which is certainly preferable to the depressing alchemy of the other instruments, but which certainly does not make for liveliness.

The bagpipe, which has been so long the companion of the lonely folk of northern moors and glens, can produce at times a certain rousing martial strain, but, even then, a wailing air creeps into the music like a Scotch mist. Its very reels and strathspeys, which ought to be jolly enough, only sound to me like elaborate complaints against life; their transitory snatches of gaiety are obviously forced. At all other times, the bagpipe is frankly pessimistic, and laments its very existence.

There is probably some technical reason why these instruments produce such doleful tones. Perhaps our sophisticated ears rebel against their peculiar harmonies and discords. But it is certainly curious that mouth-organs, concertinas, tin-whistles, and the rest, so beloved of simple people, should be intolerable to so many of us. Is it that we have no miseries to express in sound? Or is it that our optimism is so brittle that we dare not submit it to the onslaught of this strange music? I do not know.

All that I do know is that at the present moment I am sitting in my armchair before a bright fire, depressed beyond belief by the sound that floats through my window; while outside, in the cold, there stands a small boy, holding a mouth-organ in his numbed hands and bravely sliding his lips over the cold metallic edges of the thing; and by this time he is probably as gay as I am miserable.

Thus the personal essayist talks to us—as our friend, with no need to stand on ceremony. Loosely organized, flowing as smoothly as the mind and pen, the personal essay is a relaxed form, usually brief and tentative in tone, for it is searching for answers, not giving them. The writer is sharing his or her thoughts with us; they may not even be rational thoughts, and this the writer will freely admit. Why should the "strange music" of a mouth organ send one into a "fog of depression"? "I do not know," says Priestley, implicitly returning the question: Do *you* know? Have *you* ever been unaccountably moved by some slight, seemingly innocuous circumstance? The personal essay's musings may linger unresolved in the mind of the reader.

A Protest

Another kind of personal response involves a protest against something going on in the world—an issue, an attitude—that the writer finds objectionable. One such piece is James Thurber's personal response to a verbal habit that annoyed him. In this essay Thurber establishes a tone of dour humor, thereby maintaining that double vision that characterized his response to life: he was forever laughing with tears in his eyes or bristling with amused and amiable irritation.

The Spreading "You Know"[2]

JAMES THURBER

The latest blight to afflict the spoken word in the United States is the rapidly spreading reiteration of the phrase *"you* know." I don't know just when it began moving like a rainstorm through the language, but I tremble at its increasing garbling of meaning, ruining of rhythm, and drumming upon my hapless ears. One man, in a phone conversation with me last summer, used the phrase thirty-four times in about five minutes, by my own count; a young matron in Chicago got seven *"you* knows" into one wavy sentence, and I have also heard it as far west as Denver, where an otherwise charming woman at a garden party in August said it almost as often as a whippoorwill says, "Whippoorwill." Once, speaking of whippoorwills, I was waked after midnight by one of those feathered hellions and lay there counting his chants. He got up to one hundred and fifty-eight and then suddenly said, "Whip—" and stopped dead. I like to believe that his mate, at the end of her patience, finally let him have it.

My unfortunate tendency to count *"you* knows" is practically making a female whippoorwill out of me. Listening to a radio commentator, not long ago, discussing the recent meeting of the United Nations, I thought I was going mad when I heard him using "you know" as a noun, until I realized that he had shortened United Nations Organization to UNO and was pronouncing it, you know, as if it were *"you* know."

A typical example of speech *you*-knowed to death goes like this. "The other day I saw, you know, Harry Johnson, the, you know, former publicity man for, you know,

[2]Copyright © 1961 James Thurber. From *Lanterns and Lances*, published by Harper and Row. Originally printed in *The New Yorker*. Reprinted by permission of Helen Thurber.

the Charteriss Publishing Company, and, you know, what he wanted to talk about, strangely enough, was, you know, something you'd never guess. . . ."

This curse may have originated simultaneously on Broadway and in Hollywood, where such curses often originate. About twenty-five years ago, or perhaps longer, theatre and movie people jammed their sentences with "you know what I mean?" which was soon shortened to "you *know?*" That had followed the over-use, in the 1920's, of "you see?" or just plain "see?" These blights often disappear finally, but a few have stayed and will continue to stay, such as "Well" and "I mean to say" and "I mean" and "The fact is." Others seem to have mercifully passed out of lingo into limbo, such as, to go back a long way, "Twenty-three, skiddoo" and "So's your old man" and "I don't know nothin' from nothin'" and "Believe you me." About five years ago both men and women were saying things like "He has a new Cadillac job with a built-in bar deal in the back seat" and in 1958 almost everything anybody mentioned, or even wrote about, was "triggered." Arguments were triggered, and allergies, and divorces, and even love affairs. This gun-and-bomb verb seemed to make the jumpiest of the jumpy even jumpier, but it has almost died out now, and I trust that I have not triggered its revival.

It was in Paris, from late 1918 until early 1920, that there was a glut—an American glut, to be sure—of "You said it" and "You can say that again," and an American Marine I knew, from Montana, could not speak any sentence of agreement or concurrence without saying, "It *is,* you *know.*" Fortunately, that perhaps original use of *"you know"* did not seem to be imported into America.

I am reluctantly making notes for a possible future volume to be called *A Farewell to Speech* or *The Decline and Fall of the King's English.* I hope and pray that I shall not have to write the book. Maybe everything, or at least the language, will clear up before it is too late. Let's face it, it better had, that's for sure, and I don't mean maybe.

An Appreciation

In an opposite temper, the writer may express a warm personal response to an aspect of life—to solitude, for example, which poet-novelist May Sarton assures us is not loneliness, but rather "the salt of personhood."

Rewards of Living a Solitary Life[3]

MAY SARTON

The other day an acquaintance of mine, a gregarious and charming man, told me he had found himself unexpectedly alone in New York for an hour or two between appointments. He went to the Whitney [Museum of American Art] and spent the "empty" time looking at things in solitary bliss. For him it proved to be a shock nearly as great as falling in love to discover that he could enjoy himself so much alone.

What had he been afraid of, I asked myself? That, suddenly alone, he would discover that he bored himself, or that there was, quite simply, no self there to meet? But having taken the plunge, he is now on the brink of adventure; he is about to be launched into his own inner space, space as immense, unexplored and sometimes frightening as outer space to the astronaut.

[3]From *The New York Times,* 8 April 1975. © 1975 by The New York Times Company. Reprinted by permission.

His every perception will come to him with a new freshness and, for a time, seem startlingly original. For anyone who can see things for himself with a naked eye becomes, for a moment or two, something of a genius.

With another human being present vision becomes double vision, inevitably. We are busy wondering, what does my companion see or think of this, and what do I think of it? The original impact gets lost, or diffused.

"Music I heard with you was more than music." Exactly. And therefore music *itself* can only be heard alone. Solitude is the salt of personhood. It brings out the authentic flavor of every experience.

"Alone one is never lonely: the spirit adventures, waking/In a quiet garden, in a cool house, abiding single there."

Loneliness is most acutely felt with other people, for with others, even with a lover sometimes, we suffer from our differences, differences of taste, temperament, mood. Human intercourse often demands that we soften the edge of perception, or withdraw at the very instant of personal truth for fear of hurting, or of being inappropriately present, which is to say naked, in a social situation. Alone we can afford to be wholly whatever we are, and to feel whatever we feel absolutely. That is a great luxury!

For me the most interesting thing about a solitary life, and mine has been that for the last twenty years, is that it becomes increasingly rewarding. When I can wake up and watch the sun rise over the ocean, as I do most days, and know that I have an entire day ahead, uninterrupted, in which to write a few pages, take a walk with my dog, lie down in the afternoon for a long think (why does one think better in a horizontal position?), read and listen to music, I am flooded with happiness.

I am lonely only when I am overtired, when I have worked too long without a break, when for the time being I feel empty and need filling up. And I am lonely sometimes when I come back home after a lecture trip, when I have seen a lot of people and talked a lot, and am full to the brim with experience that needs to be sorted out.

Then for a little while the house feels huge and empty, and I wonder where my self is hiding. It has to be recaptured slowly by watering the plants, perhaps, and looking again at each one as though it were a person, by feeding the two cats, by cooking a meal.

It takes a while, as I watch the surf blowing up in fountains at the end of the field, but the moment comes when the world falls away, and the self emerges again from the deep unconscious, bringing back all I have recently experienced to be explored and slowly understood, when I can converse again with my own hidden powers, and so grow, and so be renewed, till death do us part.

The Short-Short Personal Essay

To say that the personal essay is a relaxed form is not to say that it is formless; rather, it proceeds according to a psychological rather than a logical movement. There is an idea, a mood, or a feeling lurking unexpressed in the writer's mind. He or she does not know exactly what it is, but tries to recreate it on paper. The words tumble forth. They make patterns, which the writer hopes will correspond to the pattern of the experience.

Critic Herbert Read noted that this process is comparable to musical improvisation. It is also "the counterpart of the lyric in poetry."[4] Thus we have such brief utterances—spontaneous, intimate, evanescent—as Logan Pearsall Smith's *Trivia,* reprinted below. These are miniature essays that capture, in little space, a fleeting moment of time, a mood, a state of mind, an unexpected but unforgettable upsurge of feeling. Note that sometimes the writer addresses us directly ("I fade from your vision, Reader . . ."); sometimes he soliloquizes, as in a diary ("I secretly write this Book, which They will never read"). In either case, we *hear* the writer's voice.

All Trivia[5]

LOGAN PEARSALL SMITH

Under an Umbrella

From under the roof of my umbrella I saw the washed pavement lapsing beneath my feet, the news-posters lying smeared with dirt at the crossings, the tracks of the busses in the liquid mud. On I went through this world of wetness. And through what long perspectives of the years shall I still hurry down wet streets—middle-aged, and then, perhaps, very old? And on what errands?

Asking myself this question I fade from your vision, Reader, into the distance, sloping my umbrella against the wind.

They

Their taste is exquisite; They live in Palladian houses, in a world of ivory and precious china, of old brickwork and stone pilasters. In white drawing-rooms I see Them, or on blue, bird-haunted lawns. They talk pleasantly of me, and Their eyes watch me. From the diminished, ridiculous picture of myself which the glass of the world gives me, I turn for comfort, for happiness to my image in the kindly mirror of those eyes.

Who are They? Where, in what paradise of palace, shall I ever find Them? I may walk all the streets, ring all the door-bells of the World, but I shall never find Them. Yet nothing has value for me save in the crown of Their approval for Their coming— which will never be—I build and plant, and for Them alone I secretly write this Book, which They will never read.

Green Ivory

What a bore it is, waking up in the morning always the same person. I wish I were Unflinching and emphatic, and had big, bushy eyebrows and a Message for the Age. I wish I were a deep Thinker, or a great Ventriloquist.

I should like to be refined-looking and melancholy, the victim of a hopeless passion; to love in the old, stilted way, with impossible Adoration and Despair under the pale-faced Moon.

I wish I could get up; I wish I were the world's greatest living Violinist. I wish I had lots of silver, and first Editions, and green ivory.

[4]Herbert Read, *Modern Prose Style* (Boston: Beacon Press, 1952), p. 66.
[5]From *All Trivia* by Logan Pearsall Smith, copyright, 1933, 1934, by Harcourt Brace Jovanovich, Inc.; copyright, 1961, 1962 by John Russell. Reprinted by permission of the publisher.

Things to Write

What things there are to write, if one could only write them! My mind is full of gleaming thoughts; gay moods and mysterious, moth-like meditations hover in my imagination, fanning their painted wings. They would make my fortune if I could catch them; but always the rarest, those freaked with azure and the deepest crimson, flutter away beyond my reach.

The ever-baffled chase of these filmy nothings often seems, for one of sober years in a sad world, a trifling occupation. But have I not read of the great Kings of Persia who used to ride out to hawk for butterflies, nor deemed this pastime beneath their royal dignity?

The Journal Entry

Many professional writers, as well as plain people who have never thought of themselves as writers, like to keep a journal: a record of observations, impressions, feelings, ideas, reflections, meditations, dreams, and memories; snatches of dialogue (spoken or overheard); brief accounts of people, places, and events. As was indicated in Chapter 14 (p. 196, "The Diary as Narration"), a journal can serve a variety of purposes and take a number of forms.

If you begin to keep a journal, you will soon find that the challenge of making regular entries stimulates the senses to see and hear more clearly, to respond and recognize. The keeper of a journal must be perpetually alive and aware of what is going on both inside and outside the self. Even a limited world bursts into vivid life when reported through the clear eyes and keen sensibilities of Sei Shōnagon, a young woman living at the imperial court in tenth century Japan. Sei Shōnagon kept a pillow book, so called because its entries, hastily dashed off at night before going to sleep, were slipped into a box placed under the pillow. The delicate and lively account of things that interested, attracted, pleased, and displeased Sei Shōnagon as she proceeded with her daily affairs is an ideal reminder of how one person, making an honest and sensitive record of his or her own life, can speak to generations that follow. This is the mark of a good journal: though it is a highly personal document, it has more than personal significance; it may be read with pleasure and profit and a quickened sense of life by people living in vastly different places and periods.

Pillow Book[6]

SEI SHŌNAGON

I Enjoy Watching

I enjoy watching the officials when they come to thank the Emperor for their new appointments. As they stand facing His Majesty with their batons in their hands, the trains of their robes trailing along the floor . . . , they make obeisance and begin their ceremonial movements with great animation.

[6]From *The Pillow Book of Sei Shōnagon*, ed. Ivan Morris (New York: Columbia University Press, 1967). Penguin edition, 1971, pp. 34, 40, 44–45, 67, 81.

Depressing Things

A dog howling in the daytime. . . . A lying-in room when the baby has died. An ox-driver who hates his oxen. A scholar whose wife has one girl after another.

Hateful Things

One is in a hurry to leave, but one's visitor keeps chatting away. If it is someone of no importance, one can get rid of him by saying, "You must tell me all about it next time"; but should it be the sort of visitor whose presence commands one's best behavior, the situation is hateful indeed. . . .

I hate the sight of men in their cups who shout, poke their fingers in their mouths, stroke their beards, and pass on the wine to their neighbors with great cries of "Have some more! Drink up!" . . .

One is just about to be told some interesting piece of news when a baby starts crying.

A flight of crows circle about with loud caws.

An admirer has come on a clandestine visit, but a dog catches sight of him and starts barking. One feels like killing the beast. . . .

A man with whom one is having an affair keeps singing the praises of some woman he used to know. Even if it is a thing of the past, this can be very annoying. . . .

I cannot stand people who leave without closing the panel behind them.

Things That Cannot Be Compared

Summer and winter. Night and day. Rain and sunshine. Youth and age. A person's laughter and his anger. Black and white. Love and hatred. The little indigo plant and the great philodendron. Rain and mist.

When one has stopped loving somebody, one feels that he has become someone else, even though he is still the same person. . . .

Things That Give a Pathetic Impression

The voice of someone who blows his nose while he is speaking.
The expression of a woman plucking her eyebrows.

Splendid Things

Chinese brocade. A sword with a decorated scabbard. The grain of wood in a Buddhist statue. Long flowering branches of beautifully colored wistaria entwined about a pine tree. . . .
The Empress's birth chamber.
Grape colored material.
Anything purple is splendid.
A large garden all covered with snow.

ASSIGNMENTS

Class Discussion and Paragraph Suggestions

(See Chapter 27 for methods of composing unified, adequately developed paragraphs.)

1. Reread the entries from *The Pillow Book* and compose an entry of your own under each of the same headings.

   Other categories in *The Pillow Book* to which you might address yourself in your own journal include:

   > Elegant Things
   > Insects
   > Unsuitable Things
   > Nothing Can Be Worse Than . . .
   > Poetic Subjects
   > Herbs and Shrubs
   > Rare Things
   > Shameful Things
   > Awkward Things
   > Times When One Should Be on One's Guard

2. The effectiveness of a personal essay depends on the authenticity of the writer's voice. Does that voice speak in a natural rhythm that you can *hear?* Is it distinctively and recognizably the writer's own? Is a suitable tone established and maintained throughout the essay? How do you derive from this tone a sense of how the writer feels about his or her subject and how he or she wants *you* to feel?

   Since the writer is the unifying thread running through the piece, it is important that he or she play a clear and consistent role. Before attempting to write your own personal essays, it will be helpful to analyze those in this chapter so that you can see exactly how these writers have achieved their special effects and made their essays work.

   a. In a sentence or two summarize the substance and what you believe to be the writer's purpose in each essay.
   b. In a sentence tell why you think the writer has or has not succeeded in achieving his or her purpose.
   c. In terms of the following rhetorical features, show how the writer establishes and maintains an attitude and tone of voice appropriate to his or her purpose.
      1. words

         > precision of nouns, verbs, adjectives
         > concreteness
         > levels of usage
         > connotation
         > repetition
         > sound

      2. sentences

         > construction (word order, economy, emphasis, main and subordinate ideas)
         > length
         > variety
         > rhythm and balance (use of parallelism, antithesis)
         > texture
         > opening and closing sentences

      3. choice of examples and illustrations
      4. citing of authorities
      5. use of images
      6. use of figurative language
      7. use of irony
      8. use of allusions
      9. smoothness of transitions

3. William Hazlitt (1778–1830), an early master of the familiar style, recorded and defined it as follows:

It is not easy to write a familiar style. Many people mistake a familiar for a vulgar style, and suppose that to write without affectation is to write at random. On the contrary, there is nothing that requires more precision, and, if I may so say, purity of expression, than the style I am speaking of. It utterly rejects not only all unmeaning pomp, but all low, cant phrases, and loose, unconnected, *slipshod* allusions. It is not to take the first word that offers, but the best word in common use; it is not to throw words together in any combinations we please, but to follow and avail ourselves of the true idiom of the language. To write a genuine familiar or truly English style, is to write as any one would speak in common conversation, who had a thorough command and choice of words, or who could discourse with ease, force and perspicuity, setting aside all pedantic and oratorical flourishes.

Comment on Hazlitt's description of the familiar style, explaining what is meant by the following terms:

   a. familiar versus vulgar
   b. unmeaning pomp
   c. low, cant phrases
   d. *slipshod* allusions
   e. the true idiom of our language
   f. ease, force, and perspicuity
   g. pedantic and oratorical flourishes

4. Write three or four short-short essays in the manner of Logan Pearsall Smith's *Trivia*. Use his titles, as listed below, or titles of your own.

Happiness	Social Success
The Sound of a Voice	Appearance and Reality
At the Window	Self-Analysis
Self-Control	A Grievance
Joy	Comfort
Terror	Talk
The Rose	The Incredible
Faces	Chairs
Reflections	Somewhere
The Stars	The Pear
The Spider	

Essay Suggestions

1. As J. B. Priestley describes his emotional response to a strain of music, describe in an essay (500–750 words) some chance occurrence that elicited a strong emotional response from you.

2. As James Thurber protests "the spreading *you know*," write an essay (500–750 words) describing your negative response to some trend or innovation in our culture.

3. Write an "appreciation"—like Sarton's "rewards"—of a particular life style or of some aspect of your life, past or present, large or small. Books have provided a subject for many fine personal appreciations, for they tend to elicit strong feelings and long-lasting attachments. A. A. Milne, for example, paid tribute to Kenneth Grahame's *The Wind in the Willows* as the kind of book a young man gives to his fiancée—and if she does not like it, he breaks the engagement. In this spirit of appreciation, you may be moved to describe the distinctive appeal of one of your childhood favorites.

4. During his lifetime Hazlitt wrote essays on the subjects listed below, most of them collected in his *Table Talk: Opinions on Books, Men, and Things.* Choose one topic and write your own piece (500–750 words).

> On Prejudice
> On Disagreeable People
> On the Want of Money
> On Reading New Books
> Of Persons One Would Wish to Have Seen
> On Going on a Journey
> On the Pleasure of Painting
> On the Ignorance of the Learned
> On the Fear of Death
> On Sitting for One's Picture
> On Fashion
> On Nicknames
> On Public Opinion
> On Personal Identity
> Dreams
> The Qualifications Necessary to Success in Life
> Envy
> Egotism
> Hot and Cold
> The Pleasure of Hating

17 What Is My Memory of X?

"It is necessary to remember and necessary to forget, but it is better for a writer to remember." So said William Saroyan in a truism worth repeating, for it points to a large body of literature built upon "remembrance of things past."

The Quality of Memory

No writer had a more prodigious memory than Thomas Wolfe, whose novels are distinguished by his genius for conjuring up sense impressions from the past: sounds, sights, odors, colors, shapes—the very texture of experience reexperienced in memory. In a remarkable and revealing account of his creative process, Wolfe described the compulsive memory which, with its shattering intensity, drove him "night and day."

The Quality of Memory[1]
THOMAS WOLFE

The quality of my memory is characterized, I believe, in a more than ordinary degree by the intensity of its sense impressions, its power to evoke and bring back

[1]Reprinted with the permission of Charles Scribner's Sons from *The Story of a Novel*, pages 31–35, by Thomas Wolfe. Copyright 1936 Charles Scribner's Sons; renewal copyright © 1964 Paul Gitlen, Administrator C.T.A.

the odors, sounds, colors, shapes, and feel of things with concrete vividness. Now [during a summer in Paris] my memory was at work night and day, in a way that I could at first neither check nor control and that swarmed unbidden in a stream of blazing pageantry across my mind, with the million forms and substances of the life that I had left, which was my own, America. I would be sitting, for example, on the terrace of a cafe watching the flash and play of life before me on the Avenue de l'Opéra and suddenly I would remember the iron railing that goes along the board-walk at Atlantic City. I could see it instantly just the way it was, the heavy iron pipe; its raw galvanized look; the way the joints were fitted together. It was all so vivid and concrete that I could feel my hand upon it and know the exact dimensions, its size and weight and shape. And suddenly I would realize that I had never seen any railing that looked like this in Europe. And this utterly familiar, common thing would suddenly be revealed to me with all the wonder with which we discover a thing which we have seen all our life and yet have never known before. Or again, it would be a bridge, the look of an old iron bridge across an American river, the sound the train makes as it goes across it; the spoke-and-hollow rumble of the ties below; the look of the muddy banks; the slow, thick, yellow wash of an American river; an old flat-bottomed boat half filled with water stogged in the muddy bank; or it would be, most lonely and haunting of all the sounds I know, the sound of a milk wagon as it entered an American street just at the first gray of the morning, the slow and lonely clopping of the hoof upon the street, the jink of bottles, the sudden rattle of a battered old milk can, the swift and hurried footsteps of the milkman, and again the jink of bottles, a low word spoken to his horse, and then the great, slow, clopping hoof receding into silence, and then quietness and a bird song rising in the street again. Or it would be a little wooden shed out in the country two miles from my home town where people waited for the street car, and I could see and feel again the dull and rusty color of the old green paint and see and feel all of the initials that had been carved out with jackknives on the planks and benches within the shed, and smell the warm and sultry smell so resinous and so thrilling, so filled with a strange and nameless excitement of unknown joy, a coming prophecy, and hear the street car as it came to a stop, the moment of brooding, drowzing silence; a hot thrum and drowsy stitch at three o'clock; the smell of grass and hot sweet clover; and then the sudden sense of absence, loneliness and departure when the street car had gone and there was nothing but the hot and drowsy stitch at three o'clock again.

Or again, it would be an American street with all its jumble of a thousand ugly architectures. It would be Montague Street or Fulton Street in Brooklyn, or Eleventh Street in New York, or other streets where I had lived; and suddenly I would see the gaunt and savage webbing of the elevated structure along Fulton Street, and how the light swarmed through in dusty, broken bars, and I could remember the old, familiar rusty color, that incomparable rusty color that gets into so many things here in America.

Wolfe's memory was, of course, a phenomenon, a miracle—cited here simply to indicate the far reaches of an ability that all of us possess to some degree. Most of us can *remember*, in other words, but only vaguely and in snatches. Images do not ordinarily loom up on their own, "in a stream of blazing pageantry." If we ask ourselves the question "What is my memory of X?" we must make a conscious and sustained effort to recover the past. It is not waiting on the surface of the mind, ready to be recalled in all its original concreteness and intensity.

Even so, those of us with a less natural endowment than Wolfe's can—by probing and pondering and digging beneath the surface layers of consciousness—recapture scattered episodes and experiences; they are there to be recalled if bidden. They do need prodding, however, and in Chapter 22, "Gathering Information," specific methods of prodding are discussed (pp. 334–36).

Remembering Childhood Experiences

Even without prodding, is there anyone who does not remember at least one teacher, classmate, incident, event, feeling or fear, pleasure or pain associated with that most impressionable period of life, that central experience of childhood—going to school?

Notice that in the essay that follows, Laurie Lee vividly recounts his rural boyhood through the judicious selection of descriptive details: the particular chants actually recited in his small village school, the exact roll call of classmates ("Walt Kerry, Bill Timbrell, Spadge Hopkins"; you can hear the names resounding in the long-ago air). By the use of such concrete sensory details (see Chapter 2, "How Can X Be Described?") the writer evokes a past reality, the "lively reek of steaming life: boys' boots, girls' hair, stoves and sweat"—the very *feel* of an experience. Only in this way can the writer put us into the situation so that we can experience it ourselves in somewhat the same way he or she did.

The Village School[2]
LAURIE LEE

The village school [in Gloucestershire in the 1920s] provided all the instruction we were likely to ask for. It was a small stone barn divided by a wooden partition into two rooms—the Infants and the Big Ones. There was one dame teacher, and perhaps a young girl assistant. . . . Our village school was poor and crowded, but in the end I relished it. It had a lively reek of steaming life: boys' boots, girls' hair, stoves and sweat, blue ink, white chalk and shavings. We learnt nothing abstract or tenuous there—just simple patterns of facts and letters, portable tricks of calculation, no more than was needed to measure a shed, write out a bill, read a swine-disease warning. Through the dead hours of the morning, through the long afternoons, we chanted away at our tables. Passers-by could hear our rising voices in our bottled-up room on the bank: "Twelve-inches-one-foot. Three-feet-make-a-yard. Fourteen-pounds-make-a-stone. Twelve-stone-a-hundred-weight." We absorbed these figures as primal truths declared by some ultimate power. Unhearing, unquestioning, we rocked to our chanting, hammering the gold nails home. "Twice-two-are-four. One-God-is-Love. One-Lord-is-King. One-King-is-George. One-George-is-Fifth . . ." So it was always, had been, would be for ever; we asked no questions; we didn't hear what we said; yet neither did we ever forget it.

[2]From *The Edge of Day: A Boyhood in the West of England* by Laurie Lee. Copyright © 1959 by Laurie Lee. Reprinted by permission of William Morrow and Company, Inc. and The Hogarth Press. (First published in Great Britain under the title *Cider with Rosie*.)

So do I now, through the reiterations of those days, recall that school-room which I scarcely noticed—Miss Wardley in glory on her high desk throne, her long throat tinkling with glass. The bubbling stove with its chink of red fire, the old world map as dark as tea; dead field-flowers in jars on the windowsills; the cupboard yawning with dog-eared books. Then the boys and the girls, the dwarfs and the cripples; the slow fat ones and the quick bony ones; giants and louts, angels and squinters—Walt Kerry, Bill Timbrell, Spadge Hopkins, Clergy Green, the Ballingers and Browns, Betty Gleed, Clarry Hogg, Sam and Sixpence, Rose and Jo—were ugly and beautiful, scrofulous, warted, ringwormed and scabbed at the knees; we were noisy, crude, intolerant, cruel, stupid and superstitious. But we moved together out of the clutch of the fates, inhabitors of a world without doom; with a scratching, licking and chewing of pens, a whisper and passing of jokes, a titter of tickling, a grumble of labour, a vague stare at the wall in a dream.

As we remember school days, so we may remember those interludes separating school years one from another—the summers of our childhood. If there was a sameness about them (every year at the beach, or at camp, or at home) they may seem, in retrospect, one single happy or unhappy blur. But if one summer was marked off from the others by an "electric" discovery, as it was for playwright Moss Hart, then that summer will stand out from the rest, never to be forgotten. To share that memorable experience with others, the writer must try not merely to tell about it, but to render it dramatically, in narrative form, as it happened. The writer must also try to conjure up many descriptive details in order to give the piece the closest possible semblance of reality, to make readers feel that they are *there*.

A Memorable Summer[3]

MOSS HART

A city child's summer is spent in the street in front of his home, and all through the long summer vacations I sat on the curb and watched the other boys on the block play baseball or prisoner's base or gutter hockey. I was never asked to take part even when one team had a member missing—not out of any special cruelty, but because they took it for granted I would be no good at it. They were right, of course. Yet much of the bitterness and envy and loneliness I suffered in those years could have been borne better if a single wise teacher or a knowledgeable parent had made me understand that there were compensations for the untough and the nonathletic; that the world would not always be bounded by the curbstone in front of the house.

One of those compensations I blundered into myself, and its effect was electric on both me and the tough world of the boys on the block. I have never forgotten the joy of that wonderful evening when it happened. There was no daylight-saving in those days, and the baseball and other games ended about eight or eight thirty, when it grew dark. Then it was the custom of the boys to retire to a little stoop that jutted out from the candy store on the corner and that somehow had become theirs through tribal right. No grownup ever sat there or attempted to. There the boys would sit,

[3]From *Act One*, by Moss Hart. Copyright © 1959 by Catherine Carlisle Hart and Joseph M. Hyman, Trustees. Reprinted by permission of Random House, Inc.

talking aimlessly for hours on end. There were the usual probings of sex and dirty jokes, not too well defined or clearly understood; but mostly the talk was of the games played during the day and of the game to be played tomorrow. Ultimately, long silences would fall and then the boys would wander off one by one. It was just after one of those long silences that my life as an outsider changed, and for one glorious summer I was accepted on my own terms as one of the tribe. I can no longer remember which boy it was that summer evening who broke the silence with a question; but whoever he was, I nod to him in gratitude now. "What's in those books you're always reading?" he asked idly. "Stories," I answered. "What kind?" asked somebody else without much interest.

Nor do I know what impelled me to behave as I did, for usually I just sat there in silence, glad enough to be allowed to remain among them; but instead of answering his question, I launched full tilt into the book I was immersed in at the moment. The book was *Sister Carrie* and I told them the story of Sister Carrie for two full hours. They listened bug-eyed and breathless. I must have told it well, but I think there was another and deeper reason that made them so flattering an audience. Listening to a tale being told in the dark is one of the most ancient of man's entertainments, but I was offering them as well, without being aware of doing it, a new and exciting experience.

The books they themselves read were the *Rover Boys* or *Tom Swift* or G. A. Henty. I had read them too, but at thirteen I had long since left them behind. Since I was much alone I had become an omnivorous reader and I had gone through the books-for-boys-series in one vast gulp. In those days there was no intermediate reading material between children's and grownups' books, or I could find none, and since there was no one to say me nay, I had gone right from *Tom Swift and His Flying Machine* to Theodore Dreiser and *Sister Carrie.* Dreiser had hit my young mind and senses with the impact of a thunderbolt, and they listened to me tell the story with some of the wonder that I had had in reading it.

It was, in part, the excitement of discovery—the discovery that there could be another kind of story that gave them a deeper kind of pleasure than the *Rover Boys*—blunderingly, I was giving them a glimpse of the riches contained outside the world of *Tom Swift.* Not one of them left the stoop until I had finished, and I went upstairs that wonderful evening not only a member of the tribe but a figure in my own right among them.

The next night and many nights thereafter, a kind of unspoken ritual took place. As it grew dark, I would take my place in the center of the stoop and, like Scheherazade, begin the evening's tale. Some nights, in order to savor my triumph more completely, I cheated. I would stop at the most exciting part of a story by Jack London or Frank Norris or Bret Harte, and without warning tell them that that was as far as I had gone in the book and it would have to be continued the following evening. It was not true, of course; but I had to make certain of my new-found power and position, and with a sense of drama that I did not know I possessed, I spun out the long summer evenings until school began in the fall. Other words of mine have been listened to by larger and more fashionable audiences, but for that tough and grimy one that huddled on the stoop outside the candy store, I have an unreasoning affection that will last forever. It was a memorable summer, and it was the last I was to spend with the boys on the block.

Similarly, Thomas Merton recalls an episode in his adolescence that left its mark on his later life.

I Fall in Love[4]

THOMAS MERTON

In three months, the summer of 1931, I suddenly matured like a weed.

I cannot tell which is the more humiliating: the memory of the half-baked adolescent I was in June or the glib and hard-boiled specimen I was in October when I came back to Oakham full of a thorough and deep-rooted sophistication of which I was both conscious and proud.

The beginning was like this: Pop wrote to me to come to America. I got a brand-new suit made. I said to myself, "On the boat I am going to meet a beautiful girl, and I am going to fall in love."

So I got on the boat. The first day I sat in a deck chair and read the correspondence of Goethe and Schiller which had been imposed on me as a duty, in preparation for the scholarship examinations at the university. What is worse, I not only tolerated this imposition but actually convinced myself that it was interesting.

The second day I had more or less found out who was on the boat. The third day I was no longer interested in the Goethe and Schiller. The fourth day I was up to my neck in the trouble that I was looking for.

It was a ten-day boat.

I would rather spend two years in a hospital than go through that anguish again! That devouring, emotional, passionate love of adolescence that sinks its claws into you and consumes you day and night and eats into the vitals of your soul! All the self-tortures of doubt and anxiety and imagination and hope and despair that you go through when you are a child, trying to break out of your shell, only to find yourself in the middle of a legion of full-armed emotions against which you have no defense! It is like being flayed alive. No one can go through it twice. This kind of a love affair can really happen only once in a man's life. After that he is calloused. He is no longer capable of so many torments. He can suffer, but not from so many matters of no account. After one such crisis he has experience and the possibility of a second time no longer exists, because the secret of the anguish was his own utter guilelessness. He is no longer capable of such complete and absurd surprises. No matter how simple a man may be, the obvious cannot go on astonishing him for ever.

I was introduced to this particular girl by a Catholic priest who came from Cleveland and played shuffleboard in his shirt sleeves without a Roman collar on. He knew everybody on the boat in the first day, and as for me, two days had gone by before I even realized that she was on board. She was traveling with a couple of aunts and the three of them did not mix in with the other passengers very much. They kept to themselves in their three deck chairs and had nothing to do with the gentlemen in tweed caps and glasses who went breezing around and around the promenade deck.

When I first met her I got the impression that she was no older than I was. As a matter of fact she was about twice my age: but you could be twice sixteen without being old, as I now realize, sixteen years after the event. She was small and delicate and looked as if she were made out of porcelain. But she had big wide-open California eyes and was not afraid to talk in a voice that was at once ingenuous and independent and had some suggestion of weariness about it as if she habitually stayed up too late at night.

To my dazzled eyes she immediately became the heroine of every novel and I all

---

[4]From *Seven Storey Mountain* by Thomas Merton, copyright 1948, by Harcourt Brace Jovanovich, Inc., and reprinted with their permission.

but flung myself face down on the deck at her feet. She could have put a collar on my neck and led me around from that time forth on the end of a chain. Instead of that I spent my time telling her and her aunts all about my ideals and my ambitions and she in her turn attempted to teach me how to play bridge. And that is the surest proof of her conquest, for I never allowed anyone else to try such a thing as that on me, never! But even she could not succeed in such an enterprise.

We talked. The insatiable wound inside me bled and grew, and I was doing everything I could to make it bleed more. Her perfume and the peculiar smell of the denicotinized cigarettes she smoked followed me everywhere and tortured me in my cabin.

She told me how once she was in a famous night club in a famous city when a famous person, a prince of the royal blood, had stared very intently at her for a long time and had finally got up and started to lurch in the direction of her table when his friends had made him sit down and behave himself.

I could see that all the counts and dukes who liked to marry people like Constance Bennett would want also to marry her. But the counts and dukes were not here on board this glorified cargo boat that was carrying us all peacefully across the mild dark waves of the North Atlantic. The thing that crushed me was that I had never learned to dance.

We made Nantucket Light on Sunday afternoon and had to anchor in quarantine that night. So the ship rode in the Narrows on the silent waters, and the lights of Brooklyn glittered in the harbor like jewels. The boat was astir with music and with a warm glowing life that pulsated within the dark hull and poured out into the July night through every porthole. There were parties in all the cabins. Everywhere you went, especially on deck where it was quiet, you were placed in the middle of movie scenery—the setting for the last reel of the picture.

I made a declaration of my undying love. I would not, could not, ever love anyone else but her. It was impossible, unthinkable. If she went to the ends of the earth, destiny would bring us together again. The stars in their courses from the beginning of the world had plotted this meeting which was the central fact in the whole history of the universe. Love like this was immortal. It conquered time and outlasted the futility of human history. And so forth.

She talked to me, in her turn, gently and sweetly. What it sounded like was: "You do not know what you are saying. This can never be. We shall never meet again." What it meant was: "You are a nice kid. But for heaven's sake grow up before someone makes a fool of you." I went to my cabin and sobbed over my diary for a while and then, against all the laws of romance, went peacefully to sleep.

However, I could not sleep for long. At five o'clock I was up again, and walking restlessly around the deck. It was hot. A grey mist lay on the Narrows. But when it became light, other anchored ships began to appear as shapes in the mist. One of them was a Red Star liner on which, as I learned from the papers when I got on shore, a passenger was at that precise moment engaged in hanging himself.

At the last minute before landing I took a snapshot of her which, to my intense sorrow, came out blurred. I was so avid for a picture of her that I got too close with the camera and it was out of focus. It was a piece of poetic justice that filled me with woe for months.

Of course the whole family was there on the dock. But the change was devastating. With my heart ready to explode with immature emotions I suddenly found myself surrounded by all the cheerful and peaceful and comfortable solicitudes of home. Everybody wanted to talk. Their voices were full of questions and information. They took me for a drive on Long Island and showed me where Mrs. Hearst lived and everything. But I only hung my head out of the window of the car and watched the green trees go swirling by, and wished that I were dead.

Remembering Episodes

Memories may provide us with short, self-contained narrative episodes such as Jan Myrdal relates in his *Confessions of a Disloyal European,* an autobiographical work that has been characterized as "a montage of memories." Among them are the four episodes reprinted below, which in many respects resemble short-short stories, for each one, brief as it is, encompasses character, setting, incident, and—in its own subtle way—theme.

Four Episodes[5]

JAN MYRDAL

I

Nic.

I met her in Gothenburg as the European war was ending. Her hair was short; she had been in a concentration camp. Her hair had the colour of many dyes; she had worked underground. The last time I saw her was in Oslo in 1956:

—You want to be happy? Why? You are supposed to work.

Her last letter reached me in Kabul in 1959. After that she didn't answer any letters. Coming to Scandinavia I called and asked:

—How is Nic?

—She is dead.

II

As a child when I lived in central Stockholm I was once playing in the doorway of another house. The caretaker saw me. When I heard him coming down the stairs I ran. He caught me in the street and started hitting me. He struck me in the face.

—I'll teach you, he said. You bastard.

Then he kicked me and left.

Close by a man was beating his Airedale terrier. A woman screamed at him:

—I will report you to the police.

I thought a lot about this the following days.

III

A gypsy family had tried to settle in the small town of Mariefred (Peace to Mary) where I was living. The good citizens, afraid of a drop in land prices, had tried to get them to move. The press in Stockholm had written about it. The citizens became afraid of scandal. Now there was a meeting of the town council to decide what to do. Reluctantly it was decided that they would get a house. On the way out from the meeting a middle-aged man turned to me and said:

—Gypsies! One ought to get rid of people like that.

—Fine, I said. You gas them and I will heat up my furnace.

---

[5]From *Confessions of a Disloyal European,* by Jan Myrdal. Copyright © 1968 by Jan Myrdal. Reprinted by permission of Pantheon Books, a Division of Random House, Inc.

As he was a Social Democrat, the Labour people said after that that I was antilabour.

IV

In the fall of 1947 I was in love with B. She was good-looking, intelligent and we said we thought that we had much in common. We were going steady for some time, but she did not allow me to sleep with her. In December that year I left for Belgrade. When I came back to Sweden I married another girl. In February 1949 I came to Stockholm by train from Herrljunga. Met B. Having met again we both realized that we actually were very much in love with each other. I followed her to her room and now she wanted "to give herself to me," as she expressed it.

Suddenly I remembered that I had not washed my feet for several days. There were reasons for this. I had hitchhiked up through Sweden, had spent the night at the county jail of Herrljunga, and had been put on the train to Stockholm. It was in the middle of winter and it was cold.

But as I was afraid that my feet stank—which would not correspond to the image I wanted B to have of me—I tried to find a way to escape from the situation. Unfortunately the fact that my feet (probably) stank did not strike me until B had started to undress. I could not find anything more convincing to say than that I seemed to love the girl I was married to. B was very understanding and we sat for a long time talking about self, soul and love.

And all this because I had forgotten to wash my feet. Or was it?

Remembering People

In addition to the memory of a particular period or event, the writer may recall a particular person, for people are important links to the past. Our memories of forms and faces can actually bring the past back to us. Sometimes the memory is dim, such as Elie Wiesel's memory of the elusive and haunting first friend of his childhood, an orphan who has come to symbolize—in retrospect—the writer's own fate.

The Orphan[6]

ELIE WIESEL

My first friend was an orphan. That is about all I remember about him. I have forgotten his name, how he looked, what he was like. The color of his eyes, the rhythm of his walk: these too, forgotten. Did he like to sing, to laugh, to play in the sun, to roll in the snow? I cannot remember and, sometimes, I feel a vague remorse, as if it were a rejection.

I sometimes search my memory hoping to find him again, to save him, or, at least, to restore to him a face, a past: I emerge empty-handed. While I have no difficulty seeing myself as a child again, he, the orphan, remains unreachable: an echo without voice, a shadow without reflection. Of our friendship, all that has been preserved is the sadness his presence inspired in me. Even now, discovering the orphan in each human being is enough to reopen an old wound, never fully healed.

I must have been five, maybe a little older. I had scarcely begun to go to primary school, to *heder.* Among the children whom I did not know and did not want to know, I felt myself to be, like each of them, no doubt, the victim of my parents' injustice. I made up countless illnesses so that I could stay home with my mother for just one more day, to hear her say she still loved me, that she was not going to turn me over to strangers.

Obstinate, I resisted the efforts of my old white-bearded schoolmaster, who gently persisted in wanting to teach me the Hebrew alphabet. I think it was because, like all children, I preferred remaining a child. I dreaded the universe of rigid laws which I sensed were inside those black letters whose mysterious power seizes hold of the imagination like a defenseless prey. Whoever says *a* will say *b* and before one notices it, one is already caught up in the machinery: one begins to find words satisfying, one makes gods of them. I had an obscure premonition that, once this threshold were crossed, it would be the letters of the alphabet that would, in the end, undo my innocence, impose itself between my desires and their realization.

The other pupils, as recalcitrant as I, showed the same distrust. Only the orphan was of a different breed. He never acted spoiled; he never tried the patience and kindness of our teacher. First to arrive, he was always the last to leave. He was not rowdy, he did not have tantrums. Diligent, obedient, in contrast to us, he did not feel uprooted in the narrow room with its damp walls, that room where we spent endless hours around a rectangular table, worn down by three generations of unhappy schoolboys.

His exemplary behavior could only annoy us: why did he insist on being different? After a while, I understood: he was different. His mother had died giving birth to him.

I did not know then what it meant to die. In fact, to be an orphan had, in my eyes, a kind of distinction, an honor that did not fall to everyone. Secretly, I began to envy him. Yet my attitude toward him changed. To win his trust, I shared my possessions with him, my little snacks, my presents. At home no one understood: all of a sudden I who refused to eat at every meal, began carrying off double portions.

My mother was alive and that seemed to me unjust. When I was with the orphan, I felt at fault: I possessed a wealth denied to him. And neither one of us had anything to do with it. I would have given everything to restore the balance. To redeem myself, I was ready to become not only his debtor but his admirer as well, his benefactor. For his part, he accepted my sacrifices, and I no longer remember if he thanked me for them, if he really needed them. I do not know why, but I thought he was poor. Or rather—yes, I do know why: spoiled child that I was, I saw every orphan as a *poor* orphan. I could not conceive of misfortune except in its totality: whoever lost one portion of affection, one possibility of love, lost everything.

His birthday coinciding with the anniversary of his mother's death, I heard him saying *Kaddish* in the synagogue. I had to restrain myself with all my might to keep from tearing myself away from my father and rushing over to my friend to embrace him, weeping, and repeat with him word by word the prayer which gives praise to God, who must know what he is doing when he takes away the joy of little children.

Over the years our paths separated. The orphan went his own way. I made new friends, and today I have other reasons for assuming my share of guilt, but at the root of this feeling it is always him I find.

Still I know very well that my first friend long ago ceased to be a unique case: we all belong to a generation of orphans, and the *Kaddish* has become our daily prayer. But each time death takes someone away from me, it is him, my forgotten friend, I mourn. Sometimes I wonder if he did not have my face, my fate perhaps, and if he was not already what I was about to become. Then I tell myself that I should set myself to learning the alphabet, diligently, if only to resemble him the more.

ASSIGNMENTS

Class Discussion and Paragraph Suggestions

(See Chapter 27 for methods of composing unified, adequately developed paragraphs.)

1. Consider Thomas Wolfe's "The Quality of Memory."
   a. Identify and comment on the sense impressions described by Wolfe.
   b. Evaluate the choice of words (nouns, verbs, adjectives).
   c. What special rhetorical devices (alliteration, repetition) contribute to the rhythm and momentum of Wolfe's sentences?

2. Write a paragraph (150–250 words) describing a vivid memory of some past experience. Be sure to include concrete sensual details (colors, shapes, sounds) so that the experience is not merely recounted but evoked.

3. Evaluate the use of the following rhetorical features in Laurie Lee's "The Village School":

   selection of details   parallelism
   choice of adjectives   rhythm
   repetition of words   inverted word order
   sensory images   suspended sentences
   metaphors   voice

4. Write a paragraph (150–250 words) describing your kindergarten, first grade, or second grade classroom. Try to remember as many details as possible: the physical layout, the teacher, your classmates (can you remember any specific names?), the songs you sang, the games you played.

5. Does Moss Hart's "A Memorable Summer" hold your interest? Is it a good story? Answer these questions by considering the following aspects:

   point of view   sentence construction
   conflict   sentence rhythm
   expository passages   narrative pace
   suspense   selection of details
   climax   dialogue
   the "tribe" analogy

6. Write a paragraph (150–250 words) using the following sentence from Hart's essay as your topic sentence: "Listening to a tale being told in the dark is one of the most ancient of man's entertainments." Use a memory of your own to develop the paragraph, or try to recreate the reaction of one of Hart's attentive young listeners.

7. Consider Thomas Merton's "I Fall in Love."
   a. Does the central character in this reminiscence come alive as a person? Can you respond to him? Can you identify with him?
   b. Describe the organization of this piece.
   c. Observe and comment on the writer's manner of combining inner and outer experiences.

8. Write a paragraph (150–250 words) using Merton's first sentence as your topic sentence: "In three months, the summer of 19—, I suddenly matured like a weed." Develop a coordinate sequence paragraph (see pp. 496–97) by citing *three* aspects of maturation, giving brief examples of each.

9. Consider Jan Myrdal's "Four Episodes."
   a. Summarize character, setting, incident, and theme in each of these narratives.

b. What special stylistic features distinguish these essays?

c. Explain their impact on you, as a reader.

10. Write an episode of your own. Open it with a name (comparable to Myrdal's "Nic").

11. Consider Elie Wiesel's "The Orphan."

a. Trace the steps that lead to the writer's conclusion that "we all belong to a generation of orphans." Does this conclusion seem justified to you? Esplain.

b. Comment on point of view and voice. How do they contribute to the total impact of Wiesel's "message"?

Essay Suggestions

1. Write an essay (500–1,000 words) dealing with an early memory connected with going to school.

2. In an essay (500–1,000 words) describe a period in your life, during childhood or adolescence, that remains marked off from other times by specific events, experiences, or feelings that you associate with it (like Hart's or Merton's memorable summer).

3. Write four episodes based on remembered experiences, incidents, people—each a short-short story in the manner of Myrdal's "Four Episodes."

4. In an essay (500–750 words) similar to Wiesel's "The Orphan," describe your first friend or any friend whose memory has had an impact on your life.

5. In a classic essay by Charles Lamb, "Dream Children: A Reverie," Lamb (the narrator), who is a bachelor, has a dream-experience—or reverie—in which his imagined grandchildren cluster about him to hear tales of their forebears. It is a heartwarming description, in many ways the typical fantasy of what might have been had circumstances worked out differently. In an essay (500–750 words), write a reverie in which you place yourself in a situation that might have been. End your reverie as Lamb ends his: "I found myself quietly seated in my . . . chair, where I had fallen asleep."

6. Read Dylan Thomas' "A Child's Christmas in Wales" and write an essay (750–1,000 words) describing any holiday as you remember it being celebrated by your family.

18 What Is the Value of X?

When we ask about the "value" of something, we are moving still further beyond basic explanation into the greater complexities of judgment, whereby we ask not merely "What does X do?" but "What does X do that is worth doing?" and "How well does X do it?" Here the purpose is not merely to inform but to appraise the worth, utility, importance, excellence, distinction, truth, beauty, goodness of something. To what extent does X meet or fail to meet specific standards? In an evaluative essay it is always you, the writer, who sets the standards. Even if they are standards adopted from someone else, you have made them your own. Thus, the moment you address yourself to the question "What is the value of X?" you become a critic. Whether the subject is books, movies, art, or society at large, you evaluate it in the light of your own notion of what it is and *should* be. As you can see, then, writing an evaluation is a special challenge, for the evaluation will have value only if you are open-minded, well informed, and fair—ready to back up your opinions, but not opinionated.

Evaluating Human Behavior

In the following essay, for example, the writer places a high value on an exuberant form of human behavior that most people frown upon or regard as frivolous. Virtue may be its own reward, but, as Eric Hoffer tells us, the spirit of playfulness—the indulgence in "trivial joys"—yields rewards far beyond its selfish, surface value. Hoffer supports his thesis by citing many momentous contributions to society that have issued from "idle musing"—what he calls "the playful mood."

The Playful Mood[1]
ERIC HOFFER

I have always felt that the world has lost much by not preserving the small talk of its great men. The little that has come down to us is marked by a penetration and a directness not usually conspicuous in formal discourse or writing; and one is immediately aware of its universality and timelessness. It seems strange that men should so effortlessly attain immortality in their playful moments. Certainly, some have missed immortality as writers by not writing as they talked. Clemenceau is a case in point. His books make dull and difficult reading, yet he could not open his mouth without saying something memorable. The few scraps we have of his small talk throw a more vivid light on the human situation than do shelves of books on psychology, sociology, and history. Toward the end of his life Clemenceau is reported to have exclaimed: "What a shame that I don't have three or four more years to live—I would have rewritten my books for my cook." It is also worth noting that the New Testament and the Lun Yu are largely records of impromptu remarks and sayings, and that Montaigne wrote as he spoke. ("I speak to my paper as I speak to the first person I meet.")

We are told that a great life is "thought of youth wrought out in ripening years"; and it is perhaps equally true that "great" thinking consists in the working out of insights and ideas which come to us in playful moments. Archimedes' bathtub and Newton's apple suggest that momentous trains of thought may have their inception in idle musing. The original insight is most likely to come when elements stored in different compartments of the mind drift into the open, jostle one another, and now and then coalesce to form new combinations. It is doubtful whether a mind that is pinned down and cannot drift elsewhere is capable of formulating new questions. It is true that the working out of ideas and insights requires persistent hard thinking, and the inspiration necessary for such a task is probably a by-product of single-minded application. But the sudden illumination and the flash of discovery are not likely to materialize under pressure.

Men never philosophize or tinker more freely than when they know that their speculation or tinkering leads to no weighty results. We are more ready to try the untried when what we do is inconsequential. Hence the remarkable fact that many inventions had their birth as toys. In the Occident the first machines were mechanical toys, and such crucial instruments as the telescope and microscope were first conceived as playthings. Almost all civilizations display a singular ingenuity in toy making. The Aztecs did not have the wheel, but some of their animal toys had rollers for feet. It would not be fanciful to assume that in the ancient Near East, too, the wheel and the sail made their first appearance as playthings. We are told that in one of the oldest cemeteries in the world the skeletons showed that the average age of the population at death was less than twenty-five—and there is no reason to assume that the place was particularly unhealthy. Thus the chances are that the momentous discoveries and inventions of the Neolithic Age which made possible the rise of

---

[1]From *The Ordeal of Change* by Eric Hoffer. Copyright © 1961 by Eric Hoffer. Reprinted by permission of Harper & Row, Publishers, Inc.

civilization, and which formed the basis of everyday life until yesterday, were made by childlike, playful people. It is not unlikely that the first domesticated animals were children's pets. Planting and irrigating, too, were probably first attempted in the course of play. (A girl of five once advised me to plant hair on my bald head.) Even if it could be shown that a striking desiccation of climate preceded the first appearance of herdsmen and cultivators it would not prove that the conception of domestication was born of a crisis. The energies released by a crisis usually flow toward sheer action and application. Domestication could have been practiced as an amusement long before it found practical application. The crisis induced people to make use of things which amuse.

When we do find that a critical challenge has apparently evoked a marked creative response there is always the possibility that the response came not from people cornered by a challenge but from people who in an exuberance of energy went out in search of a challenge. It is highly doubtful whether people are capable of genuine creative responses when necessity takes them by the throat. The desperate struggle for existence is a static rather than a dynamic influence. The urgent search for the vitally necessary is likely to stop once we have found something that is more or less adequate, but the search for the superfluous has no end. Hence the fact that man's most unflagging and spectacular efforts were made not in search of necessities but of superfluities. It is worth remembering that the discovery of America was a by-product of the search for ginger, cloves, pepper, and cinnamon. The utilitarian device, even when it is an essential ingredient of our daily life, is most likely to have its ancestry in the nonutilitarian. The sepulchre, temple, and palace preceded the utilitarian house; ornament preceded clothing; work, particularly teamwork, derives from play. We are told that the bow was a musical instrument before it became a weapon, and some authorities believe that the subtle craft of fishing originated in a period when game was abundant—that it was the product not so much of grim necessity as of curiosity, speculation, and playfulness. We know that poetry preceded prose, and it may be that singing came before talking.

On the whole it seems to be true that the creative periods in history were buoyant and even frivolous. One thinks of the lightheartedness of Periclean Athens, the Renaissance, the Elizabethan Age, and the age of the Enlightenment. Mr. Nehru tells us that in India "during every period when her civilization bloomed, we find an intense joy in life and nature and a pleasure in the art of living." One suspects that much of the praise of seriousness comes from people who have a vital need for a facade of weight and dignity. LaRochefoucauld said of solemnity that it is "a mystery of the body invented to conceal the defects of the mind." The fits of deadly seriousness we know as mass movements, which come bearing a message of serious purpose and weighty ideals, are usually set in motion by sterile pedants possessed of a murderous hatred for festive creativeness. Such movements bring in their wake meager-mindedness, fear, austerity, and sterile conformity. Hardly one of the world's great works in literature, art, music, and pure science was conceived and realized in the stern atmosphere of a mass movement. It is only when these movements have spent themselves, and their pattern of austere boredom begins to crack, and the despised present dares assert its claims to trivial joys, that the creative impulse begins to stir amidst the grayness and desolation.

Man shares his playfulness with other warm-blooded animals, with mammals and birds. Insects, reptiles, etc., do not play. Clearly, the division of the forms of life into those that can play and those that cannot is a significant one. Equally significant is the duration of the propensity to play. Mammals and birds play only when young, while man retains the propensity throughout life. My feeling is that the tendency to

carry youthful characteristics into adult life, which renders man perpetually immature and unfinished, is at the root of his uniqueness in the universe, and is particularly pronounced in the creative individual. Youth has been called a perishable talent,
but perhaps talent and originality are always aspects of youth, and the creative
individual is an imperishable juvenile. When the Greeks said, "Whom the gods love
die young" they probably meant, as Lord Sankey suggested, that those favored by
the gods stay young till the day they die; young and playful.

Obviously, "What is the value of X?" is the guiding question behind most
examples of critical writing and review. Whether you are concerned with
books, movies, theater, music, or dance, you are expected to tell the readers
of your evaluation whether the offering in question is any good. Naturally,
your opinion is, for the most part, exactly that—your *opinion*. This does not
mean, however, that a good review cannot be objective. "I personally do not
like courtroom drama," you might state, adding—if you want to be fair and to
inform your audience of a truth larger and more important than your own
likes and dislikes—that the courtroom scenes in one particular play are
extraordinarily well done. To be a good reviewer, you must get outside
yourself so that you see not only through your own eyes but also through the
eyes of others. (See W. H. Auden, "The Function of a Critic," pp. 96–97.)

Evaluating a Book

A good book review is informative, interpretive, and evaluative. Thus it
provides at least three kinds of information:

1. *It indicates the content and presumed purpose of the book.* The ability
to write a good summary is important here (see Chapter 19). More than that,
if your review is to be fair, you must infer from the *fact* of the book what the
author's intentions were—that is, *what* the author wanted to say and *how* he
or she wanted it to be received. If, for example, a book is about poverty in
Appalachia, you should not fault the author for lack of humor: clearly the
book is not supposed to be funny. (One is reminded here of Mark Twain's
spoofing criticism of the dictionary for its weak plot.)

2. *It describes the style.* By examining specific techniques, you can
determine how well or how poorly the author has handled the material and
how fully his or her purpose has been achieved.

3. *It judges the value of the book.* Is it any good? Do we have reason to be
glad that it was written? Was its purpose worth achieving? What contribution, if any, does it make to our store of knowledge or aesthetic pleasure?

Obviously, only the first two considerations can be dealt with objectively,
through analysis and interpretation; the third consideration depends on your
own judgment, on your opinion of what is valuable and worthy. However
you deal with these necessarily subjective aspects of reviewing, one thing is
certain: you should not use the review as a showcase for your personal tastes
and preferences, featuring these at the expense of the book itself. Your main
function is to describe the book in such a way that your readers, who
presumably have not read the book, can decide whether or not they want to

read it. In addition, you can help to illumine the work so that readers can understand and appreciate it more deeply.

Note how thoroughly and engagingly Joyce Carol Oates (herself a novelist of considerable renown) has handled her assignment to review a recently published novel.

Review of Eileen Simpson's *The Maze*[2]

JOYCE CAROL OATES

Introduction (background material)

Of course there are poetic geniuses who are utterly normal; there are poets who have been married contentedly for many years, who do not cause injury to themselves or others, and who labor to create works of art without obligatory plunges into the abyss of madness or drunkenness or sheer wanton childishness. But our attention is drawn to the others. Possibly fewer in number—the Byronic personalities outshine the rest. What interest has the "normal" for us, when the brilliant but outrageous is also a possibility? And so it is the fate of certain poets to be elevated more for their images than their work, and to be victimized by the very traits in their personalities that seem to appeal to their admirers—their wild, reckless originality, their need for constant experimentation and turbulence, their insatiable and, in a way, almost innocent egotism.

Summary of character and plot

Benjamin Bold in Eileen Simpson's novel [New York: Simon and Schuster, 1975] is a poet of probable genius. Now in early middle age, he has worked for more than 20 years with only limited recognition. He hungers for fame, fully expects it with the publication of his third book, and in the months preceding the book's publication he nearly destroys his wife and himself. Alternately charming and vicious, brilliant and stupid, Bold is a thoroughly convincing portrait of a certain type of man. He happens to be a poet in this narrative, and very "poetic" he is for the most part; but his psychology is that of the egomaniac who would subordinate everyone around him— friends, family, wife—to his own raw, ungovernable need. So passionately driven an individual often finds peace and happiness unendurable; he is cruelest to himself.

And yet irresistible. For Benjamin Bold, as seen through the eyes of his much-injured wife Rosy, is simply far more interesting than any normal man. Other men, by comparison, are tame and disappointing. A would-be lover Theo, an Englishman who has come to Harvard for a lecture series, senses the young wife's unhappiness but is ultimately rejected by her; though Benjamin is impossible, though their marriage is all but finished, Rosy's fate is to remain in love with him. Even when, at the novel's conclusion, she makes a desperate attempt to be free of him, he is still at the very center of her world. She cannot stop thinking of him. She *is* subordinate to him; he *is* clearly a superior personality.

Judgment (favorable)

There is not likely to be a first novel this season so subtly rendered and so convincing as Eileen Simpson's study of the Bolds' disinte-

[2]From *The New York Times Book Review*, 6 April 1975, pp. 1, 20. © 1975 by The New York Times Company. Reprinted by permission.

grating marriage and her portrait of Benjamin. He is not a likable person, yet one can sympathize with those who love him—they are simply fascinated by him, enchanted. They cannot and will not judge him by the standards applied to ordinary men. Rosy should detest him, should fear him, should at the very least be exasperated with him as one would be with a difficult, cruel child, but after 12 years of marriage, she considers him in these terms: "How did he look? Like a horse—a high-strung, high-mettled, high-stepping horse, reined in . . . and ready to dance, or rear up, or gallop away. His eyes darted. His nostrils flared. There was a pulse in his lean cheek." In an hour or two he will treat her badly again, but again he will be forgiven.

Rosy is in her early twenties when Benjamin Bold discovers her. She is inexperienced, charmingly naive, intensely feminine. Benjamin pursues her and overwhelms her; he will not rest until he possesses her—though, curiously enough, he claims that she isn't the type of woman he admires, and he wants to change her in a number of ways almost at once. (She has hopes of being a lawyer but he tells her that's nonsense—she is the sort of girl who wants someone to adore. He even wants to change her name, as he talked his sister into changing her name from Mildred to Iphigene.) After 12 years of their symbiotic relationship, in which Rosy functions as both a psychiatric nurse and an audience for Benjamin's poetry, Rosy is forced to realize that the marriage is through: Benjamin, on the brink of fame, wants freedom. The publication of the book will mark the end of an era. He must be free to begin a new life.

Set largely in Rome, "The Maze" takes place almost entirely inside Rosy's consciousness. Though she is in her early thirties at the time of the narrative, she strikes the reader as much younger, almost virginal. Her innocence is believable but at times frustrating, for she refuses again and again to assert herself against her husband; she is anxious to please him, so eager to forgive him even when he has behaved unforgivably, that it is only after temporarily leaving him that she realizes how stunted she is emotionally, how bankrupt of normal adult feeling. By then it is almost too late. Perhaps it is too late; at the novel's conclusion Rosy hopes only to be able to survive.

"The Maze" contains many spare, lean, highly dramatic scenes. Benjamin is always fascinating, whether drunk or sober, loving or hateful, depressed or caught up in manic high spirits. It is his novel all the way—and when he isn't present, the novel tends to lose its vitality. The hard-drinking literary community that has regrouped in Rome (most of them from Cambridge, Mass.) does not contain any characters of distinction, and Rosy's closest woman friend, Doris, chats with her mainly about clothes, hairdos and the hopes she has of manipulating her married lover into divorcing his wife and marrying her. The action of "The Maze" is not set in the seventies, or even the sixties, which helps to account for its pre-Women's Liberation tone. Rosy knows she has been victimized, and she knows that as a single woman she will be handicapped, but she does not care to see her predicament in larger, cultural terms. Had Eileen Simpson gone more deeply into her central character, we would perhaps feel more

Marginal notes:

Quotation

Further development

Characters

Plot

Setting

Literary technique

Evaluation (deeper analysis of strengths and weaknesses)

Benjamin "fascinating"; other characters undistinguished

Rosy: needs
sharper
delineation
yet is
"believable"

sympathy for Rosy. Her faithfulness to Benjamin contrasts sharply
with his compulsive faithlessness to her (for which she always for-
gives him) and her bursts of anger, so long repressed, are only
sporadic and do not seem to alter her essential adoration of her
husband.

Still Rosy is believable. She is weak, yes, but many women—and
many men—are weak. She cannot define herself except in terms of a
man and though this is a heretical predicament in 1975, it is probably
more commonplace than we think; it was certainly commonplace 20
years ago. And so Benjamin's rejection of her—at a time when she is
bedridden with a painful back injury, in London—is all the more
devastating. He requires a woman to take care of him, to nurse him
through his difficult bouts of poetry-writing and drinking, and when
she is no longer strong enough to nurse him, he must be free. The
rejection is shattering for Rosy, but it is, at least, the beginning of her
education.

Conclusion:
Author's
authority "im-
peccable";
reader will
be "deeply
. . . moved"

Eileen Simpson, a former wife of poet John Berryman, has done a
study of creativity in poets and has been a clinical psychologist. Her
authority in this novel is impeccable. Her sense of bewilderment and
anguish is beautifully communicated, and it is impossible to read
"The Maze" without being deeply and permanently moved.

In reviewing a nonfiction book you must answer at least the same three
questions as for a work of fiction: What is the content and purpose of the
book? How skillfully does the author execute his or her purpose? Was the
purpose worth achieving? The order in which you answer these questions is
not important so long as they are all covered in a systematic fashion. For
example, you have strong feelings about a book, you may announce them in
your first sentence, as critic Elizabeth Hardwick did in her review of a new
Ernest Hemingway biography, which she dismissed in her first sentence as
"bad news." In the following review, the reviewer withholds his highly
favorable judgment until paragraph three, after a long but interesting and
relevant introductory section on the content of the book itself.

Review of Bruce Mazlish's *James and John Stuart Mill*[3]

PHILIP ROSENBERG

The story of John Stuart Mill reads like a work of fiction—which in many ways it
was. From his own account of the celebrated education he received at the hands of
his father, we get an unnerving picture of a little homunculus, an artificial child
reading Greek at 3, mastering Robertson, Hume and Gibbon at 7, and returning, at
age 8, to reread Roman history "both in my old favourite, Hooke, and in Ferguson."

Almost literally he seems to have been the brain-child rather than merely the
offspring of his father, who appears to have created him by an act of mind much as a

[3]From *The New York Times Book Review*, 6 April 1975, p. 25. © 1975 by The New York Times
Company. Reprinted by permission.

novelist would. James Mill was in fact a writer, in his own day widely regarded as the best and most ardent literary promoter of Benthamism, though little read today. If, then, we tend to remember him largely as the author of John Stuart Mill, this is neither less than he deserves nor a mere figure of speech. The son himself saw the connection. "I was born in London on the 20th of May, 1806, and was the eldest son of James Mill, the author of the History of British India," he writes at the beginning of his autobiography.

"Most readers, and this includes most scholars, have not noticed what an extraordinary statement this is," M.I.T. historian Bruce Mazlish comments in "James and John Stuart Mill" [New York: Basic Books, 1975], his masterful new psychohistorical study of the Mills. "It invokes a new version of the immaculate conception, in which the mother is entirely missing; indeed, John Stuart Mill never mentions her throughout the published version of his work. Instead, we have 'book and boy' both produced by James Mill, seemingly acting alone," Mazlish acutely notes, then adds, in what may or may not be a pun, "The rest of the *Autobiography* appears to bear out this conception."

Subtitled "Father and Son in the Nineteenth Century," Professor Mazlish's book is an outstanding contribution to the relatively new discipline of psychohistory. Indeed, his subjects seem to have been perfectly chosen for the type of analysis he provides. Both were highly articulate men who left considerable records of their thought; both figured prominently in the literary and political cultures of their day. What is more, if in their writings the two Mills dealt with some of the major social issues of 19th-century England, in their lives they acted them out. As Mazlish demonstrates time and again, the Mill household was a sort of proving ground for liberal theory, a microcosm of the militantly ascendant British bourgeoisie.

The first half of the 19th century was, as we are well aware, a period of profound and dramatic change in the institutional structures of British life, which were forced to absorb the impact of rapid industrialization and urbanization. It was a time when, as John Ruskin observed, "every man's aim is to be in some more elevated sphere than his natural one, and every man's past life is his habitual scorn." Nowhere was this scorn more lucidly expressed than in the "Philosophic Radicalism" preached by Bentham and the elder Mill. In his own writings and in the writings of his followers, Bentham explained, "men at large were invited to break loose from the trammels of authority and ancestor-wisdom."

Undoubtedly none of the Benthamites applied this principle as assiduously as did James Mill, whose private resistance to the "ancestor-wisdom" embodied in his own parents reached almost Dickensian proportions. Like Bounderby in "Hard Times," James Mill so thoroughly repudiated his humble Scottish upbringing that even his closest associates knew almost nothing of his background. After his death, when his son undertook to write a biographical essay on him for the Encyclopedia Britannica, he found it necessary to search out friends from his father's youth and to bombard them with elementary questions. "The chief points," John Stuart Mill wrote in one such inquiry, "are the time and place of his birth; who and what his parents were, and anything interesting there may be to state about them: what places of education he went to: for what professions he was educated."

With material such as this to work with, Professor Mazlish is able to trace the deep and wide-ranging connections between James Mill's family situation, his writings and his social milieu. Similarly, in the two-thirds of the volume devoted to John Stuart Mill we are offered a fascinating exploration of the labyrinthine network of private pieties and rebellions that underlay his work. For example, Mill's lifelong involvement with the "woman question" has to my knowledge never been treated with such subtlety and sympathy.

With great care and precision, Mazlish unravels the tortuous and complex story of how the young John Stuart Mill learned from his father to despise his mother, Harriet Mill, and how he fell in love with the wife of John Taylor, also named Harriet; how he struggled against what he called "the harder & sterner features" of his father's teachings, and then entered into a lifelong liaison with Mrs. Taylor, which culminated after 18 years in a platonic marriage and which, in countless ways, allowed Mill to duplicate his discipleship to his father in his discipleship to her.

Through these sad and incomplete relationships, one can trace the growth of Mill's most permanent works, the essays "On Liberty" and "On the Subjection of Women." His thought, as Mazlish demonstrates, was always rooted in the subsoil of buried emotions, which at times limited his achievement and at times nourished it. If some of his unresolved tensions hindered his work as a social scientist, others facilitated his development as a social philosopher—in fact were an important part of the preconditions that made this development possible. "In Mill," Mazlish writes, "the political, the moral, and the psychological are inextricably mixed. He is a man, not just a mind."

Even more to the point, he was a mind, not just a man. It is to Mazlish's credit that his careful "unmasking" of the psychosocial forces behind Mill's thought has not blinded him to the thought in front. Too often, psychohistorical and psychobiographical analyses have tended to pay such exclusive attention to unconscious mental processes that they leave the reader with a thoroughly depressing estimate of the value of the conscious mind. They explain away what they should be explaining and end, as Richard Ellmann once remarked, by reducing "all achievement to a web of causation until we cannot see the Ego for the Id." Indeed, Professor Mazlish's preceding book, "In Search of Nixon," is as fine an example as one can find of why psychohistory has a bad name.

For this reason his study of the Mills is especially welcome, for it once again demonstrates that the application of psychoanalytic method to literature and history need not end in cynical reductionism. To be sure, there are moments when Mazlish seems to be trying to score points instead of make them; his examination of James Mill's writings, for example, is often rather slapdash and jargony. Elsewhere, too, his seriousness occasionally deserts him and he contents himself with mere labeling. But "James and John Stuart Mill" is a big book which never stays on the wrong track for long. It is shallow in places, but there are not many such places in a book which contains some of the best psychohistory this side of Erik Erikson.

Evaluating a Film

The form of a film review is like that of a book review in that the reviewer serves as intermediary between the film and the prospective viewer. This is what the film is about, you tell your readers, indicating not only basic plot line, character, and action but also what you take to be the intention of the director. You should also discuss technique (camera work, lighting, and so on) and quality of the performances (who plays what major roles and how well or how poorly they are performed). Finally, you should tell readers whether or not you think the film is worth going to see.

Review of Federico Fellini's *8½*[4]

PENELOPE GILLIATT

INTRODUC-
TION

It would be a waste of time to wonder how precisely autobiograph-ical Fellini was being when he made *8½*, his famous film about a famous film director. As he said once himself, there is a sense in which he would be autobiographical even if he were telling the life story of a sole.

What is certain is that this film is constructed so as to *seem* autobiographical, no matter what the facts are: it uses a scarcely veiled first-person as a deliberate artistic device. People are forever talking about subjective films, but the surprising thing is that noth-

Comparison

ing like *8½* has ever been done before in the cinema. The only work I can think of that has the same grim comic capacity for self-exposure is Evelyn Waugh's *The Ordeal of Gilbert Pinfold*.

OVERVIEW:
what film is
about

8½ is a rueful account of a peculiarly contemporary kind of man, imaginative, openly greedy, riddled with the bullet holes of his self-accusations, and almost dying of neurotic sloth. It has been made by a poet whose genius for film-making spills out of his ears, and I hope its courage isn't going to be dismissed because it is flamboyant and comic. Intellectuals here are hard on Fellini, especially since the words *la dolce vita* passed into the gossip-columnists' language. Sometimes they seem to feel his humor is something he should try to get over, something diminishing and vulgar: and my impression is that he would be much more respected if he would stop implying that sex can be cheerful and start concentrating on the misery of it, like Antonioni. . . .

CENTRAL
CHARAC-
TER
PLOT

The film director-hero of *8½*, played by Marcello Mastroianni, has hit an immovable creative block. Living in the bedlam of preparing for a big picture, he hasn't an idea in his head. Sets are already being built, rival actresses are acting their heads off to each other in the pretense that they have parts, but no one has seen a page of his script. His imagination keeps submerging into the past, remember-ing the huge hips of a woman he once saw doing a rhumba when he was a small boy, and the punishment he got afterward from the priests at school.

Coming up gasping from this daydream and shaking the drops off himself, he thinks perhaps he may at last have rescued something off the ocean bed. But when he timidly describes his trophies to a critic-figure who seems to be working on the film, the critic-figure sternly replies that there's no point in thinking of using this kind of child-hood memory to say something about the Catholic conscience in Italy because there's nothing for reviewers to get their teeth into. You think again of Gilbert Pinfold, who is made dogged in his illness by awful critical utterances like this and has hallucinations of wet, snarling boobies carving him up on the BBC. The man in *8½* is the real arch nitpicker, the enemy of art whom all artists would like to murder, the one so glutted that he thinks anyone in danger of

[4]From *Unholy Fools* by Penelope Gilliatt. Copyright © 1963 by Penelope Gilliatt. All rights reserved. Reprinted by permission of The Viking Press, Inc.

producing second-rate art should control himself and produce no art at all.

ANALYSIS

Like all creative people who are stuck, the director in *8½* finds himself feeling too many things at once. He is lonely for his wife, but as soon as she has arrived on the set they start to have bleak quarrels. He has also sent for his mistress, a plump, amiable girl with a mole on her chest that disconcertingly matches a spot on her eye veil, but though he feels tenderly toward her he can't help seeing her as absurd. He hates hurting his wife with his affairs, but he can't truthfully say that it stops him enjoying them: what he dreams of is not being able to give them up but of seeing his wife and dozens of mistresses sweetly getting on in a harem. This is a very, very funny sequence, and funny because it is aghast: he doesn't approve of himself at all for thinking what paradise it would be if his wife accepted polygamy and his actresses were longing to be whipped.

Example (one funny scene)

At one point, in despair, he arrives at the particularly modern notion that perfect happiness would lie in being able to tell the total truth without hurting anyone. But at other times—after he has talked to an aging cardinal in the steam room of a health spa, for instance— his dozing Catholic conscience is booted into life and he believes that happiness shouldn't be a goal anyway. Nor perhaps truth-telling, he begins to think. In the best scene in the film he is watching some screen tests with his wife, whose misery about his lying he has transcribed as justly as he can in a film character who speaks with his wife's words. But when she hears her own lines coming back at her from the screen it doesn't seem to her an offering to the truth; it strikes her as the most terrible of all her husband's betrayals.

Example ("at one point")
Example ("at other times")

Example ("the best scene")

EVALUA-TION: "en-thralling"
Performances
Technique
Theme

Anouk Aimée as the wife, gray-faced and biting her nails, gives a scrupulous performance. So does Mastroianni. Apart from him none of the actors was allowed to see a full script, which sounds like a despotic piece of director's trickery, but I see now why Fellini did it. *8½* is about the way the world looks to a humorous man on the edge of a breakdown, a world full of extravagantly self-absorbed people who seem to him more like gargoyles than human beings. By putting the actors into a vacuum, Fellini has forced them to give performances that are almost uncannily narcissistic, which is the distorion he wanted. The camera work by Gianni di Venanzo is enthralling; so is the editing, and the whole organization of the film.

Camera work

Review of Alfred Hitchcock's *Psycho*[5]

ERNEST CALLENBACH

Hitchcock is said to be very pleased with this film, and well he might be. In it he has abandoned the commercial geniality of his recent work and turned to out-and-out horror and psychopathology: there are two gruesome knife-murders portrayed in more or less full view, and an attempted third one. The film begins with a drab, matter-of-fact scene in a hotel bedroom (the girl's unwholesomeness—she later

[5]© 1960 by The Regents of the University of California. Reprinted from *Film Quarterly*, 14, No. 1 (Fall 1960), pp. 47–49, by permission of The Regents.

steals $40,000—is no doubt established equally by the fact of her being found in bed with a man, though wearing bra and half-slip, and by the fact that it is midday). It imperceptibly shifts to a level of macabre pathology, unbearable suspense, and particularly gory death. In it, indeed, Hitchcock's necrophiliac voyeurism comes to some kind of horrifying climax. Phallic-shaped knives swish past navels, blood drips into bathtubs, eyes stare in death along the floor, huge gashes appear in a man's amazed face, and so forth. So well is the picture made, moreover, that it can lead audiences to do something they hardly ever do any more—cry out to the characters, in hopes of dissuading them from going to the doom that has been cleverly established as awaiting them. (It turns out to be a slightly different doom than the audience believes; and in the third instance it is thwarted, slightly improbably: in this we see the usual Hitchcock, unbothered by problems of motivation and concerned only with the joy of giving one more turn to the screw. But on the whole one does not need, in *Psycho,* the suspension of common sense usually required to enjoy Hitchcock.)

The key to the excellent shift in levels (it is perhaps more a smooth descent, from apparent "normality" to utter ghastliness) is provided, unbelievable as it may seem, by Anthony Perkins, who in this film is revealed to be an actor after all. Instead of the rather wooden person we have seen in *Desire under the Elms* or *On the Beach,* Perkins here gives us first a charming, shy, lonely boy; then a lecherous, dangerous, frustrated youth; then a frightened, sinister, criminally insane man; and finally he is revealed (there is no real reason to conceal the final twist, which is equally horrifying if one knows about it in advance) as a psychological hermaphrodite who has killed and mummified his mother but preserved her in half of his own personality, so to speak, and who "in her person" commits the murders motivated by the sexuality or fears of the other half of his personality.

All this is explained, in the obligatory rationality-scene at the end, by a young psychologist in the police office. This scene supposedly restores the audience to some real frame of reference. Meanwhile Perkins, sitting in a nearby cell, hears his "mother's" voice in internal monologue, meditating on "her son's" fate. The camera closes in, but not too close, on his face, now utterly strange, intense, mad. (It is probably the most apt use ever made of internal monologue.)

All this is very nice, if not quite the kind of thing one would recommend to sensitive souls. It is superbly constructed, both shot-by-shot and in the over-all organization by which the shocks are distributed and built up to. (The music by Bernard Hermann, an old radio man, is conventional suspense stuff but immensely effective.) Aside from Perkins, the acting is ordinary but satisfactory. Hitchcock is said to have once remarked that "Actors are cattle," and this is all that is really required in many of his pictures. The suspense mechanism is all; style is all; deception is all. To allow the personae involved to become human beings would destroy everything, in the usual Hitchcock film. *Psycho* is better: the people are acceptable, at any rate; there is no need to make excuses for them. Still, it is the film *itself* that grips one—in these times, a remarkable achievement, and a hint that "realism" in the cinema is perhaps not so important as people think. *Psycho* is full of jokes, twists, pieces of nastiness that one would think gratuitous in any other film-maker. Hitchcock forces one to realize that these things are *the point.* How lovely, he would doubtless say, about the way Janet Leigh, a faintly playful, quite sexy broad, is done in! She gambols in the shower, like somebody in an advertisement, while in the background a figure blurred by the shower curtain enters the room, approaches, grips the edge of the curtain. . . . Then, in a flurry of quick cutting which managed to get past the censors yet remains the goriest thing seen on film in a long time, she is stabbed to death, and slumps hideously to the floor in a series of movements over which the camera lingers lovingly.

Psycho is surely the sickest film ever made. It is also one of the most technically exciting films of recent years, and perhaps an omen: only, it appears, in films whose subject-matter is trivial and sometimes phony can Hollywood film-makers find the inspiration or the freedom to make really ingenious films. The trickery of *Psycho* is more imaginative and far more elegantly contrived than the all-out seriousness of *Nun's Story,* not to mention the gigantism of *Ben-Hur.*

There is, to be sure, a "serious" subject to all seemingly trivial films, and in the case of Hitchcock the elucidation of the hidden motives upon which he has built his seemingly unimportant stories remains an intriguing job for some intrepid critic. In the meantime, anybody who likes gore, or who likes Hitchcock, will be made happy by *Psycho.* The tone of Hitchcock's recorded plug for the picture—delightfully charlatanish, reassuringly and almost smugly personal—is a perfectly sound introduction to the film.

ASSIGNMENTS

Class Discussion and Paragraph Suggestions

(See Chapter 27 for methods of composing unified, adequately developed paragraphs.)

1. Consider Eric Hoffer's "The Playful Mood."
   a. State the thesis of the piece in a single sentence.
   b. What concrete evidence does Hoffer cite to support his thesis?
   c. In what way is the opening sentence provocative? What two key words are significantly set against each other?
   d. How would you characterize the tone of this piece—authoritative, tentative, serious? Explain your answer by citing specific phrases and passages.

2. Write a one-paragraph response (150–250 words) to Hoffer's observation that "perhaps talent and originality are always aspects of youth."

3. Analyze and evaluate the reviews in this chapter by answering the following questions:
   a. Do they provide readers with sufficient information to make a sound judgment of their own?
   b. In what ways do the reviewers support their own evaluations (evidence, logical reasoning)?
   c. Describe the tone of each review and indicate whether it is appropriate. Does it win readers' "good will"?
   d. Comment on each reviewer's style and the overall readability of each review.
   e. How effective are the opening and closing sentences of each review?
   f. Outline the organization of the *James and John Stuart Mill* and *Psycho* reviews.

4. By answering the questions in exercise 3, above, analyze and evaluate three book, film, television, or drama reviews in your local newspaper or in a national magazine (such as *Newsweek, Time, Saturday Review*).

Essay Questions

1. Write an essay (500–1,000 words) in which you support or criticize Hoffer's evaluation of "The Playful Mood."

2. Write an evaluative essay (500–1,000 words) dealing with some state of being or aspect of human behavior (for example, boredom as a motivating force) or with

some changing aspect of our culture or society (for example, style in dress, the new morality, nudity in films). Organize your essay as follows:

Introduction
I. General evaluation
II. Examples and details supporting the evaluation
Conclusion

3. Write a review (500–1,000 words) of a book or a film. Be sure to indicate:

content and purpose
style and quality
value

19 How Can X Be Summarized?

How to restate briefly and accurately the main points in a body of information; how to see through to its essence; how to strip it bare of details and implications; how to condense and communicate its core meaning: this is the intellectual challenge of summarizing, a skill that some people regard as mechanical and routine, not at all creative. The truth is, however, that there is no greater challenge to the intellect and no more accurate test of understanding than the ability to filter an idea through your mind and restate it briefly in your own words. Indeed, to read and study efficiently; to do research; to take satisfactory notes; to write papers, critiques, and examinations; to grasp an idea and hold it in the mind—all require the ability to "boil down" materials to manageable scope and see their basic intention, their main points, and the relation of these points to one another. A summary, in other words, is a demanding exercise in analysis and interpretation (seeing the parts and judging which are more or less important).

Let us approach this as a significant and recurrent question, then: "How can X be summarized?" Most often the answer will constitute a *section* of an essay rather than a whole essay, although there are occasions when summary is the purpose of a piece of writing: in the "Week in Review" section of the Sunday *New York Times,* for example, and in *Time* and *Newsweek* magazines.

Before considering the summary as an independent form, however, we will note how it is used as a supplement to expository writing of all kinds: in a factual essay we summarize background information (related data and ideas, the past history of our subject); in concluding an argument we recapitulate its main points; in a literary review or critique we provide a plot summary, or *synopsis*, of the work in question.

It will be helpful, then, to review these different situations and types of material that call for summary, observing at the outset that the basis of all summary—whatever the subject matter or occasion—is careful and repeated reading of the text to be summarized and sustained critical thinking about what has been read: a process of probing to "the heart of the matter" so that it may be rendered in a clear, concise, accurate restatement.

Summarizing Ideas

Ideas and concepts often need brief restatement so that they may be reexamined in a new context. Take, for example, the following paragraph by John Stuart Mill, a section of his famous essay "On Liberty." Assume that you are writing a paper on freedom of the press and you have turned to this section with an eye toward summarizing Mill's ideas on the subject in your own paper. You would then read and reread this passage, analyzing it carefully to abstract for your own notes the main idea from Mill's total statement.

Of the Liberty of Thought and Discussion[1]
JOHN STUART MILL

The time, it is to be hoped, is gone by, when any defence would be necessary of the 'liberty of the press' as one of the securities against corrupt or tyrannical government. No argument, we may suppose, can now be needed, against permitting a legislature or an executive, not identified in interest with the people, to prescribe opinions to them, and determine what doctrines or what arguments they shall be allowed to hear. This aspect of the question, besides, has been so often and so triumphantly enforced by preceding writers, that it need not be specially insisted on in this place. Though the law of England, on the subject of the press, is as servile to this day as it was in the time of the Tudors, there is little danger of its being actually put in force against political discussion, except during some temporary panic, when fear of insurrection drives ministers and judges from their propriety; and, speaking generally, it is not, in constitutional countries, to be apprehended, that the government, whether completely responsible to the people or not, will often attempt to control the expression of opinion, except when in doing so it makes itself the organ of the general intolerance of the public. Let us suppose, therefore, that the government is entirely at one with the people, and never thinks of exerting any power of coercion unless in agreement with what it conceives to be their voice. But I deny the right of the people to exercise such coercion, either by themselves or by their government. The power itself is illegitimate. The best government has no more title to it than the worst. It is as noxious, or more noxious, when exerted in accordance with public opinion, than when in opposition to it. If all mankind minus one, were of one opinion, and only one person were of the contrary opinion, mankind would be

[1]From *Essential Works of John Stuart Mill*, edited by Max Lerner. Copyright © 1961 by Bantam Books, Inc. Used by permission.

no more justified in silencing that one person, than he, if he had the power, would be justified in silencing mankind. Were an opinion a personal possession of no value except to the owner; if to be obstructed in the enjoyment of it were simply a private injury, it would make some difference whether the injury was inflicted only on a few persons or on many. But the peculiar evil of silencing the expression of an opinion is, that it is robbing the human race; posterity as well as the existing generation; those who dissent from the opinion, still more than those who hold it. If the opinion is right, they are deprived of the opportunity of exchanging error for truth: if wrong, they lose, what is almost as great a benefit, the clearer perception and livelier impression of truth, produced by its collision with error.

Several careful readings make it clear that Mill has set forth in this paragraph one single important idea about liberty of the press, which may be summarized as follows:

> Except during time of panic, liberty of the press is reasonably safe from corrupt or tyrannical government. A greater present danger is from an intolerant majority who might try—on their own or through government pressure—to silence dissent, thereby robbing society of possible truth (if the dissenters are right), or (if they are wrong) of that clearer, livelier view of truth which emerges when it collides with error.

Sometimes the writer will make your job easier by summarizing his or her own main idea, in which case you would be wise to quote directly. Here is a summary of William James's essay on the function of higher education (pp. 94–96):

> James tells us in this essay that the humanities should teach biography ("the sifting of human creations!") because through this study we develop a "critical sense" which enables us "to know a good man when we see him."

In the expression "to know a good man when we see him" ("the best single phrase in which we can tell what [education] ought to do for us") James sums up approximately four hundred words of discourse, enabling you—by quoting him—to achieve an equivalent economy and precision of restatement.

In trying to summarize more complex ideas—for example, a proposal that contains several parts and a rationale—you must again commit yourself to several readings. You must again carefully search for the main points and the key terms that embody them, noting also recurrent words and phrases and "summing-up" sentences that might profitably be quoted. In the following proposal, educator James B. Conant suggests a new approach to an introductory science course.

The Tactics and Strategy of Science[2]
JAMES B. CONANT

Let me now be specific as to my proposal for the reform of the scientific education of the layman. What I propose is the establishment of one or more courses at the college level on the Tactics and Strategy of Science. The objective would be to give a

[2]From *On Understanding Science* by James B. Conant. Copyright © 1947 by Yale University Press. Used by permission.

greater degree of understanding of science by the close study of a relatively few historical examples of the development of science. I suggest courses at the college level, for I do not believe they could be introduced earlier in a student's education; but there is no reason why they could not become important parts of programs of adult education. Indeed, such courses might well prove particularly suitable for older groups of men and women.

The analogy with the teaching of strategy and tactics of war by examples from military history is obvious. And the success of that educational procedure is one reason why I venture to be hopeful about this new approach to understanding science. I also draw confidence from the knowledge of how the case method in law schools and a somewhat similar method in the Harvard Business School have demonstrated the value of this type of pedagogic device. The course would not aim to teach science—not even the basic principles or simplest facts—though as a by-product considerable knowledge of certain sciences would be sure to follow. Of course, some elementary knowledge of physics would be a prerequisite, but with the improvement in the teaching of science in high schools which is sure to come, this should prove no serious obstacle.

The case histories would almost all be chosen from the early days in the evolution of the modern discipline. Certain aspects of physics in the seventeenth and eighteenth centuries; chemistry in the eighteenth and nineteenth; geology in the early nineteenth; certain phases of biology in the eighteenth; others in the nineteenth. The advantages of this method of approach are twofold: first, relatively little factual knowledge is required either as regards the science in question or other sciences, and relatively little mathematics; second, in the early days one sees in clearest light the necessary fumblings of even intellectual giants when they are also pioneers; one comes to understand what science is by seeing how difficult it is in fact to carry out glib scientific precepts.

A few words may be in order as to the principles which would guide me in selecting case histories for my course in the Tactics and Strategy of Science. I should wish to show the difficulties which attend each new push forward in the advance of science, and the importance of new techniques: how they arise, are improved, and often revolutionize a field of inquiry. I should hope to illustrate the intricate interplay between experiment, or observation, and the development of new concepts and new generalizations; in short, how new concepts evolve from experiments, how one conceptual scheme for a time is adequate and then is modified or displaced by another. I should want also to illustrate the interconnection between science and society about which so much has been said in recent years by our Marxist friends. I should have very little to say about the classification of facts, unless it were to use this phrase as a straw man. But I should hope that almost all examples chosen would show the hazards which nature puts in the way of those who would examine the facts impartially and classify them accurately. The "controlled experiment" and the planned or controlled observation would be in the forefront of every discussion. The difference in methods between the observational sciences of astronomy, geology, systematic biology on the one hand, and the experimental sciences of physics, chemistry, and experimental biology on the other should be emphasized.

To what extent a course in the Tactics and Strategy of Science should take cognizance of the existence of problems in metaphysics and epistemology would depend on the outlook of the instructor and the maturity and interest of the student. Obviously the course in question would not be one on the metaphysical foundations of modern science; yet the teacher can hardly ignore completely the influence of new scientific concepts on contemporary thinking about the structure of the universe or the nature and destiny of man. Nor can one fail in all honesty to identify at least vaguely those philosophic problems which have arisen when man has sought to examine critically the basis of his knowledge about "the external world." Perhaps in collaboration with a colleague from the department of philosophy the instructor would wish to suggest the reading of extracts from the writings of certain philosophers. If so, the existence of more than one school of thought should certainly be emphasized.

As I shall show in subsequent chapters, a discussion of the evolution of new conceptual schemes as a result of experimentation would occupy a central position in the exposition. This being so, there would be no escape from a consideration of the difficulties which historically have attended the development of new concepts. Is a vacuum really empty, if so, how can you see through it? Is action at a distance imaginable? These questions at one time in the forefront of scientific discussion are well worthy of careful review. The Newtonian theory of gravitation once disturbed "almost all investigators of nature because it was founded on an uncommon unintelligibility." It no longer disturbs us because "it has become a common unintelligibility." To what extent can the same statement be made about other concepts which have played a major part in the development of modern science? When we say that the chemists have "established" that chlorophyll is essential for photosynthesis and that they also have "established" the spatial arrangements of the carbon, hydrogen, and oxygen atoms in cane sugar, are we using the word "establish" in two different senses? These and similar questions should be explored in sufficient degree to make the students aware of some of the complexities which lie hidden behind our usual simplified exposition of the basic ideas of modern science in an elementary course.

However, I cannot emphasize too often that the course in question must *not* be concerned with the fruits of scientific inquiries, either as embodied in scientific laws or theories or cosmologies, or in the applications of science to industry or agriculture or medicine. Rather, the instructor would center his attention on the ways in which these fruits have been attained. One might call it a course in "scientific method" as illustrated by examples from history, except that I am reluctant to use this ambiguous phrase. I should prefer to speak of the methods by which science has been advanced, or perhaps we should say knowledge has been advanced, harking back to Francis Bacon's famous phrase, the advancement of learning.

Before attempting to summarize this essay, we should construct a hypothetical purpose for our labor. (We should never, as mentioned earlier, write in a vacuum, but always with a definite occasion and audience in mind—a rhetorical stance.) Let us say, then, that we are taking notes on Conant's projected science course for a paper we are preparing on the function and status of science education today. We plan to use Conant's proposal as one of several illustrations of innovative suggestions offered by educators. The limited length of our paper makes it imperative that we boil down this proposal to a short paragraph. How can we do this without distorting its essential features?

One way to begin is by isolating key terms and concepts. The title is a helpful clue, for it contains the words "tactics" and "strategy." Is not Conant proposing that the introductory science course be concerned with the tactics and strategy of science—its long and difficult struggle to break through to new areas of knowledge—rather than with the fruits of such struggles— scientific knowledge, neatly classified into systems and codified into laws? Is not Conant proposing further that a "case history" method be used (note how many times this term appears)? By observing scientific discoveries "in process," says Conant, as if they were watching a drama unfold, students in introductory science will learn the true nature of the scientific enterprise, as they do *not* learn it in the conventional course.

We are not yet summarizing Conant's proposal, only exploring it to discover its main contours. We note, then, that the word "difficult" recurs frequently along with various synonyms that refer to the assembling of scientific precepts.

> The *necessary fumblings* of even intellectual giants when they are also pioneers. . . .
>
> One comes to understand what science is by seeing how *difficult* it is in fact to carry out glib scientific precepts.

Note the juxtaposition here of "difficult" and "glib." In a sense this sums up the difference between the course Conant would institute (one that would demonstrate how *difficult* it is to arrive at scientific precepts) and the conventional course (which Conant sees as a *glib*, packaged presentation of scientific facts).

> I should wish to show the *difficulties* which attend each new push forward. . . .
>
> I should hope to illustrate the *intricate* interplay between experiment, or observation, and the development of new concepts. . . .
>
> I should . . . show the *hazards* which nature puts in the way of those who would examine the facts impartially. . . .
>
> . . . There would be no escape from a consideration of the *difficulties* which historically have attended the development of new concepts.
>
> . . . make the students aware of some of the *complexities* which lie hidden behind our usual simplified exposition of the basic ideas of modern science in an elementary course.

Here again we note the juxtaposition of the two approaches: Conant's emphasis on *complexities* (difficulty) as against the *simplified* (and therefore falsified) conventional presentation.

The last paragraph of Conant's essay, though not a formal recapitulation, nonetheless sums up his case: "I cannot emphasize too often that the course in question must *not* be concerned with the fruits of scientific inquiries. . . . Rather [with] the ways in which these fruits have been attained." Clearly this is the central theme of Conant's essay, the main point of his argument in favor of a new type of science course. Recognizing this, we must plan to organize our summary around this point, adding whatever further information we interpret as important. Thus our summary of Conant's proposal (as it appears in our hypothetical paper on "Science Education Today") might read as follows:

> Conant proposes a new type of introductory science course that would be concerned not with the "fruits" of scientific inquiry (a presentation of scientific fact, neatly formulated into theory and law), but rather with the *way* these

fruits have been attained—what Conant calls the "Tactics and Strategy of Science." Rejecting the "usual simplified exposition" of the usual introductory course, which makes science seem static and "glib," Conant calls for a "case history" approach: a close study of a few historical examples of scientific discovery that would give students a realistic picture of how the scientific method works in actual practice: the countless difficulties and "necessary fumblings" that accompany every scientific advance, as well as the ultimate triumphs. Conant's introductory course would emphasize the difficulties and complexities of the scientific enterprise, and its tentativeness and ongoing dialectic. For science is always advancing, says Conant: "One conceptual scheme for a time is adequate and then is modified or displaced by another."

Summarizing Data

Just as we will frequently find occasion to summarize ideas and concepts, so we will find occasion to summarize a body of data that is relevant to our purposes and usable in our writing, provided it can be reduced to its most significant and relevant points of information. Data may be of many kinds (factual, technical, sociological, statistical, historical) and may be taken from many sources (a report, study, survey, reference work). In any case, summarizing data requires that we analyze what the data "add up to," writing not a long list of facts and figures, but rather a short indication of what they *mean*. A good working example of data summary may be seen in Margaret M. Bryant's book-length survey of *Current American Usage*. Based on information gathered over a ten-year period, this book presents its findings in the form of an individual entry for each particular usage that contains the accumulated evidence for and against it. Accompanying each entry is a concise summary, to give "the hurried reader a quick reference guide."

You, Indefinite[3]

Data: Indefinite *you* is employed most frequently when one wishes to express a principle or philosophy, referring to people in general, as in *"You* can never tell what's going to happen" and *"You* never find what *you* want when *you* look for it." Written examples are: "In 'Jane,' however, he has no more conscience than *you* can find in Somerset Maugham ..." (Brooks Atkinson, *The New York Times,* Feb. 10, 1952, Sec. 2, 1) and "And I suppose the point to be made is that, whereas *you* can have such tendencies ... as *you* have ... in the later Mann *you* find ..." (*Kenyon Review,* Winter, 1952, 150).

Indefinite *you* often occurs with *if* or *as if,* as in "Differences can be nourishing if *you* don't waste time and energy fighting them" (Hannah Lees, "How to Be Happy Though Incompatible," *Reader's Digest,* May, 1957, 46) and "Each pain was something all-encompassing now, as if someone were taking *you* and shaking you ..." (Julie Harris, "I Was Afraid to Have a Baby," *Reader's Digest,* Apr., 1957, 44). This usage with the conjunction is more frequent in written English than in common speech. According to one study (Altman), it occurred 29% of the time in written English and 10% in spoken English, whereas the use of *you* to express a general principle occurred much more frequently in spoken English. Another investigator (R. Thomas) showed that it is often found in expository writing.

Indefinite *you* is normally found in more informal writing, the type that meets the reading taste of the general public. More direct and less formal than *one,* it is established in current usage.

We and *they,* like *you,* are also established in standard usage as indefinite pronouns in informal English, as in "*We* never can tell what will happen in the future" and "*They* don't know any history today." This means "One never can tell . . ." and "One doesn't know . . ." French *on* and German *man* serve the same purpose and would be used in translating each one. See also *agreement, indefinite pronouns and they, indefinite.*

Summary: Indefinite you *is common Modern English and occurs both in speech and in expository writing.*

Summarizing Plot (Synopsis)

The ability to write a plot summary, or synopsis, underlies much writing about literature, for we cannot discuss a literary work such as a novel or play unless we are sure that the reader knows its story line—the sequence of events that constitute its action. We may relate the events in chronological order, adding neither interpretive asides nor explanations of the work's structure or underlying logic. Thus in "outline" versions of major works of literature, the summary is confined to a bare recital of unfolding events, as in the following one-paragraph summary of Chapter XXII in Book I of *Don Quixote.*

Don Quixote saw trudging towards him in the road twelve convicts linked together by a chain, manacled, and accompanied by four armed guards. Because these men were obviously not going to their destination of their own free will, the Don believed that this was a situation which called for the services of a knight-errant. He rode up and asked each convict what crime he had committed, receiving honest answers in return. Despite these accounts of roguery, the Don according to his duty as a knight-errant, requested the guards to free the men. When they refused, he attacked them. The convicts, seizing this opportune moment, broke their chain and proceeded to stone the guards who finally took to their heels. Sancho, fearing that a posse of the Holy Brotherhood would set upon himself and his master, advised the Don to get away as fast as possible. But Don Quixote gathered the criminals around him and commanded them to present themselves to his lady Dulcinea del Toboso. However, unwilling to risk apprehension and already suspicious of the sanity of a man who would free convicts, they began to pelt the Don with stones. When they had felled him, they stripped him and Sancho of a goodly portion of their clothing, then departed leaving the Don in a sullen mood and Sancho trembling for fear of the Holy Brotherhood.[4]

Naturally, all narrative details such as dialogue, description, and reflection are omitted from a one-paragraph summary. What is left is a bare-bones account of the action—a helpful tool for charting one's way through a long

[4]Paul B. Bass, *A Complete Critical Outline of Don Quixote* (Boston, Mass.: Student Outlines Co., 1957), pp. 32–33.

and involved novel such as *Don Quixote,* which contains many more details and episodes than one could possibly keep track of without a chapter-by-chapter outline. Such outlines are available in various series, such as the one cited above. Some of these publications are accurate and reliable; others are filled with errors and distortions of the original text. In any case, it is far better to make your own outlines, for in outlining a work, as was mentioned earlier, you come to see its shape and the progressive unfolding of its purpose on a far deeper and more intimate level than in reading the work alone or reading someone else's summary. Approached in this way, then, as a note form, the section-by-section plot summary is a helpful study aid.

Also useful is the overall plot summary, which sweeps across the terrain of an entire novel, reducing it to two pages, or even a single paragraph, as in the following:

Don Quixote de la Mancha, the history of, a satirical romance by Miguel Cervantes, the first part of which appeared in 1605 and the second in 1615. A kindly and simple-minded country gentleman has read the romances of chivalry until they have turned his brain. Clad in a suit of old armor and mounted on a broken-down hack which he christens Rozinante, he sets out on a career of knight-errantry, assuming the name of Don Quixote de la Mancha. For the object of his devotion he chooses a village girl, whom he names Dulcinea del Toboso and as squire he takes an ignorant but faithful peasant, Sancho Panza. The ordinary wayfarers of the Spanish roads of the seventeenth century are transformed by the knight's disordered imagination into warriors, distressed damsels, giants, and monsters. For instance, he tilts on one occasion, at the sails of a group of wind-mills, thinking them living creatures, and his attempts to right fictitious wrongs and win chivalric honor among them lead him and his squire into ludicrous and painful situations. Yet amidst their discomfitures Don Quixote retains a dignity, a certain nobility, and a pathetic idealism, and Sancho a natural shrewdness and popular humor which endear them to the reader. In the second part the interest is fully sustained, and variety is introduced by the sojourn of the pair with a duke and duchess and Sancho's appointment as governor of the imaginary island of Baratoria. At the end, Don Quixote, as the result of a dangerous illness, recovers his senses, renounces all books of chivalry, and dies penitent. The book was begun as an attack on the absurdities of the late chivalric romances, not on the essential chivalric ideals. As the work progresses it becomes a picture of human nature, its absurdities and its aspirations, its coarse materialism and lofty enthusiasm.[5]

The length of a summary does not determine its excellence. A good summary is as long as it *needs* to be in order to fulfill your purpose. It may be objective and analytic or subjective and interpretive, again depending on your purpose. You may not want to intrude any judgments or comments on the work, but simply to tell it "as it is"—in brief space.

It is more common and generally preferable to weave into the recital of bare facts an interpretive description of the work's underlying logic and theme. You will not usually summarize just to summarize, but rather to provide plot background for a literary review or literary analysis. In such cases the length of the plot summary will vary according to how important plot is in the development of your main theme, how much space is available,

[5]From *Thesaurus of Book Digests* edited by Hiram Haydn and Edmund Fuller. © 1949 by Crown Publishers, Inc. Used by permission of Crown Publishers, Inc.

and how much plot there is to summarize. Some stories have weak, virtually nonexistent plots, as the writer of the following summary notes:

Adolphe, a romance by Benjamin Constant. The story has very little incident or action. The whole plot may be summed up in a few words: Adolphe loves Eleonore, and can be happy neither with her nor without her. The beauty of the author's style and the keenness and delicacy with which he analyzes certain morbid moods of the soul have placed this work among the masterpieces of French literature. The romance is almost universally believed to be an autobiography, in which Constant narrates a portion of the adventures of his own youth.[6]

A summary that provides a background for a literary paper should not be a mere recital of happenings ("first this happened, then this, then this"). Rather, it should explain *why* things happen as they do, how events are significant, how they contribute to the pattern of the total work. The literary plot summary, in other words, should go beyond the superficial story line to analysis and interpretation. In such a summary you weave in your own view of the plot even as you recount the bare facts. This deeper dimension of plot summary can be seen in the brief three-sentence introduction to the interpretation of "Birthday Party" (p. 156), wherein B. Bernard Cohen uses interpretive adjectives in phrases like "*private* emotions of an *inconspicuous* couple," "*emotional* tension," and "*conflicting* responses." In using these adjectives, the writer is giving us a perspective on the plot in addition to a simple digest.

Summarizing Events

As was mentioned earlier, the weekly news magazines and the "Week in Review" section of the Sunday *New York Times* are devoted specifically to summarizing events in time—a week, a month, or more. A perspective of events as highlights in relation to the broad sweep of change is fundamental to a good "capsule" summary of the news, a form that helps busy readers find out quickly what is happening or has happened in the world.

The following ambitious summary, for example, attempts (in 500 words) to touch upon major historic events, "surprises," and trends during the sixties, and also to provide prophecies for the seventies. Note that the writer sums up the decade in a single term: "paradox."

The Paradox of the Sixties[7]

JAMES RESTON

This has been a century of stunning surprises, yet the resident seers and magicians here seem to think the seventies will be menacing but manageable. It is a

---

[6]From *The Reader's Digest of Books,* edited by Helen Rex Keller. Copyright, 1929, by The Macmillan Company and reprinted with their permission.

[7]From the *New York Times,* 21 December 1969. © 1969 by The New York Times Company. Reprinted by permission.

puzzler. The mood of the capital about present problems is pessimistic, but the forecasts for the coming decade are fairly optimistic.

No major war, retreat from Vietnam, probably a controlled war in the Middle East with the big powers on the sidelines, endless local and tribal conflict in Africa and maybe even in Latin America, more spheres of influence or Monroe Doctrines for the Soviet Union in Eastern Europe and for China in Southeast Asia; more people, more inflation, more trouble—in short, more of the same—but nothing apocalyptic. This seems to be the forecast of many thoughtful people in the capital.

The Historical Record

There is very little in the history of these last sixty years to justify this assumption that the human race has run out of spectacular stupidities. These sixty years started with the decline of the British and French and ended with the triumph of the Mets— with two tragic wars and endless barbarities and futilities in between.

Herman Kahn and Anthony J. Wiener have kept the boxscore on the astounding surprises that took place in the first and second thirds of the century. It started, they note, with parliamentary democracy in pretty good shape, and Christianity on the rise. The Western world felt fairly optimistic and secure. Then in the first third of the century, the following:

The Russo-Japanese War; the First World War, which devastated Europe; the collapse of the five major dynasties (Hohenzollern, Habsburg, Manchu, Romanov and Ottoman); the rise of Communism and the Soviet Union and Fascism; the Great Depression; and the intellectual influence of Bohr, de Broglie, Einstein and Freud.

The Big Surprises

The second third of the century produced even more surprises: The Second World War; mass murders and evacuations beyond all previous dreams of human depravity; the collapse of the old empires; the reunification and centralization of China and its development of nuclear weapons; the emergence of two superpowers (the U.S. and the U.S.S.R.), five large powers (Japan, West Germany, France, China and Britain); the new confrontation of Washington and Moscow in the cold war; and the emergence of new techniques, new post-Keynesian and post-Marxian economic theories.

Why, then, after all these apocalyptic events—why now when Washington is depressed about its frustrations over Vietnam, inflation, the blacks, the rebellious university whites—should thoughtful men and women here be taking a comparatively calm and even optimistic view of the seventies?

The Major Trends

Maybe it is merely wishful thinking or lack of imagination, and maybe the optimists are wrong, for there are many others who think the country and the world are hopelessly lost and divided and headed for chaos. But this does not seem to be the view of most reflective and experienced minds in the capital.

In fact, the majority seems to be suggesting that the sixties, for all the violence, defiance and confusion, were just violent and defiant and confused enough to force a reappraisal of past assumptions, and make the major powers think about adopting new attitudes and policies in defense of their vital interests.

Within their own geographical spheres of influence, the great powers are still demanding control, and in contested areas like the Middle East, they are still competing for influence in the most dangerous way, but on the big questions, which could produce a world and nuclear war, they are finally talking with a little more common sense.

The major trends elsewhere are also a little more rational. Europe is talking seriously again about cooperation and even economic integration; the war in Vietnam is not escalating but de-escalating; the Soviet Union is just worried enough about China's belligerent tone to reduce tensions in the West and avoid trouble on both fronts at the same time.

Accordingly, at least some observers think they see a new balance of power developing at the turn of the decade. The Congress is challenging the President's right to make war as he chooses; the Communist parties of the world are challenging Moscow's use of power against Czechoslovakia; the militant blacks and militant students in the United States are finding that violence by the minority produced counterviolence by the white majority.

So while all these struggles still go on, there is a feeling here that maybe they can be contained in the seventies, mainly because we learned in the sixties that violence doesn't always pay off, either at home or abroad.

ASSIGNMENTS

Class Discussion and Paragraph Suggestions

(See Chapter 27 for methods of composing unified, adequately developed paragraphs.)

1. Summarizing Ideas
   a. Like Mill's essay "On Liberty," Milton's *Areopagitica* is a defense of free press, a protest against censorship, specifically (in Milton's case) against the licensing of books and pamphlets—a practice established by law in seventeenth-century England. Read and reread the following passage from *Areopagitica;* distill from it its central idea; then write a paragraph (200–250 words) comparing it with the central idea in Mill's statement. Are the two men saying essentially the same thing? Explain.

Good and evil we know in the field of this world grow up together almost inseparably; and the knowledge of good is so involved and interwoven with the knowledge of evil, and in so many cunning resemblances hardly to be discerned, that those confused seeds which were imposed upon Psyche as an incessant labour to cull out, and sort asunder, were not more intermixed. It was from out the rind of one apple tasted, that the knowledge of good and evil, as two twins cleaving together, leaped forth into the world. And perhaps this is that doom which Adam fell into of knowing good and evil, that is to say of knowing good by evil. As therefore the state of man now is; what wisdom can there be to choose, what continence to forbear without the knowledge of evil? He that can apprehend and consider vice with all her baits and seeming pleasures, and yet abstain, and yet distinguish, and yet prefer that which is truly better, he is the true warfaring Christian.

I cannot praise a fugitive and cloistered virtue, unexercised and unbreathed, that never sallies out and sees her adversary, but slinks out of the race, where that immortal garland is to be run for, not without dust and heat. Assuredly we bring not innocence into the world, we bring impurity much rather; that which purifies us is trial, and trial is by what is contrary. That virtue therefore which is but a youngling in the contemplation of evil, and knows not the utmost that vice promises to her followers, and rejects it, is but a blank virtue, not a pure; her whiteness is but an excremental whiteness. Which was the reason why our sage and serious poet Spenser, whom I dare be known to think a better teacher than Scotus or Aquinas, describing true temperance under the person of Guion, brings him in with his palmer through the cave of Mammon, and the bower of earthly bliss, that he might see and know, and yet abstain. Since therefore the knowledge and survey of vice is in this world so necessary to the constituting of human virtue, and the scanning of error to the confirmation of truth, how can we more safely, and with less danger, scout into the regions of sin and falsity than by reading all manner of tractates and hearing all manner of reason? And this is the benefit which may be had of books promiscuously read., . . .

   b. In a paragraph of no more than 200 words sum up each of the following:
     1. The evidence cited in James O'Kane's "Whither the Black Odyssey?" (pp. 323–32) to support the writer's thesis that problems of black Americans are not basically racial.
     2. Allan Gilbert's argument for abolishing college lectures ("College Lectures Are Obsolete," pp. 282–86).
     3. The facts about marijuana as presented in "Questions About Marihuana" (pp. 178–81).
     4. One of the book or film reviews in Chapter 18.

2. Summarizing Data
   a. Write a summary (50–60 words) like the one on page 266 for each of the following entries in *Current American Usage:*

As . . . As, So . . . As[8]

Data: About the middle of the last century, one study (Rucks) shows, only 11.7% of the writers used *as . . . as* in negative statements whereas 88.3% used *so . . . as* ("She is not *so* pretty *as* her sister"); but today the situation is quite different; there has been a substantial shift to 53.6% using *as . . . as* and 46.4% using *so . . . as.* Two other studies (Winburne, Tavin) cited evidence such as the following: " . . . efficiency does not always pay *as* well *as* chance . . ." (*The Atlantic Monthly,* May, 1956, 16) and "There is not *as* much of it *as* there was . . ." (*Yale Review,* Autumn, 1955, 114); on the other hand, "But the effect was not quite *so* 1910 *as* it may sound" (*Harper's,* March, 1956, 82) and "Never had Great Britain been *so* prosperous *as* in 1955 . . ." (*The Atlantic Monthly,* May, 1956, 10).

    The use of *as . . . as* in the affirmative is well established. *As . . . as* has also become involved in an almost uncountable number of word patterns or stereotypes; *as* bright *as* day, *as* clean *as* a bone, *as* cunning *as* a fox, *as* dry *as* dust, *as* easy *as* not, *as* good *as, as* soon *as, as* sure *as* fate, *as* tight *as* a drum, not *as* young *as* she used to be (to mention a few). Occasionally one also encounters *so . . . as* in the affirmative, as in "Seldom has a novel opened *so* laboriously . . . and yet carried *so* forceful an impact . . . *as* this fictionized chronicle . . ." (*The New York Times Book Review,* Apr. 1, 1956, 17, cited by Rucks). Perhaps the inverted verb selects *so . . . as,* because the head word in the sentence, *seldom,* inverts the subject-verb order in the manner of *never.*

Preposition at End of Clause or Sentence

When John Dryden in the seventeenth century decided, on the analogy of Latin, against the propriety of placing a preposition at the end of a clause or a sentence, he set up a prejudice which has persisted to the present time.

Data: Actually, a number of constructions require the final preposition:

The final preposition may be part of the verb, especially in passive constructions, as in " . . . hardly any wind for us to *contend with"* (*Holiday,* June, 1953, 70); " . . . a recess *was* tacitly *agreed to"* (*New York Post,* May 28, 1953).

If the relative pronoun serving as the object of a preposition is omitted, the preposition invariably comes last, as in "It was the lumber company's watchman I went up there to call *on"* (*Holiday,* June, 1953, 45); cf. " . . . watchman *on whom* I went up there to call"; "Pride, dignity, conventionality became poor rags to *wrap* one's loneliness *in"* (*Ladies' Home Journal,* Mar., 1953, 110); cf. " . . . *in which to wrap* one's loneliness."

If *that* or *as* is the relative, the preposition comes last: " . . . plans *that* he really does not look *at . . ."* (*Saturday Review,* Apr. 2, 1955, 30). Observe that if *at* is removed from the end of the preceding example, *that* must be replaced by *which:* " . . . plans *at which* he really does not look . . ."

The preposition may come last because the clause it is in may be the object of a preposition, as in "Many a marriage might be saved by a timely look at what it was built *on"* (*Ladies' Home Journal,* Apr., 1953, 25), where the clause *what it was built on* is the object of the preposition *at.*

One construction, however, on which usage may vary, is illustrated in "News . . . is . . . those things that happen *about* which people are curious" (*Saturday Review,* Jan. 1, 1955, 9). Here the preposition could have come at the end, thus: " . . . which people are curious *about,"* as it actually does in the sentence "I recognized one which three of my partners had been working *on . . ."* (*ibid,* Oct. 2, 1954, 18). This sentence, likewise, could have been written: *"on* which three of my partners had been working. . . ." Quantitative evidence on this construction, as it occurs in a study of formal written English (Russell), shows an overwhelming preference for the preposition before its object: in almost 94% of the instances. In informal written English and in conversation, other studies (Dunlap, Frost, Hessel, Spanier, R. Thomas, Zavin) show that one finds more instances of the preposition at the end of the clause or sentence than in formal English. One also frequently finds the preposition at the end in questions: "But isn't this exactly what the ostrich was counting *on?"* (*New York Herald Tribune,* Nov. 30, 1952) and "What are we afraid *of?"* (*Life,* May 18, 1953, 172).

b. Write a digest or "abstract" (200 words) of Cohen's "Isaac Newton" (pp. 318–22).

3. Summarizing Plot

In a paragraph (100–150 words) summarize the plot of Dorothy Parker's "The Waltz" (pp. 162–64).

4. Summarizing Events

Write a set of three summaries (200 words each) of the week's news events, under the headings of national news, international news, and any subject that is prominent in the news at the moment (a particular country, government agency, or political figure). For sample summaries, see one of the weekly news magazines or the "Week in Review" section of the Sunday *New York Times.*

Essay Suggestions

1. Write an essay (500 words) summarizing events of the seventies to date.

2. Write an essay (500–750 words) summarizing the plot of a novel, play, or film.

3. Write an essay (500–750 words) summarizing the data or ideas presented in a nonfiction book (on science, philosophy, religion, or history, for example).

20 What Case Can Be Made For or Against X?

Aristotle said: "If it is a disgrace to a man when he cannot defend himself in a bodily way, it would be odd not to think him disgraced when he cannot defend himself with reason." It is reason—and *mainly* reason—that we must marshal when we ask the question "What case can be made for or against X?" In trying to build a case, we move beyond plain exposition into the more active and aggressive realm of argumentation, an ancient and honored form of discourse wherein the arguer tries not merely to explain but to defend or refute what logicians call a "proposition," a statement about which there may be and usually is conflict and controversy. Unlike a plain statement of fact ("John Smith is the mayor of Squedunk"), a proposition cannot be looked up, verified, and established once and for all. Instead, a proposition is debatable: it may or may not be true ("The mayor of Squedunk is corrupt and should be thrown out of office"). In making such a judgment, in asserting such a proposition, you assume the burden of proof; you must marshal evidence and exert rigorous reasoning in defense of your cause.

Thus your argument for or against a proposition represents your attempt to substantiate your own reasons for believing as you do. In presenting your case, you hope to convince your readers or listeners that you are right and to win them over to your side. In order to do this you must, of course, make sense; your facts must be believable and your logic unassailable. In addition, you must be persuasive; that is, you must make an appeal on a personal and emotional level; you must seem sincere, genuinely committed to your cause, responsible, well-intentioned, open-minded, fair, and clearly on the side of the good.

Is and *Ought* **Propositions**

We may distinguish two basic kinds of propositions: the *is* proposition (an assertion of opinion or value) and the *ought* proposition (a proposal for action). You will note in the illustrative essays in this chapter that most arguments combine the two types, thereby establishing the fundamental causal relationship that underlies most argumentation:

Because A *is* the case, B *ought* to be done.

An example of this logical formulation can be found in Woodrow Wilson's historic address to Congress in 1917, asking for a declaration of war against Germany.

Because Germany's aggressive submarine action against American commerce *is* an act of warfare against both the United States and mankind [an assertion of opinion or value], America *ought* to enter World War I [a proposal for action], which action would make the world "safe for democracy" [the projected conclusion].

President Wilson's aim in this classic example of "making a case" for a specific action was to win the assent of members of Congress, to convince them that what he asserted was true and just, worthy of wholehearted and unconditional support. To achieve his end, he drew upon many of the traditional methods of argumentation, even following—roughly—the three-part structure of the classical oration, as outlined below:

THE STRUCTURE OF ARGUMENT

I. *INTRODUCTION*

The introduction may consist of a single sentence or of several paragraphs, including one or more of the following:

A. *Exordium:* The beginning or opening words, designed to win attention and good will by introducing the case in an interesting and favorable light (a quotation, personal reference, story)

B. *Exposition or narration:* An account of the history of the case (what gave rise to the present problem; how the issues developed)

C. Direct statement of the case (the *proposition* to be proved or defended)

D. Division of proofs: An *outline* of how the evidence will be presented ("first I will explain . . . and then I will demonstrate . . .")

II. *BODY OF ARGUMENT*

A. *Confirmation* of one's case by presenting evidence in its favor:

1. facts
2. reasons
3. statistics
4. testimony of experts
5. opinions

      6. reports

      7. examples

      8. logical reasoning (deductive and inductive)

      9. analogy

  B. *Refutation* of opposing views by demonstrating that they are:

      1. untrue

      2. illogical

      3. self-contradictory

      4. ambiguous (terms are not clearly defined)

      5. dishonest (a deliberate attempt to deceive)

      6. absurd

  C. *Concession* of points to the opposition that must in fairness be conceded; reply to them and offer of alternate positions

III. *CONCLUSION*

  A. *Recapitulation* and *summary* of argument: To repeat is to reinforce points, and to make certain they have not been misunderstood.

  B. *Peroration:* A final, heightened appeal for support

Note how President Wilson's address falls into this pattern.

Woodrow Wilson Asks Congress to Declare War[1]

INTRODUC-
TION

Exordium

Narration

Gentlemen of the Congress:

I have called the Congress into extraordinary session because there are serious, very serious, choices of policy to be made, and made immediately, which it was neither right nor constitutionally permissible that I should assume the responsibility of making.

On the third of February last I officially laid before you the extraordinary announcement of the Imperial German Government that on and after the first day of February it was its purpose to put aside all restraints of law or of humanity and use its submarines to sink every vessel that sought to approach either the ports of Great Britain and Ireland or the western coasts of Europe or any of the ports controlled by the enemies of Germany within the Mediterranean. That had seemed to be the object of the German submarine warfare earlier in the war, but since April of last year the Imperial Government had somewhat restrained the commanders of its undersea craft in conformity with its promise then given to us that passenger boats should not be sunk and that due warning would be given to all other vessels which its submarines might seek to destroy, when no resistance was offered or escape attempted, and care taken that their crews were given at least a fair chance to save their lives in their open boats. The precautions taken were meager and haphazard enough, as was proved in distressing instance after instance in the progress of the

[1]Address delivered to a joint session of Congress, April 2, 1917.

cruel and unmanly business, but a certain degree of restraint was observed. The new policy has swept every restriction aside. Vessels of every kind, whatever their flag, their character, their cargo, their destination, their errand, have been ruthlessly sent to the bottom without warning and without thought of help or mercy for those on board, the vessels of friendly neutrals along with those of belligerents. Even hospital ships and ships carrying relief to the sorely bereaved and stricken people of Belgium, though the latter were provided with safe conduct through the proscribed areas by the German Government itself and were distinguished by unmistakable marks of identity, have been sunk with the same reckless lack of compassion or of principle.

(Note listing of details to support the case against Germany)

I was for a little while unable to believe that such things would in fact be done by any government that had hitherto subscribed to the humane practices of civilized nations. International law had its origin in the attempt to set up some law which would be respected and observed upon the seas, where no nation had right of dominion and where lay the free highways of the world. By painful stage after stage has that law been built up, with meager enough results, indeed, after all was accomplished that could be accomplished, but always with a clear view, at least, of what the heart and conscience of mankind demanded. This minimum of right the German Government has swept aside under the plea of retaliation and necessity and because it had no weapons which it could use at sea except those which it is impossible to employ as it is employing them without throwing to the winds all scruples of humanity or of respect for the understandings that were supposed to underlie the intercourse of the world. I am not now thinking of the loss of property involved, immense and serious as that is, but only of the wanton and wholesale destruction of the lives of noncombatants, men, women, and children, engaged in pursuits which have always, even in the darkest periods of modern history, been deemed innocent and legitimate. Property can be paid for; the lives of peaceful and innocent people cannot be. The present German submarine warfare against commerce is a warfare against mankind.

IS
Proposition 1

It is a war against all nations. American ships have been sunk, American lives taken, in ways which it has stirred us very deeply to learn of, but the ships and people of other neutral and friendly nations have been sunk and overwhelmed in the waters in the same way. There has been no discrimination. The challenge is to all mankind. Each nation must decide for itself how it will meet it. The choice we make for ourselves must be made with a moderation of counsel and a temperateness of judgment befitting our character and our motives as a nation. We must put excited feeling away. Our motive will not be revenge or the victorious assertion of the physical might of the nation, but only the vindication of right, of human right, of which we are only a single champion.

When I addressed the Congress on the twenty-sixth of February last I thought that it would suffice to assert our neutral rights with arms, our right to use the seas against unlawful interference, our right to keep our people safe against unlawful violence. But armed

IS
Proposition 2

neutrality, it now appears, is impracticable. Because submarines are in effect outlaws when used as the German submarines have been used against merchant shipping, it is impossible to defend ships against their attacks as the law of nations has assumed that merchantmen would defend themselves against privateers or cruisers, visible craft giving chase upon the open sea. It is common prudence in such circumstances, grim necessity indeed, to endeavor to destroy them before they have shown their own intention. They must be dealt with upon sight, if dealt with at all. The German Government denies the right of neutrals to use arms at all within the areas of the sea which it has proscribed, even in the defense of rights which no modern publicist has ever before questioned their right to defend. The intention is conveyed that the armed guards which we have placed on our merchant ships will be treated as beyond the pale of law and subject to be dealt with as pirates would be. Armed neutrality is ineffectual enough at best; in such circumstances and in the face of such pretensions it is worse than ineffectual: it is likely only to produce what it was meant to prevent; it is practically certain to draw us into the war without either the rights or the effectiveness of belligerents. There is one choice we cannot make, we are incapable of making: we will not choose the path of submission and suffer the most sacred rights of our nation and our people to be ignored or violated. The wrongs against which we now array ourselves are no common wrongs; they cut to the very roots of human life.

OUGHT
Proposition:
United
States
should
declare
war

With a profound sense of the solemn and even tragical character of the step I am taking and of the grave responsibilities which it involves, but in unhesitating obedience to what I deem my constitutional duty, I advise that the Congress declare the recent course of the Imperial German Government to be in fact nothing less than war against the government and people of the United States; that it formally accept the status of belligerent which has thus been thrust upon it; and that it take immediate steps not only to put the country in a more thorough state of defense but also to exert all its power and employ all its resources to bring the Government of the German Empire to terms and end the war. . . .

[In the next four paragraphs, omitted here, Wilson reviews the specific ways in which the country should mobilize: increase armed forces, raise taxes.]

BODY OF
ARGUMENT
(Marshalling
of reasons
in support of
proposi-
tions)

Reason 1:
to vindicate
world peace

While we do these things, these deeply momentous things, let us be very clear, and make very clear to all the world what our motives and our objects are. My own thought has not been driven from its habitual and normal course by the unhappy events of the last two months, and I do not believe that the thought of the nation has been altered or clouded by them. I have exactly the same things in mind now that I had in mind when I addressed the Senate on the twenty-second of January last; the same that I had in mind when I addressed the Congress on the third of February and on the twenty-sixth of February. Our object now, as then, is to vindicate the principles of peace and justice in the life of the world as against selfish and autocratic power and to set up amongst the really free and self-

against
autocratic
power

governed peoples of the world such a concert of purpose and of action as will henceforth insure the observance of those principles. Neutrality is no longer feasible or desirable where the peace of the world is involved and the freedom of its peoples, and the menace to that peace and freedom lies in the existence of autocratic governments backed by organized force which is controlled wholly by their will, not by the will of their people. We have seen the last of neutrality in such circumstances. We are at the beginning of an age in which it will be insisted that the same standards of conduct and of responsibility for wrong done shall be observed among nations and their governments that are observed among the individual citizens of civilized states.

We have no quarrel with the German people. We have no feeling towards them but one of sympathy and friendship. It was not upon their impulse that their government acted in entering this war. It was not with their previous knowledge or approval. It was a war determined upon as wars used to be determined upon in the old, unhappy days when peoples were nowhere consulted by their rulers and wars were provoked and waged in the interest of dynasties or of little groups of ambitious men who were accustomed to use their fellowmen as pawns and tools. Self-governed nations do not fill their neighbor states with spies or set the course of intrigue to bring about some critical posture of affairs which will give them an opportunity to strike and make conquest. Such designs can be successfully worked out only under cover and where no one has the right to ask questions. Cunningly contrived plans of deception or aggression, carried, it may be, from generation to generation, can be worked out and kept from the light only within the privacy of courts or behind the carefully guarded confidences of a narrow and privileged class. They are happily impossible where public opinion commands and insists upon full information concerning all the nation's affairs.

Reason 2:
to band
together
with other
democratic
nations

A steadfast concert for peace can never be maintained except by a partnership of democratic nations. No autocratic government could be trusted to keep faith within it or observe its covenants. It must be a league of honor, a partnership of opinion. Intrigue would eat its vitals away; the plottings of inner circles who could plan what they would and render account to no one would be a corruption seated at its very heart. Only free peoples can hold their purpose and their honor steady to a common end and prefer the interests of mankind to any narrow interest of their own.

Reason 3:
analogy to
Russia's
"shaking
off" of
autocratic
power

Does not every American feel that assurance has been added to our hope for the future peace of the world by the wonderful and heartening things that have been happening within the last few weeks in Russia? Russia was known by those who knew it best to have been always in fact democratic at heart, in all the vital habits of her thought, in all the intimate relationships of her people that spoke their natural instinct, their habitual attitude towards life. The autocracy that crowned the summit of her political structure, long as it had stood and terrible as was the reality of its power, was not in fact Russian in origin, character, or purpose; and now it has been shaken off and the great, generous Russian people have been added in all their naïve majesty and might to the forces that are fighting for freedom in the world, for justice, and for peace. Here is a fit partner for a League of Honor.

Reason 4:
German
spying

One of the things that has served to convince us that the Prussian autocracy was not and could never be our friend is that from the very outset of the present war it has filled our unsuspecting communities and even our offices of Government with spies and set criminal intrigues everywhere afoot against our national unity of counsel, our peace within and without, our industries and our commerce. Indeed it is now evident that its spies were here even before the war began; and it is unhappily not a matter of conjecture but a fact proved in our courts of justice that the intrigues which have more than once come perilously near to disturbing the peace and dislocating the industries of the country have been carried on at the instigation, with the support, and even under the personal direction of official agents of the Imperial Government accredited to the Government of the United States. Even in checking these things and trying to extirpate them we have sought to put the most generous interpretation possible upon them because we knew that their source lay, not in any hostile feeling or purpose of the German people towards us (who were, no doubt, as ignorant of them as we ourselves were), but only in the selfish designs of a government that did what it pleased and told its people nothing. But they have played their part in serving to convince us at last that that government entertains no real friendship for us and means to act against our peace and security at its convenience. That it means to stir up enemies against us at our very doors the intercepted note to the German Minister at Mexico City is eloquent evidence.

Reason 5:
constant
threat to
security

We are accepting this challenge of hostile purpose because we know that in such a government, following such methods, we can never have a friend; and that in the presence of its organized power, always lying in wait to accomplish we know not what purpose, there can be no assured security for the democratic governments of the world. We are now about to accept gauge of battle with this natural foe to liberty and shall, if necessary, spend the whole force of the nation to check and nullify its pretensions and its power. We are glad, now that we see the facts with no veil of false pretense about them, to fight thus for the ultimate peace of the world and for the liberation of its peoples, the German peoples included: for the rights of nations great and small and the privilege of men everywhere to choose their way of life and of obedience. The world must be made safe for democracy. Its peace must be planted upon the tested foundations of political liberty. We have no selfish ends to serve. We desire no conquest, no dominion. We seek no indemnities for ourselves, no material compensation for the sacrifices we shall freely make. We are but one of the champions of the rights of mankind. We shall be satisfied when those rights have been made as secure as the faith and the freedom of nations can make them.

(This
sentence
would
become a
rallying cry
for the Allied
Forces)

Just because we fight without rancor and without selfish object, seeking nothing for ourselves but what we shall wish to share with all free peoples, we shall, I feel confident, conduct our operations as belligerents without passion and ourselves observe with proud punctilio the principles of right and of fair play we profess to be fighting for.

I have said nothing of the governments allied with the Imperial Government of Germany because they have not made war upon us or challenged us to defend our right and our honor. The Austro-Hungarian Government has, indeed, avowed its unqualified indorsement and acceptance of the reckless and lawless submarine warfare adopted now without disguise by the Imperial German Government, and it has therefore not been possible for this government to receive Count Tarnowski, the Ambassador recently accredited to this government by the Imperial and Royal Government of Austria-Hungary; but that government has not actually engaged in warfare against citizens of the United States on the seas, and I take the liberty, for the present at least, of postponing a discussion of our relations with the authorities at Vienna. We enter this war only where we are clearly forced into it because there are no other means of defending our rights.

CONCLU-
SION
Recapitu-
lation

It will be all the easier for us to conduct ourselves as belligerents in a high spirit of right and fairness because we act without animus, not in enmity towards a people or with the desire to bring any injury or disadvantage upon them, but only in armed opposition to an irresponsible government which has thrown aside all considerations of humanity and of right and is running amuck. We are, let me say again, the sincere friends of the German people, and shall desire nothing so much as the early re-establishment of intimate relations of mutual advantage between us,—however hard it may be for them, for the time being, to believe that this is spoken from our hearts. We have borne with their present government through all these bitter months because of that friendship,—exercising a patience and forbearance which would otherwise have been impossible. We shall, happily, still have an opportunity to prove that friendship in our daily attitude and actions towards the millions of men and women of German birth and native sympathy who live amongst us and share our life, and we shall be proud to prove it towards all who are in fact loyal to their neighbors and to the government in the hour of test. They are, most of them, as true and loyal Americans as if they had never known any other fealty or allegiance. They will be prompt to stand with us in rebuking and restraining the few who may be of a different mind and purpose. If there should be disloyalty, it will be dealt with with a firm hand of stern repression; but, if it lifts its head at all, it will lift it only here and there and without countenance except from a lawless and malignant few.

Peroration

It is a distressing and oppressive duty, Gentlemen of the Congress, which I have performed in thus addressing you. There are, it may be, many months of fiery trial and sacrifice ahead of us. It is a fearful thing to lead this great peaceful people into war, into the most terrible and disastrous of all wars, civilization itself seeming to be in the balance. But the right is more precious than peace, and we shall fight for the things which we have always carried nearest our

hearts,—for democracy, for the right of those who submit to authority to have a voice in their own governments, for the rights and
liberties of small nations, for a universal dominion of right by such a
concert of free peoples as shall bring peace and safety to all nations
and make the world itself at last free. To such a task we can dedicate
our lives and our fortunes, everything that we are and everything that
we have, with the pride of those who know that the day has come
when America is privileged to spend her blood and her might for the
principles that gave her birth and happiness and the peace which
she has treasured. God helping her, she can do no other.

Locating the Issues

It is not our business here to dwell on the intrinsic merits of this historic
argument—or on the merits of any of the illustrative arguments presented in
this chapter; we shall simply note some of their logical and rhetorical
features so that we may be better equipped to make our own arguments
concerning problems that confront us today. One contemporary argument,
drawn from the field of education, is found in the more informal essay that
follows: Allan H. Gilbert's spirited case against a hallowed academic tradition, the college lecture. Here again, *is* and *ought* propositions are combined:

> Because, in an age of mass printing and sophisticated audio-visual aids, the
> lecture system of teaching *is* obsolete [assertion of opinion and value], college
> lectures *ought* to be abolished [proposal for action].

Note that here again the classic three-part division of argument is visible:
introduction, body, conclusion. Note also how carefully Gilbert has isolated
the issues involved in this controversial topic.

"Issues" may be defined as the main points of difference or opinion on
which a writer builds his or her case. Thus, locating the issues on any given
subject is the essential first step in argumentation, since the body of an
argument is generally organized according to a systematic consideration of
issues, each one coming up for review and, wherever possible, for proof.

College Lectures Are Obsolete[2]
ALLAN H. GILBERT

INTRODUC-
TION

Narration

The advertising pamphlet of a well-known American university
recently showed a picture of a professor presenting chemistry to
some hundreds of students. Except for the costumes and the ugly
angularity of the room, it might have been an academic scene in
1450, before the invention of printing. In 1766 Dr. Johnson remarked:

Quoting
authority

I cannot see that lectures can do as much good as reading the books
from which the lectures are taken.

[2]From *CEA Critic*, October 1967. Reprinted with the permission of the author and the College
English Association.

And in 1781 he still thought:

> Lectures were once useful, but now, when all can read, and books are so numerous, lectures are unnecessary.

Proposition (implicitly stated)

Yet after two hundred years, the modern professor has not overtaken Dr. Johnson. He has not discovered that printing has been invented—not to mention xerox, etc. The old-time methods are good enough for him. Academic photographers are especially amusing in that they delight in showing the most blatantly up-to-date subjects, such as physics, presented as in Abelard's Paris. Obviously this applies not to the occasional public lecture, but to the twice-a-week throughout the term.

BODY

What Is Wrong About Lectures?

Systematic review of issues: first from a negative point of view . . .

1. Even a good speaker will not always be correctly heard by his audience. Horns toot, students cough. And sometimes professors mumble. Even in the notes of graduate students the well-known Professor Fredson Bowers has appeared as Fritz and Brower, and Nike of Samothrace as the Decay of Sammy's Face.

2. What is written on a blackboard—often in professorial scribble—cannot be perfectly copied. Time presses; even modern lighting is not all-revealing; perfect vision is not universal.

3. A student trying to take excellent notes cannot think about their content; he must not lag. He is like the telegrapher of whom Edison tells. The man received, in dots and dashes, the news of Lincoln's assassination; when he went out on the street, he learned that such news had been reported. In the days of monotype composition for newspapers, I knew the man who set the gossip column for the local paper. When the paper appeared, he read it as something new to him. Such must be the mind of the student who takes notes so good that he can attain the ideal of giving back in his blue book what the lecturer has said. The Welsh professor of mediaeval literature, Dr. Ker, is said to have remarked: "How can I give less than 90 for my own words?"

4. Lectures prepared long since and read from yellowed paper cease to call on the professor's brain. His class in the morning need not call him from the idiot box in the evening. The chairman of a department in which I served once read the same lecture to a class for the third successive time. . . . It is reported of a Harvard professor that he moved to the door and put his hand on the knob for his last sentence. No student could catch him. Revision would disarrange the schedule and desecrate the sentences which, through many repetitions, the professor has come to regard as truth. He is a human tape recorder. The students are tape-receivers. . . .

5. The college lecturer seldom has a prepared audience. How often can a lecturer on Shakespeare, for example, be sure that his hearers have read the play on which he speaks? If he can read aloud, he may read to his class with profit, but then he ceases to be a lecturer. The unprepared audience (or the audience not eager to learn the subject, and not impatient of failure to help them do so) affects the lecturer. He wishes to break through their boredom. So

he tends to become an entertainer, giving a show. There is much in the story that the faculty of a well-known college for men opposes the admission of women because—evidently being old fogies—they imagine they would be deprived of the bawdy jokes supposed to amuse their captive audiences. But how often do professorial jokes illustrate the subject in hand? Or the popular lecturer turns to oratory. Newspaper pictures of some popular teachers who recently have gathered publicity by dismissal, show them making gestures suited to the soap box or the pulpit. An academic Savonarola or Billy Sunday or Graham may rouse in a few hearers an emotional desire to learn. Such a desire, when it lasts, prepares a youth to study and to seek aid from a teacher, but it is not teaching. Colleges, like the rest of life, need their share of emotion, but their primary business is intellectual. A man given over to his own convictions and beliefs is not a teacher because he cannot see both sides of a subject.

6. Especially for commuting students, attendance at lectures is a serious burden. If the teacher has lectures prepared, let them be mimeographed. Then the student can study them at home. Or let the professor require the student to read the books from which the lectures are drawn. They can be bought for less money than commuting requires; and the student is not wasting his time in a bus or automobile.

7. In the lecturer's audience, the student tends to become a mere numbered unit, deprived of power to question, much less to object. He is trained to accept the dicta of the professor—a habit worse than that of going to the library to find "a book"—author unobserved—from which to copy. At least the library offers more than one book, and even the most facile pedagogue is likely to take more pains with dicta to be printed than with those merely to be pronounced in the uncritical isolation of the lecture hall, before students who—if they wish good marks—will not murmur publicly against what they are told. The lecture inculcates passivity of mind. The student is a spectator, with no part in the game, except that he selects the lecture course because it is called a crib.

8. The book, even when mimeographed, is better than any student's notes. There are no hiatuses for sickness, empty pens, noise. As Dr. Johnson said: "If your attention fails and you miss part of a lecture, you are lost; you cannot go back as you can upon a book."

Furthermore, the best lectures are most likely to attain printing. If a professor has lectures better than any printed book or even group of printed books, can he be defended for restricting them to his own university, instead of giving them to mankind? Are we to suppose that there are in America a hundred sets of lecture notes superior to anything in print? Is not the student better off with A. C. Bradley's own vindication of Falstaff—however absurd it is—than with the Shakespeare professor's diluted version of it? If the professor cannot do better than the authors on his reading list, why not omit the lectures and attend to the reading list?

9. Something can be said for the living presence of the lecturer. But this is again revivalistic; the college lecturer is supposed to be teaching a subject. There is, too, a presence behind the written

word, usually stronger, though less immediate, than that on the platform. Does the student come to college for the personality of Professor X, or to learn? Indeed the professor who gives a course in himself is handicapped by the insignificance of his subject. "A good book is the precious life blood of a master spirit." How often are lecture-writers such spirits?

10. The important poets have been so richly annotated that even the most expert scholars can now add little detailed comment. Fortunate is the lecturer on Milton who can improve on Professor Hughes' notes. The lesser authors have been carefully worked. How many teachers of Herrick can correct any of Professor Patrick's notes, or explain difficulties he has not elucidated? As to more general comment, a lecturer may indeed warn his pupils against much that has been written on great authors, but how many lecturers are capable of anything else than riding with the tide? Poetry exists to be read; the lecture pushes it into the class of something to be talked about rather than experienced. (Non-lecture teaching is somewhat less subject to this danger.)

. . . then
from
a positive
point of
view—the
remedy

The Remedy

Perfect teaching will appear when we have teachers who have entered into their subjects and students eager to learn. With these, we would not need to bother about systems. Without them, not much can be done. We have always had, and always shall have, lawyers not aware of the nature of law, generals unaware of the nature of war, professors of physics who have not found out what their subject is, teachers of Chaucer and Dante who do not, as Benedetto Croce has said, sympathize with their authors. Yet something external can be done against lecturitis.

Citing
authority

Let a teacher who sufficiently believes in his own greatness put his lectures in print to be revised frequently as he grows wiser. Then he can abandon his robes of glory, and the student will have more accurate statements and clearer diagrams, which he can copy at his leisure, if that will implant them in his memory.

In a normal lecture course, let us suppose thirty lectures per term, and 150 students. At that rate, each student gets of the professor's public time $\frac{1}{150}$ of thirty hours, or $\frac{1}{5}$ of an hour. If the professor abandons his rostrum, he has time to meet each student individually for ten minutes a term. The student is warned to prepare. The assistants who gather about such courses are consulted on what the student may profitably ask. Some students would treasure throughout life the memory of ten minutes' serious talk with an eminent professor.

I know students at some of our large places who have gone through their four years without ever speaking on their studies with a man of professorial rank. Such undergraduates deal with junior teachers, graduate students, some of them brilliant, but many of them destined to be mediocrities or failures. Yet from the class of a thousand, the hundred and fifty with the best records can still meet the eminent professor. Such a teacher, relieved from the strain of the large lecture—not entirely removed by the loud speaker—would usually be willing to go beyond the hundred and fifty. If freed from the ceremonial lecture, the pupil has two hours a week free for studying books, mimeographed or printed, and scientific specimens. He does not—in the computer age—spend thirty hours a term writing by hand. Nothing good in the present system need be abolished. The students in the big class can still be divided into small sections, presided over by the best junior teachers the college will pay for.

CONCLU-
SION

Recapitu-
lation

Peroration

The survival of the lecture, for nearly five hundred years after the invention of printing, exhibits the unimaginative, unobserving professorial mind. Hidebound professors still read lectures to three or four students, even to one. This seems more ludicrous in nuclear physics than in the humanities, but does not reveal a more imperceptive mind. John Philip Holland, the father of the submarine, said that naval officers (who yield little to professors in holding to what has been) disliked the submarine because it provided no quarter deck to strut on. Do professors cling to lectures because they offer a rostrum to strut on and a lectern to sprawl over?

Lively and provocative as this argument is, are there not logical grounds on which its indictment of the lecture system could be challenged? Are all lectures *necessarily* read "from yellowed paper"? Are all lecturers *necessarily* "human tape recorders"? Are all students *necessarily* "human tape-receivers"? Are mimeographed copies of a lecture read by students privately in the library *necessarily* more profitable than personal delivery in a lecture? (May not students fall asleep in the library as well as the lecture hall?) What about the creative lecturer (is there such a person?) who communicates fresh insights so compellingly that students "catch fire"—as they could not from the printed page? Cannot more be said about the possibilities and value of person-to-person classroom encounter? Does the lecture *have* to be an extended monologue? Is Gilbert talking about *some* kinds of lectures and lecturers or *all* kinds (see pp. 290–91 on generalization)? Do you think a writer convinced of the merits of a lecture system could challenge Gilbert's position and, using a different set of descriptive terms and examples, write an equally lively and provocative case *for* the college lecture?

Deduction and Induction

There is no single best way of making a case for or against something. The best way depends on the particular subject and situation at hand, the particular readers being addressed, and the particular purpose in the writer's mind. These factors are relative. What are constant and predictable are the two basic lines of reasoning along which argument inevitably proceeds. They are *deduction*—inferring a particular fact from a general truth (for example, since deciduous plants are known to shed their leaves in winter, I can expect the deciduous dogwood that I planted in my yard last spring to shed its leaves this winter) and *induction*—moving from particular facts to generalizations (for example, since I have tasted thirty green apples and each one was sour, I conclude that all green apples are sour). In actual experience the two modes run into one another, as Thomas Huxley demonstrated in his essay "Thinking Scientifically" (pp. 77–79). Thus:

	1. You examine thirty green apples.
	2. Each one is sour.
(induction)	3. You generalize: green apples are sour.
	4. You pick up apple thirty-one, which is also green.
(deduction)	5. You infer that this apple—which you have not yet tasted—will also be sour.

Interdependent as they are, each mode of reasoning has distinctive features and therefore should be examined individually.

Deduction

In deductive reasoning we lay down *premises*, certain statements we know or strongly believe are true; from these premises we then derive a *conclusion*. Deduction, then, involves a closely linked *chain of reasoning:*

A   B

	A B
major premise:	All human beings are mortal.
	C A
minor premise:	Socrates is a human being.
	C B
conclusion:	Socrates is mortal.

The line of reasoning in this *syllogism* (as a three-part statement of this kind is called) is logically valid because given the two premises, the conclusion necessarily follows. In fact, the conclusion merely states *explicitly* what is already stated *implicitly* in the premises. The conclusion can then be said to derive logically and formally from the premises; in this case it points to the axiomatic truth that "things equal to the same thing are equal to each other." Thus in the example above, A equals B; C equals A; therefore ($\therefore$) C equals B.

There are formal rules for syllogisms, but we need not go into them here. Our interest is in compositional logic, not in logic per se. Furthermore, common sense—that inborn quality of mind that enables us to follow a logical line of reasoning even if we have never heard the word "logic" before—will often alert us to logical errors. We can tell, for example, that thinking is askew when the premises state that *some* of X is undesirable, and the inference drawn is that *all* of X is undesirable:

> Some people are cruel.
> John is a person.
> $\therefore$ John is cruel.

Obviously, John might not belong in the group of "cruel people." The conclusion changes "some" to "all."

This leap from "some" to "all" is an especially common logical error, or *fallacy;* most people will not specify "some" even when they mean it. Instead they will say, "People are cruel." Such a statement is patently unfair.

It can create ill feeling toward whole groups, when in truth only some members are blameworthy: because some students cheat on examinations, we should not conclude—as a sensational magazine story might maintain—that "college kids are dishonest."

Similarly, common sense tells us that another gross error has been committed in the following statement:

> All human beings are mammals.
> All monkeys are mammals.
> ∴ All human beings are monkeys.

Logicians call this "the fallacy of the undistributed middle";[3] but here again we need not name the logical flaw to see that it has been committed: we know that things belonging to the same general class are not necessarily identical. In this case, the fact that humans are mammals and monkeys are also mammals simply means that they, along with many other animals, share a larger biological category, as the logician's circular diagram shows:

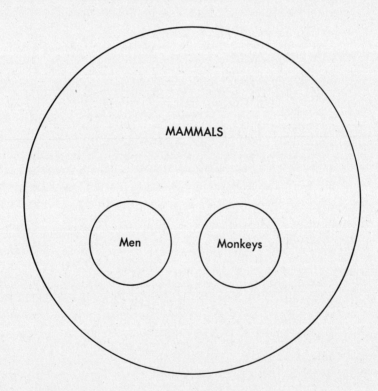

No one would fail to spot the fallacy of the undistributed middle in this example (we *know* people are not monkeys!); but the fallacy is not usually so easy to detect. Indeed it may be (and frequently is) used in a subtle and

---

[3] In logic "distributed" means that a term refers to *all* members of the class designated. Thus in the fallacy of the undistributed middle, the middle term in the syllogism ("monkeys") does not refer to *all* members of the class.

insidious way to create spurious arguments, such as that of guilt by association:

> Communists support the ABC Plan.
> Jack Smith supports the ABC Plan.
> Jack Smith is a communist.

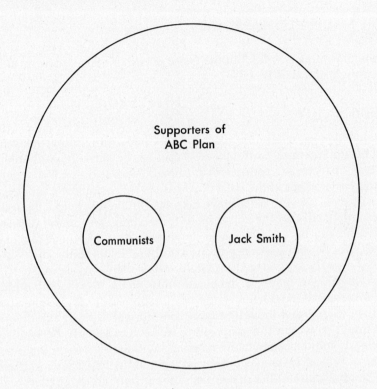

Syllogism is a logician's term, but the process of thought that it describes is hardly specialized; whenever anyone infers one idea from another, he or she is using a syllogism. If the reasoning is correct, the syllogism is valid—that is, the conclusion follows logically from the premises. But is it true? That is quite another question, since it is possible for a syllogism to be *valid* (correct in its formal reasoning) but factually *false*.

Thus the following two syllogisms are valid (given the premises, the conclusions may logically be inferred); yet the first one is nonsense and the second is patently false because the premises are false:

> All boys are unicorns.
> All unicorns are girls.
> ∴ All boys are girls.

> All people are weaklings.
> All weaklings are fools.
> ∴ All people are fools.

Clearly, it is important to examine the premises of an argument before making a judgment. If someone accuses a member of Congress of accepting graft, for example, by arguing that "it is a widely known fact that members of Congress take graft, so why should this member of Congress be any different?" it should be obvious immediately that the basic premise is open to question. *Is* it widely known and is it a *fact* that all members of Congress accept graft? The attack conceals a faulty syllogism:

> All members of Congress take graft.
> Mr. X is a member of Congress.
> ∴ Mr. X takes graft.

Yes, the reasoning is valid; but the major premise is false, thereby dictating that the conclusion will be false.

Induction

As noted above, when we reason inductively we follow the scientific method of moving from particular facts that are objectively verifiable (what we can test, observe, or experience) to a broad generalization. We see the sun rise in the east and set in the west . . . once . . . twice . . . three times . . . four . . . five . . . six . . . seven. Finally we take the "inductive leap," the assertion of the general truth that the sun rises in the east and sets in the west, and in all likelihood can be counted on to do so tomorrow, the next day, the day after that. (The scientist works with probability, not certainty; thus all scientific truths must be considered probable rather than absolute.)

A good inductive leap can be made only when a sufficient number of particular instances have been observed. This number varies from situation to situation, the perfect induction being one in which every member of the class of things to which the proposition refers has actually been observed. This is clearly impossible in many cases and unnecessary in most cases; a fair sampling of typical instances chosen at random usually leads to a reliable enough generalization. For example, fifteen sour green apples certainly provide a reasonable basis for the generalization "green apples are sour." Yet if all the apples tasted came out of one orchard, or even one group of orchards located in one section of the country, we have to wonder, "Is it just *these* green apples that are sour? Perhaps green apples in other sections of the country are as sweet as red ones." A fair sampling of apples, then, should include apples from different parts of the country, thereby eliminating the possibility that special geographical or climatic conditions produce sour green apples.

Scientific investigators require a relatively large fair sampling—perhaps hundreds, thousands, or in some cases tens of thousands of subjects (especially in medical research)—before any generalizations can safely be drawn.

In any induction, the danger to guard against is that of hasty generalizations made without a sufficient number of examples, which is perhaps the most widespread fallacy in popular thinking. Like the error in deductive reasoning that takes us from "some" to "all," this error in inductive reasoning can produce or reinforce prejudice. A person who is already prejudiced against a minority group (blacks, Jews, Chicanos) is predisposed to conclude after noting even a few "offenses" in the group that "that's the way they *all* are."

Interestingly, the tendency to "wild generalization" has been analyzed psychologically as a form of exhibitionism:

The exhibitionist desires to attract attention to himself. No one pays much attention to such undramatic statements as "Some women are fickle," or that some are liars, or "Some politicians are no better than they ought to be." But when one says that "all women are liars" this immediately attracts notice.[4]

Argument by Analogy

Another mode of reasoning, often regarded as a form of induction, is argument by analogy—the drawing, in one inductive leap, of a crucial comparison.

In urging the United States to join the Allied cause in the First World War, Woodrow Wilson pointed to the fact that Russia had done so. In comparing his proposed action for the United States with Russia's earlier action, Wilson was making an analogy, telling Congress that just as Russia wisely joined the Allied cause, so should we. The reasoning here proceeds from one specific instance to a similar specific instance, the implication being that what was a good action for one country will be a good action for another.

There is no doubt that analogical reasoning serves an important function in argumentation. It makes a point simply and economically (if Russia found it impossible to deal with Germany, why should the United States find it any easier?). Analogy is also vivid and may strike a strongly persuasive note when all direct reasoning fails. The story is told, for example, of the union organizer in the early days of the labor movement who, after reciting all rational reasons for joining the movement, finally won a prospective member by drawing a vivid and amusing analogy: "The top crowd's pressin' down! The bottom crowd's pressin' up. Whaddayou wanna be, a hamburger?"

Aside from its dramatic impact, the value of inductive analogy can be determined only by closely examining the two things being compared. Are they in fact similar in the essential characteristics relating to the conclusion? *Does the generalization underlying the analogy stand up to logical analysis?* In his book *Thinking Straight*, Monroe Beardsley points to what he calls a "simple and crude example" of how analogy may mislead.

One old gambit of the temperance orator was to say: "The delicate membranes of the stomach are like the delicate membranes of the eye; if you want to see what alcohol does to your stomach, just pour some gin in your eye." Now we may grant that there are *some* resemblances between eye tissue and stomach tissue: the question is whether these are *relevant* resemblances. In other words, the question is whether there is some true generalization like "Everything that hurts the eye will hurt

[4]Lionel Ruby, *The Art of Making Sense* (Philadelphia: J. B. Lippincott Co., 1968), pp. 254–55.

the stomach" that will allow us to infer that if gin hurts the eye it will also hurt the stomach.

So we might reply to him, "So you mean that *everything* that hurts the eye will also hurt the stomach?" He may wish to narrow the suggested generalization from "everything" to "every liquid," or in some other way. But unless he is willing to subscribe to *some* relevant generalization, he simply hasn't got what it takes to draw the conclusion he wants. We are therefore justified in saying to him, "If your argument proved anything, it would prove just as well that lemonade, vinegar, and hot coffee are bad for the stomach because they will hurt the eye. Doesn't that show that there must be important *differences* between the eye and stomach, so that what is true of one is not necessarily true of the other?"[5]

The important thing to remember about analogy, then, is this: the fact that two things are alike in some respect does not necessarily mean they are alike in others. Mental processes and bodily processes, for example, are comparable but not identical; therefore the following analogy represents a deceptive argument in favor of censorship: "We don't allow poisonous substances to be put into our foods, so why should we permit books to be published that will poison the minds of our citizens?" Do you see the dangerously authoritarian generalization that underlies this argument? It is just as unsound as the old defense of monarchy that maintained that since the earth revolved around the sun, circular motion was "natural"; consequently, by analogy, monarchy was a "natural" form of government because the subjects revolved around their monarch.[6]

Standing alone to prove a point, analogy cannot be trusted; it is useful only as a supplement to factual evidence mounted in support of a proposition. In the following essay,[7] for example, note how effectively the writer uses analogies to illuminate and reinforce his contention that in its own terms and within the context of its own premises, Marxist theory does not stand up to analysis: instead, it denies itself.

Marxism[8]

W. T. JONES

We have criticized Marxism as a theory of social causation because, of course, it was put forward as a definitive account of social change. Just as in physics a "law" is supposed to describe a necessary pattern of behavior that makes prediction and control possible, so the formula of dialectical materialism was supposed to reveal a necessary sequence of social relations. Marx the social scientist believed that what men do is not the product of "free will" but merely the expression of economic forces over which they have no control and which develop according to a purely deterministic sequence.

[5]Monroe C. Beardsley, *Thinking Straight*, 3rd ed., © 1966. Reprinted by permission of Prentice-Hall, Inc., Englewood Cliffs, New Jersey.

[6]Example cited in Bernard F. Huppé and Jack Kiminsky, *Logic and Language* (New York: Alfred A. Knopf, 1956), p. 204.

[7]Note also the use of analogy in the long paper of argumentation, "Whither the Black Odyssey?" pp. 323–32.

[8]From *A History of Western Philosophy*, by W. T. Jones, copyright 1952, by Harcourt Brace Jovanovich, Inc. and reprinted with their permission.

But Marx was not only a social scientist; he was a reformer. Now, suppose for the sake of argument that dialectical materialism is the "scientifically correct" formula describing the social process. Since the overthrow of bourgeois capitalism is inevitable, what is the point of agitating for its overthrow? If we take Marx seriously as a social scientist, Marx the reformer looks about as silly in writing his *Manifesto* urging the workers of the world to unite as we would look inviting a falling stone to fall a little faster. Of course, Marx could reply that the economic forces at work in the society of which he was a part determined that he would fight for the revolution, just as they determined that somebody else with a different economic background would fight against it. But this plunges Marxism—the theory—into the struggle about which it theorizes. It is not just a question of whether or not it is silly to try to further an inevitable end (e.g., induce the stone to fall faster), but whether, if the course of events is inevitable, "end" has anything more than a purely subjective meaning.

On the other hand, when Marx the reformer spoke, Marx the social scientist took a back seat, and we get a wholly different conception of the function of the theory and of its claim to truth. Marx the reformer was aware that the objective truth of a theory is no measure of its utility as a rallying point for aspiration and endeavor. (The Arian and orthodox theories of the Trinity are cases in point.) For Marx the reformer, Marxism was not a theory of social causation; it only pretended to be for propagandistic purposes. It was actually a call to the working class to rise and overthrow their masters, and it should be judged on the basis of its effectiveness in producing a class war from which the proletariat emerge victorious.

But why, then, did Marxism pretend to be a theory of social causation? Because, given the time, the place, and the circumstances (e.g., the "vogue" of science), men want to be assured that what they are fighting and dying for has been "scientifically" proved to be true—just as purchasers of soap or cigarettes like to be assured that "science" shows the product they use to be superior. In another age, in another country, revolutionists would not formulate their program in terms of dialectical materialism, but in terms, say, of a crusade to free the Holy Places from the infidel. It just happens that in the present age the former type of formula appeals and so provides the oppressed classes with a rationale for the revolutionary acts which one wants them to perform.

This presents a totally different picture of the social process. Far from being rigorously determined, it now appears that free will and indeterminism are predominant factors. Action, it would seem, can always alter the course of events. This would appear to rule out a science of social causation, but Marx the reformer would not be distressed: *qua* reformer, he had no interest in theory as theory. Thus, in his *Theses against Feuerbach,* Marx stated quite explicitly, "The question whether human thought can achieve objective truth is not a question of theory but a *practical* question. In practice man must prove the truth, i.e., the reality, power, and this-sidedness of his thought. The dispute over the reality or unreality of thought which is isolated from practice is a purely *scholastic* question." From this point of view, a theory proves itself true by its success in bringing about the state of affairs it describes—dialectical materialism would be a "true" theory if it incited the workers to rise and make an end of bourgeois capitalism.

It will be seen, then, that Marxism falls apart. It is impossible to ignore, as some have done, these pragmatic aspects of Marxism, but it is ridiculous to maintain, as others have, that this is the only "true" Marx. From a purely pragmatic point of view, dialectical materialism is encumbered with all sorts of impedimenta which can hardly have appealed to the working class but which Marx and Engels took very seriously— and took seriously not because they held them to be good propaganda but because they held them to be "true." This duality of point of view has persisted in Marxism to this day. On the one hand, we find a rigid and authoritarian dogmatism masquerading as a science of social causation; on the other, an extremely flexible and Machiavellian *Realpolitik,* designed to bring events which refuse to be determined by dialectic into conformity with the "fore-ordained" pattern. But it is only fair to say that Marxism is not unique in this respect; it is not the first philosophy that has combined doctrinaire self-assurance about ends with a cynical attitude toward means.

Common Logical Fallacies: A Checklist

Before citing further examples of argumentation, it will be helpful to consider some common logical fallacies, recognizing that logical flaws are not necessarily *rhetorical* flaws. In fact, logical flaws may be extremely effective in their impact on readers. Lies, if they are bold enough, generate drama and excitement; emotional appeals often touch the heart so deeply that the understanding is ignored. But these, of course, are tricks designed to fool and blind readers. Since we consider the ethics of rhetoric later on (in Chapter 24, "The Limits of Language"), we need not go into these matters here. Suffice it to say that the good argument is logically sound and intellectually honest; the good argument is based on reason and uses emotion only to reinforce reason; the good argument not only makes a case for or against its subject, it also illuminates it so that readers—whether they agree or disagree with the argument—will at least learn more about the issues.

Circular Reasoning

To assume in the premise what you are supposedly trying to *prove* in the course of your argument is to argue in a circle—or beg the question. It has been observed that "the function of logic is to demonstrate that because one thing or group of things is true, another must be true as consequence."[9] But in a circular argument there is no progression; the same thing is said in different words: "We shall always be free in America because we have a democratic form of government." This statement establishes nothing because the idea of freedom is already assumed in the word "democratic."

Equivocation

To equivocate is to change the meaning of a word in the course of an argument or to use an ambiguous word in two different senses (whether deliberately or unintentionally)—as in the following:

> Science has discovered many laws of nature. This is proof that there is a God, for a law implies the existence of a lawgiver, and God is the great Lawgiver of the universe.

Observe the confused and careless use of the word "law": it is first used with the scientific meaning of uniform behavior in nature; it is then used prescrip-

[9]See Robert Gorham Davis, "Logic and Logical Fallacies," in the *Harvard Handbook for English* (Harvard University, 1947).

tively to refer to regulations enforcible by a higher authority.[10] (For further discussion see Chapters 1 and 24.)

Evading the Issue

This fallacy takes several forms:

1. *Distraction*

The course of an argument may be turned away from the main issues by raising extraneous considerations, such as emotions or sentiments. Thus in making a case for the democratic form of government, the arguer may eulogize George Washington and the other founders of the United States, extolling their personal courage and foresight. Such distractions may divert readers' attention and make them forget the real issues.

2. *Ad hominem*

Another way to evade the issue is by directing the argument against the character of the person making the case rather than against the case itself. This fallacy is common and sinister ("You cannot trust Smith's reform bill because he has had questionable leftist leanings . . . and there is his divorce . . . and that suspicious suicide attempt. . . .").

3. *Name-Calling*

Here is still another evasive smear tactic (and verbal trick): calling an opposing view by a "bad name," thereby suggesting that it is in reality bad. Thus an attempt to improve welfare legislation may be labelled "starry-eyed idealism" or "sheer romanticism," which will turn our government into a "welfare state." (See also pp. 386–90.)

4. *Appeal to Pity*

When General Douglas MacArthur, pleading his case before the American people, cited the old refrain "Old soldiers never die, they just fade away," he was resorting to the popular and often successful ruse of making himself pitiful in order to win sympathy. Obviously, this focusing on "poor old me" is another way of evading substantive issues.

Fallacious Appeal to Authority

To cite a Nobel Prize–winning chemist as an authority on civil rights legislation is to misunderstand the meaning of the word "authority." An authority's opinion is meaningful only when it concerns his or her special field of competence; otherwise the so-called authority is simply an ordinary citizen like the rest of us—neither wiser nor more foolish.

Fallacy of the Undistributed Middle

(See "Deduction," pp. 287–90.)

---

[10]Example drawn from Lionel Ruby, *The Art of Making Sense*, pp. 32–33.

False Analogy

(See "Argument by Analogy," pp. 291–94.)

Hasty Generalization

(See "Induction," pp. 290–91.)

Non Sequitur

When a conclusion does not follow from its premises, there has obviously been a serious slip in the deductive reasoning process.

> All artists are creative.
> Jackson is an artist.
> ∴ Jackson should be subsidized.

This broken line of reasoning can be mended and made to conform to a logical pattern, but it must be thought through carefully. What the individual probably wants to say, and is obliged to say if the conclusion is to be rendered valid, is this:

> All creative artists deserve to be subsidized.
> Jackson is a creative artist.
> ∴ Jackson should be subsidized.

Both syllogisms contain the same conclusion; but in one case it does not follow from the premises, and in the other it does. To correct a non sequitur, we must remember that a conclusion is valid not in and of itself but within the context of its own terms, that is, the body of the syllogism.

Oversimplification

This is a root fallacy in which the arguer ignores the complexities of a problem so that he or she may solve it more easily.

1. *Either . . . Or*

This is a device in which the arguer states that there are two and only two alternatives in a given situation: *Either* you vote for the mayor's tax reform bill *or* you permit the city to become bankrupt. No intermediate choices are allowed, although in fact there may be many other possibilities.

2. *Post Hoc, Ergo Propter Hoc* ("After this, therefore because of this")

This error in cause-and-effect analysis was described earlier (see p. 107).

Personifying Abstractions

This fallacy represents both oversimplification and verbal distortion. It suggests that "Science tells us . . ." or "History teaches . . ." or "Poets believe . . ." as if each of these were a single person speaking with one voice instead of a complex abstraction representing many different points of view (Chapter 24, "The Limits of Language").

Substantiating Your Argument

Argumentation is by far the most demanding and comprehensive form of discourse, not only because it requires rigorous reasoning and persuasive tactics but also because it frequently embraces other forms: definition, description, comparison, analysis, narration, characterization, interpretation, reflection, and evaluation. All of them may enter into argumentation. Indeed, it is quite possible that in the course of answering question 20, "What case can be made for or against X?" you may include every form of writing cited—and some others that are not mentioned.

In "making a case," then, you should try to raise as many pertinent points as possible, for it is the content of the argument—the evidence that substantiates your position—as well as the rigor of your reasoning that will establish and prove your case. The following essay, for example, is a brief but compelling argument in favor of raising safety standards in U.S. coal mines. It is compelling because the writer cites facts and figures as well as personal opinion and experience. He clearly knows what he is talking about: he checked his information with the International Labor Office; he obtained production figures and accident rates for U.S. and foreign mines. He moves through his subject with assurance because he is thoroughly familiar with it; he does not lapse into vague generalities, nor does he simply play on emotion. Instead he combines objective data with first-hand accounts of what working in a coal mine is like. It is grim, and we are made to see how and why it is grim. We are also made to feel, with the writer, a deep compassion for the miner, whose fears are rooted in the realities of an inherently hazardous situation, but whose pride (the writer himself projects this attitude) persists in the face of all dangers. By the time we have finished reading this piece we have a deeper understanding of the coal miner's situation.

Life, and Death, in the Coal Mines[11]
DUANE LOCKARD

INTRODUC-
TION

NARRATION

BODY

Nearly thirty years ago, 350 feet beneath a West Virginia mountain, I stood paralyzed with fear when a greasy haulage motor caught fire. Having heard endless mine lore from my father and grandfather, I knew that fire in a mine was death, especially when the mine was not rockdusted to reduce the explosiveness of coal dust. I knew many miles of volatile coal dust lay in the tunnels of that mine, since I was at that moment preparing to spray the walls with tons of an incombustible matter.

We worked 24 hours that Saturday and Sunday rockdusting because the boss said the state mine inspector was coming Monday and the mine had to be prepared for him. The fire burned itself out, but not before it impressed me as deeply as any fright I ever experienced, including wartime air combat.

This memory returns as I observe the current maneuvers to prevent the raising of U.S. coal mine safety standards.

[11]From the *New York Times*, 21 June 1969. © 1969 by The New York Times Company. Reprinted by permission.

Mining is dangerous and always will be; no other industry levies a higher toll in lives and disabling accidents. To produce half a billion tons of bituminous coal last year cost the lives of 307 miners; 88 of them died in explosions and an equal number were crushed in roof falls. Besides these fatalities another 9,500 men suffered serious injuries. And an undetermined number breathed the decisive quantity of coal dust that assured their lingering death of asphyxiation from pneumonoconiosis or "black lung."

Apologists for the industry point to the reduction in the number of accidents in recent decades, and it is true that since 1930 the number of accidents has declined from 100,000 to about 10,000. Not all the reduction is due to safety advances, however, for 135,000 miners now produce as much coal as did half a million during World War II.

Does the production of coal necessitate such a cost in lives? Coal can be and long has been mined in other countries with lower accident rates. On the average Western European nations have mining fatality rates that are a third to a half of those for the United States.

The International Labor Office reports that American mining fatality rates are matched only by those for Canada, Taiwan, Korea and Turkey among the 22 nations for which it has data. Morocco and Southern Rhodesia have rates only half as high as ours, while India, Czechoslovakia, Poland, Great Britain and Yugoslavia have rates that are lower still.

Is this because American mines are more dangerous than others? I posed this question to a British mining official. He replied that on the contrary, "British mines are inherently more dangerous than yours and therefore our safety standards have to be all the higher. . . . Our rockdusting standards are very high and rigidly enforced. I believe our standards of electrical safety are higher than in the U.S. Indeed, most American machinery—if not all—that has been installed over here has had to be redesigned on the electrical side."

He concluded, "It sounds as if I'm being beastly and critical of your mining people and I would hate to be so, because we have a lot to learn from them in some matters while still trying to retain our safety standards. We have learned by experience, much of which has been bitter, and I am quite sure that it is the inherently greater danger in our mines that makes us the more careful and creates our higher standards."

Mining has changed greatly since I left it, but that dreaded top still hangs overhead always ready to avenge its loss. I recall once that my father asked me to stop shoveling while he sounded the roof with his pick-handle, listening carefully. Coal began to snap and fly just as he shouted a warning and we ran from the coal face. Within seconds the half-filled coal car, the tracks, some tools (but not the lunch buckets—I saw to their safety) disappeared in a roar of rubble and a cloud of dust. A thick layer of slate had given way, splintering huge safety posts like twigs as it came down.

Every miner is aware of this risk, as he is of explosions, and his body bears blue scars to mark each injury by a hank of coal. I never knew a miner lacking in fear of the mine nor one without a certain compensating pride.

Peroration   Too many of these brave men will be killed even with the best of safety rules, but in this technologically advanced nation need we have so much blood on our coal?

Testing Your Argument

Whatever case you may make for or against any subject, you should test your argument against the following questions:

1. Have you defined the terms? (Chapter 1, "What Does X Mean?" and Chapter 24, "The Limits of Language")
2. Have you established exactly what the argument is about? That is, have you stated the proposition *clearly* and indicated precisely what issues are to be defended and refuted?
3. Are facts and assumptions correct?
4. Have you offered sufficient evidence—facts, statistics, illustrations, testimony—that will further illuminate and substantiate each point as well as the overall position? (Chapter 22, "Gathering Information")
5. Are generalizations fair and reliable?
6. Do conclusions follow logically from the premises?
7. Have you cited reliable authorities?
8. Have you been as *precise* as possible in the treatment of the subject?
9. Is the presentation "artful," rhetorically effective, clear, well-organized? (It is well to remember that in no form of writing is it more important to use the strengths of language "to the best possible effect." Stylistic failings such as undefined terms that create ambiguity, confusing grammatical constructions, vague allusions, and pompous, clumsy, overlong sentences are guaranteed to alienate those who might otherwise be convinced. Bad writing, in other words, can kill a case as surely as lack of evidence or fallacious reasoning.)
10. Is the tone (whether serious or satiric) appropriate to the subject, the audience, the occasion, and the purpose you are trying to achieve?
11. Have you examined *every* important aspect of the case? Aristotle maintained that we should be able to argue on either side of a question—not because we are without personal conviction or commitment, but because only then can we feel certain that no aspect of the case has escaped us. Only then can we anticipate readers' (or listeners') objections and by anticipating them either avoid them or prepare an advance refutation.
12. Is the approach reasonable rather than dogmatic, rigid, unnecessarily (and irritatingly) disputatious?

In considering the last question, you might also consider the rule of that eminently practical and successful diplomat, Benjamin Franklin, who, recognizing that an overconfident and imperious manner may "lose the day," wrote the following in his autobiography:

I made it a rule to forbear all direct contradictions to the sentiments of others, and all positive assertion of my own. I even forbade myself . . . the use of every word or expression in the language that imported a fix'd opinion, such as *certainly, undoubtedly,* etc., and I adopted, instead of them, *I conceive, I apprehend,* or *I imagine* a thing to be so or so; or it *so appears to me at present.* When another asserted something that I thought an error, I deny'd myself the pleasure of contradicting him abruptly, and of showing immediately some absurdity in his proposition: and in answering I began by observing that in certain cases or circumstances his opinion would be right, but in the present case there *appear'd* or *seem'd* to me some difference, etc. I soon found the advantage of this change in my manner; the conversations I engag'd in went on more pleasantly. The modest way in which I propos'd my opinions procur'd them a readier reception and less contradiction; I had less mortification when I was found to be in the wrong, and I more easily prevail'd with others to give up their mistakes and join with me when I happened to be in the right.

And this mode, which I at first put on with some violence to natural inclination, became at length so easy, and so habitual to me, that perhaps for these fifty years past no one has ever heard a dogmatical expression escape me. And to this habit (after my character of integrity) I think it principally owing that I had early so much weight with my fellow-citizens when I proposed new institutions, or alterations in the old, and so much influence in public councils when I became a member; for I was but a bad speaker, never eloquent, subject to much hesitation in my choice of words, hardly correct in language, and yet I generally carried my points.

ASSIGNMENTS

Class Discussion and Paragraph Suggestions

(See Chapter 27 for methods of composing unified, adequately developed paragraphs.)

1. Discuss the advantages and possible disadvantages of Benjamin Franklin's advice, cited above. Do his rules preclude the kind of *confident* assertion necessary to win the reader's agreement and assent? Explain the psychological value of Franklin's approach.

2. Evaluate Woodrow Wilson's address to Congress from the point of view of its factual content, soundness of logic, and persuasive tactics.

3. Discuss Allan H. Gilbert's essay "College Lectures Are Obsolete." Consider arguments in favor of the lecture system.

4. Analyze the analogies in W. T. Jones' essay "Marxism." Indicate in what ways they enhance the argument.

5. Read the letter below and answer the questions that follow.

A Letter to the Editor

(1) With a great show of moral indignation, it was recently revealed that 47 percent of Monroe College students "cheated" on quizzes, prelims, and examinations. Since then, readers of *The Bulletin* have been deluged with pious commentaries. Isn't it about time someone asked whether our modern Puritans aren't being overly righteous in this matter? A little giving or taking of information on an examination, or the

use of a few crib notes, is not such a bad thing as some prudish minds would have us think. The very fact that so many loyal Monroe students indulge in this is evidence that it can't be very wrong.

(2) On the contrary, copying or the use of crib notes seems quite pardonable in many courses. In a course which requires remembering a lot of facts, why not use crib notes? It's only a difference of degree between using them and using some elaborate system for memorizing facts. Both are artificial means to help you remember.

(3) If we view the problem from another angle, we can see that what is so smugly denounced as "dishonesty" may actually reveal foresight—which is certainly a praiseworthy trait. If you were going into an unknown wilderness, you would take along the things you knew were needed for survival, wouldn't you? Taking crib notes into the unknown territory of an examination shows the same foresight. Now suppose also that one of your companions on this expedition desperately needed water or food or help of some sort. You'd do what you could for him, wouldn't you? Helping someone on an examination isn't any different.

(4) To put the question another way, suppose we define charity as "giving to a person in need." Isn't one, therefore, performing an act of charity during an examination when one gives some "needy" person the desired information? The fact that one isn't giving money or food doesn't make the act any less charitable.

(5) If we inquire *who* is stirring up this fuss over alleged "cheating," we find it's the faculty—in other words, the persons who have selfish interests to protect. Obviously, they flunk students to make them repeat the course and thus to keep it filled.

(6) Finally, to take a long-range view, why should colleges get all excited over what they choose to call "cheating" when there are much more urgent things for them to worry about? When the very existence of our democracy is being threatened by Communism, why fret about the source of Johnny X's information on an ancient history exam?

—Name Withheld

    a. What is the writer's main point? State the reasons given in support of it.
    b. What is the writer's implied definition of cheating? Comment on its adequacy as a definition.
    c. What is the writer's view of people who denounce cheating? What purpose does this view serve in the argument?
    d. What is the implied premise or underlying assumption of: "The very fact that so many loyal Monroe students indulge in this is evidence that it can't be very wrong?"
    e. Identify and briefly describe the fallacy in paragraph 2.
    f. What kind of argument is used in paragraph 3? Appraise its soundness.
    g. Comment on the argument presented in paragraph 4 and again in paragraph 6.

6. Outline the essays in this chapter and evaluate their rhetorical effectiveness and logical soundness.

Essay Suggestions

1. Write an essay (750–1,000 words) in which you make a case for some political program, policy, or piece of legislation that you support and would like to persuade others to support. (Try to move readers to *action*, as President Wilson moved Congress to action.)

2. In an essay (750–1,000 words) reply to Allan H. Gilbert's essay "College Lectures

Are Obsolete." Support the position or assert a contrary position in favor of the lecture system.

3. Write an essay (750–1,000 words) arguing against another aspect or procedure of our educational system that you consider obsolete or otherwise inadequate (the grading system, required courses, awarding of degrees, formal class meetings). Be sure to locate specific issues and to include in the body of your argument not only evidence in behalf of your case, but evidence refuting points of opposition.

4. In an essay (500–750 words) make a case against any -ism of your choice (atheism, romanticism, racism) by showing that it is either self-contradictory (a logical flaw) or self-defeating (a moral flaw). Use analogies to develop your argument.

Writing
a Long Paper: Research
and Organization

21 The Long Paper

For our purposes we have regarded the short paper (500–1,000 words) as one that takes its impulse from a single question and is confined to answering the question.

In this chapter we shall examine longer and more complex forms of writing in which the answer to one question involves the writer in many subsidiary questions. Specifically, we shall consider four longer papers: an extended analysis, a description-narration, an extended characterization, and an extended argument. Following each sample paper are suggestions for a term paper on a similar subject and of comparable scope—that is, one that takes its major impulse from one question but which requires you, in the course of extending your subject, to answer many of the other twenty questions posed in earlier chapters.

It will be helpful to begin by describing the term paper itself.

Form and Function of the Term Paper

A so-called term paper is a strictly academic form, named for the period of time in which the paper must be completed. It is essentially a long paper—a relatively thorough study of an aspect of a given subject—averaging 3,000 to 6,000 words and usually requiring some research. Instructors in every discipline are likely to assign term papers, on the justifiable assumption that term papers require more independent, intensive, and creative effort than any other single unit of work asked of students throughout the semester. Certainly it is true that when you prepare a term paper you generally select your own topic, locate appropriate reference materials, abstract from them what you need, and reassemble your data to conform to the new statement you wish to make, expressed in your own style. No single piece of work, then, requires more imagination and patience, more sustained intellectual effort, more persistence and rhetorical skill than this full-term research and writing project; nor does any single piece of work give the instructor a better measure of your ability to relate meaningfully and articulately to some aspect of the discipline in question.

The four essays that follow are in forms suitable for a term paper.

Extended Analysis

The Lady on the Bookcase*

JAMES THURBER

One day twelve years ago an outraged cartoonist, four of whose drawings had been rejected in a clump by *The New Yorker,* stormed into the office of Harold Ross, editor of the magazine. "Why is it," demanded the cartoonist, "that you reject my work and publish drawings by a fifth-rate artist like Thurber?" Ross came quickly to my defense like the true friend and devoted employer he is, "You mean third-rate," he said quietly, but there was a warning glint in his steady gray eyes that caused the discomfited cartoonist to beat a hasty retreat.

With the exception of Ross, the interest of editors in what I draw has been rather more journalistic than critical. They want to know if it is true that I draw by moonlight, or under water, and when I say no, they lose interest until they hear the rumor that I found the drawings in an old trunk or that I do the captions while my nephew makes the sketches.

The other day I was shoving some of my originals around on the floor (I do not draw on the floor; I was just shoving the originals around) and they fell, or perhaps I pushed them, into five separate and indistinct categories. I have never wanted to write about my drawings, and I still don't want to, but it occurred to me that it might be a good idea to do it now, when everybody is busy with something else, and get it over quietly.

Category No. 1, then, which may be called the Unconscious or Stream of Nervousness category, is represented by "With you I have known peace, Lida, and now you say you're going crazy" and the drawing entitled with simple dignity, "Home." These drawings were done while the artist was thinking of something else (or so he has been assured by experts) and hence his hand was guided by the Unconscious which, in turn, was more or less influenced by the Subconscious.

Students of Jung have instructed me that Lida and the House-Woman are representations of the *anima,* the female essence or directive which floats around in the ageless universal Subconscious of Man like a tadpole in a cistern. Less intellectual critics insist that the two ladies are actual persons I have consciously known. Between these two schools of thought lies a discouragingly large space of time extending roughly from 1,000,000 B.C. to the middle Nineteen Thirties.

---

*Copr. © 1948 James Thurber. From *The Beast in Me—and Other Animals,* published by Harcourt Brace Jovanovich. Originally printed in *The New York Times.*

"With you I have known peace,
Lida, and now you say you're going
crazy."

Home

"All right, have it your way—you
heard a seal bark."

"That's my first wife up there, and
this is the *present* Mrs. Harris."

"For the last time, you and your
horsie get away from me and stay
away!"

"The father belonged to some people who were driving through in a Packard."

"What have you done with Dr. Millmoss?"

"Touché!"

"Well, I'm disenchanted, too. We're all disenchanted."

"You said a moment ago that everybody you look at seems to be a rabbit. Now just what do you mean by that, Mrs. Sprague?"

Whenever I try to trace the true identity of the House-Woman, I get to thinking of Mr. Jones. He appeared in my office one day twelve years ago, said he was Mr. Jones, and asked me to lend him "Home" for reproduction in an art magazine. I never saw the drawing again. Tall, well-dressed, kind of sad-looking chap, and as well spoken a gentleman as you would want to meet.

Category No. 2 brings us to Freud and another one of those discouragingly large spaces—namely, the space between the Concept of the Purely Accidental and the Theory of Haphazard Determination. Whether chance is capricious or we are all prisoners of pattern is too long and cloudy a subject to go into here. I shall consider each of the drawings in Category No. 2, explaining what happened and leaving the definition of the forces involved up to you. The seal on top of the bed, then ("All right, have it your way—you heard a seal bark"), started out to be a seal on a rock. The rock, in the process of being drawn, began to look like the head of a bed, so I made a bed out of it, put a man and wife in the bed, and stumbled onto the caption as easily and unexpectedly as the seal had stumbled into the bedroom.

The woman on top of the bookcase ("That's my first wife up there, and this is the *present* Mrs. Harris") was originally designed to be a woman crouched on the top step of a staircase, but since the tricks and conventions of perspective and planes sometimes fail me, the staircase assumed the shape of a bookcase and was finished as such, to the surprise and embarrassment of the first Mrs. Harris, the present Mrs. Harris, the lady visitor, Mr. Harris and me. Before *The New Yorker* would print the drawing, they phoned me long distance to inquire whether the first Mrs. Harris was alive or dead or stuffed. I replied that my taxidermist had advised me that you cannot stuff a woman, and that my physician had informed me that a dead lady cannot support herself on all fours. This meant, I said, that the first Mrs. Harris was unquestionably alive.

The man riding on the other man's shoulders in the bar ("For the last time, you and your horsie get away from me and stay away!") was intended to be standing alongside the irate speaker, but I started his head up too high and made it too small, so that he would have been nine feet tall if I had completed his body that way. It was but the work of thirty-two seconds to put him on another man's shoulders. As simple or, if you like, as complicated as that. The psychological factors which may be present here are, as I have indicated, elaborate and confused. Personally, I like Dr. Claude Thornway's theory of the Deliberate Accident or Conditioned Mistake.

Category No. 3 is perhaps a variant of Category No. 2; indeed, they may even be identical. The dogs in "The father belonged to some people who were driving through in a Packard" were drawn as a captionless spot, and the interior with figures just sort of grew up around them. The hippopotamus in "What have you done with Dr. Millmoss?" was drawn to amuse my small daughter. Something about the creature's expression when he was completed convinced me that he had recently eaten a man. I added the hat and pipe and Mrs. Millmoss, and the caption followed easily enough. Incidentally, my daughter, who was 2 years old at the time, identified the beast immediately. "That's a hippotomanus," she said. *The New Yorker* was not so smart. They described the drawing for their files as follows: "Woman with strange animal." *The New Yorker* was nine years old at the time.

Category No. 4 is represented by perhaps the best known of some fifteen drawings belonging to this special grouping, which may be called the Contributed Idea Category. This drawing ("Touché!") was originally done for *The New Yorker* by Carl Rose, caption and all. Mr. Rose is a realistic artist, and his gory scene distressed the editors, who hate violence. They asked Rose if he would let me have the idea, since there is obviously no blood to speak of in the people I draw. Rose graciously consented. No one who looks at "Touché!" believes that the man whose head is in the air is really dead. His opponent will hand it back to him with profuse apologies, and the discommoded fencer will replace it on his shoulders and say, "No harm done, forget it." Thus the old controversy as to whether death can be made funny is left just where it was before Carl Rose came along with his wonderful idea.

Category No. 5, our final one, can be called, believe it or not, the Intentional or Thought-Up Category. The idea for each of these two drawings just came to me and I sat down and made a sketch to fit the prepared caption. Perhaps, in the case of "Well, I'm disenchanted, too. We're all disenchanted," another one of those Outside Forces played a part. That is, I may have overheard a husband say to his wife, on the street or at a party, "I'm disenchanted." I do not think this is true, however, in the case of the rabbit-headed doctor and his woman patient. I believe that scene and its caption came to me one night in bed. I *may* have got the idea in a doctor's office or a rabbit hutch, but I don't think so.

If you want to, you can cut these drawings out and push them around on the floor, making your own categories or applying your own psychological theories; or you can even invent some fresh rumors. I should think it would be more fun, though, to take a nap, or baste a roast, or run around the reservoir in Central Park.

Commentary

The above article is an extended analysis, specifically a classification. Thurber spoofingly arranges his drawings into "five separate and indistinct categories." The key to the spoof is the term "indistinct." In a serious classification, as we saw in Chapter 9, the types are divided into logically distinct categories. Thurber's classification is hardly logical in the strict sense, but, humor aside, the basic plan remains the same. The essay, then, can stand as a model of a long classification paper.

Essay Suggestions

1. Suggested Topic: Picasso's "Periods": A Chronological Overview
   Classify (in 3,000 to 5,000 words) the work of any cartoonist, artist, or writer into categories, organizing your paper around any aspect of the work that seems most relevant or illuminating (for example, basic themes, chronological development).
   For a discussion of research procedure and library sources, read Chapter 22, "Gathering Information." For a list of possible sources for the topic "Picasso's 'Periods': A Chronological Overview," see p. 357.

2. Expand one of the essay suggestions in Chapter 9 (pp. 130–31) into a paper of 3,000 to 5,000 words.

Description-Narration

In Chapter 14, "How Did X Happen?" Winston Churchill's essay "In the Battle of Hastings" is cited as an example of a historical event rendered in narrative form—that is, with the drama and excitement of a story. The following account of another historical event, the assassination of Abraham

Lincoln, drawn from Carl Sandburg's celebrated biography of Lincoln, is a more extended example of this same form, a description-narration.

The Assassination of Lincoln*

CARL SANDBURG

The play proceeds, not unpleasant, often stupid, sprinkled with silly puns, drab and aimless dialogues, forced humor, characters neither truly English nor truly American nor fetching as caricatures. The story centers around the Yankee lighting his cigar with an old will, burning the document to ashes and thereby throwing a fortune of $400,000 away from himself into the hands of an English cousin. The mediocre comedy is somewhat redeemed by the way the players are doing it. The audience agrees it is not bad. The applause and laughter say the audience is having a good time.

Mrs. Lincoln sits close to her husband, at one moment leaning on him fondly, suddenly realizing they are not alone, saying with humor, "What will Miss Harris think of my hanging on to you so?" and hearing his: "She won't think anything about it."

From the upholstered rocking armchair in which Lincoln sits he can see only the persons in the box with him, the players on the stage, and any persons offstage on the left. The box on the opposite side of the theatre is empty. With the box wall at his back and the closely woven lace curtains at his left arm, he is screened from the audience at his back and from the musicians in the orchestra pit, which is below and partly behind him.

The box has two doors. Sometimes by a movable cross partition it is converted into two boxes, each having its door. The door forward is locked. For this evening the President's party has the roominess and convenience of double space, extra armchairs, side chairs, a small sofa. In the privacy achieved he is in sight only of his chosen companions, the actors he has come to see render a play, and the few people who may be offstage to the left.

This privacy however has a flaw. It is not as complete as it seems. A few feet behind the President is the box door, the only entry to the box unless by a climb from the stage. In this door is a small hole, bored that afternoon to serve as a peephole—from the outside. Through this peephole it is the intention of the Outsider who made it with a gimlet to stand and watch the President, then at a chosen moment to enter the box. This door opens from the box on a narrow hallway that leads to another door which opens on the balcony of the theatre.

Through these two doors the Outsider must pass in order to enter the President's box. Close to the door connecting with the balcony two inches of plaster have been cut from the brick wall of the narrow hallway. The intention of the Outsider is that a bar placed in this cut-away wall niche and then braced against the panel of the door will hold that door against intruders, will serve to stop anyone from interfering with the Outsider while making his observations of the President through the gimleted hole in the box door.

At either of these doors, the one to the box or the one to the hallway, it is the assigned duty and expected responsibility of John F. Parker to stand or sit constantly and without fail. A Ward Lamon or an Eckert on this duty would probably have noticed the gimleted hole, the newly made wall niche, and been doubly watchful. If Lincoln believes what he told Crook that afternoon, that he trusted the men assigned to guard him, then as he sits in the upholstered rocking armchair in the box he believes that John F. Parker in steady fidelity is just outside the box door, in plain clothes ready with the revolver Pendel at the White House had told him to be sure to have with him.

In such a trust Lincoln is mistaken. Whatever dim fog of thought or duty may move John F. Parker in his best moments is not operating tonight. His life habit of never letting anything trouble him is on him this night; his motive is to have no motive. He has always got along somehow. Why care about anything, why really care? He can always find good liquor and bad women. You take your fun as you find it. He can never be a somebody, so he will enjoy himself as a nobody—though he can't imagine how perfect a cipher, how completely the little end of nothing, one John F. Parker may appear as a result of one slack easygoing hour.

"The guard . . . acting as my substitute," wrote the faithful Crook later, "took his position at the rear of the box, close to an entrance leading into the box. . . . His orders were to stand there, fully armed, and to permit no unauthorized person to pass into the box. His orders were to stand there and protect the President at all hazards. From the spot where he was thus stationed, this guard could not see the stage or the actors; but he could hear the words the actors spoke, and he became so interested in them that, incredible as it may seem, he quietly deserted his post of duty, and walking down the dimly-lighted side aisle, deliberately took a seat."

The custom was for a chair to be placed in the narrow hallway for the guard to sit in. The doorkeeper Buckingham told Crook that such a chair was provided this evening for the accommodation of the guard. "Whether Parker occupied it at all, I do not know," wrote Crook. "Mr. Buckingham is of the impression that he did. If he did, he left it almost immediately, for he confessed to me the next day that he went to a seat, so that he could see the play." The door to the President's box is shut. It is not kept open so that the box occupants can see the guard on duty.

Either between acts or at some time when the play was not lively enough to suit him or because of an urge for a pony of whiskey under his belt, John F. Parker leaves his seat in the balcony and goes down to the street and joins companions in a little whiff of liquor—this on the basis of a statement of the coachman Burns, who declared he stayed outside on the street with his carriage and horses, except for one interlude when "the special police officer (meaning John F. Parker) and the footman of the President (Forbes) came up to him and asked him to take a drink with them; which he did."

Thus circumstance favors the lurking and vigilant Outsider who in the afternoon gimleted a hole in the door of the President's box and cut a two-inch niche in a wall to brace a bar against a door panel and hold it against interference while he should operate.

The play goes on. The evening and the drama are much like many other evenings when the acting is pleasant enough, the play mediocre and so-so, the audience having no thrills of great performance but enjoying itself. The most excited man in the house, with little doubt, is the orchestra leader, Withers. He has left the pit and gone backstage, where, as he related, "I was giving the stage manager a piece of my mind. I had written a song for Laura Keene to sing. When she left it out I was mad. We had no cue, and the music was thrown out of gear. So I hurried round on the stage on my left to see what it was done for."

And of what is Abraham Lincoln thinking? As he leans back in his easy rocking chair, where does he roam in thought? If it is life he is thinking about, no one could fathom the subtle speculations and hazy reveries resulting from his fifty-six years of adventures drab and dazzling in life. Who had gone farther on so little to begin with? Who else as a living figure of republican government, of democracy, in practice, as a symbol touching freedom for all men—who else had gone farther over America, over the world? If it is death he is thinking about, who better than himself might interpret his dream that he lay in winding sheets on a catafalque in the White House and people were wringing their hands and crying "The President is dead!"—who could make clear this dream better than himself? Furthermore if it is death he is thinking about, has he not philosophized about it and dreamed about it and considered himself as a mark and a target until no one is better prepared than he for any sudden deed? Has he not a thousand times said to himself, and several times to friends and intimates, that he must accommodate himself to the thought of sudden death? Has he not wearied of the constructions placed on his secret night ride through Baltimore to escape a plot aimed at his death? Has he not laughed to the overhead night stars at a hole shot in his hat by a hidden marksman he never mentioned even to his boon companion Hill Lamon? And who can say but that Death is a friend, and who else should be more familiar of Death than a man who has been the central figure of the bloodiest war ever known to the Human Family—who else should more appropriately and decently walk with Death? And who can say but Death is a friend and a nurse and a lover and a benefactor bringing peace and lasting reconciliation? The play tonight is stupid. Shakespeare would be better. "Duncan is in his grave . . . he sleeps well."

Yes, of what is Abraham Lincoln thinking? Draped before him in salute is a silk flag of the Union, a banner of the same design as the one at Independence Hall in Philadelphia in February of '61 which he pulled aloft saying, "I would rather be assassinated on this spot than surrender it," saying the flag in its very origins "gave promise that in due time the weights would be lifted from the shoulders of all men, and that all should have an equal chance." Possibly his mind recurs for a fleeting instant to that one line in his letter to a Boston widow woman: "the solemn pride that must be yours to have laid so costly a sacrifice upon the altar of freedom." Or a phrase from the Gettysburg speech: "we here highly resolve that these dead shall not have died in vain."

Out in a main-floor seat enjoying the show is one Julia Adelaide Shephard, who wrote a letter to her father about this Good Friday evening at the theatre. "Cousin Julia has just told me," she reported, "that the President is in yonder upper right hand private box so handsomely decked with silken flags festooned over a picture of George Washington. The young and lovely daughter of Senator Harris is the only one of his party we see as the flags hide the rest. But we know Father Abraham is there like a Father watching what interests his children, for their pleasure rather than his own. It had been announced in the papers he would be there. How sociable it seems like one family sitting around their parlor fire. Everyone has been so jubilant for days that they laugh and shout at every clownish witticism such is the excited state of the public mind. One of the actresses whose part is that of a very delicate young lady talks about wishing to avoid the draft when her lover tells her not to be alarmed 'for there is to be no more draft' at which the applause is loud and long. The American cousin has just been making love to a young lady who says she'll never marry for love but when her mother and herself find out that he has lost his property they retreat in disgust at the left hand of the stage while the American cousin goes out at the right. We are waiting for the next scene."

And the next scene?

The next scene is to crash and blare as one of the wildest, one of the most inconceivably fateful and chaotic, that ever stunned and shocked a world that heard the story.

The moment of high fate was not seen by the theatre audience. Only one man saw that moment. He was the Outsider. He was the one who had waited and lurked and made his preparations, planning and plotting that he should be the single and lone spectator of what happened. He had come through the outer door into the little hallway, fastened the strong though slender bar into the two-inch niche in the brick wall, and braced it against the door panel. He had moved softly to the box door and through the little hole he had gimleted that afternoon he had studied the box occupants and his Human Target seated in an upholstered rocking armchair. Softly he had opened the door and stepped toward his prey, in his right hand a one-shot brass derringer pistol, a little eight-ounce vest-pocket weapon winged for death, in his left hand a steel dagger. He was cool and precise and timed his every move. He raised the derringer, lengthened his right arm, ran his eye along the barrel in a line with the head of his victim less than five feet away—and pulled the trigger.

A lead ball somewhat less than a half-inch in diameter crashed into the left side of the head of the Human Target, into the back of the head, in a line with and three inches from the left ear. "The course of the ball was obliquely forward toward the right eye, crossing the brain in an oblique manner and lodging a few inches behind that eye. In the track of the wound were found fragments of bone, which had been driven forward by the ball, which was embedded in the anterior lobe of the left hemisphere of the brain."

For Abraham Lincoln it was lights out, good night, farewell and a long farewell to the good earth and its trees, its enjoyable companions, and the Union of States and the world Family of Man he had loved. He was not dead yet. He was to linger in dying. But the living man could never again speak nor see nor hear nor awaken into conscious being.

Near the prompt desk offstage stands W. J. Ferguson, an actor. He looks in the direction of a shot he hears, and sees "Mr. Lincoln lean back in his rocking chair, his head coming to rest against the wall which stood between him and the audience . . . well inside the curtains"—no struggle or move "save in the slight backward sway."

Of this the audience in their one thousand seats knew nothing.

Major Rathbone leaps from his chair. Rushing at him with a knife is a strange human creature, terribly alive, a lithe wild animal, a tiger for speed, a wildcat of a man bareheaded, raven-haired—a smooth sinister face with glaring eyeballs. He wears a dark sack suit. He stabs straight at the heart of Rathbone, a fast and ugly lunge. Rathbone parries it with his upper right arm, which gets a deep slash of the dagger. Rathbone is staggered, reels back. The tigerish stranger mounts the box railing. Rathbone recovers, leaps again for the stranger, who feels the hand of Rathbone holding him back, slashes again at Rathbone, then leaps for the stage.

This is the moment the audience wonders whether something unusual is happening—or is it part of the play?

From the box railing the Strange Man leaps for the stage, perhaps a ten-foot fall. His leap is slightly interrupted. On this slight interruption the Strange Man in his fine calculations had not figured. The draped Union flag of silk reaches out and tangles itself in a spur of one riding-boot, throwing him out of control. He falls to the stage landing on his left leg, breaking the shinbone a little above the instep.

Of what he has done the audience as yet knows nothing. They wonder what this swift, raven-haired, wild-eyed Strange Man portends. They see him rush across the stage, three feet to a stride, and vanish. Some have heard Rathbone's cry "Stop that man!'' Many have seen a man leap from a front seat up on the stage and chase after the weird Stranger, crying ''Stop that man!''

It is a peculiar night, an odd evening, a little weird, says the audience to itself. The action is fast. It is less than half a minute since the Strange Man mounted the box railing, made the stage, and strode off.

Offstage between Laura Keene and W. J. Ferguson he dashes at breakneck speed, out of an entrance, forty feet to a little door opening on an alley. There stands a fast bay horse, a slow-witted chore boy nicknamed John Peanuts holding the reins. He kicks the boy, mounts the mare; hoofs on the cobblestones are heard but a few moments. In all it is maybe sixty or seventy seconds since he loosed the one shot of his eight-ounce brass derringer.

Whether the Strange Man now riding away on a fast bay horse has paused a moment on the stage and shouted a dramatic line of speech, there was disagreement afterward. Some said he ran off as though every second of time counted and his one purpose was to escape. Others said he faced the audience a moment, brandished a dagger still bloody from slashing Rathbone, and shouted the State motto of Virginia, the slogan of Brutus as he drove the assassin's knife into imperial Caesar: *''Sic semper tyrannis''* —''Thus be it ever to tyrants.'' Miss Shephard and others believed they heard him shriek as he brandished the dagger: ''The South is avenged!'' Others: ''The South shall be free!'' ''Revenge!'' ''Freedom!''

Some said the lights went out in the theatre, others adding the detail that the assassin had stabbed the gasman and pulled the lever, throwing the house into darkness. Others a thousand miles from the theatre said they saw the moon come out from behind clouds blood-red. It is a night of many eyewitnesses, shaken and moaning eyewitnesses.

The audience is up and out of its one thousand seats, standing, moving. Panic is in the air, fear of what may happen next. Many merely stand up from their seats, fixed and motionless, waiting to hear what has happened, waiting to see what further is to happen. The question is spoken quietly or is murmured anxiously—''What is it? What has happened?'' The question is bawled with anger, is yelled with anguish— ''For God's sake, what is it? What has happened?''

A woman's scream pierces the air. Some say afterward it was Mrs. Lincoln. The scream carries a shock and a creeping shiver to many hearing it. ''He has shot the President!'' Miss Shephard looks from the main floor toward the box and sees ''Miss Harris wringing her hands and calling for water.'' There are moanings. ''No, for God's sake, it can't be true—no! no! for God's sake!''

Men are swarming up to the edge of the stage, over the gas-jet footlights onto the stage. The aisles fill with people not sure where to go; to leave would be safe, but they want to know what has happened, what else they may see this wild night. Men are asking whether some God-damned fool has for sure tried to shoot the President. Others take it as true. The man who ran across the stage did it. There are cries: ''Kill him! Shoot him!'' On the stage now are policemen, army officers, soldiers, besides actors and actresses in make-up and costume. Cries for ''Water, water!'' Cries for ''A surgeon! a surgeon!'' Someone brings water. It is passed up to the box.

An army surgeon climbs to the stage and is lifted up and clambers over the railing into the box. Some two hundred soldiers arrive to clear the theatre. The wailing and the crazy chaos let down in the emptying playhouse—and flare up again in the street outside, where some man is accused of saying he is glad it happened, a sudden little mob dragging him to a lamppost with a ready rope to hang him when six policemen with clubs and drawn revolvers manage to get him away and put him in jail for safekeeping.

Mrs. Lincoln in the box has turned from the railing, has turned from where she saw the wild-eyed, raven-haired man vanish off the stage, sees her husband seated in the rocking chair, his head slumped forward. Never before has she seen her husband so completely helpless, so strangely not himself. With little moaning cries she springs toward him and with her hands keeps him from tumbling to the floor. Major Rathbone has shouted for a surgeon, has run out of the box into the narrow hallway, and with one arm bleeding and burning with pain he fumbles to unfasten the bar between wall and door panel. An usher from the outside tries to help him. They get the bar loose. Back of the usher is a jam of people. He holds them back, allowing only one man to enter.

This is a young-looking man, twenty-three years old, with mustache and sideburns. Charles A. Leale, assistant surgeon, United States Volunteers, who had left the army General Hospital at Armory Square, where he was in charge of the wounded commissioned officers' ward, saying he would be gone only a short time. Rathbone shows Dr. Leale his bleeding arm, "beseeching me to attend to his wound," related Leale later. "I placed my hand under his chin, looking into his eyes an almost instantaneous glance revealed the fact that he was in no immediate danger, and in response to appeals from Mrs. Lincoln and Miss Harris, who were standing by the high-backed armchair in which President Lincoln sat, I went immediately to their assistance, saying I was a United States army surgeon."

Leale holds Mrs. Lincoln's outstretched hand while she cries piteously: "Oh, Doctor! Is he dead? Can he recover? Will you take charge of him? Do what you can for him. Oh, my dear husband! my dear husband!" He soothes her a little, telling her he will do all that can possibly be done.

The body in the chair at first scrutiny seems to be that of a dead man, eyes closed, no certainty it is breathing. Dr. Leale with help from others lifts the body from the chair and moves it to a lying position on the floor. He holds the head and shoulders while doing this, his hand meeting a clot of blood near the left shoulder. Dr. Leale recalls seeing a dagger flashed by the assassin on the stage and the knife wound of Rathbone, and now supposes the President has a stab wound. He has the coat and shirt slit open, thinking to check perhaps a hemorrhage. He finds no wounds. He lifts the eyelids and sees evidence of a brain injury. He rapidly passes the separated fingers of both hands through the blood-matted hair of the head, finding a wound and removing a clot of blood, which relieves pressure on the brain and brings shallow breathing and a weak pulse. "The assassin," Leale commented later, " . . . had evidently planned to shoot to produce instant death, as the wound he made was situated within two inches of the physiological point of selection, when instant death is desired."

Dr. Leale bends over, puts a knee at each side of the body, and tries to start the breathing apparatus, attempts to stimulate respiration by putting his two fingers into the throat and pressing down and out on the base of the tongue to free the larynx of secretion. Dr. Charles Sabin Taft, the army surgeon lifted from the stage into the box, now arrives. Another physician, Dr. Albert F. A. King, arrives. Leale asks them each to manipulate an arm while he presses upward on the diaphragm and elsewhere to stimulate heart action. The body responds with an improvement in the pulse and the irregular breathing.

Dr. Leale is sure, however, that with the shock and prostration the body has undergone, more must now be done to keep life going. And as he told it later: "I leaned forcibly forward directly over his body, thorax to thorax, face to face, and several times drew in a long breath, then forcibly breathed directly into his mouth and nostrils, which expanded his lungs and improved his respirations. After waiting a moment I placed my ear over his thorax and found the action of the heart improving. I arose to the erect kneeling posture, then watched for a short time and saw that the President could continue independent breathing and that instant death would not occur. I then pronounced my diagnosis and prognosis: 'His wound is mortal; it is impossible for him to recover.'"

Commentary

Basing his account on historical fact, carefully rendered down to the smallest detail, Sandburg has given us a chillingly vivid account of this famous horror scene from history—the assassination of President Lincoln. We see him sitting in his box seat, his wife next to him whispering fondly in his ear. At that same moment a nameless Outsider is peering through the barrel of his derringer pistol. We know what is coming, yet Sandburg manages to build suspense. How does Sandburg create the almost palpable sense of immediacy and stark reality that transports us back to Ford's Theater, watching and waiting for *it* to happen: the assassination of a president? Sandburg draws on two important devices here:

1. He uses the present tense, thereby creating for us the feeling that we are present at the event. Indeed, almost every verb puts us into a vividly reconstructed present where events are unfolding before our eyes: Lincoln *leans* back in his rocker, Major Rathbone *leaps* from his chair, a woman's scream *pierces* the air.

2. He weaves in countless small details that lend further authenticity to the description. As readers, we believe this account because the writer has painted such a full picture, even allowing us a glimpse of the action onstage, and the thoughts that might have been going through Lincoln's unsuspecting mind.

More than this, the writing—sentence structure, rhythm, variety in sentence length, choice of words, general flow—is impeccable.

Essay Suggestions

1. Suggested Topic: The Assassination of Malcolm X.

   Since the assassination in 1865 of Abraham Lincoln, there have been many other assassinations, several occurring in our own time. One is the assassination of Malcolm X, a leader of the black revolution. A man with a criminal past (by his own admission a thief, drug peddler, and pimp), Malcolm X ultimately converted to the religion of Islam, which he then served with passionate intensity. Implacably anti-white at first, he was beginning to embrace a more compassionate view when an assassin shot him dead in 1965, thereby fulfilling Malcolm X's prediction that he would not live to see his autobiography in print. How did this tragedy happen? How can it be described? What were its causes and consequences? What was its larger significance? Can any comment be made on the nature of the assassin? These are some of the questions that a term paper (4,000–5,000 words) on this subject should encompass. It is essentially a description-narration; but it is also an analysis-interpretation.

   For a discussion of research procedure and library sources, read Chapter 22, "Gathering Information." For a list of possible sources for the topic "The Assassination of Malcolm X," see pp. 357–58.

2. Additional topics suitable for a description-narration (3,000–5,000 words).

> The Assassination of Mahatma Gandhi
> The Assassination of John F. Kennedy
> The Assassination of Martin Luther King
> The Assassination of Robert Kennedy

3. Write an extended narration using one of the essay suggestions in Chapter 14 (pp. 201–02).

Extended Characterization

Like the short character sketch, the extended characterization focuses on a single individual, posing the question, "What kind of person is this? what makes him or her tick?" The extra length of the extended study enables you to probe more deeply into the complexities of your subject and to compose a fuller portrait: richer in descriptive detail, illustrative episode, and possible interpretations. Even so, like the 500-word sketch, the 5,000-word character study should have a unifying thread; it should point to the quality or qualities that define the person and provide a key to his or her character (Chapter 15, "What Kind of Person is X?").

In the following essay, the writer sweeps across the life of one of the greatest scientists of all time, noting not only what kind of person he was but also what special contribution he made to humanity as a whole.

Isaac Newton*

I. BERNARD COHEN

The mind and personality of Isaac Newton challenge any historian. Newton was a strange, solitary figure, and the wellsprings of his behavior were hidden even from his contemporaries. A biographer of his time compared Newton to the River Nile, whose great powers were known but whose source had not been discovered. Nevertheless, the few facts we have about his early life do allow some speculation about Newton's character and development.

He was born prematurely, a physical weakling. It is said that he had to wear a "bolster" to support his neck during his first months, that no one expected him to live. Newton later was fond of saying that his mother had said he was so tiny at birth that he could have been put into a quart mug.

Newton's father died three months before he was born. When the boy was less than two years old, his mother remarried, and he was turned over to his aged grandmother. He lived on an isolated farm, deprived of parental care and love, without the friendly companionship and rivalry of brothers and sisters. The late Louis T. More, author of the best-known modern biography of the man, held that much of Newton's "inwardness" could be attributed to his lonely and unhappy childhood.

Born in 1642, Newton grew up in an era when England was still tasting the "terrors of a protracted and bitter civil war." Raiding and plundering parties were common. His grandmother was "suspected of sympathy to the royal forces." In the face of these real terrors and "the frights of his imagination," he could not have received much comfort from his grandmother or the hired laborers on the farm. Naturally enough, as More observed, the boy turned to "the solace of lonely meditation" and developed a strong habit of self-absorption. A girl who knew him in his youth described him as a "sober, silent, thinking lad" who "was never known scarce to play with the boys abroad, at their silly amusements."

He evidently overcame his physical weakness by the time he reached school age, for a schoolmate reported that Newton challenged a bully who had kicked him in the belly to a fight and "beat him till he would fight no more"—winning out because he had "more spirit and resolution." The bully stood high in the class, and Newton was so determined "to beat him also at his books" that "by hard work he finally succeeded, and then gradually rose to be the first in the school."

When Newton was 14, his mother took the boy back into her home, her second husband having died. She conceived the idea of making him a farmer, but the experiment proved an unqualified failure. Newton found farming totally distasteful. Instead of attending properly to his chores, he would read, make wooden models with his knife, or dream. Fortunately for science, his mother gave up the attempt and allowed him to prepare for Cambridge University.

At the age of 18, Newton entered Trinity College. In his early years at the University he was not outstanding in any way. Then he came under the influence of Isaac Barrow, a professor of mathematics and an extraordinary man. He was an able mathematician, a classicist, an astronomer and an authority in the field of optics. Barrow was one of the first to recognize Newton's genius. Soon after his student had taken a degree, Barrow resigned his professorship so that Newton might have it. Thus at 26 Newton was established in an academic post of distinction and was free to pursue his epoch-making studies.

He had already sown the seeds of his revolutionary contributions to three distinct fields of scientific inquiry: mathematics, celestial mechanics and physical optics. After his graduation from the University he had returned to his home at Woolsthorpe for 18 months of work which can fairly be described as the most fruitful 18 months in all the history of the creative imagination. Newton's subsequent life in science consisted to a large degree in the elaboration of the great discoveries made during those "golden" months. What Newton did at Woolsthorpe is best stated in his words:

"In the beginning of the year 1665 I found the method for approximating series and the rule for reducing any dignity [power] of any binomial to such a series [i.e., the binomial theorem]. The same year in May I found the method of tangents of Gregory and Slusius, and in November [discovered] the direct method of Fluxions [i.e., the elements of the differential calculus], and the next year in January had the Theory of Colours, and in May following I had entrance into the inverse method of Fluxions [i.e., integral calculus], and in the same year I began to think of gravity extending to the orb of the Moon . . . and having thereby compared the force requisite to keep the Moon in her orb with the force of gravity at the surface of the earth, and found them to answer pretty nearly. . . ."

As a by-product of his analysis of light and colors, which he had shyly kept to himself, Newton invented a reflecting telescope, to free telescopes from the chromatic aberration of refracting lenses. He made a small version of his new telescope for the Royal Society of London, and was shortly elected, at the age of 30, as a Fellow of the Royal Society, the highest scientific honor in England.

Newton was understandably overwhelmed by his sudden public recognition. He had been loath to announce his discoveries, but within a week after his election to the Society he asked permission to communicate an account of the "philosophical discovery" which had induced him "to the making of the said telescope." With a disarming lack of false modesty, he said that in his judgment he had made "the oddest, if not the most considerable detection, which hath hitherto been made in the operations of nature."

Newton's letter to the Royal Society, "containing his new theory of light and colours," was sent to London on February 6, 1672. This paper can claim a number of "firsts." It was Newton's initial publication; it founded the science of spectroscopy, and it marked the beginning of a sound analysis of color phenomena. Briefly, what Newton showed is that a prism separates white light into its component colors, associated with specific indices of refraction, and that a second prism can recombine the dispersed light and render it white again. These magnificent experiments provided a new departure for the formulation of theories about the nature of color. Yet the paper did not win for Newton the universal applause that he had sought. The Royal Society was bombarded with letters disputing Newton's conclusions. Some of the objectors were unimportant, but others were men of stature: Christian Huygens, Robert Hooke. With astonishing patience, Newton wrote careful letters answering each objection. But he won over only one of his opponents—the French Jesuit Father Pardies.

The controversy had an acid effect on Newton's personality. He vowed that he would publish no further discoveries. As he wrote later to Leibnitz: "I was so persecuted with discussions arising from the publication of my theory of light, that I blamed my own imprudence for parting with so substantial a blessing as my quiet to run after a shadow." And yet he did later continue to publish; he wanted the applause of the scientific world. This ambivalence was not overlooked by Newton's enemies. The astronomer John Flamsteed, who broke with Newton, described him as "insidious, ambitious, and excessively covetous of praise, and impatient of contradiction. . . . I believe him to be a good man at the bottom; but, through his nature, suspicious."

At Cambridge Newton was the very model of an absent-minded professor. His amanuensis, Humphrey Newton (no relative), wrote that he never knew Newton "to take any recreation or pastime either in riding out to take the air, walking, bowling, or any other exercise whatever, thinking all hours lost that were not spent in his studies." He often worked until two or three o'clock in the morning, ate sparingly and sometimes forgot to eat altogether. When reminded that he had not eaten, he would go to the table and "eat a bite or two standing." Newton rarely dined in the college hall; when he did, he was apt to appear "with shoes down at heels, stockings untied, surplice on, and his head scarcely combed." It was said that he often delivered his lectures to an empty hall, apparently with as much satisfaction as if the room had been full of students.

After the controversy, Newton withdrew from the public eye as a scientist. He served the University as its representative in Parliament and worked away in private at chemistry and alchemy, theology, physics and mathematics. He became acquainted with Leibnitz, but refused to give his great contemporary any exact information about his discoveries in mathematics. Today it is generally agreed that the calculus was discovered more or less independently by both Newton and Leibnitz, but the two men and their partisans quarreled acrimoniously over priority, and Newton accused Leibnitz of plagiarism. Newton conceived a jealous proprietary interest in every subject he studied, and almost every achievement of his creative life was accompanied by some quarrel.

In 1684 came the famous visit to Newton by the astronomer Edmund Halley. He had a problem concerning the gravitational attraction between the sun and the planets. Halley and Hooke had concluded from Johannes Kepler's accounting of planetary motions that the force of attraction must vary inversely with the square of the distance between a planet and the sun. But they had been unable to prove their idea. "What," Halley asked Newton, "would be the curve described by the planets on the supposition that gravity diminished as the square of the distance?" Newton answered without hesitation: "An ellipse." How did he know that? "Why," replied Newton, "I have calculated it." These four words informed Halley that Newton had worked out one of the most fundamental laws of the universe—the law of gravity. Halley wanted to see the calculations at once, but Newton could not find his notes. He promised to write out the theorems and proofs. Under Halley's insistent urging he completed a manuscript for the Royal Society. Thus was born the *Philosophiae Naturalis Principia Mathematica,* known ever since simply as the *Principia.*

Just before its publication a crisis arose when Hooke laid claim to the inverse-square law. Newton threatened to withdraw the climactic chapters of his work, but Halley mollified him and the great classic went to press intact. Halley's credit in this enterprise is enormous. He not only got Newton to write the work but also saw it through the press and paid the costs of publication, although he was not a wealthy man.

The *Principia* is divided into three "books." In the first Newton laid down his three laws of motion and explored the consequences of various laws of force. In the second he explored motion in various types of fluids; here he was somewhat less successful, and much of his work had to be revised in the succeeding decades. In the third he discussed universal gravitation and showed how a single law of force explains at once the falling of bodies on the earth, the motion of our moon or of Jupiter's satellites, the motions of planets and the phenomenon of tides.

One of the most vexing problems for Newton was to find a rigorous proof that a sphere acts gravitationally as if all its mass were concentrated at its center. Without this theorem, the whole theory of gravitation would rest on intuition rather than precise calculation. For instance, in the simple case of an apple falling to the ground—the occasion of the central idea of gravitation according to Newton's own account—what is the "distance between" the earth and the apple? Here the calculus came into play. Newton considered the earth as a collection of tiny volumes of matter, each attracting the apple according to the inverse-square law of gravitation. Then he summed up the individual forces and showed that the result was the same as if the earth were a point mass, as if all the matter of the earth were shrunk into a tiny region at its center.

Newton suffered some kind of "nervous breakdown" after the completion of the *Principia.* He complained that he could not sleep, and said that he lacked the "former consistency of his mind." He wrote angry letters to friends and then apologized; he protested bitterly to John Locke, for example, that the philosopher had attempted to "embroil him with women."

In 1696 Newton abandoned the academic life for the position of Warden, later Master, of the Mint. Honors for his scientific achievements continued to come to him: he was knighted in 1705 and served many years as president of the Royal Society. But the last quarter century of his life produced no major contributions to science. Some say that his creative genius had simply burned out. Others argue that after having founded the science of physical optics, invented the calculus and shown the mechanism of the universe, there just wasn't anything left for him to do in the realm of science.

Although he made no important discoveries, Newton's last years were not barren of ideas. Now famous and honored, he felt secure enough to offer many public speculations on scientific problems. He suggested various possible hypotheses as to the "cause" of gravitation and speculated on the nature of the "ether," the size of the constituent units of matter, the forces of electricity and magnetism, the cause of muscular response to the "commands of the will," the origins of sensation, the creation of the world, the ultimate destiny of man. In the century after Newton, physical experimenters followed up many of his bold speculations.

Newton is often described as the inaugurator of the "Age of Reason." Alexander Pope expressed the sentiment of his time in the famous lines:

> Nature and Nature's laws lay hid in night:
> God said, Let Newton be! and all was light.

Commentary

Note the provocative opening of this essay, which presents Newton *as a man* rather than as a scientist. Newton, the writer says, is a challenge, for he was "a strange, solitary figure"; even his contemporaries hardly knew him, though they suspected the power of his genius, one comparing him to the Nile. The advantage of such an opening paragraph is obvious: it captures the attention and interest of scientist and nonscientist alike. Because the writer of this essay humanizes his subject, the reader is moved to read on, to try to understand Newton's life—and in so doing comes to understand Newton's work as well, for in this essay Cohen has very skillfully described and evaluated the massive contribution of Newton as "the inaugurator of the 'Age of Reason,'" a man who bridged the gap between science and art. Thus the closing quotation from Pope invests the essay with an appropriately poetic tone and significance.

Essay Suggestions

1. Suggested Topic: Robert Schumann: The Triumph and the Tragedy.

   As Bernard Cohen has explored the life and work of Newton, study and write (3,000–5,000 words) about the composer Robert Schumann, whose idyllic love affair with Clara Schumann was marred by his steadily advancing mental illness. Try to find the motivational source (the key that turns the lock) of this talented but tormented figure.

   For a discussion of research procedure and library resources, read Chapter 22, "Gathering Information." For a list of possible sources for the topic "Robert Schumann: The Triumph and the Tragedy," see p. 358.

2. Additional topics for an extended characterization (3,000–5,000 words).

Copernicus	Mme. de Staël
Galileo	Mary Wollenstonecraft
Charles Darwin	Harriet Beecher Stowe
Leonardo da Vinci	John Brown
Pavlov	Ludwig van Beethoven
Benjamin Franklin	Pablo Picasso
George Sand	Albert Schweitzer
Isadora Duncan	

Extended Argumentation

Most good examples of argumentation are at least 3,000 to 5,000 words long, since it requires that many words to develop issues, marshal evidence, and construct a convincing case. The following article, written by a sociologist, argues that the plight of black people is a consequence of class and ethnic factors rather than simply of race.

Whither the Black Odyssey?*

JAMES M. O'KANE

In recent years it has become academically fashionable to analyze and interpret the plight of the lower-income black in urban ghettoes as though this were an entirely novel situation in American life. Reference has been made to the "problem of the black," as one which is intrinsically unique and fundamentally different from the predicament of all previously lower-income minority groups.

This mode of analysis implies that the difficulties which this black urbanite faces as a result of his inferior position on the lowest rungs of the social ladder are infinitely more complex, more paradoxical, and less amenable to solution than anything encountered by the Irish, the Pole, the Jew, and the Italian. The problem's specific interpretation in these terms has consequently resulted in social scientists abandoning, or at least side-stepping, the socio-historical relationships relevant to the routes of upward mobility for minority groups in American life.

The resultant myopic interpretation has subsequently led social observers to view the problem of the lower-income black as essentially a *racial* problem. Hence the black has been differentiated from previous lower-class minority groups on the basis of so-called racial differences and distinctions. The argument runs as follows: the black cannot be likened to the immigrant groups of the nineteenth century simply because of his ascribed *racial* qualities. The former slave status and legal disenfranchisement from American social life have necessitated the realization that the black is in a category distinct from all previous societal rejects. His situation and problems are unique; they are literally larger and more incomprehensible than anything of a similar vein witnessed in our history, and the old answers will be irrelevant to the amelioration of the Negro's situation.[1]

Such a position betrays not only a pessimistic, but also a tempo-centric view of the lower-income black and his supposed uniqueness at the bottom of urban society. Yet, *how* different is this urban black from his Italian counterpart of sixty years ago? *How* distinct is the so-called female centered household of the lower-income black from that of the Irish a century ago? *How* different is the inequality and discrimina-

*From *The Drew University Magazine*, Vol. 3, No. 3 (Spring 1969). Reprinted by permission. Originally published as "Ethnic Mobility and the Lower-Income Negro: A Socio-Historical Perspective" in *Social Problems*, Vol. 16, No. 3 (Winter 1969). Reprinted by permission of The Society for the Study of Social Problems.

[1]*The Report of the National Advisory Commission* has subscribed to this approach, stating: "Racial discrimination is undoubtedly the second major reason why the Negro has been unable to escape from poverty. The structure of discrimination has persistently narrowed his opportunities and restricted his prospects. Well before the high tide of immigration from overseas, Negroes were already relegated to the poorly paid, low status occupation. . . . European immigrants, too, suffered from discrimination, but never was it so pervasive as the prejudice against color in America which has formed a bar to advancement, unlike any other." *Report of the National Advisory Commission on Civil Disorders* (New York: Bantam Books, 1968), pp. 278–79.

tion which the black ghettoite presently faces from that of his Jewish predecessors? Basically the differences are secondary. To become absorbed in analyzing only the differences between these groups implies a certain degree of ignorance of the structural supports of ethnic and class mobility which have been similar for all the minority groups in American urban life.

Presently it might indeed be more fruitful to view the plight of the lower-income urban black in terms of *class* and *ethnic* factors rather than *racial* factors. The social unrest and turmoil evident in the urban ghettoes are consequences of lower-class membership and, to that degree, are not specifically related to racial factors. John and Lois Scott in a recent article have paraphrased this relationship:

> Most racial antipathy in America is not pure racism but derives from the disdain of higher classes for those below them. The tragedy of race in this country . . . is that visible genetic differences, superficial in themselves, have become generally reliable clues to a person's class position—his education, his income, his manners. . . . Events of the last 20 years have done much to modify the legal and political aspects of this subordination, but the more general effects of the past remain: black Americans are disadvantaged and poor, and their culture—so much a "culture of poverty"—is offensive to more affluent classes.[2]

The lower-income black thus represents the most recent ethnic group in urban America and, like his forerunners from other ethnic minorities, has migrated from agricultural poverty to industrial poverty. Essentially he has moved from the lowest position in an agricultural caste society to the lowest position in an urban class system; in the former environment caste characteristics exerted primary importance while in the latter they are secondary and of limited consequence in either defining or labeling the plight of the black.

The black, like all the lower ethnic minorities in America's past, comes from an agricultural background. He has been forced from the land and consequently drawn to the cities primarily because of agricultural technology and impoverishment which have destroyed his economic usefulness in an agricultural society. In this respect he differs little from the Irish, the Pole, and the Southern Italian. To observe that each came from a different historical, social, and cultural heritage does not alter the fact that their primary reasons for migration were similar.

So also with the lower-income black. It is of little concern to the unemployed Harlemite that his great-grandfather was a slave. His concerns are with survival in a modern urban metropolis. To dwell solely on the past glories and past humiliations of the black, of his African heritage, of his slave status and freedom from bondage, is an irrelevant point. All the immigrant minorities had similar exposures to cultural pride and historical trauma, yet this heritage had little to do with their realistic position in poverty. Each of these minorities also fought and pushed its way into a dominant American society which had made it quite evident that the group concerned was not socially acceptable. The Irish, the Jews, and the Italians—all faced the reality of exclusion from the dominant middle-class society, yet each in turn maneuvered its way into the economic, political, and social mainstream. There is no reason to suggest that the black will not do similarly, for if the lessons of history are correct, he will be successful.

Yet how is the black slum dweller to move away from his socially inferior lower class position? Through what methods will he be able to partake of the status and affluence of the middle class dominant groups? What routes of upward social mobility lie open to him? The historical and social realities of America's past suggest

[2]John F. Scott and Lois H. Scott, "They Are Not So Much Anti-Negro As Pro–Middle Class," *New York Times Magazine*, 24 March 1968, p. 46.

answers to these questions, for, strangely enough, the lessons of our own history provide us with the clues necessary for the understanding of the present situation.

One factor remains constant: no minority group ever achieved acceptance through dependence upon the benevolence and good will of the dominant American society. Each of the immigrant groups started at the bottom of American society and eventually forged its way into economic, political, and—ultimately—social equality with the dominant society. They had not been invited, and it has been adequately documented that their presence was ridiculed and resented in America. Naturally there were those few voices in the established society which bemoaned the cruel and harsh treatment of the immigrant minorities, yet these dissenters from middle-class propriety were too few and too powerless to effect any real change. Hence, the Irish and the Jews, the Italians and the Slavs—all faced the same basic dilemma of removing themselves from the poverty of the lower class and simultaneously gaining a foothold in the door of the socially accepted classes.

However, the socially approved routes of upward mobility bear little semblance to the daily reality of life in the slums. Being economically and socially ostracized, the newcomers were forced into seeking routes of upward mobility which were not totally explainable in terms of the Horatio Alger form of success. Prejudice and discrimination prevented these minority groups from succeeding in the acceptable manner and consequently other forms or modes of mobility evolved. But what were these routes of mobility? What form did they take?

Each of the minority groups utilized three core modes of movement from the lower classes to the dominant society, each of which is interrelated and interdependent. These can be identified as labor, crime, and politics. Each of these offered a route of upward mobility to the newcomers and their children. This is not to imply that no other modes were present. Hence, for specific ethnic groups such as the Irish, the clergy became an "occupational" source of prestige and power. For other groups, particularly the black and Puerto Rican, professional sports and entertainment became alternative methods of success.[3]

Yet these alternative forms served as corollary forms of mobility while the primary forms remained labor, crime, and politics. In discussing the progress of the immigrants and their relationship to the Anglo-Saxon Establishment, E. Digby Baltzell in *The Protestant Establishment* writes, "as the traditional ways to wealth and respectability in business or the professions were more or less monopolized by Protestant Americans of older stock, many of the more talented and ambitious members of minority groups found careers in urban politics, in organized crime, or for those of the Catholic faith, in the hierarchy of the church."[4] Thus the analysis of ethnic upward mobility somehow encompasses the relationships between these three factors of labor, crime, and politics.

Labor

The economic expansion of the nineteenth century provided the most obvious channel of upward mobility for the recent immigrants, for it was this industrial

---

[3]Oscar Handlin writes, "In the theatre, art, music and athletic worlds, talent was more or less absolute; and discrimination was much less effective than in other realms. This accounted for the high incidence among Negroes and Puerto Ricans to seek these pursuits as a way up; and it accounted also for the popularity and high status among them of prize fighters, musicians and the like, a popularity of which the incidence of reference in magazines and newspapers is a striking index." Oscar Handlin, *The Newcomers* (Garden City: Doubleday, 1962), p. 72.

[4]E. Digby Baltzell, *The Protestant Establishment* (New York: Vintage, 1966), p. 49.

expansion which required the abundant supply of cheap and unskilled labor. Each of the ethnic minorities had been forced through societal exclusion to work at the most menial and underpaid types of employment—digging canals, working in the garment sweatshops, building subways and railroads, working in unskilled construction, and literally thousands of other tasks which had been deemed economically and socially unfit for the dominant classes. Yet these jobs provided the newcomer with a relative degree of economic security, a ray of hope perhaps not for himself but possibly for his children. Certainly he was mistreated and underpaid, yet his meager, but growing, savings and primitive accumulation enabled him to initiate the ever-so-slow process of mobility from the ethnic slum and the conditions of pauperization. In time, each of the minorities accepted this pattern and subsequently realized that the American norms of thrift, hard work, advancement, and progress were integral parts of the American ethos. As Handlin points out, they were the keys to status and respectability in the new nation and the immigrant's desire for upward mobility necessarily required the internalization of these ideals.[5] Hence, labor in the unskilled and semi-skilled professions provided the immigrant with a beginning from which he could at least maintain himself and his immediate family. Physical labor was in economic demand and it furnished the newcomer with the "tool" necessary for an entry into the labor market.

The plenitude of unskilled labor enabled the immigrant to place himself, however unequally, on the lowest rung of the social class ladder, but at least he was on the ladder. Hence stable unskilled employment became the basic requirement for the subsequent mobility of all the nation's ethnic minorities. Without such economic usefulness, upward mobility would have been conceivably impossible. Yet this marginal employment did not function in a social vacuum, for simultaneously there existed and prospered two other modes of ethnic mobility—ethnic crime and ethnic politics.

Ethnic Crime and Ethnic Politics

It would be fruitless and unrealistic to speak of the ethnic political movements of the nineteenth and early twentieth centuries without realizing the close connection between these movements and the criminal organizations of that era. Ethnic crime and ethnic political structures formed a symbiotic relationship which is perhaps best epitomized by the success of Tammany Hall in New York City. In his book, *The Gangs of New York,* the noted social observer Herbert Asbury comments on this relationship:

> The political geniuses of Tammany Hall were quick to see the practical value of the gangsters, and to realize the advisability of providing them with meeting and hiding places, that their favor might be curried and their peculiar talents employed on election days to assure government of, by and for Tammany. . . . The underworld thus became an important factor in politics, and under the manipulation of the worthy statement the gangs of the Bowery and Five Points participated in a great series of riots which began with the spring election disturbances of 1834 and continued, with frequent outbreaks, for half a score of years.[6]

Ethnic crime and ethnic politics thus formed a working alliance which dates from the earlier part of the nineteenth century and has continued to the present. In New York, the Irish ranked as the most noteworthy of the early immigrant groups in both politics and crime, and their political and criminal expertise has subsequently been duplicated and imaginatively expanded by the Jews and the Italians. As each of these groups attained success and renown in politics and crime, so also did the entire

[5]Handlin, p. 19.
[6]Herbert Asbury, *The Gangs of New York: An Informal History of the Underworld* (New York: Knopf, 1929), p. 37.

ethnic group maneuver into the dominant society. Once established, in the new acceptable class, the ethnic group no longer depended on the functional relation of crime and political structure and, correspondingly, the lower ranks of the political structure and underworld activities came into the hands of those groups still struggling to remove themselves from the lower class. As Daniel Bell has phrased it, crime is the "American way of life."[7]

New immigrant groups wasted little time in realizing the potential value of success, not only in the political sphere, but simultaneously in the criminal sphere, for political affiliations and connections provided the legal immunity so essential to the survival of criminals. In turn the influence of the gangster could be noted in his provision of financial backing for political ventures, in his physical "support" for the growing trade union movement, and, perhaps most important of all, in his power to dissuade unwelcome individuals and groups from political competition with the forces in power. Realistically, then, it remains historically and socially significant that some of the earliest leaders of urban political machines were, at the same time, the leaders of the more important gangs of that era.

Commenting on this symbiotic relationship between political parties and gangsters, Richard Cloward and Lloyd Ohlin write, in *Delinquency and Opportunity:*

> The gangsters and racketeers contributed greatly to the coffers of political parties and were rewarded with immunity from prosecution for their various illegal activities. As the political power of the ethnic or nationality group increased, access to legitimate opportunities became enlarged and assimilation facilitated. . . . Blocked from legitimate access to wealth, the immigrant feels mounting pressures for the use of illegal alternatives.[8]

Accordingly, a working relationship emerged in each of the ethnic groups between crime and politics. As Oscar Handlin and Will Herberg both discuss, illegality provided an attractive means of upward mobility and social advancement, and its success was insured through an established, though sometimes tenuous and uneasy relation to the local neighborhood political structure. The vast majority of the specific ethnic groups worked their way out of the lower classes by saving their "pennies and dimes" and eventually, in two or three generations, their descendants achieved middle-class status and respectability.[9]

Productive labor was but one factor. Concurrent with it there existed the profound impact of ethnic crime and politics which supplied the finances and the political acumen necessary for the mobility of the entire group. Ethnic consciousness and ethnic solidarity were thus created, the cultural heroes of each of these groups being both the political bosses and the gangsters. These "models" demonstrated to the masses of the lower class that an individual could achieve success and power and that the ethnic group itself, as a collective entity, constituted a force with which the dominant elites would have to reckon.[10]

[7]Daniel Bell, "Crime as an American Way of Life," *Antioch Review,* 13 (Sept. 1953), 131–54.

[8]Richard Cloward and Lloyd Ohlin, *Delinquency and Opportunity* (Glencoe: Free Press, 1960), p. 196.

[9]Handlin, p. 26; see also Herberg's discussion of the immigrant groups and political development, in Will Herberg, *Protestant, Catholic, Jew* (Garden City: Doubleday Anchor, 1960), p. 17.

[10]Boss Joseph Maloney, Alderman of "Cornerville" bitterly recognized this, stating, "Then the Italians will always vote for one of their own. We recognized them when we didn't need to. They didn't have many votes, and we could have licked them everytime, but we gave them Italian representatives. We did it for the sake of the organization. But they wouldn't stick by us. The Italian people are very undependable. You can't trust them at all. They play a dirty game too. I estimate that now there are between eight hundred and a thousand repeaters in Cornerville every election. I've tried to stop that, but you can't do it. You can't tell one Italian from another." William Whyte, *Street Corner Society* (Chicago: U. of Chicago, 1955), p. 95. See also, Baltzell, p. 217, for a discussion of Al Capone as a folk hero and his relationship to the American value of non-conformity.

Implications

What about the black? How do the channels of employment, crime, and politics affect his opportunities for upward mobility? What relationship, if any, exists between the lessons of historical mobility and the conditions of black lower-income life?

The answers to these questions are both interrelated and complex; it would be an oversimplification and, indeed, a gross misrepresentation of reality to say that the black should pursue these routes of mobility. The fact remains that he *is* pursuing these routes. It takes no profound insight to see that in crime and politics the black has been working his way into the higher positions of power. Yet, like the Jew and the Italian before him, he has been forced to contend with the established criminal and political elites, for mobility in the political and the criminal realm is demonstrably as difficult, if not more so, than mobility in the occupational realm. Thomas Pettigrew, in an article entitled, "Negro American Crime," has written " . . . as with other minority groups who find discriminatory barriers blocking their path towards the mainstream of success-oriented America, many Negroes turn to crime. Crime may thus be utilized as a means of escape, ego-enhancement, expression of aggression, or upward mobility."[11]

Political considerations are also operative. The recent black political successes in Gary, Indiana and Cleveland, Ohio underscore the contention that the traditional path of ethnic political power is being utilized. Among both black militants and moderates there is a growing awareness that the key to success lies not in violence and disorder but rather in political mobility. In a recent interview, in *The New York Times,* Timothy Still, the late president of the United Community Corporation of Newark, stated:

> Newark is a city that is 60 percent colored, and we are going to inherit this city. And so we cannot let fools destroy the city we are going to inherit. The guys who were trying to start all this trouble were those who were lost, hopeless, those who had no chance. I can understand their feelings, but you can't destroy the whole city. It is *our* city, and we are not going to let you do that.[12]

Still's comments point to the increasing recognition on the part of the black community of the need for political awareness and political power. Black power and black consciousness thus can be considered as necessary intermediary means to the politicalization of the black population.[13] If present demographic projections hold true, the major urban centers of America will be predominantly black and consequently the population base for black political leverage will be present. Ethnic solidarity thus becomes the key to the subsequent political power and political mobility of the entire group. Again, the lessons of America's past are in evidence, for the black is presently actualizing what other minorities historically have accomplished.

A closer examination of the employment route, however, reveals the presence of one all-important factor which has blocked the potential for upward mobility for the black. Unlike all his predecessors, the lower-income black faces one enduring fact of

[11]Thomas Pettigrew, "Negro American Crime," in *A Profile of the Negro American* (Princeton: Van Nostrand, 1964), p. 156.

[12]Fred Cook, "It's Our City, Don't Destroy It," *New York Times Magazine,* 30 June 1968, p. 31.

[13]For a recent appraisal of the relationship between black power and the Negro community see, Seymour Leventman, "Black Power and the Negro Community in Mass Society," paper presented at the annual meeting of the American Sociological Association, Boston, August 1968.

UNEMPLOYMENT RATE FOR NON–WHITE WORKERS AS PERCENT
OF RATE FOR WHITE WORKERS, 1948–1967
(Persons 16 years and over)

Year	Unemployment Rate		Non-white Rate as Percent of White
	White	Non-white	
1948	3.2	5.9	169
1949	5.6	8.9	159
1950	4.9	9.0	184
1951	3.1	5.3	171
1952	2.8	5.4	193
1953	2.7	4.5	167
1954	5.0	9.9	198
1955	3.9	8.7	223
1956	3.6	8.3	231
1957	3.8	7.9	208
1958	6.1	12.6	207
1959	4.8	10.7	223
1960	4.9	10.2	208
1961	6.0	12.4	207
1962	4.9	10.9	222
1963	5.0	10.8	216
1964	4.6	9.6	209
1965	4.1	8.1	198
1966	3.3	7.3	221
1967	3.4	7.4	218

Source: *Manpower Report, 1967,* U.S. Department of Labor (Washington, D.C.: Government Printing Office, 1967).

contemporary economic structure—the relative disappearance of unskilled occupations. The lower-income Negro increasingly can be classified as economically useless.[14] Economic and technological developments since World War II have eliminated precisely those positions which the black might have utilized as leverage for subsequent mobility. Without these jobs he cannot even hope to climb the class ladder. Without them he has little chance of removing himself from the lower class, for employment in these occupations constitutes the barest minimum necessary for ethnic mobility. In *Problems and Prospects of the Negro Movement,* Herbert Hill has emphasized this factor:

> Optimistic assumptions regarding the Negro's progress in American society must be reexamined in the light of the Negro's current economic plight. The great mass of Negroes, especially in the urban centers, are locked in a permanent condition of poverty. This includes the long-term unemployed as well as the working poor, who have only a marginal economic existence and who increasingly are forced into the ranks of the unemployed.[15]

Hence, structural considerations of employment and its impact upon the black has created the present societal chaos so evident in our urban centers. An analysis of the condition of unemployment over the past two decades reflects this structural problem—one which statistically is growing more chronic over the years. Unemployment statistics illustrate the situation of the non-white worker, and his plight has increased

[14]For an interesting article dealing with the economics of uselessness of the lower-income Negro see, Sidney M. Willhelm and Edwin Powell, "Who Needs the Negro?," *Transaction,* 1 (Sept.–Oct. 1964), 3–6.

[15]Herbert Hill, "Racial Inequality in Employment: The Patterns of Discrimination," in *Problems and Prospects of the Negro Movement,* eds. R. Murphy and H. Elinson (Belmont, California: Wadsworth, 1966), p. 86.

significantly from the plight of the white worker since 1948, the first year when such statistics were available for persons over 16 years of age.

However, class factors are evident in the employment situation confronting the black. The unavailability of unskilled jobs does not affect the middle-class black and, to that degree, its members participate in the economic and social prosperity so characteristic of contemporary American society. The black has been victimized not primarily by his color, nor by his former slave status, but by his lower-class position. In this he remains no different from his Puerto Rican, Mexican-American, or Appalachian white counterpart. All are substantially represented in the lower class, and upward mobility is increasingly very difficult due to the economic structural forces beyond their control. Thus, the degree that unemployment in the unskilled jobs diminishes, to the same degree will the lower-income black be cut-off from the possibilities of upward mobility.

The recent urban disorders in scores of cities have underscored this problem of class. In many of the cities, the rioters demonstrated the same hostility towards middle-class blacks as they did towards white policemen, firemen, and business proprietors. It should also be emphasized that lower-income blacks were not the only group to participate in urban disorders, for New York City, in the summer of 1967, and Paterson, New Jersey, in the summer of 1968, witnessed small scale outbreaks among the lower-income Puerto Rican community.

The rigidity of lower-class positioning and the increasing uncertainty of upward mobility thus create tensions in those individuals cut-off from the prospects of improving their societal lot. Given the proper environment, these tensions erupt in violence and destruction. As the Riot Commission has pointed out, the typical rioter was *better* educated, *better* informed, and geographically *more stable* than the non-rioter of the same neighborhood.[16] He perhaps had more reason to hope for subsequent upward mobility, yet the inevitable workings of an economic structure which cannot, or will not, use his labor has confronted him with the realities of the American class structure. His behavior bears the marks of vengeance, of lashing back at a society which has promised him much yet has removed the routes to the rewards. It may be surmised that the non-rioter comprises an American variation of the Marxian "lumpenproletariat"—that group which has been so suppressed that appeals to revolution and retaliation become meaningless and hollow.

The problems and the styles of life encountered in the lower-income black are not basically distinguishable from those of other ethnic groups, past or present. Certainly his family structure, his beliefs, and his values are different from those of the middle class. Yet, how distinct are these same traits from other lower-income ethnic groups such as the Puerto Rican? The similarities found in our current lower-class ethnic minorities greatly outweigh the differences and to magnify the differential styles and values of these respective groups is to place undue emphasis for poverty and deprivation on the wrong factors.

Currently, the black comprises the most important ethnic group in the urban lower class. His problems and tragedies are those of preceding ethnic minorities, yet the profound economic changes in American society have greatly complicated his status and his potential for mobility. These changes have produced the disorders of Watts, Detroit, Newark, and Washington. In turn the unskilled black's relative economic marginality has created the impetus for the proliferation of many of the socio-psychological problems of the ghetto with its underlying culture of poverty, its

---

[16]*The Report of the National Advisory Commission on Civil Disorders,* pp. 128–35.

irrelevant educational system, its so called multi-problem families, and its forced exclusion from affluent America through economic dysfunction.

Racial considerations add little to the analysis of these issues; all too often they act as smokescreens which mask the real problems. If race and racial considerations exerted primary importance, it would increasingly be difficult to interpret the values and styles of life of the black *middle-class* population. These values are vastly different from the black lower class, yet they are essentially similar to the values and life styles of the white middle-class population. The gap thus exists between the classes, not the races; it is between the white and black middle class on one hand, and the white and black lower class on the other. Skin color and the history of servitude do little to explain the present polarization of the classes.

Social class thus assumes a primary position in defining and explaining the relationship between upward mobility and the behavior of specific ethnic groups, while racial stigmatization can be considered as relatively secondary in importance. Class differentials, not racial differentials, explain the presence and persistence of poverty in the ranks of the urban black. It thus becomes superfluous to speak of the problem in moral terms, in the rhetoric of brotherly love and social equality. However noble these answers may be, they ignore the reality of ethnic mobility, for no group has ever achieved parity unless it followed the well-traversed route of labor, crime, and politics. Only *after* each of the groups achieved relative success and power in these ventures were they "accepted." Social acceptance and social integration were the last steps, and perhaps the easiest steps, in the long journey from the bottom. In contemporary America, many well-meaning individuals and groups have placed the cart before the horse. They have argued for social acceptance first, from which ultimately should come economic equality, political power, etc., rather than the converse. To argue in this manner merely aggravates the situation, for it deflects the forces of change from the economic and structural considerations and wastes them in moral reform and spiritual catharsis.

The Head Starts, the community action programs, the educational pilot projects function yet they remain unrelated to the roots of the problem of poverty in the black ghettoes. The facts speak for themselves: none of the existing programs attack the problem at its structural foundation, employment. What difference does it make if all these programs do not create employment for the presently unskilled? What contribution is made by a Job Corps that trains youth for non-existing jobs? What difference does it really make for a lower-income Negro to get a high school diploma when the available statistics suggest that his unemployment rate remains disproportionately higher than whites with or without the diploma? These are the crucial questions which must be answered if the black is to move in American society. His odyssey is essentially no different from that of previous ethnic minorities; it only remains for American society to provide the employment necessary to make the journey productive and rewarding.

BIBLIOGRAPHY

Asbury, Herbert. *The Gangs of New York: An Informal History of the Underworld.* New York: Alfred A. Knopf, 1929.

Baltzell, E. Digby. *The Protestant Establishment.* New York: Vintage Books, 1966.

Bell, Daniel. "Crime as an American Way of Life." *Antioch Review,* 13 (Sept. 1953), 131–54.

Cloward, Richard, and Lloyd Ohlin. *Delinquency and Opportunity.* Glencoe, Ill.: The Free Press, 1960.

Cook, Fred. "It's Our City, Don't Destroy It." *New York Times Magazine,* 30 June 1968, pp. 31 ff.

Handlin, Oscar. *The Newcomers.* Garden City, N.Y.: Doubleday Anchor Books, 1962.

Herberg, Will. *Protestant, Catholic, Jew.* Garden City, N.Y.: Doubleday Anchor Books, 1955.

Hill, Herbert. "Racial Inequality in Employment: The Patterns of Discrimination." *Problems and Prospects of the Negro Movement.* Eds. R. Murphy and H. Elinson. Belmont, Calif.: Wadsworth Co., 1966.

Leventman, Seymour. "Black Power and the Negro Community in Mass Society." Paper presented to the Annual Meeting of the American Sociological Association, Boston, August 1968.

Pettigrew, Thomas. *A Profile of the Negro American.* Princeton, N.J.: Van Nostrand Co., 1964.

Report of the National Advisory Commission on Civil Disorders. New York: Bantam Books, 1968.

Scott, John, and Lois H. Scott. "They Are Not So Much Anti-Negro As Pro–Middle Class." *New York Times Magazine,* 24 March 1968, pp. 46ff.

Whyte, William. *Street Corner Society.* Chicago: University of Chicago Press, 1955.

Willhelm, Sidney, and Edwin Powell. "Who Needs the Negro?" *Transaction,* 1 (Sept.– Oct. 1964), 3–6.

OTHER SOURCES CONSULTED*

Baltzell, E. Digby. *Philadelphia Gentlemen, The Making of a National Upper Class.* Glencoe, Ill.: The Free Press, 1958.

Bell, Daniel. *The End of Ideology.* Glencoe, Ill.: The Free Press, 1960.

Cahan, Abraham. *The Rise of David Levinsky.* New York: Harper and Brothers, 1917.

Glazer, Nathan, and Daniel Moynihan. *Beyond the Melting Pot.* Cambridge, Mass.: The M.I.T. Press, 1963.

Gordon, Milton. *Assimilation in American Life.* New York: Oxford University Press, 1964.

Hansen, Marcus Lee. *The Problem of the Third Generation Immigrant.* Rock Island, Ill.: Augustana Historical Society, 1938.

Higham, John. *Stranger in the Land: Patterns of American Nativism 1860–1925.* New Brunswick, N.J.: Rutgers University Press, 1955.

Hofstadter, Richard. *The Age of Reform.* New York: Vintage Books, 1960.

Liebow, Eliot. *Tally's Corner.* Boston: Little, Brown and Company, 1967.

Solomon, Barbara. *Ancestors and Immigrants: A Changing New England.* Cambridge, Mass.: Harvard University Press, 1956.

Commentary

In this piece, as in the shorter examples of argumentation cited in Chapter 20, "What Case Can Be Made For or Against X?" the structure of the argument follows the conventional form: introduction, body, and conclusion. Note too that in supporting his case for an ethnic approach to black problems, the writer touches on many of our other twenty questions:

1. He describes the past and present status of blacks in the United States.
2. He compares their problems and life style with those of other minority groups.

*This list refers to works consulted or read by the writer, but not used directly in the article.

3. He traces the causes and consequences of their problems.
4. He summarizes opposing views.
5. He explains how other minorities have achieved upward mobility (a process analysis).
6. He cites numerous facts, details, and statistics.
7. He interprets these facts, details, and statistics in the light of his propositions.

After supporting his main *is* proposition throughout the body of his argument (namely that black people are victimized not so much by their color as by their lower-class status, their poverty), the writer moves on at the end of his argument to infer from the *is* proposition an *ought* proposition: the problems of blacks *ought* to be attacked not on a social level but at their roots, at the level of employment. The writer draws to a conclusion with a series of provocative rhetorical questions ("Why bother training blacks for non-existent jobs?"). He concludes with a brief recapitulation of his position: "[The blacks'] odyssey is essentially no different from that of previous ethnic minorities; it only remains for American society to provide the employment necessary to make the journey productive and rewarding."

Essay Suggestions

1. Suggested Topic: "Whither the Black Odyssey?": A Reply.

    If you disagree with this interpretation—if you believe that the present problems faced by black ghetto-dwellers are qualitatively different from those faced by other dispossessed minority groups in this country; if you believe that their African heritage and former slave status have created in black Americans a distinct identity that cannot be dealt with apart from the racial issue; and if you believe that we are more likely to solve the problems of poverty and deprivation among blacks by approaching the problem from a racial rather than economic point of view—you could write a reply to this article in which you explain how and why the position of blacks differs from that of other minorities in our nation's history. How can blacks expect to achieve "upward mobility," if that is their goal? What are their aspirations? How may they best achieve them?

    The author of "Whither the Black Odyssey?" has called on many sources to support his position, as his footnotes and bibliography indicate. In order to write a substantial reply (4,000–5,000 words), you must do the same. For a discussion of research procedure and library resources, read Chapter 22, "Gathering Information." For a list of possible sources for the topic "'Whither the Black Odyssey?': A Reply," see pp. 358–59.

2. Write an extended argumentation (3,000–5,000 words) for an unorthodox interpretation and solution to one of these problems:

    urban blight
    inflation
    rising crime rate
    rising divorce rate
    drug abuse and addiction
    the Middle East conflict
    unemployment
        or
    address yourself to a matter of current concern such as women's liberation

22 Gathering Information

In an article entitled "What Every Writer Must Learn," poet John Ciardi pointed out that "good writers deal in information." All writers who want their pieces to have substance and texture build upon solid information that they have obtained from one or more of the following sources:

1. remembering
2. observing
3. thinking
4. research

In this chapter we shall consider these sources separately, noting how you may best proceed in each case, noting also that most often you will turn to more than one source for your materials.

Remembering Facts

As was noted in Chapter 17, "What Is My Memory of X?" novelist Thomas Wolfe could remember with shattering clarity events of his childhood and early youth: they came back to him unsolicited, in their minutest, most vivid detail. Because most of us do not have this gift of total recall, we must make a conscious and sustained effort to conjure up the past so that we can reproduce it on paper with a degree of reality and vividness.

Take a typical memorable event; for example, let us say you once almost drowned. That should provide the ingredients for an exciting narrative account—but maybe not. It depends on how accurately you can recall specific details. If you are a careful writer, you will strain to remember and render in vivid images the specific sensations and impressions associated with the original experience—the water bubbling in your ears as you went down ... down ... the sound of voices in the distance ... (how did they sound—*exactly?*). You know that you can make your experience live again on paper only if you activate those small, telling details that capture its essence. Thus, you will spend hours gathering information from the deepest recesses of your memory. You know that it is all buried there *somewhere* and that if you persist in your digging you will recover it. You know, too, that this is not an easy task but a formidable discipline.

Interestingly, many conscious procedures, even rituals, have been worked out by people who want, for a variety of reasons, to prod their memories. Two of these are worth mentioning here, for they may be adapted to the writer's purpose. They arise from the group workshops in creativity and "direct experience workshops" conducted by psychotherapist Ira Progoff.[1] Although these workshops have a larger than literary purpose ("They are designed," says Dr. Progoff, "to expand awareness and evoke the unlived creative potential of the individual"), their methods can be applied to retrieving one's past experience so that it may be recreated realistically on paper. In his workshop sessions, Dr. Progoff tries "to help the individual extend the time dimension of his personality so that he can feel the movement and direction of his life from the outside." Thus at one workshop session Dr. Progoff addressed the group as follows:

> Let's put ourselves in adolescence ..., make it early adolescence, pre-sexual awareness. Ask yourself "How did I feel then? Were there any special experiences that stand out in my mind? Funny? Sad? Strange? How did I feel about myself? About life? About my relation to life? What was my image of myself in those days?" Let yourself be carried back ... relax and think ... try to remember ... people ... images ... events.... Just speak out when you *do* remember.... Tell us what it was like.

We can simulate a creativity workshop by assembling a small group of people (five or six classmates, let us say) who will systematically set out to evoke memories, their own and one another's. Actually there are many ways to conduct such a session: the participants might take turns free associating, letting their minds wander at will and telling their stories as they think of them, or as other people's stories remind them of their own. Or the session might be structured by having one person present a problem, like the following:

> There's an intersection: two roads going in different directions; one road is taken, one is not. Relax and think of yourself on the road, any kind of road that will lead into a crossroad. Get the feeling of being there, walking along,

[1] Dr. Progoff, formerly a special lecturer on depth psychology at Drew University, now director of Dialogue House in New York City, has conducted workshops at universities and study centers across the country.

thinking, feeling, coming to the intersection, trying to decide which way to go
... *which way will it be?* What happens? What is there on the road you finally
take? *Why* do you take it? Just speak out as it comes to you on that road. . . .

There is still another way student writers may adapt workshop methods to
their own purpose: by keeping an intensive journal (as workshop members
call it), a psychological notebook in which they enter significant images or
thoughts, flashes of memory, dreams, ideas, feelings, fears. "The purpose of
the notebook," says Dr. Progoff, "is to give the individual a tangible procedure by which he can enter the depth of himself and [thereby] re-experience
his existence from an inward point of view." It is this tangible procedure of
reexperiencing one's existence *inwardly* that can be most helpful to you as a
writer. You should make daily entries in your notebook; then, after a few
days, read the entries at your leisure, ponder their significance, try to recover
those half-forgotten details that are often the key to a whole experience.

Take that most trite of trite topics, for example, which students and
teachers alike ridicule as a nonsubject—"My Summer Vacation." Everyone
expects a paper written under this heading to be slapdash and dull, *but does
it have to be?* Is a visit to the Grand Canyon dull, for example, if it is seen
with the seeing eye? If you have really looked? If you have experienced it
genuinely in your own person and remembered not only the familiar outward spectacle but your own inward response as well? When approached in
this way—with a sense of the self at the center of the experience ("Let me
tell you, reader, what it was like; I have a purpose in writing this piece")—an
account of your summer vacation at the Grand Canyon, or anywhere, will not
be a bore to yourself or your readers.

One last point should be mentioned in this section. Writing an essay that
authentically recreates one of your own experiences not only gains the
instructor's commendation but also, and more important, gains for *you* a
portion of your own life seen again from a deeper and more meaningful
perspective. And in doing this you are, in a sense, *extending* your life; for it
may be that you will see your experiences for the first time in their true
shape; it may be that you will probe for the first time into their true and full
significance.

Observing Facts

Just as memory may be probed and prodded, so the power of observation
may be extended and sharpened by making a conscientious and deliberate
effort to gain more than a general impression of something—a place, event,
person, object. Anyone can get a general impression merely by being present
at an event. But this is not enough for the writer; in fact, to merely look is not
enough, as was pointed out in Chapter 2, "How Can X Be Described?" and
Chapter 14, "How Did X Happen?" Looking must be *purposive;* all senses
must be alert to precise details: the exact color, texture, shape, smell,
temperature, or tactile sensation of a place or an object; the exact appearance
of a person—facial expressions, hand gestures, body movements, tones of

voice; the exact event as it occurred and the way people reacted to it and to one another. These are the raw materials that must register in your consciousness if you are to gather facts from observations and write a realistic account of how something happened, or what someone or something was like. Not everyone is a highly sensitive receptor, to be sure, but you can at least *try* to see more than you would ordinarily see if you made no special effort.

Actually, observation, like charity, begins at home, in our immediate surroundings. Because professional writers realize this, they are—in an important sense—always "on duty," always gathering information, making mental notes, noticing this or that detail that might provide material at some future time.

Let us say that you have decided to write a piece about a single special place—the campus library. Since you are a regular visitor and pass it daily, you regard this as a relatively simple, straightforward assignment. Are you ready, then, to sit down and start writing? Not at all. Not until you have looked at it with the conscious intention of seeing this structure with fresh eyes, as if you had never seen it before. Only then will you discover that in truth *you have never seen it before*, in any richness or sharpness of detail. Chances are that on each previous visit—numerous as they were—you only glossed over its general contour and main features. In just this way New Yorkers observe their own huge New York Public Library on Fifth Avenue and Forty-second Street. Naturally, everyone notices the stately white columns that frame the entrance, and the famous reclining stone lions. But how many observers note that there are precisely *six* columns and that the lions are *angled* slightly toward each other? How many of those who look, look still more closely—over the heads of the lions—at the maxims engraved on the building itself: BUT ABOVE ALL THINGS TRUTH BEARETH AWAY THE VICTORY (on the right), and BEAUTY OLD YET EVER NEW, ETERNAL VOICE AND INWARD WORD (on the left). The careful observer will note still another detail: over the revolving doors of the main entrance are three plaques pointing out that this library is in actuality *three separate libraries* housed in one building, a fact that most New Yorkers are unaware of, even though it appears in bold lettering on the face of the building that many thousands of them pass every day of the week.

A famous teacher of the art of observation was Louis Agassiz, the great nineteenth-century naturalist, who began his course in zoology by presenting his students with a dead fish, insisting they they *look at it*. And so they would for an entire morning, after which Agassiz would return, asking "Well, what is it like?" As the students recited what they had seen (fringed gill-arches, fleshy lips, lidless eyes), Agassiz's face would reflect disappointment. "Keep looking," he would finally say—and leave them to their observations for the afternoon. One student who had been looking for days and days and days, later described the experience as follows:

I was piqued. I was mortified. Still more of that wretched fish! But now I set myself to my task with a will, and discovered one new thing after another, until I saw how just the Professor's criticism had been. The afternoon passed quickly; and when, towards its close, the professor inquired:

"Do you see it yet?"

"No," I replied, "I am certain I do not, but I see how little I saw before."

"That is next best," said he, earnestly, "but I won't hear you now; put away your fish and go home; perhaps you will be ready with a better answer in the morning."[2]

For eight solid months Agassiz would entreat his pupils to "look at your fish"; he had them compare it with other fish in the same family, note resemblances and differences, detect the orderly arrangement of parts, and finally see the parts in relation to the whole and the whole in relation to an overall principle or law. Indeed, the lesson in looking ended only after Agassiz had warned his students never to be satisfied with isolated observations, no matter how apt they might be, for as Agassiz believed, "facts are stupid things until brought into connection with some general law."

Thinking: Inferences and Interpretations

In order to see a "general law" behind a set of particular details, we must carry the process of observation a step further: we must go beyond looking to *thinking;* we must observe and analyze each particular, and then move on through a chain of reasoning to a valid and correct inference about the nature of the whole. To draw an inference, to see one truth as following from another: this is still another way of gathering information for a piece of writing.

Not everyone is equally adept at formulating original interpretations, but as was suggested in the section on argumentation, everyone of normal intelligence is capable of moving in a logical progression from one thought or observation to another. William Blake aspired to see the world in a grain of sand—an essentially poetic insight, to be sure; but also a *cerebral* one, arrived at through rigorous thinking and through a leap or inference from the facts as observed in a grain of sand to a larger truth of nature.

We have already made a brief survey of logical procedures in Chapter 20, "What Case Can Be Made For or Against X?" At this point it is worth simply repeating that we do not have to be logicians to think logically. All that is needed is a practical compositional logic that enables us to interpret materials correctly, to make sound and interesting conjectures, to draw provocative, *defensible* conclusions, and—at the higher reaches—to weld old ideas into new patterns: to reassess, recreate, and synthesize. Such is the work of the creative thinker and writer. An extraordinary example of this creativity is the French essayist, Michel de Montaigne (1533–92), who at the age of forty-seven shut himself up in his library "with only his own thoughts" so that he might spend the rest of his life committing his musings to paper (thereby creating the essay form). Was Montaigne a man of vast erudition? In his own

[2]Samuel H. Scudder, "Look at Your Fish," *Every Saturday*, 4 April 1874.

words, he never "bit his nails" over Aristotle or mastered any single branch of knowledge. "What does it avail us," he once asked, "to have a stomach full of food if it does not digest, if it does not become transformed within us, if it does not increase our size and strength?" Thus Montaigne's erudition was characterized not so much by a vast store of accumulated knowledge (he was convinced everything had already been thought) but rather by the way he *transformed knowledge* through his own mental operations—his inferences and interpretations.

Research

The fourth method of gathering information for expository writing is through research. To be a good researcher you must be part scholar, part reporter: you must be able to locate within the libraries accessible to you those printed and manuscript sources that contain the facts you need, and you must have a kind of nose for news, the ability to see which of the facts you encounter in your reading best serve your purpose and which must be discarded because they do not contribute to the special thesis of your piece. This screening process is evidence that invention does not end when research begins, for even as you are gathering the special information that will constitute the substance of your paper, you are rounding it out and reshaping it. You may even revise your original thesis somewhat in the light of the materials you collect during this active research period; although you will try not to revise it too drastically—not unless the emerging facts show that your central thesis is not true or that it will not work. Otherwise the central thesis or intention of your paper serves as your guide to what is relevant and therefore usable in the materials you uncover.

Most often you will gather more information for a research paper than you end up using. This may seem wasteful, but it is really a necessary part of research procedure because you are learning about your subject, developing a perspective on your materials and an awareness of the context from which they are drawn. Without this broader view, you may not be able to distinguish what is relevant from what is not. Furthermore, all the facts that you know about your subject—even those that do not appear in the finished piece—contribute to its total impact, for they give you confidence in your knowledge of your subject and authority in your writing.

At the same time, you must not allow yourself to get bogged down in research. There is a point at which you must decide "this is enough"—even if it does not seem *quite* enough. In most cases, no matter how conscientiously you have explored your subject, there will be some aspect of it you would like to pursue further, something else you would like to know. Arbitrarily but firmly you must call an end to research and move on to the writing. In most cases, of course, you will begin writing (however tentatively) while you are still doing research—setting up a possible beginning, a strong conclusion, or some self-contained middle section.

The necessity of limiting research to what is feasible within the allotted time has been aptly commented upon by Charles Schultz, creator of the famous "Peanuts" comic strip. Because Schultz believes that a comic strip should constantly introduce the reader to "new areas of thought and endeavor," which "should be treated in an authentic manner," he is constantly engaged in research:

I never draw about anything unless I feel I have a better than average knowledge of my subject. This does not mean that I am an expert on Beethoven, kite-flying, or psychiatry, but it means that as a creative person, I have the ability to skim the surface of such subjects and use just what I need.[3]

To skim the surface of a subject and dip down only where and when there is usable information pertinent to your purpose—this is a skill you should try to cultivate so that you may cope with the thousands of pages contained in the hundreds of volumes you will be consulting during your college years.

Major Reference Sources

Let us now move into the library itself to see what major reference sources are available and how the precise source you need can best be located when you need it. This is an important aspect of research technique: that you be able to find what you want as quickly as possible, without wasting time looking up information that bears only a peripheral relationship to your subject. Library materials are roughly of two kinds: primary and secondary. "Primary" refers to basic, first-hand sources: original manuscripts, letters, diaries, journals, notebooks, research reports written by the researchers themselves, statistics issued by the people who compiled them, reports of interviews, and so on. Articles and books are considered primary if the content is essentially original with the authors. Secondary materials are largely derivative in that they are assembled from a variety of outside sources. Thus all major reference works such as encyclopedias and almanacs are secondary; so are essays, articles, and books whose major purpose is to report on, analyze, or interpret the findings of original researchers. Actually many works are primary in one sense, secondary in another—that is, they offer their own findings and interpretations built upon someone else's findings and interpretations. Thus the terms "primary" and "secondary" are relative rather than absolute. Though primary sources are obviously more reliable, undergraduate students work most of the time with secondary sources.

We shall make a brief survey here of the major reference sources[4] you are

[3]Charles M. Schulz, "But a Comic Strip Has to *Grow*," *Saturday Review*, 12 April 1969, pp. 73–74.

[4]The main emphasis in the following discussion is on *categories* of reference works, with only representative examples of the works themselves, since a listing of all reference sources would occupy a whole volume. Indeed, such a volume is available in all libraries as the standard, annotated guide to reference materials:

Winchell, Constance M. *Guide to Reference Books*. 8th ed. Chicago: American Library Association, 1967.

likely to need during the academic years ahead—and in later years as well, when your professional work or your duties as a citizen (determined to *write* that letter to the editor, and not just talk about it!) may send you to the reference room of your local library to gather information on a given subject.

It will be helpful to begin with a definition of a reference book:

A reference book, as generally understood, is a book to be consulted for some definite information rather than for consecutive reading. In such books, the facts are usually brought together from a vast number of sources and arranged for convenient and rapid use.

Reference tools serve the inquirer in two ways. They may supply the information directly, as in encyclopedias, directories, almanacs, and similar works, or they may point the way to the place where the information is found, the function of the many ingenious bibliographies and indexes now available.[5]

A reference book differs from an ordinary book, then, in that it is not read sequentially. The researcher turns to it with a special purpose in mind, thumbing as quickly as possible to the place that will provide the information he or she needs.

In the sections that follow, reference materials are grouped under seven main headings:

1. General Reference Books
   A. Encyclopedias
   B. Biographical Works
   C. Dictionaries
   D. Yearbooks and Almanacs
   E. Atlases and Gazetteers
   F. Books of Curious Facts
2. Special Reference Books
3. General Bibliographies
4. Periodical Indexes and Abstracts
   A. General Indexes

First Supplement, 1965–1966. Second Supplement, 1967–1968.

For a handy, quick guide suitable for your own reference shelf, you should buy one of the following inexpensive paperbacks:

Barton, Mary Neill, and Marion V. Bell. *Reference Books: A Brief Guide for Students and Other Users of the Library.* 6th ed. Baltimore: Enoch Pratt Free Library, 1966.

Galin, Saul and Peter Spielberg. *Reference Books: How to Select and Use Them.* New York: Random House, 1969.

Gates, Jean Key. *Guide to the Use of Books and Libraries.* New York: McGraw-Hill Book Company, 1969.

McCormick, Mona. *Who-What-When-Where-How-Why Made Easy.* A *New York Times* Book. Chicago: Quadrangle Books, 1971.

Morse, Grant W. *A Concise Guide to Library Research.* New York: Washington Square Press, Inc., 1967.

Murphy, Robert W. *How and Where to Look It Up.* New York: McGraw-Hill Book Company, 1958.

[5]Mary Neill Barton and Marion V. Bell, *Reference Books: A Brief Guide for Students and Other Users of the Library* (Baltimore: Enoch Pratt Free Library, 1966), p. 7.

    B. Special Subject Indexes
    C. Abstracts
5. Government Publications
6. Pamphlets
7. Card Catalogue

As the definition above points out, there are two broad types of reference works: those that give information about a subject and those that tell you where to find information. The first two categories discussed below (general and special reference books) are concerned exclusively with direct sources of information, in most instances the logical place to begin research.

1. GENERAL REFERENCE BOOKS

When you have finally found your topic and are ready to gather information, you would be wise to turn at the outset to the most general sources available, for they will provide a helpful overview of the subject, a description of its essential nature and its scope. More than that, they will verify whatever facts you have on hand and fill in further details, thereby bringing you up-to-date on your subject and either reinforcing your interest in it or (equally helpful) discouraging you, if your preliminary study shows that the subject is not as promising as it seemed.

A. ENCYCLOPEDIAS

The best—and best-known—all-around reference work is the encyclopedia, which provides background materials for almost any field of knowledge. Do you want to know about white supremacy in Africa? the fiscal crisis of Catholic parochial education? the world's consumption of raw materials? All these questions call for initial consultation with a broad treatment of the subject. This is exactly what the encyclopedia offers in the form of a relatively short, condensed article, in many cases written by a specialist and signed.

The best general encyclopedias include the following:

> *The New Encyclopaedia Britannica: A Survey of Universal Knowledge.* 30 vols. Chicago: Encyclopaedia Britannica, Inc., 1974.
> Supplemented annually by the *Britannica Book of the Year.*
>
> *Encyclopedia Americana* (International Edition). 30 vols. New York: Encyclopedia Americana Corp., 1975.
> Supplemented annually by the *Americana Annual.*
>
> *Chamber's Encyclopaedia.* New rev. ed. Oxford and New York: Pergamon Press, 1967.
> Supplemented annually by Chamber's *Encyclopaedia World Survey.*
>
> *Collier's Encyclopedia.* 24 vols. New York: Crowell-Collier, 1970.
> Supplemented by *Collier's Year Book.*

Special Note:
Whatever encyclopedia you use, several facts are worth remembering:
1. Although the major encyclopedias are not thoroughly revised each year,

most of them undergo a process of continuous revision whereby each printing embodies some changes. In most cases, therefore, the information gathered from a reputable encyclopedia is relatively up-to-date. For up-to-the-minute information, however, you must consult a periodical—an abstract, article, or news report. (These are described below under "Periodical Indexes and Abstracts.")

2. Every encyclopedia contains an explanation of its own code: its abbreviations, a key to the initials on the signed articles, index conventions, and so on. This code should be consulted at the outset of research so that the information that is gathered may be fully understood.

3. The major encyclopedias contain bibliographies (lists of other works on a given subject or other places where information may be obtained), plus a detailed index, usually located in the last volume. Researchers are not always aware of these supplementary aids; the main index, in particular, is often ignored by the student who hurriedly turns to the main entry where, in truth, most of the needed information can be found. But proper use of the encyclopedia also involves cross-referencing. If your topic is the chateau country of France, for example, you should follow each of the suggested cross-references to individual chateaux as they are mentioned in the main entry (Amboise, Chenonceaux) and then you should proceed—on your own—to look up other entries that *might* provide more information: you might investigate individual kings, for example, who built or restored chateaux (Charles VIII, Louis XII, Francis I), or you might turn to the individual towns in which chateaux are located. Your ingenuity at cross-referencing may determine whether your paper contains simply the usual and expected information, or that extra dimension that raises it above the ordinary.

B. BIOGRAPHICAL WORKS

If your topic involves a prominent person or persons (a historical character, an inventor, a literary figure), then you must begin your research by compiling biographical data. General biographical works may be universal in scope (like the first two listed below) or they may be limited to individuals of a particular nationality, geographical location, or professional position. For our purposes—in fact for most purposes—the main distinction is whether the person in question is living or dead.

PERSONS LIVING

Current Biography, 1940–date. New York: Wilson, 1940–date.
   Published monthly and cumulated into annual volumes, each of which contains lively profiles of about 400 new personalities.

Who's Who, 1849–date. London: Black, 1849–date.
   Published annually, this famous dictionary of notable living Englishmen and a few distinguished persons of other countries gives brief facts and addresses.

Who's Who in America, 1899/1900–date. Chicago: Marquis, 1899–date.
   This American counterpart of the British *Who's Who* is published every other year, along with a supplementary *Who's Who of American Women*, 1958–date. (See also separate volumes of *Who's Who* that cover different regions of the United States: *Who's Who in the East*, *Who's Who in the South and Southwest*, *Who's Who in the Midwest*, and so on. See also volumes covering

various other nations such as *Who's Who in Australia, Who's Who in Modern China, Who's Who in Latin America.*)

Other contemporary biographical sources are organized according to profession and include such volumes as the following:

American Men and Women of Science
The Directory of American Scholars
Twentieth Century Authors
Contemporary Authors
Who's Who in American Politics
Dictionary of Scientific Biography

PERSONS NO LONGER LIVING
Dictionary of American Biography. 20 vols. New York: Scribner, 1927–1972.
   Also includes Index and Supplements I–IV.
   Long, detailed articles, written by prominent scholars and accompanied by a bibliography of sources (most of them primary), chronicle the lives and accomplishments of distinguished Americans. See also *Facts About the Presidents, American Authors* (1600–1900), and *Notable American Women, 1607–1950.*

Dictionary of National Biography. Ed. Leslie Stephen and Sir Sidney Lee. London: Smith, Elder and Co., and Oxford University Press, 1885–date.
   The British counterpart of (and model for) the *Dictionary of American Biography* (D.A.B.), the D.N.B. is the most complete and accurate guide to the lives of important Britons of the past.
   (See also such helpful sources as *Who Was Who, British Authors of the Nineteenth Century, British Authors Before 1800, European Authors, 1000–1900,* and *World Authors: 1950–1970.*)

PERSONS LIVING AND DEAD
Webster's Biographical Dictionary. Springfield, Mass.: G. & C. Merriam Company, 1969.
Chambers's Biographical Dictionary. Rev. ed. New York: St. Martins, 1969.
(See also entries under individual names in the general encyclopedias and see *Biography Index,* described below under "Periodical Indexes and Abstracts.")

C. DICTIONARIES
   At the outset of research it is wise to look up key terms in order to find out their conventional boundaries of meaning. Will you want to stay within these boundaries or will you want to use certain terms in an unorthodox sense, either more or less restricted than usual? As we saw in Chapter 1, "What Does X Mean?" we can vary word usage provided we indicate at the outset that we are using the term in a special sense, one that meets the particular needs of the paper.
   Before we can make any such statement, however, we must see what the dictionary—preferably an unabridged dictionary—has to say. We may even find it necessary to find out how the meaning of a particular word has changed over the years: maybe a past meaning will be specially relevant to our purpose; maybe it will be worth adopting or adapting. To provide information of this kind there are four good standard dictionaries: three are general, one historical.

Webster's Third New International Dictionary of the English Language. 3rd
ed. unabridged. Ed. Philip Gove. Springfield, Mass.: Merriam, 1961.
One of the great English dictionaries—the first to be published under the
direct and commanding influence of modern linguistic science—*Webster's
Third* contains almost half a million words, 100,000 of which are new entries or
new meanings for older entries. Some early critics maintained that this dictionary would never replace Webster's more traditional Second Edition (1934), but
it has.

The Random House Dictionary of the English Language. Unabridged ed. Ed.
Jess Stein. New York: Random House, 1966.
A computer-produced, highly legible dictionary containing 260,000 words.

The American Heritage Dictionary of the English Language. Ed. William
Morris. New York: American Heritage Publishing Co., Inc., and Boston:
Houghton Mifflin Co., 1969.
An entirely new and highly readable dictionary, copiously illustrated.

New English Dictionary on Historical Principles. Ed. Sir James A. H. Murray.
10 vols. and supplement. Oxford: Clarendon Press, 1888–1933. Reissued,
1933, in 13 vols. under the title *Oxford English Dictionary* (OED).
(See also the one-volume *Oxford University Dictionary,* 3rd ed., revised with
addenda and corrections. Oxford: Clarendon Press, 1959.)
This great dictionary, the most scholarly lexicographical achievement in the
English language, which took years of cooperative scholarship to complete,
was compiled on a different plan and serves a different purpose from that of the
ordinary dictionary. It traces the history of every word in the language (its
meaning, spelling, pronunciation) from the time it first appeared as an English
word (perhaps 800 years ago) to the present, giving illustrations of its usage at
the various stages of its career.

D. YEARBOOKS AND ALMANACS

Yearbooks and almanacs, published each year, contain a wealth of general
information and statistics, much of it based on primary materials drawn from
government bulletins and abstracts.

Facts on File, A Weekly Digest of World Events with Cumulative Index. New
York: Facts on File, Inc., 1930–date.
An extremely helpful, time-saving weekly digest of the news, arranged
under such headings as world affairs, arts, economy, science, education, religion. It has been said that *Facts on File* is a *current* encyclopedia, keeping the
reader abreast of the latest developments in all fields, particularly in the
United States.
(See also *Keesing's Contemporary Archives,* a weekly diary of world events,
published in London but worldwide in scope.)

The New York Times Encyclopedic Almanac. New York: The New York
Times, 1970–date.
Comprehensive and reliable, this recently introduced encyclopedic almanac
offers all the useful features of an almanac (statistics on every phase of American life, from the Supreme Court to sports) based on the research and educational resources of the *New York Times.* Issued annually.

The World Almanac and Book of Facts. New York: Newspaper Enterprise
Association, 1868–1876, 1886–date.

*Statesman's Year-Book: Statistical and Historical Annual of the States of the
World.* London: Macmillan, 1864–date.
An exceptionally useful manual containing information and statistics on the

governments of the world—their rulers, constitutions, forms of government, population, commerce, state finance, defense, production, industry.

(See also the Worldmark *Encyclopedia of the Nations* (1971), which provides supplementary materials to the *Statesman's Year-Book* and presents helpful information on the newer countries and on famous persons in each country's history. See also yearbooks for individual countries and continents, such as *Europa Year Book: A World Survey, Canadian Almanac and Directory, South American Handbook.*)

E. ATLASES AND GAZETTEERS

There are general and special atlases, some of which are listed below:

GENERAL
Hammond Medallion World Atlas
Rand McNally Commercial Atlas
Rand McNally Cosmopolitan World Atlas
McGraw-Hill International Atlas
The Times Atlas of the World

SPECIAL
Atlas of American History
Atlas of World History
Atlas of the Historical Geography of the United States
Atlas of the Sky

A gazetteer is a dictionary of places that provides information about history, population, trade, industry, cultural institutions, natural resources. See, for example:

Columbia-Lippincott Gazetteer of the World
Webster's New Geographical Dictionary
The Times Index-Gazetteer of the World

F. BOOKS OF CURIOUS FACTS

Odd bits of out-of-the-way information can be located in such books of "curious facts" as those listed below:

Douglas, George William. *The American Book of Days*. Rev. ed. New York: Wilson, 1948.
   An account of the history and observance of American holidays, local festivals, and anniversaries of such events as the world's first balloon ascension. (For the British equivalent see Chambers, Robert. *Book of Days, A Miscellany of Popular Antiquities*. 2 vols. Edinburgh: Chambers, 1863–64.)

Kane, Joseph Nathan. *Famous First Facts*. 3rd ed. New York: Wilson, 1964.
   Records famous "firsts" in the United States: events, discoveries, inventions, etc.

Funk & Wagnalls Standard Dictionary of Folklore, Mythology and Legend. Ed. Maria Leach. New York: Funk & Wagnalls, 1972.
   A vast and comprehensive work dealing with all aspects of world culture: gods, heroes, tales, customs, beliefs, songs, dances, demons, folklore of animals and plants.

Walsh, William Shepard. *Curiosities of Popular Customs and of Rites, Ceremonies, Observances, and Miscellaneous Antiquities*. Philadelphia and London: Lippincott, 1898.

Descriptions of popular customs and celebrations in different countries of the world.

Walsh, William Shepard. *Handy Book of Curious Information Comprising Strange Happenings in the Life of Men and Animals, Odd Statistics, Extraordinary Phenomena and Out-of-the-Way Facts Concerning the Wonderlands of the Earth.* Philadelphia and London: Lippincott, 1913.
(See also *Walsh's Handy Book of Literary Curiosities,* 1909.)

Wheeler, William Adolphus. *Familiar Allusions: A Handbook of Miscellaneous Information.* 5th ed. Boston: Houghton, 1890.

Radford, E., and M. A. Radford. *Encyclopedia of Superstitions.* Ed. and rev. by Christina Hole. London: Hutchinson, 1961.
(See also A *Treasury of American Superstitions.*)

2. SPECIAL REFERENCE BOOKS

In addition to general references, there are many special reference works devoted to individual fields such as history, political science, and literature. Each of these fields has its own body of materials—encyclopedias, handbooks, indexes, abstracts, almanacs, yearbooks, dictionaries, and so on—that can be located through a general reference guide like Constance Winchell's standard *Guide to Reference Books* or one of the smaller "pocket guides." These overall subject guides are your single most helpful research aid, for they acquaint you with the major writings in your chosen field, listing not only encyclopedias and handbooks but also bibliographies, abstracts, and periodical indexes that tell you where you can find further information (discussed below under "Periodical Indexes").

How many subject areas have their own reference shelf of special materials? It would be impossible to list them all here, for there are separate reference works devoted to almost every discipline, activity, profession, occupation, and recreation; there are handbooks and encyclopedias concerned with every field and every field-within-a-field that one can imagine. We can suggest only some of the more common subject headings under which special reference works are likely to be listed:

SUBJECT HEADING	REPRESENTATIVE REFERENCE WORKS
Philosophy	*Encyclopedia of Philosophy*
Psychology	*Annual Review of Psychology*
Religion	*Encyclopedia of Religion and Ethics* (See separate encyclopedias for Catholic, Jewish, etc.)
Social Sciences	*Sources of Information in the Social Sciences* *International Encyclopedia of the Social Sciences* *Dictionary of Sociology* *Biennial Review of Anthropology* (See separate reference works in political science, economics, law, education, etc.)
Physical Sciences	*The Harper Encyclopedia of Science* *McGraw-Hill Encyclopedia of Science and Technology*

	A *Guide to the Literature of Chemistry* The *International Dictionary of Applied* *Mathematics* *Encyclopaedic Dictionary of Physics* *Glossary of Geology and Related Sciences*
Natural Sciences	*The Encyclopedia of Biological Sciences* *Gray's Manual of Botany* *Mammals of the World* *Glossary of Genetics and Other Biological Terms*
Technology	*McGraw-Hill Encyclopedia of Science and* *Technology* A *Guide to Information Sources in Space Science* *and Technology* (See separate reference works under medical science, engineering, agriculture, business, etc.)
Fine Arts	*Encyclopedia of World Art* A *Guide to Art Reference Books* *Grove's Dictionary of Music and Musicians* *Encyclopedia of Jazz*
Literature	*The Reader's Adviser: A Guide to the Best in* *Literature* (See also bibliographies, dictionaries, directories, handbooks, biographies, criticisms, history, drama, poetry, fiction, etc.; see also national literatures: English, American, French, etc.)
Language and Linguistics	*The World's Chief Languages* *Language in Culture and Society* A *History of the English Language*[6] *Dictionary of Linguistics*
History	*An Encyclopedia of World History* *Oxford Classical Dictionary* (See under historical periods: ancient, medieval, etc.; also national histories: English, American, etc.)

3. GENERAL BIBLIOGRAPHIES

Formal bibliographies are very much like subject guides in that they also list books and other written materials according to author and subject. Thus Winchell's *Guide to Reference Books* also functions as an annotated bibliography, for it includes brief notes and comments about each title listed. A formal bibliography (one that is published independently, not merely appended to a scholarly article or an encyclopedia entry) is an end in itself, a rigorously and systematically organized listing of the literature on a given subject.

A bibliography, then, is a list and nothing but a list. As such it is extraordinarily useful, for it indicates how much material exists on a subject

---

[6]This book, by scholar-historian Albert Baugh, is an example of a textbook so comprehensive that it may be regarded as a reference work.

and where it is available. It also suggests—either implicitly in the title of the work listed or explicitly in an annotation—which articles and books bear most directly on a topic. Thus a good bibliography saves you time and effort, for it helps you to begin your research with the most useful and pertinent works. Equally important, it enables you to check the literature on your subject so that you will know what has already been done and what remains to be done.

There are several master bibliographies that you should be familiar with and refer to early in your research.

> *Bibliographic Index: A Cumulative Bibliography of Bibliographies.* New York: H. W. Wilson Company, 1938–.
> An indispensable tool for anyone compiling a bibliography in a particular subject, especially if the subject is somewhat obscure.
> *World Bibliography of Bibliographies.* 4th ed., rev. and enl. Ed. Theodore Besterman. Geneva: Societas Bibliographica, 1965–66.
> A monumental work that includes 117,000 separately published bibliographies arranged according to subject.
> *Subject Guide to Books in Print: An Index to the Publishers' Trade List Annual.* New York: Bowker, 1957–. Annual.
> *United States Catalog.* 4th ed. New York: Wilson, 1928. Supplemented by *Cumulative Book Index,* 1928–date. New York: Wilson, 1933–date.
> *Library of Congress Catalog.* Washington, D.C.: Library of Congress, 1955–.

4. PERIODICAL INDEXES AND ABSTRACTS

When you want to find out the latest information on a given subject (the influence of drugs on mental alertness, critical opinion of a current production of *King Lear,* new facts about the moon, and so on), you must turn to periodical indexes that list articles, reports, reviews, essays, news stories, speeches, bulletins, and editorials that have been printed in periodicals— journals, magazines, and newspapers. In some cases, you may want to turn to this resource immediately, for what is new about your subject may be the most important thing you need to learn; it may be the core of your paper and your reason for writing it.

This is what you can expect from the periodical indexes, then: to be put in touch with the most recent and up-to-date information. In that special type of index known as an "abstract," you will also find a brief summary of what is contained in the articles and essays.

Major periodical indexes can be divided into general and specialized (according to subject areas).

A. GENERAL INDEXES

> *The Readers' Guide to Periodical Literature.* New York: Wilson, 1905–date.
> *Social Science Index* and *Humanities Index.* New York: Wilson, 1974–date.
> Formerly known as *Social Sciences and Humanities Index,* 1965–1974.
> *New York Times Index,* New York: New York Times Corp., 1851–date.
> *Essay and General Literature Index,* New York: Wilson, 1900–date.
> *Book Review Digest.* New York: Wilson, 1905–date.
> *Book Review Index.* Detroit: Gale Research, 1965–date.

B. SPECIAL SUBJECT INDEXES

Here again, it is impossible to list all the separate indexes devoted to particular subjects. To locate the particular one most useful to your purpose, it is wise to consult one of the general guides to the literature such as Winchell's *Guide to Reference Books* (mentioned earlier), or the less formal but eminently readable *How and Where to Look It Up*.

A few representative subject indexes are:

> *Applied Science and Technology Index.* New York: Wilson, 1958–date.
> Formerly *Industrial Arts Index*, 1913–58.
> *Art Index.* New York: Wilson, 1929–date.
> *Business Periodicals Index.* New York: Wilson, 1958–date.
> *Education Index.* New York: Wilson, 1929–date.
> *Film Literature Index*, 1973–date.
> *Index of Religious Periodical Literature.* Ed. American Theological Library Assn. Princeton, N.J.: Princeton Theological Seminary, 1953–date.
> *The Music Index.* Detroit: Information Service, Inc., 1949–date.
> *Public Affairs Information Service Bulletin.* New York: Public Affairs Information Service, 1915–date.
> *Psychological Index*, 1894–1935. 42 vols. Princeton, N.J.: Psychological Review Co., 1895–1936. (Continued by *Psychological Abstracts*)

C. ABSTRACTS

> *Abstract of English Studies*
> *America: History and Life: A Guide to Periodical Literature* (with abstracts)
> *Biological Abstracts*
> *Chemical Abstracts*
> *Historical Abstracts*
> Now being published in two parts: *Modern Abstracts, 1775–1914;* and *Twentieth Century Abstracts, 1914*–date.
> *Mathematical Reviews*
> *Mineralogical Abstracts*
> *Psychological Abstracts*
> *Religious and Theological Abstracts*
> *Science Abstracts* (physics and electrical engineering)
> *Sociological Abstracts*

5. GOVERNMENT PUBLICATIONS

The United States government is probably the largest and most versatile publisher in the world, printing and processing in a single year more books, booklets, periodicals, newsletters, leaflets, films, and filmstrips; more annual reports, research documents, transcripts (of Congressional hearings, for example), manuals, handbooks, bibliographies, indexes, dictionaries, catalogues, checklists, and statistical compilations than any single commercial publisher or any foreign government.

Few people are aware of the enormous amount of information available through the Government Printing Office, either free or at very low cost. A brief listing of recent titles suggests how far-ranging this information is: *Science and the City, Mini-gardens for Vegetables, Family Budgeting, The Nature of Ocean Beds, Raising Raccoons, Home Construction, Space, National Parks, Living Death: The Truth About Drug Addiction, FDA* (Food and Drug Administration) *on Oral Contraceptives, Story of the Mississippi Chocktaws, Pocket Guide to Japan, Fables from Incunabula to the Present.* In truth, there are few fields not touched on by government publications, especially in the areas of history, travel, and the social, physical, and biological sciences.

To tap this rich source of information, most of it authoritative and up-to-date primary source material, you should be familiar with the main bibliographies and indexes issued by the government and some of the more recent and important guides.[7]

> U.S. Superintendent of Documents. *Monthly Catalog of United States Government Publications,* Washington, D.C.: Government Printing Office, 1895–date.
>
> *Price Lists of Government Publications.* Washington, D.C.: Government Printing Office, 1898–date.
>
> U.S. Bureau of the Census. *Statistical Abstract of the United States.* Washington, D.C.: Government Printing Office, 1878–date.
>> This matchless compendium of statistics covers the political, social, economic, and industrial organization of the country, including vital statistics, and figures on population, immigration, finance, employment, etc. It is the basic source of statistical information of all kinds from which most other sources (yearbooks, almanacs) get their information.
>
> Jackson, Ellen. *Subject Guide to Major United States Government Publications.* Chicago: American Library Association, 1968.
>> Covers important government publications from the earliest period to the publication date, arranged by subject.
>
> Leidy, W. Philip. *A Popular Guide to Governmental Publications.* 4th ed. New York: Columbia University Press, 1976.
>> Covers the most popular government publications issued 1961–66, arranged by subject.
>
> Schmeckebier, Lawrence F., and Roy B. Eastin. *Government Publications and Their Use.* 2nd rev. ed. Washington, D.C.: Brookings Institute, 1969.
>> Contains descriptions of catalogues and indexes, bibliographies, Congressional publications, constitutions (federal and state), court decisions, Presidential papers, etc.

6. PAMPHLETS

Pamphlets deserve to be treated in a separate category because, like government publications, they are often ignored by the student researcher who is unaware of their importance, or even their existence. Pamphlets serve the important function of bridging a time gap until current information on a given topic can be gathered into book form.

Many reputable organizations and institutions, such as the Mental Health Association, the public affairs offices of colleges and universities,

---

[7]It should be pointed out that libraries organize their government materials differently: some catalogue them in the regular card catalogue, as they would any other library material; others keep them in a separate file, or official United States government depository, classifying them as "Government Documents" or "Government Publications." The reference librarian can explain the system used in the individual library.

and the American Civil Liberties Union, regularly publish pamphlets in order to keep the public abreast of their activities and achievements.

The best way to locate a pamphlet dealing with a given subject is through the Pamphlet or Vertical File of the library or, if your library integrates pamphlets into its general collection, in the regular card catalogue under the appropriate subject heading. You can expect to find materials on current and controversial subjects such as racial conflicts, drug addiction, alcoholism, civil disobedience, and pollution.

In working with pamphlets, you should be particularly alert for evidence of bias. Extremist political groups, for example, often distribute pamphlets that seem to be informative but are really propagandist. These should be viewed with appropriate suspicion.

Some of the more noteworthy pamphlet series are cited below:

Public Affairs Pamphlets
Published by the nonprofit Public Affairs Committee to keep the American public informed on vital economic and social problems.

Headline Series
Published by the nonprofit, nonpartisan Foreign Policy Association to stimulate wider interest in world affairs.

Editorial Research Reports
Individual monographs dealing with vital contemporary issues.

National Industrial Conference Board
This nonprofit fact-finding board publishes studies on scientific research in the fields of business economics and management.

American Universities Field Staff Publications
A continuing series on current developments in world affairs issued by the nonprofit American Field Staff, Inc.

National Bureau of Economic Research
Publishes scientific reports on current economic problems.

Center for the Study of Democratic Institutions
A nonprofit, nonpartisan educational institution, the Center publishes articles dealing with basic problems in a democratic society.

7. CARD CATALOGUE

The card catalogue is exactly that: a catalogue of 3 x 5 index cards, filed alphabetically in pull-out drawers that line the walls of the main circulation room in your library. This catalogue is the index to the library, for each card represents a library holding—a book, booklet, periodical—and contains such vital facts as author, title, subject, publisher, place and date of publication, number of pages. For each library holding there are usually three cards: one indexed under the author's name, one under the title of the book, the third under the subject. (A typical card is shown opposite.)

It is impossible to overestimate the importance of the card catalogue, because it tells you not merely what has been published on your subject but what is actually available in your own library.

Learning how to use the card catalogue is not difficult. It requires no special sleuthing to turn to the "Man–Mut" drawer to locate books on the

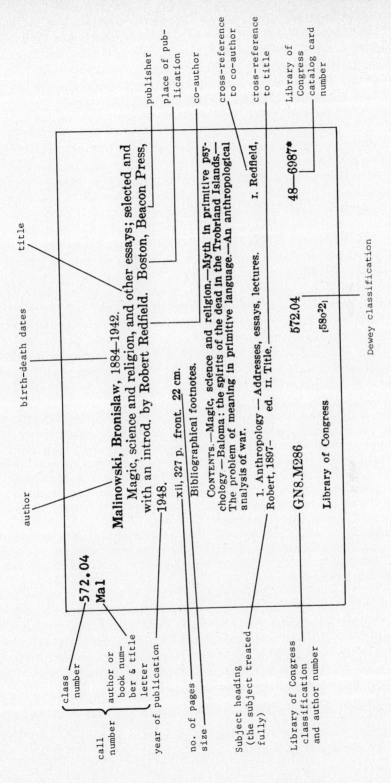

author

birth-death dates

title

publisher

place of publication

co-author

cross-reference to co-author

cross-reference to title

Library of Congress catalog card number

Malinowski, Bronislaw, 1884–1942.

Magic, science and religion, and other essays; selected and with an introd. by Robert Redfield. Boston, Beacon Press, 1948.

xii, 327 p. front. 22 cm.

Bibliographical footnotes.

CONTENTS.—Magic, science and religion.—Myth in primitive psychology.—Baloma: the spirits of the dead in the Trobriand Islands.—The problem of meaning in primitive language.—An anthropological analysis of war.

1. Anthropology — Addresses, essays, lectures.   I. Redfield, Robert, 1897–   ed. II. Title.

GN8.M286   572.04   48—6987*

Library of Congress   [58o²²]

class number

author or book number & title letter

year of publication

no. of pages

size

Subject heading (the subject treated fully)

Library of Congress classification and author number

Dewey classification

call number {

572.04
Mal

subject of "Money"; or the "Gut–Hil" drawer for a novel by "Hemingway"; or "Fez–Fos" if the title of the novel you want is *For Whom the Bell Tolls.* What does take some thought, however, is tracking down *all* the material in the library that pertains to your subject, for this is not always evident from a first quick look under the obvious main headings. Here again you must be aware of various subheadings under which relevant works may be listed. Some subheadings are indicated on the main entry card itself as illustrated on page 353 ("Anthropology—Addresses, essays, lectures"). For further information you can refer to these subject cards. In addition to being ingenious about subheadings, you must be imaginative and knowledgeable enough about your subject to figure out alternate designations. If it is "cinema techniques" you want to know about, for example, then surely you should think of turning to "Motion Pictures," "Film," or perhaps "Movies." By referring to *Subject Headings . . . of the Library of Congress,* a large volume owned by most libraries and installed near the card catalogue, you will get an idea of the variety of cross-references possible for most subjects.

One of the main limitations of the card catalogue is that it generally includes only the main subject matter of a book, not all the subjects discussed in the book. Thus, as one librarian-author reminds us, "a book on North American Indians might contain a very useful discussion of wampum, but few card catalogues would have a subject card for this book indexed under wampum."[8] What to do, then, to tap resource material *within* books themselves?

There are a number of other guides to a library's contents which you should learn to use. For example, you may find that your reference librarian has his own card catalogue, developed out of his own experience. That is, he will have carded for his own use the best sources of information on many different subjects. These may include subjects which are important but about which few or no special books have been written. Through his years of answering people's queries he has found sources containing the needed information, and he has carded these sources. Most librarians will be glad to let you use their special card files.

In addition, . . . most special collections in libraries have their own card catalogues, both complementing and supplementing the main catalogue. In a number of such catalogues the index of subjects is considerably more detailed than it is in the main library catalogue.[9]

Helpful as it is to become aware of special catalogues, you should concentrate on the regular catalogue, especially that single main entry card, which generally provides you with enough information to decide whether or not a book is worth fetching from the stacks. *Note date of publication:* Maybe the work is too old to be useful. *Note author:* Is he or she known to you? Is he or she reputable? Is his or her book likely to be a trustworthy treatment of the

[8]Robert W. Murphy, *How and Where to Look It Up* (New York: McGraw-Hill Book Company), p. 33.
[9]Ibid.

subject? *Note publisher:* Is it a reputable press or a fly-by-night, pay-for-publication-yourself "vanity" press that publishes anything? *Note number of pages:* Maybe the book is too long or too short for your purposes. *Note the exact wording of the title and subtitle:* Maybe the tone of the book is all wrong.

Final Note: Having become acquainted on your own with the main resources of the library, you need not feel guilty about addressing difficult questions to the reference librarian, whose job is to guide researchers in areas where they cannot find their own way. Indeed, reference librarians are themselves repositories of vast information concerning the resources of the particular library in which they work and of the resources to be found locally as well as in the nation at large. When necessary, they can help you obtain materials through interlibrary loan, or, if this is not possible, they may suggest alternate materials.

Gathering Information for Short Papers

The weekly, biweekly, or semiweekly writing assignment that usually runs from 500 to 1,000 words often requires library research. Let us take an average 500–750-word paper (two to three pages) and call it a "short" paper. Information for this average writing assignment can be gathered in approximately three to four hours of library research, with an equal amount of time allowed for writing the paper and revising. Thus the average writing assignment requires from six to eight hours of total effort. Since virtually all writing assignments have a deadline, they are thereby self-limiting: what needs to be done, in other words, becomes a function of what *can* be done within the prescribed time. You should keep this in mind, for it puts the paper in perspective and helps you make a realistic assessment of how much you can hope to cover and what you can accomplish. (It has been said that even a work of art is "never finished, but abandoned.")

Let us consider how you might go about gathering information for four possible topics, each an answer to a specific question:[10]

1. How Does X Compare to Y?
   Title: The Peace Corps—Then and Now
   LIST OF POSSIBLE SOURCES:
   Encyclopedia Americana
   Government publications (See "Federal Depository" in college library, which contains recent government reports, pamphlets, bulletins, programs, etc.)
   Public Affairs Information Service Bulletin (PAIS)

[10]Not all references listed need be consulted in each instance; sometimes one or two provide sufficient information. Although it is obvious, it might also be mentioned that in most cases you should also look into the card catalogue under appropriate headings. Although you may not have time to read a whole book on a subject, you may find separate chapters directly pertinent to your purpose.

New York Times Index
Readers' Guide to Periodical Literature

2. What Is the Present Status of X?
   Title: A New View of the Soul[11]

   LIST OF POSSIBLE SOURCES:

   Encyclopedia of Philosophy
   The Dictionary of Religious Terms
   Encyclopedia of Religion and Ethics
   The New Schaff-Herzog Encyclopedia of Religious Knowledge
   Handbook of Denominations in the United States
   Religious and Theological Abstracts

3. How Is X Made or Done?
   Title: How Artificial Snow Is Made

   LIST OF POSSIBLE SOURCES:

   Science News Yearbook (annual)
   Encyclopaedia Britannica
   McGraw-Hill Encyclopedia of Science and Technology
   (see supplementary yearbooks)
      or
   Van Nostrand's Scientific Encyclopedia
   Weather and Climate
   Applied Science and Technology Index
   Readers' Guide to Periodical Literature

4. What Case Can Be Made For or Against X?
   Title: The Case Against Multiple Choice Tests

   LIST OF POSSIBLE SOURCES:

   Encyclopedia of Educational Research
   Mental Measurements Yearbook
   Psychological Abstracts
   Education Index
   Readers' Guide to Periodical Literature
   Card catalogue (under "Educational Tests," "Testing," etc.)

Gathering Information for Long Papers

Three of the long papers reprinted in Chapter 21, "The Long Paper"—
"The Assassination of Lincoln," "Isaac Newton," and "Whither the Black
Odyssey?"—were written only after the writers had spent not merely three
or four hours but perhaps thirty or forty hours in the library. You may not be
able to devote that much time to a term paper assignment, but you should
plan on at least fifteen to twenty hours of research for a paper that will run

---

[11]This topic could be treated briefly, or it could easily be extended into a long piece dealing
with different concepts of the soul at different periods in history or among different religions.
See *Handbook of Denominations in the United States* and encyclopedias and dictionaries of the
various religions.

between 3,000 and 5,000 words. It is impossible, of course, to set exact specifications; the demands of the subject vary, as does the background information of the writer.

Following is a list of possible sources for the term paper topics suggested after each of the selections in Chapter 21. They will give an indication of the extent of research necessary for a typical term paper.

Term Paper 1: An Extended Analysis
   Title: Picasso's "Periods": A Chronological Overview

1. Biographical sources
    Chambers's Biographical Dictionary, rev. ed.
    Webster's Biographical Dictionary
2. Encyclopedias and dictionaries
    Encyclopedia of World Art
    Encyclopedia of Modern Art
    Dictionary of Art and Artists
    Dictionary of Art
    Dictionary of Modern Painting
3. Bibliographies and indexes
    Readers' Guide to Periodical Literature (for articles in national magazines)
    New York Times Index
    The Art Index
    A Guide to Art Reference Books
4. Picasso's artistic development—some specific works
    Ashton, Dore. *Picasso on Art*. New York: Viking Press, 1972.
    Barr, Alfred H., Jr. *Picasso: Fifty Years of His Art*. Rev. and enl. ed. New York: Museum of Modern Art, 1974.
    Chevalier, Denis. *Picasso: Blue and Rose Periods*. New York: Crown, 1969.
    Gallwitz, Klaus. *Picasso at 90: The Late Work*. New York: Putnam, 1971.
    Schiff, G., ed. *Picasso in Perspective*. Englewood Cliffs, N.J.: Prentice-Hall, 1974.
5. Card catalogue
    For individual biographies, check under "Picasso, Pablo." For background information, check under "Art History," "Modern Art," "Twentieth-Century Art."

Term Paper 2: A Description-Narration
   Title: The Assassination of Malcolm X
        (Since this topic is of relatively recent occurrence [1965], you will need to use recent references.)

1. Biographical sources
    Current Biography
    Who Was Who in America
    Biography Index
2. Newspaper and magazine accounts
    New York Times Index
    Readers' Guide to Periodical Literature

3. Essays and commentaries in journals, anthologies, etc.
   Essay and General Literature Index
   Social Science and Humanities Index
   America: History and Life: A Guide to Periodical Literature
4. Card catalogue
   See under Malcolm X: Biography, Bibliography.

5. Reference Books
   Black American Reference Book
   Encyclopedia of Islam

Term Paper 3: An Extended Characterization
Title: Robert Schumann: The Triumph and the Tragedy

1. Encyclopedias and dictionaries
   Harvard Dictionary of Music
   Grove's Dictionary of Music and Musicians
   Encyclopedia of Concert Music
   The International Cyclopedia of Music and Musicians
   (These references contain bibliographies.)
2. Biographical dictionaries and guides
   Baker's Biographical Dictionary of Musicians
   Great Composers, A Biographical and Critical Guide
3. Bibliographies and indexes
   Music Reference and Research Materials: An Annotated Bibliography (1967)
   Music Index
   Social Sciences and Humanities Index
   See also *Subject Guide to Books in Print*
4. Card catalogue
   Check under "Schumann, Robert" for individual biographies.

Term Paper 4: An Extended Argument
Title: "Whither the Black Odyssey?": A Reply

1. General background survey
   Encyclopedia Americana
2. Guides and handbooks
   The Negro in the United States: A Research Guide
   The Black American Reference Book
   The Negro Almanac
3. Card catalogue: see under
   Afro-Americans and/or Negroes
   Afro-Americans. History
   Afro-Americans. Bibliography
   Under this last heading you are likely to find such pertinent materials as the following:
   Work: A Bibliography of the Negro in Africa and America (1928)
   Bibliography of Negro History (1963)
   The Negro in the United States: A Selected Bibliography (1970)
4. Indexes
   Index to Periodical Articles by and About Negroes (1950–date)

Public Affairs Information Service Bulletin
America: History and Life
New York Times Index
Readers' Guide
Psychological Abstracts
Sociological Abstracts

5. Miscellaneous

Government publications
Pamphlets
Negro Yearbook

Note-Taking

The importance of familiarizing yourself with the library's major reference tools cannot be overstated; but at the same time it must be admitted that the vast resources of the Library of Congress itself would be of little use if you did not know how to extract from them the information you needed. In order to develop your particular topic into a sound and informative paper, you must know how to take good notes, for they are obviously the foundation on which the paper itself will be constructed. When the time comes to sit down and write the paper—when a certain point must be made, or certain data provided—if you have taken good notes you need simply thumb through them and there the needed information will be. *The writing process is a lot easier when you have taken accurate, ample, and well-organized notes.* If you have not, you are in serious trouble, for without good notes it is impossible to write a good research paper, just as it is impossible to build a strong and attractive building if the individual bricks are not themselves strong and attractive.

It is worthwhile, then, to devote special attention to note-taking, a skill closely related to writing in that the good note-taker does not mindlessly copy a paragraph of text, word for word. On the contrary, you must actively *think* about what you read and try to figure out exactly what it means and how it may contribute to your topic. Only after you have figured out its possible usefulness to your purpose are you ready to put pencil to pad— preferably a small 3 x 5 or 5 x 8 pad (or cards) where you can enter separate points on separate pages, thereby saving yourself the trouble later on of leafing through the dense, cluttered, and unclassified materials of a notebook.

Each note should be written in your own words (unless the passage deserves to be quoted verbatim) and carefully labeled (in the upper right-hand corner of the page, or wherever you choose—according to the special category of information that it deals with). Thus a note card or page might read as shown in the sample cards on the following page:

Card 1

Poe / Early Years

The only major American writer of his time to spend part of
childhood at school in England. Apparently healthy: a good
athlete; boxer; represented his school at racing competition;
story often told of how he could swim up to six miles, against
the tide and under a hot June sun. Also a top student with
a "keen disciplined mind." Yet as reminiscences from school-
mates indicate, he was "not popular in the usual sense of the
word." (p. 84)

Quinn's EAP, pp. 65-85

Card 2

Poe / Personal Appearance

Neat and tidy, nervous in manner. Slender and dark: "His hair
was dark as a raven's wing. So was his beard--which he always
kept shaved." (p. 53) Broad forehead; long slender neck which
"made him appear, when sitting, rather taller than he really
was." (p. 54) Slender arms and hands, gracefully tapered: "In
fact, his hands were truly remarkable for their roseate softness
and lily-like, feminine delicacy." (p. 56) Oval face, violet
eyes with long lashes, strong chin, even white teeth: "really
handsome...especially when he smiled." (p. 57) Strange smile:
"...there was this peculiarity about his smile...it did not
appear to be the result of gladness of heart altogether...but
...of that apollonian disdain which seemed to say, what you
'see through a glass darkly, I behold through the couched eyes
of an illuminated Seer.'"

- Chivers' Life of Poe, pp. 53-58

Card 3

Poe / Theory of Poetry

Poe saw "Beauty" as the proper province of the poem and
"Sadness" as the proper tone:
Beauty of whatever kind, in its supreme
development, invariably excites the
sensitive soul to tears. Melancholy
is thus the most legitimate of all the
poetical tones.

Philos. of Comp., p. 198

By classifying your notes as you go along, you are actually creating order out of the chaos of materials that confront you; without this preliminary organizing you would probably be overcome by the incredible bulk of sheer verbiage. You cannot take it *all* down—but you do not need it all. You need only what relates to your topic, and presumably you have made at least a tentative decision about your topic and its main headings. Your notes, then, will pick up these headings, and perhaps even break them down into smaller subheadings (for example, Poe/Early years/Relationship with mother), so that you can later sort related page headings into separate groups (an "early years" group subdivided into "relationship with parents," "school," "early influences"; a "theory of poetry" group; a "marriage" group; a "drinking problem" group; a "financial reverses" group). When notes are organized in this way, it is relatively easy to see the total paper taking shape, even before you have begun writing. You can also judge your materials more easily: see where you have enough information (on Poe's theory of poetry, let us say) and where there are confusing "gaps" (Was Poe a dipsomaniac or a drunkard? Is there a difference between the two?). Thus it becomes possible, simply by examining a particular grouping of notes, to see that in one area more information is needed, whereas in other areas the research is apparently complete.

If you are conscientious in your note-taking, you will probably end up with more notes than you actually use, but if you are reasonably selective along the way, you will not pile up an unscalable mountain of information.

Beyond what has already been said about being a thoughtful rather than a passive note-taker, there are a few principles of note-taking that should be mentioned:

1. Avoid taking notes too soon—during the preliminary background reading period in encyclopedias, for example. You may want to get down certain basic facts, figures, and dates about your subject, but beyond this it is generally best to hold your pencil until you have the overall feel of your subject. More specialized references, which you will turn to later, will probably provide more timely and profound information; *then* you will want to begin note-taking in earnest, but not before.

2. Read reference materials at different rates and levels of intensity, depending on how promising they seem. It may be necessary merely to skim page after page of a book, without taking a single note; then you may come upon a section or a separate article so relevant and reliable that you must pause two or three times per page to take notes.

3. Just as you deal with different types of references, so you must take different types of notes: you may simply record relevant facts or ideas, summarizing them in your own words; another type of note may be a direct word-for-word copy of a quotation you would like to use; still another may include not only the data gleaned from reading, but your own comment on it: your own responses and observations as they strike you during your reading. It is wise to jot these down immediately, while the thought is with you; it is also wise to set off your own remarks

in brackets, or in some other way, so that you can distinguish later between what your authority said and what you said.

4. In general, try to compress and summarize information that you take down from a reference source so that when you are ready to use this information, you will have no alternative but to fill out the idea in your own words. This reduces the possibility of inadvertent plagiarism (see the next section, "Avoiding Plagiarism").

5. Very important: the first time you use a new source, make out a complete citation slip on which you enter *all* the documentary information you will need for footnotes and bibliography (for example, "Davidson, Edward H. *Poe: A Critical Study.* Cambridge, Mass.: Harvard University Press, 1957"). Having done this, you need not repeat all the information about the work on each page of notes; in fact, some simple code like "Davidson, p. 8" or "David., p. 8" or "David./8" or even "D/ 8" is sufficient—so long as you can understand your own abbreviations later.[12]

6. Finally, a suggestion that may seem trivial but is actually important: never take notes on both sides of the paper. Unfailingly, when you are at the writing stage, looking for a specific point of information, it will be on the *other* side of the page you are looking at—where you cannot find it! (See "Gumperson's Law," p. 120.) To avoid a frustrating shuffle from one side of a sheet to the other, then, write on only one side of a note page.

Avoiding Plagiarism

Plagiarism is an ugly practice which most students try to avoid, but may inadvertently commit if they are not aware of what plagiarism *is*. There should be no uncertainties on this score, however, for the offense is serious.

[12]Note that on each sample card on page 360, the source is cited in short-hand form. The full citations for Cards 1,2, and 3 would be noted on separate 3 × 5 bibliography cards:

```
Quinn, Arthur Hobson.  Edgar Allen Poe, A Critical
Biography.  New York:  Appleton-Century-Crofts,
1941.
```

```
Chivers' Life of Poe. Ed. Richard Beale Davis.
New York: E. P. Dutton & Co., 1952.
```

```
Poe, Edgar Allen. "The Philosophy of Composition,"
Graham's Magazine (Apr. 1846), rpt. in James A.
Harrison, ed., The Complete Works of Edgar Allen
Poe. Vol. XIV.  New York: AMS Press, Inc., 1965,
pp. 193-208.
```

Plagiarism is literally a crime, a form of theft in which one person steals the words of another—in ignorance, perhaps, of the fact that "phraseology, like land and money, can be individual personal property, protected by law."[13] Plagiarism can also involve ideas: you might take someone else's ideas, put them into your own words, and say they are yours. But they are *not* yours, and courtesy as well as honesty requires that this fact be acknowledged with a simple phrase such as "according to":

> *According to Northrop Frye,* the writer's ability to shape life into a literary form comes not from life but from previous contact with literature. This point is made in Frye's essay "Nature and Homer."

Even if it seems to you, after having read it, that you could have thought of that idea yourself, remember that *you did not*—and that you therefore owe a credit line to Mr. Frye, whether you have used his exact words or not. You have borrowed his idea. As a conscientious writer, you must always be on guard against violations of this kind. You should be aware, for instance, that it was not anybody-at-all or nobody-in-particular, but *specifically* H. L. Mencken who maintained that "No quackery has ever been given up by the American people until they have had a worse quackery to take its place." This observation, with its fine cynical edge, was passed along by Gilbert Seldes in *The Stammering Century,* a history of quacks and cultists in nineteenth-century America. Seldes credited Mencken with the statement even though it is not a direct quotation and Seldes was not even certain whether Mencken made the remark in print or in private conversation.

Another subtle and often unwitting form of plagiarism involves *slightly changing* someone else's statement (substituting a different word here and there, shifting phrases, inverting clauses) and then presenting the passage as one's own. Here again it is important to recognize that this is not permissible. A paraphrase in your own language and style still deserves to be credited.

Most students realize, as mentioned above, that they must use quotation marks when an exact sentence or two is picked up, but they may not realize that this holds true even for a simple phrase, in fact even for a single word: if that word is significant, it should be placed in quotes. It was the critic Gilbert Murray, for example, who wrote an essay called "Literature and Revelation." If you were to follow Murray in this—that is, to treat literature as "revelation" and introduce the term as such into your writing, with all the richness of meaning that accompanies it, you should credit Murray: "Another way to view literature, as Gilbert Murray has pointed out, is as 'revelation.'" (A footnote should indicate precisely in what article Murray said this.)

It is possible, of course, for you to arrive independently at an idea such as Murray's. "I just thought up that idea myself," you might say. "I wrote about literature as revelation because that's the way I saw it. I don't even know who Gilbert Murray is." The point is that you *should* know; you should know who has written on your chosen subject before you did; you should have read Murray's essay as part of a routine check of the literature in the

---

[13]Craig B. Williams and Allan H. Stevenson, *A Research Manual* (New York: Harper & Row, 1963), p. 126.

Essay and General Literature Index or one of the literary bibliographies listed according to topic. After all, it stands to reason: very few ideas are totally original. The honest and conscientious writer—student and professional alike—realizes this and therefore always begins a piece of writing by searching the literature to see what has already been said on his or her projected subject. By conducting this preliminary search of the literature, you gain two advantages: you stimulate your own thinking and possibly learn something new; you also find out what has already been written. Knowing this, you will not naïvely present as new and original an idea that is, in fact, old and familiar (as many seemingly fresh ideas turn out to be). This does not mean that no one can write about literature as revelation because Murray has already done so. It *does* mean that anyone writing on the subject should know what Murray said at an earlier date, and go on from there.

To summarize: credit should be given in the following instances—either in a footnote or in the body of text:

1. When you directly quote someone else
2. When you use someone else's ideas or opinions (unless they are common knowledge)
3. When you use someone else's examples
4. When you cite statistics or other facts gathered by someone else
5. When you present evidence or testimony taken from someone else's argument

Footnotes and Bibliography

Footnotes and bibliographies provide a set procedure for crediting your sources, telling readers exactly where you obtained information on your subject. In order to simplify and standardize the process of documentation, most writers use one of two established forms, either that set forth in the University of Chicago's *A Manual of Style* or that in *The MLA* (Modern Language Association) *Style Sheet*. These two do not differ radically from each other, nor is one better than the other. The writer simply chooses the one that serves his or her purpose better (writers in the sciences tend toward the University of Chicago style, those in the humanities toward the MLA). You should determine which one you want to use (or are required to use) and use it consistently throughout.

As an undergraduate, you need not concern yourself with the intricacies of footnoting; you need only learn the basic forms required to document your term papers. The following section should provide adequate guidance.

Footnotes

As was mentioned in the section on plagiarism, all information taken from a source, whether it is summarized, paraphrased, or quoted, should be documented in a footnote. Footnotes should be numbered consecutively throughout the paper and be placed at the bottom of the page on which the reference occurs or in a list at the end of the paper. (Instructors generally indicate their preference in this matter.)

Footnotes are also used for explanations and additional comments that you wish to include but that you think would interrupt the continuity of thought in your text. (See p. 355 for an example of an informational footnote.) You are free to develop your own style for this kind of footnote.

Documentary footnotes should include the following information, listed in the order cited.

BOOKS

Author's or authors' names in normal order

Title of book, underlined (If reference is to a particular section of a book, as in footnote 8 below, it precedes the book title and is enclosed in quotation marks.)

Editor's or translator's name in normal order (See exception in footnote 6 below.)

Edition used if several have been published

Series name if any

Place, publisher, and date of publication

Volume number in Roman numerals

Page number or numbers (If a volume number precedes a page number, the abbreviation "p." or "pp." is not used.)

ENCYCLOPEDIAS

Author's or authors' names in normal order (If the author is identified.)

Title of article exactly as it appears in the encyclopedia

Name of encyclopedia, underlined

Latest copyright date

Volume number in Roman numerals

Page number or numbers without "p." or "pp."

PERIODICALS

Author's or authors' names in normal order

Title of article in quotation marks (If no author is specified, this item comes first.)

Name of periodical, underlined

Volume number in Arabic numbers (See exception in footnote 2 below.)

Date of issue in parentheses (See exception in footnote 2 below.)

Page number or numbers without "p." or "pp." (If the volume number is not cited, "p." or "pp." precedes the page number.)

For the conventions of punctuation in footnotes see the examples below.

Examples of the most common types of documentary footnotes are cited below. Their form is based on *The MLA Style Sheet*.

SAMPLE FOOTNOTES—FIRST REFERENCES
BOOKS

[1]Kenneth B. Clark, *Dark Ghetto: Dilemmas of Social Power* (New York: Harper & Row, 1965), p. 14.
[one author]

[2]George Eaton Simpson and J. Milton Yinger, *Racial and Cultural Minorities: An Analysis of Prejudice and Discrimination,* 3rd ed. (New York: Harper & Row, 1965), p. 345.
[two authors; book that has gone through several editions]

[3]Emmette S. Redford et al., *Politics and Government in the United States,* 2nd ed. (New York: Harcourt Brace Jovanovich, 1968), p. 385.
[four or more authors]

[4]Bertolt Brecht, *Collected Plays,* ed. Ralph Manheim and John Willett (New York: Pantheon, 1970), I, 63.
[edited work; work in more than one volume]

[5]Carl Sandburg, *Abraham Lincoln: The War Years* (New York: Harcourt Brace Jovanovich, 1939), II, 95.
[work in more than one volume]

[6]Brooks Atkinson, ed., *The Sean O'Casey Reader: Plays, Autobiographies, Opinions* (New York: St. Martin's Press, 1968), p. 797.
[another way to handle an edited work]

[7]André Boucourechliev, *Schumann,* trans. Arthur Boyars, Evergreen Profile Book 2 (New York: Grove Press, 1959), p. 47.
[translation; book in a series]

[8]Linda Harrison, "On Cultural Nationalism," in *The Black Panthers Speak,* ed. Philip S. Foner (Philadelphia: J. B. Lippincott & Co., 1970), p. 151.
[article in an edited collection]

ENCYCLOPEDIAS

[1]"Schumann, Robert Alexander," *Encyclopaedia Britannica,* 1971, XIX, 1188.
[unsigned article; title is given as it appears in the encyclopedia]

[2]Daniel Gregory Mason, "Robert Schumann," *The International Cyclopedia of Music and Musicians* (New York: Dodd, Mead & Co., 1958), p. 1684.
[signed article]

MAGAZINES

[1]Joseph Stanley-Brown, "My Friend Garfield," *American Heritage,* 22 (Aug. 1971), 52.
[signed article]

[2]"Pity the Poor Porpoise," *Newsweek,* 6 Sept. 1971, p. 60.
[unsigned article; weekly magazine]

Note: *The MLA Style Sheet* suggests abbreviating the titles of periodicals such as *PMLA (Publications of the Modern Language Association).* Your instructor will tell you whether such abbreviations are desirable or acceptable in your paper.

NEWSPAPERS

[1]Russell Baker, "A Timid Question," *New York Times,* 31 Aug. 1971, p. 33.
[signed article]

[2]*New York Times,* 31 Aug. 1971, p. 18.
[unsigned article]

GOVERNMENT BULLETINS

[1]*The Foreign Assistance Program: Annual Report to the Congress for Fiscal Year 1970* (Washington, D.C.: Government Printing Office, 1971), p. 22.

[2]*Preserving Our Air Resources,* New York State Department of Health, 1968, p. 10.

SAMPLE FOOTNOTES—SECOND REFERENCES

Second or later references should be as brief as is consistent with clarity. Following are some acceptable forms for such references.[14]

BOOKS

[1]Clark, p. 15.

[Only one book by Clark is referred to in the paper.]

[2]Ibid.

[Reference is to the same page of the same book cited in the preceding footnote.]

[3]Ibid., p. 22.

[Reference is to a different page of the same book cited in the preceding footnote.]

[4]Clark, *Dark Ghetto*, p. 15.

[Two or more books by Kenneth B. Clark are referred to in the paper; therefore it is necessary to use a short form of the title to distinguish between them. A short form of the title is now preferred to the old and elusive "op. cit."]

[5]Kenneth B. Clark, p. 22.

[Another author named Clark is referred to in the paper; therefore it is necessary to distinguish between the two names.]

[6]Simpson and Yinger, p. 346.

[7]Redford et al., p. 386.

[8]Brecht, p. 65.

[9]Sandburg, p. 96.

[10]Sandburg, III, 86.

[If more than one volume of the Sandburg work is cited, it is necessary to give the volume number with each citation.]

ENCYCLOPEDIAS

[1]"Schumann, Robert Alexander," p. 1189.

[2]"Schumann, Robert Alexander," *Encyclopaedia Britannica*, p. 1189.

[Repetition of the name of the encyclopedia is necessary if an article with the identical title from another encyclopedia is used.]

MAGAZINES

[1]Stanley-Brown, p. 53.

[2]Stanley-Brown, "My Friend Garfield," p. 53.

[Repetition of the title is necessary if more than one article by Stanley-Brown is referred to.]

[3]"Pity the Poor Porpoise," p. 60.

NEWSPAPERS

[1]Baker, p. 33.

[2]*New York Times*, p. 18.

[3]*New York Times*, 31 Aug. 1971, p. 18.

[If more than one issue of the *New York Times* is referred to, it is necessary to repeat the date.]

GOVERNMENT BULLETINS

[1]*The Foreign Assistance Program*, p. 23.

[2]*Preserving Our Air Resources*, p. 9.

[14]These second references follow the order of the first references above, but second references are not given for all the works cited under "First References."

Bibliographies

The form of bibliographies is the same as that for footnotes with the following exceptions:

1. The name of the author (or of the first author if there are more than one) is given last name first ("Brown, Frank"). Entries in a bibliography are listed in alphabetical order by author. Frequently a bibliography is subdivided into "Books Consulted," "Periodicals," "Encyclopedias," and so on.
2. If the work is in more than one volume, the number of volumes is given.
3. No page references are given for books, but full page references are given for articles in periodicals and encyclopedias.
4. A bibliography may be titled simply "Bibliography" or, if the writer prefers, "List of Works Consulted," "Sources," and so on. (See pp. 331–32 for an example.)

The following examples cover most of the common usages and illustrate the conventions of punctuation in bibliographies:

BOOKS

Atkinson, Brooks, ed. *The Sean O'Casey Reader: Plays, Autobiographies, Opinions.* New York: St. Martin's Press, 1968.
Boucourechliev, André. *Schumann.* Trans. Arthur Boyars. New York: Grove Press, 1959. (Evergreen Profile Book 2)
Brecht, Bertolt. *Collected Plays.* Ed. Ralph Manheim and John Willett. Vol. I. New York: Pantheon, 1970.
Clark, Kenneth B. *Dark Ghetto: Dilemmas of Social Power.* New York: Harper & Row, 1965.
Harrison, Linda. "On Cultural Nationalism." *The Black Panthers Speak.* Ed. Philip S. Foner. Philadelphia: J. B. Lippincott & Co., 1970.
Redford, Emmette S., et al. *Politics and Government in the United States.* 2nd ed. New York: Harcourt Brace Jovanovich, 1968.
Sandburg, Carl. *Abraham Lincoln: The War Years.* 4 vols. New York: Harcourt Brace Jovanovich, 1939.
Simpson, George Eaton, and J. Milton Yinger. *Racial and Cultural Minorities: An Analysis of Prejudice and Discrimination.* 3rd ed. New York: Harper & Row, 1965.

ENCYCLOPEDIAS

Mason, Daniel Gregory. "Robert Schumann." *The International Cyclopedia of Music and Musicians.* New York: Dodd, Mead & Co., 1958, pp. 1683–87.
"Schumann, Robert Alexander." *Encyclopaedia Britannica,* 1971.

MAGAZINES

"Pity the Poor Porpoise." *Newsweek,* 6 Sept. 1971, p. 60.
Stanley-Brown, Joseph. "My Friend Garfield." *American Heritage,* 22 (Aug. 1971), 49–53, 100–01.

NEWSPAPERS

Baker, Russell. "A Timid Question." *New York Times,* 31 Aug. 1971, p. 33.
New York Times, 31 Aug. 1971, p. 18.

GOVERNMENT BULLETINS

The Foreign Assistance Program: Annual Report to the Congress for Fiscal Year 1970. Washington, D.C.: Government Printing Office, 1971.
Preserving Our Air Resources. New York State Department of Health, 1968.

ASSIGNMENTS

1. Preparing Bibliographies
   a. Prepare a bibliography of general references you would consult in order to write a short essay (500–750 words) on one of the following topics:

   Why the Taj Mahal Was Built
   A Brief History of the Alligator
   Four Types of American Prisons
   Carrie Nation: A Character Study
   The Facts About Smoking
   The Function of the Pituitary Gland
   The Present Status of Pop Art
   What Is Propaganda?
   The Poverty Program: Then and Now
   A Critical Estimate of Edward Albee

   b. Prepare a bibliography of eight to twelve reference works you would consult in preparation for writing a term paper on one of the following:
      1. The Case Against (or for) Capital Punishment
      2. A Critical Estimate of Tennessee Williams
      3. Hiroshima in Retrospect (an analysis and evaluation of causes and consequences)
      4. The Lincoln and Kennedy Assassinations: A Comparative Study

2. Take notes on the following essays, treating them as if they were source materials for a paper you are writing on a related subject:

   John C. Pallester, "The Grasshopper" (p. 50)
   David Randolph, "Five Basic Elements of Music" (p. 63)
   John Kord Lagemann, "How to Get More Work Done" (p. 84)
   W. H. Auden, "The Function of a Critic" (p. 96)
   George Stade, "Football—The Game of Aggression" (p. 153)
   I. Bernard Cohen, "Isaac Newton" (p. 318)
   James M. O'Kane, "Whither the Black Odyssey?" (p. 323)

23 Organizing the Paper

Having found your topic and gathered sufficient information (invention), you face your next and in some ways most bedeviling challenge, *how to handle your materials:* how to sort, select, and classify categories of information; how to isolate main points and weave in supporting details; how to determine what should go where—and why. This second stage of the writing process is referred to in classical rhetoric as "disposition" or "arrangement"—the organization of the whole into an orderly sequence of parts. Whether you do it on paper in carefully worked out detail or only roughly in your head, you must plan your paper so that it will flow smoothly and logically from one point to another, moving steadily in its intended direction.

Natural Order

In examining the twenty questions that generate topics, we noted that some kinds of writing are, in a sense, self-organizing. A simple analysis, for example, breaks a subject down into its component parts or types, which are then—quite naturally—listed in a series (part one, part two, and so on). Similarly, an analysis of a process (how something is done or made) is inevitably organized chronologically (first this, then this, then this). A description is usually arranged according to space (left to right, north to south), and narration naturally organizes itself according to time (chronological sequence, flashback, and so on). In such cases the materials determine how they should be developed. You need only recognize the imperatives of your topic and fulfill them; the piece organizes itself.

Logical Order

This is not always the case, however. In constructing a comparison, for example (Chapter 10, "How Does X Compare to Y?"), you must make a conscious decision about its structure: Should you compare the totalities X and Y (comparison of wholes)? Should you break them down and systematically examine elements of each (comparison of parts)? Should you compare likenesses and differences (comparison of parts)? The decision rests on your own logical determinations: Which ordering principle will best promote your purpose by exhibiting your points in their clearest and sharpest light?

Note, for example, that in "Marrying Absurd" (p. 173), Joan Didion— responding to the question "What are the facts about Las Vegas weddings?"—has organized her wide variety of details and examples under three main headings:

1. What is required
2. What people expect
3. What Las Vegas offers

[Plus conclusion: Description of a typical Las Vegas wedding]

In this essay, as in most exposition and all argumentation, the ordering of parts is purely logical. The writer works out his or her own pattern of ideas— establishing causal connections, making inferences, drawing conclusions. If the reasoning process is sound, then the essay will seem as inevitably ordered as the steps of a natural process.

The Working Outline

A practical approach to organization is expressed in such reminders as E. B. White's, "Before beginning to compose something, gauge the nature and extent of the enterprise and work from a suitable design." White's reasoning is simple and convincing:

Design informs even the simplest structure, whether of brick and steel or of prose. You raise a pup tent from one sort of vision, a cathedral from another. This does not mean that you must sit with a blueprint always in front of you, merely that you had best anticipate what you are getting into.[1]

Journalist John Gunther also believed in anticipating "what you are getting into." Before he had written a single page of his voluminous *Inside Asia,* he

[1]E. B. White, "An Approach to Style," William Strunk and E. B. White, *The Elements of Style,* 2nd ed. (New York: The Macmillan Co., 1972), p. 63.

had projected thirty-five chapters; he ended up with thirty-six. "It is always a good thing," he suggested, "to have a firm structure in mind." This is helpful advice, for without a structure or goal in mind, the writer resembles the harried gentleman who reportedly jumped on his horse and rode off in all directions.

Let us face a deeper truth about organization: it is not accomplished, as some people think, with a strict outline that establishes once and for all the shape of the final paper. "One's plan is one thing," said Henry James, "and one's result another." As was mentioned earlier, invention is an ongoing process. It spills over into the research stage and the organizing and writing stages as well. The writer continues to make discoveries. Writing itself is discovery, and the outline, to cite James again, is but "the early bloom of one's good faith." You must allow for, indeed expect, later blooms as well. In this sense the outline should be viewed not as a permanent form but as a working guide, pointing the way in a given direction but amenable to change when you happen on new and better possibilities.

Keeping this in mind, let us see how you might draw up an outline for a representative term paper topic—an extended analysis of hypnosis that will include information on its function, present status, and value. Whether the paper is to be 2,000 or 10,000 words, certain inevitable categories will suggest themselves:

1. definition (What constitutes the hypnotic state?)
2. history (the phenomenon of hypnosis as observed through the centuries)
3. hypnotic technique
4. hypnotic behavior
5. uses of hypnotism (medicine, dentistry, psychotherapy)
6. abuses and dangers of hypnotism (unqualified hypnotists)
7. autohypnosis
8. individual susceptibility to hypnosis
9. recent experimental evidence
10. posthypnotic suggestion
11. misconceptions about hypnosis
12. current scientific opinion of hypnosis

Certainly these twelve categories will be useful during the note-taking stage when you group your information under specific headings. Later on, however, when you organize your material, you will undoubtedly find twelve categories unwieldy and repetitious. Thus you will have to condense the categories into three or four main headings under which you will list various subheadings. Thus the working outline might look something like this:

Tentative title: "What Is Hypnotism? or The Continuing Mystery of Hypnosis"

Introduction: A general statement about hypnotism, a subject that has intrigued people for centuries and that remains mysterious despite the probings of modern science

I. What hypnotism is (brief description of psychological and physiological state)

II. History

    A. Ancient observations, superstitions, etc.

    B. Eighteenth and nineteenth centuries: beginning of scientific study (Mesmer, Charcot)

III. Hypnotism today: what we know

    A. The hypnotic trance

        1. How induced

            a. Classical techniques (gazing at fixed object, etc.)

            b. Drugs (sodium pentothal, etc.)

            c. Autohypnosis

        2. How subject reacts *(cite examples)*

            a. Hypnotic anaesthesia (insensitivity to pain)

            b. Hallucinations

            c. Age regression

            d. Unusual muscular strength and rigidity

            e. Organic effects (blisters, etc.)

            f. Social behavior

        3. Posthypnotic suggestions

    B. Hypnotic subjects

        1. Variations in individual susceptibility

        2. Variations in "how far" people go under hypnosis

            a. Antisocial acts (crime, etc.)

            b. Destructive acts

    C. Uses of hypnotism

        1. Medicine *(weave in evidence from recent scientific studies)*

        2. Dentistry

        3. Psychotherapy *(cite examples)*

    D. Abuses and possible dangers *(weave in stories to illustrate)*

        1. Hypnotism as "entertainment"

        2. Unqualified hypnotists (unable to awaken subject, etc.)

Conclusion: Summary of significance of hypnotism; speculation on possible future applications

A working outline helps not only to channel ideas as you write, but also to check beforehand on their logical progression. Does section three logically follow section two, or should the order be reversed? Should part of the introduction be transferred to the conclusion? Is the first part of the middle section too long in comparison to the second part? And so on. By studying the outline carefully, much as an architect studies a blueprint, you can see whether the structure is likely to hold together: whether the parts are clearly and consistently related and whether they are soundly and strategically developed, each in its proper proportion. By checking and improving a paper in the outline stage you can save yourself hours of reworking and rewriting later on.

Intuitive Order

Still another method of organizing a piece of writing is by intuition—that is, according to an internal "voice" and rhythm that dictates how a subject is to be treated. What should be said first, second, third? What is the proper point of view, the appropriate tone, the right word? The structure of such a piece follows the contours of the writer's musings, which may have their own natural logic. Similarly, the mood is established not by any premeditated plan, but simply by following feelings and setting them down as they are felt—with no conscious organization. Approached in this way, as critic Herbert Read wrote, an essay is an informal "attempt at the expression of an idea or a mood or feeling lurking unexpressed in the mind . . . an attempt to create a pattern in words which shall correspond with the idea, mood or feeling."[2]

Read wrote further that this process is comparable to musical improvisation; it is also "the counterpart of the lyric in poetry." Thus we have such free and spontaneous pieces as Logan Pearsall Smith's "Trivia" and J. B. Priestley's "On a Mouth-Organ." Obviously it is the writer's intimate relationship to the subject and his or her desire to explore with readers an essentially "inner experience" that make an intuitive ordering of materials not only appropriate but inevitable. In such cases, as in the writing of a poem, it is in the act of writing itself that the writer discovers what he or she wants to say.

It should be added here that only certain subjects and certain informal forms lend themselves to this approach; a term paper, for example, usually would *not* fall into this category.

Getting Started

Many students complain that getting started is the most difficult job in writing. The opening section is least likely to come naturally. It is an important section, however, for it is the place where the attention of readers must be captured. A provocative introduction that arouses curiosity or establishes the importance of the subject will encourage them to read on into the body of the piece. Provided it is not a mere trick to entice readers—provided it creates an honest and appropriate expectation of what will follow—a provocative introduction may be viewed as a valid and valuable rhetorical device.

There are many types of introductions. Note that each of the following examples prepares readers for the piece by raising a central issue, making a meaningful observation, creating a mood, or defining a key term.

1. A quotation or meaningful allusion:

"I have traveled a good deal in Concord," said the stationary pilgrim Henry Thoreau. Today his descendants move from country to country instead, some

[2]Herbert Read, *Modern Prose Style* (Boston: Beacon Press, 1952), p. 66.

seeking wisdom, some seeking academic credit, some only fun. Indeed, a latter day Children's Crusade is upon us. No crusaders are sold into slavery, but nobody can say whether any will reach Jerusalem.

—Hans Rosenhaupt, "The New Children's Crusade, or
Going to Jerusalem on a Grant"

William Congreve's opinion that hell has no fury like a woman scorned can fairly be expanded by the alteration of a word. For "woman" read "author"; the cries of exasperation from aggrieved writers come shrieking down the centuries.

—Ivor Brown, "Critics and Creators"

Pascal once remarked that the entire face of the world was changed by the shape of Cleopatra's nose. Almost two thousand years later the entire face of history was nearly changed by the shape of another nose. In the fall of 1831 the twenty-two-year-old divinity student, Charles Darwin, was about to sail as an unpaid naturalist on his Majesty's ship, the *Beagle*. But Captain Fitzroy, who commanded the *Beagle,* hesitated to take Darwin along because he judged, from the shape of Darwin's nose, that the young man had "neither the mentality nor the energy" to become a good scientist.

—Henry Thomas and Dana Lee Thomas, "Charles Robert Darwin"

2. A short narration:

Nine days before his death Immanuel Kant was visited by his physician. Old, ill and nearly blind, he rose from his chair and stood trembling with weakness and muttering unintelligible words. Finally his faithful companion realized that he would not sit down again until the visitor had taken a seat. This he did, and Kant then permitted himself to be helped to his chair and, after having regained some of his strength, said "Das Gefühl für Humanität hat mich noch nicht verlassen"—"The sense of humanity has not yet left me." The two men were moved almost to tears. For, though the word *Humanität* had come, in the eighteenth century, to mean little more than politeness or civility, it had, for Kant, a much deeper significance, which the circumstances of the moment served to emphasize: man's proud and tragic consciousness of self-approved and self-imposed principles, contrasting with his utter subjection to illness, decay and all that is implied in the word "mortality."

Historically the word *humanitas* has had two clearly distinguishable meanings. . . .[3]

—Erwin Panofsky, "The History of Art as a Humanistic Discipline"

A young medical student at Pisa was kneeling in the Cathedral. There was silence over the vast auditory save for the annoying rattle of a chain. A sacristan had just filled a hanging oil lamp and had carelessly left it swinging in the air. The tick-tack of the swinging chain interrupted the student's prayer and started him upon a train of thought that was far removed from his devotions.

Suddenly he jumped to his feet, to the amazement of the other worshipers. A flash of light had descended upon him in the rhythm of the swinging lamp. It seemed to him that this rhythm was regular, and that the pendulum of the rattling chain was

---

[3]From *Meaning in the Visual Arts* by Erwin Panofsky. Copyright © 1955 by Erwin Panofsky. Reprinted by permission of Doubleday and Company, Inc.

taking exactly the same time in each of its oscillations although the distance of these oscillations was constantly becoming less and less.

Was this evidence of his senses correct? If so, he had hit upon a miracle. He must rush home and find out immediately whether he had suffered an illusion or discovered one of the great truths of nature.

When he arrived home, he hunted up two threads of the same length and attached them to two pieces of lead of the same weight. He then tied the other ends of the threads to separate nails and was ready for his experiment. He asked his godfather, Muzio Tedaldi, to help him in this experiment. "I want you to count the motions of one of the threads while I count the motions of the other."

The old man shrugged his shoulders. "Another of Galileo's crazy ideas," he mumbled to himself. But he agreed to help.

Galileo took the two pendulums, drew one of them to a distance of four hands' breadth and the other to a distance of two hands' breadth from the perpendicular, and then let them go simultaneously. The two men counted the oscillations of the two threads, and then compared notes. The total was exactly the same—one hundred counts in each case. The two threads, in spite of the great difference in their starting points, had arrived at the same point at the same time.

And thus, in the swinging motion of the cathedral oil lamp, Galileo had discovered the rhythmic principle of nature which today is applied in the counting of the human pulse, the measurement of time on the clock, the eclipses of the sun and the movement of the stars.[4]

> —Henry Thomas and Dana Lee Thomas, "Galileo Galilei"

3. A provocative question, observation, or line of dialogue:

The attitude of some citizens is like that of a mother who said to her son, "Why do you want to be a physicist, John? Isn't there enough trouble in the world already?"

> —Joel H. Hildebrand, "The Care and Feeding
> of Creative Young Minds"

"Now tell me," said the lady, "all about yourself."

> —J. B. Priestley, "All About Ourselves"

4. A definition of a key term:

"Alienation," a term once confined to philosophy, law, psychiatry and advanced literary criticism, has entered the daily vocabulary. Newspaper editorials refer without quotes or elucidation to the alienation of the slum dweller, the drug addict, the vanguard painter; popular fiction writers rely on readers to recognize the symptoms of alienation as a motive for adultery or murder. Alienage, or strangeness, is understood to be not only a condition (as of foreigners) but a process. As they say in the health drives, it can happen to anyone.

> —Harold Rosenberg, "It Can Happen to Anyone"

5. A striking contrast:

Not often in the story of mankind does a man arrive on earth who is both steel and velvet, who is as hard as rock and soft as drifting fog, who holds in his heart and mind the paradox of terrible storm and peace unspeakable and perfect.

---

[4]From *Living Biographies of Great Scientists* by Henry Thomas and Dana Lee Thomas. Copyright 1941 by Doubleday & Company, Inc. Reprinted by permission of the publishers.

Here and there across centuries come reports of men alleged to have these contrasts. And the incomparable Abraham Lincoln, born 150 years ago this day, is an approach if not a perfect realization of this character.

> —Carl Sandburg, "Lincoln, Man of Steel and Velvet"

6. A direct statement:

Where readers may be assumed to have interest in and some knowledge of the subject, writers may announce their purpose directly, with no preparation or buildup:

The film "Hiroshima, Mon Amour," which is getting a good deal of attention in this country, deserves to be viewed—and reviewed—from a number of perspectives. But I have noticed that reviewers have all tended *not* to explore its moral substance, what the vernacular would call its "message." This is remarkable when a film's message is expressed as urgently as this one's is, and even more remarkable when it is expressed with success *cinematically,* when it is perfectly fused with a web of images and sounds. Here is a film that contradicts the widely-held assumption that messages and good esthetics are incompatible.

> —Amitai Etzioni, "Hiroshima in America"

It might well dismay the intelligent reader to be informed at the outset that the years 1600–60 were an age of transition. But while every period in history deserves, and doubtless has received, that illuminating label, there are some periods in which disruptive and creative forces reach maturity and combine to speed up the normal process of change. In the history of England, as in that of Europe at large, the seventeenth century is probably the most conspicuous modern example, unless we except our own age, of such acceleration.

> —Douglas Bush, "The Background of the Age"

Critics permit themselves, for this or that purpose, to identify literature with great books, with imaginative writing, with expressiveness in writing, with the non-referential and non-pragmatic, with beauty in language, with order, with myth, with structured and formed discourse—the list of definitions is nearly endless—with verbal play, with uses of language that stress the medium itself, with the expression of an age, with dogma, with the *cri de coeur,* with neurosis. Now of course literature is itself and not another thing, to paraphrase Bishop Butler; yet analogies and classifications have merit. For a short space let us think of literature as sentences.

> —Richard Ohmann, "Literature as Sentences"

Ending the Paper

At one point in her adventures in Wonderland, Alice is advised to "begin at the beginning, keep going until you get to the end, and then stop." In some cases it is possible for you to do exactly the same thing: to stop when you have finished saying what you want to say. Your piece (especially if it is a short paper) ends where your last thought ends, creating its own sense of completeness and finality. In other cases, however (usually in a long paper), a formal conclusion of some kind is needed: a recapitulation of the main points; a heightened restatement of the thesis or argument (what the ancients called a "peroration"); a summing-up quotation; a reference to an idea or event mentioned earlier. Any one of these devices (and there are many other suitable equivalents) signals readers that the piece is coming to an end: *Pay close attention; here are my final words on the subject.*

Unquestionably the end is an emphatic position, for the final words impress themselves more forcibly on readers' minds than any others. Similarly, the mood at the end of a piece strongly influences—and may even determine—readers' final feeling about what they have read.

Since there are no standard endings, you must depend on your own judgment in ending your paper. You must compose a conclusion that is appropriate to the subject and purpose of your piece. One helpful procedure is to set aside, at an early stage of research or writing, some information or a passage of quoted material that might serve as a concluding statement. This ending should not open up a whole new aspect of the subject (it is too late for that), nor should it raise additional questions that you cannot answer. Rather, the ending should tie the paper together so that readers experience a sense of satisfaction, both rational (a unit of discourse has reached a logical conclusion) and emotional (the end *feels* like the end).

ASSIGNMENTS

1. Indicate in outline form the structure of the following essays:

   Bruce Catton, "Grant and Lee" (p. 135)
   A. M. Rosenthal, "No News from Auschwitz" (p. 148)
   George Stade, "Football—the Game of Aggression" (p. 153)
   Allan H. Gilbert, "College Lectures Are Obsolete" (p. 282)
   I. Bernard Cohen, "Isaac Newton" (p. 318)
   James M. O'Kane, "Whither the Black Odyssey?" (p. 323)

2. Evaluate the opening and closing paragraphs of the above essays. What special devices for opening and closing are used? Are they effective? Can you suggest alternate opening and closing paragraphs that would be equally, or perhaps even more, effective?

Principles of Style: A Guide

24 The Limits of Language

Language Is Removed from Reality

In his Second Meditation, the French philosopher René Descartes complained that "words often impede me." It is difficult to imagine what unutterable insights, what wordless thoughts (if such is possible) this most original of thinkers was contemplating when he made this paradoxical complaint—a complaint echoed a hundred years later in a great comic-tragic line by T. S. Eliot: "I gotta use words when I talk to you."

Yes, we all "gotta use words." Philosophers and scientists have demonstrated that without the ordering convention of words, we would be overwhelmed by what William James called the "blooming, buzzing confusion" of real life—the world "out there" where nothing stands still long enough to be named; where "Stately Nature" is in actual, measurable fact a dynamic, ongoing process, and "objects" are really "events" flowing into one another by insensible gradations. Our words are still-cameras that artificially freeze reality, making us believe that it conforms to the linear, cause-and-effect structure of our language. But it does not. Language is removed from reality and, in fact, imposes a pattern on reality that is essentially a distortion. Semanticist Alfred Korzybski vividly illustrates this point:

If we take something, anything, let us say the object ... called "pencil" and enquire what it represents ... we find that the "scientific object" represents an "event," a mad dance of "electrons," which is different every instant, which never repeats itself, which is known to consist of extremely complex dynamic processes of very fine structure, acted upon by and reacting upon the rest of the universe, inextricably connected with everything else and dependent on everything else. If we enquire *how many characteristics* we should ascribe to such an event, the only possible answer ... is that we should ascribe to an event infinite numbers of characteristics ... [1]

Clearly it is impossible to ascribe to an event an infinite number of characteristics: there is not enough time; there are not enough words. In order, then, to cope with the world "out there" (and the world within as well, for there is a "mad dance of 'electrons'" going on within as well as outside us), we must change it; we must somehow stop the world long enough to make contact with it and with one another. So we select and simplify, with the help, first of all, of our senses, which compress time, mass, motion, light, and sound so that we are cut off from much of what is going on. What is, in reality, an incessant process, we see simply as an object. And we call that object by a name, thereby simplifying still further. These dancing atoms we designate "rock"; that vast mass of gases spinning in space we designate "star"; and so on. We name these things, in other words, as if they were fixed entities, unchanging from one moment to the next.

But obviously *the word is not the thing*—only a pale and distorted version of the thing. The thing itself is beyond our grasp to know or talk about. In addition to scientists, philosophers, and semanticists, poets and writers emphasize this point; for they too sense that in talking about the world—as opposed to directly experiencing it—we somehow shape it into something different:

> In the way you speak
> You arrange, the thing is posed
> What in nature merely grows.[2]
> —Wallace Stevens, "The Idea of Order at Key West"

Similarly, a character in a Virginia Woolf novel laments the artificial and deceptive tidiness that language imposes on actual experience:

[How] tired I am of phrases that come down beautifully with all their feet on the ground! Also, how I distrust neat designs of life that are drawn upon half sheets of notepaper. I begin to long for some little language such as lovers use, broken words, inarticulate words, like the shuffling of feet on the pavement.

Life is indeed more a shuffling on pavement than a neat landing with both feet solidly on the ground. Note that in indicating this truth, Woolf has abandoned ordinary language in favor of metaphor, which, as we shall see later, is often more effective than a direct statement in describing certain kinds of insights and experiences:

[1]Alfred Korzybski, *Science and Sanity*, 3rd ed. (Lakeville, Conn.: Institute of General Semantics, 1948), p. 387.
[2]Copyright 1936 and renewed 1964 by Holly Stevens Stephenson. Reprinted from *The Collected Poems of Wallace Stevens* by permission of Alfred A. Knopf, Inc.

Words strain,
Crack and sometimes break, under the burden,
Under the tension, slip, slide, perish,
Decay with imprecision. . . . [3]

—T. S. Eliot, "Burnt Norton" in *Four Quartets*

Words Are Generalizations

It is the nature of language, then, to both help and hinder us in our attempt to know the world. It helps by freezing the infinite, ongoing process of reality into fixed, finite objects. It also helps by enabling us to generalize about these objects, for, as was pointed out above, we could not have a name for every separate object in the world; every idea, every thought that passes through the mind of every person; every feeling, every sensation, every emotion; and so on. To make our world intelligible, we must bunch things together into categories so that every word (with the exception of proper nouns) is a class word or generalization, representing not one particular idea, object, or person, but a whole class of ideas, objects, or persons.

Thus verbs are class words; each one points to a class of actions characterized by certain features: "to jump" is to engage in an action marked by a propulsive leap from the ground, repeated in bobbing, bouncing up-and-down movements of the legs and entire body. All actions sharing these particular features are thereby classified, categorized, abstracted, and generalized in the verb "jump." Likewise, nouns name a cluster of qualities that "sum up" an object, for example, a "dog": a furry, barking, four-legged, carnivorous domesticated mammal. Every noun represents a list of qualities that, according to the abstracting process of our own minds, a group of objects have in common. Even function words like "and" and "to" perform a class function in that "and" joins together like grammatical elements and "to" indicates relationship.

Words, then, are simply "convenient capsules of thought" that tell us what the members of a class have in common ("house"), but do not tell us anything about the differences (how my house differs from yours and a dozen other houses on the street). As T. S. Eliot observed, "The particular has no language."

Here is a curious predicament indeed. Our most important means of communication is characterized by the most frustrating of limitations: its generalizing tendency is always drawing us away from the particular thing we want to say. To achieve particularity, we must actively and constantly counteract this inherent resistance of language; we must use all the devices against it that we can command, else we shall end up in realms of abstraction wherein no one knows exactly what anyone else is talking about. This happens all too often when we deal with abstract words such as the word "nature." It was once demonstrated that Western philosophers were using this word in no less than thirty-nine different senses and that it was on

[3]From *Four Quartets* by T. S. Eliot. Reprinted by permission of Harcourt Brace Jovanovich, Inc.

occasion being used two or three different ways on the same page. What, then, is meant by "nature"? Anyone using words at this level of abstraction should follow Cicero's counsel that every rational discourse begin with a definition.

We should also note here that this generalizing tendency of language has played into the hands of the prejudiced by enabling them to make sweeping statements and judgments about whole groups of people, treating them as if they were a single entity rather than an aggregate of individuals ("All Southerners are reactionary"). A group may be identified on the basis of race, religion, political affiliation, geographical location, nationality—whatever. The fallacy lies in not seeing that each member of a group—*any* group—is different from every other member, is indeed unique. Semanticist Alfred Korzybski has suggested that, as an exercise, we remind ourselves of this fact by adding index numbers to our general nouns. Then we would see, he says, that cow_1 is not cow_2; $Italian_1$ is not $Italian_2$; Jew_1 is not Jew_2; $politician_1$ is not $politician_2$. Apart from such obvious and harmless generalizations as "Cows give milk" or "Jews are a minority group," we should then avoid sweeping pronouncements.

Language Is Subjective

Another limit of language is that it is one of the most intensely subjective of media. No one can speak with total objectivity; there is no such thing as neutral language. The first person singular, whether or not it appears explicitly as "I," is implicit in every statement we make. Thus physicist P. W. Bridgeman observed:

When I make a statement, even as cold and impersonal a statement as a proposition of Euclid, it is I that am making the statement, and the fact that it is I that am making the statement is part of the picture which is not to be discarded. And when I quote you it is I that am doing the quoting.[4]

"We never get away from ourselves," concludes Bridgeman. "The brain that tries to understand is itself part of the world that it is trying to understand." No wonder then that we never "transcend the human reference point." Words are always filtered through the mind and emotions of the person using them, so that he or she alone endows them with their special meaning for that situation; he or she has something "in mind." What is it? How can we find out? In a sense we cannot. As news commentator Edward R. Murrow once remarked, "We are all prisoners of our own experience." During the lifetime each of us has spent with words, we have related them in personal ways to our own experiences; we have made them our own. Consequently, no two people respond to the same word in precisely the same way.

[4]P. W. Bridgeman, "The Way Things Are," in *The Limits of Language,* ed. Walker Gibson (New York: Hill and Wang, 1962), p. 42.

At the sound of the word "car," for instance, you and I would immediately focus our attention on a four-wheeled vehicle—a "car." There is no special ambiguity in the term. Still, from the moment the word is pronounced, it might evoke an utterly different image in your mind and in mine; an utterly different internal response. Let us say you are a racing fan. Thus the mere mention of "car" sets your pulse beating faster as you recall (all in a flash and perhaps not even consciously) moments of high adventure and excitement on the speedway. But to me, prone to carsickness, the word "car" instantly conjures up a touch of nausea.

In their classic study of semantics, *The Meaning of Meaning*, C. K. Ogden and I. A. Richards constructed a "triangle of meaning" to illustrate the subjectivity of language. Semanticist Bess Sondel later "animated" and commented upon the diagram as follows:

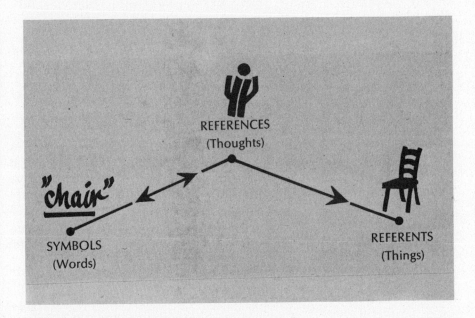

At the peak of the "triangle" is a human being. Here is either the user of words—the person who has selected the words—or the recipient of the words who must, from his perspective, entertain those words.

There is no base in this "triangle."

There is no direct relation between words and things.

Consider yourself at the peak of that "triangle." As you use the word "chair," if your thoughts and mine are directed to the same object out there in the world, then you and I come together—we communicate through the use of the word "chair." We "understand" each other.[5]

But let us say that your thoughts and mine are *not* directed toward the same object. As we have seen, words are so general that they cannot automat-

[5]Bess Sondel, *The Humanity of Words* (New York: World Publishing Co., 1958), pp. 48–49.

ically conjure up identical "referents" in different minds. Before they are referred outward to the real thing, words make a trip through the nervous system of a human being. Thus, as the triangle of meaning makes clear, the circuit of meaning is not completed until words are filtered through the mind of an individual. The thought, then, stands between the word and the thing, even as the cartoon person at the peak of the triangle is spatially located between the Words and the Things they refer to "out there" in the external world.

It is the nature of language, then, and the nature of the human constitution to prevent us from ever achieving *total* communication. We can only do the best we can with what we have, and what we have, as we have seen, is flawed. Words distort reality, and we distort words by being inescapably subjective. We are also inescapably emotional in that words never come to us as pure thought, but always as thought encased in emotion, sensation, attitude, mood, memory.

Denotation and Connotation

These associated overtones of meaning are called the *connotations* of a word, as opposed to the agreed-upon, more or less formal dictionary definition or *denotation*. All words, no matter how bloodless they seem on the surface—words such as "circular" or "flat"—are nonetheless capable of evoking emotional responses. Some words, of course, are richer in connotation than others. Take the word "house," for example, a relatively straightforward term referring to a dwelling place, a physical structure. Now take the word "home"; it too refers to a dwelling place, but the connotations of this word suggest the special place it is: the place where the family lives, where, as Robert Frost wrote, "when you have to go there they have to take you in." On Christmas and Easter vacations, you do not go to a house; you go home.

Many words change in connotation over time. The word "discrimination," for example, was once an admiring reference to a person's taste. Today, however, it might suggest that the person is a bigot. Similarly, the word "propaganda" once suggested a reliable and trustworthy source of information; now it implies slanting and deception. One may play semantic games by juggling with the connotations of words, as in Bertrand Russell's famous "I am firm; you are stubborn; he is pig-headed." All three terms have more or less the same *core* meaning (denotation); by cleverly manipulating the *overtone* of meaning (connotation), the user can shade his or her statement into a commendation or a criticism. Consider the following pairs of words, which have essentially the same denotation—but do they mean the same thing?

debate	dispute
relax	loaf
reflect	daydream
carefree	unconcerned
statesman	politician
sweet	saccharine
childlike	childish

antique	old-fashioned
slender	skinny
voluptuous	fat
restrained	repressed
chatting	yakking
intellectual	egghead

In most contexts the connotations of the words in the left column would be favorable, whereas those in the right would be less favorable. You can see how useful and dangerous a tool connotation can be in the hands of those who would like to misinform without really lying. To cite a small and relatively innocuous example from the mass media: during the 1940s a news magazine, openly Republican in policy, would refer repeatedly to Democratic President Truman's friends as "cronies" (suggesting backroom, poker-playing types). Later, when Republican President Eisenhower was in office, however, the magazine spoke solemnly and respectfully of the president's "long-time associates" (suggesting dignified colleagues in high political office).

One of the strangest, most tragic accounts of mistaken connotation comes out of the Second World War. It involves a reply reportedly received through the official news agency of Japan in response to the surrender ultimatum issued by the Allies at Potsdam. The reply contained the Japanese word *mokusatsu,* which the Domei agency translated into the English word "ignore," thereby implying that the Emperor's regime would not consider surrender under any circumstances. In truth, however, the word *mokusatsu* suggests that one is not flatly dismissing or *ignoring* but only "reserving an answer until a decision is reached." If this careless translation of *mokusatsu,* which failed to incorporate the special connotations of this word, did in fact "confirm America's resolve to drop the atomic bomb, the error may well have been the most costly linguistic blunder in human history."[6]

Extending the Limits

In recognizing the limits of language we can begin extending them as well; we can begin making effective compensations. Aldous Huxley once noted that although no complete solution is possible for the problems posed by language, the alternative need not be despair (the either-or fallacy). We can approach a language problem, the ambiguity of words, for example, "armed with suitable equipment to deal with it." In this way ambiguous words may be "considerably clarified"; a more modest goal than absolute clarity, to be sure, but with this advantage: it is obtainable.

Aristotle said that "it is the mark of an educated man to look for precision in each class of things just so far as the nature of the subject admits." No better counsel could be adopted by the writer, for without precision there is no possibility of communication. Sometimes we *think* we are communicat-

[6]Michael Girsdansky, *The Adventure of Language,* rev. and ed. Mario Pei (New York: Fawcett Publications, 1967), p. 88.

ing because words are going back and forth. But this is no test of communication; people can and often do talk at cross-purposes, answering questions that have not been asked, attacking arguments that have not been proposed. In other words, people can and often do talk *at* each other, without realizing that they are not talking about the same thing, without even knowing precisely what they *are* talking about:

> "The Heart sees farther than the Head," says Debater A.
> "Oh, no," protests Debater B. "That's a blatantly Romantic notion."
> "I don't think it's at all Romantic. It's an Experiential Truth that's been Demonstrated time and time again."
> "I regard it as Immature and Dangerous. All Thought and Action should be Controlled by the Head."

Is there a real argument going on here? Who can tell? Who can even know what the debaters are talking about until they specify what they mean by such abstractions as "Romantic" (one of the most protean terms in all of literature, criticism, history, art, and popular usage). And what is an "Experiential Truth" in this context? In what sense is it "Dangerous?"

In "A Note on Methods of Analysis," Professor Herbert J. Muller warns against discussions of this kind:

> The assertion that the Heart sees farther than the Head gets us nowhere, until we specify what kind of thing it sees better, under what circumstances, for what purposes—always remembering that heart and head see in conjunction, and are not engaged in a seeing contest.

The crucial test of communication, then, is not whether words are going back and forth, but whether ideas are being exchanged. Is there a crossing-over between one mind and another? A giving and receiving, not just a giving of information? After all, communication is a circular and not a linear process. The case for precision cannot be made too emphatically—or too early. Thus it has been included here as one means of extending that most serious of all limits of language: its tendency to raise us to realms of abstraction where no one knows precisely what anyone else is talking about.

In *The Meaning of Meaning*, Ogden and Richards set up a "new science of symbolism" in which they rejected all general words that have no "concrete referent"—no object, situation, or event that could be pointed to as the external "thing" for which the word stands. Such words ("faith," "loyalty," "beauty") are not real symbols, said Ogden and Richards, but only expressions of emotion, not appropriate in a "language of fact."

> This distinction between symbolic and emotive language is not intended by these authors to depreciate emotive language. Emotive language is conceded by Ogden and Richards to have its usefulness in the communication process. It may be used, they say, to evoke desired attitudes in others or to incite others to action of one kind or another. But emotive language has no place in the new science of symbolism.
> Ogden and Richards are interested only in the correspondence of words and

thoughts and things, and the language of science is set up as the exemplar of their theories. In the language of science, the words refer specifically and definitely and accurately to things, and this without the intrusion of the reporter's attitudes. A reporter doesn't say *It's hot today.* He says *The temperature is ninety degrees according to that thermometer.* The language of science is symbolic language at its best.[7]

Obviously Ogden and Richards set standards for a "language of fact" that the nonscientist may find overly rigid and restrictive (and that some scientists, like Bridgeman, quoted on p. 384, do not agree with). Even so, when you are writing an expository essay, the primary purpose of which is to inform and explain, you should take careful note; for by observing rigorous standards of fact you will sharpen your prose. You will also develop the important habit of distrusting the lofty abstractions and sweeping generalizations that give the *sound* of meaning but not the substance.

Using Language to Deceive

To review briefly: we have seen that the nature of language and our own human nature are such that communication can never be more than approximate; we never deliver an idea directly (mind-to-mind) without contamination. Under the best of circumstances and with the best of intentions our words can constrain, constrict, and even distort meaning. Imagine, then, what happens when circumstances are *not* of the best and when intentions are *not* honest, when a deliberate attempt is being made to deceive.

This is the problem to which professional semanticists address themselves, for they recognize that we use language not only to formulate our highest ideals and aspirations but also to justify our basest motives and our meanest behavior. Thus semanticists like Stuart Chase warn against "the tyranny of words": linguistic manipulations by advertisers, propagandists, demagogues, who try to control our behavior by stirring emotion rather than thought, thereby eliciting an uncritical conditioned response. In these cases language is being used for directive rather than communicative purposes; for words that convey absolutely no information may direct us, as by hypnosis, to vote for candidate A rather than B ("He's the one!"), or to buy a car that will make us "Feel Like a Million."

Developing Semantic Sophistication

Our only protection against manipulations of this kind is our own semantic sophistication. We must be able to see through verbal tricks; we must recognize that language lends itself to subtle misrepresentation and sinister manipulation. If we are not aware of this, we will surely be victimized by it.

[7]Sondel, p. 44.

Note how the dictator in the following story misuses language to promote his own dark purposes:

A dictator rules a land. In the morning he orders that the able-bodied men of three villages be required to crush rock and construct roads of it. They are to work indefinitely and without pay. All other villagers, old men, all women and children, are lined up and machine-gunned. All of the villagers' goods are confiscated.

In the evening the dictator speaks over the radio, telling of his morning's work. He says, "I have readjusted the population proportion in the north. I have arranged for the more rapid and efficient improvement of our country's transportation system. I have arranged to have available a greater per capita supply of the basic necessities of life."

The populace cheers.[8]

Obviously, the populace does not know what it is cheering *for*. People think they have been given the facts, but in truth they have been grievously misled. They are both uninformed and misinformed.

In our reading and listening, then—as in our writing—we must develop semantic sophistication; we must test words against the rigorous standards of fact (referents). Unless we do we become symbol worshippers. It is easy to become a symbol worshipper because most of the time most of us do not and cannot adhere to the strict language of fact that scientists and semanticists recommend. Instead we may get so caught up in the connotations of a word that we refuse to accept a fact that does not concur with our feelings. Thus a young woman was heard to protest a news story about a lady who had murdered her child, maintaining that it was "impossible for a *Mother* to do such a thing!"

We can extend the semantic limits of language only by extending the limits of our own critical intelligence. We must not allow ourselves to be mesmerized by words. Only if we understand how language works, and how it may be worked against us, can we hold our own against those who would deceive and mislead. The ultimate aim is to bring about a more intelligent use of language for human ends.

Writing Versus Speech

There remains but one aspect of language to touch upon: the special limits of writing (words on paper) as opposed to speech (words in the air). Both are language, of course, and both are therefore subject to the limits inherent in the medium itself and in ourselves. But writing deserves special attention, for it is a special way of using language that has its own obvious strengths (it endures, for one thing, while speech drifts off into empty space), and its own not-so-obvious, very serious limitations.

Writing is flat, one-dimensional. Try raising your voice on paper. Well,

[8]John Lord, *Experiments in Diction, Rhetoric, Style* (New York: Holt, Rinehart and Winston, 1960), p. 61.

maybe you can manage that with capital letters: LOOK, I'M RAISING MY VOICE. Very good. Now try raising your eyebrows on paper. Ah, you are stuck! But surely you are familiar with this gesture; it is so expressive that it has become part of our language: to raise one's eyebrows is to be disapproving, skeptical—or something like that. It is impossible to translate into words the unstudied eloquence of that gesture—or other gestures like it: lowering one's eyes, closing them, lifting, narrowing, fluttering, rolling, winking. One can carry on an extended conversation with the eyes.

This is true of all the expressive features that supplement the spoken word: facial expressions (pursing the lips in stubborn defiance); body movements (a shrug of the shoulders); and most important, variations in the voice ("Is he *crazy?*" versus "Is *he* crazy!"). Loudness, stress, pitch, pause: all these expressive features, and many more, enter into every spoken sentence and impart to it a distinctive tone and point of view—all of which are absent on the written page where words stand alone, bearing the full burden of meaning.

Thus written English, an "artificial dialect of speech," as linguist Harold Whitehall called it, "must be so managed that it compensates for what it lacks." To begin with, it must be more carefully organized than talk, for in discussing a subject orally, we may shift back and forth, digress, repeat ourselves, and even fall into contradiction. The other person is there to issue a direct challenge ("But you said earlier it was an ethical question, and now you're saying it's basically psychological"); or to ask a question ("I don't understand what you mean by 'diminishing returns.' Would you explain that term?"); or to pick up cues ("That half-smile on your face suggests that you are not completely serious. . . ."). The reader, sitting alone with an article or book, has no such opportunity to observe signs or to ask for further information; nor does the writer have a second chance to clarify a point or to safeguard a meaning.

Thus the writer must be more painstaking than the speaker. As Quintilian said centuries ago, the writer must aim not merely "at being possible to understand, but at being impossible to misunderstand." And this writers must do in the absence of personality and without the assistance of gestures, tone of voice, timing. In truth, writers can never make up for the many deficiencies of writing as compared to speaking; they can only make amends. Specifically, they can try to anticipate the reader's questions and possible points of confusion; they can also organize the material carefully so that point follows point in reasonable, understandable, logical sequence.

Still a third consideration: the writer must be more concise and compressed than the speaker. A group of people can enjoy two or three hours of conversation, during which time tens of thousands of words pass back and forth; but few people would be willing to spend an equal number of hours reading an equivalent number of words on a subject, if their book did not provide substantially more information than their conversation. For the writer, then, economy is an imperative: *every word must tell.*

Of course, writing has its advantages as well as its shortcomings. For the reader there is the opportunity to proceed slowly or rapidly and to reread what he or she does not understand or would like to understand better. Reading is a private and in some ways more thoughtful activity than listening; certainly it provides an opportunity for greater concentration.

From the writer's point of view, too, there are obvious advantages to writing. There is the possibility of revision: what he or she does not say well in the first rough draft, the writer can improve in a later polishing; and the reader will never see the earlier, less successful effort. In conversation or impromptu speech, we think as we talk, talk as we think—at the rate of about 200 to 300 words a minute. The pace of writing can be adjusted to the needs of the writer, who can think, brood, rearrange, reclassify, rephrase, and delete as the writing goes along—a stuttering and stammering process that would be totally unacceptable in speech.

ASSIGNMENTS

1. Language and Reality
   a. It has been observed that nothing ever happens "again"; the word "again" is a verbal fiction. In a paragraph (150–250 words), explain why this is so, citing other verbal fictions in our language and indicating why most words distort reality.
   b. Virginia Woolf distrusted language because, as she said, it draws neat designs of life on notepaper. In a short essay (150–250 words), explain what you think she means by this, comment on her metaphor, and indicate your own sense of how well or poorly language represents ("re-presents") life.

2. The Generalizing Tendency of Language
   a. There are various ways to make language more precise: by quantifying (for example, instead of saying "a large crowd," saying "about 2,000 people"), exemplifying, illustrating, explaining, defining, describing. Using one of the opening sentences suggested below (all generalizations), write a paragraph (150–250 words) in which you provide specific referents for the general term or suggest specific applications to specific situations:
      1. Lincoln claimed that all *progress* may be laid to *discontent*.
      2. "A hungry man," said Montaigne, "would be very foolish to seek to provide himself with a fine garment, rather than a good meal: we must speed to what is *most urgent*."
      3. Balthasar Gracián once wrote that women are *realists* and men are *romanticists*.
      4. The show was *wonderful*.
      5. Everyone should *work*.
      6. "*Pleasure*" is the main motive for human *action*.

   b. Write two versions of a paragraph based on an activity (such as *eating, dancing, writing poetry*) or a concept *(loyalty, beauty, justice)*. In version one, use as many general and emotive words as you wish; in version two, confine yourself exclusively to "the language of fact."

3. The Subjectiveness of Language
   To what extent are we "prisoners of our own experience"? Write a one-paragraph "response" to one or more of the following terms and compare your response with that of another student who has written on the same subject.

auto racing	reading poetry	fighting a lost cause
divorce	a second chance	wounded vanity
falling in love	a salesman	lying
death	a dog	apologizing
writing a paper	hearing a sermon	parting
ballet	making a mistake	dissent

4. Connotations

   a. Consider the following words, all with good connotations. Cite for each a bad counterpart: a word that means approximately the same thing denotatively but *not* connotatively.

cautious	satisfied	leader
courageous	passion	cooperation
retaliation	discuss	independent
compromise	individualist	patriotism
liberty	clever	reformer
subtle	dissent	nonconformist

   b. After conducting a detailed study of dictionaries and *Roget's Thesaurus*, black author and actor Ossie Davis concluded that "the English language was his enemy":

In *Roget's,* he counted 120 synonyms for "blackness," most of them with unpleasant connotations: blot, blotch, blight, smut, smudge, sully, begrime, soot, becloud, obscure, dingy, murky, threatening, frowning, foreboding, forbidden, sinister, baneful, dismal, evil, wicked, malignant, deadly, secretive, unclean, unwashed, foul, blacklist, black book, black-hearted, etc. Incorporated in the same listing were words such as Negro, nigger, and darky.

In the same *Roget's,* Mr. Davis found 134 synonyms for the word "white," almost all of them with favorable connotations: purity, cleanness, bright, shining, fair, blonde, stainless, chaste, unblemished, unsullied, innocent, honorable, upright, just, straightforward, genuine, trustworthy, honesty, etc. "White" as a racial designation was, of course, included in this tally of desirable terms.

No less invidious than black are some of the words associated with the color yellow: coward, conniver, baseness, fear, effeminacy, funk, soft, spiritless, poltroonery, pusillanimity, timidity, milksop, recreant, sneak, lily-livered, etc. Oriental people are included in the listing.[9]

Commenting on this report, Norman Cousins speaks of a "language of prejudice," which not only reflects the way we think about minorities in this country, but actually influences our thoughts:

People in Western cultures do not realize the extent to which their racial attitudes have been conditioned since early childhood by the power of words to ennoble or condemn, augment or detract, glorify or demean. Negative language infects the subconscious of most Western people from the time they first learn to speak. Prejudice is not merely imparted or superimposed. It is metabolized in the bloodstream of society. What is needed is not so much a change in language as an awareness of the power of words to condition attitudes. If we can at least recognize the underpinnings of prejudice, we may be in a position to deal with the effects.[10]

Contemplate the above observation, adding your own observations on an alleged "language of prejudice," indicating also whether you agree or disagree with the idea that this language "infects the subconscious" of a nation and thereby promotes prejudice.

[10]Ibid.

25 Choosing Words

Despite the limitations of language (as discussed in the previous chapter), words are the writer's only tool. It is not surprising then that the professional writer is forever preoccupied with and even obsessed by words, not simply their meaning but their sound, shape, texture, configuration, rhythm. Like strains of melody presenting themselves unbidden to the composer, words whirl about in the writer's mind, resound in the inner ear, impinge on the consciousness—as if they were palpable beings with lives of their own. Indeed, some writers even personify words, as the Mexican poet Octavio Paz has done in his observation that

the easiest thing in the world is to break a word in two. At times the pieces continue to live with a frantic life, ferocious, monosyllabic. It's wonderful to throw that handful of newborns into the circus: they jump, they dance, they bound and rebound, they scream tirelessly, they raise their colored banners.

Ordinary people do not have this almost mystical affinity for words; they do not see them as "colored banners," but rather as conveyors of meaning. And properly so, for it is here that our concern should begin: with words that convey meaning most simply, clearly, and forcefully. Thus, as Lincoln said in his second Inaugural Address:

With malice toward none, with charity for all, with firmness in the right as God gives us the right, let us strive on to finish the work we are in, to bind up the nation's wounds, to care for him who shall have borne the battle and for his widow and his orphan, to do all which may achieve and cherish a just and lasting peace among ourselves and with all nations.

Note the simplicity of the diction here; each word is *right* because it is appropriate not only to the speaker, but also to his subject and to the occasion for the address. There are no long, pretentious adjectives, no vague terms, no clichés, no fiery declamations. The inspired eloquence of the utterance can best be appreciated when we read George Orwell's more formal but flat paraphrase:

We want to terminate this conflict and have an equitable peace. We do not desire a vindictive peace but one that will restore the country to unity. We believe that we are right and are determined to gain the victory and have a fair peace. After the cessation of hostilities we must not forget to take care of the veterans and the dependents of those killed or wounded in the struggle.

We cannot—on order or even on exhortation—increase our sensitivity to words or enlarge our word-stock. As we read and pay attention to words, as words assume a prominent place in our thinking, only then will the right word be available when it is needed, only then will the struggle for that word seem worthwhile. In the meantime, however, you can improve your writing by committing yourself to certain broad categories of words: to the natural word as opposed to the pretentious or trite; to the concrete word as opposed to the vague; to the exact word as opposed to the approximate. We shall consider each of these in turn.

The Natural Word

Bertrand Russell once advised the young writer never to use a long word if a short one will do. This somewhat sweeping dictum ignores those notable exceptions where a long word has a better sound or helps to establish a better rhythm in the sentence. Even so, the general principle has merit. Certainly we should avoid such pomposities as that reported of Samuel Johnson, who remarked casually and naturally of a comedy he had just seen that "It has not wit enough to keep it sweet." Disturbed by the simplicity of this statement, Dr. Johnson hastily amended it to "It has not vitality enough to preserve it from putrefaction."

We can forgive Dr. Johnson the lapse he viewed as a correction, for the sonorous, elevated style he used was accepted, or at least tolerated, in his time. Today, however, it is unthinkable, absurd. Modern prose style is straightforward and relaxed, designed to capture the rhythms of everyday speech, to serve readers rather than to impress them, to talk to them rather than to pontificate. The modern prose stylist, as Bonamy Dobrée points out in *Modern Prose Style,* "is trying to be more honest with himself," is aiming at a style "that will faithfully reflect [the] mind as it utters itself naturally."

In this sense, the unknown author of Ecclesiastes was writing in a modern vein when composing the following verse:

I returned, and saw under the sun, that the race is not to the swift, nor the battle to the strong, neither yet bread to the wise, nor yet riches to men of understanding, nor yet favour to men of skill; but time and chance happeneth to them all.

In his essay "Politics and the English Language" George Orwell praises this passage as an example of "good English"—simple, direct, concrete, smoothly flowing, harmonious, *natural*. By way of contrast Orwell offers a stiff, jargon-ridden variation, written by an imaginary but "typical" bad writer, a stylist of "the worst sort":

Objective considerations of contemporary phenomena compel the conclusion that success or failure in competitive activities exhibits no tendency to be commensurate with innate capacity, but that a considerable element of the unpredictable must invariably be taken into account.

"This is a parody," Orwell admits, "but not a very gross one." He goes on to explain why Ecclesiastes is preferable:

It will be seen that I have not made a full translation. The beginning and ending of the sentence follow the original meaning fairly closely, but in the middle the concrete illustrations—race, battle, bread—dissolve into the vague phrase "success or failure in competitive activities." This had to be so, because no modern writer of the kind I am discussing—no one capable of using phrases like "objective consideration of contemporary phenomena"—would ever tabulate his thoughts in that precise and detailed way. . . . Now analyse these two sentences a little more closely. The first contains forty-nine words but only sixty syllables, and all its words are those of everyday life. The second contains thirty-eight words of ninety syllables: eighteen of its words are from Latin roots, and one from Greek. The first sentence contains six vivid images, and only one phrase ("time and chance") that could be called vague. The second contains not a single fresh, arresting phrase, and in spite of its ninety syllables it gives only a shortened version of the meaning contained in the first.[1]

In an attempt to be "formal" and to seem properly "authoritative," many of us are trapped into writing stiff, dehumanized prose such as that which Orwell parodies. We must guard against it, repress any impulse to use a word such as "transpire," for example, when we simply mean "take place." We must also repress the tendency to write phrases like "objective consideration of contemporary phenomena" or "commensurate with innate capacity" or "considerable element of the unpredictable." One need only read these passages aloud and *listen* to them to know that they are hardly faithful reflections of "the mind as it utters itself naturally."

---

[1]George Orwell, *Shooting an Elephant and Other Essays* (New York: Harcourt Brace Jovanovich, 1945), pp. 84–85.

The Concrete Word

We have already discussed the generalizing tendency of language (see pp. 383–84), which leads us away from clear, unambiguous statement. We saw that one word like "nature," for example, may have as many as thirty-nine specific referents. In addition to raising semantic problems and even dangers, general and abstract terms cause rhetorical problems, for they create dense, lifeless prose lacking in precision and energy. We cannot avoid such prose altogether, for a certain amount of classifying of ideas and experiences is necessary to all discourse. Nonetheless, every time we choose a word we can make a determined effort to be as specific and concrete as the subject will allow. In his *Philosophy of Style*, Herbert Spencer suggested that we avoid sentences like: "In proportion as the manners, customs, and amusements of a nation are cruel and barbarous, the regulations of their penal code will be severe." Instead, said Spencer, we should write a sentence like: "In proportion as men delight in battles, bull-fights, and combats of gladiators, will they punish by hanging, burning, and the rack."

The point to keep in mind is that most people do not think in general or abstract terms but in concrete particulars. Thus when readers encounter generalizations or abstractions, they tend to translate them into specific images of their own choosing. Conscientious writers, of course, do not want readers filling in their prose for them. Thus they write in concrete images of their own choosing. It is no accident that in Antony's speech over Caesar's body, Shakespeare—who wanted to excite in his audience the utmost horror—has Antony talk in the most highly particularized language: "those honorable men [not who merely *killed* Caesar, but] whose *daggers* have *stabbed* Caesar."[2]

The following examples illustrate another way in which the general may be rendered more specific, the abstract more concrete, by adding details:

Example: My father and I argue about everything.
Improvement: My father and I argue about everything from politics and civil rights to the relationship between parents and children.

Example: She looked sensational.
Improvement: She looked sensational in her new purple knit pantsuit, long dangling earrings, and brown leather thong-sandals.

The Accurate Word

In order to use words with any exactness, you must be painstaking. The first word that comes to mind is not always the best one, and it does not help much to try to clarify your meaning by rephrasing what you have just written, prefacing it with "in other words" or "that is to say." The precisely right word used in precisely the right place will say once and for all what needs to be said.

[2]Richard Whately, *Elements of Rhetoric* (Boston and Cambridge: James Munroe and Company, 1854), p. 322.

It is difficult to discuss "right" words in the abstract, for they depend on specific writing situations. Some general principles, however, may be set down.

1. Make certain that the word you choose is literally correct and used in the customary way. In the following examples the writers have made nearly right but ultimately wrong choices:

Example:	Her selfishness is prevalent throughout the story.
Improvement:	Her selfishness is *evident*. . . .
Example:	There is a sadness that emits from the character's every action.
Improvement:	There is a sadness that *issues*. . . .
Example:	I banged my fist on the table, thereby instilling pain throughout my arm.
Improvement:	I banged my fist on the table, thereby *inflicting*. . . .
Example:	They are utterly ignorant to her fears.
Improvement:	They are utterly ignorant *of* her fears.
Example:	I found his poems unmeaningful.
Improvement:	I found his poems *meaningless*.
Example:	He became bitter when the job he was promised never happened.
Improvement:	. . . never *materialized*.
Example:	The fishing trip had a remedial effect on their spirits.
Improvement:	The fishing trip had a *restorative* effect. . . .

2. Choose a word that is appropriate in tone and level of usage (formal, informal, colloquial, slang). Although modern prose style tends to be informal and relaxed, you should not introduce words that are clearly out of place in the context of your piece. Certainly anyone with the slightest sensitivity to words will recognize that the verb in the following sentence is ill-chosen.

> Plato's dialogues stuff the student's mind with new ideas.

The verb "stuff" in this sentence clearly has the wrong tone and the wrong connotation. One may *stuff* one's mouth with food or *stuff* a bag with equipment, but readers of Plato do not have their minds *stuffed*.

Similarly, in the following sentence there is an awkward combination of three different levels of usage: formal, informal, and slangy:

> Students remember that despite the multitudinous tasks that confront them, they must somehow get their work done; they cannot permit themselves to goof off, even for a day.

Today there are no fixed rules governing correctness; slang expressions and colloquialisms are often included in so-called formal writing. As the National Council of Teachers of English announced in 1952, "All usage is relative." The correct or best expression always depends on many factors:

what is being said (a description of a soccer scrimmage or stoic philosophy); how it is said (written or spoken); to whom it is said and on what occasion (a bull session with a roommate or a presentation of a paper before an honors committee). Ultimately, you must exercise your own taste and judgment, your sense of what is appropriate, acceptable, and comfortable in a given context.

Two recent reference works may be consulted by writers who cannot make up their minds about a specific usage:

Margaret Nicholson, *A Dictionary of American-English Usage* (New York: Oxford University Press, 1957).
    This American adaptation of H. W. Fowler's *Modern English Usage* strikes a sensible balance between purism and permissiveness.

Margaret M. Bryant, *Current American Usage* (New York: Funk & Wagnalls, 1962).
    A survey of 240 disputed points of usage, this book is readable and extremely helpful because it is based on how words are *in fact* being used today, rather than on how the author feels they *should* be used.

3. Choose a word that has suitable connotations. Your own sensitivity to words must be your guide here.

Example:	In their simple-mindedness, children are free of racial and religious prejudice.
Problem:	"Simple-mindedness" suggests that children are ignorant, that they simply do not understand the complexities of the situation—and that if they did, they too would be prejudiced.
Improvement:	In their *innocence,* children are free of racial and religious prejudice. ("Innocence" is preferable here because it suggests—as the writer wanted to suggest—purity rather than ignorance.)

Example:	In his novels Faulkner lashes out at racial prejudice.
Problem:	"Lashes out" implies violence and lack of control.
Improvement:	In his novels Faulkner *attacks* racial prejudice. ("Attack" does not carry the connotation of uncontrollable fury but rather of a more measured, thoughtful, and even *righteous* action against an opposing evil.)

4. Whenever possible, choose the *single exact* word in place of a series of words.

Example:	He was introducing considerations that had nothing to do with the case.
Improvement:	He was introducing *extraneous* considerations.

Example:	They cut themselves off from the main group.
Improvement:	They *detached* themselves from the main group.

Example:	There are many factors contributing to the deficiencies in my writing, the most outstanding one being my unwillingness to work.
Improvement:	Many factors contribute to my writing deficiencies, most notably my *laziness.*

5. Avoid ill-sounding combinations of words. Although good readers read silently, they "hear" the sounds of the words. Inadvertent rhymes and words that have the same sound but different meanings (homonyms) are distracting and should be avoided.

Example:	Another explanation of his motivation can be found in his observation that ...
Problem:	Too many "-*tion*" endings.

Example:	Those who lean toward leniency ...
Problem:	Awkward repetition of "*lean*"-sound.

Example:	The sole purpose of his soul-searching address was ...
Problem:	Homonyms.

Example:	It must be clear that the fear of the atmosphere ...
Problem:	Inadvertent rhyme.

6. Avoid awkward variations. "Repetition is bad," said Mark Twain, "but inexactness is worse." Guard against using an inexact or awkward variation of a word simply to avoid repetition.

Example:	Having considered Faulkner's vision, let us now go on to a consideration of the characters who exemplify the theory.
Improvement:	Repeat the word "vision" in place of "theory."

7. Avoid quaint and archaic terms.

Example:	We should treat the medium of writing with respect, nay with reverence.
Improvement:	We should treat the medium of writing with respect, *even* (or "as well as" or "indeed") with reverence.

8. Avoid clichés.

Example:	It was a deep dark secret that I would not for the life of me have revealed to a soul; certainly not to any Tom, Dick, or Harry that happened by, like a ship passing in the night.

Clichés

A cliché may be defined as an expression that was once original and apt—a new and vivid metaphor, perhaps—but that acquired "an unfortunate popularity" and has been used and used and used. The *Oxford English Dictionary* calls the cliché "a stereotyped expression, a commonplace phrase." We might add to this definition the adjectives "trite," "hackneyed," "overworked," "worn out"—"a coin so battered by use as to be defaced."[3]

Clichés appear in many varieties:

[3] George Baker, cited in Eric Partridge, *A Dictionary of Clichés* (New York: E. P. Dutton & Co., 1963), p. 2. This is a book everyone should own, for it lists more than 2,000 words, phrases, and familiar expressions that are better "left unsaid": to "lend an ear," "cook someone's goose," "make the supreme sacrifice"; to be "up in arms," "fit for a king," "on the horns of a dilemma," "under the thumb of," or "in the lap of the gods."

Some are foreign phrases *(coup de grâce; et tu, Brute)*. Some are homely sayings or are based on proverbs ("You can't make an omelet without breaking eggs," *blissful ignorance*). Some are quotations ("To be or not to be, etc."; "Unwept, unhonored, and unsung"). Some are allusions to myth or history *(Gordian knot, Achilles' heel)*. Some are alliterative or rhyming phrases *(first and foremost, high and dry)*. Some are paradoxes *(in less than no time, conspicuous by its absence)*. Some are legalisms *(null and void, each and every)*. Some are playful euphemisms *(a fate worse than death, better half)*. Some are figurative phrases *(leave no stone unturned, hit the nail on the head)*. And some are almost meaningless small change *(in the last analysis, by the same token)*.[4]

We cannot banish clichés altogether from our speech and writing; but they should be weeded out with patience and diligence before they destroy all possibility of meaningful discourse. Stock phrases are the enemy of thought; we repeat them mechanically without thinking about what we are saying. Thus the cliché can lead to a kind of mass No-Think.

Because the reader or listener participating in the No-Think of the cliché expects the language to proceed according to a set pattern, we can extract humor by twisting or reversing the pattern and thereby thwarting the expectation. Thus wits have come up with: "She's as pure as the driven slush"; "You pays your money and you takes your Joyce"; "It is better to have loved and lost then never to have lost at all"; "None but the brave desert the fair"; "Bachelors never make the same mistake once"; "Work is the curse of the drinking class." Bergen Evans has said that these anticlichés are "golden transmutations of some of the world's dullest lead."

Figures of Speech

As discussed earlier (Chapter 24, "The Limits of Language"), language is an abridgment of reality. There are not enough words in any language to express the infinite variety of human ideas, feelings, and experiences. Because we instinctively recognize this, we try to expand and strengthen our power of expression by creating new ways of saying what we mean, specifically by using figures of speech—nonliteral expressions of meaning in which we say one thing in terms of something else.

> I think a poet is just a tree—
> it stands still and rustles its
> leaves; it doesn't expect to lead
> anyone anywhere.
> —Boris Pasternak

The bases of figures of speech are comparison and association, and their purpose is to add freshness, vividness, and immediacy to our utterance and to enhance its meaning.

[4]Theodore Bernstein, *The Careful Writer* (New York: Atheneum, 1965), p. 104.

When I say, for instance, "That a good man enjoys comfort in the midst of adversity"; I just express my thought in the simplest manner possible. But when I say, "To the upright there ariseth light in darkness"; the same sentiment is expressed in a figurative style; a new circumstance is introduced; light is put in the place of comfort, and darkness is used to suggest the idea of adversity. In the same manner, to say, "It is impossible, by any search we can make, to explore the divine nature fully," is to make a simple proposition. But when we say, "Canst thou, by searching, find out God? Canst thou find out the Almighty to perfection? It is high as heaven, what canst thou do? deeper than hell, what canst thou know?" This introduces a figure into style; the proposition being not only expressed, but admiration and astonishment being expressed together with it.[5]

Because figures of speech issue from the deepest recesses of the imagination, they cannot be learned. You can simply note the figures of other writers and hope that in sensitizing yourself and giving free play to your own imagination, you too will be inspired to create word-pictures. Let us examine, then, some of the more common forms of figurative language.

Metaphor (identification of one thing with another)

To an imaginative person, what is a map? The silhouette of a chimera or a spot of colour? Trivial comparisons are futile, so be careful. What is South America? A pear upside down.
—Adolfo Costa Du Rels, *Bewitched Lands*

In his financial operations, Monsieur Grandet was part tiger and part boa constrictor. He would crouch in ambush watching his prey until it was time to spring with open jaws; then, having swallowed the gold, he would slowly digest it, like a snake, impassive, methodical, cold to any human touch.
—Honoré de Balzac, *Eugénie Grandet*

(Note also the simile here: "*like* a snake"; see "simile," below.)

Living was a field of grain blowing in the wind on the side of a hill. Living was a hawk in the sky. Living was an earthen jar of water in the dust of the threshing with the grain flailed out and the chaff blowing. Living was a horse between your legs and a carbine under one leg and a hill and valley and a stream with trees along it and the far side of the valley and hills beyond.
—Ernest Hemingway, *For Whom the Bell Tolls*

No man is an island, entire of itself; every man is a piece of the continent, a part of the main.
—John Donne, *Meditation XVII*

Rhetorical question

If gold ruste, what shall iren do?
—Geoffrey Chaucer, *The Canterbury Tales,* Prologue

[5]Hugh Blair, *Lectures on Rhetoric and Belles Lettres* (Brooklyn: Printed by Thomas Kirk, 1812), Lecture XIV.

Implicit or
submerged
metaphor

Youth is the time to go flashing from one end of the world to the other both in mind and body; to try the manners of different nations; to hear the chimes at midnight.

—Robert Louis Stevenson

Outside the weather was winter, the trees medieval presences arching gray through gray.

—John Updike, "Museums and Women"

About the middle of the nineteenth century, in the quiet sunshine of provincial prosperity, New England had an Indian summer of the mind; and an agreeable reflective literature showed how brilliant that russet and yellow season could be.

—George Santayana, *Character and Opinion
in the United States*

A kind of splendid carelessness goes with surpassing power. The labor of the file was not for Aeschylus as it was not for Shakespeare.

—Edith Hamilton, *The Greek Way to Western Civilization*

Simile
(comparison
of one thing
with another
joined by
"like" or
"as")

Unfortunately Justice is like a train that's nearly always late.

—Yevgeny Yevtushenko, *A Precocious Autobiography*

His whole appearance had an amazing, sparkling freshness, like a newly cut bunch of lilacs and the morning dew still in their leaves.

—Yevgeny Yevtushenko, *A Precocious Autobiography*

Their prose—Tolstoy's sentences, heavy as blocks of granite; Chekhov's rhythms, soft as autumn leaves; Dostoievsky's moaning and quivering like telegraph wires at night—revealed itself to me in all its beauty of language and depth and richness of meaning.

—Yevgeny Yevtushenko, *A Precocious Autobiography*

Human potentialities, so poignant and literally crucial in adolescence really are trapped and vitiated in a mass society. But American society, just because it is so very mass is attached to mass institutions like a factory to its parking lot, or a church to its graveyard.

—Edgar Z. Friedenberg, *Coming of Age in America*

Personification
(attribution
of human char-
acteristics to
inanimate
objects or
ideas)

Wit is a lean creature with a sharp inquiring nose, whereas humor has a kindly eye and comfortable girth.

—Charles Brooks, "Wit and Humor"

Falseness withered in her presence, hypocrisy left the room.

—Adlai Stevenson, eulogizing Eleanor Roosevelt

The songbirds might all have been brooded and hatched in the human heart. They are typical of its highest aspirations, and nearly the whole gamut of human passion and emotion is expressed more or less fully in their varied songs. Among our own birds there is the song of the hermit thrush for devoutness and religious serenity; that of the wood thrush for the musing, melodious thoughts of twilight; the song sparrow's for simple faith and trust, the bobolink's for hilarity and glee, the mourning dove's for hopeless sorrow, the vireo's for all-day and everyday contentment, and the nocturne of the mockingbird for love. Then there are the plaintive singers and the half-voiced, inarticulate singers. The note of the wood pewee is a human sigh; the chickadee has a call full of unspeakable tenderness and fidelity. There is pride in the song of the tanager, and vanity in that of the catbird. There is something distinctly human about the robin; his is the note of boyhood.

> —"John Burroughs' America: Selections from the Writings
> of the Hudson River Naturalist"

Death came for her, ashamed of itself.
> —Bertolt Brecht, *Brecht on Brecht*

ASSIGNMENTS

1. Render the following sentences in concrete or specific terms that will create a more vivid impression in the reader's mind.

    a. She seemed happy.
    b. She seemed lovely.
    c. She seemed intelligent.
    d. She seemed rebellious.
    e. She seemed tired.
    f. She seemed angry.
    g. She seemed restless.
    h. She seemed frightened.
    i. She seemed nervous.
    j. The countryside was beautiful.
    k. The city was awful.
    l. The campus was in a turmoil.
    m. The dormitory was noisy.
    n. The room was crowded.
    o. He had the patience of Job.

2. Improve the following sentences by changing one or more words.

    a. The park is rather circular, with momentous oak trees.
    b. The reversal of Robert Jordan in *For Whom the Bell Tolls* is Frederic Henry in *A Farewell to Arms.*
    c. Thomas Wolfe was abhorred by what he saw in society.
    d. One notices the author's occupation with this theme.
    e. He carries out his life in accordance with Faulkner's vision of fate and moral responsibility.
    f. The memory of Ben's death was so vivid that Wolfe was able to duplicate it in his novel with all its poignancy.
    g. The most beneficial source was *The International Index.*
    h. The room seemed to him to have too much in it.
    i. Many writers are too flowery and superfluous, so that the point they are trying to convey is lost in the garbage of irrelevant material.
    j. For a complete terminology of a word, see an unabridged dictionary.
    k. Oftentimes I yearn for the good old days.

l. The speaker of the poem relates how he felt the loss of the pleasures he had once enjoyed.

m. Hemingway looked very deeply into the nature of courage.

n. He was admired for his stubborn principles.

o. Mrs. Compson's last speech in *The Sound and the Fury* reiterates our assumptions about her.

p. Most high school students are all the same.

q. Words are one of the most essential sophistications humanity has devised.

3. Try to revitalize the following clichés by creating a "play" or "twist" on the words.

a. Home is where the heart is.

b. It never rains but it pours.

c. The more the merrier.

d. As ye sow, so shall ye reap.

e. Hell hath no fury like a woman scorned.

f. All work and no play makes Jack a dull boy.

g. A fool and his money are soon parted.

h. Spare the rod and spoil the child.

i. People who live in glass houses shouldn't throw stones.

j. Beggars can't be choosers.

26 Improving Sentences

We learn in school how to compose paragraphs and essays, but we master the grammar of the sentence in early childhood, long before we are even conscious of the learning process. Whether it issues from our tongue or pen, the sentence appears as a spontaneous creation of the individual consciousness, a result of a lifetime's experience with language, not just the needs of the moment. Thus no one can tell someone else how to write a sentence, for by the time we are writing sentences (certainly by the time we have reached college), a habit pattern has already been established. We call this habit pattern our "style," our characteristic way of expressing ourselves, and however unsatisfactory and frustrating we may find it ("I know I don't write well!"), we tend to cling to the way we have written before. This is natural and should be admitted at the outset. What we can hope to do, and what this chapter will try to accomplish, is to indicate specific ways in which you can take a sentence you have written and rewrite it to better effect so that it will be a more accurate and successful rendition of what you want to say.

It is a formidable job, improving one's sentences, but it can be done by anyone who takes the trouble to contemplate them critically—that is, to see how they actually work on paper and what options are available for effective change and revision. Only in this way can you improve your writing style, for the rhetorical strengths that contribute to what we call "readability" operate principally on the level of the sentence. No matter how apt and interesting a subject is, no matter how carefully it is visualized and organized, no matter how soundly it is developed, it cannot be turned into a good essay unless the writer has embodied each element of thought in a clear, tight, reasonably smooth-flowing, easy-to-follow series of forceful, graceful sentences.

Logically we may think in paragraphs or units of thought, but concretely we spin out our ideas sentence by sentence—subject/verb/object by subject/verb/object. This is the typical English prose sentence, which we vary instinctively as we feel a need for change in rhythm and pace. The reader receives ideas sentence by sentence, reaching out from subject to predicate and trying to remember the various modifications and qualifications set down along the way. Every sentence advanced beyond the primer stage of "See John run!" contains more than a bald subject committed to a particular action. There are always conditions and descriptions woven into the assertion that deepen and enrich its core meaning.

Dr. Samuel Johnson said that "most men think indistinctly and therefore cannot speak with exactness." To some extent this is true, but it is also true that your special function as a writer is to overcome this human deficiency. Before setting down your thoughts on paper, you have a special obligation to probe your mind until you see your ideas clearly as a distinct and unified whole. It is then your special obligation to try out different forms for each sentence to see which one most exactly reproduces the idea as it exists in your mind. Only after you have made clear thinking *visible on paper* are you justified in claiming the time and attention of a reader.

We shall approach the subject of the sentence first by reviewing its basic grammar and then by considering six basic rhetorical features of the sentence that provide a foundation for clarity and readability: unity, coherence, emphasis, economy, vigor, and rhythm. Upon this foundation each writer can build those subtler qualities of prose tone and style that best suit the needs and purposes of the individual piece and person. Every writer, student as well as professional, is entitled to his or her own style, just as everyone is entitled to his or her own personality (of which writing style is a reflection). The only imperative is that style begin with the minimum rhetorical proficiency without which a piece of writing, no matter how modest in purpose or limited in scope, is doomed to failure. Throughout this discussion, suggestions and illustrations will be cited from the lectures of the eighteenth-century rhetorician Hugh Blair, whose observations on writing and on the improvement of style, although they were published in 1783, have yet to be surpassed.

The Basic Grammar of the Sentence

Grammar, very simply, is the structure of a language or the study of how a language works. In reviewing the basic grammar of the sentence, we shall move from a consideration of the various kinds of words to a discussion of the ways in which words are combined to form phrases, clauses, and sentences. The section concludes with a review of the principles of sentence correctness.

Types of Words

Words are conventionally divided into eight categories, the so-called parts of speech: nouns, pronouns, verbs, adjectives and adverbs (modifiers), prepositions and conjunctions (connectives), and interjections. It will be helpful to review each of these in turn, except for the interjection, a word that is grammatically unrelated to the rest of the sentence, merely expressing an attitude or emotion (*"Oh,* I'm going to be late!" *"Ah,* what a relief!")

Nouns and Pronouns

A noun is conventionally defined as the name of a person, place, or thing (object, animal, idea, or quality). Thus:

> The *woman* is busy.
> The *Girl Scout* is helpful. [compound noun]
> The *city* is beautiful.
> The *cat* is purring.
> The *thought* is well expressed.
> Her *beauty* is dazzling.

A pronoun is conventionally defined as a word that takes the place of, or refers to, a noun.

> *She* is busy.
> *It* is beautiful.
> *They* are quarreling.
> *Anyone* can learn to swim.

In sentences, nouns and pronouns can function in any of the following ways:

> as a subject (The *horse* pulled the carriage.)
> as a direct or indirect object (The girl gave her *father* the *book.*)
> as the object of a preposition (Give the book to *him.*)
> as a subject complement (The man is a *laborer.*)
> as an object complement (The girl called the writer a *fraud.*)
> as an appositive (The speaker, a *socialist,* outlined the program.)
> as a modifier (She gave *her* book to *John's* mother.)
> as the subject of a participle (We saw the *table* being broken.)
> as the object of a participle (Finding her *pencil,* she began to write.)
> as the object of a gerund (Making *bread* is one of my hobbies.)
> as the subject of an infinitive (Jack wanted *her* to win the match.)
> as the object of an infinitive (We tried to catch the *ball.*)
> in direct address (*Girls,* please be ready on time.)
> in absolute constructions (The *storm* over, we left.)

Pronouns and—to a lesser extent—nouns undergo *inflection,* a change of form to indicate their specific meaning or grammatical function in the sentence. The inflectional form of a noun or pronoun is referred to as its *case:* a subject (except the subject of an infinitive or of a participle) is required to be in the *subjective,* or nominative, case (*woman/she*); an object is required to be in the *objective* case (*woman/her*). The *possessive,* or genitive, case form is indicated in nouns by the use of an apostrophe and in pronouns by a change in form *(woman's/hers)*.

Nouns and some indefinite pronouns vary their case form only to show possession:

> The *girl's* book was lost on the train.
> *Anybody's* mother would have felt the same way.

The following six pronouns require different and distinctive forms in all three cases:

Subjective	I	we	he, she	they	who
Possessive	my (mine)	our (ours)	his, her	their	whose
			(hers)	(theirs)	
Objective	me	us	him, her	them	whom

Several other principles of case should be kept in mind:

1. The personal pronouns *it* and *you* are inflected only to show possession: *its, your, yours*.

2. A pronoun used in apposition should be in the same case as the noun or pronoun to which it is in apposition.

> They put the blame on the two of us, John and *me*.

3. The case of a pronoun is determined by its function in its own clause.

> She will invite *whoever* can come. [pronoun subject of clause]
> She will invite *whomever* she wants. [pronoun object of clause]
> I will talk to *whoever* is in the office. [pronoun subject of clause]

4. The case of a pronoun following *than, as,* or *but* is determined by whether the pronoun is the subject or object of the verb that follows, whether that verb is explicitly stated or only implied.

> She is older than *I* [am].
> They call her more often than [they call] *me*.
> Everyone applauded but *I* [did not applaud].

Exceptions: In informal usage the conjunctions *than* and *but* are often regarded as prepositions; in such instances it is permissible to use the objective case of the pronoun.

> She is taller than *him*.
> Everyone applauded but *me*. [analogous to . . . *except me.*]

5. In standard written English the pronoun *whom* is consistently used when its position in the sentence requires the objective case.

> The student *whom* he advised has finally registered. [*Whom* is direct object of *advised*.]
> To *whom* are you addressing that question? [*Whom* is object of preposition *to*.]

Exceptions: In informal usage—in speech or when the pronoun opens the sentence (where the subjective case is normally the rule)—the use of *who* has become acceptable, indeed idiomatic.

Who did I see you with last night?
She is a student *who* I admire greatly.

In many instances it is possible to avoid the controversy and confusion that surround the use of *who/whom* by simply editing the pronoun out of the sentence.

She is a student I admire greatly.
Are you talking about any particular writer? [rather than the correct but awkward-sounding *Whom are you talking about?*]

On similar grounds, writers who object to the conventionally correct use of the subjective case for a pronoun used as subject complement of the linking verb *be* ("Can it be *they?*") can sidestep the issue by recasting the sentence ("Do you hear them coming?"). "It's me" (as opposed to the grammatically pure "It is I") has already been established as an idiom.

Verbs

Verbs are conventionally defined as words that assert action or state of being. A more precise definition would incorporate the fact that verbs *predicate* some action of the subject; that is, they make a statement ("She worked hard"), ask a question ("Are you coming?"), or issue a command or direction ("Fold the batter into a cakepan"). A verb, then, is a word that functions in the sentence as the predicate or as part of the predicate.

Kinds of Verbs

Verbs are of two kinds: transitive and intransitive. A *transitive* verb requires an object to complete its meaning.

The speaker announced his subject.

An *intransitive* verb does not require an object to complete its meaning.

They moaned and cried.

Linking verbs (sometimes called "state of being" verbs)—for example *feel, seem, be, appear, become, smell, taste*—are considered intransitive because they serve merely to connect or "link" a subject with its subject complement.

She felt happier than ever.
He was becoming anxious.
It smelled terrible.

The same verb may sometimes be used transitively or intransitively.

Mary paints pictures. [transitive]
Mary paints beautifully. [intransitive]

Tense

Verbs are inflected to indicate tense, or time. Basically there are six tenses:

Present: She *asks* no questions.
Past: She *asked* no questions.
Future: She *will ask* no questions.
Present Perfect: She *has asked* no questions.
Past Perfect: She *had asked* no questions.
Future Perfect: She *will have asked* no questions.

A present tense verb is often used to express universal truth ("All people are mortal") or habitual action ("He longs for final answers").

Voice

Verbs may be cast in active or passive voice. A verb in the *active* voice has a direct object.

The police officer *put* a parking ticket on the car.

A verb is in the *passive* voice when the object is converted to the subject by casting the verb into a phrase consisting of a form of the verb *to be*, followed by a past participle.

A parking ticket *was put* on the car.
The car *was given* a parking ticket.

Note that the subject of a verb cast in the active voice performs an action, while the subject of a verb cast in the passive voice receives an action.

Mood

Verbs are also inflected to indicate the manner or mode—the mood—in which an action or state of being is conceived. The English language has four basic moods:

Indicative: makes a statement or assertion (The car needs repair.)
Interrogative: asks a question (Does the car need repair?)
Imperative: issues a command, request, or directive (Repair the car.)
Subjunctive: suggests actions that are probable, possible, or contrary to fact or desire. Once used in a variety of constructions, the subjunctive mood is now used in a limited number of forms:
in the present and past tense of the verb *to be* (If I *were* you, I would repair the car.)
in *that* clauses pertaining to parliamentary motions, or in recommendation, resolution, demand, or command:

I move that the car *be* repaired.
She recommended that he *repair* the car.
Resolve that this car *be* repaired.

Modifiers

Variety and nuance in sentences are achieved primarily by adding modifying words, phrases, and clauses. Basically, there are two types of modifiers: adjectival and adverbial.

Adjectives

Adjectives are words that modify (qualify, quantify, describe, or limit) nouns and pronouns.

The *four* women waved their *red* scarves.

Frequently, a word that ordinarily functions as another part of speech may be converted to adjectival use.

In order to lose weight, she went to a *milk* farm.

Here the word *milk*, normally a noun and sometimes a verb ("She *milked* the cow"), is being used as an adjective. Similarly, nouns in the possessive case ("*Gloria's* room," "the *boy's* trousers") and such pronouns as *this, that, her, our, your* may serve an adjectival function ("*Our* clothes are wet"); so may certain phrases and clauses, as we shall see.

Adverbs

Adverbs are words that modify (qualify, quantify, describe, or limit) verbs, adjectives, or other adverbs.

He drank his milk *slowly*.
The milk was *terribly* sour.
He drank his milk *very* slowly.

In addition, adverbs may modify gerunds, participles, and infinitives (see p. 416).

Adverbs generally indicate place (*nowhere, here*), definite time (*now, yesterday*), indefinite time (*often, always, seldom, never*), degree (*very, exactly, quite, almost*), and manner (*quietly, softly, stealthily*).

Sometimes a so-called adverb of modality may qualify an entire sentence:

Clearly, that man is incompetent.
Surely you don't mean that.
I *certainly* do mean it.

Many adverbs are formed simply by adding *-ly* to an adjective: *rapid* (adjective), *rapidly* (adverb). However, there are many adverbs that do not have a final *-ly*, as is shown above in the list of adverbs signifying place, time, and manner. Still other adverbs have the same form as their corresponding adjectives. The word *slow*, for instance, may be used as either adjective or adverb. Contrary to what many people think, the road sign "Go Slow" is grammatically correct. (*Slowly* may be used as an adverb but not as an adjective.)

Connectives

As the term suggests, connectives serve mainly to connect other words in the sentence and to show their relationship. Having no lexical meaning of their own apart from their function in the sentence, the two major kinds of connectives, prepositions and conjunctions, are often called "function words."

Prepositions

Prepositions connect nouns or noun equivalents to show how they are related to some other part of the sentence or to the whole sentence.

> She walked *into* the room two minutes *before* class ended.
> *Up* the street a man was watering his lawn.

The preposition and the noun (which may have its own modifiers) constitute a modifying unit, the noun serving as the so-called object of the preposition.

There are many prepositions in the English language (*out, in, to, toward, under, over, between, in front of, in back of,* and so on), and their use is generally established by idiom and usage. Sometimes usage is so lax and regionally determined that one may communicate the same idea by using different prepositions ("I got *up* from the bed," "I got *down* from the bed," "I got *out* of bed"). Those who are curious and would like to know more about prepositions may consult an entire book on the subject: Frederick T. Wood, *English Prepositional Idioms* (New York: St. Martin's Press, 1967).

One rule, however, has no exceptions: a pronoun following a preposition must be in the objective case. Many people violate this rule by using the expression "between you and *I*" in the belief that *I* is somehow more elegant than plain *me*. To avoid such overcompensation, it may be helpful to think of the analogous expression "between *us*," for which "between *we*" would never be used.

There is an old prohibition against ending a sentence with a preposition, which grew out of a mistaken belief that English grammar must imitate Latin grammar. Winston Churchill is said to have dismissed this "rule" as "the sort of English up with which I will not put." Indeed, rigid adherence to it could result in such nightmarish sentences as the following, supposedly addressed by a nursemaid to her young charge: "What did you choose that book to be read aloud out of for?" And it has been suggested that the child might have come back with: "What did you bring this book I don't like to be read aloud to out of from up for?"[1] As a general guideline, use a final preposition if the sentence sounds more natural and idiomatic and is not thereby robbed of its proper emphasis.

Conjunctions

Acting as function words, conjunctions connect words, phrases, or clauses. There are two kinds of conjunctions: coordinating and subordinating.

Coordinating conjunctions (and, but, or, nor, for, yet) connect two words or word groups of equal grammatical rank.

> The girl *and* the boy were skating.
> It is a warm *but* cloudy day.
> Did you open the front door *or* the living room window?

---

[1]Cited in Sir Ernest Gowers, *The Complete Plain Words*, rev. Sir Bruce Fraser (London: Her Majesty's Stationery Office, 1973), p. 131.

In using a coordinating conjunction, make certain that the elements on both sides of the conjunction are of equal rank: if two single words are joined by the conjunction, they should be the same part of speech; if two word groups are joined, both should be either phrases or clauses (see the discussion of parallelism on pp. 450–52).

Subordinating conjunctions (*if, since, because, when, although,* and so on) connect sentence elements that are of unequal rank—specifically, main and subordinate clauses—and show their relationship. The following list presents the most commonly used subordinating conjunctions, grouped according to the specific relationships they establish.

Comparison: *than, as . . . as, likewise*

>   She has no more feeling than a stone.

Condition: *if, unless, whether, as long as, provided that*

>   If the rain continues, the picnic will be postponed until Saturday.

Concession or contrast: *though, although, even though*

>   Although the archeologists dug steadily for six months, they failed to find any artifacts.

Degree or comparison: *as, just as, as much as, as . . . as, than*

>   They carried as much food and water to the survivors as they could.
>   John ranked higher on the College Boards than Jim had ranked last year.

Manner: *as, as if, as though*

>   She studied for the exam as she had been instructed.

Place: *where, wherever*

>   Wherever you go in California, you are certain to see spectacular scenery.
>   I found my gloves where I had left them.

Purpose: *so that, in order that*

>   I have written full instructions on the board so that the exam can begin on time.

Reason or cause: *because, since, as*

>   They laughed because they were enjoying themselves.

Time: *when, until, before, while, since, as*

>   While they were attending the lecture, fire broke out in the basement.

Conjunctive adverbs simultaneously connect main clauses and provide an adverbial modifier. The chief conjunctive adverbs include single words (*however, furthermore, thus, therefore, indeed, consequently, nonetheless, moreover*) and transitional phrases (*for example, in addition, in fact, on the other hand, on the contrary, at the same time, that is*). In contrast to subordinating conjunctions, conjunctive adverbs generally relate two main clauses and are preceded by a semicolon rather than a comma (see the punctuation review in Chapter 28, p. 503).

Relationships of Words

Phrases

A phrase is a group of words that functions as a unit but does not contain a subject and a predicate. A phrase may be classified according to its own construction and according to the part of speech whose function it performs.

Prepositional Phrase

A prepositional phrase is introduced by a preposition; it functions as an adjective or adverb.

Adjectival: modifies a noun or pronoun

> The girl *in the bright green dress* entered the room.
> Her yellow hat, *with its purple feathers,* attracted our attention.

Adverbial: modifies a verb, adverb, or adjective

> The man walked *through a long, dark tunnel.*
> Drive carefully *on icy streets.*
> The bread was still hot *from the oven.*

Verbal Phrase

A verbal phrase consists of a verb form plus other words; it functions as a noun or an adjective.

Gerundive: often called a "verbal noun"; always ends in *-ing;* functions as a noun, taking objects, complements, or modifiers.

> *Stealing someone else's lines* is plagiarism.
> *Stealing with a grand flourish* is still stealing.
> *Dancing the polka* is my favorite exercise.

Participial: often called a "verbal adjective"; modifies a noun or pronoun.

> The woman *banging on the door* was obviously terrified.
> *Having been rejected,* he plunged into a depression.

Infinitival: functions as a noun, an adjective, or an adverb.

> *To attempt more* is *to achieve less.*
> *To have made more pressing demands* would have cost him his job.
> Jan is an artist *to be admired.*
> The meat was marinated *to make it tastier.*

Clauses

A clause is a group of related words containing both a subject and a predicate and forming a sentence or part of a sentence.

Subordinate Clauses

Like a phrase, a subordinate clause is a group of related words which functions as a unit but cannot stand alone. The most helpful way to identify a subordinate (or dependent) clause is to distinguish it from a main (or independent) clause. Like a sentence, a main clause contains a subject and predicate and can stand alone:

A sixteen-year-old can get a permit when he or she is accompanied by a parent.

In the above sentence only the first clause, the main clause, can stand alone:

A sixteen-year-old can get a permit.

The second clause *cannot* stand alone:

. . . when he or she is accompanied by a parent.

The sense of this statement depends on the rest of the sentence; therefore it is clearly a subordinate (dependent) clause.

Subordinate clauses may be used as adjectives, adverbs, or nouns.

An *adjective clause* modifies a noun or a pronoun and is generally introduced by a relative pronoun (*who, whom, which, that*) or by a relative adverb (*where, when, why*):

This pen, *which I found in the library*, belongs to Lee.
The store *where I bought the dress* is closed for the afternoon.
She is a girl *I cannot understand.* [relative pronoun *whom* omitted]

An *adverbial clause* is introduced by a subordinating conjunction, which indicates the exact relationship between the subordinate idea and the main idea:

His friends gave a party *when he returned.*
She agreed to go *although she had grave reservations.*

A *noun clause* functions like a noun and—like an adjective clause—is generally introduced by *who, whom, which, that;* also by *whichever, whoever, whomever, where, when, why.*

Whoever telephoned for an appointment this morning has just called back.
He said *that he would arrive at noon.*
    or
He said *he would arrive at noon.* [conjunction *that* may sometimes be omitted]

Using subordinate clauses effectively will enhance your writing greatly, enabling you to combine facts in varied sentence patterns which show more exact relationships than the mere stringing together, in a coordinate sequence, of one idea after another.

Coordination: I went downtown and it rained.
Subordination: When I went downtown, it rained.

Main Clauses

Main (or independent) clauses can stand alone as simple, separate sentences.

> The man called my name, and I called his name in return.
> They have made sensible plans; furthermore, they know how to implement them.
> No higher praise can be given than this: he was a man who lived by principle.

The Sentence

A sentence is a group of words containing a subject and a predicate. The subject names the person, thing, or concept spoken about. The subject of a sentence can be identified by asking, "Who or what is doing the action?" The predicate—a verb plus its object and complement, if any—makes an assertion about that person, thing, or concept. The verb can be identified by asking, "What is the action?" The object can be identified by asking, "Who or what receives the action?"

Six Basic Sentence Patterns

The three most important patterns of the English sentence are:

1. a subject and a verb

Subject	Verb
The girl	laughed.
Lions	roar.
The boy	is shouting.

2. a subject, an action verb, and one or two objects

Subject	Verb	Object	Object
Cats	drink		milk.
The boy	called	her	a heroine.
Duane	bought	her	a necklace.

3. a subject, a linking verb, and a complement (a linking verb is one which does not indicate action but merely links the subject with descriptive words that complete its meaning; hence the words that follow such verbs are called *complements*).

Subject	Verb	Complement
Einstein	was	a genius.
The boy	will become	a scientist.
The lion	seems	hungry.
The coat	felt	heavy.

To the above patterns three more may be added. These are not as frequently used, but they are equally important in that they represent variations on the usual order and relation of subject and predicate.

4. Passive pattern: the object in an active sentence is converted to the subject.

Subject	Passive Verb	Object
Milk	is drunk	by cats.
She	was called	a heroine by the boy.
Her necklace	was bought	by Duane.

5. Impersonal pattern: the real subject of the sentence follows the verb, while an "anticipatory" subject (*it, there*) precedes the verb.

Subject	Verb	Complement	Subject
It	is	unlikely	that they will protest.
There	was		an echo.
There	will be		a good turnout.

6. Imperative pattern: the subject, though not explicitly stated, is "understood" to be *you*.

Verb	Object or Complement
Stop.	
Answer	my question.
Do not start	any trouble.
Be	good.

Upon these six basic patterns most English sentences are built. An inversion such as *Him I don't like* (rather than the normal *I don't like him*) provides emphasis by its very irregularity or deviation from the norm. Questions also represent a variation of normal patterning, the most common being the inversion of subject and verb (used in conjunction with *be, have, shall, will, can, may, must, ought, need*):

Was she there?
Must I stay?

Structural Types

Sentences may also be classified on the basis of their grammatical structure: simple, compound, complex, compound-complex.

Simple: a sentence containing only one subject and one predicate—that is, one main clause, with no subordinate clauses. Such a sentence may contain modifying phrases, however.

I decided to go home.
Tired and rejected, I decided to go home.

Compound: a sentence containing at least two subjects and two predicates—that is, two or more main clauses, with no subordinate clauses. A compound sentence is actually two independent sentences linked by a semicolon and/or by a coordinating conjunction (*and, but, for, or, nor, yet*) or conjunctive adverb (*however, therefore*, and so on).

> She was a sophomore; he was a junior.
> She wanted to leave the stage, but the audience would not stop applauding.
> The reviews of the show were poor; however, the word-of-mouth reports were excellent.

The compound sentence is useful when you wish to express two thoughts that are of approximately equal value or that are contrasting or opposing aspects of a single idea. The pairing of independent clauses into a compound sentence provides a structure that clarifies the relationship between the clauses.

Complex: a sentence containing one main clause and one or more subordinate clauses.

> Although the reviews of the show were poor, the word-of-mouth reports were excellent.

A complex sentence should be used when you wish to show more precisely the relationship between ideas—specifically, when you wish to give greater stress or importance to one part of the sentence. In such cases it is advisable to subordinate grammatically that which is actually subordinate or less important. (See "Working Toward Emphasis," pp. 444–47.)

Compound-complex: a sentence containing at least two main clauses and at least one subordinate clause.

> When the flowers arrived, she placed them into a large vase; thus she enjoyed the rest of the afternoon, gazing at her fragrant gift.

Basic Principles of Sentence Correctness

Agreement of Subject and Verb

1. A verb should agree with its subject in person and number.

> Many zoo animals [third person plural subject] live [plural verb] in crowded cages.
> She [third person singular subject] lives [third person singular verb] in the country.

2. Two or more subjects connected by *and* require a plural verb.

> A noun and a verb are needed in a sentence.

Exception: When two singular subjects connected by *and* present a single idea, the verb may be singular.

> His pride and joy is his new car.
> Ham and eggs is my favorite breakfast.

3. When two or more subjects are connected by *or, either . . . or,* or *neither . . . nor,* the verb agrees with the subject nearest to it.

> Either the men or the woman is guilty.
> Neither Jim nor his brothers are guilty.

4. A collective noun referring to a group as a unit requires a singular verb; a collective noun referring to individuals in a group acting separately requires a plural verb.

> The class is attentive.
> The class are going their separate ways.
>
> The public is easy to reach.
> The public are writing letters to the radio station.

5. Nouns plural in form but singular in meaning require a singular verb.

> The news is bad.
> Economics is a popular subject.
> Politics is an art.
> Any system of ethics has its inconsistencies.
> *The Magnificent Ambersons* is a fine film.

6. Words stating time, money, fractions, weight, and amount are generally singular and require a singular verb.

> Thirty days is a long time.
> Five dollars is the price.
> Two-thirds of nine is six.
> Twenty pounds is not considered excessive.
> Twelve miles is a long walk.

7. A prepositional phrase that follows a subject does not affect the number of the verb.

> The size of the pictures in the album is small.
> The cost of his pranks was paid by his parents.

8. A relative pronoun used as a subject may be either singular or plural, depending on the number of its antecedent.

> John is one of those men who always complain. [antecedent of *who* is *men*]
> John is the only one of those men who always complains. [antecedent of *who* is *one*]

9. Singular pronouns require singular verbs: *each, everyone, everybody, anyone, anybody, someone, somebody, no one, nobody, one, another, anything, either, neither.*

> Each of the boys is gifted.
> Neither of the candidates shows any promise.

The pronoun *none* is singular or plural according to context.

> None of the students was willing to reply.
> None of the students were able to attend.

10. *Every* and *many a* before a word or series of words should be followed by a singular verb.

> Every man, woman, and child in town is invited.
> Many a girl in this situation has given up.

11. A singular subject followed by *with, in addition to, as well as,* and *including* requires a singular verb.

> The woman, as well as the three men in the car, was injured.
> Jane, as well as Jim, is leaving for the weekend.

12. In *here is/here are* and *there is/there are* constructions, the noun following the verb is considered the real subject and therefore determines the person and number of the verb. A singular subject obviously requires a singular verb:

> Here is your coat.

Similarly, a plural subject requires a plural verb:

> There are thirty students in the class.

When the first element of a compound subject is singular, the choice between a singular or plural verb is a matter of taste:

> There was [or *were*] joy and tears in her eyes.

Agreement of Pronoun and Antecedent

1. A pronoun should agree with its antecedent in person, number, and gender.

> The chairman [third person, singular, masculine] submitted his [third person, singular, masculine] report.
> The women [third person, plural, feminine] left their [third person, plural] coats in the closet.
> Mary and John [compound subject] handed in their [plural] papers.
> The sales pitch for aspirin [third person, singular, neuter] emphasized its [third person, singular, neuter] pain-killing properties.

2. Collective nouns that refer to a group as a unit require singular pronouns; those that refer to individuals in a group acting separately require plural pronouns.

> The jury announced its verdict.
> The audience applauded their hero.
> As a finale, everyone threw their hats in the air.

3. The words *each, either, neither, somebody, anybody, nobody, someone, anyone,* and *no one* require a singular pronoun; *everyone* and *everybody* take a singular or plural pronoun, depending on meaning.

> Nobody knew where to find his coat.
> No one can call his judgment infallible.
> Everybody reported their grades.
> Each member of the cast knows his role.

Since English has no single pronoun to indicate both male and female, *he* has traditionally been used to refer to both genders. This usage is essentially inaccurate, however, because the reference may be to a woman as well as a man. One way to avoid this problem is to pluralize.

> All the members of the cast know their roles.

Another possibility is to say simply:

> Someone left his or her book in class.

4. The impersonal *one* may be followed by *his*.

> One should watch his manners.

An alternate and more conservative usage provides more consistency and accuracy:

> One should watch one's manners.

5. *Who* refers to persons, *which* to things, and *that* to persons or things. The importance of definite, unambiguous pronoun reference cannot be overemphasized; for further discussion and illustrations, see "Working Toward Coherence," pp. 427–39.

Sentence Integrity: Conventions and Exceptions

Conventions

A standard English sentence contains a complete subject and predicate. Violations of the standard confuse the reader and suggest that the writer has been careless and negligent. Therefore the following should be avoided:

1. Careless or indefensible sentence fragment
   a. Treating a participial phrase or verbal as if it were a whole sentence

   > *Wrong:*   Calling frantically to the men on the pier, and pointing to the injured swimmer.

   In this case the participial phrases should be replaced by at least one verb:

   > *Correct:*   He called frantically to the men on the pier, pointing to the injured swimmer.
   >   or
   >   Calling frantically . . ., he pointed. . . .

   > *Wrong:*   She wanted to get *A*'s in all her subjects. Being competitive and ambitious.

   Being is a verbal; the participial phrase modifies *she*.

   > *Correct:*   Being competitive and ambitious, she wanted to get *A*'s in all her subjects.

   b. Treating a subordinate clause as if it were a main clause.

   > *Wrong:*   They wanted to return home as quickly as possible. Where they knew they would be welcome.

   The *where* clause is subordinate and should be joined to its main clause by a comma.

   > *Correct:*   They wanted to return home as quickly as possible, where they knew they would be welcome.

2. Comma splice

This violation of sentence integrity is committed when a connective comma (rather than a period, semicolon, or coordinating conjunction) is used between two main clauses (or sentences), thereby "splicing" the sentence and creating what is called a "run-on" sentence.

Wrong: She simply could not answer the question, it confused her completely.

Correct: She simply could not answer the question. It confused her completely.

> or

She simply could not answer the question; it confused her completely.

> or

She simply could not answer the question, for it confused her completely.

In some cases a comma splice is committed when a comma rather than a semicolon is used before a conjunctive adverb (*however, therefore, thus, nevertheless,* and so on).

Wrong: I wanted to go, however, I could not raise the fare.

Correct: I wanted to go; however, I could not raise the fare.

3. Fused sentence

This violation of sentence integrity consists in writing two sentences with no punctuation between them (no period or semicolon) and no coordinating conjunction.

Wrong: She got to the game on time that kind of punctuality was unusual for her.

Correct: She got to the game on time. That kind of punctuality was unusual for her.

> or

She got to the game on time; that kind. . . .

Exceptions

Divergence from the standard complete sentence is acceptable when you are trying to achieve some special effect, as in the following instances.

1. In the case of the imperative, where the subject is "understood."

Don't go. [subject "understood" to be *you*]

2. An answer to a question.

Was she angry? Not at all.

3. An exclamation.

Never!
What a joy!

4. Part of running dialogue.

"They looked the other way. Didn't want to know the truth."

5. A descriptive word or phrase, set off for emphasis.

The mountains were lofty and ice-capped. An awesome sight.

6. Part of a stream of consciousness in which the thought processes naturally flow in fragments.

This late age of the world's experience had bred in them all, all men and women, a well of tears. Tears and sorrows; a perfectly upright and stoical bearing.

—Virginia Woolf, *Mrs. Dalloway*

7. Appositional sentences, especially where they are used as transitions:

No money, no food.
To return to my original topic, racism.

Let us turn now to the six rhetorical features that are essential to the clarity and readability of a sentence: unity, coherence, emphasis, economy, vigor, and rhythm.

Working Toward Unity

A sentence, however elaborated by modifications and qualifications, should be essentially about *one* thing.

For the very nature of a Sentence implies one proposition to be expressed. It may consist of parts, indeed; but these parts must be so closely bound together as to make the impression upon the mind of one object, not of many.

—Blair, Lecture XI

Thus the reader, who can accommodate only one idea at a time (this being a universal human limitation), can grasp the writer's one idea before moving on to the next. A sentence is unified, then, if it clearly conveys its one main idea; a sentence is not unified if it tries to crowd in so many details that no single idea emerges as *the* idea of the sentence. Similarly, a sentence is not unified if its parts are illogically arranged or if there is needless shifting within the sentence from one subject to another. Let us now consider each of these impediments to sentence unity.

Avoiding Overcrowding

When we talk about unity, we are actually concerned with something inside the writer: his or her idea as it forms in the mind and takes shape on paper. Is it one unified idea that takes a clearly defined shape? Or do many ideas—only vaguely related and vaguely expressed—crowd into one another to form an amorphous mass that buries rather than exhibits its meaning, as in the following sentence?

We think that there is footloose in society, in the enthusiasms with which people become missionaries for the various things in which they take a deep personal interest, a great capacity for helping the other fellow along, and we believe that any leisure-time service should consider its function not alone to the promotion of specific activities, such as athletics, or the arts, but that we should consider as a leisure-time field, in which a great many will find happy outlets for their energies, the pursuit of information or of intellectual culture, not as a matter of schooling but as a matter of post-school avocational interest, and that others can only be served by affording organized outlets for their own leisure enjoyment, in being helpfully identified with causes and movements which are appealing to them, in capacities of service to their group as individuals, or to society at large.

—"Youth . . . Leisure for Living"

To convert this gibberish into well-formed phrases and clauses, we must first isolate the main point, focus it sharply, and state it clearly. Then we must organize the details so that they follow in an orderly sequence. At the same time, we must eliminate meaningless generalities ("post-school avocational interest"). Having done all this, we are ready to convert these "notes" into an intelligibly written statement. In this case we will need more than one sentence:

Improvement: Most people appear to enjoy helping other people: notice how enthusiasts (say, tennis players) try to convert others to their pastime. A leisure-time agency could easily utilize this natural missionary impulse by building a program of social service into its regular program of athletic and cultural activities. Such a program would provide an organized outlet for people who want to do good for individuals in their own communities or for society at large.

Avoiding Piled-Up Phrases

Like the overcrowded sentence (of which it is a variation), the sentence with too many prepositional phrases, one piled on top of the other, confuses the reader because no single coherent idea emerges. There is no rule concerning the number of prepositional phrases that can comfortably be accommodated in a sentence. Suffice it to say that a long string of phrases generally produces a loose, rambling effect. In such cases the writer should eliminate some of the phrases and replace others with single adjectives or adverbs.

Example: Words are the efforts made by an individual to crystallize his or her ideas and thoughts in order to express them in a manner suitable to the mind of a rational creature.

Improvement: Words represent an individual's effort to crystallize and express his or her ideas in a rational manner (or simply "rationally").

Avoiding Illogical Arrangement

Long, rambling sentences are not the only violators of unity. The following short sentence also fails to convey meaning because the hodgepodge arrangement of words on paper simply does not add up to one unified, well-thought-out idea. Indeed, it is impossible to infer from the following exactly what the writer *meant*—or was trying to say.

> If one moves into the sentient, aware sense of intellectual self-development, here too are found barriers to attainment.

Meaningless, confused, illogical, roundabout sentences generally issue from one of two problems: either your thoughts are tangled, or they are not coming out on paper as clearly as you envisioned them. In either case you must work with the sentence itself, examining it critically word by word and asking, "Does it make the clear, logical, unified statement that I have in mind? If not, how can I make it say what I want it to say and not something else?" Only after you have answered these questions can you begin to revise your sentences so that they will convey meaning effectively, so that they will not fall apart in the reader's mind. The writer of the sentence cited above has to rethink the idea itself because the form it took on paper does not make a logical statement.

Another kind of illogical arrangement that may be classified as a violation of unity grows out of a careless, illogical combination of subject and predicate. Rhetoricians call this "faulty predication," a very common problem, illustrated by the following:

> The first step in hiking is comfortable shoes and light clothing.

The writer of this sentence should have asked, as he or she critically reread the first draft, "Are shoes and clothing steps in hiking?" Of course not. The sentence should read:

> The first step in preparing for a hike is to get comfortable shoes and light clothing.
> or
> Before setting out on a hike, one should put on comfortable shoes and light clothing.

Neither of the improved versions is a model of rhetorical splendor, but at least each states a simple idea clearly and accurately, whereas in the original sentence the predicate does not sensibly complete the meaning initiated by the subject.

Working Toward Coherence

A sentence is a sequence of separate words and word clusters—that is, phrases and clauses. How these words are arranged on paper determines what they mean. A careful and skillful arrangement in which the separate parts fit together to form a cohesive structure is clear; an arrangement in which the parts are loosely and haphazardly thrown together or set down as they happen to enter the writer's mind is unclear, perhaps incomprehensible. Working toward coherence, then, means improving the structure of the sentence so that the meaning flows logically and smoothly from one sentence element to the next, thereby enabling the reader to follow and grasp the exact contour of the writer's thoughts as well as its bare substance.

To be able to improve the structure of a sentence, however, we must first understand its dynamic. How does the sentence work? How is it composed? Here we may turn to a modern rhetorician, Francis Christensen, who has formulated what he calls "a generative rhetoric of the sentence" in which he demonstrates that writing a sentence is essentially an "additive" process, that is, a building or adding on to a basic unit.[2] In a paragraph, the basic unit is a topic or lead sentence; in a sentence, the basic unit is a main clause. Like a topic sentence, a main clause is generally stated in general or abstract terms to which the writer adds specific modifiers (subordinate clauses, adjective clusters, verb clusters, prepositional phrases) that expand and enrich the meaning of the predication. Thus a "cumulative sentence," like a "cumulative paragraph," comes into being through the addition or accumulation of specific details.

Specifically, there are six basic ways in which we may add to or expand a minimal sentence:

1. Compounding the base or "head" term in a subject/verb/complement pattern:

   Example: Fresh fruit is good.
   Head word: fruit
   Expansion: Fresh fruit and vegetables are good.

2. Juxtaposing appositive phrases to the head term:

   Expansion: Fresh fruit, a rare treat in any season, is good.

3. Using verbals or verbal phrases (participles, gerunds, infinitives) in the subject/verb/complement pattern:

   Expansion: Oozing with natural juices, fresh fruit is good.

4. Using noun clauses to serve as the subject or complement in the subject/verb/complement pattern:

   Expansion: Whoever eats fresh fruit says that it is good.

5. Using an adjective or adjective clause to modify the head term of the subject or complement in the subject/verb/complement pattern:

   Expansion: Wherever it comes from, fresh fruit is good.

[2]Francis Christensen, "A Generative Rhetoric of the Sentence," in *Notes Toward a New Rhetoric* (New York: Harper & Row, 1967), pp. 1–23.

6. Using an adverb or adverb clause to modify the verb in the subject/verb/complement pattern:

Expansion: Fresh fruit is always good.

Christensen points out that "What you wish to say is found not in the noun but in what you add to qualify the noun. . . . The noun, the verb, and the main clause serve merely as a base on which the meaning will rise. The modifier is the essential part of any sentence."[3] The sentence, then, like the paragraph (as we shall see in the next chapter), frequently exhibits "levels of generality." An example will make this clear:

```
1 He dipped his hands in the bichloride solution and shook them, (main clause)
  2 a quick shake, (noun cluster)
    3 fingers down (absolute—a verb cluster with its own subject)
      4 like the fingers of a pianist above the keys. (prepositional phrase)
                              —Sinclair Lewis (cited in Christensen, p. 9)
```

Here is another, longer example:

```
  2 Calico-coated (adjective cluster)
  2 small-bodied (adjective cluster)
    3 with delicate legs and pink faces in which their mismatched eyes rolled wild
      and subdued (prepositional phrase)
1 they huddled, (main clause)
  2 gaudy, motionless and alert, (adjective series)
  2 wild as deer, (adjective cluster)
  2 deadly as rattlesnakes, (adjective cluster)
  2 quiet as doves. (adjective cluster)
                              —William Faulkner (cited in Christensen, p. 9)
```

It may seem strange to see a sentence laid out in this almost mathematical manner, but it is important to recognize that a well-constructed sentence lends itself to schematization, for any well-constructed sentence has a plan or design. The practiced writer frequently creates the design spontaneously as the product of a well-ordered and trained mind, accustomed to bending words to its will. Just as frequently, however, the design is a result of the careful reworking and polishing of a rough first draft.

In any case, it is well to keep Christensen's schema in mind, for it describes more accurately than the traditionally "diagrammed" sentence how we actually write: we accumulate information as we go along; word follows word on the page; they unite into clusters, phrases, clauses; separate parts combine to form a total statement—a sentence.

The possible methods of expanding a sentence are legion. The simplest example of the "additive process" is the joining of assertions to form a compound sentence:

I eat / and / I drink.

[3]Christensen, p. 25.

Or we may amplify a basic point through a series of modifying details:

> The girl / who had won the scholarship / was celebrating / at a house party / when her parents arrived / to congratulate her.

You should experiment with various alternatives to determine which works best in a given situation. Most important, you should aspire to coherence—a sentence in which the main clause and its added elements flow smoothly and logically into one another, with no interruption or obstacle.

To begin working toward coherence of this kind you must avoid the pitfalls listed below, each of which involves carelessness or misplacement of an added element.

Avoiding Misplaced Modifiers

It was a misplaced modifier that created the amusing song title of some years ago, "Throw Mama from the Train a Kiss." Similarly, it was a misplaced modifier (plus a few missing words) that produced the inadvertently humorous letter written by a serviceman's wife to the welfare service at Lackland Air Force Base: "In accordance with your instructions, I have given birth to twins in the enclosed envelope."

Word order is the principal grammatical process of the English language (the difference in meaning between "Dog bites man" and "Man bites dog" is simply a matter of how identical words are positioned); therefore it is vital that the writer arrange words on paper so that they show accurate relationships. Modifiers should be near the terms they modify, and related ideas should be close together; otherwise they may latch on to some other sentence element where they will not make sense.

Notice how easily the following sentences—each containing a misplaced modifier—can be improved either by repositioning the modifier or by restructuring the sentence slightly so that the reader can readily see what words and word groups are intended to go together:

Example: He saw an accident which he reported yesterday.
Problem: What does "yesterday" modify—the accident or the time of the report?

Improvement: He saw an accident yesterday, which he immediately reported.
               or
               He immediately reported the accident (which) he saw yesterday.

Example: She was the kind of girl who could accept the fact that she was pigeon-toed with a smile.
Improvement: She was the kind of girl who could accept with a smile the fact that she was pigeon-toed.

Example: He was born while the Korean War was in progress in the United States.
Improvement: He was born in the United States while the Korean War was in progress.

In improving sentences with a dangling modifier, the writer must either change the placement of the modifier or revise the syntax of the main clause in the sentence.

Example: Having just returned from a long cruise, the city seemed unbearably hot.

Problem: In *A Dictionary of American-English Usage*, Margaret Nicholson cites this as an example of the often inadvertently funny dangling participle. "The city had not been on the cruise," Nicholson points out—thereby voicing the English teacher's classic protest. Participles must be attached to the noun responsible for the action or they will "dangle." On this ground she revises the sentence to read:

Improvement: Having just returned from a long cruise, we found the city unbearably hot.

A prohibitive attitude toward the dangling participle will be familiar to almost all students, for the construction has long been universally condemned—unfairly so, according to many contemporary writers on usage and style who point out that in most instances the so-called dangling modifier (it may be a gerund or an infinitive as well as a participle) is often modifying the entire main clause, not just the single noun subject. Thus, according to Bergen and Cornelia Evans in *A Dictionary of Contemporary American Usage* (New York: Random House, 1957), it is not misleading or unclear to say "Looking at the subject dispassionately, what evidence is there?" They claim that "this is the idiomatic way of making statements of this kind and any other construction would be unnatural and cumbersome."

The general principle to follow is simply this: if the meaning is obscured or made absurd by a dangling modifier, it should be rewritten so that the sentence makes immediate sense. The reader should never be required to reread the sentence in order to get it right. Thus, in order to be absolutely free of ambiguity, a sentence such as "After finishing college, my family moved to New York" should be improved to read "After I finished college, my family moved to New York."

Avoiding Mixed Constructions

There are times when a writer begins a sentence with one construction in mind and then, somewhere along the way, carelessly shifts to another.

Example: Students know that by getting together to discuss a problem how they can avoid violence.

Improvement: Students know that by getting together to discuss a problem they can avoid violence.

The second version of this sentence is an improvement because the second half of the sentence fulfills the expectation raised in the first half—namely that the subordinating conjunction "that" will be followed by a new subject and predicate. These grammatical terms may mean little or nothing to the average reader who has either forgotten or never really understood grammatical terminology, but the reader nonetheless responds to structural signs.

Thus a reader unconsciously knows that in a sentence beginning "I believe that . . ." a subject and predicate will follow.

> I believe that someone is knocking at the door.
>> or
> I believe that Harry will call.
>> *not*
> I believe that how hard you try is good.

In this last sentence, as in the example cited above, the subordinating conjunction "that" is followed by a second subordinating conjunction, "how." The result is momentary confusion in the reader's mind, for halfway along in the sentence the signals have been abruptly shifted. The implied promise of the sentence has not been fulfilled; the reader's expectations have been thwarted.

It is important to avoid this kind of awkwardness in sentence construction. Actually it is carelessness rather than ignorance that creates such problems, for all native speakers have a deep awareness of the basic structure of English. If you doubt this, consider Lewis Carroll's famous "Jabberwocky" from *Through the Looking-Glass*, which begins:

> 'Twas brillig and the slithy toves
> Did gyre and gimble in the wabe:
> All mimsy were the borogoves,
> And the mome raths outgrabe.

When Alice hears these lines she says: "Somehow it seems to fill my head with ideas—only I don't know exactly what they are!" Actually, the ideas are *patterns*—the structural or grammatical meanings that stand out unmistakably because the lexical meanings have been obliterated. That is, the words themselves do not mean anything, but the *forms* of the words and their arrangement within the line stir the mind to vague recognition. Let us see how this works. First of all, there are certain real words that frame the nonsense words. The verse starts with "it was" ("'Twas"). Ask yourself, what kind of word could follow "'Twas" in this particular line? Certainly not a verb. "'Twas *walked*"? Nobody would ever combine such words in English. Our intuition leads us to such expressions as "it was *lovely*," or "it was *dangerous*," or "it was *special*." Which is to say that "brillig" is probably an adjective and "slithy" is obviously another adjective followed by the noun "toves."

> 'Twas beautiful and the happy girls
> Did dance and frolic in the snow:

Some such statement is being made here. We know it; we feel it; it could not be otherwise. Whatever particular words you might choose to fill in here, they would all have the same *form:* they would be adjective, adjective, noun/verb, verb, noun. The same principles apply to the next two lines:

All mimsy were the borogoves,
And the mome raths outgrabe.

All (adjective) were the (noun),
And the (adjective) (noun) (verb).

All happy were the carolers,
And the young boys rejoiced.

How do we know and why do we feel that these kinds of words fit into these particular places? As modern linguists point out,[4] we are responding here to the structural or grammatical meanings that we learned as children, long before we could read or write. We heard words in certain positions within an utterance: the subject came first, followed by an action, then by an object or adjective. We learned to identify the territories where we could expect to encounter one or another form. In other words, we learned the basic grammatical process of the English language: word order.

We also learned that certain kinds of words changed in set ways; some might have an *s* sound attached to the end, and when they did certain other words would change their form to be in *agreement* with them. Thus we feel that "borogoves" is plural; it has an *s* ending, and the verb that precedes it is a verb that goes with a plural noun. If "borogoves" were singular, the verb preceding it would be "was," not "were."

It does not matter what the individual word denotes here: "borogoves" could mean "cars" or "handkerchiefs." In either case—in *any* case—the structural or grammatical meaning (the terms are interchangeable) remains constant: an *s* ending signals plurality, and an alteration in verb form signals a particular relationship between the verb and the noun. Collectively these changes in form are known as *inflection*. Inflection is the second most important structural device in the English language.

There is a third formal device. Function words such as "the," "and," "by" have no concrete meaning when they stand alone but serve an important function within the context of a sentence. There they help to indicate how substantive words—that is, words with a full referential meaning—such as "water" and "sink" are related: "The water is *in* the sink"; "The shoes are *under* the bed." Function words are *determiners*, or *formal markers*, that help us to identify other words in the sentence and indicate how other words are functioning: as verbs? nouns? adjectives? After all, what a word *is* depends on how it functions in the sentence: one may *jump* across a puddle (verb); one may take a big *jump* (noun); or one may watch a referee at a basketball game toss up a *jump* ball (adjective).

When we find a "the" or "a" preceding words such as "toves" or "wabe," we know that they are words to which an *s* can be added, words that we, using traditional terminology, call "nouns." Thus when we substitute for "borogoves" we automatically do so with another noun. Similarly, by using the function word "and" at the beginning of the fourth line—"and the mome

---

[4]See W. Nelson Francis, "Revolution in Grammar," *Quarterly Journal of Speech*, October 1954.

raths outgrabe"—the writer is telling us that the fourth line conveys a parallel assertion to the assertion in line three, "All mimsy were the borogoves." The past tense "were" (rather than "are") in line three is therefore carried over, by virtue of the connective "and" (a conjunction), to line four. The "borogoves *were*," and the "mome raths" also appear to have completed some action in the past.

The purpose of this long explanation has been to demonstrate that you need not be familiar with the complexities of English grammar to write well-constructed sentences. What you must do is follow your own unconscious knowledge of how words are "signaled" so that you may fulfill the reader's expectations.

Avoiding Other Kinds of Shifts

We have seen that any change in the pattern of a sentence that surprises and stops the reader—even for a fraction of a second—or that disappoints an expectation set up in the early part of the sentence is a violation of coherence, the "sticking together" of the parts that makes the sentence a sound, consistent, and easy-to-read unit. In addition to shifts in the basic pattern of the sentence that produce hybrid constructions, there are other kinds of shifts. They are not as obviously bad as those described above, but equally unnecessary and undesirable because they break up the flow and therefore the coherence of the sentence. These are shifts in voice, tense, mood, and person; we shall consider each of them in turn.

Shift in Voice

Example: When the townspeople heard that the mayor had resigned, a general meeting was called.

Problem: In the above sentence the writer has needlessly shifted from active to passive voice—and this, in turn, has involved a shift in subject from "townspeople" to "meeting." Both of these shifts interfere with the smooth, natural flow of the sentence.

Improvement: When the townspeople discovered that the mayor had resigned, they called a general meeting.

(See "Using Active Voice," pp. 447–48.)

Shift in Tense

Example: They come into the room and began opening up the books that are on the table.

Problem: The writer shifts carelessly from present to past to present tense.

Improvement: They come into the room and begin opening up the books that are on the table.

or

They came into the room and began opening up the books that were on the table.

Shift in Mood

Example: First discuss the problem; then you should take action.

Problem: A needless shift in mode or mood—from imperative, which issues a command or request, to subjunctive, which expresses obligation.

Improvement: First discuss the problem; then take action.

Shift in Person

Example: A student should know the provisions of the Civil Rights Act, for one cannot be a good citizen unless you keep up with current legislation.

Problem: The writer shifts from "student" to "one" to "you."

Improvement: A student should know the provisions of the Civil Rights Act, for he or she cannot be a good citizen unless he or she keeps up with current legislation.

or

You should know the provisions of the Civil Rights Act, for you cannot be a good citizen unless you keep up with current legislation.

Blair sums up the case against unnecessary shifts:

During the course of the Sentence, the scene should be changed as little as possible. We should not be hurried by sudden transitions from person to person, nor from subject to subject. There is commonly, in every Sentence, some person or thing, which is the governing word. This should be continued so, if possible, from the beginning to the end. . . . Should I express myself thus:

After we came to anchor they put me on shore, where I was welcomed by all my friends who received me with the greatest kindness.

In this Sentence, though the objects contained in it have a sufficient connexion with each other, yet by this manner of representing them, by shifting so often both the place and the person, *we* and *they* and *I* and *who,* they appear in such a disunited view that the sense of connexion is almost lost. The Sentence is restored to its proper unity . . . in . . . the following manner:

Having come to anchor, I was put on shore, where I was welcomed by all my friends and received with the greatest kindness.[5]

Avoiding Unclear References

Still another violation of sentence coherence grows out of unclear pronoun reference, a common flaw in student writing. "Reference" suggests that the meaning of a pronoun depends on its antecedent. Strictly speaking, a pronoun is a word used in place of a noun; therefore unless the reader knows precisely what noun or noun clause, what overall idea the pronoun is replacing, the sentence will be neither clear nor coherent.

Example: The women were stopped and questioned by company guards. They then went to the police who refused to protect them. This attitude has also been reported in other towns.

[5]Note the dangling modifier here. Do you find it offensive? Can a person ("I") "come to anchor"? See the discussion on page 431.

Problem: The direct antecedent of "they" in the second sentence is "guards." Yet (as we realize on a second reading) the pronoun is supposed to refer to "women." Still another problem: "This attitude" is not clear. Does the writer mean "this *hostile* attitude"—or what? The pronoun references do not provide a clear and definite guide to meaning because the writer has been careless about antecedents of the personal pronoun and has not supplied enough information to indicate precisely what the demonstrative adjective "this" refers to. It is up to the writer to say *specifically* what he or she means here. The reader should not be asked to fill in a noun and adjectives.

Improvement: After being stopped and questioned by company guards, the women went to the police, who refused to protect them. A similar indifference on the part of the police has been reported in other towns.

Another unclear, ambiguous reference:

Example: Jim's father was president of the college, which gave him considerable prestige.

Problem: Does "him" refer to Jim's father? Technically it does, but is that what the writer means? (The reference of "which" is also vague.)

Improvement: Because his father was president of the college, Jim enjoyed considerable prestige.

Avoiding Unnecessary Splits

Sentence flow or coherence is impaired by the careless separation or splitting of words that belong together, as in the following examples:

Subject Split from Its Verb
Example: Zodomirsky, shocked and grieved at the death of Mariana, becomes a monk.
Improvement: Shocked and grieved at the death of Mariana, Zodomirsky becomes a monk.

Verb Split from Its Object
Example: She sipped slowly and contentedly the warm cocoa.
Improvement: Slowly and contentedly she sipped the warm cocoa.

Verb Split from Its Auxiliaries
Example: He had long ago known the woman.
Improvement: He had known the woman long ago.
or
Long ago he had known the woman.

It should be pointed out here that not all splits are bad. Sometimes, as in the following sentence, the writer deliberately suspends the predication—the signal of the sentence's direction—without losing the flow or continuity of thought.

"Alienation," a term once confined to philosophy, law, psychiatry, and advanced literary criticism, has entered the daily vocabulary.

Using Precise Connectives

Generally speaking, a sentence can be neither coherent nor logical if the writer has not provided precise connectives—that is, conjunctions such as "and," "but," "or," "therefore," "since," "although," and "consequently." These words indicate how the parts of the sentence are related in the writer's mind. Thus the reader looks to these words for a sign of what direction the sentence will take. These words prepare the reader for what is to come; if used accurately, they predict the writer's intent.

To demonstrate, here is a simple exercise in logical predication:[6]

I read the book (,) (;)
- and
- or
- because
- however
- therefore
- after
- although
- consequently

Each of these connectives suggests the type of particulars that will follow "I read the book":

and—Like the plus sign (+) in arithmetic, the coordinating conjunction "and" suggests an addition of comparable (or coordinate) importance:

I read the book and I enjoyed it.
 or
I read the book and I wrote a letter.

As Frank C. Flowers wrote,

In both sentences, the added clauses involve balanced AGENT–ACT sequences. The balance would be disturbed logically if the sentence were to read "I read the book, and Tom is a senior." The two thoughts do not seem to "add" as parts of a normal context. There seems to be no reason why these two expressions should be joined. Logicians would say of the second thought *"non sequitur"*. . . "it does not follow logically."

or—This coordinating conjunction signals that an alternative rather than a simple addition is about to follow:

I read the book, or at least *tried* to read it.

because—This subordinating conjunction anticipates a causal relationship:

I read the book because it was assigned.

Here again the connective prepares the reader for a particular type of statement—a reason *why*. Should this explanation fail to appear in the

[6]Adapted from Frank C. Flowers, "Logic and Composition," in *Practical Linguistics for Composition* (New York: The Odyssey Press, 1968), pp. 77–83.

second half of the sentence, the sentence falls apart in the reader's mind (as it has in the writer's). Witness the following example, which produces gibberish:

I read the book because suntan lotion prevents sunburn.

however—This connective (called a conjunctive adverb) functions like the simple conjunction "but"; it predicts a qualification of, or contrast to, what might be expected:

I read the book, but I did not enjoy it.
  or
I read the book; however, I did not enjoy it.

therefore—This conjunctive adverb tells the reader that "I read the book" and provides a reason for what follows:

I read the book; therefore I understand these issues.

after—Connectives such as "after" and "before" alert the reader to the introduction of a time element:

I read the book after I had talked to the professor.
  or
I read the book after dinner.

although—Like "however," this conjunction foretells qualification and contrast, a possible reversal of expectations:

I read the book, although I did not want to.

consequently—Like "therefore," this term signals reason and result, suggesting (however faintly) a time element—that is, the consequences resulting over a period of time:

I read the book; consequently I was able to lead the class discussion on Friday.

Avoiding Weak Connectives

In addition to using connectives precisely, you should avoid small, loose connectives that detract from the impact of a statement. As an example, we may look at Wilson Follett's observation in *Modern American Usage* on the use of "as."

The novice's resort to *as* with the meaning *since* or *because* is always feeble. It makes trivial what follows. Webster (1934 edition) remarks: "*As* assigns a reason even more casually than *since.*" What is worse, the untrained or heedless writer turns to this weak subordinating link to introduce a co-ordinate clause or what should be his main clause. In either case he ruins emphasis. *It was a comparatively unproductive year, as he was dogged by ill health and domestic worries.* For *as* read *for.*

Similarly, the word "so" is a loose connective, more suited to rambling conversation than to writing.

> So I told him I was so angry I could barely contain myself. And so he finally admitted he was so sorry he could hardly stand it. And so I said "forget it." So we made up and so I'm seeing him again tonight.

Where "so" is used as an intensifier ("I was so happy") it can usually be eliminated without loss, for like most so-called intensifiers ("I really was happy," "I truly was so very happy") it does not work.[7] In fact, it may produce a reverse effect by creating uneasiness and suspicion. "Exactly how happy is so happy?" the reader may wonder. "Why is the writer being vague and seemingly inarticulate and insistent?"

The use of "so" to introduce a clause of purpose or a clause of result is equally ineffective, although the usage is clearly established in informal conversation.

> I wanted to see the town so I asked them to take me along.
> The glass was broken so I had to get another.

Even here the link provided by "so" is weak and can be made more emphatic by using "so that."

> The glass was broken so that I had to get another.

Better still, the first half of the sentence can be subordinated.

> Because (or since) the glass was broken, I had to get another.

Working Toward Economy

Loose writing is often said to be a reflection of loose thinking; if so, verbosity is a root flaw. Frequently, however, loose writing is a sign not so much of loose thinking as of not enough work, specifically not enough reworking and revising of the original sentence. That first spontaneous overflow simply cannot be trusted to convey meaning in a clear, concise, and effective manner. "With years of practice," as editor Norman Cousins has observed, "a man may be able to put down words swiftly and expertly. But it is the same kind of swiftness that enables a cellist, after having invested years of effort, to negotiate an intricate passage from Haydn."[8]

Those of us who are not experts will probably need more than one try at most sentences, for people are naturally wordy. Indeed, as George Orwell observed in "Politics and the English Language," "It is easier—even quicker once you have the habit—to say *In my opinion it is not an unjustifiable assumption that* than to say *I think*."

We cannot very well trim our conversation as we go along, nor can we go

---

[7]See "Avoid ineffective intensifiers," p. 441.
[8]Norman Cousins, *Present Tense: An American Editor's Odyssey* (New York: McGraw-Hill Book Company, 1967), p. 479.

back and edit it. When we write, however, we can and must do exactly that: we must return to the sentences we have written and rework, recast, rewrite them until they are lean, crisp, and concise, free of what Flaubert so justifiably deplored as fatty deposits. Such "tight" sentences have far more impact on the reader: "'Beware the anger of a quiet man' is superior to 'A quiet man's anger is especially to be feared,' for the same reasons and in the same way that a short, straight shaft is better than a long, crooked one in most machine operations."[9]

Admittedly it is always harder to condense than to write; still there are concrete ways to go about the "boiling down" process: we can eliminate unnecessary words, and we can condense long sentence elements into shorter ones. Let us consider each of these devices in turn.

Eliminating Unnecessary Words

Avoid indirect expressions

Example: Probably the *Encyclopaedia Britannica* would provide one with the choicest information since it spends almost five pages expounding upon Shelley. (20 words)

Improvement: The *Encyclopaedia Britannica,* with five full pages on Shelley, is probably the best source. (14 words)

Example: Without words and what they communicate both connotatively and denotatively, human beings would be reduced to the level of lower primates. (21 words)

Improvement: Without language human beings would be reduced to the level of the lower primates. (14 words)

Example: The agnostic is one who holds that he has no knowledge of God; indeed that the human mind is incapable of knowing whether there is or is not a God. (30 words)

Improvement: An agnostic maintains that the human mind has no way of knowing [or "cannot know"] whether or not God exists. (14–17 words)

Avoid useless repetition

Example: He sees not only the world of man, but instead he also sees the world of God.

Improvement: He sees both the world of man and the world of God.

Example: The main portion of the story dealt with Robert Peel's political life, an aspect of his life that was very active.

Improvement: The main portion of the story dealt with Robert Peel's very active political life.

Example: The average person in high school is a combination of both of these types, having a balance of both of these types of characteristics.

Improvement: The average high school student combines the characteristics of both types.

[9]Jackson Burgess, "Sentence by Sentence," *College Composition and Communication* 14 (Dec. 1963).

Avoid negative phrasing
Example: I find myself not in complete agreement with you.
Improvement: I disagree with you.

Example: I do not have much faith in his honesty.
Improvement: I distrust him.

Example: She was not very often on time.
Improvement: She usually arrived late.
                         or
                 She usually was late.

Example: I do not expect to be misunderstood.
Improvement: I expect to be understood.

Avoid loose, inexact verbs
Example: He felt that the best way to avoid temptation was to get her to leave.
Improvement: He felt that the best way to avoid temptation was to make her leave.

Avoid ineffective intensifiers ("really") and qualifiers ("rather")
Example: A *Farewell to Arms* was the novel which really first made Hemingway a commercial success.
Improvement: A *Farewell to Arms* was Hemingway's first commercially successful novel.

Example: The most powerful force in all the world is love.
Improvement: The most powerful force in the world is love.

Example: He was a somewhat quiet man.
Improvement: He was a quiet man.

Avoid anticipatory phrases such as "it is," "there was"[10]
Example: It is for the above-mentioned reasons that I abandoned the project.
Improvement: For the above-mentioned reasons I abandoned the project.

Example: There were crowds of people milling about.
Improvement: Crowds of people were milling about.

Example: The reason that he voted for the independent candidate was that she had an antiwar record.
Improvement: He voted for the independent candidate because she had an antiwar record.

Avoid redundance
Example: Her dress was pink in color.
Improvement: Her dress was pink.

Example: The professor introduced a new innovation.
Improvement: The professor introduced an innovation.

[10]This principle generally applies, although with notable exceptions: specifically when the extra words contribute to the rhythm of the sentence or when they help to build the sentence toward an appropriately emphatic climax.

Avoid deadwood (words that carry no meaning)

Example: In many cases students are now working along the lines of discussing controversial issues with the administration.

Improvement: Many students are now discussing controversial issues with the administration.

Example: He is working in the interest of political unity.

Improvement: He is working toward political unity.

Example: That society is an interesting one.

Improvement: That society is interesting.

Example: She was aware of the fact that he had not returned her paper.

Improvement: She was aware that he had not returned her paper.

Here is a list of common deadwood expressions that pad rather than add to the meaning of a sentence:

along the lines of	in the interest of
to the extent that	of the nature of
the fact that	owing to the fact that
seems to me to be	with reference to
of the character that	tends to be
on the level of	may be said to be

Note how easily many such useless and cumbersome expressions can be abbreviated.

at that time	then
at some future time	after
in the event that	if
is aware of	knows
by virtue of	through
owing to the fact that	because
in spite of the fact that	despite
he is a man who	he
is likely to	may
was of the opinion that	believed
the question as to whether	whether
to be desirous of	to want
the great percentage of	most
to be deficient in	to lack
in a slow manner	slowly
there is no doubt that	undoubtedly
it may be assumed that	supposedly
as an example	
or	
an example is	for example
to take into consideration	to consider

Condensing Long Sentence Elements

Reduce predications

Example: If we follow such a policy it may have the desired effect of convincing the U.S.S.R. that we mean business.

Improvement: Following this policy may convince the U.S.S.R. that we mean business.

Subordinate independent clauses

Example: Honor was important to both Stamm and Zodomirsky, and as a result of it they were both hurt.
Improvement: Because honor was important to both Stamm and Zodomirsky, they were both hurt.

Example: In many cases, people have trouble finding ways to use up idle time. This is especially true of Sundays, when they have been removed from the cares of work.
Improvement: Many people have trouble using idle time, especially on Sundays, when they do not have to work.

Example: It has been shown throughout history that some people are ahead of their time. Such is the case with Galileo and Newton.
Improvement: Throughout history some people, like Galileo and Newton, have been ahead of their time.

Example: In the second section complications are introduced by Mariana. She begs Zodomirsky not to duel. This begging causes Zodomirsky to face a conflict between his honor as a man and his love for Mariana.
Improvement: In the second section complications are introduced by Mariana, who begs Zodomirsky not to duel, thereby creating in him a conflict between honor and love.

Reduce clause to phrase or adjective

Example: Einstein, who was one of the most brilliant men of all time, behaved in a manner that was warm and human.
Improvement: Einstein, one of the most brilliant men of all time, was a warm human being.

Example: After his working day was completed, he stopped in at the same tavern which he visited nightly.
Improvement: Every night after he finished work, he stopped in at [or "went to"] the same tavern.

Example: I picked up the papers which were on the desk.
Improvement: I picked up the papers on the desk.

Example: He was introducing considerations which had nothing to do with the case.
Improvement: He was introducing extraneous considerations.

Reduce phrase to adjective

Example: This passage from the Bible is noted for its style, which is simple and eloquent.
Improvement: This biblical passage is noted for its simple eloquence.

In summary, we should aspire to spareness and leanness of style, taking care not to go to the other extreme of making our style so spare as to be telegraphic:

We shall always find our Sentences acquire more vigour and energy when ... retrenched: provided always that we run not into the extreme of pruning so very close, as to give a hardness and dryness to style. For here, as in all other things, there is a due medium. Some regard, though not the principal, must be had to fullness and swelling of sound. Some leaves must be left to surround and shelter the fruit.

—Blair, Lecture XII

Working Toward Emphasis

In a properly emphatic sentence every word and every group of words are given what Blair calls "due weight and force." The clues as to what is most important in the sentence and what is less important can to some extent be built into the grammatical construction of the sentence. Main ideas can be placed in the main clause and subordinate ideas can be placed in a subordinate clause. Important elements can also be placed in emphatic positions in a sentence so that they make a deeper impression on the reader's mind. Let us consider each of these grammatical constructions in turn.

Putting Main Idea in Main Clause

It is an oversimplification to say that the main idea should always be placed in the main clause, and subordinate points in the subordinate clause; but it represents a helpful technique that can be easily demonstrated. If, for example, you have two points of information to present in a sentence—(1) that you were walking in the park, and (2) that you saw a thief steal a woman's purse—you certainly would want to emphasize the second point for that is clearly the *news* of the sentence: that you were witness to a theft. Thus you would be wise to subordinate the background information by placing it in a subordinate rather than in a coordinate position:

Example: I was walking in the park and I saw a man snatch a woman's purse.

Problem: This coordinate construction distributes importance equally to both halves of the sentence. Actually, however, the two halves are not equal and should not be made to seem so. The first clause should be made subordinate.

Improvement: As I was walking in the park, I saw a man snatch a woman's purse.

This second form makes it clear that you just happened to be walking in the park at the time of the incident. The incident itself, the point of your statement and the part that you will develop in succeeding sentences, is that you saw a purse snatched. By embodying the greater importance of this point in your grammatical construction, you are focusing attention where it belongs and moving the reader toward completion of the story you have initiated.

In general, ideas should not be indiscriminately connected by the coordinating conjunction "and." This produces a loose, unemphatic statement that—at the extreme—can sound childlike: "I was walking in the park and I saw a man take a lady's purse and I ran to a policeman and he asked me what the man looked like and I said he was very tall and. . . ."

Using Emphatic Positions

You can also achieve proper emphasis in a sentence by positioning important elements as Blair suggests:

[Another principle] for promoting the Strength of a Sentence . . . is to dispose of the capital [important] word or words in that place of the Sentence where they will make the fullest impression. That such capital words there are in every Sentence on which the meaning principally rests, every one must see; and that these words should possess a conspicuous and distinguished place is equally plain. Indeed, that place of the Sentence where they will make the best figure, whether the beginning or the end or sometimes even in the middle cannot, as far as I know, be ascertained by any precise rule. This must vary with the nature of the Sentence. . . . For the most part, with us, the important words are placed in the beginning of the Sentence. So Mr. Addison:

> The pleasures of the imagination, taken in their full extent, are not so gross as those of sense, nor so refined as those of the understanding.

And this, indeed, seems the most plain and natural order, to place that in the front which is the chief object of the proposition we are laying down. Sometimes, however, when we intend to give weight to a Sentence, it is of advantage to suspend the meaning for a little, and then bring it out full at the close:

> Thus [says Mr. Pope] on whatever side we contemplate Homer, what principally strikes us is his wonderful invention.

—Blair, Lecture XII

Thus, the beginning of the sentence and, especially, the end are the emphatic positions. In the unfolding of a sentence, as in the unfolding of an essay, the last words stand out and impress themselves most forcibly on the reader. To fail to take advantage of this, to allow a sentence to trail off with empty qualifying phrases, insignificant afterthoughts, or weak monosyllables such as "it," "was," "done," "is," "etc.," is not only to ignore an extremely important psychological resource but also to create a sense of anticlimax, of a sentence continuing past its natural and proper end.

Example: The advances of the future must be made in the moral as well as the technological sphere, according to the commencement speaker.

Improvement: According to the commencement speaker, the advances of the future must be made in the moral as well as the technological sphere.

Example: Hawthorne was haunted throughout his life by the evil deeds his ancestors had done.

Improvement: Hawthorne was haunted throughout his life by the evil deeds of his ancestors.

Example: The word is the basic unit of language and what we communicate with.

Improvement: The word is the basic unit of language with which we communicate.

Note that in the last example the final preposition has been moved to a less prominent middle position. This was done not because the final preposition is in itself bad, as the old rule proclaims ("Never end a sentence with a preposition"), but rather because it is an unemphatic word that ends the sentence weakly. Actually, where idiom demands it, a final preposition is acceptable:

I did not know what to put it in.

Where idiom does not demand a final preposition, however, it should be avoided, along with all small "inconsiderable words" as Blair terms them, referring to adverbs, participles, conjunctions.

For besides the want of dignity which arises from those monosyllables at the end, the imagination cannot avoid resting for a little on the import of the word which closes the sentence; and as those prepositions [and other weak words] have no impact of their own but only serve to point out the relations of other words, it is disagreeable for the mind to be left pausing on a word which does not by itself produce any idea nor form any picture in the fancy.

—Blair, Lecture XII

Varying Normal Word Order

Because the normal and familiar pattern of the English sentence is subject/verb/object ("I don't like him"), any variation in this pattern calls attention to itself and thereby emphasizes the point being expressed ("Him I don't like"). The second sentence intensifies the predication because it wrenches subject and object out of their expected positions. The subject no longer opens the sentence; the object no longer follows the verb. Instead the word "him" opens the sentence—an unusual location for a pronoun in the objective case. Clearly, then, this sentence informs the reader that this is no ordinary dislike, just as this is no ordinary sentence. The inexperienced writer might try to get the point across by using weak intensifiers ("I really dislike him very very much"); the simple transposition of pronouns is far more economical and successful.

Achieving emphasis through transposition is not necessarily a conscious process. The strength of our feelings often dictates a spontaneous switching of terms:

That I cannot believe!

Oh, the troubles I've had!

Never will I do that again!

We can also make conscious use of this device in such simple transpositions as the ones listed below, all of them effective as emphasizers of what might otherwise be mundane observations.

Cold was the night.

Come winter and we'll see the fall of snow.

Of this plan, he knew nothing.

First a warning, musical; then the hour, irrevocable. [referring to Big Ben striking]
—Virginia Woolf, *Mrs. Dalloway*

Working Toward Vigor

Closely allied to economy and emphasis is vigor: a lean, tightly constructed sentence with movement and energy built into its structure. Such a sentence, as Bishop Whately wrote long ago, will "stimulate attention, excite the Imagination, and . . . arouse the feelings."[11] A vigorous sentence will probably be written in the active rather than in the passive voice and will contain a strong, substantial verb rather than a weak, colorless verb such as "is," "was," "does," or "has."

Using Active Voice

"Voice" indicates whether the subject of a sentence acts or is acted upon, whether the subject is the doer of the action or the receiver.

I hit the ball.

This is active voice because the subject, "I," is the actor or doer.

The ball was hit.

This is passive voice because the subject, "ball," receives the action of being hit.

Once we are aware of the distinction between active and passive voice, we cannot fail to see that in general the active voice is more lively and assertive than the passive, which tends—as the term "passive" suggests—to lack immediacy.

Example: The test was taken by the students.
Improvement: The students took the test.

Example: College students were recruited by the township and a new
                project was begun.
Improvement: The township recruited college students and set up a new
                project.

Sentences in the active voice are stronger and more emphatic for two reasons. First, they are more economical: the active voice generally requires

[11]Richard Whately, *Elements of Rhetoric* (Boston and Cambridge: James Munroe and Company, 1854).

fewer words. Second, the *real* subject is emphasized because it is also the *grammatical* subject: "students" in the first example above is the *real* subject of the sentence, not "test." But we should also recognize that in some cases the passive voice is preferable: when the doer of the action is unknown ("The house was robbed"); when the receiver of the action, rather than the doer, has to be emphasized ("Shoplifters will be prosecuted"); and in formal report writing, where it is conventional for a writer to be anonymous ("The test was run and the following results obtained").

Despite these important exceptions, you should try, whenever possible, to strengthen and enliven your sentences by converting unnecessary and awkward passives into the active voice.

Concentrating Activity in Verbs

The second way to invigorate a sentence is to concentrate its action in substantial, well-chosen verbs, avoiding wherever possible weak verbs such as "is," "was," "has," and "does." Shakespeare habitually used strong verbs rather than the weak state-of-being forms ("is" and "was"). When he did use them, he exacted from them their deepest existential meaning: "To be or not to be, that is the question."

The careless writer often uses a weak, roundabout verb form or inadvertently wastes the action of the sentence on a noun.

Example: He felt an obvious hatred for the new recruit.
Improvement: He obviously hated the new recruit.

Example: Thoreau became a complete recluse from society in his shack at Walden Pond.
Improvement: Thoreau secluded himself in his shack at Walden Pond.

Example: In this anthology are some of the best haiku and tanka verse ever written.
Improvement: This anthology contains some of the best haiku and tanka verse ever written.

Example: There were two contributing factors to this situation.
Improvement: Two factors contributed to this situation.

Example: There was a car moving in circles around the speedway.
Improvement: A car moved in circles around the speedway.
or
A car circled the speedway.

Note that when we exploit the peculiar power of the verb to invigorate a sentence, we have at the same time tightened the sentence by reducing the number of words and phrases. We have also pinpointed the action of the sentence on one vivid verb, instead of wasting it on a noun ("Thoreau became a recluse") or a participle ("a car moving").

Choosing Concrete, Specific Words

A third way to promote vigor in the sentence is to use words that are specific and concrete rather than general and abstract ("the tall, red-haired soldier at the end of the line" rather than "that man over there"). (See Chapter 25, "Choosing Words.")

Working Toward Rhythm

Although rhythm is usually associated with poetry, it is a feature of prose writing as well. Indeed, anyone who has ever listened to a sentence read aloud knows that it is a unit not only of meaning but also of rhythm and sound. There is no better guide to good writing than the ear, because what sounds good usually reads well. Conversely, what is jarring, overly intricate, or unpronounceable is usually hard to read and just as hard to understand. Thus it is wise to test your sentences on your ear, to *listen* to the sound of the words—both individually and in combination—and to *feel* their rising and falling action. As one writer has noted,

an author who would please or move his readers will often wish to do so by sound as well as sense. Here rhythm becomes important. Feeling tends to produce rhythm; and rhythm, feeling. Further, a strong rhythm may have a hypnotic effect, which holds the reader, as the Ancient Mariner held the wedding guest; prevents his attention from wandering; and makes him more suggestible.[12]

It should be admitted that basically prose rhythm defies strict analysis and is probably "dictated by some inner pressure, hardly felt at the time, just as the rhythms of poetry seem to come into the head almost unbidden."[13] We may speculate that rhythm is associated with physical sensations: the writer's rate of breathing, heartbeat, pulse, metabolism. Similarly for the reader, a good sentence meets what Flaubert called "the needs of respiration." The sentence must "breathe" correctly—provide pauses where needed, change of pace, slowing down, speeding up. "A good sentence," Flaubert concluded, "should be like a good line of poetry, *unchangeable,* just as rhythmic, just as resonant."

Certainly the musical quality of the sentence cannot be denied, but neither can it be described easily in a short space. It will suffice to quote Blair once again, for his observations on "harmony"—though brief—are germane:

Let us consider agreeable sound, in general, as the property of a well-constructed Sentence. . . . This beauty of musical construction in prose, it is plain, will depend upon two things; the choice of words, and the arrangement of them.

I begin with the choice of words; on which head, there is not much to be said, unless I were to descend into a tedious and frivolous detail concerning the powers of the several letters, or simple sounds, of which Speech is composed. It is evident, that words are most agreeable to the ear which are composed of smooth and liquid sounds, where there is a proper intermixture of vowels and consonants; without too

[12]F. L. Lucas, *Style* (New York: Macmillan, 1962), p. 215.
[13]Marjorie Boulton, *The Anatomy of Prose* (London: Routledge and Kegan Paul Ltd., 1954), p. 68.

many harsh consonants rubbing against each other; or too many open vowels in succession, to cause a hiatus, or disagreeable aperture of the mouth. It may always be assumed as a principle, that whatever sounds are difficult in pronunciation, are, in the same proportion, harsh and painful to the ear. Vowels give softness; consonants strengthen the sound of words. The music of Language requires a just proportion of both; and will be hurt, will be rendered either grating or effeminate by an excess of either. Long words are commonly more agreeable to the ear than monosyllables. They please it by composition, or succession of sounds which they present to it: and, accordingly, the most musical languages abound most in them. Among words of any length, those are the most musical, which do not run wholly either upon long or short syllables, but are composed of an intermixture of them; such as, *repent, produce, velocity, celerity, independent, impetuosity.*

The next head, respecting the Harmony which results from a proper arrangement of the words and members of a period, is more complex, and of greater nicety. For, let the words themselves be ever so well chosen, and well sounding, yet, if they be ill disposed, the music of the Sentence is utterly lost. . . . In English, we may take, for an instance of a musical Sentence, the following from Milton, in his Treatise on Education:

> We shall conduct you to a hill-side, laborious indeed, at the first ascent; but else, so smooth, so green, so full of goodly prospects, and melodious sounds on every side, that the harp of Orpheus was not more charming.

Every thing in this Sentence conspires to promote the Harmony. The words are happily chosen; full of liquid and soft sounds; *laborious, smooth, green, goodly, melodious, charming:* and these words so artfully arranged, that were we to alter the collocation of any one of them, we should, presently, be sensible of the melody suffering. For, let us observe, how finely the members of the period swell one above another. "So smooth, so green,"—"so full of goodly prospects, and melodious sounds on every side;"—till the ear, prepared by this gradual rise, is conducted to that full close on which it rests with pleasure;—"that the harp of Orpheus was not more charming."

—Blair, Lecture XIII

Rhythm and harmony are matters too complex to contemplate here with any thoroughness. We shall simply consider four basic rhetorical devices that contribute to the rhythmic and euphonious arrangement of sentence elements: (1) parallel construction; (2) balanced antithesis; (3) order of climax; (4) variation in sentence length, pattern, and type.

Parallel Construction

More than any other single resource available to the writer, parallel construction—repetition of sentence elements ("I came, I saw, I conquered")—provides a basis for rhythm in prose. Listen to these familiar words from Lincoln's Gettysburg Address: " . . . we cannot dedicate, we cannot consecrate, we cannot hallow this ground." Rhythmically, this sentence approaches poetry, as we can hear by noting the measured beat in each clause:

        ′ × ×   ′ × ×
we cannot dedicate,

        ′ × × ′ × ×
we cannot consecrate,

        ′ × × ′ ×   ×   ′
we cannot hallow this ground.

Or, if you wish to stress different syllables:

        × ′   ′   ′ × ×
we cannot dedicate,

        × ′   ′   ′ × ×
we cannot consecrate,

        × ′   ′   ′ ×   ×   ′
we cannot hallow this ground.

The casting of like ideas in like grammatical form improves a sentence on almost every count. It tightens, enlivens, and unifies. It also makes the sentence more emphatic and coherent, because likeness of form enables the reader to recognize more readily likeness of content: each item in a parallel series announces itself as a companion to the others—a comparable action:

> They were walking, running, leaping. (three participles)

Because the meaning of such a sentence is reinforced by its structure and rhythm, a direction issued in parallel form is easier to grasp:

> Walk, do not run, to the nearest exit. (two imperative verbs)

Similarly, a longer sentence that contains a series of observations or many details and qualifications is held together by a framework of parallelism.

> The only advice . . . that one person can give another about reading is to take no advice, to follow your own instincts, to use your own reason, to come to your own conclusions.
>
> —Virginia Woolf, *The Second Common Reader*

(Note the series of four infinitives: "to take . . . , to follow . . . , to use . . . , to come. . . .")

> Jealousy of Mr. Elliot had been the retarding weight, the doubt, the torment. That had begun to operate in the very hour of first meeting her in Bath; that had returned, after a short suspension, to ruin the concert; and that had influenced him in every thing he had said and done, or omitted to say and do, in the last four-and-twenty hours.
>
> —Jane Austen, *Persuasion*

(Note that in the first sentence above the three complements of "had been" are nouns presented in order of rising intensity: "weight," "doubt," "torment." In the second, longer sentence the parts are held in place by the three long "that" clauses, in the last of which there is parallelism within the parallel: "every thing he had said and done, or omitted to say and do. . . .")

Parallelism combined with repetition of key words produces an especially tight and emphatic rhythmic unit.

No fact, however interesting, no image, however vivid, no phrase, however striking, no combination of sounds, however resonant, is of any use to a poet unless it fits: unless it appears to spring inevitably out of its context.
—Northrop Frye, "New Directions from Old"

The careless and inexperienced writer is apt to overlook both the semantic and rhythmic significance of arranging like ideas in parallel form. He or she does not realize that when the items themselves correspond to one another, the reader expects to find the words in corresponding form and is disappointed if they are not.

Example: They liked to go to the movies, hiking in the mountains, and on long rainy days they would sleep the whole afternoon.

Problem: The writer has expressed three comparable activities in three different grammatical forms: an infinitive phrase, a participial phrase, and a clause.

Improvement: They liked to go to the movies, to hike in the mountains, and on long rainy days to sleep the whole afternoon.
or
They liked going to the movies, hiking in the mountains, and— on long rainy days—sleeping the whole afternoon.

Example: The course grade is based on three factors: what you do in the final examination, writing a term paper, and classwork.

Problem: Here again, three ideas of equal importance are expressed in three different grammatical forms: a relative clause, a participial phrase, and a single noun.

Improvement: The course grade is based on three factors: a final examination, a term paper, and classwork.

Balanced Antithesis

It has long been recognized that when two ideas stand in opposition to each other, the contrast or tension between them (the "is" versus the "is not"; the "either . . . or") can be emphasized by setting them forth in a form of parallelism called *balanced antithesis*.

Either we live by accident and die by accident; or we live by plan and die by plan.
—Thornton Wilder, *The Bridge of San Luis Rey*

The tragedy of life is not that man loses but that he almost wins.
—Heywood Broun

Talent, Mr. Micawber has; money, Mr. Micawber has not.
—Charles Dickens, *David Copperfield*

(Note that Dickens has achieved further emphasis by inverting normal word order.)

The force and binding power of balanced antithesis rest basically on parallel constructions in which key words are repeated in an opposite

context. Note the impact, for example, of President Kennedy's famous statement.

Ask not what your country can do for you; ask what you can do for your country.

One way to emphasize a balanced antithesis is to pair words through
alliteration:

Both poems are didactic: one preaches, one praises.

Yonder is one whose years have calmed his passions but not clouded his reason.
—Samuel Johnson, *Rasselas*

As Herbert Read noted, "used with discretion [balanced antithesis] adds
point and vivacity to expression; but when abused it becomes tedious and
artificial."[14]

Order of Climax

But in a larger sense we cannot dedicate, we cannot consecrate, we cannot hallow
this ground.

Note that, in addition to casting this sentence in a parallel construction,
Lincoln carefully organized its three verbs in climactic order, moving from
the least commitment ("to dedicate" is to set aside ground); to a deeper
commitment ("to consecrate" is to declare the ground sacred); to the very
deepest commitment ("to hallow" is to perpetually honor the ground as
holy). Thus, Lincoln fulfilled the requirements of a rhythmic as well as a
properly emphatic statement; he did not allow his sentence to fall off at the
end. Indeed, he arranged the verbs so that they would grow both in meaning
and in rhythmic impact. The importance of rising action cannot be over-
stressed, for it rests on the natural human expectation that items in a series
will intensify as they progress. Surely it was this recognition that led Jane
Austen in the sentence cited earlier to describe jealousy in progressively
more oppressive terms: first as a "retarding weight," then as a "doubt," and
finally as a "torment." To reverse the order (a "torment," a "doubt," a
"retarding weight") would create an anticlimax—a letdown instead of a
buildup. Thus, as Blair wrote, the writer should always make certain that the
"members" of a sentence

go on rising and growing in their importance above one another. This sort of
arrangement . . . is always a beauty in composition. From what cause it pleases is
abundantly evident. In all things we naturally love to ascend to what is more and
more beautiful, rather than to follow the retrograde order. Having had once some
considerable object set before us, it is with pain we are pulled back to attend to an

[14]Herbert Read, *English Prose Style* (Boston: Beacon Press, 1955), p. 40.

inferior circumstance. . . . The same holds in melody . . . : that a falling off at the end always hurts greatly. For this reason particles, pronouns, and little words, are as ungracious to the ear, at the conclusion, as I formerly showed they were inconsistent with strength of expression. It is more than probable that the sense and sound here have a mutual influence on each. That which hurts the ear seems to mar the strength of meaning; and that which really degrades the sense, in consequence of this primary effect appears also to have a bad sound.

—Blair, Lecture XIII

Variation in Sentence Length, Pattern, and Type

A succession of declarative sentences written in the conventional subject/verb/object order, with an average length of fourteen to twenty words, or two lines apiece, would produce a droning monotone. After a while the sameness of rhythm and pattern, the lack of emphasis, would dull the reader's senses and send his or her attention elsewhere. Note the tiresome succession of short, choppy sentences in the following paragraph:

> Hemingway's works abound in war, violence, and death. Hemingway had firsthand experience with all three. He took in two world wars. He also participated in smaller wars. They made him see death without disguise. He had no heroic illusions. [Note gap in thought here.] Life and death were intermingled in the minds of his characters.

Most writers intuitively vary sentence length because the mind in the process of composition tends to express itself in unequal "waves" of thought. Note in the following paragraph, for example, how John Steinbeck's sentences range in length from three words to forty-two:

Sentence Length

Average (27 words)   When I was very young and the urge to be someplace else was on me, I was assured by mature people that maturity would cure this itch.

Short (12 words)   When years described me as mature, the remedy prescribed was middle age.

Average (25 words)   In middle age I was assured that greater age would calm my fever and now that I am fifty-eight perhaps senility will do the job.

Short (3 words)   Nothing has worked.

Average (20 words)   Four hoarse blasts of a ship's whistle still raise the hair on my neck and set my feet to tapping.

Long (42 words)   The sound of a jet, an engine warming up, even the clopping of shod hooves on pavement brings on the ancient shudder, the dry mouth and vacant eye, the hot palms and the churn of stomach high up under the rib cage.

Average (15 words)   In other words, I don't improve; in further words, once a bum always a bum.

Short (6 words)   I fear the disease is incurable.

—John Steinbeck, *Travels with Charley*

Similarly, most writers tire of the typical declarative sentence and vary the pattern of their prose with the addition of a rhetorical question, an imperative, an exclamation.

I hate to hear people saying, "He is young, he must wait; he will get plenty of chances." How do they know? Could Keats have waited, or Shelley, or Byron, or Burns?

—J. A. Spender, *The Comments of Bagshot*

Writers also tire of the usual subject/verb/object pattern and automatically alter it so that sentences open differently—sometimes with the subject, other times with a prepositional phrase, an adverb, a subordinate clause.

Sometimes in history, a nation collapses not because of its own flaws but because of the attacking nation's tremendous strength. Was this but the latest example? For years, from Berlin, I had watched Nazi Germany's mercurial rise in military might, which the sleeping democracies in the West did little to match. I had followed, too, at firsthand, Hitler's cynical but amazingly successful diplomacy, which had so easily duped the West and paved the way for one quick military conquest after another. But still the French debacle was quite incomprehensible. Not even the German generals I had talked with in Berlin expected it.

—William Shirer, *The Collapse of the Third Republic*

The most dramatic wrenching of normal word order occurs in the so-called suspended sentence, wherein the writer postpones the predication to the end of the sentence, thereby achieving a kind of "suspense."

The fighter who stays in the ring as long as he can stand on his feet, the man who keeps his business alive while his clothes are threadbare and his stomach empty, the captain who clings to his ship while there is a plank left afloat—that is Washington.

—W. E. Woodward, *George Washington, the Image and the Man*

Because the reader does not know what a suspended sentence is about until the end, he or she will surely get lost or simply give up along the way unless the writer establishes a rhythmic unity that holds the sentence together and moves it toward its climax. This can be achieved only by observing strict parallelism, as in the following example:

How is it that I, who had the biggest Big League Gum collection in the East, who can still recite the lineup of the 1931 World Series (though there isn't much demand for it), who missed supper rather than miss the ball scores on WOR at 7 P.M., who never read the great novels because of a boyhood spent reading baseball news and "The Baseball Magazine" instead—how is it that I, the despair of my parents for an addiction that shut out almost every other field of knowledge, the bane of my sisters for the simulated major league doubleheaders that I played against the side of the house every day with a rubber ball, can hardly bring myself to follow the game today?

—William Zinsser, *Pop Goes America*

Sentences like these gain enormously in emphasis and vigor by virtue of their suspension—the "long and steady climb upward over successive terraces of clauses,"[15]—followed by the final swift descent to the point of the sentence, its predication. Certainly the reader is caught up in the cadence of such a sentence, so that a whole new dimension of rhythmic as well as mental response is elicited.

Not all sentences, it should be said, are as dramatically suspended as the above examples. Frequently the writer introduces a short delay, using words that may seem unnecessary but that serve a rhythmic purpose.

It was not until the other day, when I returned on a visit to Coney Island, that I recalled an important episode of my youth which had been buried all these years.
—Isaac Rosenfeld, in "Coney Island Revisited"

At first we might deplore the seemingly useless "It was" opening of the above sentence. But if we study it more carefully, we will see that this normally poor construction works here; it enables the writer to build a short rhythmic suspense that has more impact than the direct and economical and flat alternative:

> I recalled an important, long-buried episode of my youth the other day when I returned on a visit to Coney Island.

It is commonly supposed, and to some extent true, that a series of short, simple sentences conveys an impression of speed, whereas longer sentences, as Herbert Read noted, "give an air of solemnity and deliberation to writing."[16] Actually, long sentences may move swiftly, provided they are well constructed and flow smoothly and harmoniously from one word group to another. Take the two virtuoso examples that follow:

1. This sentence closes Lytton Strachey's biography of Queen Victoria:

Perhaps her fading mind called up once more the shadows of the past to float before it, and retraced, for the last time, the vanished visions of that long history—passing back and back, through the cloud of years, to older and ever older memories—to the spring woods of Osborne, so full of primroses for Lord Beaconsfield—to Lord Palmerston's queer clothes and high demeanor; and Albert's face under the green lamp, and Albert's first stag at Balmoral, and Albert in his blue and silver uniform, and the Baron coming in through a doorway, and Lord M. dreaming at Windsor with the rooks cawing in the elmtrees, and the Archbishop of Canterbury on his knees in the dawn, and the old King's turkey-cock ejaculations, and Uncle Leopold's soft voice at Claremont, and Lehzen with the globes, and her mother's feathers sweeping down towards her, and a great old repeater-watch of her father's in its tortoise-shell case, and a yellow rug, and some friendly flounces of sprigged muslin, and the trees and the grass at Kensington.
—Lytton Strachey, *Queen Victoria*

---

[15] Stephen Potter, *Our Language* (London: Books, Ltd., 1950).
[16] Read, *English Prose Style*, p. 35.

This long sentence moves back steadily in time, as the writer imagines the queen's "fading mind" moving back through memory to retrace the "vanished visions" of her long life. As her memories pass "back and back, through the cloud of years," so this single sentence moves back and back in a continuous flow of images. One long life is thus encompassed in one long tightly organized sentence that captures in its unity the unity and rhythm of the life it describes.

2. Here is another seemingly endless descriptive sentence, this one suspended:

If the eyes are too big, and they are twice too big, and if they surround a nose that cannot be subdivided, and if the body parts might have been assembled by a weary parent on Christmas Eve, and if the teeth are borrowed from a rabbit soliciting carrots, and if the voice could summon sentry dogs, and if she does not walk so much as lurch, glide and jerk in continuing peril of collapsing like a rag doll dismissed by a bored child, and if on top of that she is saddled with being Judy Garland's first of three children by her second of five marriages, then how can the bearer of these oddments, how can this girl put together in the Flea Market, how can Liza Minnelli, at 23, threaten to become the major entertainment figure that she is becoming?[17]

This sentence is clearly an amusement as well as a description. By piling *if*-clause upon *if*-clause, the writer has tried to intensify the mystery ("Who is this strange creature?" we wonder), and by building on a repetitive "and if . . . and if," he has established an almost breathless musical refrain, moving us, we are led to expect, to some sort of crescendo. Instead, the sentence falls off at the end, contrary to conventional principles of emphasis and harmony. Nonetheless, the sentence succeeds almost despite itself, for it brings us down to earth, again rhythmically. The subject, after all, is not of momentous import (note that most of the words are short and simple); the writer's weak ending seems to tell us that he knows he has been a bit overdramatic, but he has been writing in a spirit of fun. There is clearly a tongue-in-cheek element in this sentence. It is in itself a little essay, light and playful in tone.

Forging a Better Style

As Blair points out in the following passage, the best way to forge a better style is to write slowly and carefully, never aiming directly for speed. At the same time, we must not be too plodding.

Many rules concerning style I have delivered, but no rules will answer the end, without exercise and habit. At the same time, it is not every sort of composing that will improve style. This is so far from being the case, that by frequent, careless, and hasty composition, we shall acquire certainly a very bad style; we shall have more

---

[17]Thomas Thompson, "Judy's Daughter Wants to Be Liza," *Life*, 17 October 1969.

trouble afterwards in unlearning faults, and correcting negligences, than if we had not been accustomed to composition at all. In the beginning, therefore, we ought to write slowly and with much care. Let the facility and speed of writing, be the fruit of longer practice. Says Quintilian, with the greatest reason, "I enjoin, that such as are beginning the practice of composition, write slowly and with anxious deliberation. Their great object at first should be, to write as well as possible; practice will enable them to write speedily. By degrees, matter will offer itself still more readily; words will be at hand; composition will flow; every thing as in the arrangement of a well-ordered family, will present itself in its proper place. The sum of the whole is this; by hasty composition, we shall never acquire the art of composing well; by writing well, we shall come to write speedily."

We must observe, however, that there may be an extreme, in too great and anxious care about words. We must not retard the course of thought, nor cool the heat of imagination, by pausing too long on every word we employ. There is, on certain occasions, a glow of composition which should be kept up, if we hope to express ourselves happily, though at the expense of allowing some inadvertencies to pass. A more severe examination of these must be left to be the work of correction. For, if the practice of composition be useful, the laborious work of correcting is no less so: it is indeed absolutely necessary to our reaping any benefit from the habit of composition. What we have written, should be laid by for some little time, till the ardour of composition be past, till the fondness for the expressions we have used be worn off, and the expressions themselves be forgotten; and then, reviewing our work with a cool and critical eye, as if it were the performance of another we shall discern many imperfections which at first escaped us. Then is the season for pruning redundances; for weighing the arrangement of sentences; for attending to the juncture and connecting particles; and bringing style into a regular, correcting and supported form. This *"Limoe Labor,"* must be submitted to by all who would communicate their thoughts with proper advantage to others; and some practice in it will soon sharpen their eye to the most necessary objects of attention, and render it a much more easy and practicable work than might at first be imagined.

—Blair, Lecture XIX

ASSIGNMENTS

1. Compose appropriate second halves for the sentence below, using each of the connectives and indicating what kind of relationship each of them signals.

   I went to class (,) (;)   and
                               because
                               however
                               therefore
                               after
                               although
                               consequently
                               or
                               but
                               hence
                               since
                               so that
                               so . . . that

indeed
likewise
moreover
specifically
yet
as if

2. Locate the weaknesses in the following sentences, and rewrite each sentence to improve it.

   a. Just as scientific progress has dispelled the belief that an "evil spirit" causes the headache, so has it replaced the former cure of boring holes in the skull with aspirin.
   b. There are more single women than men in the United States, according to the Census Bureau.
   c. Most of the churches have large congregations that are rather wealthy.
   d. In 1870 Pavlov conducted an investigation of the pancreatic nerves and was awarded a gold medal for it.
   e. One old cottage in particular attracted my attention. It was a huge white structure with four gables, one at each corner.
   f. Milton, who was one of the most scholarly men of all time, devoted a good part of his life to activities in the sphere of politics.
   g. She began singing in a coffeehouse in Boston at the age of nineteen.
   h. The author's central purpose is a view of human behavior.
   i. It is important to keep in mind what sin and guilt meant in Hawthorne's use.
   j. He was a man of heroic soul, keen intellect, and quiet wit.
   k. There is a noticeable lack of friends in his life.
   l. On returning to the deck, the sea became dark and turbulent.
   m. The French engineers proposed an alternative plan. Their plan called for the construction of a semicircular dam two hundred fifty feet wide which cost eighty million dollars.
   n. Today's American woman is envied by other women. The main basis for this is her supposed freedom to live as she chooses. This may include such things as travel, studying in college and graduate school, and even day-to-day attire.
   o. There are two basic means of communication of which one is speaking and the other is the use of the written word.
   p. The English hate frogs, but the French love frogs and hate the English, and cut off their hind legs and consider them a great delicacy.
   q. The next morning he was found lying on the floor by a cleaning woman.

3. Comment on the following passages and indicate what factors contribute to their rhetorical effectiveness.

   a. When youth is gone, every man will look back upon that period of life with infinite sorrow and regret. It is the bitter sorrow and regret of a man who knows that once he had a great talent and wasted it, of a man who knows that once he had a great treasure and got nothing from it, of a man who knows that he had strength enough for everything and never used it.

   —Thomas Wolfe

   b. The world of Homer is unbearably sad because it never transcends the immediate moment; one is happy, one is unhappy, one wins, one loses, finally one dies. That is all. Joy and suffering are simply what one feels at the moment; they have no meaning beyond that; they pass away as they came; they point in no direction; they change nothing. It is a tragic world but a world without guilt for its tragic flaw is not a flaw in human nature, still less in an individual character, but a flaw in the nature of existence.

—W. H. Auden, Introduction to *The Portable Greek Reader*

c. Our literature is filled with young people like myself who came from the provinces to the Big Cave, seeking involvement in what one always thought from the outside was a world of incomparable wonder, hoping for some vague kind of literary "fulfillment." In the 1960s, as always since New York became our literary and journalistic marketplace, there would be thousands of them clustered around the great axis of publishing, newspapering, and broadcasting, starting out at minuscule salaries, living in unfamiliar, claustrophobic walk-ups, fighting the dread and alien subways twice a day, coming to terms with the incredible noise and crowdedness. Most of them would not "make it"; the more resourceful and talented might.

Why did we come? Not because the materials for our work did not exist in those places we knew best. Not merely for fame and money and success, for these also some of us could have had, and perhaps in more civilized ways, in places far removed from New York. Not even because we wanted to try ourselves in the big time, and out of curiosity to see how good the competition was. We had always come, the most ambitious of us, because we *had* to, because the ineluctable pull of the cultural capital when the wanderlust was high was too compelling to resist.

—Willie Morris, *North Toward Home*

d. I who am blind can give one hint to those who see—one admonition to those who would make full use of the gift of sight: Use your eyes as if tomorrow you would be stricken blind. And the same method can be applied to the other senses. Hear the music of voices, the song of a bird, the mighty strains of an orchestra, as if you would be stricken deaf tomorrow. Touch each object you want to touch as if tomorrow your tactile sense would fail. Smell the perfume of flowers, taste with relish each morsel, as if tomorrow you could never smell and taste again. Make the most of every sense; glory in all the facets of pleasure and beauty which the world reveals to you through the several means of contact which Nature provides. But of all the senses, I am sure that sight must be the most delightful.

—Helen Keller, *Three Days to See*

e. They went down to the camp in black, but they come back to the town in white; they went down to the camp in ropes, they came back in chains of gold; they went down to the camp with their feet in fetters, but came back with their steps enlarged under them; they went also to the camp looking for death, but they came back from thence with assurance of life; they went down to the camp with heavy hearts, but came back with pipe and tabor playing before them.

—John Bunyan, *Life and Death of Mr. Badman*

f. We sailed early in January, and for nearly a year we wandered from country to country. I saw Egypt. I saw the Pyramids, at noon and at sunset, by moonlight, and at sunrise. I saw the Tombs of the Kings, and the great Temple at Karnak. I saw the lovely vanished Temple of Philae. I saw the coast of Asia Minor, and the harbor of Smyrna. I sailed on the Aegean Sea. I saw the Isles of Greece, and the Acropolis. I saw the Golden Horn in the sunrise, and the minarets and the cypresses of Constantinople. I saw Italy. I saw Switzerland. I saw Paris. I saw London. I saw England in summer. I saw the frozen lakes of Norway, and the midnight sun over the ice fields.

—Ellen Glasgow, *The Woman Within*

27 Writing Paragraphs

The Paragraph as a Cage of Form

When we talk about writing the paragraph, we are talking about the act of writing itself, the actual at-the-desk, word-by-word, sentence-by-sentence writing situation. You are not then thinking about rhetorical principles, but rather about the rush of ideas whirling about in your mind. How can you commit them to paper, capture them, as Archibald MacLeish said, in a "cage of form"? MacLeish's image refers to poetry, but it applies equally to the paragraph, for it is in the paragraph—the major message unit of the piece— that you unfold your ideas, one by one, as your mind dictates and your pen flows.

In this sense it may be said that we write in paragraphs. True, the writing process proceeds sentence by sentence; but the sentence is never written in isolation, only within the context of the paragraph. Certainly we think in paragraphs, or units of thought that we block out as we write, indenting every so often when it seems "time" to do so. Interestingly, this intuitive approach works well, for studies have shown that most people instinctively begin a new paragraph at the right place: where there is a change or turn of thought, a shift from one phase of the subject to another.

From the standpoint of its basic function, the paragraph is both a convenience and a convention. Physically it serves an important purpose by breaking up a solid mass of print that would otherwise tire readers' eyes and tax their patience.

Recognized as a logical and rhetorical unit as well as a mechanical structure, the paragraph has been described as "a small group of thoughts that hang together."[1] Although they are part of a larger whole, these thoughts generally constitute a self-contained unit that makes sense by itself. Each paragraph or series of paragraphs marks off a stage in the development of the writer's thought. Thus each paragraph in a well-written essay can be justified as such: the writer made it a paragraph because it is a meaningful unit of the total discourse. Paragraph indentations, then, help readers by indicating the organization and development of the writer's thought as it moves from one aspect of the subject to another.

Paragraph Division

Many paragraphs dictate their own boundaries, especially if the writer is working from an outline. In a short paper each heading often turns out to be one or two paragraphs; in a longer paper the subheadings frequently constitute or at least suggest paragraph divisions. Of course paragraph breaks are generally determined by the topic itself. In fact it is a common and generally wise practice to open a paragraph with a *topic sentence*—a sentence that announces the main or base idea on which the entire paragraph will be constructed, the idea that will determine what belongs and what does not belong in the paragraph. Both writer and reader benefit from topic sentences, for they keep the discourse moving in a single, logical line of development.

In the short essay that follows, note that the first sentence is, in fact, an introductory (topic) paragraph listing the three elements that will make up the whole; each of these elements is then embodied in a topic sentence of its own, serving as a base for further amplification and illustration within the paragraph. The essay ends with a fourth paragraph which comments on the preceding three and with a final, one-sentence paragraph (like the one-sentence paragraph that opens the essay) in which a summing-up statement is made.

Studying Music in India[2]

RAVI SHANKAR

Guru, vinaya, sadhana—these three words form the heart of the musical tradition of India.

Guru, as many people now know, means master, spiritual teacher, or preceptor. We give a very important place to the *guru,* for we consider him to be the representation of the divine. There is a saying—

Pani piye chhanke
Guru banaye janke

[1] Marjorie Boulton, *The Anatomy of Prose* (London: Routledge and Kegan Paul Ltd., 1954), p. 41.

[2] From *My Music, My Life* by Ravi Shankar. Copyright © 1968, by Kinnara School of Indian Music, Inc. Reprinted by permission of Simon and Schuster, Inc.

—which means that one should drink water only after it has been filtered, and one should take a *guru* only after one feels sure of the decision. The choice of the *guru,* to us, is even more important than choosing a husband or a wife. A potential disciple cannot make a hasty decision to take just any teacher as his *guru,* nor should he break the bond between *guru* and *shishya,* once the *ganda* or *nara* ceremony, the initiation, which symbolically binds the two together for life, has taken place.

Vinaya means humility; it is the complete surrendering of the self on the part of the *shishya* to the *guru.* The ideal disciple feels love, adoration, reverence, and even fear toward his *guru,* and he accepts equally praise or scoldings. Talent, sincerity, and the willingness to practice faithfully are essential qualities of the serious student. The *guru,* as the giver in this relationship, seems to be all-powerful. Often, he may be unreasonable, harsh, or haughty, though the ideal *guru* is none of these. Ideally, he should respond to the efforts of the disciple and love him almost as his own child. In India, a Hindu child, from his earliest years, is taught to feel humble toward anyone older than he or superior in any way. From the simplest gesture of the *namaskar,* or greeting (putting the hands palm to palm in front of the forehead and bowing), or the *pranam* (a respectful greeting consisting of touching the greeted person's feet, then one's own eyes and forehead with the hands held palm to palm) to the practice of *vinaya* or humility tempered with a feeling of love and worship, the Hindu devotee's vanity and pretension are worn away. . . .

The third principal term associated with our music is *sadhana,* which means practice and discipline, eventually leading to self-realization. It means practicing with a fanatic zeal and ardent dedication to the *guru* and the music. If the student is talented, sincere, faithful to his *guru* and devoted in his practicing, and if the *guru* is teaching with utmost dedication and not being miserly with his knowledge, there is a distinct pattern for learning Indian music. The student must begin by acquiring the most basic techniques of the voice or instrument. In vocal music, this skill is achieved by assiduously practicing first one note, trying to produce correct breathing, voice, and pitch control. Students both of vocal and of instrumental music then learn scales and *paltas* (also called *alankars*). *Paltas* are short melodic figures performed in sequential order with a scale and *tala* framework in different tempi. Then, the *sargams* must be learned—the various fixed compositions sung to the note-names. In some fixed compositions *talas* and tempi can be varied, and in others no *tala* is used at all. The student also learns various other fixed compositions called *bandishes,* which include songs in different styles sung to a meaningful text, slow or fast instrumental pieces *(gats),* or some melodic phrases in a variety of melodic motions and tempi *(tans).*

This elementary training, for a talented and persevering student, should last not less than five years, very much like the elementary training for any Western musical discipline. This means the student should practice every day for at least eight hours. In Western music, of course, the student has a visual advantage. That is, much of his learning can be taken from books, without the close supervision of a teacher. But with Indian music, for the first five or six years, the student relies completely on the guidance of his *guru*. This is because the *guru* teaches everything to the *shishya* individually and directly, according to our ancient oral traditions, for very rarely do we use textbooks or manuals. Then, little by little, the student learns to improvise, and he works at it until he feels free and confident with a *raga*. From this point on, the aspiring musician must draw completely from within himself—from his own methodical musical training and his feelings and inspirations. As his musicianship grows, he acquires first a high degree of proficiency in the technical side of playing and then an ability to follow his imagination in whatever musical direction it leads. His technique must be highly enough developed to enable him to render instantaneously the mental pictures that flash before his mind's eye. It is such an exhilarating feeling to grasp a fresh idea and perform it spontaneously! Even after the student has become a fairly proficient performer and has created his own musical personality, he goes back to his *guru* from time to time for an evaluation of his development and to be inspired by new ideas. A true *guru* never stops growing musically and spiritually himself and can be a constant source of inspiration and guidance to the loving disciple.

So, starting from the very beginning, I would estimate that it requires at least twenty years of constant work and practice to reach maturity and a high standard of achievement in our classical music.

Paragraphing does not always correspond so neatly to joints in the structure of thought, for in addition to logic there are many considerations that enter into the division of prose into paragraphs. Indeed, "thought movement itself," as rhetorician Paul C. Rodgers has pointed out, "submits to very flexible partitioning; hence the size of a given logical paragraph frequently reflects secondary influences."[3] The narrow-column format of a newspaper, for example, and readers' demand that they be able to skim the page and get the news almost at a glance, require short, varied paragraphs. (They should all be short but not *equally* short.) Normally, however, you should not fragment your ideas by chopping them up into a series of consistently short paragraph units. We can see immediately that a typewritten page containing four or more paragraphs needs reworking: the writer either has not developed his or her ideas sufficiently or has failed to respect their unity and flow.

Strictly formal considerations may also enter into paragraph division, "as when paragraphs are paired off for contrast or comparison or knit into some larger pattern involving paragraphs as units."[4]

Similarly, a paragraph may be set off for a particular purpose: as an introduction, a conclusion, or a transition from one aspect of thought to another. Such paragraphs may contain only one or two sentences, but they nonetheless deserve to stand alone.

Finally, we must consider emphasis, rhythm, and tone. A short paragraph, for example, isolates a piece of information and thereby stresses it; it may also contribute to the rhythmic sweep of your essay and the particular tone you hope to establish. A philosophic essay may contain relatively long, detailed paragraphs that reinforce the unity, flow, and continuity of thought; a light essay may embody its scattered and tentative ideas in shorter, less formally structured paragraphs. As always, you must consider not only your subject but your readers as well. Will a demandingly long and bulky paragraph discourage them? If so, it may be advisable to divide a normal unit of thought into two units—that is, to develop one topic sentence over two

---

[3]Paul C. Rodgers, Jr., "A Discourse-Centered Rhetoric of the Paragraph," *College Composition and Communication*, 17 (Feb. 1966), 5.
[4]Ibid.

paragraphs—as the writer of the following narrative has done, clearly to increase readability:

In any journey there are three separate and recognizable stages. First there is the setting-out, the more-or-less anxious business of organizing the expedition and getting it off complete and on time. Then there is the journey itself, with its satisfying sense of achievement in each mile travelled. This is the most peaceful stage for the travellers, since we hand ourselves over as so much baggage to be passively transported. Even in a motor-car which we drive ourselves we are only a part of the steering-wheel: we have only to propel the car; and even driving across London in the rush hour is wonderfully soothing, for instance, compared with getting a family off on summer holiday.

The third stage of the journey is less definite and more variable. It begins imperceptibly as we near the end, and we recognize the transition by a growing impatience to arrive. We are no longer travelling, but impatiently covering the distance which still separates us from where we want to be. However it is not the number of miles remaining which decides our impatience: it is their proportion of the whole. On a journey of a hundred miles, at forty-nine we are still placid travellers.

—Nan Fairbrother, *The House in the Country*

Similarly, the writer of the following piece has promoted readability by distributing a single idea—that is, by developing one topic sentence ("Sebastiana was devoted to Tanguy, in a silent, inarticulate way")—over four relatively short paragraphs, each bringing out a different nuance of feeling:

Sebastiana was devoted to Tanguy, in a silent, inarticulate way. She watched over him and took care of him. Every day, during the midday break, everyone saw her arrive with "the kid's" dinner. She had a half-hour's walk each way to bring him his food, but she was determined he must get something hot inside him. She always managed to get something which she considered a "luxury"—a slice of ham, perhaps, or a little cheese. She arrived proudly carrying her bundle and sat on a big stone, in the shade, beside Tanguy. Other workers used to have jokes at her expense, and tell her she was "past the age for that kind of thing." She let them talk, and did not even take the trouble to reply. She was desolate at seeing Tanguy so ill and dejected, and she continued to look after him with extraordinary tenderness.

She spent a great deal of time finding classical music for him in the radio programs, pretending to adore Bach and Beethoven. In the evening, after Tanguy had come home, they would sit before dinner in the little courtyard and chat. When he was reading the paper or listening to music, she sat quietly, without moving or speaking.

They never expressed their affection openly. Sebastiana's love remained dumb; like Gunther, she never gave external reality to her tender feelings except through the unimpeachable eloquence of her actual behavior. She lived for Tanguy as she would have lived for her own son, watched over him while he slept, took care of his clothes, gave him the kind of food he liked best (as far as she could), and tried to find amusements for him. On Sundays they sometimes picnicked on the beach, well away from the crowd.

He told her about everything. She listened in silence and smiled at him tenderly. All her understanding came from her heart, for she was the maternal instinct personified. Tanguy, on his part, loved and admired her because she was fair and honest. He loved her uncalculating generosity and her tranquil expression. She was sensible rather than clever, but she almost always knew what was right.[5]

In summary, then, it may be said that paragraph divisions proceed primarily by logic and secondarily by physical, rhythmical, tonal, formal, and other rhetorical criteria. There is no simple formula by which to describe the architecture of the paragraph. "To indent," as Rodgers concluded, "is to interpret." And if you follow the indentation with a topic sentence that announces the new thought about to be developed, you are interpreting your ideas that much more explicitly and clearly.

Paragraph Unity

Insofar as the average paragraph treats a relatively self-contained idea, we may accept the common view of the paragraph as a miniature essay, which, like the full-length essay, answers a specific question posed by the writer. If the essay itself is a unified whole, then the individual questions posed at the paragraph level are but aspects of the larger questions posed by the piece. Whether each question is specifically embodied in the topic sentence, or merely implied in the direction of the discourse at a certain stage of its development, you confront the same imperative: to answer *that* question which you have raised and no other. In the paragraph, then, as in the essay, you are obliged to work toward unity—singleness of subject. The substance of the paragraph (like the substance of the total piece) should be about what it is supposed to be about; it should make the points you set out to make and not some other points that happen to occur to you as you are writing. It should, in other words, stick to its subject and not wander off into irrelevant side issues. A paragraph is unified when it contains only those elements that contribute to the realization of its main idea.

No quality is more central to good exposition than unity, for it is only through a series of unified paragraphs, clearly and systematically related to one another, that a good piece of writing—whether a short essay or a long book—can result.

It is worthwhile, then, to consider the problem of paragraph unity in detail and to examine some representative paragraphs. Take the following paragraph, for example, drawn from an article on cabaret life in contemporary Germany. At the point in the article where this paragraph occurs, the writer clearly wanted to draw a contrast between East and West Berlin cabarets. Note how she characterizes the contrast in her opening topic sentence— "striking and pathetic"—and how she then presents details and reasons which support and explain that single idea—and no other.

[5] From *Child of Our Time* by Michael del Castillo. Copyright © 1958 by Frederick Muller, Ltd. Reprinted by permission of Alfred A. Knopf, Inc.

The difference between West Berlin cabarets and the one cabaret in East Berlin is striking and pathetic. To begin with, the Distel is not a cabaret at all, but a little theater; there are no little tables; and since smoking is not allowed and one cannot order drinks, coffee, or frankfurters during the performance, the whole *gemutlich* atmosphere is lost. No one feels impelled to join in the choruses, or even to laugh very loudly. There is a feeling of discipline—not to be confused with the universal Central European solemnity about the arts—which is infinitely out of place and depressing, for the cabaret is just the place where discipline should be thrown to the wind.

—Sarah Gainham, "The Political Cabarets"

Here is a longer paragraph written by a Shakespearean scholar. Note that once again the main idea is stated in the opening sentence, followed by restatement in the second and third sentences, followed by examples. This, as we shall see, is a recurrent paragraph pattern: idea followed by illustrations or examples.

The easiest way to bring home to oneself the nature of the tragic character is to compare it with a character of another kind. Dramas like *Cymbeline* and the *Winter's Tale,* which might seem destined to end tragically, but actually end otherwise, owe their happy ending largely to the fact that the principal characters fail to reach tragic dimensions. And, conversely, if these persons were put in the place of the tragic heroes, the dramas in which they appeared would cease to be tragedies. Posthumus would never have acted as Othello did; Othello, on his side, would have met Iachimo's challenge with something other than words. If, like Posthumus, he had remained convinced of his wife's infidelity, he would not have repented her execution; if, like Leontes, he had come to believe that by an unjust accusation he had caused her death, he would never have lived on, like Leontes. In the same way the villain Iachimo has no touch of greatness. But Iago comes nearer to it, and if Iago had slandered Imogen and had supposed his slanders to have led to her death, he certainly would not have turned melancholy and wished to die. One reason why the end of the *Merchant of Venice* fails to satisfy us is that Shylock is a tragic character, and that we cannot believe in his accepting his defeat and the conditions imposed upon him. This was the case where Shakespeare's imagination ran away with him, so that he drew a figure with which the destined pleasant ending would not harmonise.

—A. C. Bradley, *Shakespearean Tragedy*

Clearly, then, you achieve unity in the paragraph when you recognize and respect the thrust of your own idea, whether it is explicitly stated or only implied. The following passage demonstrates vividly how every detail in a unified paragraph contributes to the total effect—in this case an image of "disgust." Note that the topic sentence is the third sentence of the paragraph, the first two sentences serving as an introduction.

Whoever writes about his childhood must beware of exaggeration and self-pity. I do not want to claim that I was a martyr or that Crossgates was a sort of Dotheboys Hall. But I should be falsifying my own memories if I did not record that they are largely memories of disgust. The overcrowded, underfed, underwashed life that we led was disgusting, as I recall it. If I shut my eyes and say "school," it is of course the physical surroundings that first come back to me: the flat playing-field with its cricket pavilion and the little shed by the rifle range, the draughty dormitories, the dusty splintery passages, the square of asphalt in front of the gymnasium, the raw-looking pinewood chapel at the back. And at almost every point some filthy detail obtrudes itself. For example, there were the pewter bowls out of which we had our porridge. They had overhanging rims, and under the rims there were accumulations of sour porridge, which could be flaked off in long strips. The porridge itself, too, contained more lumps, hairs and unexplained black things than one would have thought possible, unless someone were putting them there on purpose. It was never safe to start on that porridge without investigating it first. And there was the slimy water of the plunge bath—it was twelve or fifteen feet long, the whole school was supposed to go into it every morning, and I doubt whether the water was changed at all frequently—and the always-damp towels with their cheesy smell: and, on occasional visits in the winter, the murky sea-water of the local Baths, which came straight in from the beach and on which I once saw floating a human turd. And the sweaty smell of the changing-room with its greasy basins, and, giving on this, the row of filthy, dilapidated lavatories, which had no fastenings of any kind on the doors, so that whenever you were sitting there someone was sure to come crashing in. It is not easy for me to think of my schooldays without seeming to breathe in a whiff of something cold and evil-smelling—a sort of compound of sweaty stockings, dirty towels, faecal smells blowing along the corridors, forks with old food between the prongs, neck-of mutton stew, and the banging doors of the lavatories and the echoing chamber-pots in the dormitories.[6]

The most common violation of unity is the inclusion of material in one paragraph that should be either put in a separate paragraph or dropped altogether. The best way to test for unity is to reread the first draft of each paper to make certain that no extraneous material has crept in during the writing stage. It is necessary to be very critical at this time, examining each point of information and each turn in the development of thought to make sure that it belongs where it is and that each point picks up the preceding point and leads to the next in a natural, logical movement. Indeed it may be said of every structural element (sentence, paragraph, essay, chapter, book) that it is never a haphazard concourse of ideas but rather "a careful record of a mind moving toward a preconceived goal." It is this principle in action, the meticulous development of a single idea through its various stages, that gives a work organic unity—oneness of aim in all its parts.

Developing the Paragraph

In addition to sticking to your subject, you must say enough about it to give your readers a sense of inclusiveness, a clear, well-rounded, and reasonably complete picture of the matter at hand. As Edgar Allan Poe said of the poem

[6]From "Such, Such Were the Joys" in *Such, Such Were the Joys* by George Orwell, copyright, 1945, 1952, 1953, by Sonia Brownell Orwell. Reprinted by permission of Harcourt Brace Jovanovich, Inc., and Martin Secker & Warburg.

and short story, so we may say of any piece of prose writing, that "a certain degree of duration" is necessary to produce a given effect. Frequently, Poe's purpose in his fiction was to produce an emotional effect such as horror or fear; the expository writer tries to produce in his or her readers something quite different—the intellectual effect or state of understanding. In both cases, however, duration, or extended treatment, is required—that is, systematic development of an idea beyond the mere mention of it. The question of development, then, is concerned with fullness of information, fleshing out the bare bones of thought so that the reader knows precisely what the writer means.

We cannot generalize about how much readers should be told at any given stage of exposition. You yourself must decide, paragraph by paragraph, how best to amplify a unit of meaning so that readers are not left with unanswered questions and gaps in thought and reasoning. To avoid these problems, you must provide supporting data that will fill in the boundaries of an idea: details, facts, examples, analogies, anecdotes, reasons, illustrations, quotations. These are the supporting materials of paragraph development, and although they may be arranged in an infinite number of ways, there are certain recurrent patterns that you should be familiar with. Some of these are discussed and illustrated below.

From General to Specific

Simplistic as it may seem, there is truth in the notion of the paragraph as a block of prose introduced by a topic sentence containing a main idea that is developed in the remaining sentences of the paragraph through specific details, examples, reasons, and so on. Studies of professional writing indicate that this deductive pattern of paragraph development (that is, movement from a general statement to specific examples or explanations of that statement) does in fact characterize much of English prose. Note, for example, how the following paragraphs, drawn from different sources, exemplify this "from general to specific" principle of order.

1. *General idea developed by specific examples.* An example is a representative member of a group; therefore examples serve to illustrate a general principle and—if they are plentiful enough—to support and possibly prove it.

Many of the Founding Fathers were passionate lovers or practitioners of music. Jefferson used to rise at five in the morning to practice the violin; his expense books record many a purchase of "the latest minuets" and of fiddle strings for string-quartet sessions; and he was well acquainted with the technique and construction of various instruments. Samuel Adams organized the people of Boston into secret singing clubs to stir up enthusiasm for independence. And Thomas Paine wrote at least two fine songs, "The Liberty Tree" and "Bunker Hill." In addition to having made a famous ride, Paul Revere might go down in history as having been the engraver of the first volume of original hymns and anthems ever published in this country. And Benjamin Franklin—most versatile of all—not only was a writer of ballad verses and a music publisher, but even invented a new musical instrument— the glass Armonica, for which Gluck, Mozart, and Beethoven composed a number of pieces.

—Elie Siegmeister, "Music in Early America"

A surprising number of the people of Hiroshima remained more or less indifferent about the ethics of using the bomb. Possibly they were too terrified by it to want to think about it at all. Not many of them even bothered to find out much about what it was like. Mrs. Nakamura's conception of it—and awe of it—was typical. "The atom bomb," she would say when asked about it, "is the size of a matchbox. The heat of it is six thousand times that of the sun. It exploded in the air. There is some radium in it. I don't know just how it works, but when the radium is put together, it explodes." As for the use of the bomb, she would add, "Shikata ga nai," a Japanese expression as common as, and corresponding to, the Russian word "nicheve": "It can't be helped. Oh, well. Too bad." Dr. Fujii said approximately the same thing about the use of the bomb to Father Kleinsorge one evening, in German: "Da ist nicht zu machen. There's nothing to be done about it."

—John Hersey, *Hiroshima*

2. *General idea developed by specific details.* Details are the component parts that make up a whole—the individual steps in a procedure, the particular aspects of an image or impression. Details include factual data of all kinds: statistics, evidence, direct quotations. They answer the questions "How?" and "What?"

Scientists have learned to supplement the sense of sight in numerous ways. In front of the tiny pupil of the eye they put, on Mount Palomar, a great monocle 200 inches in diameter, and with it see 2000 times farther into the depths of space. Or they look through a small pair of lenses arranged as a microscope into a drop of water or blood, and magnify by as much as 2000 diameters the living creatures there, many of which are among man's most dangerous enemies. Or, if we want to see distant happenings on earth, they use some of the previously wasted electromagnetic waves to carry television images which they re-create as light by whipping tiny crystals on a screen with electrons in a vacuum. Or they can bring happenings of long ago and far away as colored motion pictures, by arranging silver atoms and color-absorbing molecules to force light waves into the patterns of the original reality. Or if we want to see into the center of a steel casting or the chest of an injured child, they send the information on a beam of penetrating short-wave X rays, and then convert it back into images we can see on a screen or photograph. Thus almost every type of electromagnetic radiation yet discovered has been used to extend our sense of sight in some way.

—George R. Harrison, "Faith and the Scientist"

He had altered. His eyes had lost a little of the brilliance which used to strike one so forcibly, and his face was no longer ascetically thin. His hair had turned white, of course, and this made his beard look less sparse. The body covered by the sand-colored tunic was as frail as ever; but his cheeks had filled out and taken on a pinkness which gave him a somewhat artificial air. There was still a strong hint of

mischief in his expression, however, and his dry laugh supplied the finishing touch—
he looked and sounded like some old scholar whose wisdom had led him to discover
the virtues of poverty. . . .

—Jean Lacouture, *Ho Chi Minh*

3. *General idea developed by specific reasons.* There are three kinds of reasons: opinions, judgments, deductions. Reasons answer the question "Why?" Reasons are acceptable and respectable only if they are founded on established fact, close observation and experience, or logical analysis.

The life of a student in India is much more difficult than anything we know in this country. Lack of material resources hampers most of the students at every turn. An overwhelming majority of them live at home, if they have homes, in conditions—by any standards we know—of miserable poverty. Often they have too little to eat, very little to wear, almost never any money to spend on the small things which we take so much for granted in our country. More serious is the fact that they can rarely afford to buy books for study, nor do their libraries have resources remotely comparable with those of our institutions. Beyond this, instruction is frequently anything but inspiring, and study is constrained and limited because the student is required by law to pass an annual examination which puts a high premium on memory work—an examination, set by an outside examining authority, to which each year many more are called than can possibly be chosen. And if a student persists in the face of repeated difficulty and finally in time earns a degree, there is the further debilitating consideration that his chances of finding an appropriate job are frighteningly slim. Yet so great is his inner drive and so bright his hope that the Indian student desires education beyond all else, and perseveres.

—Nathan M. Pusey, *The Age of the Scholar*

In outward appearance Canada is very definitely a North American, not a European land. It possesses the vast spaces and distances that are likely to be one of the strongest impressions of the European who visits the United States. And many regions of Canada suggest northward extensions of the United States. We have, to be sure, no equivalent for the distinctive French community, closely knit by bonds of race and religion, that one finds in the Province of Quebec. But the tranquil prosperous farming country of the Upper St. Lawrence is not very different from the neighboring districts of New England and New York. And Canada's prairie provinces—Manitoba, Saskatchewan, Alberta—have much in common with Kansas and Iowa and the Dakotas.

—William Henry Chamberlain, "Canada and Ourselves"

4. *General idea developed by specific illustration.* An illustration is a narrative example of anecdote that embodies an idea in an action. In illustration, in other words, something happens (the distinguishing mark of all narration). The writer may develop his or her point with one paragraph-length illustration or with several short ones.

"Omit needless words!" cries the author on page 17, and into that imperative Will Strunk really put his heart and soul. In the days when I was sitting in his class, he omitted so many needless words, and omitted them so forcibly and with such eagerness and obvious relish, that he often seemed in the position of having shortchanged himself—a man left with nothing more to say yet with time to fill, a radio prophet who had outdistanced the clock. Will Strunk got out of this predicament by a simple trick: he uttered every sentence three times. When he delivered his oration on brevity to the class, he leaned forward over his desk, grasped his coat lapels in his hands, and, in a husky, conspiratorial voice, said, "Rule Thirteen. Omit needless words! Omit needless words! Omit needless words!"

—William Strunk, Jr., and E. B. White, *Elements of Style*

Never in the history of English letters has there been a more dedicated participant in the literary feuds of his day than the great and cantankerous Dr. Samuel Johnson, who stomped noisily through eighteenth-century London, demolishing arguments and smashing reputations with enormous vigor and gusto. Usually his verbal abuse was enough to smite the unworthy, but sometimes the impatient Doctor resorted to physical violence. ("There is no arguing with Johnson," the novelist, Oliver Goldsmith, said, "for when his pistol misses fire he knocks you down with the butt end of it.") Once, when a waiter used his dirty fingers instead of the proper tongs to drop a lump of sugar into the Doctor's tea, Johnson tossed the glass through the window and was about to do the same with the waiter, when a friend appeared and calmed him. On another occasion, the manager had placed a chair on a side stage especially for Dr. Johnson's use. Another man, finding the seat empty, sat in it, and then made the unpardonable error of failing to relinquish it to its rightful holder. Faced with this effrontery, the powerful Dr. Johnson simply picked up the chair, with the man still in it, and threw both chair and occupant into the pit.

—Myrick Land, *The Fine Art of Literary Mayhem*

Clearly, the particularizing of general ideas clarifies and enlivens a subject as well as developing it. Factual details and an analysis of reasons give texture to writing and lend substance, authenticity, and authority to general observations. Examples embody the generalization and thereby illuminate it; nothing is more encouraging to the reader plowing through difficult material than the two words "for example," since the example frequently clarifies the straight exposition that preceded it. Similarly an anecdote or illustration enlivens discourse by "acting out" ideas and facts in the form of a story.

Some particularizing procedures are simpler than others. For example, the paragraph on the Founding Fathers' love of music can easily be diagrammed, because each sentence is, in fact, an example of the general idea set forth in the topic sentence.

General idea: Founding Fathers loved music

Jefferson . . .
Adams . . .
Paine . . .
Revere . . .
Franklin . . .

The paragraph on scientists' ability to supplement the sense of sight is only a little more complex. Here again each sentence following the opening sentence provides concrete information as to *how* scientists perform their feats. Only in the last sentence does the writer repeat his generalization. Thus the paragraph (a kind of "sandwich") may be diagramed as follows:

General idea: Scientists supplement sight in numerous ways

    Way 1
    Way 2
    Way 3
    Way 4
    Way 5

Terminator: Summing-up restatement

Not all paragraphs are as neatly representative of a type as these. Many writers mix supporting examples, reasons, and details, as in the following paragraph. In it Norman Podhoretz explains, through a series of vividly recounted details, presented anecdotally, precisely why he finds Norman Mailer "extraordinary."

The better I got to know Mailer personally—and we became very close friends—the more extraordinary I found him. He was, as the saying goes, a walking bag of contradictions: pugnacious in temperament and yet of a surpassing sweetness of character; foolish beyond belief about people, and yet unbelievably quick to understand the point of what anyone was up to; obsessed with fame, power, and rank, and yet the freest of any man I had ever encountered of snobbishness in any of its forms. Like most famous writers, he was surrounded by courtiers and sycophants, but with this difference: he allowed them into his life not to flatter him but to give his radically egalitarian imagination a constant workout. He had the true novelist's curiosity about people unlike himself—you could see him getting hooked ten times a night by strangers at a party—and his respect for modes of life other than his own was so great that it often led him into romanticizing people and things that might legitimately have been dismissed as uninteresting or mediocre. He would look into the empty eyes of some vapid upper-class girl and announce to her that she could be the madam of a Mexican whorehouse; or he would decide that some broken-down Negro junkie he had met in a Village dive was a battalion-commander at heart. Mailer assumed in the most straightforward way that everyone was out for all the power he could get at every minute of the day, and that from the most casual confrontation between two people, one emerged with a victory and the other with a defeat; he even had a hypochondriacal theory involving the birth and death of cells to cover for the assumption. He himself wanted everything: he would "settle for nothing less" than making a revolution in the consciousness of his time, *and* earning millions of dollars, *and* achieving the very heights of American celebrityhood. He respected the position of celebrityhood precisely as he respected people, sometimes romanticizing a particular "office," but never making the more common and worse mistake of underestimating how much it took to get anywhere big in America or pooh-poohing the qualities of mind and character required for staying on top.[7]

Similarly, the following paragraph mixes its supporting materials by incorporating into an extended illustration a mass of statistical data that if pre-

[7]From *Making It*, by Norman Podhoretz. Copyright © 1967 by Norman Podhoretz. Reprinted by permission of Random House, Inc.

sented directly would be dull. When presented within the frame of a story, however, the facts and figures come alive. It is the concreteness and specificity of the illustrative story—dealing with a family in a specific place, paying a stated amount of money for a prefabricated ranch house—that demonstrates the truth of the general observation.

Investigating home-buying habits in the Midwest, I found that most home buyers do not compute the burden they are undertaking when a home is offered to them on a long-term mortgage. In Toledo, Ohio, a salesman and his wife proudly showed me their customized pre-fab ranch house which they said they had just bought for $19,500. Did they have a mortgage? Yes, it was a thirty-year kind for $17,000. How much was their interest rate? The husband said, "Gosh, I don't know . . . 4½ per cent I think." His wife thought it was 6 per cent. Their difference in guesses could make a difference of nearly $6,000 in the total cost. Actually, it turned out, they were paying 5½ per cent interest. The one thing they did know was that their monthly payment was $96.53. We quickly multiplied that figure by the 360 months they had committed themselves to pay it, and added on the $2,500 cash down payment. The result was a figure that plainly dismayed them: $37,250.80. That was the real price of their home, not $19,500.

—Vance Packard, *The Waste Makers*

Levels of Generality

The paragraph pattern of "general to specific" has recently been amended by the rhetorician Francis Christensen, who has observed that in the paragraphs of professional writers, as in their sentences (Chapter 26, "Improving Sentences"), a far more subtle pattern is actually at work—an "additive" or "cumulative" method of expanding the paragraph at "varying levels of generality."[8] This means that one sentence (usually the first, "topic" sentence) will contain a statement that provides a base for discussion; the sentences that follow represent an ebb and flow between the general and the particular. It will be rewarding to examine this method, for it clarifies still further how paragraphs work. To be sure, Christensen's inductive approach is not the only possible approach to paragraph analysis today, but it is demonstrably practical. It enables us to see the many shapes paragraphs take and to appreciate the variability and viability of the form. Such insights surely enable us to use the form with greater control and skill.

Strictly speaking, the well-constructed, well-developed paragraph may assume an indefinite number of forms: it is impossible to encompass all possible paragraphs in a single description. But basically, Christensen has written, the paragraph is "a sequence of structurally related sentences."

By a sequence of structurally related sentences I mean a group of sentences related to one another by coordination and subordination. If a first sentence of a paragraph is the topic sentence, the second is quite likely to be a comment on it, a

---

[8]Francis Christensen, *Notes Toward a New Rhetoric* (New York: Harper & Row, 1967), pp. 52–81.

development of it, and therefore subordinate to it. The third sentence may be coordinate with the second sentence (as in this paragraph) or subordinate to it. The fourth sentence may be coordinate with either the second or third (or with both if they themselves are coordinate, as in this paragraph) or subordinate to the third. And so on.[9]

The typical paragraph, then, opens with a "base" or topic sentence to which other sentences are added; the first may simply be a comment, the second an example, the third another example (detail or reason), the fourth another comment, and so on. The significant point Christensen makes is that the movement of the paragraph is not necessarily in a straight line from general to specific. Indeed, he writes, "Following a paragraph is more like a dance than a dash. The topic sentence draws a circle, and the rest of the paragraph is a pirouette within that circle."

In the properly unified paragraph, then, all the sentences deal with the same subject but at various levels of generality. A comment, for example, will be subordinate to the base sentence on which it is commenting; an explanation or example of the comment will be subordinate to the comment, and so on. The paragraph moves and takes shape in terms of how each added sentence relates—either coordinately or subordinately—to the sentence that precedes it. We can see that the topic sentence is like the base clause of the additive sentence (Chapter 26, "Improving Sentences") in that "it is the sentence on which all the others depend: the sentence whose assertion is supported or whose meaning is explicated or whose parts are detailed by the sentences added to it."

If the added elements all have the same structure and the same relationship to the topic sentence, then Christensen calls the sequence in that paragraph "coordinate," and likens the paragraph to a two-level sentence:

Two-level sentence

   1 [Lincoln's] words still linger on the lips—
     2 eloquent and cunning, yes
     2 vindictive and sarcastic in political debate,
     2 ripping and ribald in jokes,
     2 reverent in the half-formed utterance of prayer.
            —Alistair Cooke (cited in Christensen, p. 59)

Coordinate sequence paragraph

   1 This is the essence of the religious spirit—the sense of power, beauty, greatness, truth infinitely beyond one's own reach, but infinitely to be aspired to.
     2 It invests men with pride in a purpose and with humility in accomplishment.
     2 It is the source of all true tolerance, for in its light all men see other men as they see themselves, as being capable of being more than they are, and yet falling short, inevitably, of what they can imagine human opportunities to be.

[9]Ibid., p. 57.

2 It is the supporter of human dignity and pride and the dissolver of vanity.
2 And it is the very creator of the scientific spirit; for without the aspiration to understand and control the miracle of life, no man would have sweated in a laboratory or tortured his brain in the exquisite search after truth.
—Dorothy Thompson (cited in Christensen, p. 59)

Note that in this type of paragraph all supporting sentences are structurally alike (note, also, that the Founding Fathers paragraph on pages 470–71 follows this same pattern).

In a subordinate sequence the sentences added to the topic sentence are structurally different and have different relationships to the topic sentence and to each other. Christensen compares this type of paragraph to a multi-level sentence:

Multilevel sentence

1 A small Negro girl develops from the sheet of glare-frosted walk,
2 walking barefooted,
3 her brown legs striking and recoiling from the hot cement,
4 her feet curling in,
5 only the outer edges touching.
—Cited in Christensen, p. 60

Subordinate sequence paragraph

1 The process of learning is essential to our lives.
2 All higher animals seek it deliberately.
3 They are inquisitive and experiment.
4 An experiment is a sort of harmless trial run of some action which we shall have to make in the real world; and this, whether it is made in the laboratory by scientists or by fox-cubs outside their earth.
5 The scientist experiments and the cub plays; both are learning to correct their errors of judgment in a setting in which errors are not fatal.
6 Perhaps this is what gives them both their air of happiness and freedom in these activities.
—J. Bronowski (cited in Christensen, p. 60)

By viewing the paragraph as a linked sequence of sentences—as in the above examples—Christensen provides a quick and useful test of paragraph unity, one which we can easily apply to our own writing. As we reread the first draft of a paragraph we have written, we can ask, "Does every sentence (that is, every link in the sequence) connect with the sentence that precedes it and the sentence that follows?" If not, if a sentence is neither coordinate with any sentence before it nor subordinate to the sentence immediately preceding it, then it does not belong in the paragraph (it breaks the sequence) and should either be moved elsewhere or set off in parentheses. In these cases, as Christensen puts it, "the paragraph has begun to drift from its moorings, or the writer has unwittingly begun a new paragraph."

Purely coordinate or subordinate paragraph sequences are, as we might expect, not as common as a mixed sequence in which subordinate elements are added to a basically coordinate sequence or vice versa. Some examples follow.

Mixed sequence, based on coordination

1 The atmosphere that stirs expectation, that tantalizes the secret hunches that all theater-goers have, is composed of many things, some tangible and some not so very.
  2 Titles count.
    3 ("Sixth Finger in a Five Finger Glove" is not a good title; "The Strong Are Lonely" is not a good title; "Bells Are Ringing" is a good title.)
  2 Personalities count.
    3 (I've always liked that nice Walter Pidgeon.)
  2 Subject matter counts.
    3 (Do I want to see a play tonight about treachery in a prison camp?)
  2 Timing counts.
    3 (I may want to see a play about treachery in a prison camp next year, or I may have wanted to see one last year, but—tonight?)
  2 Circumstances count.
    3 (Is it Eugene O'Neill's last play, and what did he say about his family?)
  2 Curiosity counts.
    3 (What in heaven's name can "The Waltz of the Toreadors" be like?)
  2 The curve of the moon counts.

                    —Walter Kerr, "How to Beat the Critics"

Mixed sequence, based on coordination

1 It is commonplace that most artists of outstanding originality and creative power have met lack of appreciation or abuse in their lifetimes.
  2 We know that Beethoven's latest and finest works seemed to his contemporaries to be meaningless meanderings of senility aligned with deafness, that Rembrandt's paintings were judged to be "Gothic and crude" by the autocrats of good taste in France.
  2 We know the obloquy which the Post-Impressionist painters were required to face.
    3 Even in 1925 Cézanne was described by one American critic as "commonplace, mediocre, and a third-rate painter," and in 1934 his work was characterized by another as "meager and unfulfilled art," while an English critic of some prominence has published his judgement that when you have seen one you have seen them all.
  2 We know the indignation which was aroused at the beginning of the century by the new enthusiasm for African sculpture.
  2 We remember the bewildered ridicule of "modern" music—Stravinsky and Bartók, even of Scriabin and Sibelius—which is now accepted and "placed."
  2 We remember the controversies aroused by D. H. Lawrence and James Joyce, the repudiation of Eliot, Pound, Auden.
[Summing-up] This is not a new thing in critics who have led the vociferous opposition to the new.

                    —Harold Osborne, *Aesthetics and Criticism*

Mixed sequence, based on subordination

1 Whether we like it or not, ours is an Age of Science.
  2 It is also, like every other epoch of history, an Age of Private Experience.
    3 In this second half of the twentieth century what can a writer do about these inescapable historical facts?
    3 And what, as a conscientious literary artist and a responsible citizen, ought he to do about them?
      4 His first duty, of course, is to write as well as he can.
        5 Much of our experience comes to us, so to say, through the refracting medium of art.
          6 If that art is inept, our experience will be vulgarized and corrupted.
          6 Along with unrealistic philosophy and religious superstition, bad art is a crime against society.
      4 The writer's next duty is to learn something, if only superficially and in patches, about the methods and results of advancing science.
        5 This knowledge should then be correlated with private experience and the shared traditions of culture, and the amalgam should be treated as a new kind of raw material for the creation of new varieties of the familiar literary forms.

—Harper's

Mixed paragraphs such as these are especially interesting and worthy of close study, for as Christensen says, they suggest "careful calculation of what could be left to the reader and what must be made more explicit." Obviously those points that contain several subordinate sentences are being treated at greater length because the writer feels that they need clarification or emphasis. The inclusion of subordinate categories of information (details, examples) provides the additional "mass" that tells the reader "take note: this is difficult; it needs further explaining" or "this is important and therefore should be lingered over."

The determination of how much the reader must be told at any point—where an added subordinate sentence is necessary or where another coordinate statement might clarify or emphasize an important idea—is left to the judgment of the individual writer. There is no formula that spells out the proper proportions of a paragraph. Even so, the writer can benefit enormously by familiarity with the "additive" approach, for very often all that is needed to improve a passage of prose is further development or amplification at a given level. Thus, says Christensen, "there is nothing arbitrary or unnatural about urging the student to add levels, usually of a lower order of generality, in order to produce a texture rich enough to contain and display his subject."[10]

Similarly, John Lord wrote in his study of the paragraph that "all good writing is a constant weaving up and down between the concrete and the

[10]Francis Christensen, "Symposium on the Paragraph," *College Composition and Communication*, 17 (May 1966), 60–88.

abstract, as well as a constant forward movement from a beginning through a middle to an end."[11]

Finally, it is worth noting that a paragraph may stand on its own with no topic sentence per se, in fact with no announced statement of its theme:

> 2 In Spain, where I saw him last, he looked profoundly Spanish.
>> 3 He might have passed for one of those confidential street dealers who earn their living selling spurious Parker pens in the cafés of Málaga or Valencia.
>>> 4 Like them, he wore a faded chalk-striped shirt, a coat slung over his shoulders, a trim, dark moustache, and a sleazy, fat-cat smile.
>>> 4 His walk, like theirs, was a raffish saunter, and everything about him seemed slept in, especially his hair, a nest of small, wet serpents.
>> 3 Had he been in Seville and his clothes been more formal, he could have been mistaken for a pampered elder son idling away a legacy in dribs and on drabs, the sort you see in windows along the Sierpes, apparently stuffed.
> 2 In Italy he looks Italian; in Greece, Greek: wherever he travels on the Mediterranean coast, Tennessee Williams takes on a protective colouring which melts him into his background, like a lizard on a rock.
> 2 In New York or London he seems out of place, and is best explained away as a retired bandit.
>> 3 Or a beach comber: shave the beard off any of the self-portraits Gauguin painted in Tahiti, soften the features a little, and you have a sleepy outcast face that might well be Tennessee's.
>
> —Kenneth Tynan (cited in Christensen, pp. 71–72)

In this paragraph, the three level 2 sentences are clearly coordinate, but there is, as Christensen notes, "no superordinate sentence to umbrella them; that is, there is no level 1, no topic sentence. With paragraphs such as this the topic can usually be inferred from the preceding paragraph." Indeed, very often the structure and impetus of an idea carries over from paragraph to paragraph so that no formal transition or topic sentence is needed.

In summary, then, it may be said about this most crucial subject of development that each paragraph unit (or each series of units) should have sufficient "duration" to do full justice to its subject; it should also develop its thought (answer its question) systematically, with a variety of materials that give the paragraph substance and texture (levels of generality); and it should not drop the thought (leave that aspect of the answer) until, as Herbert Read wrote, it has been "seen in all profitable lights."[12] Furthermore, these thoughts should be developed at a steady, reasonably accelerated pace so that the writing *flows*. To quote Read again:

> There is about good writing a visual actuality. It exactly reproduces what we should metaphorically call the contour of our thought. The metaphor is for once exact: thought has a contour or a shape. The paragraph is the perception of this contour or shape.

[11]John Lord, *The Paragraph: Structure and Style* (New York: Holt, Rinehart and Winston, 1964), p. 73.

[12]Herbert Read, *English Prose Style* (Boston: Beacon Press, 1955), p. 54.

The writer has toward his materials, words, the same relation that an artist, say a modeller, has toward his material, clay. The paragraph is a plastic mass, and it takes its shape from the thought it has to express: its shape *is* the thought."[13]

Achieving Coherence

Coherence literally means "sticking together." Thus a piece of writing is coherent when all its parts stick together, when the individual words, phrases, and sentences are so arranged and connected that a clear pattern of thought emerges. The word "pattern" is important here. Words, like pictures, must fall into a pattern before they can be recognized and understood. Indeed, in a sense, words *are* pictures of a state of affairs. To continue this analogy, ask: Would we recognize a picture if it had no visible order, proportion, or composition, if the parts were not firmly held together by the canvas backbone? We would not only not recognize it, we would not even call it a picture but a jigsaw puzzle that had to be reassembled into a meaningful visual whole.

Readers, who are, as E. B. White once wrote, "always in trouble," have no time and certainly no inclination to play games, to reassemble verbal parts; they must accept the writer's composition as they read it. If there are missing pieces (important points not mentioned) or corners cut so that the pieces do not interlock (gaps in thought, puzzling jumps from one idea to another), then readers cannot see the shape of the writer's thought.

As a conscientious writer, then, you must try to communicate more than the basic raw material of your ideas; you must try to communicate relationships: Why does point three follow point two and not vice versa? Does the example cited at the end of the paragraph illustrate the whole paragraph or only the last point? Is the second point the cause or the effect of the first? And what does reason three have to do with reason two? Are they of equal importance, or is one subordinate to the other? You should allow for no guesswork; you should make certain not only that your readers can share the main idea of your paragraph (unity), but also that they can follow your particular train of thought from beginning to end (coherence).

Coherence in writing is accomplished basically in three ways:

1. By arranging material in a logical sequence.
2. By providing transitions from one idea to another.
3. By maintaining a consistent tone and point of view.

We have already discussed the most common ordering principle: the deductive or analytic—that is, movement from the general to varying levels of the specific. It is worth mentioning that this order is occasionally reversed, so that the paragraph opens with a series of specific details that culminate in a general statement. This is an inductive or synthetic paragraph. The following is an example:

[13] Ibid., p. 61.

Ivy's red skin was flecked with tiny freckles, like rust spots, and in each of his hard cheeks there was a curly indentation, like a knot in a tree-hole,—two permanent dimples which did anything but soften his countenance. His eyes were very small, and an absence of eyelashes gave his pupils the fixed, unblinking hardness of a snail's or a lizard's. His hands had the same swollen look as his face, were deeply creased across the back and knuckles, as if the skin were stretched too tight. He was an ugly fellow, Ivy Peters, and he liked being ugly.

—Willa Cather, *A Lost Lady*

In addition to the ordering principles of general to specific and specific to general, there are other orders that determine a paragraph pattern: time, space, and order of emphasis.

Time Order

Material can be arranged according to *when* it happened (past or present, early to late, old to new), or in what order it should be done (first do this, then that, and finally this). Narration, historical accounts, the steps in a process, directions or instructions have to be presented in the order in which they happen or should happen.

As an example of this type of ordering, here is an account of the final moments in the life of Mary, Queen of Scots. The writer takes us to the scaffold and allows us to witness the event minute by minute:

She laid her crucifix on her chair. The chief executioner took it as a perquisite, but was ordered instantly to lay it down. The lawn veil was lifted carefully off, not to disturb the hair, and was hung upon the rail. The black robe was next removed. Below it was a petticoat of crimson velvet. The black jacket followed, and under the jacket was a body of crimson satin. One of her ladies handed her a pair of crimson sleeves, with which she hastily covered her arms; and thus she stood on the black scaffold with the black figures all around her, blood-red from head to foot.[14]

It should be mentioned that chronological order does not necessarily imply an uninterrupted movement forward in time. You may begin with an important or exciting event and weave in background by interrupting the ongoing development of the story to dip into the past for some crucial or illuminating details. In other words, you may organize your material in whatever time sequence best suits the subject and purpose of your paragraph (or essay), as long as the presentation proceeds in an orderly manner that readers can follow.

Spatial Order

Just as some material lends itself to a presentation in time, other material calls for a presentation in space. Here again there are no rigid rules prescrib-

---

[14]James Anthony Froude, "The Execution of Mary Queen of Scots," *History of England from the Fall of Wolsey to the Defeat of the Spanish Armada* (New York: AMS Press, 1969).

ing one spatial pattern over another. It is important that writers visualize the effect they are trying to achieve and that they then set about achieving that effect in a systematic manner. They should be clear in their own minds where the narrator stands (point of view), and proceed according to a natural or logical principle of progression (left to right, far to near, bottom to top). Note that in the following paragraph from *The Adventures of Huckleberry Finn*, Mark Twain blends a time and space pattern. Huck is a stationary observer, describing what he sees as the day breaks over the water.

The first thing to see, looking away over the water, was a kind of dull line—that was the woods on t'other side; you couldn't make nothing else out; then a pale place in the sky; then more paleness spreading around; then the river softened up away off, and warn't black any more, but gray; you could see little dark spots drifting along ever so far away—trading-scows, and such things; and long black streaks—rafts; sometimes you could hear a sweep creaking; or jumbled-up voices, it was so still, and sounds come so far; and by and by you could see a streak on the water which you know by the look of the streak that there's a snag there in a swift current which breaks on it and makes that streak look that way; and you see the mist curl up off the water, and the east reddens up, and the river, and you make out a log cabin in the edge of the woods, away on the bank on t'other side of the river, being a wood-yard, likely, and piled by them cheats so you can throw a dog through it anywheres; then the nice breeze springs up, and comes fanning you from over there, so cool and fresh and sweet to smell on account of the woods and the flowers; but sometimes not that way, because they've left dead fish laying around, gars and such, and they do get pretty rank; and next you've got the full day, and everything smiling in the sun, and the song-birds just going to it!

Order of Climax or Emphasis

As mentioned earlier, when presenting a series of items or ideas, it is generally best to arrange them in ascending order of importance or value. The rhetorical justification rests on what appears to be a law of human nature: that we intuitively build to a climax, passing from the least to the most, with the last-mentioned item impressing itself most forcibly on our minds. Thus if a third or fourth item is weak, we say that it is anticlimactic; we have built up to something and then fallen off. Attempting to order your materials emphatically, you might begin by embedding in your topic sentence a specific fact or situation which you then unfold by degrees, working steadily toward a culmination or resolution. Or you might simply move from what is expected and obvious to what is unexpected and surprising—as in the following paragraph:

As Americans are drawn more and more into overseas travel and service abroad, we are advised to be ready for something called "culture shock." Culture shock, roughly defined, is the total psychological discomfort one feels in foreign situations where every human function is dealt with somewhat differently. Big differences, such as language, are obvious; it is not too hard to make allowances for them and adjust to them. But the many, many tiny differences between life in the United States and life abroad—like the taste of the coffee, the value of time, or the smells—are more insidious. Bit by bit, their effects pile up in the pit of the emotions until they all become too much to be endured. Suddenly, unexpectedly, we have had it.

—Donald Lloyd, "The Quietmouth American"

It should be mentioned here that the building-up order of climax is not always suitable. Sometimes one item is so obvious and all-important that it must be stated at the outset—directly after the topic sentence—just as an overwhelmingly strong reason in support of an argument often must be presented first if it is not to be conspicuous by its absence, thereby distracting readers, who may keep wondering why the writer does not say the obvious. Thus in the following paragraph, the writer quite properly presents his most important explanation first:

Some people are astonished to find that such primitive transportation as dog traction is still used. Why? Probably the most important reason is economy. A dog team can be assembled without expenditure of too much money. Pups appear in the normal course of events. The team becomes self-supporting since it enables the owner to become a more efficient hunter, especially of seals and caribou. The environment furnishes food for the team and food and clothing for the hunter and his family. A vehicle such as a weasel, snow-buggy, or motor toboggan requires cash capital for the initial investment and for spare parts, gasoline, and oil. Most Eskimos are relatively wealthy in meat and animal products but desperately poor in money. A recent comparison of motor toboggans and dog teams in the Canadian Arctic showed that, considering weight only of food or fuel needed per mile, the dog teams were more efficient. And—very important—a team can be started in thirty-below-zero weather without preheating, using explosive ether for starting fluid, or "burning" one's hands on the cold steel.

Transitional Expressions or Devices

The word "transition" means passing over. Thus transitional guides are connectives (symbols, words, phrases; sometimes whole sentences and paragraphs) that make possible a smooth "passing over" from one idea to the next. Transitions are made by referring to what has been said before, establishing cause-and-effect connections, looking ahead to what will be said, referring to the present, marking time and place, qualifying, comparing, contrasting. These and other common transitional devices are briefly described below in categories that necessarily overlap to some extent:

Referring back: as we have seen, on the whole, as mentioned above, as stated previously, as I have said, it seems then

Looking ahead: then, later, next, after, afterward, thereafter, finally, now, consequently, to sum up

Establishing causal connections: the result, in conclusion, to conclude, because, for, since, consequently, accordingly, hence, thus, therefore

Time markers: now, then, later, soon, before, next, afterward, finally, meanwhile, thereafter, at the same time

ace markers: here, there, at this point, below, beside, next to, behind, in
nt, outside, inside

Comparing and establishing degree: and, similarly, in like manner, in the
same way, just as, so . . . that, also, more than, less than, beyond this

Qualifying, conceding, or contrasting: but, nevertheless, on the other
hand, however, despite this, still, on the contrary, conversely, if, as if,
granted that, unless, whether, anyhow, although, even though, yet

Adding and intensifying: first, second, third; a, b, c; 1, 2, 3; to repeat, in
addition, moreover, and, also, still, again, similarly, furthermore, finally,
really, indeed

Introducing an illustration: thus, to illustrate, for example, for instance

Repeating a key word: This device keeps the main idea before the
reader's attention and carries the thread of meaning throughout a passage.

Using synonyms: Instead of repeating a key word so that it becomes
monotonous, you may use suitable synonyms that continue the same
thought.

Using proper pronoun reference: Another substitute for the repetition of
key nouns and another way of connecting ideas is to use pronouns in place of
nouns.

Maintaining same subject throughout paragraph: It is often possible to
continue the same subject from sentence to sentence, thereby maintaining a
steady focus throughout the paragraph.

Establishing repetitive or parallel sentence patterns: In addition to
repeating key words and ideas, you may repeat the grammatical structure of
your sentences, thereby reinforcing the unity of your thoughts and promoting their flow.

Linking of last sentence of one paragraph with first sentence of next: This
is a natural, frequently intuitive method of maintaining coherence between
paragraphs. Sometimes connecting words are needed (such as "then again"
or "on another occasion"), but sometimes the direction of the thought provides its own continuity.

Note in the following paragraph (cited earlier) how many transitional
words and devices have been used to "tie up" the paragraph into a cohesive
whole: to keep readers aware throughout of the writer's intent, to let them
know what is coming next (an additional bit of information, a contrast, an
effect):

	The life of a *student* in India is much more diffi-cult than anything we know in this country. Lack of	
Repetition	material resources hampers most of the *students* at every turn. An overwhelming majority of *them* live	
Pronoun reference	at *home,* if *they* have *homes,* in conditions—by any standards we know—of miserable poverty. Often	
Intensification and word repetition	*they* have too *little* to eat, *very little* to wear, almost never any money to spend on the small things which we take so much for granted in our country.	Parallel phrases

More serious is the fact that they can rarely afford to buy books for study, nor do their libraries have resources remotely comparable with those of our institutions. *Beyond this,* instruction is frequently anything but inspiring, and study is constrained and limited because the student is required by law to pass an annual *examination* which puts a high premium on memory work—an *examination,* set by an outside examining authority, to which each year many more are called than can possibly be chosen. *And* if a student persists in the face of repeated difficulty *and finally* in time earns a degree, there is the *further debilitating consideration* that his chances of finding an appropriate job are frighteningly slim. *Yet so* great is his inner drive and *so* bright his hope that the Indian student desires education *beyond* all else, and perseveres.
—Nathan M. Pusey, *The Age of the Scholar*

Left margin labels:
Comparison and pronoun reference
Additive/time marker
Repetition (parallel structure)

Right margin labels:
Compar (degree)
Repetition
Conjunction (additive) Comparison (degree) and synonyms
Conjunction (contrast) Comparison

Now let us examine a passage of prose and observe how the writer has included many transitional signals (thirty-five) to keep readers moving steadily from beginning to end in a straight line of connected statements, each following logically from the one preceding it and each telling readers accurately what they can expect next (an "and" suggesting another item of equal value; a "however" suggesting contrast; a "because" anticipating a reason).

Place marker — But the plays we are concerned with *here pursue*

ends quite different from *those* of the conventional — *Pronoun reference*

Causal connection — play and *therefore use* quite different methods. — *Parallel (to "pursue")*

Pronoun reference — *They* can be judged only by the standards of the

Theatre of the Absurd, which it is the purpose of

Demonstrative adjective — *this* book to define and clarify.

It must be stressed, *however,* that the dramatists — *Contrast*

Place marker — whose work is *here* presented and discussed under

the generic heading of the Theatre of the Absurd do

not form part of any self-proclaimed or self-con-

Synonym (for "dramatists") — scious school or movement. *On the contrary,* each — *Contrast*

of the *writers* in question is an individual who

	regards himself as a lone outsider, cut off and	
·onoun eference	isolated in his private world. *Each* has his own	Parallel structure
	personal approach to both subject matter and	
	form; his own roots, sources, and background. *If*	Qualifying condition
Additives	they *also,* very clearly *and* in spite of *themselves,*	Reflexive pronoun
Causal connection	have a good deal in common, *it* is *because their*	Pronoun reference
Comparison of degree	work *most* sensitively mirrors and reflects the	Additive "and's" plus parallel structure
	preoccupations and anxieties, the emotions and	
	thinking of an important segment of their contem-	
Transitional phrase (looking back)	poraries in the Western world.	
	This is not to say that their works are representa-	Pronoun reference
	tive of mass attitudes. It is an oversimplification to	
	assume that any age presents a homogeneous pat-	
Pronoun reference	tern. *Ours* being, *more than most others,* an age of	Comparison of degree
Pronoun reference	transition, *it* displays a bewilderingly stratified pic-	Additive and time marker
	ture: medieval beliefs *still* held and overlaid by	
	eighteenth-century rationalism and mid-nine-	Parallel (to "held and overlaid")
	teenth-century Marxism, *rocked* by sudden vol-	
	canic eruptions of prehistoric fanaticisms and pri-	
Pronoun reference	mitive tribal cults. *Each of these* components of the	
	cultural pattern of the age finds *its* characteristic	Pronoun reference
	artistic expression. The Theatre of the Absurd,	
Contrast	*however,* can be seen as the reflection of what	
	seems the attitude most genuinely representative	
	of our own time's contribution.	
	The hallmark of *this attitude* is its sense that the	Demonstrative adjective plus repetition of "attitude"

Parallel "that" clauses

certitudes and unshakable basic assumptions of former ages have been swept away, that they have been tested and found wanting, that they have been discredited as cheap and somewhat childish illusions. The decline of religious faith was masked until the end of the Second World War by the substitute religions of faith in progress, nationalism, and various totalitarian fallacies. *All this* was shattered by the war. By 1942, Albert Camus was calmly putting the question why, since life had lost all meaning, man should not seek escape in suicide.[15]

Pronoun reference

Consistency of Tone

A third factor in a coherent paragraph or essay is the *tone*—specifically the tone of voice—that emerges from the written page. It is your voice, the voice of the writer, selecting, arranging, spinning out your story in terms of how you feel about it (angry, amused, disdainful, admiring). However bloodless the subject, all writing is, as pointed out in the introduction to this book, a *human* activity. Therefore there is always a voice involved in a passage of prose, however formal or muted it may be.

Simply stated, tone is a function of your attitude toward your subject and your readers. How do you want them to take your statement: as a formal explanation, a personal impression, an emotional attack, a lament, a joke? It is not merely what you say but the *way* that you say it that enters into the total meaning of a piece of writing and either reinforces or violates its coherence.

To maintain a consistent tone and point of view, you must begin with mechanical decisions concerning who is speaking (a first-person "I"? an impersonal "one"? an unbiased "he or she"?) and then consider whether the statement should be made in the present or past tense, the active or passive voice. On a deeper level, you must consider who your readers are; having visualized them, you will know what kind of usage would be most appropriate (should you say "conflagration" or "fire"?). On a still deeper level you must define the particular effect you are trying to create with your words

[15]From *The Theatre of the Absurd* by Martin Essling, copyright © 1961, 1968, 1969 by Martin Essling. Reprinted by permission of Doubleday & Company, Inc.

(should you call a woman "thin," "skinny," or "scrawny"?). These mechanical and semantic considerations must be accompanied by a searching of your own mind to ensure that you have a clear idea of how *you* feel about what you are saying and how you want your readers to feel and think.

Note in the following scatterbrained account of New York City that the writer fails to maintain consistency either in tone or point of view: the person shifts from "I" to "one" to "you"; tenses and voice change throughout; the writer gasps colloquially over a "hunk of engineering" and then comments pompously on what is "therapeutically preferable." The paragraph is poorly written on many counts, not the least of which is failure to establish and maintain an appropriate tone.

> Although I was born and raised in New York, it still seems to me an exciting city. One can see beautiful sights no matter where you travel, especially up the West Side Highway where I saw the George Washington Bridge eloquently span the Hudson River from New York to New Jersey. What a hunk of engineering! All kinds of recreational activities are offered by New York: at Madison Square Garden you could be a spectator of almost any sport one is interested in: basketball, hockey, boxing. As for participating sports (which are, psychiatrists maintain, therapeutically preferable), I can't imagine any that you wouldn't be able to take up: bowling, tennis, horseback riding, ad infinitum. A veritable cornucopia of cultural activities also awaits the visitor to New York: theatres where thespians from all over the country—nay, the globe—exhibit their talents in plays that rival the splendor of the glorious age of Greek drama; museums which I had the opportunity to visit all my life and were always educational and are also interesting; concerts which are always well-attended by New Yorkers as well as a multitude of outsiders who will be eager to see their favorite artists in the flesh. No kidding, New York is an exciting city.

As a more sustained and successful example of tone, examine the following series of three paragraphs on the subject of "why men marry." The sentences are short and clipped, the words carefully chosen for their biting edge. The writer does not say in so many words that men would be better off not marrying, but does he leave any doubt that that is precisely what he thinks?

Men marry for a variety of reasons, few of them self-appreciated and self-apprehended. The reasons they believe they marry for are seldom the real ones. Men, even quite young men, often marry for no other reason than that they are lonely and seek a consoling companionship. Older men frequently marry not because they are immediately lonely or seek companionship but because they fear loneliness in their later years. This is particularly—almost inevitably—true in cases where the man is alone in the world, without living parents or close relatives. He is, like a child, afraid of the dark that lies ahead. Love, money, all the other usual theoretical considerations, have nothing to do with his marrying or with the woman he marries. He just wants to get married, and that is that.

"Love at first sight—there is no other kind of love, for all men's analysis," an eminent Viennese psychologist has lately observed. Although the illustrioso's remark has been widely ridiculed, there is a deal of truth in it. If it isn't love, or at least something quickly leading to love, at first sight, it isn't love. It may be respect or admiration, or understanding, or camaraderie, or animal magnetism, or anything else of the sort, but it is not love. And it is this first sight, impromptu emotional galvanism that often draws men into marriage without the slightest sober reflection on such matters as have occupied the Viennese Professor Baber's solemn inquiry. A man's eye has much oftener propelled him into wedlock than his heart, and both combined have sucked him into matrimony twenty thousand times oftener than his cerebrum.

Men also marry out of disappointment. The beaten man, the humiliated man, the disappointed man, the man who has taken it on the chin in one way or another, is a veritable gull for almost any woman gunning for a mate. And this is even more true in the case of women. The woman who has been hurt, the woman who has been disappointed, is ready to take on the first even faintly eligible man who comes her way.[16]

There is no simple or single formula for maintaining an appropriate tone throughout a unit of writing; your own sensitivity plus a keen awareness of rhetorical stance (your relation to your subject and your audience) must be your guide.[17] It is worth repeating, however, that the tone of modern prose style is, on the whole, natural and informal, for, as mentioned earlier, most expository writers are using the rhythms of normal, everyday speech.

With these principles as a general guide, you must check for violations of tone in the paragraphs of the piece you are writing. If a flippantly irreverent term—ill-suited to the context of your subject—slips into a sentence during the writing stage, it should be deleted during a later rewriting or revision. So too should a ponderous or overly elaborate phrase be eliminated from a light informal piece, or a strongly emotional outburst be toned down in a serious argument.

Choice of words and phrases, levels of usage, length and rhythm of sentences, juxtaposition of details, and other such rhetorical devices combine to produce the special tone of the paragraph. It is up to you to forge the tone you feel is appropriate, and, having forged it, you should—in the name of coherence—maintain that tone throughout, as in the following examples:

Straight exposition: objective, informative, and detached

As the paragraph evolved throughout the centuries from simple graphic mark to complex verbal structure, the word *paragraph* itself came to have three major and distinct meanings. Its earliest meaning signified a graphic mark or character in a variety of forms placed in the margin or in the text itself to direct attention to a particular part of the text. Later the paragraph came to be understood as a division of discourse introduced either by a paragraph mark or indentation. The word now designates a prose structure capable of organic internal arrangement.

—Virginia Burke, *The Paragraph in Context*

Informal exposition: subjective, witty

One can argue over the merits of most books, and in arguing understand the point of view of one's opponent. One may even come to the conclusion that possibly he is

[16]From *The World of George Jean Nathan*, edited by Charles Angoff. Reprinted by permission of Mrs. George Jean Nathan.
[17]See pages 9–10.

right after all. One does not argue about *The Wind in the Willows.* The young man gives it to the girl with whom he is in love, and if she does not like it, asks her to return his letters. The older man tries it on his nephew, and alters his will accordingly. The book is a test of character. We can't criticize it, because it is criticizing us. As I wrote once: It is a Household Book; a book which everybody in the household loves, and quotes continually; a book which is read aloud to every new guest and is regarded as the touchstone of his worth. But I must give you one word of warning. When you sit down to it, don't be so ridiculous as to suppose that you are sitting in judgment on my taste, or on the art of Kenneth Grahame. You I don't know. But it is you who are on trial.

—A. A. Milne, Introduction to *The Wind in the Willows*

Nonfiction narration: reflective, personal

There are in this world some very strange individuals whose thoughts are even stranger than they are.

In our house in Warsaw—No. 10 Krochmalna Street—and sharing our hallway, there lived an elderly couple. They were simple people. He was an artisan, or perhaps a peddler, and their children were all married. Yet the neighbors said that, despite their advanced years, these two were still in love. Every Sabbath afternoon, after the *cholent,* they would go for a walk arm in arm. In the grocery, at the butcher's—wherever she shopped—she spoke only of *him: "He* likes beans . . . *he* likes a good piece of beef . . . *he* likes veal . . ." There are women like that who never stop talking about their husbands. He, in turn, also would say at every opportunity, "My wife."

—Isaac Bashevis Singer, "The Sacrifice," *In My Father's Court*

Critical review: breezy, sarcastic

Her (Bette Davis') first husband lacked professional drive and had to be divorced. Her second husband, toward whom she still feels tender, died. She paid alimony to get shet of her third. She and her fourth husband, Gary Merrill, were happy for a long time. But he fell out of love with her, she says, because "for three years I was solely a wife and mother." She had become a confirmed homebody with cleaning rag and stirring spoon, like Old Mother Hubbard or Old Dutch Cleanser. Now Miss Davis is thoroughly disillusioned. "Power is new to women," she says with the solemn authority of a sociologist, but she does see a "swing towards a matriarchal society." Three swings out, I hope.

—Brooks Atkinson, *Brief Chronicles*

ASSIGNMENTS

1. a. Analyze each of the following paragraphs, considering
      1. topic sentence
      2. main idea or purpose of paragraph
      3. basic materials of development
      4. ordering principle (general to specific, specific to general)
      5. transitional devices
      6. tone and point of view
      7. pace

   b. In order to see their structure more clearly, diagram these paragraphs (as the Founding Fathers paragraph is diagrammed on page 473) or arrange and number them according to Christensen's "levels of generality" (see pages 475–80).

1. The line between the fancy and the plain, between the atrocious and felicitous, is sometimes alarmingly fine. The opening phrase of the Gettysburg address is close to the line, at least by our standards today, and Mr. Lincoln, knowingly or unknowingly, was flirting with disaster when he wrote "Four score and seven years ago." The President could have got into his sentence with plain "Eighty-seven," a saving of two words and less of a strain on the listeners' powers of multiplication. But Lincoln's ear must have told him to go ahead with four score and seven. By doing so, he achieved cadence while skirting the edge of fanciness. Suppose he had blundered over the line and written, "In the year of our Lord seventeen hundred and seventy-six." His speech would have sustained a heavy blow. Or suppose he had settled for "Eighty-seven." In that case he would not have got into his introductory sentence too quickly; the timing would have been bad.

—William Strunk and E. B. White, *The Elements of Style*

2. Out on Safaris, I had seen a herd of Buffalo, one hundred and twenty-nine of them, come out of the morning mist under a copper sky, one by one, as if the dark and massive, iron-like animals with the mighty horizontally swung horns were not approaching, but were being created before my eyes and sent out as they were finished. I had seen a herd of Elephant travelling through dense Native forest, where the sunlight is strewn down between the thick creepers in small spots and patches, pacing along as if they had an appointment at the end of the world. It was, in giant size, the border of a very old, infinitely precious Persian carpet, in the dyes of green, yellow, and black-brown. I had time after time watched the progression across the plain of the Giraffe, in their queer, inimitable, vegetative gracefulness, as if it were not a herd of animals but a family of rare, long-stemmed, speckled gigantic flowers slowly advancing. I had followed two Rhino on their morning promenade, when they were sniffing and snorting in the air of the dawn—which is so cold that it hurts in the nose—and looked like two very big angular stones rollicking in the long valley and enjoying life together. I had seen the royal lion, before sunrise, below a waning moon, crossing the grey plain on his way home from the kill, drawing a dark wake in the silvery grass, his face still red up to the ears, or during a midday-siesta, when he reposed contentedly in the midst of his family on the short grass and in the delicate, spring-like shade of the broad Acacia trees of his part of Africa.[18]

3. What are qualities that make language live? *Feeling* is one. A writer's ability to feel life deeply, to be responsive to it. Then *power over language,* the gift to use words significantly and to form them in ways to give them meaning and impact. Also the quality of *style,* a writer's personal way with words, as intimate a part of a good writer as the size and shape of his nose. *Knowledge* is another quality that elevates writing into literature, so that the reader is memorably informed and made aware of new worlds. *Insight* is still another quality—a writer's ability to illuminate experience, to light up the dark places so that the reader sees life more clearly. And lastly what Dobie calls *perspective,* so that in reading one is aware of relationships both in space and time.

—Lawrence Clark Powell, *The Little Package*

[18] From *Out of Africa,* by Isak Dinesen. Copyright 1937 and renewed 1965 by Rungstenlundfonden. Reprinted by permission of Random House, Inc. Reprinted by permission of Putnam & Company Ltd., British Commonwealth publishers.

4. The Negro's search for equality has followed closely the classic pattern of most revolutions. Crane Brinton, Harvard's distinguished professor of history, notes in his study of the subject that there are at least three principal requisites for the birth of a revolution. First, revolution most often takes place in a society that is economically progressive, but in which the fruits of progress are not distributed evenly throughout the population. This is certainly true of U.S. society, and of the Negro's place in it. Secondly, the government should either be corrupt or else ineffective in trying to institute reforms. The Federal government today is hardly corrupt, nor is it ineffective. But it certainly did very little to help the Negro during the ninety years between emancipation and the beginning of his American revolution. A third condition is that the upper classes, and especially the upper-class intellectuals, have enough leisure to develop social consciousness and take up causes. Leisure born of rising affluence, of course, is a mark of American society today, and the Negro has in fact drawn much support from upper-class sympathizers and intellectuals (he has, however, perhaps drawn more from young college students). Brinton also found that a revolution flourishes best when the country is not involved in any international conflict, which tends to distract attention from the cause. This is one condition lacking in the Negro revolution, since the United States has become deeply involved in war in Vietnam. In fact, the Vietnam war is cited by civil-rights leaders as one very specific reason why the Negro's revolt has slowed: many of those who once worried about the Negro's plight now worry about the war.[19]

5. The chronicler of Petrarch's life must record high hopes coupled with bitter disappointments. The poet spent a lifetime lyricizing an idealized and unattainable love, finally concluding that "Commerce with women, without which I had sometimes thought I could not live, I now fear more than death. . . . When I reflect on what woman is, a temptation quickly vanished." He worked for the restoration of an imperial Rome, only to decide that it was a city which sold for gold the blood of Christ. He wanted an ivory tower in which to write masterpieces, but wandered restlessly through a dozen towns on a lifetime odyssey, which Bishop retraced in preparing his book. (Mrs. Bishop's pen impressions of these towns illustrate and enhance the volume.) He sought to emulate Virgil by rallying Italy to greatness with an epic poem on Scipio Africanus, only to have contemporaries hoot at it and tempt him to burn it. He strove for immortality through erudite works in Latin, but he won it with Italian rimes to a woman he had never touched.

—Robert J. Clements, "Laurels in Lieu of the Lady"

6. The rehearsal studio of a ballet company is something of a cross between a convent and a prize fight gym. Before the dancers go into action, they paw a resin box in a corner, like fighters, and when they make their way about the room between classes or rehearsal sessions, they are apt—even the most petite of ballerinas—to walk with a pugilist's flat-footed but springy gait, shoulders swaying with a bit of swagger, arms hanging loosely. There is the acrid sweat smell of the gym, and the same formidable presence of lithe, steel-muscled, incredibly trim and capable bodies ruthlessly forcing themselves to become even trimmer and more capable. But there is also an aura of asceticism, of spirituality—a spirituality achieved paradoxically, by means of single-minded concentration of the body. The mirror covering one whole wall from ceiling to floor would seem to speak of gross vanity, but the dancers, though they may have embarked on their careers from vain motives, have learned to

---

[19]From *Black and White* by William Brink and Louis Harris. Copyright © 1966, 1967, by Newsweek, Inc. Reprinted by permission of Simon and Schuster.

rid themselves of conceit when they work. They use the mirror dispassionately, measuring their reflected selves with almost inhuman objectivity against the conception of an ideal to which they have dedicated their lives. The ideal, of course, is that of a particular kind of beauty, a centuries-old, thoroughly artificial way of moving, which, when shaped into ballets by a choreographer, becomes art of a special sort—an elusive, evanescent art, as fleeting as fireworks or soap bubbles, that nevertheless has the power not only to entrance beholders but even, in some mysterious manner, to convey an experience of lasting significance.[20]

7. The attitude toward slavery of those much-admired classical Greeks is curious. Certainly there were great thinkers among the Athenians, but the lot of the slave never engaged their sympathy. Reading Plato's *Republic* or Aristotle's *On Politics,* one can easily come to think what nasty people those Greeks were. Somehow they just could not see that the "slave mentality" that they so despised was the product, not of the kind of people made into slaves, but of the system. As the great sociologist, William Graham Sumner, remarked in *Folkways,* "If any man, especially a merchant, who went on a journey incurred a great risk of slavery, why was not slavery a familiar danger of every man, and therefore a matter for pity and sympathy?" The woes of slavery were certainly often enough pictured in the tragedies, but the inequities of the system never worried the philosophers.

—L. Morston Bates, "On Being Mean"

8. The parlor, a room in which to have conversation, not only derived etymologically from the French verb *parler,* but took its airs and graces from what was called in the early part of the last century "the French taste." In polite urban circles anything French was considered more fashionable than anything English, and it was not until late in the century, when the "parlor" had become the butt of ridicule and rich Americans were buying titled Englishmen as husbands for their daughters, that the British expression "drawing room" came into polite usage in America. In general the parlor meant a room set apart for formal occasions; for entertaining acquaintances, rather than intimate friends, and clergymen on their rounds of parish calls. The word was ubiquitous, and even in the log houses of the frontier, which consisted of two square cabins joined by a breeze way or dog-trot, the room in which the family entertained guests (as opposed to the "family room," where the family cooked and ate and some of it slept) was called the parlor.

—"The Parlor," *American Heritage*

9. While Boston and little Concord were moving forward, Salem, like most of the other seaports, stricken by the War of 1812, had lapsed into quietude and decay. Beside its dilapidated wharves, where grew the fat weeds, the windlass chanty and the caulker's maul no longer broke the silence. The water-side streets were no longer thronged with sailors, "all right" for shore, with their blue jackets and checked shirts, their well-varnished hats and flowing ribbons, with bundles under their arms from the cannibal isles, or from India or China. One seldom heard the lively "Cheerily, men!" while all hands joined in the chorus. The grass choked chinks of the cobble-stones over which drays had clattered. An occasional bark or brig discharged its hides. One saw some Nova Scotia schooner, drawn up at Derby's Wharf, unloading a cargo of firewood. A few idle seafaring men leaned against the posts, or sat on the planks, in the lee of some shabby warehouse, or lolled in the long-boats on the strand. But the great days of the port were a tale that was told, over and over, by the

[20]From p. 3 in *Balanchine* by Bernard Taper. Reprinted by permission of Harper & Row, Publishers.

ancient skippers, who dozed away their mornings at the custom house, with their chairs tilted against the wall.

—Van Wyck Brooks, *The Flowering of New England: 1815–1865*

10. I only once came in contact with real destitution. Louise and her husband, the roofer, lived in a room in the Rue Madame, a garret right at the top of the house; she had a baby and I went to visit her with my mother. I had never set foot in a building of this kind before. The dreary little landing on which there were a dozen identical doors made my heart sink. Louise's tiny room contained a brass bedstead, a cradle, and a table on which stood a small oil stove; she slept, cooked, ate, and lived with her husband and child between these four walls; all around the landing there were families confined to stifling little holes like this; the comparative promiscuity in which I myself had to live and the monotony of bourgeois life oppressed my spirits. But here I got a glimpse of a universe in which the air you breathed smelled of soot, in which no ray of light ever penetrated the filth and squalor: existence here was a slow death. Not long after that, Louise lost her baby. I cried for hours: it was the first time I had known misfortune at first hand. I thought of Louise in her cheerless garret without her baby, without anything: such terrible distress should have shaken the world to its foundations. "It's not right!" I told myself. I wasn't only thinking of the dead child but also of that sixth-floor landing. But in the end I dried my tears without having called society in question.[21]

11. Stupidity: at one time my sister and I used to accuse other children of stupidity when we found them dull and boring; now there were many grown-ups, and in particular our school-teachers, who were so accused. Unctuous sermons, all kinds of solemn twaddle, grand words, inflated turns of phrase, and any pompous affectation was "stupidity." It was stupid to attach importance to trifles, to persist in observing conventions and customs, to prefer commonplaces and prejudices to facts. The very height of stupidity was when people fatuously believed that we swallowed all the righteous fibs that were dished out to us. Stupidity made us laugh; it was one of our never-failing sources of amusement; but there was also something rather frightening about it. If this duncelike dullness had won the day we would no longer have had the right to think, make fun of people, experience real emotion, and enjoy real pleasures. We had to fight against it, or else give up living.[22]

2. Study the paragraphs in the following selections.

    a. Note how each paragraph functions in the whole unit of discourse.

    b. Note the main idea, method of development, ordering principle, transitional devices, tone, and pace of the individual paragraphs.

1. The lyrical fragment "Kubla Khan" (fifty-odd rhymed and irregular verses of exquisite prosody) was dreamed by the English poet Samuel Taylor Coleridge on a summer day in 1797. Coleridge writes that he had retired to a farm near Exmoor; an indisposition obliged him to take a sedative; sleep overcame him a few moments after he had read a passage from Purchas describing the construction of a palace by Kubla Khan, the emperor who was made famous in the West by Marco Polo. In the dream the lines that had been read casually germinated and grew; the sleeping man perceived by intuition a series of visual images and, simultaneously, the words that

[21]From Simone de Beauvoir, *Memoirs of a Dutiful Daughter* (New York: Harper & Row, 1959). Harper Colophon edition, p. 131.

[22]Ibid., p. 123.

expressed them. After a few hours he awoke with the certainty that he had composed, or received, a poem of about three hundred verses. He remembered them with singular clarity and was able to write down the fragment that is now part of his work. An unexpected visitor interrupted him and afterward he was unable to remember any more. To his no small surprise and mortification, although he still retained "some vague and dim recollection of the general purport of the vision, yet, with the exception of some eight or ten scattered lines and images, all the rest had passed away like the images on the surface of a stream into which a stone has been cast, but, alas! without the after restoration of the latter!" Coleridge wrote.

Swinburne felt that what he had been able to salvage was the supreme example of music in the English language, and that to try to analyze it would be like trying to unravel a rainbow (the metaphor belongs to John Keats). Summaries or descriptions of poetry whose principal virtue is music are useless and would only defeat our purpose; so then let us merely remember that Coleridge was given a page of undisputed splendor in a dream.

Although the case is quite extraordinary, it is not unique. In the psychological study *The World of Dreams* Havelock Ellis has compared it to the case of the violinist and composer, Giuseppe Tartini, who dreamed that the Devil (his slave) was playing a prodigious sonata on the violin; when the dreamer awoke he played *Trillo del Diavolo* from memory. Another classic example of unconscious cerebration is that of Robert Louis Stevenson; as he himself has related in his "Chapter on Dreams," one dream gave him the plot of *Olalla* and another, in 1884, the plot of *Jekyll and Hyde*. Tartini undertook to imitate the music he had heard in a dream. Stevenson received outlines of plots from his dreams. More akin to Coleridge's verbal inspiration is the inspiration attributed by the Venerable Bede to Caedmon *(Historia ecclesiastica gentis Anglorum,* IV, 24). The case occurred at the end of the seventh century in the missionary and warring England of the Saxon kingdoms. Caedmon was an uneducated herdsman and was no longer young; one night he slipped away from a festive gathering because he knew that they would pass the harp to him and he knew also that he could not sing. He fell asleep in the stable near the horses, and in a dream someone called him by name and told him to sing. Caedmon replied that he did not know how to sing, but the voice said, "Sing about the origin of created things." Then Caedmon recited verses he had never heard before. He did not forget them when he awoke, and was able to repeat them to the monks at the nearby monastery of Hild. Although he did not know how to read, the monks explained passages of sacred history to him and he ruminated on them like a clean animal and converted them into delightful verses. He sang about the creation of the world and man and the story of Genesis; the Exodus of the children of Israel and their entrance into the Promised Land; the Incarnation, Passion, Resurrection, and Ascension of the Lord; the coming of the Holy Spirit; the teaching of the Apostles; and also the terror of the Last Judgment, the horror of Infernal Punishments, the delights of Heaven, and the graces and punishments of God. He was the first sacred poet of the English nation. Bede wrote that no one equaled him because he did not learn from men, but from God. Years later he foretold the hour of his death and awaited it in sleep. Let us hope that he met his angel again.[23]

2. There is one word which, if we only understand it, is the key to Freud's thought. That word is "repression." The whole edifice of psychoanalysis, Freud said, is based upon the theory of repression. Freud's entire life was devoted to the study of the

---

[23] From *Other Inquisitions* by Jorge Luis Borges, translated by R. L. Simms. Reprinted by permission of University of Texas Press.

phenomenon he called repression. The Freudian revolution is that radical revision of traditional theories of human nature and human society which becomes necessary if repression is recognized as a fact. In the new Freudian perspective, the essence of society is repression of the individual, and the essence of the individual is repression of himself.

The best way to explore the notion of repression is to review the path which led Freud to his hypothesis. Freud's breakthrough was the discovery of meaningfulness in a set of phenomena theretofore regarded, at least in scientific circles, as meaningless: first, the "mad" symptoms of the mentally deranged; second, dreams; and third, the various phenomena gathered together under the title of the psychopathology of everyday life, including slips of the tongue, errors and random thoughts.

Now in what sense does Freud find meaningfulness in neurotic symptoms, dreams and errors? He means, of course, that these phenomena are determined and can be given a causal explanation. He is rigorously insisting on unequivocal allegiance to the principle of psychic determinism; but he means much more than that. For if it were possible to explain these phenomena on behavioristic principles, as the result of superficial associations of ideas, then they would have a cause but no meaning. Meaningfulness means expression of a purpose or an intention. The crux of Freud's discovery is that neurotic symptoms, as well as the dreams and errors of everyday life, do have meaning, and that the meaning of "meaning" has to be radically revised because they have meaning. Since the purport of these purposive expressions is generally unknown to the person whose purpose they express, Freud is driven to embrace the paradox that there are in a human being purposes of which he knows nothing, involuntary purposes, or, in more technical Freudian language, "unconscious ideas." From this point of view a new world of psychic reality is opened up, of whose inner nature we are every bit as ignorant as we are of the reality of the external world, and of which our ordinary conscious observation tells us no more than our sense organs are able to report to us of the external world. Freud can thus define psychoanalysis as "nothing more than the discovery of the unconscious in mental life."

But the Freudian revolution is not limited to the hypothesis of an unconscious psychic life in the human being in addition to his conscious life. The other crucial hypothesis is that some unconscious ideas in a human being are incapable of becoming conscious to him in the ordinary way, because they are strenuously disowned and resisted by the conscious self. From this point of view Freud can say that "the whole of psychoanalytic theory is in fact built up on the perception of the resistance exerted by the patient when we try to make him conscious of his unconscious." The dynamic relation between the unconscious and the conscious life is one of conflict, and psychoanalysis is from top to bottom a science of mental conflict.

The realm of the unconscious is established in the individual when he refuses to admit into his conscious life a purpose of desire which he has, and in doing so establishes in himself a psychic force opposed to his own idea. This rejection by the individual of a purpose or idea, which nevertheless remains his, is repression. "The essence of repression lies simply in the function of rejecting or keeping something out of consciousness." Stated in more general terms, the essence of repression lies in the refusal of the human being to recognize the realities of his human nature. The fact that the repressed purposes nevertheless remain his is shown by dreams and neurotic symptoms, which represent an irruption of the unconscious into consciousness, producing not indeed a pure image of the unconscious, but a compromise between the two conflicting systems, and thus exhibiting the reality of the conflict.

Thus the notion of the unconscious remains an enigma without the theory of repression; or, as Freud says, "We obtain our theory of the unconscious from the theory of repression." To put it another way, the unconscious *is* "the dynamically unconscious repressed." Repression is the key word in the whole system; the word is chosen to indicate a structure dynamically based on psychic conflict.[24]

3. The Kingdom of Didd was ruled by King Derwin. His palace stood high on the top of the mountain. From his balcony, he looked down over the houses of all his subjects—first, over the spires of the noblemen's castles, across the broad roofs of the rich men's mansions, then over the little houses of the townsfolk, to the huts of the farmers far off in the fields.

It was a mighty view and it made King Derwin feel mighty important.

Far off in the fields, on the edge of a cranberry bog, stood the hut of the Cubbins family. From the small door Bartholomew looked across the huts of the farmers to the houses of the townsfolk, then to the rich men's mansions and the noblemen's castles, up to the great towering palace of the King. It was exactly the same view that King Derwin saw from his balcony, but Bartholomew saw it backward.

It was a mighty view, but it made Bartholomew Cubbins feel mighty small.

—Dr. Seuss, *The Hats of Bartholomew Cubbins*

4. Southern characters in local color stories judge almost everyone in terms of his ability to work. In sentimental eulogies of plantation life, the argument that Negroes are too lazy to care for themselves is used to defend slavery. One Page character shouts, "George Washington a slave! Madame, you misapprehend the situation. *He* is no slave. I am the slave, not only of him but of three hundred more as arrogant and exacting as the Czar, and as lazy as the devil." The southern apologists also argue that the Negro's unwillingness to work hard made slavery an expensive and impractical method of cultivating land. One mistress of a large plantation "had heard some talk of the government buying the negroes from their owners and setting them free. She ardently hoped this would be done, for she was sure they could then be hired cheaper than they could be owned and provided for."

Only laziness automatically makes a poor, white man into a poor white. Johnston's petty Dan Hickson, in "A Case of Spite," is trash because he won't work, just as his wife is respectable because she "slaves herself." When "good" Negroes refer condescendingly to white trash, the whites' laziness is usually mentioned. Henry, the best slave on the plantation which serves as setting for "The Whipping of Uncle Henry," objects to Cobb, the new overseer, because Cobb is too lazy to work in the fields, as we are led to infer that the absent owner does. According to Henry, "Thar ain't no pore white trash in all this valley country as low down as all . . . [Cobb's] layout." Mrs. Pelham, the owner's wife, recognizes that Henry has assessed the overseer correctly. She says to herself, "Nobody kin hate a lazy, good-fer-nothin' white man like a nigger kin" (p. 49). Henry proves his superiority to Cobb by refusing to follow Cobb's orders, instead doing the work of three men in clearing a field by himself.

—Merrill Maguire Skaggs, *The Folk of Southern Fiction*

28 Revising and Editing

Once the first draft of a piece of writing has been committed to paper, you are entitled to a sense of accomplishment and relief. Random thoughts have been assembled and shaped into a new, cohesive whole; words have been wrenched from your mind—externalized at last—and set down *there* on paper. The worst is over. But the best still lies ahead, and that generally requires another wave of energy and painstaking effort. This final stage is called revision, literally a "looking again" at the piece to see how and where it can be strengthened and improved. Inserting needed changes—tightening a sentence here and there; replacing a word or an uncertain fact; repositioning a modifier; moving one paragraph up and another one down a page; checking the mechanics of punctuation, spelling, and so on—constitutes the vital next-to-last step in the writing process. The last step is proofreading. Because you are bound to make typing mistakes—to reverse letters, leave out words, misspell others—you should *always* read over your paper one last time, with an eye to "editing out" those inadvertent but inevitable errors.

At this final stage in the writing process it is helpful to view your manuscript as if it had been written by someone else; as if you, the writer, were just another reader making your way through the piece, following the train of thought step by step. One way to achieve the objectivity required of a good editor is to set the finished piece aside. Returning to it after a few days, you will find that you have "gone cold," that you can see the piece with fresh eyes and are capable of spotting and correcting problems you had not even noticed in the heat of the composing process.

An Editing Checklist

This checklist of the principles discussed in Chapters 24–27 may be applied to your own or to someone else's writing. As an editor, you need the kind of distance and objectivity that the following questions will help you to achieve. To answer the questions you will have to reexamine the finished work, and thus discover weaknesses which can be converted into strengths.

Content

Does the writer have something to say?

Is it said with relative completeness—that is, with a sufficient number of specific details, examples, reasons, illustrations, and so on?

Does the writer project authority—that is, a grasp of the material?

Is the subject interesting?

Is the presentation convincing?

Is the chosen subject worth writing about—that is, is it a suitable choice and does the treatment have some substance?

Organization

Does the piece have a good and appropriate opening?

Does the piece have a fitting conclusion that gives a sense of closure, of completeness?

Are the materials arranged in logical and readable order?

Is the organizing principle clear and well-focused?

If not, how could the organization be improved?

Are there sufficient transitions so that the piece flows smoothly, without jarring gaps or unexpected turns of thought?

Tone

Is the point of view or tone appropriate to the subject, projected audience, and purpose of the writer?

Has the tone been consistently maintained throughout the piece?

Style

Paragraphs: Are they unified, coherent, and sufficiently developed?

Do they contain clearly stated topic sentences?

Do succeeding sentences develop the topic sentence in an ongoing progression, varying the level of generality to produce a rich texture that provides adequate exposition of the subject?

Are concluding sentences appropriate and emphatic?

Sentences: Are they clear and graceful?

Has the writer skillfully used such rhetorical devices as economy, parallelism, coordination and subordination, order of climax, sentence variation, alliteration, balanced antithesis?

Has the writer avoided violations of sentence integrity such as the following (see pp. 423–24)?

Careless or indefensible sentence fragments
Comma splices
Fused or run-on sentences

Has the writer avoided basic grammatical and rhetorical violations such as the following?

Unnecessary splits (see p. 436)
Dangling or otherwise misplaced modifiers (see pp. 430–31)
Failure in subject—verb agreement (see pp. 420–21)
Faulty parallelism (see pp. 450–53)
Unnecessary shifts in subject (see p. 435)
Faulty or ambiguous pronoun references (see pp. 435–36)
Mixed constructions (see pp. 431–34)

Words: Are they aptly and accurately chosen, with a sensitivity to connotation?

Has the writer used synonyms to avoid unnecessary repetition?
Has the writer avoided jargon and clichés?

Mechanics

Has the writer observed the established conventions of spelling, punctuation, capitalization, and so on?

The rest of this chapter will provide a brief review of mechanical considerations.

Punctuation Review: Four Main Functions

The following chart demonstrates at a glance the fundamental principles of sentence punctuation; it is followed by a brief summary of the main points of punctuation usage.

Punctuation Chart

1. Sentence. Sentence.
2. Main clause; main clause.
3. Main clause: main clause.

4. Main clause, $\begin{Bmatrix} \text{and} \\ \text{or} \\ \text{but} \\ \text{for} \\ \text{nor} \end{Bmatrix}$ main clause.

5. Main clause; $\begin{Bmatrix} \text{so that} \\ \text{therefore} \\ \text{however,} \\ \text{then} \end{Bmatrix}$ main clause.

6. Main clause subordinate clause.
7. Subordinate clause, main clause.
8. Introductory word or phrase, main clause.
9. Main clause subordinate clause; main clause.
10. Main clause; subordinate clause, main clause.

As you can see, the rules of punctuation are neither numerous nor complicated. They must be adhered to *with exactness,* however, for as linguist Harold Whitehall has pointed out, "The traditional purpose of punctuation is to symbolize by means of visual signs the patterns heard in speech."[1] In other words, punctuation marks do the work of vocal inflections in conveying critical distinctions in meaning, as between "He's a great guy!" and "He's a great guy?"

Punctuation marks serve readers in much the same way that road signs serve drivers: they let readers know where they are and keep them moving in the right direction. Whitehall has noted that the most important function of punctuation is "to make grammar graphic" and that it fulfills this function in four ways:[2]

1. by *linking* parts of sentences and words

   semicolon
   colon
   dash
   hyphen

2. by *separating* sentences and parts of sentences

   period
   question mark
   exclamation point
   comma

3. by *enclosing* parts of sentences

   paired commas
   paired dashes
   paired parentheses

[1] Harold Whitehall, *Structural Essentials of English* (New York: Harcourt Brace Jovanovich, 1956), p. 119.
[2] Ibid.

paired brackets
paired quotation marks

4. by *indicating* omissions

apostrophe
omission period or dot
triple periods or dots

Let us consider each of these marks in its turn.

Linking Punctuation

Use a semicolon (;)

1. To link main clauses that could otherwise occur as separate sentences, especially if they are parallel in structure and emphasis:

   I insisted on a camping trip; no other vacation interested me.

2. To link word groups containing heavy internal punctuation:

   My department chairman, John Webster, plans to travel through most of southern Europe; through all of the Near East; and, if he has the time, along the northern, western, and southern coasts of Africa.

3. To link main clauses joined by a conjunctive adverb:

   I mailed in a deposit; however, I received no reply.

4. To precede words, phrases, or abbreviations such as *namely, for instance, i.e., e.g.,* which provide a summary or explanation of what has gone before in the sentence:

   A writer should follow a specific principle of organization; for example, time order, space order, order of climax.

According to Whitehall, the semicolon distributes emphasis more or less equally between the preceding and following statements; whereas the colon throws emphasis forward toward the following statement.

Use a colon (:)

1. To introduce a summary or a list; generally the introductory clause should be a main clause (see p. 418):

   He carried a suitcase filled with books: the plays of Shakespeare, the novels of George Eliot, the poems of Keats, the essays of Montaigne, and the collected cartoon strips of Charles Schultz.

2. To introduce an extended quotation (use a comma if the quotation is a single sentence or part of a sentence):

   He said: "I cannot begin to think about returning home. My work is barely under way; in fact, today I had my first chance to examine the data. The preliminary findings are certainly promising."

3. To introduce a formal statement or question:

The committee met to consider a sobering question: What shall we do if the president resigns?

Whitehall explains that the dash, unlike the anticipatory colon, throws the reader's attention back to the original statement.

Use a dash (—; typed as a double hyphen with no spacing:- -)

1. To introduce a final clause that summarizes, explains, amplifies, or provides an unexpected addition to what has gone before.

Freedom of speech, freedom of worship, freedom from want, freedom from fear—these form the foundation of a democratic state.

He was modest, shy, simply dressed—and absolutely obsessed with the subject of sex.

2. To indicate a break in thought or in speech:

Periodically—I'd say about every two months—he writes me to ask for a loan.
I—I don't know what to say.

3. To stress or reinforce an idea:

She was good—too good.

Use a hyphen (-)

1. To indicate continuation of a word divided at the end of a line. (Always check the dictionary to make certain you are dividing the word where the syllables break.)
2. To link the elements of compound numbers from twenty-one to ninety-nine and to link the elements of fractions:

sixty-eight dollars
two-thirds of a nation

3. To link nouns or modifiers which are being used in a compound sense:

It was a well-run school.
The year-end dinner-dance was a great success.

Many formerly hyphenated words have become fused into single units, such as *seaweed* and *bookkeeper*. Where there is no precedent, the best policy is to hyphenate when you feel that hyphenation will make your meaning clearer.

Separating Punctuation

Use a period (.)

1. To separate declarative subject-predicate sentences (including mild commands) from sentences which follow. One can *hear* the end of a

declarative sentence, for there is a distinct drop in the voice from high to low pitch:

The lake is light blue.
Do not be late.

2. To conclude a statement which may not be in conventional subject-predicate form but which clearly falls in pitch and thereby generates a pause:

The more, the merrier.

Use a question mark (?)

1. To separate questions and quoted questions from their following context. Because the grammatical meaning of the question mark is "answer needed," it should be used to indicate all forms of query:

Did she say that?
She said what?
Can you pass the course? is the main question.
He asked me, "Are you leaving tonight?"

2. To express more than one query in the same sentence:

Did she say that? or you? or who?

Use an exclamation point (!)

1. To separate exclamatory sentences expressing surprise, incredulity, admiration, or other strong emotion from their following context:

How lovely!
What a surprise!
I can't believe it!
O Lord, save thy people!

Use a comma (,)

1. To separate elements in a sentence that might cause confusion or fail to make sense if considered in combination:

Instead of hundreds, thousands came.
To Mary, Clark was very friendly.
What the answer is, is hard to say.
Out of every hundred, fifty were rejected.

2. To separate main clauses that are joined by a coordinating conjunction (*and, but, or, nor, for*):

She attended all the lectures, but she could not get to the laboratory sessions.

3. To separate introductory words, phrases, or dependent clauses from the main clause and thereby to facilitate reading:

Luckily, she arrived in time.
Up to that time, she had never taken a math course.

Before gathering shells, we went for a swim.
Although he intended no harm, his behavior created chaos in the classroom.

4. To separate words, phrases, or clauses in a series:

The blonde, pretty, somewhat plump girl said her name was Nancy.
They wanted bread, cheese, salami, and wine.
He looked after the baby, cleaned, and cooked.
After looking through my desk, after phoning the lost and found office, after
   questioning everyone in the building, I finally found my notebook.
I came, I saw, I conquered.[3]

5. To set off nonrestrictive[4] or parenthetical words, phrases, or clauses in
   a sentence:

The financial risk, he reported, was enormous.
Chapter One, which deals with definition, serves as an introduction to all
   forms of discourse.
but: The chapter which deals with definition serves as an introduction to all
   forms of discourse. [No comma is necessary here because the clause *which
   deals with definition* is restrictive—that is, essential to identify the chapter
   being referred to.]

6. To set off words or phrases in apposition:

That man, the owner of the bookstore, will never reduce his prices.

7. To set off words or phrases in contrast:

He needs sympathy, not anger.

8. To set off absolute expressions:

The course having ended, the students prepared to leave the campus.
   [nominative absolute]
Indoors or out, tennis is a healthful sport. [absolute phrase]
Well, let's get started. [mild interjection]
We don't have a chance, do we? [echo question]

9. To indicate the omission of an "understood" verb in a compound
   sentence:

Byron was a poet; Beethoven, a composer.
My brother lives in New Jersey; my sister, in New York.

10. To set off a noun or phrase in direct address:

Madame President, the vote has been counted.

---

[3]When a complete predication is made in two or three words, or when the predications form a
unit of expression (such as a proverb or familiar saying), commas may be used in place of periods
or semicolons.

[4]Restrictive modifiers are those which are essential to the meaning of a sentence ("The woman
who snatched the purse was arrested"). Nonrestrictive modifiers are not essential but merely
elaborative; they could be eliminated without altering the basic meaning of the sentence ("The
woman who snatched the purse was arrested, *while her husband stood by, unable to help*").

11. To set off *Yes* and *No* when used at the beginning of a sentence:

    No, I cannot leave the building.

12. To separate a direct quotation from its context:

    "I cannot go," she told him.

13. To separate elements in dates and place names:

    She was born December 15, 1945, in Sioux City, Iowa, and lived there for ten years.

14. To separate initials or the abbreviations of academic degrees from the rest of a sentence:

    Brown, J. S., and Jones, B. D., are listed in the student directory.
    Thomas Hale, M.D., and James Hale, D.D.S., will open their clinic next week.

Do *not* use a comma

1. To separate compound predicates or pairs of words, phrases, or dependent clauses joined by a coordinating conjunction:

   She was born in Sioux City and lived there for ten years.
   Do you want cake or pie?
   I tried to call or to come as quickly as possible.
   Students who want to pass the course but who are unable to grasp basic concepts must attend review sessions.

2. To separate two nouns, one of which identifies the other; in such cases the appositive is so closely related to the noun as to be considered a part of it:

   The booklet "Fixing Furniture" is on the coffee table.
   My sister Jane leaves for school on Monday.
   Carter's boat *The Nautilus* will be ready in June.

3. To separate an appositive which is part of a name:

   I remember reading about Richard the Lion-Hearted.

4. To separate an appositive which contains several words in a series, punctuated by commas; in such instances use dashes instead:

   We looked for them—John, Harry, Jim, and Kate—for almost four hours.

5. To separate the month and year in a date:

   The bridge will be opened in June 1979.

Enclosing Punctuation

Enclosing punctuation consists of paired commas, dashes, parentheses, brackets, and quotation marks, all of which "are used to enclose elements outside the main structure of a sentence. They represent a triple scale of enclosure, in which paired commas enclose elements most closely related to the main thought of the sentence and parentheses those elements least closely related."[5] Paired dashes enclose elements whose connection falls between the two extremes of closeness. Brackets are essentially a special kind of parentheses, and quotation marks are used mainly to enclose direct reports of spoken words.

Use paired commas (, . . . ,)

1. To enclose nonrestrictive sentence elements—that is, elements that are not essential because they do not identify the word they modify, but merely add information about it:

   The boat, which was red, sank under the first wave.
   but: The boat which we built ourselves sank under the first wave.

2. To enclose interpolated or transitional words or phrases:

   The truth, as a matter of fact, is none of your business.
   Your report, I conclude, is based on secondary sources.
   That notion, however, has no basis in fact.

Use paired dashes (— . . . —)

1. To enclose elements that are not as closely related to the main thought of the sentence as are those contained within paired commas, but not as incidental to the main thought as are those enclosed within parentheses:

   My subject—related to anthropology, yet not strictly anthropological—concerns a tribe of New Zealanders now almost extinct.

2. To provide emphasis or suspense:

   She said—and she must have known it all along—that he had won first prize.

3. To mark a sudden break or abrupt change in thought:

   If I fail the boards—which heaven forbid!—I will have to take them again next year.
   He said—and no one could contradict him—that the dates had been miscalculated.

4. To replace paired commas when the enclosed word group contains heavy comma punctuation:

   A representative from each department—English, History, Zoology, Political Science, Anthropology, and Psychology—attended the meeting.

[5]Whitehall, *Structural Essentials of English,* p. 128.

Use paired parentheses (...)

1. To enclose material clearly not part of the main thought of the sentence, and not a grammatical element of the sentence, yet important enough to be included:

   The standard Austen text (based on a collation of the early editions by R. W. Chapman) should be cited in the footnotes.

2. To enclose an explanatory word or phrase that is not part of the main statement:

   The unconscious (not to be confused with the subconscious) was definitively explored by Sigmund Freud.

3. To enclose references and directions:

   The data (see Chart 13) indicate that the incidence of polio is decreasing.

4. To enclose the numbering elements of a series:

   The aims of the new party were (1) to gather together local dissidents; (2) to formulate common goals; and (3) to promote these goals through political activism.

5. To enclose figures repeated to ensure accuracy:

   Enclosed is fifty dollars ($50.00) to cover the cost of our tickets.

Use paired brackets [...]

1. To insert additions or comments in a quoted passage:

   "She [Edith Wharton] addressed herself to the novel of manners."
   She testified that she had, as she put it, "never seen the man in her life [I actually saw them together in the cafeteria last week] nor even heard his name spoken."

2. To enclose *sic,* indicating that an error in a quotation has been noted but not changed:

   "Zelda Fitzgerald's *Save Me the Waltz* was published in 1934 [*sic*]."

Use paired quotation marks (" ...")

1. To enclose direct quotations (use paired single quotation marks to enclose a quotation within a quotation):

   The reply was a firm "Yes."
   Jim said, "I am leaving," but she refused to believe him.
   "When I asked her to come home," he explained, "she told me, 'Never again.'"

2. To enclose technical terms used in a nontechnical context.

   His tendency to "disassociate" suggested a possible psychological disorder.

3. To enclose terms used in an idiomatic or deprecatory sense, such as hackneyed expressions, slang, sarcasm (such usage should be sparing):

   The "reward" was a ten-dollar fine.
   She appeared to think it was "the thing to do."

4. To enclose words used as words (an alternative is to italicize such words; see p. 515):

   How hot is "hot"?

5. To enclose titles of plays, essays, short stories, short poems, chapters of a book, newspaper and magazine articles:

   I suggest that you read Milton's "Lycidas."
   Is Dorothy Parker's "The Waltz" really about a waltz?

Remember the proper positioning of quotation marks:

1. Quotation marks are always used *in pairs;* for every opening quotation mark, there must be a closing one.

2. Quotation marks always go outside commas and periods:

   She said, "Let's go now," and then I heard a crash.
   She heard someone say, "The party is over."

3. Quotation marks always go inside semicolons and colons:

   He told me plainly, "It was all your fault"; but I knew better.
   She wanted to "pack them all up": the books, the furniture, the equipment.

4. Quotation marks may go inside or outside the question marks and exclamation points, depending on the intended meaning:

   He asked me, "Where are my books?" [The question mark applies only to the quotation.]
   Did he really say, "Those are my books"? [The question mark does not apply to the quotation, but rather to the whole sentence.]
   but: Did he really ask you, "Where are my books?" [A second question mark is not used after the quotation mark.]
   He said, "What a great book!" [The exclamation point applies only to the quotation.]
   How wonderful it was to hear him say, "You have passed the course"! [The exclamation point does not apply to the quotation, but rather to the whole sentence.]

Punctuation Indicating Omissions

Use an apostrophe (')

1. To indicate contractions or omitted letters:

   you've (you have)
   o'clock (of the clock)
   it's (it is)

2. To form plurals of letters, figures, symbols, and words used as words:

> She received three A's.
> Her *e*'s and *l*'s look alike.
> The beginning writer has trouble making *8*'s.
> His *and*'s are usually *&*'s.

3. To indicate the possessive case of nouns and pronouns:

   a. Add *'s* to form the possessive case of all singular nouns:

   > cat's, girl's, man's, lady's, Jones's, Keats's, Dickens's

   When a noun ends in an *s* sound, the option exists of adding only an apostrophe, omitting the second *s*. In such instances be sure to place the apostrophe *after* the *s* that is part of the noun:

   > Keats' *or* Keats's [not *Keat's*]
   > Jones' *or* Jones's [not *Jone's*]
   > James' *or* James's [not *Jame's*]

   The choice of which form to use depends on how it sounds (does "Dickens's novels" *sound* better to your ear than "Dickens' novels"?) Whenever the addition of an *s* creates real difficulty in pronunciation, add only the apostrophe:

   > Aristophanes', Mars', mistress'

   b. Add an apostrophe alone to form the possessive of most plural nouns:

   > boys', hats', sailors', musicians'

   Nouns that end in *s* in the singular must add *es* for the plurals; to form the possessive, place the apostrophe after the final *s:*

   > The Joneses' books are for sale.
   > Ladies' hats are on the fourth floor.

   The relatively few plurals which do not end in *s* must add *s* to form the possessive:

   > people's, men's, women's, children's, oxen's, mice's

   c. Add *'s* to the final word of compound nouns:

   > secretary-treasurer's report
   > brother-in-law's room [singular possessive]
   > brothers-in-law's rooms [plural possessive]

   d. Add *'s* only to the last noun to show joint possession in a series of nouns:

   > soldiers and sailors' home
   > Tom, Dick, and Harry's apartment

   e. Add *'s* to each noun to show separate possession in a series of nouns:

   > Tom's, Dick's, and Harry's apartments

f. Add an apostrophe or *'s* to the last component of an indefinite pronoun:

somebody else's desk
others' classes

4. To indicate the omission of initial centuries in dates:

the class of '45

Do *not* use an apostrophe

1. To form the possessive of personal pronouns:

his, hers, theirs, its, whose

Do not confuse the possessive pronoun *its* with the contraction *it's* ("it is"):

Its wing is broken.
It's a broken wing.

Similarly, do not confuse the possessive pronoun *whose* with the contraction *who's* ("who is"):

Who's on the telephone?
Whose telephone should I use?

2. To form plurals of spelled-out numbers and of words that already contain an apostrophe:

threes and fours
a list of don'ts

Do add *'s*, however, if it makes the plural easier to read:

which's and *that*'s

3. After words ending in *s*, such as names of countries and other organized bodies that are more descriptive than possessive:

United Nations Assembly
United States policy
merchants market

4. To form the simple plural of a noun:

The Smiths and Joneses arrived late. [*not* The Smith's and Jones's arrived late.]

5. To show possessive case of an inanimate object:

the woman's leg
but: the leg of the chair

Some idioms have been established in the possessive (*a hair's breadth*); some organizations composed of people may be referred to in the possessive *(the company's retirement plan, the city's streets);* and some expressions of time may be cast in the *'s* possessive *(a week's work, a month's salary, today's paper).* But general usage dictates that the possessive case should not be cast in the *'s* form for inanimate objects. Thus *the door of the car* is preferable to *the car's door; the emblem on his shirt* to *the shirt's emblem; the living room of the house* to *the house's living room.*

Use an omission period or dot (.)

1. To indicate abbreviation:

   Mr. L. B. Matthews
   B.A., M.S., M.D., Ph.D.
   R.F.D.
   U.S.

   When a sentence ends with an abbreviated word, use only one period to punctuate both the abbreviation and the sentence:

   Please send my packages C.O.D.

Do *not* use an omission period

1. After Roman numerals:

   III   IV   XXX

2. After the word *percent* (for *per centum).*
3. With abbreviated names of well-known government agencies, labor organizations, and the like:

   NIH (National Institute of Health)
   WAC (Women's Army Corps)
   UMW (United Mine Workers)

Use triple periods or dots, called ellipsis (. . .)

1. To indicate omission of words or phrases from a quoted text:

   "On the other hand, when Marx the reformer spoke, . . . we got a wholly different conception of the function of the theory and of its claim to truth."
   "The ultimate aim is to bring about a more intelligent use of language. . . ."
   [The first period punctuates the sentence, and the last three periods indicate the omission of the words that followed in the original text.]

2. To indicate omission in content, in order to leave something to the reader's imagination or to create an atmosphere (use sparingly to avoid a mannered effect):

   They rowed on . . . past the meadow . . . past the old decaying castle . . . on and on they rowed.

General Mechanics

Capitalization

1. Capitalize the first word of every sentence of a direct quotation, and, generally, of each line of a poem.

2. Capitalize all proper nouns—the names of persons, places, and official organizations:

   Abraham Lincoln
   Paris, France
   Union Station [but: *the railroad station in Washington*]
   British Commonwealth: the Commonwealth [but not when used in a general sense: *a commonwealth of nations*
   Bureau of the Census; the Census Bureau [but not when used in a general sense: *the census bureau in Laurel*]

3. Capitalize the names of specific geographic locations and features:

   the North Atlantic states, the East, the South [but not when used merely to indicate direction or position: *north, south, east, west*]
   the Promised Land
   the Continent [but not when merely descriptive: *continental boundaries*]

4. Capitalize days, months, holidays, historic events:

   Monday, January, Fourth of July, War of 1812

5. Capitalize titles of all books—literary works, official publications, documents, formal acts and treaties:

   The Oxford Companion to English Literature [do not capitalize prepositions, conjunctions, or articles within a title]
   American Journal of Science
   Treaty of Ghent

6. Capitalize specific school courses:

   Survey of English Literature [but not general subject areas: *math, science, literature*]

7. Capitalize titles preceding names and the names of offices when they are used as titles:

   Doctor Smith [but not an occupation itself: *doctor, engineer, chemist*]
   Ambassador George [but not when used in a general sense: *ambassador-at-large*]
   President Lincoln [*President* and *Presidency* are always capitalized when they refer to the office of President of the United States; the term is *not* capitalized when used in a general sense: *the president of a college*]

Italics

Use italics (underline)

1. To indicate the titles of books, plays, newspapers, magazines, works of art, the names of ships and aircraft:

Madame Bovary, Othello, the Boston *Globe, The New Yorker,* the *Mona Lisa,* the *Queen Mary,* the *Spirit of St. Louis*

2. To indicate foreign words and phrases:

ad hoc	*bonjour*
ad infinitum	*mañana*
faux pas	*Zeitgeist*

3. To indicate words or phrases used as words or phrases (quotation marks may be used instead of underlining, but whichever form you use, be consistent throughout):

How hot is *hot?*
He said *honey* so many times that it began to sound like a nonsense word.

Abbreviations and Contractions

Abbreviations should be avoided except where convention specifically dictates their usage. Contractions, a form of abbreviation whereby an apostrophe replaces an omitted letter (*you're* for *you are*), should also be avoided except in dialogue or in informal essays, where contractions provide the more relaxed and natural tone suitable for such writing.

Abbreviations may be used to designate

1. Established titles and degrees:

Mr., Mrs., Ms., Dr., B.A., Ph.D.

2. Time:

It was 4:30 a.m.

3. Established organizations or agencies:

UNESCO, CIA, CARE

4. Certain standard foreign phrases:

i.e. (that is)
e.g. (for example)
etc. (and so on)

Do *not* abbreviate

1. Professional titles:

Professor [not *Prof.*]
President [not *Pres.*]

2. Names of days, months, or periods of time:

Tuesday [not *Tues.*]
February [not *Feb.*]
years [not *yrs.*]

3. Names of nations, states, streets, avenues, and so on:

United States [not *U.S.*]
12 Selma Drive [not *Dr.*]

4. Holidays

Christmas [not *Xmas*]

5. Weights and measures

pounds [not *lbs.*]
feet [not *ft.*]

Numbers

Although usage varies somewhat, the following is a reasonably reliable guide to the use of numbers.

1. Use numbers for dates, street addresses, telephone and social security numbers and the like, chapters of a book, decimals, percentages, and fractions (in a mathematical context; see item 5, below):

   January 22, 1970 [not *January 22nd*]
   Chapter 14
   .12
   12 percent
   ¼, ⅓ [not *¼th, ⅓rd*]

2. Use numbers to indicate measurement or weight:

   The room was 14 × 12 feet.
   She weighed 115 pounds.

3. Use numbers in a sentence containing a series of figures:

   He calculated the following totals: 18, 14, 12, 19, and 15.

4. Use numbers to indicate time, always adding *a.m.* or *p.m.*:

   The meeting adjourned at 4:15 p.m.

5. Use words when no more than two words are required to pronounce a figure:

   twelve, forty-two, nine thousand, one-half, ten million
   Jane is twenty years old.

6. Use numbers when more than two words are required to pronounce a figure:

   $10.86; 9,842; 354

7. Never begin a sentence with a number:

   Twelve students were reported missing. [not *12 students*...]
   In 1912 he had his first success. [not *1912 marked* ...]

Spelling

Because English spelling is not only not phonetic but also exasperatingly irregular, we must trust to memory and to the clear mental picture of words that most of us gain during our many years of schooling and independent reading. There are many intelligent people, however, who simply cannot retain the image of the correct spelling of a word. Whatever the reason for this inability, a simple prescription is in order: a dictionary or comparable word guide must always be kept within easy reach. There is no overemphasizing the importance of accurate spelling. Anything less than complete accuracy tends to brand the writer as careless and unreliable, if not subliterate: so strong is the concern about spelling in American schools and in the society at large.

Spelling is a basic aspect of the mechanics of writing, and you are therefore expected to provide your readers with correctly spelled words. Even one spelling error creates a distraction from the substance of your paper and may cause your readers to doubt your carefulness and reliability.

In addition to consulting a dictionary regularly, you may find it helpful to study the following list of commonly misspelled words in order to check your memory and to reinforce correct practice.

101 Commonly Misspelled Words

absence
all right
already
analogous
appalled
apparatus
argument
ascendance

balance
believe
benefited
breath (compare *breathe*)

cemetery
changeable
choose (compare *chose*)
committed
consensus
correspondent

defensible
definite
dependent
desirable
development

devise (compare *device*)
disappearance
disastrous
dissension

effect (compare *affect*)
embarrass
environment
exaggerate
exhilarate
existence
exorbitant

friend
fulfilled

governor
grammar
grievous
guarantee

harass
height

independent
ingenious

interpretation
interruption
irresistible
its (compare *it's*)

judgment

likable
loneliness
lose

maintenance
mathematics
miscellaneous
mischievous
misspell
movable

necessary
neighbor
ninety
noticeable

occasionally
occurrence
occurred

offense

omitted

parallel

parceled

peculiar

persistent

persuade

polluted

possession

preceding

preferable

preferred

prejudice

principal (compare *principle)*

privilege

questionnaire

quite (compare *quiet)*

receive

recommend

recurrence

referring

relevant

repetition

resemblance

reverence

rhyme

seize (compare *siege)*

separate

similar

stationary (compare *stationery)*

succeed

than (compare *then)*

their (compare *there)*

tyranny

whose (compare *who's)*

your (compare *you're)*

INDEX

7
8
D 9
E 0
F 1
G 2
H 3
I 4